Human Impact on the Natural Environment

D1334635

Human Impact on the Natural Environment

Past, Present and Future

Andrew S. Goudie
St. Cross College and the School of Geography and the Environment,
University of Oxford,
Oxford, UK

Eighth Edition

ASKHAM BRYAN
COLLEGE
LEARNING RESOURCES

This edition first published 2019

© 2019 John Wiley & Sons Ltd

Andrew Goudie (1e, 1981), Andrew Goudie (2e, 1986), Andrew Goudie (3e, 1990), Andrew Goudie (4e, 1993), Andrew Goudie (5e, 2000), Andrew Goudie (6e, 2006), John Wiley & Sons, Ltd (7e, 2013)

All rights reserved. No part of this publication may be reproduced, stored in a retrieval system, or transmitted, in any form or by any means, electronic, mechanical, photocopying, recording or otherwise, except as permitted by law. Advice on how to obtain permission to reuse material from this title is available at http://www.wiley.com/go/permissions.

The right of Andrew S. Goudie to be identified as the author of this work has been asserted in accordance with law.

Registered Office(s)

John Wiley & Sons, Inc., 111 River Street, Hoboken, NJ 07030, USA

John Wiley & Sons Ltd, The Atrium, Southern Gate, Chichester, West Sussex, PO19 8SQ, UK

Editorial Office

9600 Garsington Road, Oxford, OX4 2DQ, UK

For details of our global editorial offices, customer services, and more information about Wiley products visit us at www.wiley.com.

Wiley also publishes its books in a variety of electronic formats and by print-on-demand. Some content that appears in standard print versions of this book may not be available in other formats.

Limit of Liability/Disclaimer of Warranty

While the publisher and authors have used their best efforts in preparing this work, they make no representations or warranties with respect to the accuracy or completeness of the contents of this work and specifically disclaim all warranties, including without limitation any implied warranties of merchantability or fitness for a particular purpose. No warranty may be created or extended by sales representatives, written sales materials or promotional statements for this work. The fact that an organization, website, or product is referred to in this work as a citation and/or potential source of further information does not mean that the publisher and authors endorse the information or services the organization, website, or product may provide or recommendations it may make. This work is sold with the understanding that the publisher is not engaged in rendering professional services. The advice and strategies contained herein may not be suitable for your situation. You should consult with a specialist where appropriate. Further, readers should be aware that websites listed in this work may have changed or disappeared between when this work was written and when it is read. Neither the publisher nor authors shall be liable for any loss of profit or any other commercial damages, including but not limited to special, incidental, consequential, or other damages.

Library of Congress Cataloging-in-Publication Data

Names: Goudie, Andrew, author.
Title: Human impact on the natural environment : past, present and future /
 by Andrew S. Goudie, St. Cross College and the School of Geography and the
 Environment, University of Oxford, Oxford, UK.
Other titles: Human impact
Description: Eighth edition. | Hoboken, NJ, USA : Wiley, [2018] | Includes
 bibliographical references and index. |
Identifiers: LCCN 2018008627 (print) | LCCN 2018009296 (ebook) | ISBN
 9781119403920 (pdf) | ISBN 9781119403739 (epub) | ISBN 9781119403555 (pbk.
 : alk. paper)
Subjects: LCSH: Nature–Effect of human beings on.
Classification: LCC GF75 (ebook) | LCC GF75 .G68 2018 (print) | DDC
 304.2–dc23
LC record available at https://lccn.loc.gov/2018008627

Cover Design: Wiley
Cover Image: © Johner Images/Getty Images

Set in 9.5/11.5pt Minion Pro by SPi Global, Chennai, India
Printed and bound in Singapore by Markono Print Media Pte Ltd

10 9 8 7 6 5 4 3 2 1

Contents

Preface to the Eighth Edition

It is now three-and-a-half decades since the first edition of this book appeared, and only around 14% of the literature cited in this new edition pre-dates 1981. Indeed, this is the most thoroughly revised edition that I have produced. This period has seen a remarkable transformation in interest in the impact that humans are having on the environment, together with an explosion of knowledge. In this edition, I have made substantial changes to the text, figures, tables, and references, and have tried to provide updated statistical information. I have also divided the book into sections, which I hope will facilitate cross-referencing. The original stimulus for writing this book came from that greatest of editors, the late John Davey, to whom I shall always be indebted.

About the Companion Website

This book is accompanied by a companion website:

www.wiley.com/go/goudie/human-impact-natural-environment

The website includes:

- Powerpoints of all figures and tables from the book for downloading
- A web-only Glossary

1

Introduction

CHAPTER OVERVIEW

In this chapter the first issue that is addressed is the development of ideas over the last 300 years about the relationship between humans and their environment and in particular the development of ideas about how humans have changed their environment. The historical theme continues with a brief analysis of the changes that have taken place in human societies from prehistoric times onwards, culminating in the massive impacts that humans have achieved over the last three centuries and in particular during the so-called 'Great Acceleration' since the Second World War.

1.1 The Development of Ideas

To what extent have humans transformed their natural environment? This is a crucial question which became very important in the seventeenth and eighteenth centuries (Grove and Damodaran, 2006) as Western Europeans became aware of the ravages inflicted in the tropics by European overseas expansion. It was a theme that intrigued the eighteenth-century French natural historian, Count Buffon, in his colossal series, *L'Histoire Naturelle*. He can be regarded as the first Western scientist to be concerned directly and intimately with the human impact on the natural environment (Glacken, 1967). He contrasted the appearance of inhabited and uninhabited lands.

Studies of the torrents of the European Alps, undertaken in the late eighteenth and early nineteenth centuries, deepened immeasurably the realization of human capacity to change the environment. Jean-Antoine Fabre and Alexandre Surell studied the flooding, siltation, erosion, and division of watercourses brought about by deforestation in these mountains (Ford, 2016). Similarly Horace-Bénédict de Saussure showed that Alpine lakes had suffered a lowering of water levels in recent times because of deforestation. In Venezuela, Alexander von Humboldt concluded that the lake level of Lake Valencia in 1800 (the year of his visit) was lower than it had been in previous times, and that deforestation, the clearing of plains, irrigation, and the cultivation of indigo, were among the causes of the gradual drying up of the basin

(Cushman, 2011). Comparable observations were made by the French rural economist, Jean-Baptiste Boussingault (1845). He returned to Lake Valencia some 25 years after Humboldt and noted that the lake was actually rising. He described this reversal to political and social upheavals following the granting of independence to the colonies of the erstwhile Spanish Empire. The freeing of slaves had led to a decline in agriculture, a reduction in the application of irrigation water, and the re-establishment of forest.

Boussingault also reported some pertinent hydrological observations that had been made on Ascension Island in the South Atlantic:

> In the Island of Ascension there was an excellent spring situated at the foot of a mountain originally covered with wood; the spring became scanty and dried up after the trees which covered the mountain had been felled. The loss of the spring was rightly ascribed to the cutting down of the timber. The mountain was therefore planted anew. A few years afterwards the spring reappeared by degrees, and by and by followed with its former abundance. (Boussingault, 1845: 685)

Charles Lyell, in his *Principles of Geology*, one of the most influential of all scientific works, referred to the human impact and recognized that tree-felling and drainage of lakes and marshes tended 'greatly to vary the state of the habitable surface'. Overall, however, he believed that the

Human Impact on the Natural Environment: Past, Present and Future, Eighth Edition. Andrew S. Goudie.
© 2019 John Wiley & Sons Ltd. Published 2019 by John Wiley & Sons Ltd.
Companion website: www.wiley.com/go/goudie/human-impact-natural-environment

forces exerted by people were insignificant in comparison with those exerted by nature:

> If all the nations of the earth should attempt to quarry away the lava which flowed from one eruption of the Icelandic volcanoes in 1783, and the two following years, and should attempt to consign it to the deepest abysses of the ocean they might toil for thousands of years before their task was accomplished. Yet the matter borne down by the Ganges and Burrampooter, in a single year, probably very much exceeds, in weight and volume, the mass of Icelandic lava produced by that great eruption. (Lyell, 1835: 197)

Lyell somewhat modified his views in later editions of the *Principles* (Lyell, 1875), largely as a result of his experiences in the United States, where recent deforestation in Georgia and Alabama had produced numerous ravines of impressive size (Figure 1.1).

One of the most important physical geographers to show concern with our theme was Mary Somerville (1858) (who clearly appreciated the unexpected results that occurred as man 'dextrously avails himself of the powers of nature to subdue nature'):

> A farmer sees the rook pecking a little of his grain, or digging at the roots of the springing corn, and

poisons all his neighbourhood. A few years after he is surprised to find his crop destroyed by grubs. The works of the Creator are nicely balanced, and man cannot infringe his Laws with impunity. (Somerville, 1858: 493)

This is in effect a statement of one of the basic laws of ecology, much championed by Alexander von Humboldt (see Wulf, 2015): that everything is connected to everything else and that one cannot change just one thing in nature.

Considerable interest in conservation, climatic change, and extinctions arose amongst European colonialists who witnessed some of the consequences of Western-style economic development in tropical lands (Grove, 1997). However, the extent of human influence on the environment was not explored in detail and on the basis of sound data until George Perkins Marsh (Figure 1.2) published *Man and Nature* (1864), in which he dealt with human influence on the woods, the waters, and the sands. The following extract illustrates the breadth of his interests and the ramifying connections he identified between human actions and environmental changes:

> Vast forests have disappeared from mountain spurs and ridges; the vegetable earth accumulated beneath the trees by the decay of leaves and fallen trunks, the soil of the alpine pastures which skirted

Figure 1.1 A newly formed ravine or gully that developed at Milledgeville, Georgia, USA, following deforestation. *Source:* Lyell (1875: 338).

Figure 1.2 George Perkins Marsh (1801–1882). *Source:* from the Library of Congress Prints and Photographic Division, Washington DC, http://loc.gov/pictures/resource/cwpbh.02223/ (accessed January 2018).

and indented the woods, and the mould of the upland fields, are washed away; meadows, once fertilized by irrigation, are waste and unproductive, because the cisterns and reservoirs that supplied the ancient canals are broken, or the springs that fed them dried up; rivers famous in history and song have shrunk to humble brooklets; the willows that ornamented and protected the banks of lesser watercourses are gone, and the rivulets have ceased to exist as perennial currents, because the little water that finds its way into their old channels is evaporated by the droughts of summer, or absorbed by the parched earth, before it reaches the lowlands; the beds of the brooks have widened into broad expanses of pebbles and gravel, over which, though in the hot season passed dryshod, in winter sealike torrents thunder; the entrances of navigable streams are obstructed by sandbars, and harbours, once marts of an extensive commerce, are shoaled by the deposits of the rivers at whose mouths they lie; the elevation of the beds of estuaries, and the consequently diminished velocity of the streams which flow into them, have converted thousands of leagues of shallow sea and fertile lowland into unproductive and miasmatic morasses. (Marsh, 1965: 9)

More than a third of the book is concerned with 'the woods'; Marsh does not touch upon important themes like the modifications of mid-latitude grasslands, and he is much concerned with Western civilization. Nevertheless, employing an eloquent style and copious footnotes, Marsh, the versatile Vermonter, stands as a landmark in the study of environment (Thomas, 1956; Lowenthal, 2000, 2013).

Marsh, however, was not totally pessimistic about the future role of humankind or entirely unimpressed by positive human achievements:

New forests have been planted; inundations of flowing streams restrained by heavy walls of masonry and other constructions; torrents compelled to aid, by depositing the slime with which they are charged, in filling up lowlands, and raising the level of morasses which their own overflows had created; ground submerged by the encroachment of the ocean, or exposed to be covered by its tides, has been rescued from its dominion by diking; swamps and even lakes have been drained, and their beds brought within the domain of agricultural industry; drifting coast dunes have been checked and made productive by plantation; sea and inland waters have been repeopled with

fish, and even the sands of the Sahara have been fertilized by artesian fountains. These achievements are far more glorious than the proudest triumphs of war . . . (Marsh, 1965: 43–44)

Elisée Reclus (1873), an anarchist and one of the most prominent French geographers of his generation, was an important influence in the USA and recognized that the 'action of man may embellish the earth, but it may also disfigure it; according to the manner and social condition of any nation, it contributes either to the degradation or glorification of nature' (p. 522). Reclus (1871) also displayed a concern with the relationship between forests, torrents, and sedimentation.

In 1904 the German geographer Ernst Friedrich coined the term 'Raubwirtschaft', which can be translated as 'economic plunder', 'robber economy' or, more simply, 'devastation'. He believed that destructive exploitation of resources leads of necessity to foresight and to improvements, and that after an initial phase of ruthless exploitation and resulting deprivation human measures would, as in the old countries of Europe, result in conservation and improvement. This idea was opposed in the USA by Carl Sauer (1938) and Joe Russell Whitaker (1940), the latter pointing out that some soil erosion could well be irreversible (p. 157):

It is surely impossible for anyone who is familiar with the eroded loessial lands of northwestern Mississippi, or the burned and scarred rock hills of north central Ontario, to accept so complacently the damage to resources involved in the process of colonization, or to be so certain that resource depletion is but the forerunner of conservation.

Nonetheless Friedrich's concept of robber economy was adopted and modified by the great French geographer, Jean Brunhes, in his *Human Geography* (1920). He recognized the interrelationships involved in anthropogenic environmental change (p. 332): 'Devastation always brings about, not a catastrophe, but a series of catastrophes, for in nature things are dependent one upon the other.' Moreover, Brunhes acknowledged that the 'essential facts' of human geography included 'Facts of Plant and Animal Conquest' and 'Facts of Destructive Exploitation'. At much the same time other significant studies were made of the same theme. Nathaniel Shaler of Harvard (*Man and the Earth*, 1912) was very much concerned with the destruction of mineral resources (a topic largely neglected by Marsh).

Sauer led an effective campaign against destructive exploitation, reintroduced Marsh to a wide public, recognized the ecological virtues of some so-called primitive peoples, concerned himself with the great theme of domestication, concentrated on the landscape changes that resulted from human action, and gave clear and far-sighted warnings about the need for conservation (Sauer, 1938: 494):

> We have accustomed ourselves to think of ever expanding productive capacity, of ever fresh spaces of the world to be filled with people, of ever new discoveries of kinds and sources of raw materials, of continuous technical progress operating indefinitely to solve problems of supply. We have lived so long in what we have regarded as an expanding world, that we reject in our contemporary theories of economics and of population the realities which contradict such views. Yet our modern expansion has been affected in large measure at the cost of an actual and permanent impoverishment of the world.

The theme of the human impact on the environment has, however, been central to some historical geographers studying the evolution of the landscape. The clearing of woodland (Darby, 1956; Williams, 2003), the domestication process (Sauer, 1952), the draining of marshlands (Williams, 1970), the introduction of alien plants and animals (McKnight, 1959), and the transformation of the landscape of North America (Whitney, 1994) are among some of the recurrent themes of a fine tradition of historical geography.

In 1956, some of these themes were explored in detail in a major symposium volume, *Man's Role in Changing the Face of the Earth* (Thomas, 1956). Kates et al. (1990: 4) write of it:

> *Man's role* seems at least to have anticipated the ecological movement of the 1960s, although direct links between the two have not been demonstrated. Its dispassionate, academic approach was certainly foreign to the style of the movement . . . Rather, *Man's role* appears to have exerted a much more subtle, and perhaps more lasting, influence as a reflective, broad-ranging and multidimensional work.

In the last five decades many geographers have contributed to, and been affected by, the phenomenon which is often called the environmental revolution or the ecological movement. The subject of the human impact on the environment, dealing as it does with such matters as environmental degradation, pollution, and desertification, has close links with these developments, and is once again a theme in many textbooks and research monographs in geography (see Turner et al., 1990; Meyer, 1996; Middleton, 2013).

Concerns about the human impact have become central to many other disciplines and to the public, particularly since the early 1970s, and a range of major developments in literature, legislation, and international debate have taken place (Table 1.1). The concepts of global change or global environmental change have developed. Wide use of the term 'global change' seems to have emerged in the 1970s but in that period was used principally, though by no means invariably, to refer to changes in international social, economic, and political systems (Price, 1989). It included such issues as proliferation of nuclear weapons, population growth, inflation and matters relating to international insecurity, and decreases in the quality of life. Since the early 1980s the concept of global change has taken on another meaning which is more geocentric in focus. This can be seen in the development of the International Geosphere-Biosphere Programme: A Study of Global Change. This was established in 1986 by the International Council of Scientific Unions, 'to describe and understand the interactive physical, chemical and biological processes that regulate the total Earth system, the unique environment that it provides for life, the changes that are occurring in this system, and the manner in which they are influenced by human activities'. The term 'global environmental change' has in many senses come to be used synonymously with the more geocentric use of 'global change'. As Castree (2015) has stressed, global change has become a major research thrust, and it can provide a major focus for a more integrated discipline of Geography (Goudie, 2017).

Table 1.1 Some environmental milestones.

1864	George Perkins Marsh, *Man and Nature*
1892	John Muir founds Sierra Club in USA
1903	President Theodore Roosevelt establishes a federally protected wildlife refuge at Pelican Island, Florida. The first of fifty-three wildlife sanctuaries he creates as president
1905	The Bureau of Forestry in the Department of Agriculture becomes the US Forest Service
1916	USA National Park Service established
1935	Establishment of Soil Conservation Service in USA
1949	USA National Trust for Historic Preservation created
1956	*Man's Role in Changing the Face of the Earth*
1961	Establishment of World Wildlife Fund
1962	Rachel Carson's *Silent Spring*
1969	Friends of the Earth established
1970	US Environmental Protection Agency created

Table 1.1 (Continued)

1971	Greenpeace established
1971	Ramsar Treaty on International Wetlands
1972	United Nations Environmental Programme (UNEP) established
1972	*Limits to Growth* published by Club of Rome
1973	Convention on International Trade in Endangered Species (CITES)
1974	F.S. Rowland and M. Molina warn about CFCs and ozone hole
1975	Worldwatch Institute established
1979	Convention on Long-Range Transboundary Air Pollution
1980	IUCN's World Conservation Strategy
1985	British Antarctic Survey finds ozone hole over Antarctic
1986	International Geosphere Biosphere Programmme (IGBP)
1987	World Commission on Environment and Development (Brundtland Commission). *Our Common Future*
1987	Montreal Protocol on substances that deplete the ozone layer
1988	Intergovernmental Panel on Climate Change (IPCC) established
1989	Global Environmental Facility
1992	Earth Summit in Rio and Agenda 21
1993	United Nations Commission on Sustainable Development
1994	United Nations Convention to Combat Desertification
1996	International Human Dimensions Programme on Global Environmental Change
1997	Kyoto Protocol on greenhouse gas emissions
2001	Amsterdam Declaration
2002	Johannesburg Earth Summit
2002	Introduction of the term 'Anthropocene'
2007	United Nations Bali Climate Change Conference
2010	United Nations Copenhagen Climate Change Conference
2010	Nagoya Biodiversity Summit and International Year of Biodiversity
2012	Rio + 20 United Nations Conference on Sustainable Development
2015	Paris Conference on Climate Change
2015	28th Meeting of the Parties to the Montreal Protocol to phase out HFCs
2015	China introduces Environmental Protection Law

In addition to the concept of global change, there is an increasing interest in the manner in which biogeochemical systems interact at a global scale, and an increasing appreciation of the fact that the Earth is a single system. Earth System Science has emerged in response to this realization (see Steffen et al., 2004). Earth System *Science*, a modern manifestation of Global Change which concentrates on modelling, treats the Earth as an integrated system and seeks a deeper understanding of the physical, chemical, biological, and human interactions that determine the past, current, and future states of the Earth's lithosphere, hydrosphere (including the cryosphere), biosphere, and atmosphere. While it has its antecedents in the work of people like Humboldt (see Wulf, 2015; Stott, 2016), it came into prominence in the last two decades of the twentieth century. It has emerged in response to (1) the realization that biogeochemical systems operate globally and (2) an increasing appreciation that Earth is a single system. It includes societal dimensions and the recognition that humanity plays an ever-increasing role in global change. It represents humans as internal components of the Earth system not just an external 'forcing agent'.

1.2 The Anthropocene

Early in this millennium, Crutzen and colleagues introduced the term 'Anthropocene' (e.g. Crutzen, 2002; Steffen et al., 2007; Röckstrom et al., 2009), as a name for a new epoch in Earth's history – an epoch when human activities have 'become so profound and pervasive that they rival, or exceed the great forces of Nature in influencing the functioning of the Earth System' (Steffen, 2010). In the last three hundred years, they suggest, we have moved from the Holocene into the Anthropocene. They identify three stages in the Anthropocene. Stage 1, which lasted from c. 1800 to 1945, they call 'The Industrial Era'. Stage 2, which extends from 1945 to c. 2015, they call 'The Great Acceleration', and Stage 3, which may perhaps now be starting, is a stage when people have become aware of the extent of the human impact and may thus start stewardship of the Earth System. Good reviews of the Anthropocene concept are provided by Castree (2014a, b, c).

However, it has been argued that the Anthropocene was initiated much more than three centuries ago. Indeed, one of the great debates surrounding the Anthropocene is when it started and whether it should be regarded as a formal stratigraphic unit with the same rank as the Holocene (Waters et al., 2016). Walker et al. (2015), for example, raise the possibility that the Anthropocene might be designated a unit of lesser rank, and hence could become a subdivision of the Holocene rather than an epoch in its own right. On the other hand, there are those who think the Anthropocene should

ASKHAM BRYAN
COLLEGE
LEARNING RESOURCES

replace the Holocene, which would become downgraded and reclassified as the final stage of the Pleistocene (Lewis and Maslin, 2015). Conversely, there are those who think the Anthropocene only started with the Industrial Revolution and that 1800 AD is a logical start date for the new epoch (Steffen et al, 2011; Zalasiewicz et al., 2011). At the other end of the spectrum, there are archaeologists (Balter, 2013), who believe that substantial human impacts go back considerably further. They have drawn attention to the deep history of widespread human impacts (Ellis et al. 2013a, b; Albert, 2015; Braje, 2015; Piperno et al., 2015). Smith and Zeder (2013) argued that the Anthropocene started at the Holocene/Pleistocene boundary (around 10,000 years ago), with the first domestication of plants and animals and the development of agriculture and pastoralism (see Section 1.5). Certini and Scalenghe (2011) preferred to place the lower boundary at around 2000 years ago when major civilizations flourished.

Foley et al. (2013) proposed the term 'palaeoanthropocene' for the period between the first signs of human impact and the start of the Industrial Revolution, whereas Glikson (2013) suggested a sub-division of the Anthropocene into three phases. He regarded the discovery of ignition of fire (see Section 2.3) as a turning point in biological evolution and termed it the Early Anthropocene. The onset of the Neolithic he referred to as the Middle Anthropocene, while the onset of the industrial age since about 1750 AD he called the Late Anthropocene. Ruddiman (2014) argued that early deforestation and agriculture caused large greenhouse gas (carbon dioxide and methane) emissions slightly later, but nevertheless quite early in the Holocene.

Lewis and Maslin (2015) reviewed the evidence for a 'golden spike' which might provide an incontrovertible, globally relevant mark in the sedimentary record for the start of the Anthropocene. They proposed that there were two candidates. The first of these is a dip in atmospheric CO_2 levels around 1610 as recorded in high-resolution Antarctic ice cores, while the second is a spike in ^{14}C concentrations in 1964 (associated with atom bomb testing prior to test bans coming into force) as recorded within tree-rings of a dated pine in Poland. The 1610 dip in CO_2 values, which they regarded as the most convincing golden spike, resulted from the arrival of Europeans in the Americas. This led to a large decline in the indigenous population, the accompanying near-cessation of farming, a reduction in fire use, and the regeneration of over 50 million hectares of forest, woody savanna, and grassland. This caused a carbon uptake by vegetation and soils and a reduction in atmospheric CO_2 levels. In similar vein, Rose (2015) postulated that a stratigraphic marker for the start of the Anthropocene was provided by spheroidal carbonaceous fly-ash particles (SCPs),

which are by-products of industrial fossil-fuel combustion. He found that data from over 75 lake sediment records showed a global, synchronous, and dramatic increase in particle accumulation starting in c. 1950, driven by the increased demand for electricity and the introduction of fuel-oil combustion, in addition to coal, as a means to produce it. He argued that SCPs are morphologically distinct and, being solely human in origin, provide an unambiguous marker. In contrast, Gale and Hoare (2012) argued that the worldwide diachroneity of human impact makes it impossible to establish a single chronological datum for the start of the Anthropocene, and the validity of a search for these sorts of golden spike has been rejected by Hamilton (2015). Thus the controversy rumbles on, though a large number of earth and environmental scientists are now firm in their opinion that the Anthropocene Epoch can be so defined (Waters et al., 2016).

The huge increase in interest in the study of the human impact on the environment and of global change has not been without other great debates and controversies, and some have argued that environmentalists have overplayed their hand (see e.g. Lomborg's *The Skeptical Environmentalist*, 2001) and have exaggerated the amount of environmental harm that is being caused by human activities. There has also been much debate about whether or not the Anthropocene is an era for hope (a 'Good Anthropocene') or an era of impending disaster (a 'Bad Anthropocene') (see Dalby, 2016).

In this book, I take a long-term perspective and seek to show the changes that mankind has caused to a wide spectrum of environmental phenomena. The current fixation with global warming should not blind us to the importance of other aspects of global change, including deforestation, desertification, salinization, pollution, and the like (Slaymaker et al., 2009).

1.3 The Development of Human Population and Stages of Cultural Development

During the history of humans on Earth, there have been some key milestones in cultural and technical development (Goudie and Viles, 2016):

Years before present (log scale)	Driving force
100	The Great Acceleration Internal combustion engine Industrial revolution European colonization of Americas, Australia, etc.

1000	Peopling of New Zealand, Madagascar, Oceania, etc.
	The classical era
	Secondary products revolution
	Irrigation
	Metals and mining
	Settlements and urbanization
	Domestication, agriculture, land clearance
10,000	Pleistocene extinctions
	Peopling of Americas and Australia
	Dying out of Neanderthals
100,000	Modern humans
1,000,000	Use of fire and stone tool manufacture
	Arrival of *Homo*

Some six or so million years ago, primitive human precursors or hominids appear in the fossil record (Wood, 2002). The earliest remains of a small, bipedal hominim, *Sahelanthropus tchadensis*, have been found in Chad (Brunet el al., 2002). Studies in Turkana, Kenya, have recently identified evidence of early hominin tool-making activity at Lomekwi 3, a 3.3-million-year-old archaeological site (Harmand et al., 2015). The oldest remains of *Homo* have been found either in sediments from the rift valleys of East Africa (as in the Afar region of Ethiopia) (Villmoare et al., 2015) or in caves in South Africa. The first recognizable human, *Homo habilis*, evolved about 2.5–2.8 million years ago, more or less at the time that the Pleistocene ice ages were developing in mid-latitudes. Since that time the human population has spread over virtually the entire land surface of the planet (Oppenheimer, 2003) (Figure 1.3). *Homo* may have reached Asia by around two million years ago (Zhu et al., 2008b) and Europe not much later (Moncel, 2010). In southern Europe there are stone tools in Italy associated with *Homo* that date back to 1.3–1.7 Ma (Arzarello et al., 2007) and also in Spain (Carbonell et al., 2008). In north-west Europe and Britain the earliest dates for human occupation are >0.78 Ma (Parfitt et al., 2010). Modern humans, *Homo sapiens*, have generally been thought to have appeared in Africa around 160,000 years ago (Stringer, 2003; White et al., 2003), though an even earlier date of c. 300, 000 years is possible based on remains from Morocco (Richter et al., 2017). They then spread 'out of Africa' to other parts of the world.

Table 1.2 gives data on recent views of the dates for the arrival of humans in selected areas. The dates for Australia are controversial, and they range from c. 40,000 years to as much as 150,000 years, but with a date of c. 50,000 years ago being widely accepted (Balme, 2013; Clarkson et al., 2017; Veth et al., 2017). There is also

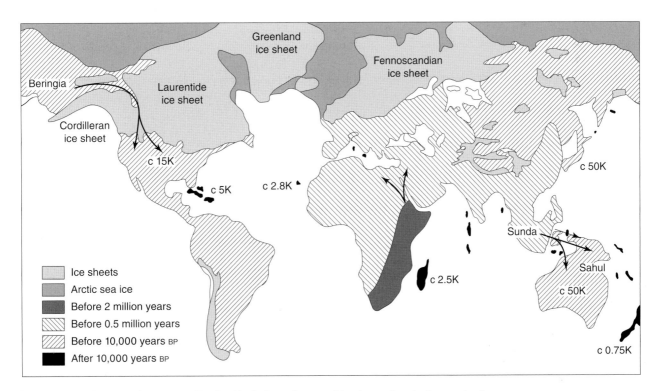

Figure 1.3 The human colonization of Ice Age Earth. Dates for some islands are given in thousands of years.

Table 1.2 Dates of human arrivals.

Area	Source	Date (years BP)
Africa	Klein (1983)	2,700,000–2,900,000
China	Huang et al. (1995)	1,900,000
Georgian Republic	Gabunia and Vekua (1995)	1,600,000–1,800,000
Java	Swisher et al. (1994)	1,800,000
Europe	Moncel (2010)	c. 1,500,000
Britain	Parfitt et al. (2010)	c. 790,000
Japan	Ikawa-Smith (1982)	c. 50,000
Australia	Geyer et al. (2017)	c. 65,000
North America	Goebel et al. (2008)	15,000
Peru	Keefer et al. (1998)	12,500–12,700
Ireland	Edwards (1985)	9,000
Taiwan	Rolett et al. (2010)	5000
Caribbean	Siegel et al. (2015)	5000
Balearic Islands	Burjachs et al. (2017)	4300
Remote Oceania	Matisoo-Smith (2015)	3000
Canary Islands	de Nascimento et al. (2015)	2800–2500
Polynesia	Kirch (1982)	2,000
Madagascar	Crowley (2010)	2500
New Zealand	Lowe (2008)	750

considerable uncertainty about the dates for humans arriving in the Americas (Goebel et al., 2008; Amick, 2016). Many authorities have argued that the first colonizers of North America, arrived via the Bering land-bridge from Asia around 12,000 years ago. However, some earlier dates exist for the Yukon (Bourgeon et al., 2017), and Florida (Halligan et al., 2016), and these perhaps imply an earlier phase of colonization. Indeed, very recently, Holen et al. (2017) claim to have found evidence of human butchering of mastodon bones in southern California, dating back to as much as 130,000 years ago. The settlement of Oceania took place relatively late, with colonization of the western archipelagos of Micronesia and eastern Melanesia taking place at c. 3500–2800 BP, of central and eastern Micronesia at 2200–2000 BP, and of eastern and southern Polynesia at 1100–700 BP (Anderson, 2009).

Estimates of population levels in the early stages of human development (Figure 1.4a) are imprecise and uncertain. At the peak of the Last Glacial Maximum around 20,000 years ago, the population of the old world

was possibly between about 2 and 8 million (Gautney and Holliday, 2015). Human population estimates for the Holocene are diverse and controversial (Boyle et al., 2011). The mid-Holocene value was between 5 and 24 million, the value at the end of the Roman period was c. 200 million, the late medieval value was between c. 400 and 500 million, and the value at the start of the Industrial Revolution was around 900–1000 million. The total has now passed 7000 million.

Before the agricultural 'revolution' some 10,000 years ago, human groups were hunters and gatherers. Population densities were low, and the optimum territory for a band of hunter-gatherers in the Middle Eastern wood-land–parkland belt would have been 300–500 square kilometres, while in the drier regions it would have been 500–2000 square kilometres (Bar-Yosef, 1998). However, the agricultural revolution probably enabled an expansion of the total human population to 500 million by AD 1650. It is since that time, helped by the medical and industrial revolutions and developments in agriculture and colonization of new lands, that human population has exploded, reaching about 1,000 million by AD 1850, 2,000 million by AD 1930, and 4,000 million by AD 1974. Victories over various diseases (e.g. smallpox, cholera, malaria) have caused marked decreases in death-rates throughout the non-industrial world, but death-rate control has not in general been matched by birth control. Thus the annual population growth rate in the late 1980s in South Asia was 2.64%, Africa 2.66%, and Latin America (where population increased fourteenfold between 1850 and 2000), 2.73%. In the period from 2005–2010 these rates had slowed down substantially, with Latin America down to 1.2% and Africa to 2.2%. The global annual growth in population has over the last decade been around 75–77 million people (Figure 1.4b).

The history of the human impact, however, has not been a simple process of increasing change in response to linear population growth over time, for in specific places at specific times there have been periods of reversal in population growth and ecological change as cultures have collapsed, wars occurred, diseases struck, and habitats been abandoned. Denevan (1992), for example, has pointed to the decline of Native American populations in the new world following European entry into the Americas. This created what was 'probably the greatest demographic disaster ever'. The overall population of the Western Hemisphere in 1750 was perhaps less than a third of what it may have been in 1492, and the ecological and atmospheric consequences were legion (see Section 1.2). It is certainly dangerous to think that in all places the human impact has shown a continually increasing trajectory, for there are many examples of ravages in one era being followed by phases of restoration, recovery, and stability in another. Trimble

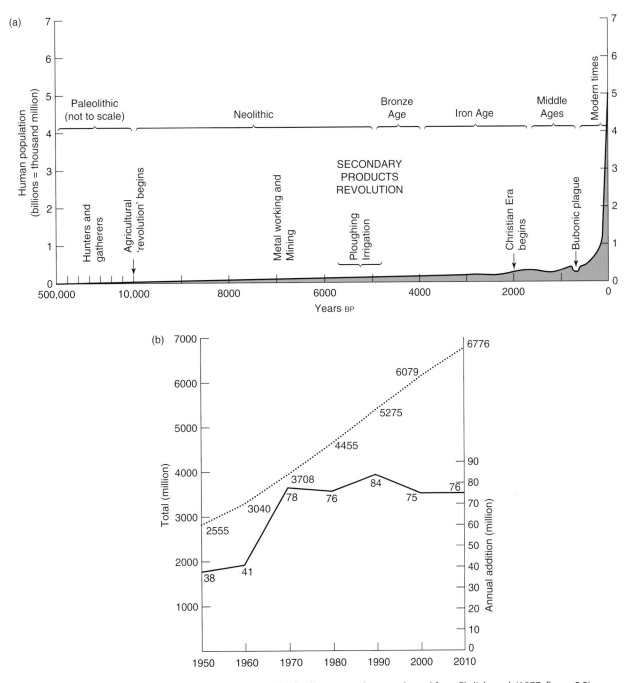

Figure 1.4 (a) The growth of human numbers for the past half million years. *Source:* adapted from Ehrlich et al. (1977: figure 5.2). (b) Annual growth of world population since 1950. *Source:* based on UN data.

(2013) demonstrates this in the context of the land use and land degradation history in the American Midwest.

The evolving impact of humans on the environment has often been expressed in terms of a simple equation:

$$I = P\,A\,T$$

where I is the amount of pressure or impact that humans apply on the environment, P is the number of people, A is the affluence (or the demand on resources per person),

and T is a technological factor (the power that humans can exert through technological change). P, A, and T have been seen by some as 'the three horsemen of the environmental apocalypse' (Meyer, 1996: 24). There may be considerable truth in the equation and in that sentiment; but as Meyer points out, the formula cannot be applied in too mechanistic a way. The 'cornucopia view', indeed, sees population not as the ultimate depleter of resources but as itself the ultimate resource capable of causing change for the better. There are cases where strong population growth has appeared to lead to a reduction in environmental degradation (Tiffen et al., 1994). Likewise, there is debate about whether it is poverty or affluence that creates deterioration in the environment. On the other hand many poor countries have severe environmental problems and do not have the resources to clear them up, whereas affluent countries do. Conversely it can be argued that affluent countries have plundered and fouled less fortunate countries, and that it would be environmentally catastrophic if all countries used resources at the rate that the rich countries do. Similarly, it would be naïve to see all technologies as malign, or indeed benign. Technology can be a factor either of mitigation and improvement or of damage. Sometimes it is the problem (as when ozone depletion has been caused by a new technology – the use of chlorofluorocarbons) and sometimes it can be the solution (as when renewable energy sources replace the burning of polluting lignite in power stations).

In addition to the three factors of population, affluence, and technology, environmental changes also depend on variations in the way in which different societies are organized and in their economic and social structures (see Meyer, 1996: 39–49 for an elaboration of this theme). For example, the way in which land is owned is a crucial issue. The controls of environmental changes caused by the human impact are thus complex and in many cases contentious, but all the factors discussed play a role of some sort, at some places, and at some times.

We now turn to a consideration of the major cultural and technical developments that have taken place during the past two to three million years. Takács-Sánta (2004) argued that there have been six major transformations in the history of the human transformation of the environment: the use of fire, the development of language, the birth of agriculture, the development of cities and states, European conquests since the fifteenth century AD, and the Technological-Scientific Revolution, with the emergence of fossil fuels as primary energy sources. In this book, three main phases will form the basis of the analysis: the phase of hunting and gathering; the phase of plant cultivation, animal keeping and metal working; and the phase of modern urban and industrial society, culminating in the Great Acceleration. These developments are treated in much greater depth by Simmons (1996) and Ponting (2007).

1.4 Hunting and Gathering

The supposed uniqueness of humans as tool makers has been seen as false because of recent studies which have shown that wild monkeys are capable of flaking stone

Figure 1.5 The Olduvai Gorge in Tanzania – one of the great sites for the investigation of early man (ASG).

tools (Proffitt et al., 2016). Nonetheless, the oldest records of human activity and technology are pebble tools which consist of a pebble with one end chipped into a rough cutting edge. At Dikika in Ethiopia there is evidence for stone-tool-assisted consumption of meat at 3.42–3.24 Ma (McPherron et al., 2010). At Lake Turkana in northern Kenya, and the Omo Valley in southern Ethiopia, a tool-bearing bed of volcanic material has been dated by isotopic means at about 2.6 million years old, another from Gona in the north-east of Ethiopia at about 2.5 million years old (Semaw et al., 1997), while another bed at the Olduvai Gorge in Tanzania (Figure 1.5) has been dated by similar means at 1.75 million years. Indeed, these very early tools are generally termed 'Oldowan'.

As the Stone Age progressed the tools became more sophisticated, varied, and effective, and Figure 1.6 shows some beautiful Palaeolithic hand axes from Olorgesailie in East Africa. Greater exploitation of plant and animal resources became feasible. Stone may not, however,

Figure 1.6 A cluster of Palaeolithic hand axes from Olorgesailie in East Africa (ASG).

have been the only material used. Sticks and animal bones, the preservation of which are less likely than stone, are among the first objects that may have been used as implements, although the sophisticated utilization of antler and bone as materials for weapons and implements appears to have developed surprisingly late in pre-history. There is certainly a great deal of evidence for the use of wood throughout the Palaeolithic Age and by modern and hunter-gatherer communities, for ladders, fire, pigment (charcoal), the drying of wood, and digging sticks. Tyldesley and Bahn (1983: 59) went so far as to suggest that 'The Palaeolithic might more accurately be termed the "Palaeoxylic" or "Old Wood Age", and experiments have shown the efficiency of wooden hunting tools in comparison with ones made of stone' (Waguespack et al., 2009).

The building of shelters and the use of clothing became a permanent feature of human life as the Palaeolithic period progressed, and permitted habitation in areas where the climate was otherwise not congenial. European sites from the Mousterian of the Middle Palaeolithic have revealed the presence of purposefully made dwellings as well as caves, and by the Upper Palaeolithic more complex shelters were in use, allowing people to live even in the tundra lands of Central Europe and Russia.

Another feature of early society which seems to have distinguished humans from the surviving non-human primates was their seemingly omnivorous diet. Whereas the great apes, though not averse to an occasional taste of animal food, are predominately vegetarian, our Palaeolithic ancestors, including *Homo sapiens*, lived as hunter-gatherers, eating wild animal-source foods (lean meats, internal organs, bone marrow, but no dairy) and uncultivated plant-source foods (mostly fruits, vegetables, and nuts). One consequence of enlarging the range of their diet was that, in the long run, humans were able to explore a much wider range of environments. Another major difference that set humankind above the beasts was the development of communicative skills such as speech. Until hominids had developed words as symbols, the possibility of transmitting, and so accumulating, culture hardly existed. Animals can express and communicate emotions, never designate or describe objects.

Very early on in their history humans started using fire (Glikson, 2013; Bowman, 2014; Albert, 2015) (Figure 1.7). This, as we shall see (Sections 2.3–2.6), is a major agent by which humans have influenced their environment (Kinoshita et al., 2016). The date at which it was first deliberately employed is a matter of ongoing controversy (Caldararo, 2002; Gowlett, 2016). In South Africa, Beaumont (2011) and Berna et al. (2012) found some traces of repeated burning events from Acheulean

Figure 1.7 Fire was one of the first and most powerful tools of environmental transformation employed by humans. The high grasslands of southern Africa may owe much of their character to regular burning, as shown here in Swaziland (ASG).

cave sediments dating back to more than a million years ago. In East Africa, Gowlett et al. (1981) claimed to find evidence for deliberate manipulation of fire from over 1.4 million years ago. In Murcia, Spain, there is evidence for use of fire in the early Palaeolithic between c. 780,000 and 980,000 years ago (Rhodes et al., 2016). After c. 400,000 years ago (i.e. in the Middle Pleistocene) evidence for the association between humans and fire becomes compelling (Shimelmitz et al., 2014).

It is apparent from many parts of the world that even small hunter-gatherer populations can cause great environmental changes through the use of fire (Lightfoot and Cuthrell, 2015). As Pyne (1982: 3) has written:

> It is among man's oldest tools, the first product of the natural world he learned to domesticate. Unlike floods, hurricanes or windstorms, fire can be initiated by man; it can be combated hand to hand, dissipated, buried, or 'herded' in ways unthinkable for floods or tornadoes.

He went on to stress the implications that fire had for subsequent human cultural evolution (p. 4):

> It was fire as much as social organisation and stone tools that enabled early big game hunters to encircle the globe and to begin the extermination of selected species. It was fire that assisted hunting and gathering societies to harvest insects, small game and edible plants; that encouraged the spread of agriculture outside the flood plains by allowing for rapid landclearing, ready fertilization, the selection of food grains, the primitive herding of grazing animals that led to domestication, and the expansion of pasture and grasslands against climate gradients; and that, housed in machinery,

powered the prime movers of the industrial revolution.

Overall, compared with later stages of cultural development, early hunters and gatherers had neither the numbers nor the technological skills to have a very substantial effect on the environment. Besides the effects of fire, early cultures may have caused some diffusion of seeds and nuts, and through hunting activities (see Section 3.7) may have had some dramatic effects on animal populations, causing the extinction of many great mammals (the so-called 'Pleistocene overkill'). Locally some eutrophication may have occurred, and around some archaeological sites phosphate and nitrate levels may be sufficiently raised to make them an indicator of habitation to archaeologists today (Holliday, 2004). Equally, although we often assume that early humans were active and effective hunters, they may well have been dedicated scavengers of carcasses of animals which had either died natural deaths or been killed by carnivores like lion.

It is salutary to remember, however, just how significant this stage of our human cultural evolution has been. As Lee and DeVore (1968: 3) wrote:

Of the estimated 80,000,000,000 men who have ever lived out a life span on earth, over 90 per cent

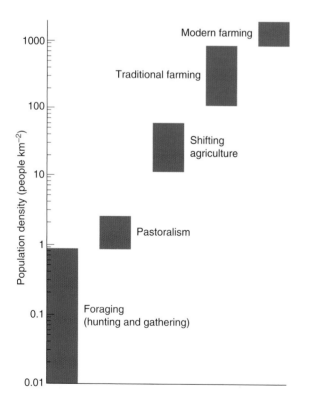

Figure 1.8 Comparison of carrying capacities of foraging, pastoralist, and agricultural societies.

have lived as hunters and gatherers, about 6 per cent have lived by agriculture and the remaining few per cent have lived in industrial societies. To date, the hunting way of life has been the most successful and persistent adaptation man has ever achieved.

Figure 1.8 indicates the very low population densities of hunter/gatherer/scavenger groups in comparison with those that were possible after the development of pastoralism and agriculture.

1.5 Humans as Cultivators and Keepers

Humans have been foragers rather than farmers for around 95% of their history, but during the end of the Pleistocene major changes were afoot. It is possible to identify some key stages of economic development that have taken place since then (Table 1.3). For example around 14,000–15,000 years ago, in the Middle Eastern region, now consisting of Jordan, Syria, Israel, Palestine, and Lebanon, the hunting folk – the Natufians – in addition to their hunting, began to build permanent houses of stone and wood, they buried their dead in and around them with elaborate rituals, gathered in communities of up to several hundred people, ground up wild cereals with pestles and mortars, and made tools and art objects from animal bones (Bar-Yosef, 1998; Barker, 2006; Balter, 2010). Then, round the beginning of the Holocene, about 10,000 years ago, the Natufians and other groups in various other parts of the world began to domesticate rather than to gather food plants and to keep, rather than just hunt, animals. This phase of human cultural development is well reviewed in Roberts (2014). By taking up farming and domesticating food plants, they reduced enormously the space required for sustaining each individual by a factor of the order of 500 at least (Sears, 1957: 54) and population densities could thus become progressively greater (Figure 1.9). As a consequence we see shortly thereafter, notably in the Middle East, the establishment of the first major settlements – towns.

It is now recognized that some hunters and gathers had considerable leisure and did not need to develop agriculture to avoid drudgery and starvation. Moreover, some believe that the mobile hunter-gatherer lifestyle was far more attractive than a sedentary one, which creates problems of refuse disposal, hygiene, and social conflict (Mithen, 2007). However, there is no doubt that through the controlled breeding of animals and plants humans were able to develop a more reliable and readily expandable source of food and thereby create a solid and secure basis for cultural advance, an advance which included civilization and the 'urban revolution' of Childe

Table 1.3 Five stages of economic development.

Economic stage	Dates and characteristics
Hunting-gathering and early agriculture	Domestication first fully established in south-western Asia around 7500 BC; hunter-gatherers persisted in diminishing numbers until today. Hunter-gatherers generally manipulate the environment less than later cultures, and adapt closely to environmental conditions
Riverine civilizations	Great irrigation-based economies lasting from c. 4000 BC to 1st century AD in places such as the Nile Valley and Mesopotamia. Technology developed to attempt to free civilizations from some of the constraints of a dry season
Agricultural empires	From 500 BC to around 1800 AD a number of city-dominated empires existed, often affecting large areas of the globe. Technology (e.g. terracing and selective breeding) developed to help overcome environmental barriers to increased production
The Atlantic-industrial era	From c. 1800 AD to today a belt of cities from Chicago to Beirut, and around the Asian shores to Tokyo, form an economic core area based primarily on fossil fuel use. Societies have increasingly divorced themselves from the natural environment, through air conditioning for example. These societies have also had major impacts on the environment
The Pacific-global era	Since the 1960s there has been a shifting emphasis to the Pacific Basin as the primary focus of the global economy, accompanied by globalization of communications and the growth of multinational corporations

Source: adapted from Simmons (1993: 2–3).

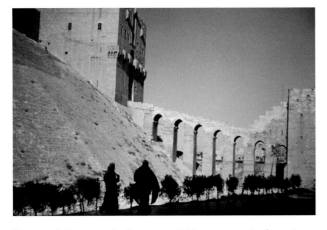

Figure 1.9 The growth of towns and cities was a major factor in the transformation of the environment. This image is of the Citadel in Aleppo, Syria. Aleppo is an ancient metropolis, and one of the oldest continuously inhabited cities in the world; it may have been inhabited since the 6th millennium BCE (ASG).

(1936) and others. Indeed, Isaac (1970) termed domestication 'the single most important intervention man had made in his environment'; and Harris (1996) regarded the transition from foraging to farming as 'the most fateful change in the human career'. Diamond (2002) termed it 'the most momentous change in Holocene human history', while Mithen (2007: 705) has said that 'The origins of farming is the defining event of human history – the one turning point that has resulted in modern humans having a quite different type of lifestyle and cognition to all other animals and past types of humans'.

A distinction can be drawn between cultivation and domestication. Whereas cultivation involves deliberate sowing or other management, and entails plants which do not necessarily differ genetically from wild populations of the same species, domestication results in genetic change brought about through conscious or unconscious human selection. This creates plants that differ morphologically from their wild relatives and which may be dependent on humans for their survival.

The origin of agriculture remains controversial (Scarre, 2005; Barker, 2006; Barker and Goucher, 2015). Some early workers saw agriculture as a divine gift to humankind, while others thought that animals were domesticated for religious reasons. They argued that it would have been improbable that humans could have predicted the usefulness of domestic cattle before they were actually domesticated. Wild cattle are large, fierce beasts, and no one could have foreseen their utility for labour or milk until they were tamed – tamed perhaps for ritual sacrifice in connection with lunar goddess cults (the great curved horns being the reason for the association). Another major theory – the demographic hypothesis – was that domestication was produced by crowding, possibly brought on by a combination of climatic deterioration (alleged post-Glacial progressive desiccation) and population growth. Gordon Childe's 'oasis propinquity hypothesis' held that increasing desiccation brought wild animals and plants into ever closer relationships, from which symbiosis and ultimately domestication emerged (Renfrew, 2006). Such pressure, may have forced communities to intensify their methods of food production. Current palaeo-climatological research tends not to support this interpretation, but that is not to say that other severe climatic changes could not have played a role (Sherratt, 1997).

Sauer (1952) believed that plant domestication was initiated in South-East Asia by fishing folk, who found that lacustrine and riverine resources would underwrite a stable economy and a sedentary or semi-sedentary life style. He surmises that the initial domesticates would be multi-purpose plants set around small fishing villages to provide such items as starch foods, substances for toughening nets and lines and making them water-resistant, and drugs and poisons. He suggested that 'food production was one and perhaps not the most important reason for bringing plants under cultivation'.

Yet another model was advanced by Jacobs (1969) which turned certain more traditional models upside down. Instead of following the classic pattern whereby farming leads to village which leads to town which leads to civilization, she proposed that one could be a hunter-gatherer and live in a town or city, and that agriculture originated in and around such cities rather than in the countryside. Her argument suggests that even in primitive hunter-gatherer societies particularly valuable commodities such as fine stones, pigments, and shells could create and sustain a trading centre which would possibly become large and stable. Food would be exchanged for goods, but natural produce brought any distance would have to be durable, so meat would be transported on the hoof for example, but not all the animals would be consumed immediately; some would be herded together and might breed. This might be the start of domestication. Indeed, settlements may have been a cause of agriculture rather than a consequence (Watkins, 2010).

Another hypothesis – the feasting hypothesis – is based on the idea that in many societies, those wishing to achieve rank and status do so by throwing feasts. The adoption of cultivation and the husbanding of domestic animals made it possible for ambitious individuals to produce increasing amounts of food which would give them an advantage in social competition (Hayden, 1995). It is also possible that as humans developed art and equipment to process plants, they developed new ideas and saw cultivation and domestication as a means of social prestige (Mithen, 2007). In other words, the origins of agriculture 10,000 years ago may perhaps be explained by a fundamental change in the way in which the human mind conceived of nature.

The process of domestication and cultivation was also once considered a revolutionary system of land procurement that had evolved in only one or two hearths and diffused over the face of the earth, replacing the older hunter-gathering systems by stimulus diffusion. It was felt that the deliberate rearing of plants and animals for food was a discovery or invention so radical and complex that it could have developed only once (or possibly twice) – the so-called 'Eureka model'. In reality, however, the domestication of plants occurred at approximately the same time in widely separated areas (Table 1.4). As Barker (2006: 412) has written:

> probably many more societies than commonly envisaged, in all parts of the world, started to engage in different kinds of animal and/or plant husbandry at or soon after the transition to the Holocene – in South-West Asia, South Asia,

Table 1.4 Dates which indicate that there may have been some synchroneity of plant domestication in different centres.

Centre	Dates (000 years BP)	Plant
Mesoamerica	10.7–9.8 9.0	Squash-pumpkin
		Bottle gourd
		Maize
Near East	11.0–9.3	Fig tree
		Emmer wheat
		Two-rowed barley
		Einkorn wheat
		Pea
		Lentil
		Flax
Far East	11.0–7.0	Broomcorn millet
		Rice
		Gourd
		Water chestnut
Andes	9.4–8.0	Chilli pepper
		Common bean
		Ullucu
		White potato
		Squash and gourd

East Asia, Island South-East Asia, several parts of the Americas, and North Africa (and who knows when in tropical West Africa?). Independent of one another (at the regional scale, that is) and in many different ways, very many societies arrived at solutions to living in the transformed landscapes they were encountering which we can recognize as the beginnings of systematic husbandry.

So, the balance of botanical and archaeological evidence seems to suggest that humans started experimenting with domestication and cultivation of different plants at different times in different parts of the world (Figure 1.10) (Mithen, 2007; Fuller et al., 2014; Larson et al., 2014). It has been argued that domestication of plants can be divided into three stages: (i) *gathering*, in which people gathered annual plants from wild stands; (ii) *cultivation*, in which wild plant genotypes were systematically sown in fields of choice; and (iii) *domestication*, in which mutant plants with desirable characteristics were raised (Weiss et al., 2006). Cultivation is the essential stage, as the repetitive cycle of sowing, collecting, and sowing of wild plants which it involves gives rise to genotype accumulation that leads on to domestication.

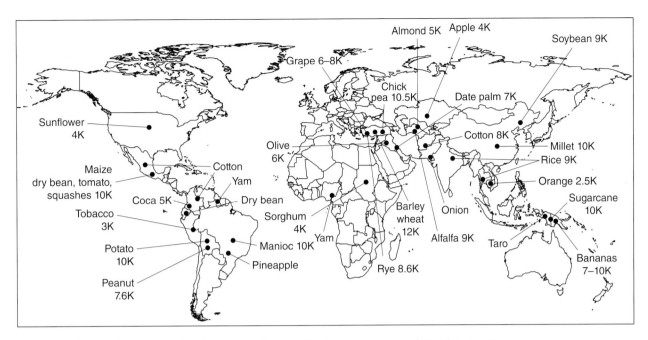

Figure 1.10 A map of the centres of origin for selected crops with details of the dates of their domestication.

The dates for the first evidence of domestication tend to have become earlier in recent years, and the first steps towards domestication of crops in the eastern Mediterranean lands and the so called 'Hilly Flanks' of the Middle East may have taken place around 12,000 BP (Before Present) (Zeder, 2008; Özkan et al., 2011). The so-called founder crops were three cereals (emmer wheat, einkorn wheat, and barley), four types of pulse, and flax. Flax (*Linum usitatissimum*), although it may have initially been domesticated as a source of oil, represents the earliest known domesticated fibre (linen) in the archaeological record. It was domesticated from 'pale flax' (*Linum bienne*), a wild plant which grows across south-west Asia, north Africa, western and southern Europe. The grape was also domesticated in the Middle East at c. 6000–8000 BP (Myles et al., 2011) and the date palm was domesticated in southern Mesopotamia around 7000 BP (Tengberg, 2012). With regard to olives, although early exploitation and use of wild olive trees (namely oleasters) has been documented since the Neolithic from the Near East to Spain, it is usually accepted that the domestication of the olive tree began in the north-east Levant approximately 6000 years ago (Besnard et al., 2013). Nonetheless, recent syntheses of sites of plant domestication on a global basis (Meyer et al., 2012) have shown the importance of such centres as China, South-East Asia, and the Americas (Dillehay et al., 2007; Pickersgill, 2007). The earliest domestication of rice occurred in China (though the exact locations are a matter of debate) after c. 9000 BP (Liu et al., 2007; Fuller et al., 2009), while evidence for

cotton domestication occurs in Baluchistan (Pakistan) at c. 8000 BP (Moulherat et al., 2002). The domestication of millet in China has been extended back to 10,000 BP (Lu et al., 2009). In Mesoamerica maize, beans, squashes, and the potatoes may have been domesticated as early as 10,000–9000 BP (Zizumbo-Villarreal and Colunga-García Marín, 2010; Ovchinnikova et al., 2011).

The locations and dates for domestication of some important domestic animals are shown in Figure 1.11. Note that the domestication of sheep, goats, pigs, and cattle took place in the Near East and neighbouring areas round about 10,500–9000 BP, with the cat following shortly thereafter (Driscoll et al., 2009). However, the animal that was first domesticated, probably because of its utility for hunting, was the dog, *Canis familiaris*, which was probably domesticated by c. 16,000 BP (Galibert et al., 2011), possibly in southern China (Pang et al., 2009), Central Asia (Shannon et al., 2015), or in Western Eurasia (Frantz et al., 2016). The horse was first domesticated in the steppes of Kazakhstan at c. 5500 BP (Outram et al., 2009), while the chicken was domesticated at several centres in south and South-East Asia (Tixier-Boichard et al., 2011), including the Indus Valley and China (Liu et al., 2006). The donkey was domesticated from the wild ass in north-east Africa and possibly Yemen about 5000 BP (Kimura et al., 2011; Rosenbom et al., 2015), and the water buffalo was domesticated during the Neolithic in various regions in south and eastern Asia (Yang et al., 2008). The pig may have been independently domesticated not only in the Middle East but also in China (Amills, 2011). The domestication of

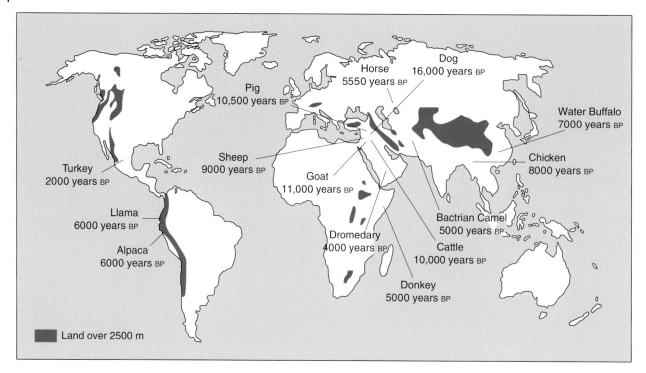

Figure 1.11 The places of origin, with approximate dates, for the most common domesticated animals.

the dromedary camel took place rather late in human history, most likely at the transition between three and four thousand BP (Orlando, 2016), while the wild bactrian camel, whose range extended from the great bend of the Yellow River in north-western China through Mongolia to central Kazakhstan, may have been domesticated about 5000 BP (Ji et al., 2009).

There are various pathways by which animal domestication occurred (Larson and Fuller, 2014). One is the *Commensal Pathway*. This does not begin with intentional action on the part of people to bring wild animals into their camps. Instead, as people manipulated their immediate surroundings, different populations of wild animals would have been attracted to elements of the human niche, including human food waste and/or smaller animals that were also attracted to the refuse. Examples of these animals include dogs, cats, pigeons, and guinea pigs. A second pathway is the *Prey Pathway*. Each step along the trajectory, from wild prey to game management, to herd management, to directed breeding, may have been guided by a desire to increase the supply of a resource that had been diminished by hunting. This applied particularly to larger meat-providing animals, such as sheep, goats, and cattle. A third pathway is the *Directed Pathway*. This was the only pathway that began with a deliberate objective to domesticate a species. Species, such as donkeys and camels, were deliberately brought into the human niche for reasons such as their utility as sources of transport.

It was the Near East, and in particular the Hilly Flanks, that was especially important for both plant and animal domestication (Bar-Yosef, 1998; Abbo et al., 2010; Zohary et al., 2012). Wild progenitors were numerous in the area, including those of wheat, barley, flax, lentils, olives, peas, sheep, goats, cows, and pigs – a list that includes what are still the most valuable crops and livestock of the modern world (Diamond, 1997, 2002; Morris, 2010).

An important and slightly later development in agriculture was irrigation (Figure 1.12) and the adoption of

Figure 1.12 Irrigation using animal power, as here in Rajasthan, India, is an example of the use of domesticated stock to change the environment (ASG).

riverine agriculture. Amongst the earliest evidence of artificial irrigation is the mace-head of the Egyptian Scorpion King which shows one of the last pre-dynastic kings ceremonially cutting an irrigation ditch around 5050 BP (Butzer, 1976), although it is possible that irrigation at Sumer in Iraq started even earlier. Irrigation in the American south-west may date back 3000 years (Damp et al., 2002). There are problems of establishing dates for the inception of irrigation in Mesopotamia and elsewhere in the Middle East, but their scale has increased over the last 3000 years (Wilkinson and Rayne, 2010).

A major difference has existed in the development of agriculture in the Old and New Worlds; in the latter there were few counterparts to the range of domesticated animals which were an integral part of the former (Sherratt, 1981). A further critical difference was that in the Old World the secondary applications of domesticated animals were explored. This has been termed 'The Secondary Products Revolution' (Greenfield, 2010). The plough was particularly important in this process (Figure 1.13) – the first application of animal power to the mechanization of agriculture. Closely connected to this was the use of the cart, which both permitted more intensive farming and enabled the transportation of its products. Furthermore, the development of textiles from animal fibres afforded, for the first time, a commodity which could be produced for exchange in areas where arable farming was not the optimal form of land use. Finally, the use of animal milk provided a means whereby large herds could use marginal or exhausted land, encouraging the development of the pastoral sector with transhumance or nomadism. Organic residues preserved in pottery vessels have provided direct evidence for early milk use in the Neolithic period in the Near East and south-eastern Europe, North Africa, Denmark, and the British Isles, and have demonstrated the early production of cheese (Dunne et al., 2012; Salque et al., 2013).

This Secondary Products Revolution therefore had radical effects, and the change took place over quite a short period. The plough was invented some 5000 years ago, and was used in Mesopotamia, Assyria, and Egypt. The wheeled cart was first produced in the Near East in the fourth millennium BC, and rapidly spread from there to both Europe and India (Figure 1.14) during the course of the third millennium. The development of other means of transport preceded the wheel. Sledge-runners found in Scandinavian bogs have been dated to the Mesolithic period (Cole, 1970: 42).

The origins of seafaring are difficult to establish. On the one hand by c. 800,000 years ago, people seem to have crossed a deep water strait between Bali and Lombok in South-East Asia, and humans crossed a 100 kilometre-wide strait to reach Australia by c. 50,000

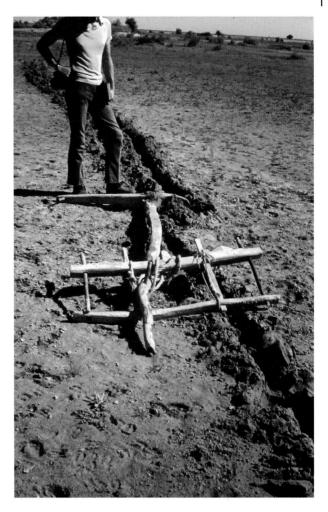

Figure 1.13 The development of ploughs provided humans with the ability to transform soils. This simple type is in Pakistan (ASG).

Figure 1.14 In the Secondary Products Revolution, cattle, such as these in Haryana, India, were used as beasts of burden, for pulling ploughs, and as a source of products such as leather (ASG).

years ago (Broodbank, 2006; Erlandson 2010; Balme, 2013). However, in the Mediterranean world there is very little firm evidence of any maritime activity until the late Pleistocene (Knapp, 2010) and this is also the time when humans may have navigated down the coast of the Americas (Erlandson et al., 2011). Neolithic people undertook a 130 kilometre open sea voyage to reach Taiwan by c. 5000 years ago (Rolett et al., 2011). Indeed, by the Neolithic era humans had developed boats, floats, and rafts that were able to cross to Mediterranean islands and sail the Irish Sea. Dugout canoes could hardly have been common before polished stone axes and adzes came into general use during Neolithic times, although some paddle and canoe remains are recorded from Mesolithic sites in northern Europe. The middens of the hunter-fishers of the Danish Neolithic contain bones of deep-sea fish such as cod, showing that these people certainly had seaworthy craft with which to exploit ocean resources.

Both the domestication of animals and the cultivation of plants have been among the most significant causes of the human impact. Pastoralists have had many major effects – for example, on soil erosion – and nomadic pastoralists are probably more conscious than agriculturalists that they share the earth with other living things. That said, heavily grazed lands tend to have considerably lower infiltration capacities than those found in ungrazed lands and this can change the nature and density of vegetation cover, thereby affecting erosion rates, including wind erosion (Aubault et al., 2015).

Agriculturalists, on the other hand, deliberately transform nature in a sense which nomadic pastoralists do not. Their main role has been to simplify the world's ecosystems. Thus in the prairies of North America, by ploughing and seeding the grasslands, farmers have eliminated a hundred species of native prairie herbs and grasses, which they replace with pure stands of wheat, corn, or alfalfa. On a world basis (see Harlan, 1976) such simplification is evident. For example, today four crops (wheat, rice, maize, and potatoes) at the head of the list of food supplies contribute more tonnage to the world total than the next twenty-six crops combined. This simplification may reduce the stability of ecosystems (but see Section 13.6).

The spread of agriculture has transformed land cover at a global scale. As Table 1.5 shows, there have been great changes in the area covered by particular biomes since pre-agricultural times. It is possible (Ruddiman, 2014) that mid-Holocene deforestation and land-cover change, including rice irrigation in China, modified global climates by releasing carbon dioxide and methane into the atmosphere, and by altering albedo (He et al., 2014). Even in the last three hundred years the areas of cropland and pasture have increased by around five- to sixfold (Goldewijk, 2001).

1.6 Mining and Metals

One further development in human cultural and technological life, which was to increase human power, was the mining of ores and the smelting of metals (Roberts et al., 2009). Neolithic cultures used native copper from the eighth millennium BC onwards, but evidence for its smelting occurs at Catal Hüyük in Turkey and in Jordan from the sixth millennium BC (Grattan et al., 2007) and in Serbia from the fifth millennium BC (Radivojević et al., 2010). The spread of metal working into other areas was rapid particularly in the second half of the fifth millennium (Muhly, 1997) and by 2500 BC bronze products were in use from Britain in the west to northern China in the east. The smelting of iron ores may date back to the

Table 1.5 Estimated changes in the areas of the major land cover types between pre-agricultural times and the present.*

Land cover type	Pre-agricultural area	Present area	Percent change
Total forest	46.8	39.3	−16.0
Tropical forest	12.8	12.3	−3.9
Other forest	34.0	27.0	−20.6
Woodland	9.7	7.9	−18.6
Shrubland	16.2	14.8	−8.6
Grassland	34.0	27.4	−19.4
Tundra	7.4	7.4	0.0
Desert	15.9	15.6	−1.9
Cultivation	0.0	17.6	+1760.0

* Figures are given in millions of square kilometres.
Source: from J.T. Matthews (personal communication), in Meyer and Turner (1994). With permission of Cambridge University Press.

late third millennium BC. Metal working required enormous amounts of wood and so led to deforestation and erosion, as in parts of China (Li et al., 2011) and Africa (Lupo et al., 2015). It also caused contamination of sediments as early as the mid-Holocene (Grattan et al., 2016). Metallurgy was also invented independently in the Andean area (Peru and Bolivia), with the use of gold starting about 4000 years ago and of copper about two thousand years ago (Serneels, 2017).

In recent decades fossil-fuelled machinery has allowed mining activity to expand to such a degree that in terms of the amount of material moved its effects are reputed to rival the natural processes of erosion. Taking overburden into account, the total amount of material moved by the mining industry globally was estimated by Young (1992) as at least 28 billion tonnes – about 1.7 times the estimated amount of sediment carried each year by the world's rivers. However, the rate at which many major minerals are being mined is steadily increasing. This can be illustrated by the statistics for iron ore. In 1974 the world figure was c. 900 million tonnes. By 2012 this figure had risen to 3000 million tonnes, an increase of more than three times. The comparable figures for coal are 3000 million tonnes in 1974, and 7924 million tonnes in 2012, an increase of 2.6 times (http://www.bgs.ac.uk/mineralsuk/statistics/home.html, accessed December 2017). In China, there has been a huge increase in the production of aggregates for cement manufacture, and China is currently using more cement in three years than the USA used in the whole of the twentieth century (https://www.washingtonpost.com/news/wonk/wp/2015/03/24/how-china-used-more-cement-in-3-years-than-the-u-s-did-in-the-entire-20th-century/?utm_term=.60b7f8d7219a, accessed December 2017). The environmental impacts of mineral extraction are diverse but extensive, and relate not only to the process of excavation and removal, but also to the processes of mineral concentration, smelting, and refining (Table 1.6). For instance, in mining areas, increased weathering leads to increased export of ions in stream flows. This is the case in the Appalachian coal mining area of the eastern USA. Here excess overburden from mountain-top mining is disposed of in constructed fills in small valleys adjacent to the mining site. Leachate from these increases the downstream concentrations of major ions (Lindberg et al., 2011; Griffith et al., 2012; Hopkins et al., 2013a). In areas with underground mining, acidic metal-rich mine drainage can develop as a result of accelerated oxidation of iron pyrite (FeS_2) and other sulphidic minerals resulting from the exposure of these minerals to both oxygen and water, as a consequence of the mining and processing of metal ores and coals (Raymond and Oh, 2009). Mining also had an impact on stream sediments and channel forms, as is evident for gold mining areas in Australia (Lawrence et al., 2016).

Table 1.6 Environmental impacts of mineral extraction.

Activity	Potential impacts
Excavation and ore removal	• Destruction of plant and animal habitat, human settlements, and other features (surface mining)
	• Land subsidence (underground mining)
	• Increased erosion: silting of lakes and streams
	• Waste generation (overburden)
	• Acid drainage (if ore or overburden contain sulphur compounds) and metal contamination of lakes, streams, and groundwater
Ore concentration	• Waste generation (tailings)
	• Organic chemical contamination (tailings often contain residues of chemicals used in concentrators)
	• Acid drainage (if ore contains sulphur compounds) and metal contamination of lakes, streams, and groundwater
Smelting/ refining	• Air pollution (substances emitted can include sulphur dioxide, arsenic, lead, cadmium, and other toxic substances
	• Waste generation (slag)
	• Impacts of producing energy (most of the energy used in extracting minerals goes into smelting and refining)

Source: Young (1992: table 5). Reproduced with permission of Worldwatch Institute.

1.7 Modern Industrial and Urban Civilizations

Although humans may have constructed modest communal settlements before the adoption of domestication (Watkins, 2010), it was within a few thousand years of the uptake of cereal agriculture that people began to gather into ever-larger settlements (cities) and into more institutionalized social formations (states). After around 6000 BP cities developed in the basins of the Tigris and Euphrates, and more followed by c. 5000 BP elsewhere in the Middle East (Figure 1.9), in the coastal Mediterranean, the Nile Valley, the Indus plain, and coastal Peru. Subsequently, cities evolved which had considerable human populations. It has been estimated that Nineveh may have had a population of 700,000, that Augustan Rome may have had a population of around one million, and that Carthage (Figure 1.15a), at its fall in 146 BC, had 700,000 (Thirgood, 1981). Another large city of the Roman Empire was Leptis Magna in modern-day Libya (Figure 1.15b). Such cities would have already exercised a considerable influence on their environs, but this influence was never as extensive as that of the last

(a)

(b)

Figure 1.15 (a) Carthage, in northern Tunisia, was one of the great cities of the ancient world, while in Libya (b) the Romans also built the city of Leptis Magna (ASG).

Figure 1.16 Urbanization (and, in particular, the growth of large conurbations such as Kuwait) is an increasingly important phenomenon. Urbanization causes and accelerates a whole suite of environmental problems (ASG).

few centuries; for the modern era, especially since the late seventeenth century, has witnessed the transformation of, or revolution in, culture and technology – the development of major industries. This, like domestication, has reduced the space required to sustain each individual and has increased the intensity with which resources are utilized.

Modern science and modern medicine have compounded these effects, leading to accelerating population increase even in non-industrial societies. Urbanization has gone on apace (Figure 1.16), and it is now recognized that large cities have their own environmental problems (Cooke et al., 1982) and environmental effects (Douglas, 1983). Cities can be conceived of as landforms, with special landforming processes, including concrete speleothem formation and sinkhole collapse (Dixon et al., 2017). Urban ecology, a transdisciplinary enterprise that integrates ecological, geographical, planning, and social sciences (Wu, 2014) has become a major research area (Douglas and James, 2014). Urban areas are hubs for

people, infrastructure, and commerce, requiring extensive resources and putting intense pressure on the environment. They account for about 60% of all residential water use, 75% of energy use, 80% of the wood used for industrial purposes, and 80% of human greenhouse gas emissions. As Haase et al. (2014: 414) remark, 'Understanding how urban ecosystems work, how they change, and what limits their performance can add to the understanding of ecosystem change and governance in an ever more human-dominated world'. As Table 1.7 shows, the world now has some enormous urban agglomerations. By 2015 there were over 500 urban areas with a population greater than 1 million, and 12 with a population over 20 million. The urban population in 2014 accounted for 54% of the total global population, up from 34% in 1960 (http://www.who.int/gho/urban_health/situation_trends/urban_population_growth_text/en/, accessed December 2017).

Cities, in turn, have large ecological footprints. They suck in resources and materials and export vast amounts of waste, so that it is now possible to use such terms as 'urban hydrology', 'urban ecology', and 'urban geomorphology' (Gurnell et al., 2007). In China, new urban areas are being created by removing mountaintops, as is the case with New Lanzhou City. Cities have their own range of internal environmental impacts and characteristics, and these are referred to elsewhere in this book (Table 1.8) and some of their wildlife impacts are discussed by Goddard et al. (2010) and Aronson et al. (2014).

Another major development was the perfecting of sea-going ships in the sixteenth and seventeenth centuries. This was part of our industrial and economic transformation, and was the time when mainly self-contained but developing regions of the world coalesced so that the ecumene became to all intents and purposes

Table 1.7 World's urban agglomerations of ten million or more inhabitants in 2016.

Agglomeration	Country	Population
1 Guangzhou	China	47,700,000
2 Tokyo	Japan	39,500,000
3 Shanghai	China	30,900,000
4 Jakarta	Indonesia	28,100,000
5 Delhi	India	26,400,000
6 Seoul	South Korea	24,400,000
7 Karachi	Pakistan	24,300,000
8 Manila	Philippines	23,300,000
9 Mumbai	India	23,200,000
10 Mexico City	Mexico	22,100,000
11 New York	United States	22,000,000
12 São Paulo	Brazil	21,800,000
13 Beijing	China	21,100,000
14 Osaka	Japan	17,800,000
15 Dhaka	Bangladesh	17,600,000
15 Los Angeles	United States	17,600,000
17 Lagos	Nigeria	17,100,000
18 Krung Thep	Thailand	16,900,000
18 Moskva	Russia	16,900,000
20 Al-Qāhirah (Cairo)	Egypt	16,800,000
21 Kolkata	India	16,000,000
21 Buenos Aires	Argentina	15,800,000
23 London	United Kingdom	14,400,000
24 Istanbul	Turkey	14,300,000
25 Tehran	Iran	13,700,000
26 Johannesburg	South Africa	13,400,000
27 Rio de Janeiro	Brazil	12,700,000
28 Paris	France	12,400,000
29 Tianjin	China	11,400,000
30 Kinshasa	Democratic Republic of the Congo	10,600,000
31 Bengaluru	India	10,576,167
32 Chennai	India	10,400,000
33 Nagoya	Japan	10,300,000
34 Lahore	Pakistan	10,200,000
35 Xiamen	China	10,000,000

Table 1.8 Urban environments.

Phenomenon	Discussion in this book (section)
Accelerated salinization	4.3
Areas of land reclamation and offshore islands	6.3
Biodiversity	3.3
Channelisation and burying of streams	6.8
Ground levelling for airports, etc.	6.2
Ground subsidence caused by fluid extraction	6.4
Groundwater augmentation and extraction	5.5
Increased sediment loads during construction	4.26
Landslides produced by building on slopes	6.12
Pits produced by excavation of building materials	6.2
Pollution of air	2.19 and 7.14
Pollution of soil (e.g. by heavy metals)	4.18
Pollution of water	5.6
Runoff generation and floods from storm drains,	
sewers & impermeable surfaces	5.3.6
Soil transformation (compaction, addition of rubble,	
loss of organics, etc.)	4.14
Sulphation and other forms of weathering	6.12
Urban animals	3.3
Urban heat island effect	7.11
Waste dumps and landfill	6.3

continuous. The invention of the steam engine in the late eighteenth century, and the internal combustion engine in the late nineteenth century, massively increased human access to energy and lessened dependence on animals, wind, and water. The number of tractors in the world as a whole increased from 0.3 million in 1920 to over 26 million in 2000 (McNeill, 2000: table 7.2). The invention of the gasoline-powered chainsaw, especially after 1950, was another important development. This cutting-edge technology allowed humans to fell trees 100 or 1000 times faster than with axes (McNeill, 2000: 307).

1.8 The Great Acceleration

The twentieth century was a time of extraordinary change (McNeill and Engelke, 2016). The human population soared from 1.5 to 6 billion, the world's economy increased fifteenfold, the world's energy use thirteen to fourteenfold, freshwater use ninefold, and the irrigated area fivefold. In the hundred centuries from the dawn of agriculture to 1900, McNeill (2003) calculated that humanity only used about two-thirds as much energy (most of it from biomass) that it used it the twentieth century. Indeed, he argued that humankind used more energy in the twentieth century than in all preceding human history put together. In addition he suggests that the seas surrendered more fish in the twentieth century than in all previous centuries, and that the forest and woodland area shrank by about 20%, accounting for perhaps half the net deforestation in world history. This is also a topic that has been discussed by Waters et al. (2016), who draw attention to the rapid development in the use of artificial materials. For example, the manufacture of new organic polymers (plastics), which were initially developed in the early years of the twentieth century, rapidly grew from the 1950s to an annual production of around 380 Tg by 2015 (Geyer et al., 2017). Likewise, concrete, which the Romans invented, has become the primary building material since the Second World War. The period from 1995 to 2015 accounts for more than half of the 500,000 Tg of concrete ever produced, and may be equivalent to around 1 kg m^{-2}.

One measure of the extent of the human impact is the human appropriation of net primary production (HANPP) as a percentage of the total amount of net primary productivity (NPP) generated on land. There is a considerable range of estimates of HANPP as a percentage of NPP, but Imhoff et al. (2004) give a global figure of around 20%, but also point to great differences between the continents, with values ranging from c. 6.1% for Latin America to 80.4% for south-central Asia. Humans have appropriated a large amount of the world's biomass for their own use and Smil (2011) has estimated that through harvesting, deforestation, and conversion of grasslands and wetlands, humans have reduced the stock of global terrestrial plant mass by as much as 45% in the last 2000 years, with a third of this being achieved in the twentieth century.

To conclude, we can recognize certain trends in human manipulation of the environment which have taken place in the modern era. The first of these is that the ways in which humans are affecting the environment are proliferating, so that we now live on what some people have argued is a human-dominated planet (Vitousek et al., 1997). For example, nearly all the powerful pesticides post-date the Second World War, and the same applies to the construction of nuclear reactors. Secondly, environmental issues that were once locally confined have become regional or even global problems. An instance of this is the way in which substances such as DDT, lead, and sulphates are found at the poles, far removed from the industrial societies that produced them. This is one aspect of increasing globalization. Thirdly, the complexity, magnitude, and frequency of impacts are probably increasing; for instance, a massive modern dam like that at Aswan in Egypt (opened in 1970) or the Three Gorges Dam in China (opened in 2003) has very different impacts from a small Roman one. Finally, compounding the effects of rapidly expanding populations is a general increase in per capita consumption and environmental impact (Myers and Kent, 2003) (Table 1.9). Energy resources are being developed at an ever-increasing rate, giving humans enormous power to transform the environment, not least in China (see Section 13.4). Increasing amounts of energy are also being harvested from hydropower schemes, which require the construction of major dams (Zarfl et al., 2015), the consequences of which for river flow and sediment trapping are very major. At least 3700 dams, each with a capacity of more than 1 megawatts, are currently either planned or under construction, primarily in countries with emerging economies. Particular concern has been expressed about the potential impacts of rampant dam construction across the Amazon basin, especially on its floodplains and the oceanic waters into which it flows (Latrubesse et al., 2017).

Table 1.9a Some indicators of change in the global economy from 1950–2015.

World indicator	1950	2005	Change(xn)	2015	Change (xn)
Grain production (million tonnes)	631	2008	3.18	2473	3.92
Meat production (million tonnes)	44	264	6.0	259	5.88
Coal consumption (million tonnes of oil equivalent)	1074	2597	2.42	3839	3.57
Oil consumption (million tonnes)	470	3861	8.21	4331	9.21
Natural gas consumption (million tonnes of oil equivalent)	171	2512	14.69		–
Car production (million)	8.0	46	5.75	91	11.38
Bike production (million)	11	124	11.27		–
Human population (million)	2555	6469	2.53	7349	2.88

Table 1.9b Scale of changes between 1890s and 1990s (modified and updated from McNeill, 2005: tables 1 and 2).

Indicator	Increase (x)
Freshwater use	9
Marine fish catch	35
Cropland	2
Irrigated area	5
Pasture area	1.8
Carbon dioxide emissions	17
Sulphur dioxide emissions	13
Lead emissions	8
Cattle population	4
Goat population	5
Pig population	9
World industrial output	40
World energy use	13
Coal production	7
Urban population	13
World economy	14

Figure 1.17 (a) World energy consumption since 1860, based on data from the United Nations. (b) World energy consumption since 1965 showing the role of different sources. (c) World energy consumption by part of world, based on data from BP Statistical Review of World Energy, 2015. *Source:* https://www.bp.com/content/dam/bp/pdf/energy-economics/statistical-review-2015/bp-statistical-review-of-world-energy-2015-full-report.pdf (accessed January 2018).

Figure 1.17a shows worldwide energy consumption since 1860 on a per capita basis, while Figures 1.17b and c show energy consumption since 1965 in terms of sources and regions. It is important to recognize, however, that there are huge differences in the likely environmental impacts of different economies in different parts of the world. The environmental impact, as measured by the so-called ecological footprint, is twelve times greater, for example, for the average American than for the average Indian (Wackernagel and Rees, 1995). On a global basis, our ecological footprint, according to the 2010 WWF *Living Planet Report*, doubled between 1961 and 2007.

Modern technologies have immense power output. A pioneer steam engine in AD 1800 might rate at 8–16 kilowatts. Modern railway diesels top 3.5 megawatts, and a large aero engine 70 megawatts. Figure 1.18 shows how the human impact on six 'component indicators of the biosphere' has increased over time. This graph is based on work by Kates et al. (1990). Each component indicator was taken to be 0% for 10,000 BP) and 100% for 1985. They then estimated the dates by which each component had reached successive quartiles (that is, 25, 50, and 75%) of its total change at 1985. They believe that about half of the components have changed more in the single generation since 1950 than in the whole of human history before that date. McNeill (2000) provides an exceptionally fine picture of all the changes in the environment that humans achieved in the twentieth century, while Steffen et al.

(2015) show the trends of various socio-economic and environmental indicators from 1750 onwards, illustrating the dramatic changes during what supporters of the Anthropocene concept call the 'Great Acceleration.'

Humans now play a very substantial role in major biogeochemical cycling, including the nitrogen cycle. For example, human activities now convert more N_2 from the atmosphere into reactive forms than all of the Earth's

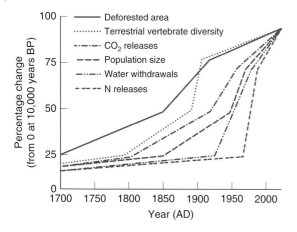

Figure 1.18 Percentage change (from assumed zero human impact at 10,000 BP) of selected human impacts on the environment.

Table 1.10 Types of global environmental change.

Type	Characteristic	Examples
Systemic	Direct impact on globally functioning system	(a) Industrial and land use emissions of 'greenhouse' gases (b) Industrial and consumer emissions of ozone-depleting gases (c) Land cover changes in albedo
Cumulative	Impact through worldwide distribution of change Impact through magnitude of change (share of global resource)	(a) Groundwater pollution and depletion (b) Species depletion/genetic alteration (biodiversity) (a) Deforestation (b) Industrial toxic pollutants (c) Soil depletion on prime agricultural lands

Source: from Turner et al. (1990: table 1). Reproduced with permission of Elsevier.

terrestrial processes combined (Galloway et al., 2008; Rockström et al., 2009). This is achieved through four processes: industrial fixation of N_2 to ammonia, agricultural fixation of N_2 via cultivation of leguminous crops, fossil-fuel combustion, and biomass burning. Much of this reactive N_2 eventually ends up in the environment, polluting waterways and coastal zones, and changing the species composition of grasslands (Stevens et al., 2015). Atmospheric deposition of N has been reported to have negative impacts on a range of European habitats, including acid grasslands and steppes. It has the potential to enrich the N content of soils, resulting in increased plant growth and hence competition for light. Reductions in biodiversity can result (Stevens et al., 2010; Zhang et al., 2014).

Above all, as a result of the escalating trajectory of environmental transformation it is now possible to talk about *global* environmental change. There are two components to this (Turner et al., 1990): systemic global change and cumulative global change. In the systemic meaning, 'global' refers to the spatial scale of operation and comprises such issues as global changes in climate brought about by atmospheric pollution. This is a topic discussed at length in Chapters 7–12. In the cumulative meaning, 'global' refers to the areal or substantive accumulation of localized change, and a change is seen to be 'global' if it occurs on a worldwide scale, or represents a significant fraction of the total environmental phenomenon or global resource. Both types of change are closely intertwined. For example, the burning of vegetation can lead to systemic change through such mechanisms as carbon dioxide release and albedo modification, and to cumulative change through its impact on soil and biotic diversity (Table 1.10). It is for this reason that we now talk of Earth System Science and recognize the complex

interactions that take place at a multitude of scales on our planet (Steffen et al., 2004) (see also Section 13.3).

1.9 Methods of Study

A range of techniques has been employed in trying to establish the timing and the extent of the human impact on the environment and to try and disentangle human and natural drivers of change. These include analyzing evidence from cores from lakes (Mills et al., 2017), ice cores (Barbante et al., 2017) bogs and the like, which can give a long-term, often well-dated, high-resolution picture of environmental change which, when compared with data on potential drivers of change, can be used to identify the human roles (e.g. O'Hara et al., 1993). Among these analyses are those of pollen, which can be used to identify, *inter alia*, vegetation change and the introduction of domesticated crops (Rösch and Lechterbeck, 2016), those of diatoms (Smol and Stoermer, 2010) which can be used to infer changes in water pH and of acid rain, and those of ostracods (Jones et al., 2015), which are especially useful for investigating changes in lacustrine environments. Faecal remains, including spherulites, may mark the introduction of grazing by domestic stock (Henry et al., 2017). Palaeosols with a distinct human signature may also be utilized (e.g. Beach et al., 2015). Related to this is the presence of anthropogenic materials, such as artefacts, coal, fly ash, slag, human-generated isotopes, or pottery, in sedimentary sequences (e.g. Tang et al., 2015; Grimley et al., 2017). Also important has been the collection of historical and archival material (Trimble and Cooke, 1991; Trimble, 2008b), including old ground photographs of, for example, vegetation type (Brusca et al., 2013), glaciers, gullies, soil erosion, debris flows, and arroyos (Cerney, 2010; Webb et al., 2010; Frankl et al., 2011), and the use of sequential maps and remotely sensed images (e.g. Bakoariniaina et al., 2006). The study of sequences of air photographs has particular value (Micheletti et al., 2015). In recent years several technological developments have led to enhanced resolution and coverage of datasets on, for example, topography and its change over time, which allow an unprecedented insight into the changing face of the Earth and the human imprints upon it. Equally, long-term monitoring, when it exists, can indicate the timing and scale of landscape changes (Burt, 1994)

and of phenomena such as water pollution, ozone depletion, and soil erosion. We have learnt much about the state of the biosphere from long-term censuses of, for example, common bird species. Numerical modelling is an increasingly important approach to understanding of systems behaviour and the prediction of possible future changes (e.g. Nearing et al., 2005), with, for example, GCMs (Global Circulation Models) being vital for creating future climatic scenarios. As discussed in Section 8.1, such models are not without limitations. In the area of hydrology, literally hundreds of studies have employed SWAT (Soil & Water Assessment Tool), which is a river basin scale model developed to quantify the impact of land management practices in large, complex watersheds (Douglas-Mankin et al., 2010).

Guide to Reading

Baker, A.R.H. (2003) *Geography and History, Bridging the Divide.* Cambridge: Cambridge University Press. Chapter 3 contains a valuable and perceptive discussion of environmental geographies and histories.

Barker, G. (2006) *The Agricultural Revolution in Prehistory: Why Did Foragers Become Farmers?* Cambridge: Cambridge University Press. An impressive assessment at a global scale of what drove foragers to become farmers near the transition to the Holocene.

Barker, G. and Goucher, C. (eds) (2015) *The Cambridge World History: Volume 2, A World with Agriculture, 12,000 BCE–500 CE.* Cambridge: Cambridge University Press. A major compilation on the history of agriculture, which includes discussions of domestication, pastoralism, etc.

Cuff, D.J. and Goudie, A.S. (eds) (2009) *The Oxford Companion to Global Change.* New York: Oxford University Press. A multi-author encyclopedia of global change.

Diamond, J. (1997) *Guns, Germs and Steel.* London: Chatto and Windus. A lively review of human history over the last 13,000 years.

Douglas, I. and James, P. (2014) *Urban Ecology: An Introduction.* London: Routledge. A wide-ranging discussion of the multiple impacts that urbanization has had.

Goudie, A.S. (ed.) (1997) *The Human Impact Reader: Readings and Case Studies.* Oxford: Blackwell. A collection of key papers on many of the themes discussed in this book.

Goudie, A.S. and Viles, H. (1997) *The Earth Transformed.* Oxford: Blackwell. An introductory treatment of the human impact, with many case studies.

Goudie, A.S. and Viles, H.A. (2016) *Geomorphology in the Anthropocene.* Cambridge: Cambridge University Press. A discussion of the Anthropocene concept and the ways in which the geomorphological environment has changed.

Govorushko, S.M. (2011) *Natural Processes and Human Impacts.* Heidelberg: Springer. A highly comprehensive and well-illustrated survey.

Meyer, W.B. (1996) *Human Impact on the Earth.* Cambridge: Cambridge University Press. A good point of entry to the literature that brims over with thought-provoking epigrams.

Middleton, N.J. (2013) *The Global Casino.* London: Routledge. The fifth edition of an outstanding introductory text by a geographer, which is well illustrated and clearly written.

Morris, I. (2010) *Why the West Rules – For Now.* London: Profile Books. A massive survey of the patterns of development since prehistory and how they have varied in the west and the east.

Oppenheimer, S. (2002) *Out of Eden: Peopling of the World.* London: Constable. A very accessible account of human development in prehistory.

Ponting, C. (2007) *A New Green History of the World.* London: Penguin. The second edition of an engaging and informative treatment of how humans have transformed the Earth through time.

Scarre, C. (ed.) (2005) *The Human Past: World History and The Development of Human Societies.* London: Thames & Hudson. A splendid account of current ideas about the evolution of humans and human societies.

Simmons, I.G. (1996) *Changing the Face of the Earth: Culture, Environment and History* (2nd edn).

Oxford: Blackwell. A characteristically amusing and perceptive review of many facets of the role of humans in transforming the Earth, from an essentially historical perspective.

Simmons, I.G. (1997) *Humanity and Environment: A Cultural Ecology.* Harlow: Longman. A broad account of some major themes relating to humans and the environment.

Steffen, W. and 10 others (2004) *Global Change and the Earth System.* Berlin: Springer. A multi-author, high-level, Earth System Science-based overview of environmental change at a global scale.

Turner, B.L. II (ed.) (1990) *The Earth as Transformed by Human Action.* Cambridge: Cambridge University Press. A great analysis of global and regional changes over the past 300 years.

2

The Human Impact on Vegetation

CHAPTER OVERVIEW

Humans have done much to transform the vegetation cover of the Earth. From very early times, they have used fire to modify the environment. Also important has been grazing by domestic livestock. However, it is deforestation that has been the most potent cause of change. Humans have also modified or contributed to the character of some major biomes, including secondary forests, desert margins, savannas, prairies, lowland heaths, and Mediterranean shrublands. Other major changes have been caused by the introduction of alien species around the world, species that sometimes invade explosively, and by pollution episodes. Finally, attention is drawn to changes in genetic composition.

2.1 Human Impacts on Nature

Humans now have the greatest biomass or anthropomass of any species and it is an order of magnitude greater than the mass of all terrestrial mammals alive today (Smil, 2011). Before discussing how this vast mass of humans has had an impact on vegetation, let us consider the sorts of ways in which humans have modified nature – both vegetation and animals, for changes in the one have an impact on the other, and *vice versa*. In any event, many of the factors promoting change are similar or overlap. If we restrict ourselves to current trends and pressures, three reports are of particular interest. First, in 2010, the Royal Botanic Gardens at Kew produced a report on 'Plants at Risk' (http:www.kew.org/science/plants-at-risk/) in which an attempt was made to summarize what were the world's most endangered plant habitats and to identify what the main threats were to plant life. As Figure 2.1a shows, the most endangered habitats are tropical wet forests, with almost two-thirds of plant species endangered. Areas least suitable for conversion to agriculture, such as wetlands and deserts, contain the smallest proportions of threatened plant species, with 4% and 0.5% of threatened species respectively. Some of the threats to plant life are natural, accounting for 18.7% of the total (Figure 2.1b). These include natural disasters as well as the intrinsic characteristics of some species, such as limited dispersal ability, restricted range, or poor reproduction. The biggest human threats, which account for 81.3% of the total, are agriculture, harvesting, and other types of development. Secondly, the Zoological Society of London produced a report on global threats to animals (Baillie et al., 2010), and Figure 2.2, based on their work, shows the threats posed to various types of organism and also population trends in fish, amphibians, reptiles, birds, and mammals since 1970. Agriculture and aquaculture emerge as the most important type of threat. Thirdly, in 2016, a group of organizations in the UK, concerned with nature conservation, examined the great range of factors that were impacting on the state of the flora and fauna. This was the 'State of Nature Report' (Hayhow et al., 2016). Table 2.1 illustrates both the range of human impacts involved and their positive and negative effects. The main impacts were associated with (1) intensive management of agricultural land, (2) climate change, (3) low-intensity management of agricultural land, (4) increasing management of other habitats, (5) hydrological change (e.g. drainage), (6) urbanization, (7) habitat creation (e.g. of wetlands), (8) increasing plantation forest area, (9) decreasing forest management, and (10) decreasing management of other habitats.

Although there are hopeful signs of an increasing concern with protection and conservation of nature (see Section 13.5), threats persist, and as Watson et al. (2017) have pointed out, there have been alarming losses,

Human Impact on the Natural Environment: Past, Present and Future, Eighth Edition. Andrew S. Goudie.
© 2019 John Wiley & Sons Ltd. Published 2019 by John Wiley & Sons Ltd.
Companion website: www.wiley.com/go/goudie/human-impact-natural-environment

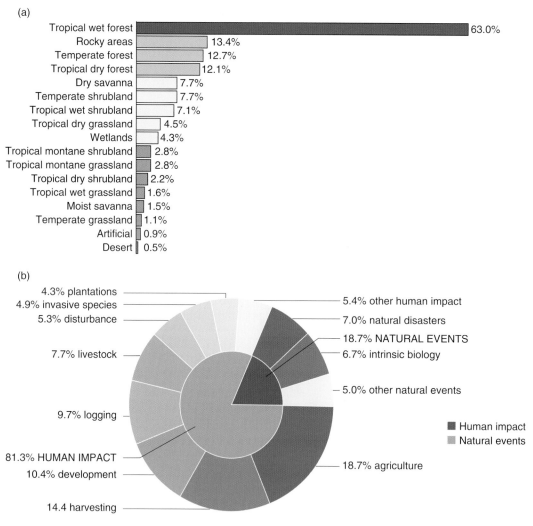

Figure 2.1 (a) Percentage of plant species at risk for different biomes and (b) the main threats, both natural and human. *Source:* adapted from Kew, *Plants at Risk* (2010).

comprising one-tenth (3.3 million km²) of global wilderness areas (i.e. biologically and ecologically largely intact landscapes that are mostly free of human disturbance) over the last two decades, particularly in the Amazon (30%) and central Africa (14%). They also assessed increases in the protection of wilderness over the same time frame and showed that these efforts are failing to keep pace with the rate of wilderness loss, which is nearly double the rate of protection. The rate of increase in the human footprint has slowed in recent years (Venter et al., 2016) but there are still some hotspots of human impact where effects on biodiversity are especially high. As with animals (see Section 3.8), these hotspots of biodiversity deserve particular attention in terms of protection and conservation. Meta-analyses (Van der Ent and Lambers, 2016) indicate about 20 global biodiversity hotspots with >3000 plant species per 10,000 km². The top five localities with >5000 species per 10,000 km², covering just 0.2% of the Earth's land area surface, but

harbouring 6.2% of total plant diversity, are: (i) Costa Rica-Chocó; (ii) Atlantic Brazil; (iii) Tropical Eastern Andes; (iv) Northern Borneo; and (v) New Guinea. Although most biodiversity hotspots are in moist tropical regions, as in south-east Asia (Hughes, 2017), there are also regions with a Mediterranean climate that are extremely species-rich: the South African Cape (*fynbos*), California (*chaparral*) in the United States, and the sandplains of south-western Australia. Some islands (see Section 3.5) are also global centres of diversity and endemicity, notably New Caledonia, Madagascar, and the islands of the Malesian archipelago.

2.2 Vegetation Change: Introduction

Humankind has possibly had a greater influence on plant life than on any of the other components of the environment (Ellis, 2011). We have appropriated a large amount of the world's biomass for our own use (Haberl et al., 2007), and Smil (2011) has estimated that through harvesting, deforestation, and conversion of grasslands and wetlands, humans have reduced the stock of global terrestrial plant mass by as much as 45% in the last 2000 years, with a third of this being achieved in the twentieth century. Through the many changes humans have brought about in land use and land cover they have modified soils (Meyer and Turner 1994) (see Chapter 4), changed the quality and quantity of some

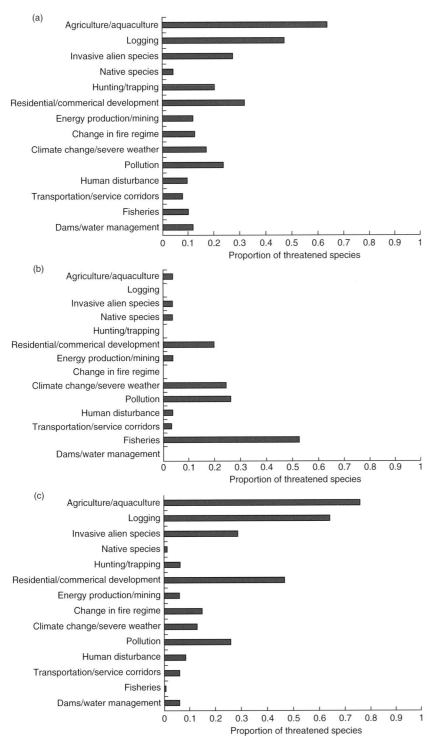

Figure 2.2 Global threats to (a) vertebrates, (b) marine fish, (c) amphibians, (d) reptiles, (e) mammals, and (f) birds. *Source:* adapted from Baillie et al. (2010).

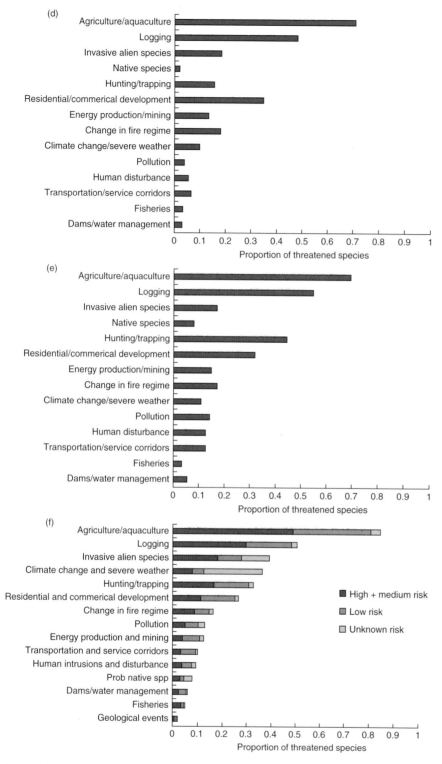

Figure 2.2 (Continued)

natural waters (see Chapter 5), affected geomorphic processes (see Chapter 6), and influenced climates (see Chapter 7). Indeed, the nature of whole landscapes has been transformed by human-induced vegetation change (Figure 2.3). Following Hamel and Dansereau (1949, cited by Frenkel, 1970) we can recognize five principal degrees of interference – each one increasingly remote from pristine conditions. These are:

Table 2.1 Why is nature changing in the UK?

1) **Intensive management of agricultural land**

   Positive factors

   Increased winter survival of some species that eat autumn-sown crops

   Negative factors

   Abandonment of mixed farming systems

   Switch from spring to autumn sowing, reducing food and habitat for many species

   Intensification of grazing regimes

   Increased use of pesticides and fertilisers

   Loss of marginal habitats, such as ponds and hedgerows

2) **Climate change**

   Positive factors

   Northward expansion of species (often with loss in southern parts of their ranges)

   Increased winter survival of some species due to milder temperatures

   Negative factors

   Loss of coastal habitat due to sea level rise

   Increases in sea temperatures adversely affecting marine food webs

   Changes in seasonal weather patterns, such as winter storms and wetter springs

3) **Low-intensity management of agricultural land**

   Positive factors

   Introduction of wildlife-friendly farming through agri-environment schemes

   Negative factors

   Abandonment and reduced grazing, leading to the loss of some habitats

4) **Increasing management of other habitats**

   Positive factors

   Conservation management, often by reinstating traditional methods

   Negative factors

   Increased grazing pressure

5) **Hydrological change**

   Negative factors

   Drainage of wetlands, upland bogs, fens, and lowland wet grasslands

   Over-abstraction of water

6) **Urbanization**

   Negative factors

   Loss of green space, including parks, allotments, and gardens

   Loss of habitats, including lowland heathland to development

   Loss of wildlife-rich brownfield sites

7) **Habitat creation**

   Positive factors

   Creation of new wetlands through conservation work and as a by-product of mineral extraction

   Planting of new broadleaved and mixed woodland

8) **Increasing plantation forest area**

   Positive factors

   Increased habitat area for species using coniferous plantations and woodland edges

   Negative factors

   Loss of the habitat that plantations replace, particularly lowland heaths and upland habitats

9) **Decreasing forest management**

   Negative factors

   Cessation of traditional management practices, such as coppicing, leading to the loss of varied age structure and open habitats within woodland

10) **Decreasing management of other habitats**

   Negative factors

   Abandonment of traditional management, including grazing, burning, and cutting, which is crucial for the maintenance of habitats such as heathland and grassland

Source: Hayhow et al. (2016: 12 and 13).

1) *Natural habitats*: those that develop in the absence of human activities.
2) *Degraded habitats*: those produced by sporadic, yet incomplete, disturbances; for example, the cutting of a forest, burning, and the non-intensive grazing of natural grassland.
3) *Ruderal habitats*: where disturbance is sustained but where there is no intentional substitution of vegetation. Roadsides are an example of a ruderal habitat.
4) *Cultivated habitats*: when constant disturbance is accompanied by the intentional introduction of plants.
5) *Artificial habitats*: which are developed when humans modify the ambient climate and soil, as in greenhouse cultivation.

An alternative model for classifying the extent of human influence on vegetation is provided by Westhoff (1983), who adopts a four-part scheme:

1) *Natural*: a landscape or an ecosystem not influenced by human activity.
2) *Sub-natural*: a landscape or ecosystem partly influenced by humans, but still belonging to the same (structural) formation type as the natural system from which it derives (for example, a wood remaining a wood).
3) *Semi-natural*: a landscape or ecosystem in which flora and fauna are largely spontaneous, but the vegetation structure is altered so that it belongs to another formation type (for example, a pasture, moorland, or heath deriving from a wood).
4) *Cultural*: a landscape or ecosystem in which flora and fauna have been essentially affected by human agency in such a way that the dominant species may have

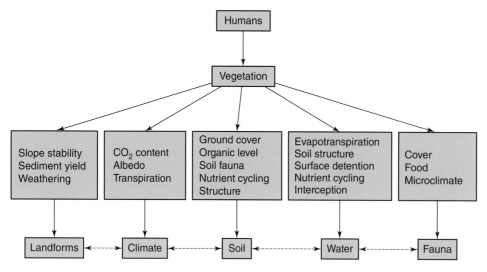

Figure 2.3 Some ramifications of human-induced vegetation change.

been replaced by other species (for example, arable land).

In this chapter we shall be concerned mainly with degraded and ruderal habitats, or sub-natural and semi-natural habitats. However, first we need to consider some of the processes that human societies employ, notably: fire, grazing, and the physical removal of forest.

2.3 The Use of Fire

Humans are known to have used fire since Palaeolithic times (see Section 1.4). They have done so for a great variety of reasons: to clear forest for agriculture, to improve grazing land for domestic animals, or to attract game; to deprive game of cover; to drive game from cover in hunting; to kill or drive away predatory animals, ticks, mosquitoes, and other pests; to repel the attacks of enemies, or burn them out of their refuges; for cooking; to expedite travel; to burn the dead and raise ornamental scars on the living; to provide light; to transmit messages via smoke signalling; to break up stone for tool-making; to protect settlements or encampments from great fires by controlled burning; to satisfy the sheer love of fires as spectacles; to make pottery and smelt ores; to harden spears; to provide warmth; to make charcoal; and to assist in the collection of insects such as crickets for eating. Indeed fire is still much used, especially by pastoralists such as the cattle-keepers of Africa, and by shifting agriculturalists. For example, the Malaysian and Indonesian *ladang* and the *milpa* system of the Maya in Latin America involved the preparation of land for planting by felling or deadening forest, letting the debris dry in the hot season, and burn-

ing it before the commencement of the rainy season. With the first rains, holes were dibbled in the soft ash-covered earth with a planting stick. This system was suited to areas of low population density with sufficiently extensive forest to enable long intervals of 'forest fallow' between burnings. Land which was burned too frequently became overgrown with perennial grasses, which tended to make it difficult to farm with primitive tools. Land cultivated for too long rapidly suffered a deterioration in fertility, while land recently burned was temporarily rich in nutrients.

The use of fire, however, has not been restricted to primitive peoples in the tropics. Remains of charcoal are found in Holocene soil profiles in Britain (Moore, 2000); large parts of North America appear to have suffered fires at regular intervals prior to European settlement (Parshall and Foster, 2002); and in the case of South America the 'great number of fires' observed by Magellan during the historical passage of the Strait that bears his name resulted in the toponym, 'Tierra del Fuego'. Indeed, says Sternberg (1968: 718): 'for thousands of years, man has been putting the New World to the torch, and making it a "land of fire". Given that the native American population may have been greater than once thought, their impact, even in Amazonia, may have been appreciable (Denevan, 1992), and the pattern of trees in the region may still reflect the deliberate planting of trees that they undertook (Levis et al., 2017). North American Indians were also not passive occupants of the land. They managed forests extensively creating 'a dynamic mosaic containing patches of young and old trees, interspersed with patches of grass and shrubs' (Bonnichsen et al., 1999: 442). As a result, some North American forests, prior to European settlement, were open and park-like, not dark and dense.

Figure 2.4 The pindan bush of north-western Australia, composed of *Eucalyptus*, *Acacia* and grasses, is frequently burned. The pattern of the burning shows up clearly on Landsat imagery. *Source:* NASA.

Fire (Figure 2.4) was also central to the way of life of the Australian aboriginals, including those of Tasmania (Hope, 1999), and the carrying of fire sticks was a

common phenomenon. As Blainey (1975: 76) has put it, 'Perhaps never in the history of mankind was there a people who could answer with such unanimity the question: "have you got a light, mate?" There can have been few if any races who for so long were able to practise the delights of incendiarism.' That is not to say that aboriginal burning necessarily caused wholesale modification of Australian vegetation in pre-European times. That is a hotly debated topic (Kohen, 1995).

In neighbouring New Zealand, Polynesians carried out extensive firing of vegetation in pre-European settlement times after their arrival in c. 1280 AD (McWethy et al., 2009), and hunters used fire to facilitate travel and to frighten and trap a major food source – the flightless, hapless moa. The fires continued over a period of about a thousand years up to the period of European settlement (Mark and McSweeney, 1990). The changes in vegetation that resulted were substantial. The forest cover was reduced from about 79% to 53%, and fires were especially effective in the drier forests of central and eastern South Island in the rain shadow of the Southern Alps. Pollen analyses (Figure 2.5) show dramatically the reduction in tall trees and the spread of open shrubland following the introduction of the widespread use of fire by the Maoris (McGlone and Wilmshurst, 1999).

Figure 2.5 Summary percentage pollen diagram, Lake Rotonuiaha, eastern North Island, New Zealand, showing the changes in vegetation brought about in Maori and European times. *Source:* from McGlone and Wilmshurst (1999: figure 1). Reproduced with permission from Elsevier.

2.4 Fires: Natural and Anthropogenic

Although people have used fire for all the reasons that have been mentioned, before one can assess the role of this facet of the human impact, one must ascertain how important fires started by human action are in comparison with those caused naturally, especially by lightning (Bowman et al., 2011). Some natural fires may result from spontaneous combustion, for in certain ecosystems heavy vegetal accumulations may become compacted, rotted, and fermented, thus generating heat. Other natural fires can result from sparks produced by falling boulders and by landslides (Booysen and Tainton, 1984). In the forest lands of the western United States about half the fires are caused by lightning. Lighting starts over half the fires in the pine savanna of Belize, Central America, and about 8% of the fires in the bush of Australia, while in the south of France, nearly all the fires are caused by people. Indeed, fires deliberately caused by arson are the prime cause of conflagrations in Mediterranean Europe (Ganteaume et al., 2013).

One method of gauging the long-term frequency of fires (Clark et al., 1997; Marlon et al., 2012) is to look at fire scars in tree rings and charcoal in lake sediments. In the USA fires occurred with sufficient frequency over wide areas to have effects on annual tree rings and lake cores every 7 to 80 years in pre-European times. The frequency of fires in different environments tends to show some variation. Rotation periods may be in excess of a century for tundra, 60 years for boreal pine forest, 100 years for spruce-dominated ecosystems, 5 to 15 years for savanna, 10 to 15 years for chaparral, and less than 5 years for semi-arid grasslands (Wein and Maclean, 1983). Fire prevalence can be increased by vegetation change, and in the Great Basin and Mojave Desert of the USA the invasion of non-native annual grasses such as the drooping brome, *Bromus rubens*, has created a more or less continuous fuel bed following years of heavy rainfall (Brooks and Matchett, 2006; Pierson et al., 2011). Similarly, in northern Australia, the invasion by a big African grass called gamba (*Andropogon gayanus*) has increased fire intensity in recent decades because of its great biomass in comparison with native grasses (Setterfield, 2010). Fire frequency can also be increased by changes in land use and land cover, as appears to be the case in Patagonia, where a substantial increase followed the arrival of European-Chilean farmers during recent centuries (Holz and Veblen, 2011). At a global scale, biomass burning showed a marked increase in the nineteenth century, and at that time direct anthropogenic activities became the dominant driver of global fire activity trends (Pechony and Shindell, 2010). On the other hand, in the western USA, because of human activities that include fire suppression, fire activity has declined in some areas since the late 1800s so that given the present climate there is what they call a 'fire deficit'. At a global scale, remote sensing has shown that the burned area declined by nearly one-quarter between 1998 and 2015 ($-24.3 \pm 8.8\%$, or $-1.35 \pm 0.49\%$ year^{-1}). Large decreases occurred in tropical savannas of South America and Africa and grasslands across the Asian steppe. The main reason for this appears to have been a shift towards more capital-intensive agriculture, driven by population increases, socio-economic development, and demand for agricultural products from regional and global markets. This has led to fewer and smaller fires (Andela et al., 2017).

2.5 Some Consequences of Fire Suppression

Given that fire has long been a feature of many ecosystems, and irrespective of whether the fires were or were not caused by people, it is clear that any deliberate policy of fire suppression might have important consequences for vegetation (Sherriff and Veblen, 2006; Kasischke et al., 2010). Fire exclusion in the Ponderosa pine forests of the Cascade Mountains in the USA over the last hundred years caused compositional and structural changes (Taylor, 2010). Rigid fire-protection policies have often had undesirable results (Bonnichsen et al., 1999) and as a consequence many foresters stress the need for 'environmental restoration burning'. One of the best ways to prevent the largest forest fires is to allow the small and medium fires to burn (Malamud et al., 1998). In Alaska, fire suppression policies, particularly adjacent to urban settlements, meant that the area burned from human-ignited fires fell from 26% for the 1950s and 1960s to 5% for the 1990s and 2000s (Kasischke et al., 2010).

Fire suppression, as has already been suggested, can magnify the adverse effects of fire. The position has been well stated by Sauer (1969: 14):

> The great fires we have come to fear are effects of our civilization. These are the crown fires of great depths and heat, notorious aftermaths of the pyres of slash left by lumbering. We also increase fire hazard by the very giving of fire protection which permits the indefinite accumulation of inflammable litter. Under the natural and primitive order, such holocausts, that leave a barren waste, even to the destruction of the organic soil, were not common.

In the coniferous forests of the middle upper elevations in the Sierra Nevada Mountains of California fire protection since 1890 has made the stands denser, shadier, and less park-like, and sequoia seedlings have decreased in number. In the high altitude mountains of the western USA the whitebark (*Pinus albicaulis*) has suffered from the expansion of fire-intolerant species (Larson and Kipfmueller, 2012), and the same has happened to Douglas fir (*Pseudotsuga menziesii*) in south-western Oregon (Messier et al., 2012). Likewise, at lower elevations the Mediterranean semi-arid shrubland, called chaparral, has had its character changed. The vegetation has increased in density, the amount of combustible fuels has risen, fire-intolerant species have encroached, and vegetation diversity has decreased, resulting in a monotony of old-age stands, instead of a mosaic of different successional stages. Unfavourable consequences of fire suppression have also been noted in Alaska (Oberle, 1969), where it has been found that when fire is excluded from many lowland sites an insulating carpet of moss tends to accumulate and raise the permafrost level. In the Kruger National Park, in South Africa, fires have occurred less frequently after the establishment of the game reserve, when it became uninhabited by natives and hunters. As a result, bush encroachment has taken place in areas that were formerly grassland, and the carrying capacity for grazing animals has declined. Controlled burning has been reinstituted as a necessary game-management operation.

However, following the severe fires that ravaged America's Yellowstone National Park in 1988, there was considerable debate as to whether the inferno, the worst since the park was established in the 1870s, was the result of a policy of fire suppression. Without such a policy the forest would burn at intervals of 10–20 years because of lightning strikes. Could it be that the suppression of fires over long periods of, say, 100 years or more, allegedly to protect and preserve the forest, led to the build-up of abnormal amounts of combustible fuel in the form of trees and shrubs in the understory? Should a programme of prescribed burning be carried out to reduce the amount of available fuel?

Fire suppression policies at Yellowstone did indeed lead to a critical build-up in flammable material. However, other factors must also be examined in explaining the severity of the fire. One of these was the fact that the last comparable fire had been in the 1700s, so that the Yellowstone forests had had nearly 300 years in which to become increasingly flammable. In other words, because of the way vegetation develops through time (a process called succession) very large fires may occur every 200–300 years as part of the natural order of things (Figure 2.6). Another crucial factor was that the weather conditions in the summer of 1988 were abnormally dry, bringing a great danger of fire. As Romme and Despain (1989: 28) remarked:

It seems that unusually dry, hot and windy weather conditions in July and August of 1988 coincided with multiple ignition in a forest that was at its most flammable stage of succession. Yet it is unlikely that past suppression efforts greatly exacerbated the Yellowstone fire. If fires occur naturally at intervals ranging from 200 to 400 years, then 30 or 40 years of effective suppression is simply not enough for excessive quantities of fuel to build up. Major attempts at suppression in the Yellowstone forests may have merely delayed the inevitable.

Certainly, studies of the long-term history of fire in the western USA have shown the great importance of climatic changes at the decennial and centennial scales in controlling fire frequency during the Holocene (Whittock et al., 2003; Marlon et al., 2012). There is also evidence that an increase in the severity of forest fires in the mountains of California and Nevada has taken place since the mid-1980s, partly because of the availability of combustible materials following fire suppression but also possibly because of a more favourable climate for the generation of large fires (Miller et al., 2009). Figure 2.7 shows the increasing area burned in Arizona and New Mexico since 1916, while Figure 2.8 shows the increasing area burned in Canada since 1960.

2.6 Some Effects of Fire on Vegetation

The effects which fires have on the environment depend very much on their size, duration, and intensity. Some fires are relatively quick and cool, and only destroy ground vegetation. Other fires, crown fires, affect whole forests up to crown level and generate very high temperatures. In general forest fires are hotter than grassland fires. Perhaps more significantly in terms of forest management, fires which occur with great frequency do not attain too high a temperature because there is inadequate inflammable material to feed them.

There is evidence that fire has played an important role in the formation of various major types of vegetation (e.g. savanna, pine forests, etc.) and in influencing the operation of ecosystems (Crutzen and Goldammer, 1993; O'Connor et al., 2011). Fire may assist in seed germination. For example, the abundant germination of dormant seeds on recently burned chaparral sites has been reported by many investigators, and it seems that some seeds of chaparral species require scarification by fire. The better germination of those not requiring scarification may be related to the removal by fire of competition, litter and some substances in the soils which are toxic to plants. Fire alters seedbeds. If litter and humus removal

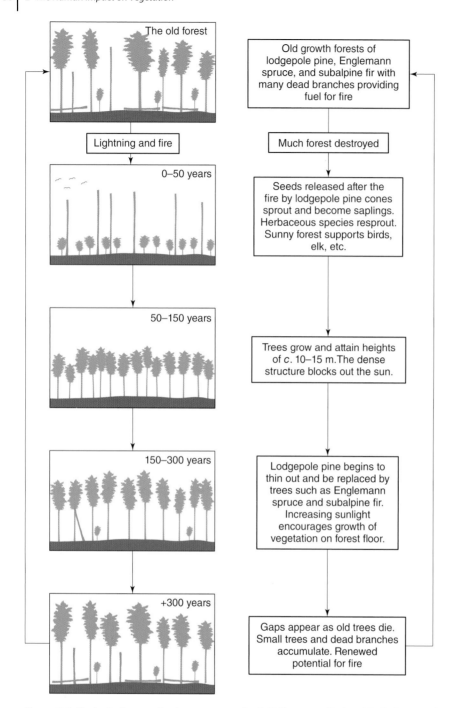

Figure 2.6 Ecological succession in response to fire in Yellowstone National Park. *Source:* adapted after Romme and Despain (1989: 24–25), heavily modified.

are substantial, large areas of rich ash, bare soil, or thin humus may be created. Some trees, such as Douglas fir and the giant sequoia (*Sequoiadendron giganteum*), benefit from such seedbeds. Fire sometimes triggers the release of seeds (as with the Jack pine, *Pinus bankdiana*) and seems to stimulate the vegetative reproduction of many woody and herbaceous species. Fire can control

forest insects, parasites, and fungi – a process termed 'sanitization'. It also seems to stimulate the flowering and fruiting of many shrubs and herbs, and to modify the physicochemical environment of the plants. Mineral elements are released both as ash and through increased decomposition rates of organic layers. Above all, areas subject to fire often show greater species diversity, which

Figure 2.7 The increasing annual area burned by wildfires in Arizona and New Mexico. This has commonly been attributed to accumulated living and dead forest fuels that have accumulated since fire suppression began early in the twentieth century. *Source:* http:/forestfire.nau.edu/statistics.htm (accessed January 2018).

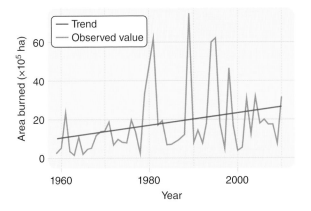

Figure 2.8 The increasing wildfire trend recorded in Canada since the 1960s. *Source:* Fire regime, Forest Change indicators, Canadian Forest Service. Reproduced with the permission of the Minister of Natural Resources Canada, 2017, http://www.nrcan.gc.ca/forests/climate-change/forest-change/17780 (accessed January 2018).

is a factor that tends to favour stability. Fire may also influence climate by changing surface albedo and releasing greenhouse gases into the atmosphere and also cause the degradation of permafrost.

One can conclude by quoting at length from Pyne (1982: 3), who provides a detailed and scholarly analysis of the history of cultural fires in America:

> Hardly any plant community in the temperate zone has escaped fire's selective action, and, thanks to the radiation of *Homo sapiens* throughout the world, fire has been introduced to nearly every landscape on earth. Many biotas have consequently so adapted themselves to fire that, as with biotas frequented by floods and hurricanes, adaptation has become symbiosis. Such ecosystems do not merely tolerate fire, but often encourage it and even require it. In many environments fire is the most effective form of decomposition,

the dominant selective force for determining the relative distribution of certain species, and the means for effective nutrient recycling and even the recycling of whole communities.

2.7 The Role of Grazing

Many of the world's grasslands have long been grazed by wild animals like the bison of North America or the large game of East Africa, but the introduction of pastoral economies based on domestic stock has also affected their nature and productivity (Figure 2.9).

Light grazing may increase the productivity of wild pastures. Nibbling, for example, can encourage the vigour and growth of plants, and in some species, such as the valuable African red grass, *Themeda triandra*, the removal of coarse, dead stems permits succulent sprouts to shoot. Likewise the seeds of some plant species are

Figure 2.9 Intensive grazing by domestic stock, such as these cattle near Belo Horizonte in Brazil, has a major influence on many biomes, including grasslands and savannas (ASG).

spread efficiently by being carried in cattle guts, and then placed in favourable seedbeds of dung or trampled into the soil surface. Moreover, the passage of herbage through the gut and out as faeces modifies the nitrogen cycle, so that grazed pastures tend to be richer in nitrogen than ungrazed ones. Also, like fire, grazing can increase species diversity by opening out the community and creating more niches.

On the other hand, heavy grazing may be detrimental. Excessive trampling when conditions are dry will reduce the size of soil aggregates and break up plant litter to a point where they are subject to removal by wind. Trampling, by puddling the soil surface, can accelerate soil deterioration and water erosion as infiltration capacity is reduced. Heavy grazing can kill plants or lead to a marked reduction in their level of photosynthesis. In addition, when relieved of competition from palatable plants or plants liable to trampling damage, resistant and usually unpalatable species expand their cover. Thus in the western USA poisonous burroweed (*Haploplappius* spp.) has become dangerously common, and many woody species have intruded. These include the mesquite (*Prosopis juliflora*), the big sagebrush (*Artemisia tridentata*), the one-seed juniper (*Juniperus monosperma*) and the Pinyon pine. Grover and Musick (1990) saw shrubland encroachment by creosote bush (*Larrea tridentata*) and mesquite as part and parcel of desertification and indicate that in southern New Mexico the area dominated by them has increased several fold over the last century. This has been as a result of a corresponding decrease in the area's coverage of productive grasslands. They attributed both tendencies to excessive livestock overgrazing at the end of the nineteenth century, but pointed out that this was compounded by a phase of rainfall regimes that were unfavourable for perennial grass growth.

It is evident then that the semi-arid grasslands of south-western North America have changed dramatically over the last 150 years as a result of the encroachment of native woody species such as mesquite. Van Auken (2000: 207) concluded: 'The major cause of the encroachment of these woody species seems to be the reduction of grass biomass (fire fuel) by chronic high levels of domestic herbivory coupled to a reduction of grassland fires, which would have killed or suppressed the woody plants to the advantage of the grasses.'

There are many reasons why excessive grazing can lead to shrub dominance (Archer et al., 1999):

1) Livestock may effectively disperse woody plant seeds, particularly those of some leguminous shrubs and arborescents.

2) Utilization of grasses increases chances for germination and early establishment of woody seedlings.
3) Concomitant reductions in transpirational leaf area, root biomass, and root activity associated with grazing of grasses can:
   a) increase superficial soil moisture to enhance woody seedling establishment and growth of shallow-rooted woody species;
   b) increase the amount of water percolating to deeper depths and benefit established woody species with deep root systems;
   c) increase nutrient availability to woody plants; and
   d) release suppressed populations of established tree or shrub 'seedling reserves'.
4) Grazing increases mortality rates and decreases plant basal area, seed production, and seedling establishment of palatable grasses.
5) Grazing may also increase susceptibility of grasses to other stresses such as drought. These factors would combine to increase the rate of gap formation and available area for woody plant seedling establishment, especially in post-drought periods.
6) Herbaceous species may be replaced by assemblages that compete less effectively with woody plants.
7) Reduction of the biomass and continuity of fine fuel may reduce fire frequency and intensity.
8) Invading woody species are often unpalatable relative to grasses and forbs and are thus not browsed with sufficient regularity or severity to limit establishment or growth.
9) Lower soil fertility and alterations in physicochemical properties occur with loss of ground cover and subsequent erosion. This favours N_2-fixing woody plants (e.g. *Prosopis*, *Acacia*) and evergreen woody plant growth forms that are tolerant of low nutrient conditions.

In Australia the widespread adoption of sheep grazing after European settlement led to significant changes in the nature of grasslands over extensive areas. In particular, the introduction of sheep led to the removal of kangaroo grass (*Themeda australis*) – a predominantly summer-growing species – and its replacement by essentially winter-growing species such as *Danthonia* and *Stipa*. Also in Australia, not least in the areas of tropical savanna in the north, large herds of introduced feral animals (e.g. cattle, horse, dromedary, and sambar deer) have resulted in overgrazing and alteration of native habitats (see Section 3.2). As they appear to lack significant control by predators and pathogens, their densities, and thus their effects, became very high (Freeland, 1990).

Similarly in Britain many plants are avoided by grazing animals because they are distasteful, hairy, prickly, or even poisonous (Tivy, 1971). The persistence and spread of bracken (*Pteridium aquilinium*) on heavily grazed rough pasture in Scotland is aided by the fact that it is slightly poisonous, especially to young stock. The success of bracken is furthered by its reaction to burning, for with its extensive system of underground stems (rhizomes) it tends to be little damaged by fire. The survival and prevalence of shrubs such as elder (*Sambucus nigra*), gorse (*Ulex* spp.), broom (*Sarothamus scoparius*), and the common weeds ragwort (*Senecio jacobaea*) and creeping thistle (*Cirsium arvense*), in the face of grazing, can be attributed to their lack of palatability.

The role of grazing in causing marked deterioration of habitat has been the subject of further discussion in the context of upland Britain. In particular, Darling (1956) stressed that while trees bring up nutrients from rocks and keep minerals in circulation, pastoralism means the export of calcium phosphate and nitrogenous organic matter. The vegetation gradually deteriorates, the calcicoles disappear and the herbage becomes deficient in both minerals and protein. Progressively more xerophytic plants come in: *Nardus stricta* (mat grass), *Molinia caerulaea* (purple moor grass), *Erica tetralix* (cross-leaved heath), and then *Scripus caespitosa* (deer grass). However, this is not a view that has received universal support (Mather, 1983). Studies in several parts of upland Britain have shown that mineral inputs from precipitation are very much greater than the nutrient losses in wool and sheep carcasses. During the 1970s the idea of upland deterioration was gradually undermined.

In general terms it is clear that in many part of the world the grass family is well equipped to withstand grazing. Many plants have their growing points located on the apex of leaves and shoots, but grasses reproduce the bulk of fresh tissue at the base of their leaves. This part is least likely to be damaged by grazing and allows regrowth to continue at the same time that material is being removed.

Communities severely affected by the treading of animals (and indeed people) tend to have certain distinctive characteristics. These include diminutiveness (since the smaller the plant is, the more protection it will get from soil surface irregularities); strong ramification (the plant stems and leaves spread close to the ground); small leaves (which are less easily damaged by treading); tissue firmness (cell-wall strength and thickness to limit mechanical damage); a bending ability; strong vegetative increase and dispersal (for example, by stolons); small hard seeds which can be easily dispersed, and the production of a large number of seeds per plant (which is particularly important because the mortality of seedlings is high under treading and trampling conditions).

2.8 Deforestation

Deforestation is one of the great processes of landscape transformation (Williams, 2003). On a global basis, Richards (1991: 164) calculated that since 1700 about 19% of the world's forests and woodlands have been removed. Over the same period the world's cropland area has increased by over four-and-a-half times, and between 1950 and 1980 it amounted to well over 100,000 km^2 per year.

However, controversy surrounds the meaning of the word 'deforestation' and this causes problems when it comes to assessing rates of change and causes of the phenomenon (Williams, 1994). It is best defined (Grainger, 1992) as 'the temporary or permanent clearance of forest for agriculture or other purposes'. According to this definition, if clearance does not take place then deforestation does not occur. Thus, much logging in the tropics, which is selective in that only a certain proportion of trees and only certain species are removed, does not involve clear felling and so cannot be said to constitute deforestation. However, how 'clear' is clear? Many shifting cultivators in the humid tropics leave a small proportion of trees standing (perhaps because they have special utility). At what point does the proportion of trees left standing permit one to say that deforestation has taken place? This is not a question to which there is a simple answer. There is not even a globally accepted definition of forest, and the UN's Food and Agriculture Organization (FAO) defined forest cover as greater than 10% canopy cover, while the International Geosphere Biosphere Programme (IGBP) defined it as greater than 60%.

The deliberate removal of forest is one of the most long-standing and significant ways in which humans have modified the environment, whether achieved by fire or cutting. Pollen analysis shows that temperate forests were removed in Mesolithic and Neolithic times and at an accelerating rate thereafter. The example of Easter Island in the Pacific is salutary, for its deforestation at an unsustainable rate caused the demise of the culture that created its great statues (Flenley et al., 1991). Since pre-agricultural times world forests have declined approximately one-fifth, from five to four billion hectares. The highest loss has occurred in temperate forests (32–35%), followed by sub-tropical woody savannas and deciduous forests (24–25%). The lowest losses have been in tropical evergreen forests (4–6%) because many of them have for much of their history been inaccessible and sparsely populated (World Resources Institute, 1992: 107).

In Britain, Birks (1988) analyzed dated pollen sequences to ascertain when and where tree pollen values in sediments from upland areas drop to 50% of their

Holocene maximum percentages, and takes this as a working definition of 'deforestation'. From this work he identified four phases:

1) *3700–3900 years BP*: north-west Scotland and the eastern Isle of Skye.
2) *2100–2600 years BP (the pre-Roman Iron Age)*: Wales, England (except the Lake District), northern Skye, and northern Sutherland.
3) *1400–1700 years BP (post-Roman)*: Lake District, southern Skye, Galloway, and Knapdale-Ardnamurchan.
4) *300–400 years BP*: the Grampians and the Cairngorms.

Sometimes forests are cleared to allow agriculture; at other times to provide fuel for domestic purposes, or to provide charcoal or wood for construction; sometimes to fuel locomotives, or to smoke fish; and sometimes to smelt metals. The Phoenicians were exporting cedars as early as 4600 years ago (Mikesell, 1969) both to the Pharaohs and to Mesopotamia. Attica in Greece was laid bare by the fifth century BC and classical writers allude to the effects of fire, cutting, and the destructive nibble of the goat. The great phase of deforestation in Central and Western Europe, described by Darby (1956: 194) as 'the great heroic period of reclamation' occurred from c. AD 1050 onwards for about 200 years. In particular, the Germans moved eastwards: 'What the new west meant to young America in the nineteenth century, the new east meant to Germany in the Middle Ages' (Darby, 1956: 196). The landscape of Europe was transformed (Kaplan et al., 2009), just as that of North America, Australia, New Zealand, and South Africa was to be as a result of the European expansions, especially in the nineteenth century. Temperate North America underwent particularly brutal deforestation (Williams, 1989), and lost more woodland in 200 years than Europe did in 2000. The first colonialists arriving in the *Mayflower* found a continent that was wooded from the Atlantic seaboard as far as the Mississippi River (Figure 2.10). The forest originally occupied some 170 million hectares. Today only about 10 million hectares remain.

Fears have often been expressed that the mountains of High Asia (for example in Nepal) have been suffering from a wave of deforestation that has led to a whole suite of environmental consequences, which include accelerated landsliding, flooding in the Ganges Plain, and sedimentation in the deltaic areas of Bengal. Ives and Messerli (1989) doubted that this alarmist viewpoint is soundly based and argued (p. 67) that 'the popular claims about catastrophic post-1950 deforestation of the Middle Mountain belt and area of the high mountains of the Himalayas are much exaggerated, if not inaccurate'.

Likewise, some workers in West Africa have interpreted 'islands' of dense forest in the savanna as the relics of a once more extensive forest cover that was being rapidly degraded by human pressure. More recent research (Fairhead and Leach, 1996), however, suggests that this is far from the truth and that villagers have in recent decades been extending rather than reducing forest islands (Table 2.2). There are also some areas of Kenya and Ethiopia (Nyssen et al., 2009) in East Africa where, far from recent population pressures promoting vegetation removal and land degradation, there has been an increase in woodland since the 1930s.

2.9 Tropical Forests

With regard to the tropical rain forests, the researches of Flenley and others (Flenley, 1979) have indicated that forest clearance for agriculture has been going on since at least 3000 BP in Africa, 7000 BP in South and Central America, and possibly since 9000 BP or earlier in India and New Guinea. Recent studies by archaeologists and palaeoecologists have tended to show that prehistoric human activities were rather more extensive in the tropical forests than originally thought (Willis et al., 2004).

The causes of the present spasm of deforestation in the tropics (Figure 2.11) are complex and multifarious and are summarized in Grainger (1992) and Table 2.3. He also provides a review of the problems of measuring and defining loss of tropical forest area (Grainger, 2008). Indeed, there are very considerable difficulties in estimating rates of deforestation in part because different groups of workers use different definitions of what constitutes a forest and what distinguishes rain forest from other types of forest. There is thus some variability in views as to the present rate of rain forest removal and this is brought out in the debate between Achard et al. (2002) and Fearnside and Lawrance (2003). FAO estimates (Lanly et al., 1991) showed that the total annual deforestation in 1990 for 62 countries (representing some 78% of the tropical forest area of the world) was 16.8 million ha, a figure significantly higher than the one obtained for these same countries for the period 1976–1980 (9.2 million ha per year). Myers (1992) suggested that there was an 89% increase in the tropical deforestation rate during the 1980s (compared with an FAO estimate of a 59% increase). He believed that the annual rate of loss in 1991 amounted to about 2% of the total forest expanse.

The change in forest area on a global basis in the 1990s is shown in Table 2.4a. These FAO data indicate ongoing deforestation in Africa, parts of Asia and the Pacific, Latin America, and the Caribbean, and the stable or slightly reducing amount of deforestation in Europe, West Asia, and North America (Figure 2.12).

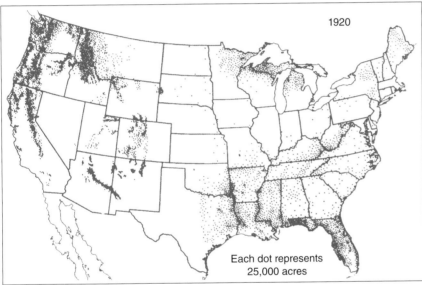

Figure 2.10 The distribution of American natural forest in 1620 and 1920. *Source:* adapted from Williams (1989).

Table 2.2 Estimates of deforestation since 1900 (millions of hectares).

Country	Orthodox estimate of forest area lost	Forest area lost according to World Conservation Monitoring Centre	Forest area lost according to Fairhead and Leach (1996: table 9.1)
Côte d'Ivoire (Ivory Coast)	13	20.2	4.3–5.3
Liberia	4–4.5	5.5	1.3
Ghana	7	12.9	3.9
Benin	0.7	12.9	3.9
Togo	0	1.7	0
Sierra Leone	0.8–5	6.7	*c.*0
Total	**25.3–30.2**	**48.6**	**9.5–10.5**

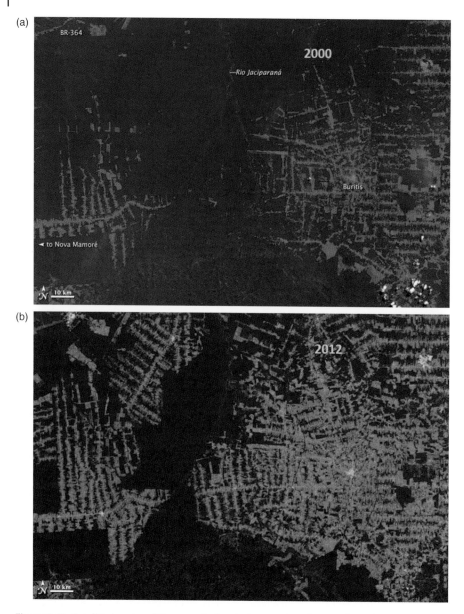

Figure 2.11 Satellite images of the spread of agriculture and settlement through part of the Amazonian rainforest in the state of Rondônia in western Brazil in (a) 2000, (b) 2012. *Source:* NASA Earth Observatory.

The recent net gain in Asia is due to massive reforestation in China. There was, however, a considerable variation in the rate of forest regression in different areas within the tropics (Figure 2.13), with some areas under relatively modest threat, e.g. western Amazonia, the forests of Guyana, Surinam, and French Guyana, and much of the Zaire Basin in central Africa (Myers, 1983 and 1984). Some other areas were being exploited so fast that it was feared that minimal areas would soon be left, for example, in: the Philippines, peninsular Malaya, Thailand, Australia, Indonesia, Vietnam, Bangladesh, Sri Lanka, Central America, Madagascar, West Africa, and eastern Amazonia. Annual rates of deforestation in Amazonia have, however, shown some reduction since c. 2004 (Figure 2.14).

An examination of rates of deforestation in selected hot spots was provided by Achard et al. (2002) (Table 2.4b and c). They suggested that the annual deforestation rate for rainforests was 0.38% for Latin America, 0.43% for Africa, and 0.91% for South-East Asia, but that the hot spot areas can have rates that are much greater (e.g. up to 5.9% in central Sumatra and up to 4.7% in Madagascar). These rates were not as high as those of Myers, but were still extremely rapid. The current annual rate of loss exceeds 5% in the eastern lowlands of Sumatra and the peatlands of Sarawak

Table 2.3 The causes of deforestation.

A) Immediate causes – land use

1) Shifting agriculture
   (a) Traditional long-rotation shifting cultivation
   (b) Short-rotation shifting cultivation
   (c) Encroaching cultivation
   (d) Pastoralism
2) Permanent agriculture
   (a) Permanent staple crop cultivation
   (b) Fish farming
   (c) Government-sponsored resettlement schemes
   (d) Cattle ranching
   (e) Tree crop and other cash crop plantations
3) Mining
4) Hydro-electric schemes
5) Cultivation of illegal narcotics

A) Underlying causes

1) Socio-economic mechanisms
   (a) Population growth
   (b) Economic development
2) Physical factors
   (a) Distribution of forests
   (b) Proximity of rivers
   (c) Proximity of roads
   (d) Distance from urban centres
   (e) Topography
   (f) Soil fertility
3) Government policies
   (a) Agriculture policies
   (b) Forestry policies
   (c) Other policies

Source: from Grainger (1992). Reproduced with permission of Earthscan/Routledge (T&F) – Informa

(Miettingen et al., 2011). In Indonesia and Malaysia one of the main causes of forest disappearance is the rapidly expanding removal of forest for palm oil cultivation (Wicke et al., 2011). Production and demand for palm oil has soared in recent years (Figure 2.15). On the other hand, the rate of deforestation in Brazilian Amazonia, while still high, may have become reduced by almost three-quarters since 2004 (Regalado, 2010; Malingreau et al., 2012).

Hansen et al. (2013) reported the results of a satellite-based survey of world forest cover change. Earth observation satellite data were used to map global forest loss (2.3 million km^2) and gain (0.8 million km^2) from 2000 to 2012 at a spatial resolution of 30 m. The tropics were the only climate domain to exhibit a trend, with forest loss increasing by 2101 km^2 per year. They reported that Brazil's well-documented recent reduction in deforestation, which as annual forest loss decreased on average 1318 km^2/year, was offset by increasing forest loss elsewhere. Increased annual loss of Eurasian tropi-

cal rainforest (1392 km^2/year), African tropical moist deciduous forest (536 km^2/year), South American dry tropical forest (459 km^2/year), and Eurasian tropical moist deciduous (221 km^2/year) and dry (123 km^2/year) forests more than offset the slowing of Brazilian deforestation.

The rapid loss of rain forest is potentially extremely serious, because as Poore (1976: 138) stated, these forests are a source of potential foods, drinks, medicines, contraceptives, abortifacients, gums, resins, scents, colorants, specific pesticides, and so on. Their removal may contribute to crucial global environmental concerns (e.g. climatic change and loss of biodiversity), besides causing regional and local problems, including lateritization, increased rates of erosion, and accelerated mass movements. The great range of potential impacts of tropical deforestation is summarized in Table 2.5.

Some traditional societies have developed means of exploiting the rain forest environment which tend to minimize the problems posed by soil fertility deterioration, soil erosion, and vegetation degradation. Such a system is known as shifting agriculture (*swidden*). The tropical rain forest and the swidden plots have certain common characteristics. Both are closed cover systems, in part because in swidden some trees are left standing, in part because some tree crops (such as banana, papaya, areca, etc.) are planted, but also because food plants are not planted in an open field, crop-row manner, but helter-skelter in a tightly woven, dense botanical fabric. It is, in Geertz's words (1963: 25) 'a miniaturized tropical forest'. Secondly, swidden agriculture normally involves a wide range of cultigens, thereby having a high diversity index like the rain forest itself. Thirdly, both swidden plots and the rain forest have high quantities of nutrients locked up in the biotic community compared to that in the soil. The primary concern of 'slash-and-burn' activities is not merely the clearing of the land, but rather the transfer of the rich store of nutrients locked up in the prolific vegetation of the rain forest to a botanical complex whose yield to people is a great deal larger. If the period of cultivation is not too long and the period of fallow is long enough, an equilibrated, non-deteriorating, and reasonable productive farming regime can be sustained in spite of the rather impoverished soil base upon which it rests.

Unfortunately this system often breaks down, especially when population increase precludes the maintenance of an adequately long fallow period. When this happens, the rain forest cannot recuperate and is replaced by a more open vegetation assemblage ('derived savanna') which is often dominated by the notorious *Imperata* savanna grass which has turned so much of South-East Asia into a green desert. *Imperata cyclindrica* (also called cogongrass) is a tall grass which springs up from rhizomes

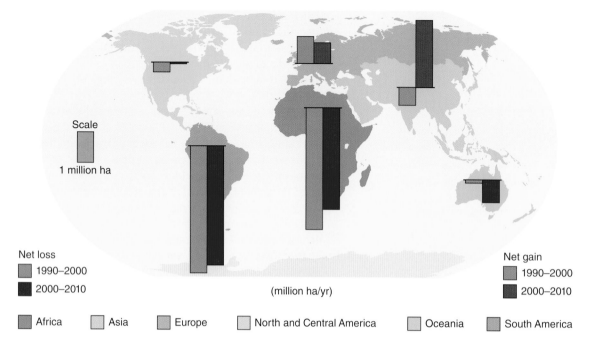

Scale

1 million ha

Net loss
- 1990–2000
- 2000–2010

(million ha/yr)

Net gain
- 1990–2000
- 2000–2010

Africa   Asia   Europe   North and Central America   Oceania   South America

Figure 2.12 Change in forest area by region, 1990–2010. *Source:* UNEP and FAO data, in Figure 3.4 in Geo5.

and is highly invasive. Because of its rhizomes it is fire-resistant, but since it is a tall grass it helps to spread fire (Gourou, 1961).

One particular type of tropical forest ecosystem coming under increasing pressure from various human activities is the mangrove forest (Polidoro et al., 2010) (Figure 2.16). Mangroves are a coastal intertidal wetland forest composed of halophytic trees and shrubs. Mangroves cover just 0.1% of the Earth's continental surface but are nonetheless of extreme importance, not least because they and their associated soils and sediments are hugely important stores of carbon (Atwood et al., 2017). They contain approximately 70 vegetation species in 40 genera. Associated with this vegetation are a plethora of coastal and terrestrial fauna, including fish, crustaceans, snakes, and mammals and these ecosystems constitute a reservoir, refuge, feeding ground, and nursery for many useful and unusual plants and animals. In particular, because they export decomposable plant debris into adjacent coastal waters, they provide an important energy source and nutrient input to many tropical estuaries. In addition they can serve as buffers against the erosion caused by tropical storms – a crucial consideration in low-lying areas like Bangladesh. In spite of these advantages, mangrove forests are being degraded and destroyed on a large scale in many parts of the world, either through exploitation of their wood resources or because of their conversion to single-use systems such as agriculture, aquaculture,

salt-evaporation ponds, or housing developments. While the dominant threats to mangroves differ nationally and regionally, aquaculture has traditionally been seen as a leading cause of mangrove deforestation throughout the tropics, and globally it is responsible for just over half of mangrove declines. More recently, the expansion of oil palm plantations (see Section 2.9) has accounted for 16% of their loss in South-East Asia between 2000 and 2012 (Friess, 2016). While loss in South-East Asia is largely due to direct land-cover conversion, in regions such as Africa, indirect causes of degradation dominate. These include harvesting for charcoal and construction materials, and indirect ecosystem stressors such as organic pollution from rapidly expanding peri-urban areas. Data from FAO suggest that the world's mangrove forests, which covered 19.8 million ha in 1980, have now been reduced to only 14.7 million ha, with the annual loss running at about 1% per year (compared to 1.7% a year from 1980 to 1990) (http://www.fao.org/DOCREP/005/Y7581E/y7581e04.htm) (accessed December 2017). However, some areas are now being relatively well protected, including the Sundarbans of Bangladesh. Friess (2016) reported that deforestation rates in some parts of the world have decreased over the last decade. For example, while in the 1970s–1990s it was assumed that mangroves in South-East Asia were being lost at an annual rate of c. 1% per year, recent analyses suggest that this has decreased to c. 0.2%.

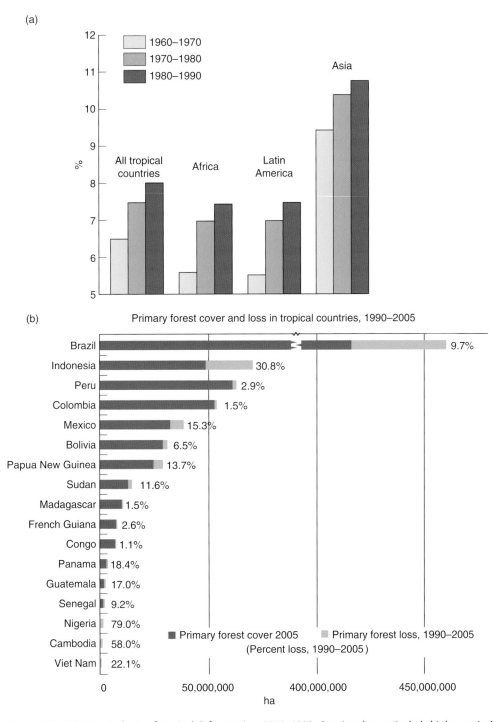

Figure 2.13 (a) Estimated rate of tropical deforestation, 1960–1990, showing the particularly high rates in Asia. *Source:* adapted from *World Resources, 1996–97*. (b) Primary forest cover and loss in selected tropical countries, 1990–2005. *Source:* based on FAO data.

2.10 The Forest Transition

Deforestation is not an unstoppable or irreversible process. What is called the 'forest transition' has taken place in some parts of the world. This is a shift from net deforestation to net reforestation. The forest transition is now being recognized in some developing countries including Vietnam, China, and India (Mather, 2007; Meyfroidt and Lambin, 2008), but has also been a feature of many European and other developed countries (Rudel et al., 2005, 2010; Meyfroidt and Lambin, 2009). Around the Mediterranean Sea, for instance, farmland abandonment has been widely reported, caused by national and international migrations and because market conditions made farming unprofitable in areas with steep slopes, small field sizes, and with difficulties for access and mechanization (García-Ruiz et al., 2011). While the environmental impacts of deforestation are widely recognized, the forest transition also entails less well-known ecological effects, such as the change of fire regimes or the loss of habitats in increasingly homogeneous agro-forest landscapes (Cervera et al., In press). In the United Kingdom, the area of woodland rose from 1.2 million ha in 1924 to over 3 million ha in 2010 (Figure 2.17). In the United States the forested area has increased substantially since the 1930s and 1940s, though it is possible that some authors have exaggerated the extent of abandoned agricultural land and the amount of forest regrowth that has occurred (Ramankutty et al., 2010). Nevertheless, this 'rebirth of the forest' (Williams, 1988) has a variety of causes: new timber growth and planting was rendered possible because the old forest had been removed, forest fires have been suppressed and controlled, farmland has been abandoned and reverted to forest, and there has been a falling demand for lumber and lumber-derived products. It is, however, often very difficult to disentangle the relative importance of grazing impacts, fire, and fluctuating climates in causing changes in the structure of forested landscapes. In some cases, as, for example, the Ponderosa pine forests of the American south-west, all three factors may have contributed to the way in which the park-like forest of the

Table 2.4a Change in forested land 1990–2000 by region.

	Total land area (million ha)	Total forest 1990 (million ha)	Total forest 2000 (million ha)	% of land forested in 2000	Change 1990–2000 (million ha)	% change per year
Africa	2,963.3	702.5	649.9	21.9	−52.6	−0.7
Asia and the Pacific	3,463.2	734.0	726.3	21.0	−7.7	−0.1
Europe	2,359.4	1,042.0	1,051.3	44.6	9.3	0.1
Latin America and the Caribbean	2,017.8	1,011.0	964.4	47.8	−46.7	−0.5
North America	1,838.0	466.7	470.1	25.6	3.9	0.1
West Asia	372.4	3.6	3.7	1.0	0.0	0.0
World	**13,014.1**	**3,960.0**	**3,866.1**	**29.7**	**−93.9**	**−0.24**

Source: compiled from FAO (2001).
Note: numbers may not add due to rounding.

Table 2.4b Top ten countries reporting the greatest annual net loss of forest area, 2010–2015.

Country	Annual forest area net loss (thousand ha)	Rate (%)
1) Brazil	984	0.2
2) Indonesia	684	0.7
3) Myanmar	546	1.8
4) Nigeria	410	5.0
5) United Republic of Tanzania	372	0.8
6) Paraguay	325	2.0
7) Zimbabwe	312	2.1
8) Democratic Republic of the Congo	311	0.2
9) Argentina	297	1.1
10) Bolivia	289	0.5

Source: Reproduced with permission of Food and Agriculture Organization of the United Nations.

Table 2.4c Top ten countries reporting the greatest annual net gain in forest area, 2010–2015.

Country	Annual forest area net gain (thousand ha)	Rate (%)
1) China	1542	0.8
2) Australia	308	0.2
3) Chile	301	1.8
4) United States of America	275	0.1
5) Philippines	240	3.3
6) Gabon	200	0.9
7) Lao People's Democratic Republic	189	1.0
8) India	178	0.3
9) Viet Nam	129	0.9
10) France	113	0.7

Source: http://www.fao.org/3/a-i4793e.pdf (accessed December 2017). Reproduced with permission of Food and Agriculture Organization of the United Nations.

Figure 2.14 Forest loss in Brazilian Amazonia (ha), 1998–2017. *Source:* https://news.mongabay.com/2017/10/deforestation-drops-16-in-the-brazilian-amazon/ (accessed January 2018).

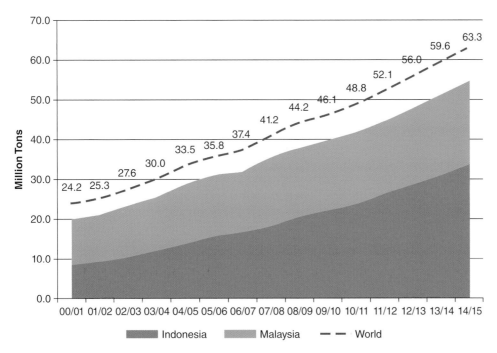

Figure 2.15 Area of palm oil harvested in Indonesia, Malaysia and the World 2000–2015. *Source:* http://pecad/fas.usda.gov/highlights/2014/09/SEAsia/index.htm (accessed August 2016).

Table 2.5 The consequences of tropical deforestation.

1) Reduced biological diversity
   (a) Species extinction
   (b) Reduced capacity to breed improved crop varieties
   (c) Inability to make some plants economic crops
   (d) Threat to production of minor forest products
2) Changes in local and regional environments
   (a) More soil degradation
   (b) Changes in water flows from catchments
   (c) Changes in buffering of water flows by wetland forests
   (d) Increased sedimentation of rivers, reservoirs etc.
   (e) Possible changes in rainfall characteristics
3) Changes in global environments
   (a) Reduction in carbon stored in terrestrial biota
   (b) Increase in carbon dioxide content of atmosphere
   (c) Changes in global temperature and rainfall patterns by greenhouse effects
   (d) Other changes in global climate due to changes in land surface processes

Source: from Grainger (1992). Reproduced with permission of Earthscan/Routledge (T&F) – Informa

Figure 2.16 Mangrove swamps are highly productive and diverse ecosystems that are being increasingly abused by human activities (ASG).

nineteenth century has become significantly denser and younger today (Savage, 1991). Even when forest recovery occurs, the type of forest that develops may not compositionally be the same as it was prior to clearance. Rhemtulla et al. (2009) compared forests for three time slices in Wisconsin (mid-1800s, 1930s, 2000s) and documented the recovery of forests since the peak agricultural extent that occurred in the 1930s. They found that in the south of the state, maples and other shade-tolerant trees were thriving in areas which prior to clearance had been dominated by oak forests and savannas. In southern Wisconsin the original savanna ecosystems were maintained through a frequent low-intensity fire regime. Such fires are now suppressed so that the forests are succeeding towards species that are less fire resistant and more shade tolerant. Paulson et al. (2016) undertook a

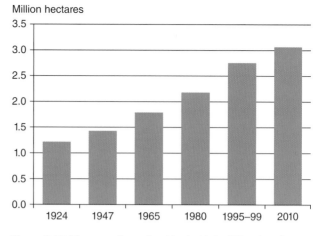

Million hectares

Figure 2.17 The area of woodland in the United Kingdom from 1924 to 2009. *Source:* based on Forestry Commission statistics in http://webarchive.nationalarchives.gov.uk/2016015160709/http://www.ons.gov.uk/ons/rel/environmental/environmental-accounts/2011/sumforestry.html (accessed January 2018).

survey of vegetation change in the Great Lakes region. Here fire and windfall originally dominated as disturbance agents, driving dynamics in prairies, savannas, and in many forested ecosystems. However, fire suppression over the last century has radically lengthened fire-return intervals. Community composition has changed dramatically since the mid-nineteenth century. Preferred timber species (e.g. *Pinus strobus* and *Tsuga canadensis*) and fire-adapted species (e.g. *Quercus macrocarpa* and *Pinus banksiana*) have declined across the region, while aspen (*Populus* spp.) and/or maple (*Acer* spp.) have consistently increased. Oak savannas became closed forests and aspen and maple now dominate much of the region.

2.11 Secondary Rain Forest

When an area of rain forest that has been cleared for cultivation or timber exploitation is abandoned by humans, the forest begins to regenerate; but for an extended period of years the type of forest that occurs – secondary forest – is very different in character from the virgin one it replaces. The features of such secondary forest, which is widespread in many tropical regions and accounts for as much as 40% of the total forest area in the tropics, have been summarized by Brown and Lugo (1990) and Corlett (1995).

Firstly, secondary forest is lower and consists of trees of smaller average dimensions than those of primary forest; but since it is comparatively rare that an area of primary forest is clear-felled or completely destroyed by fire, occasional trees much larger than average are usually found scattered through secondary forest. Secondly, very young secondary forest is often remarkably regular and uniform in structure, though the abundance of small climbers and young saplings gives it a dense and tangled appearance which is unlike that of primary forest and makes it laborious to penetrate. Thirdly, secondary forest tends to be much poorer in species than primary, and is sometimes, though by no means always, dominated by a single species, or a small number of species. Fourthly, the dominant trees of secondary forest are light-demanding and intolerant of shade, most of the trees possess efficient dispersal mechanisms (having seeds or fruits well adapted for transport by wind or animals), and most of them can grow very quickly. The rate of net primary production of secondary forests exceeds that of the primary forests by a factor of 2 (Brown and Lugo, 1990). Some species are known to grow at rates of up to 12 m in three years, but they tend to be short-lived and to mature and reproduce early. One consequence of their rapid growth is that their wood often has a soft texture and low density.

There is an increasing number of studies of the nature of secondary forests of differing ages and of the rates at which regrowth can occur (Chazdon et al., 2007). For example, Gehring et al. (2005), working in central Amazonia, calculated that 25 years of regrowth restored half of the mature forest biomass, and they estimated that 75% would be restored after 175 years. Goosem et al. (2016) found that in north-east Australia, secondary forests contained important plant diversity for conservation, particularly in older sites, but that even the oldest secondary forests (60 years old) did not converge with the species composition and diversity of mature forests. Bonnell et al. (2011) working in East Africa, established that it would take 95–112 years for structural recovery of logged areas to approach that of adjacent mature forest, but considerably longer for the original species composition to occur. Liebsch et al. (2008) estimated that it might take about one to four thousand years for a secondary forest to reach the endemism levels that exist in mature forests. This was a finding similar to that of Chai and Tanner (2011) working in Jamaica. They found that it would take one or two centuries for tree density and basal area to match that of old-growth forests but that even longer periods would be required to fully recover original species composition. However, secondary forests can be species rich, though the composition of species will not be the same (Finegan, 1996). They become more species rich with age and in eastern Brazil Piotto et al. (2009) showed that more than half the species found in a 40-year-old secondary forest were shared with the neighbouring old growth forests.

Secondary forests should not be dismissed as useless scrub. All but the youngest secondary forests are probably effective at preventing soil erosion, regulating water supply, and maintaining water quality (see, for example, Wilby and Gell, 1994). They provide refuge for some flora and fauna and can provide a source of timber, albeit generally of inferior quality than derived from primary forest.

2.12 The Human Role in the Creation and Maintenance of Savanna

Savannas (Figure 2.18) are 'unique among the world's biomes because they are the only major one defined by the coexistence of two major plant forms – grasses and trees' (Laris, 2011: 1067). They are extremely widespread in low latitudes (Harris, 1980), covering about 18 million km^2 (an area about 2.6 million km^2 greater than that of the tropical rain forest). They occupy about 65% of the African continent and are home to a fifth of the global human population and a large portion of the world's ungulates. Their origin has been the subject of great contention in the literature of biogeography (Furley, 2016), though most savanna research workers agree that no matter what savanna origins may be, the agent which seems to maintain them is intentional or inadvertent burning. As with most major vegetation types a large number of interrelated factors are involved in causing savanna (Mistry, 2000), and too many arguments about origins have neglected this fact (Figure 2.19). Confusion has also arisen because of the failure to distinguish clearly between predisposing, causal, resulting, and maintaining factors (Hills, 1965). It appears, for instance, that in the savanna regions around the periphery of the Amazon basin, the climate *predisposes* the vegetation towards the development of savanna rather than forest. The geomorphic evolution of the landscape may be a *causal* factor; increased laterite development a *resulting* factor; and fire, *a maintaining* factor.

Originally, however, savanna was envisaged as a predominantly natural vegetation type of climatic origin (see, for example, Schimper, 1903). According to supporters

Figure 2.18 A tropical savanna in the Kimberley District of north-west Australia (ASG).

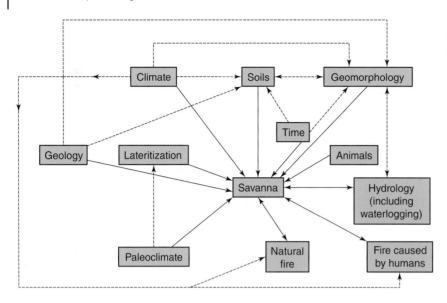

Figure 2.19 The interrelated factors involved in the formation of savanna vegetation.

of this theory, savanna is better adapted than other plant formations to withstand the annual cycle of alternating soil moisture: rain forests could not resist the extended period of extreme drought, while dry forests could not compete successfully with perennial grasses during the equally lengthy period of large water surplus (Sarmiento and Monasterio, 1975). Strong correlations have been established between the degree of woody cover in African savannas and the amount of mean annual precipitation (Sankaran et al., 2008).

Other workers have championed the importance of edaphic (soil) conditions, including poor drainage, soils which have a low water-retention capacity in the dry season, soils with a shallow profile due to the development of a lateritic crust, and soils with a low nutrient supply (either because they are developed on a poor parent rock such as quartzite, or because the soil has undergone an extended period of leaching on an old land surface). Associated with soil characteristics, ages of land surfaces, and degree of drainage is the geomorphology of an area. This may also be an important factor in savanna development. Soil moisture is certainly a major control of vegetation patterns in the savannah landscapes of West Africa, as is bedrock lithology (Duvall, 2011).

Some other researchers – for example, Eden (1974) – found that savannas are the product of former drier conditions (such as late Pleistocene aridity) and that, in spite of a moistening climate, they have been maintained by fire. Fire is certainly important in maintaining and originating some savannas (Murphy and Bowman, 2012). This is suggested by the fact that many savanna trees are fire resistant. Periodic fires maintain the structure of a savanna by preventing the transition to dense woodland or forest, and fire differentiates between areas with a high and a low tree cover, especially in regions

with rainfall between 1000 and 2000 mm per year (Staver et al., 2011). There are also many observations of the frequency with which, for example, African herdsmen and agriculturists burn over much of tropical Africa and thereby maintain grassland. Savannas are the most frequently burned ecosystems in the world (Beerung and Osborne, 2006). Certainly the climate of savanna areas is conductive to fire for, as Gillon (1983: 617) put it, 'Large scale grass fires are more likely to take place in areas having a climate moist enough to permit the production of a large amount of grass, but seasonally dry enough to allow the dried material to catch fire and burn easily.'

Some savannas are undoubtedly natural, for pollen and isotopic analysis in South America shows that savanna vegetation was present before the arrival of humans. The origin of modern savannah biomes dates back to the late Miocene, c. 8 million years ago (Beerung and Osborne, 2006). Savannas first began to spread across Africa at that time and a major hypothesis for explaining this vegetation change is the increase in C_4 grasses, promoting fire, and the evolution and spread of mammal browsers (Charles-Dominique et al., 2016). In South Asia, C4 vegetation had extended across all South Asia by the Late Miocene (Ratnam et al., 2016).

Many modern savannas, however, are 'nature–society hybrids' (Duvall, 2011). Even natural savannas, when subjected to human pressures, change their characteristics. For example, the inability of grass cover to maintain itself over long periods in the presence of heavy stock grazing may be documented from many of the warm countries of the world. Heavy grazing tends to remove the fuel (grass) from much of the surface. The frequency of fires is therefore significantly reduced, and tree and bush invasion take place. As Johannessen (1963: 111) wrote: 'Without intense, almost annual fires, seedlings of trees and shrubs are able to invade the savannas where the grass sod has been opened by heavy grazing … the age and size of the trees on the savannas usually confirm the relative recency of the invasion.' In the case of the savannas of interior Honduras, he reports that they only had a scattering of trees when the Spaniards first encountered them, whereas now they have been invaded by an assortment of trees and tall shrubs.

Such bush or shrub encroachment, which can be defined as 'The suppression of palatable grasses and herbs by encroaching woody species often unpalatable to domestic livestock' (Ward, 2005: 101), is a serious cause of rangeland deterioration in savanna regions (Roques et al., 2001), not least in South Africa (Wigley et al., 2009) and the Kalahari in Botswana (Dougill et al., 2016). It also occurs in South America and Australia (Stevens et al., 2017). This woody encroachment involves an increase in woody biomass, stem densities, or woody cover. The encroaching woody species include both indigenous and exotic woody species, and thus bush encroachment actually includes two kinds: (1) the proliferation of indigenous woody plant species and (2) the invasion of exotic/alien woody species (Belayneh and Tessema, 2017). However, some communal land users recognize that bush encroachment can be advantageous by providing increased woody resources for building and firewood and increased browse availability (Wigley et al., 2009). It is extremely expensive to remove established dense scrub cover by mechanical means, though some success has been achieved by introducing animals that have a browsing or bulldozing effect, such as goats, giraffes, and elephants. A prime cause of bush encroachment, it is often asserted, is overgrazing, especially around cattle watering points and near settlements (Moleele et al., 2002; Gil-Romera et al., 2011). This reduces the vigour of favourable perennial grasses, which tend to be replaced, as we have seen, by less reliable annuals and by woody vegetation. Annual grasses do not adequately hold or cover the soil, especially early in the growing season. Thus runoff increases and topsoil erosion occurs. Less water is then available in the topsoil to feed the grasses, so that the woody species, which depend on deeper water, become more competitive relative to the grasses which can only use water within their shallow root zones. The situation is exacerbated when there are few browsers in the herbivore population and, once established, woody vegetation competes effectively for light and nutrients. Increasing levels of grazing also reduce fuel load, making fire less intense and thus less damaging to trees. Deliberate reductions in fire use can have a similar effect and enable trees and shrubs to flourish (Ratnam et al., 2016). Conversely, fire frequency can be increased because of

the spread of invasive grasses (Foxcroft et al., 2010; Setterfield et al., 2010). As we saw earlier, tree encroachment can also be caused by invasion of exotic plants. Drier tracts of fine-leafed spiny savannas in both South Asia and South-East Asia have been heavily invaded by *Prosopis juliflora,* which originates from the Americas, and which transforms open tree–grass landscapes into woody thickets, often with extensive bare ground (Ratnam et al., 2016). The same has happened in the Baringo region of Kenya, where dense stands of the mesquite *Prosopis juliflora,* introduced in Kenya in 1973 through a governmental initiative to restore quarries near Mombasa, strongly reduce the availability of pasture and crop land and also increasingly restrict the physical access of both humans and animals to lake shores and river banks. Other trees have also expanded in the Baringo area, including various Acacias, such as *Acacia mellifera* (Vehrs, 2016).

Another example of human interventions modifying savanna character is through their effects on savanna-dwelling mammals such as the elephant. They are what is known as a 'keystone species' because they exert a strong influence on many aspects of the environment in which they live (Waithaka, 1996). They diversify the ecosystems which they occupy and create a mosaic of habitats by browsing, trampling, and knocking over bushes and trees. They also disperse seeds through their eating and defecating habits and maintain or create water holes by wallowing. All these roles are beneficial to other species. Conversely, where human interference prevents elephants from moving freely within their habitats and leads to their numbers exceeding the carrying capacity of the savanna, their effect can be environmentally catastrophic. The reintroduction of elephants into an area has been found to cause extirpation of some woody species (O'Connor, 2011). Equally, if humans reduce elephant numbers in a particular piece of savanna, the savanna may become less diverse and less open, and its water holes may silt up. This will be to the detriment of other species. One further major anthropogenic impact on savannas that has been recognized is the practice of afforestation, involving the planting of exotic eucalypt and pine monocultures, especially in Brazil, Colombia, Nigeria, Congo, and China (Fernandes et al., 2016). In other countries, savannas are being afforested for the production of other commodities, such as fruit in China and palm oil in Latin America. In Colombia, for instance, the area occupied by oil palm plantations more than doubled over the last ten years.

Finally, tree densities in some savannas appear to have increased in recent decades (Buitenwerf et al., 2012) as a possible response to increased atmospheric carbon dioxide levels (Bond and Midgley, 2012; Stevens et al., 2017).

2.13   The Spread of Desert Vegetation on Desert Margins

One of the most contentious and important environmental issues of recent years has been the debate on the question of the alleged expansion of deserts (Middleton and Thomas, 1997) and the use of the term 'desertification' (Behnke and Mortimore, 2016). This was first used but not formally defined by Aubréville (1949), and for some years the term 'desertization' was also employed, for example by Rapp (1974: 3) who defined it as: 'The spread of desert-like conditions in arid or semi-arid areas, due to man's influence or to climatic change'. There has been some variability in how 'desertification' itself is defined. Some definitions stress the importance of human causes, while others have suggested that climatic changes and fluctuations have played a role.

It is also by no means clear how extensive desertification is or how fast it is proceeding. Indeed, the lack of agreement on the former makes it impossible to determine the latter. As Grainger (1990: 145) remarked in a well-balanced review, 'Desertification will remain an ephemeral concept to many people until better estimates of its extent and rate of increase can be made on the basis of actual measurements.' He continued (p. 157): 'The subjective judgements of a few experts are insufficient evidence for such a major component of global environmental change … Monitoring desertification in the drylands is much more difficult than monitoring deforestation in the humid tropics, but it should not be beyond the ingenuity of scientists to devise appropriate instruments and procedures.'

The United Nations Environment Programme (UNEP) has played a central role in the promotion of desertification as a major environmental issue, as is made evident by the following remark by Tolba and El-Kholy (1992: 134):

> Desertification is the main environmental problem of arid lands, which occupy more than 40 per cent of the total global land area. At present, desertification threatens about 3.6 billion hectares – 70% of potentially drylands, or nearly one-quarter of the total land area of the world. These figures exclude natural hyper-arid deserts. About one sixth of the world's population is affected.

However, in their book *Desertification: Exploding the Myth*, Thomas and Middleton (1994) have discussed UNEP's views on the amount of land that is desertified. They state:

> The bases for such data are at best inaccurate and at worst centred on nothing better than guesswork. The advancing desert concept may have been useful as a publicity tool but it is not one that represents the real nature of desertification processes. (Thomas and Middleton, 1994: 160)

Their views have been trenchantly questioned by Stiles (1995), but huge uncertainties do indeed exist.

There are relatively few reliable studies of the rate of supposed desert advance. Lamprey (1975) attempted to measure the shift of vegetation zones in the Sudan (see Figure 2.20) and concluded that the Sahara had advanced by 90 to 100 km between 1958 and 1975, an average rate of about 5.5 km per year. However, on the basis of analysis of remotely sensed data and ground observation, Helldén (1985) found sparse evidence that this had in fact happened. One problem is that there may be very substantial fluctuations in biomass production from year to year. This has been revealed by meteorological satellite observations of green biomass production levels on the south side of the Sahara (Dregne and Tucker, 1988).

--·--·--·-- Limit of Khartoum's exploitation of wood and charcoal
— — — — Approximate desert boundary

Figure 2.20 Desert encroachment in the northern Sudan 1958–1975, as represented by the position of the boundary between sub-desert scrub and grassland in the desert. *Source:* adapted from Rapp et al. (1976: figure 8.5.3). Also shown is the expanding wood and charcoal exploitation zone south of Khartoum, Sudan. *Source:* adapted from Johnson and Lewis (1995: figure 6.2).

The spatial character of desertification is also the subject of some controversy (Helldén, 1985). Contrary to popular rumour, the spread of desert-like conditions is not an advance over a broad front in the way that a wave overwhelms a beach. Rather, it is like a 'rash' which tends to be localized around settlements. It has been likened to Dhobi's itch – a ticklish problem in difficult places. Fundamentally, as Mabbutt (1985: 2) has explained, 'the extension of desert-like conditions tends to be achieved through a process of accretion from without, rather than through expansionary forces acting from within the deserts'. This distinction is important in that it influences perceptions of appropriate remedial or combative strategies, which are discussed in Goudie (1990). Figure 2.21 shows two models of the spatial pattern of desertification. One represents the myth of a desert spreading outward over a wide front, while the other shows the more realistic pattern of degradation around routes and settlements.

The role of overgrazing in promoting desertification is significant and in Jordan its effects have been identified as early as the mid-Holocene (Henry et al., 2017).

However, there are debates about grazing's role in causing rangeland deterioration (Middleton, 2016). Wood-cutting is another extremely serious cause of vegetation decline around almost all towns and cities of the Sahelian and Sudanian zones of Africa. Many people depend on wood for domestic uses (cooking, heating, brick manufacture, etc.), and the collection of wood for charcoal and firewood is an especially serious problem in the vicinity of urban centres. This is illustrated for Khartoum in Sudan in Figure 2.20. Likewise, the installation of modern boreholes has enabled rapid multiplication of livestock numbers and large-scale destruction of the vegetation in a radius of 15–30 km around boreholes. Given this localization of degradation, amelioration schemes such as local tree-planting may be partially effective, but ideas of planting green belts as a 'cordon sanitaire' along the desert edge (whatever that is) would not halt deterioration of the situation beyond this Maginot line. The deserts are not invading from without; the land is deteriorating from within. Nonetheless, proposals for the creation of 'green walls' are still made, the latest being for a strip of forest 15 km wide and 7675

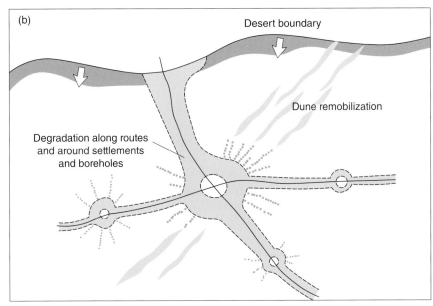

Figure 2.21 Two models of the spatial pattern of desertification: (a) The myth of desert migration over a wide front. (b) The more local development of degradation around routes, settlement, and boreholes.

km long stretching from Dakar to Djibouti (Minassian, 2011).

There has been considerable debate as to whether the vegetation change and environmental degradation associated with desertization is irreversible. In many cases, where ecological conditions are favourable because of the existence of such factors as deep sandy soils or beneficial hydrological characteristics, vegetation recovers once excess pressures are eliminated. There is evidence of this in arid zones throughout the world where temporary or permanent enclosures have been set up (Le Houérou, 1977). The speed of recovery will depend on how advanced deterioration is, the size of the area which is degraded, the nature of the soils and moisture resources, and the character of local vegetation. It needs to be remembered in this context that much desert vegetation is adapted to drought and to harsh conditions, and that it often has inbuilt adaptations which enable a rapid response to improved circumstances. Nonetheless, in certain specific circumstances recovery is slow and so limited that it may be appropriate to talk of 'irreversible desertization'. In North Africa, decades after the end of hostilities, wheel tracks and degraded vegetation produced in World War II are still present in the desert. Some desert surfaces, such as those covered by lichens, are easily destroyed by vehicular traffic but take a long time to recover (Figure 2.22).

The causes of desertification are also highly controversial and diverse (Table 2.6). The question has been asked whether this process is the result of (i) temporary drought periods of high magnitude, (ii) a long-term climatic change towards aridity (either as alleged post-glacial progressive desiccation or as part of a 200-year cycle), (iii) anthropogenic climatic change, or (iv) human action degrading the biological environments in arid zones. There is little doubt that severe droughts do take place,

Figure 2.22 A lichen field, near Swakopmund in Namibia, shows the effects of vehicular traffic. Such scars can take a long time to recover (ASG).

and that their effects become worse as human and domestic animal populations increase. The devastating drought in the African Sahel from the mid-1960s caused greater ecological stress than the droughts of 1910–1915 and 1944–1948, largely because of the increasing anthropogenic pressures.

It is evident that it is largely a combination of human activities with occasional series of dry years that leads to presently observed dryland deterioration. The process also seems to be fiercest not in desert interiors, but on the less arid marginal areas around them. It is in semi-arid areas – where biological productivity is much greater than in extremely arid zones, where precipitation is frequent and intense enough to cause rapid erosion of unprotected soils, and where humans are prone to mistake short-term economic gains under temporarily favourable climatic conditions for long-term stability – that the combination of circumstances particularly conductive to desert expansion can be found. It is in these marginal areas that dry farming and cattle rearing can be a success in good years, so that susceptible areas are ploughed and cattle numbers become greater than the vegetation can support in dry years. In this way, a depletion of vegetation occurs which sets in train such insidious processes as water erosion and deflation. The vegetation is removed by clearance for cultivation, by the cutting and uprooting of woody species for fuel (Figure 2.23), by over-grazing, and by the burning of vegetation for pasture and charcoal. Cow dung may be used for fuel rather than for fertilizing the ground (Figure 2.24).

These tendencies towards bad land-use practices result in part from the restrictions imposed on many nomadic societies through the imposition of national boundaries across their traditional migration routes, or through various schemes implemented for political and social reasons to encourage their establishment in settled communities. Some of their traditional grazing lands have been taken over by cash-crop farmers. The traditional ability to migrate enabled pastoral nomads and their cattle to emulate the natural migration of such wild animals as wildebeest and kob, and thereby to make flexible use of available resources according to season and according to yearly variations in rainfall. They could also move away from regions that had become exhausted after a long period of use. As soon as migrations are stopped and settlements imposed, such options are closed, and severe degradation occurs (Sinclair and Fryxell, 1985).

The suggestion has sometimes been made that not only are deserts expanding because of human activity, but that deserts themselves are created by human activity. There are authors who have suggested, for example, that the Thar Desert of India is a post-glacial and

Table 2.6 Some examples of causes and consequences of desertification.

Trigger factor	Consequences
Direct land use • Overcultivation (decreased fallows, mechanized farming) • Overgrazing • Mismanagement of irrigated lands • Deforestation (burning, fuel & fodder collection) • Exclusion of fire	Physical processes affected • Decline in soil structure, water permeability, depletion of soil nutrients and organic matter, increases susceptibility to erosion, compaction of soil, sand dune mobilization • Loss of biodiversity and biomass, increased soil erosion via wind and water, soil compaction from trampling, increased runoff, sand dune mobilization • Causes water logging and salinization of soil, hence lower crop yields, possible sedimentation of water reservoirs • Promotes artificial establishment of savanna vegetation, loss of soil-stabilizing vegetation, soil exposed and eroded, increases aridity, increased frequency of dust storms, sand dune mobilization (e.g. Ethiopia is losing approx. 1000 million tonnes of topsoil per year) • Promotes growth of unpalatable woody shrubs at the expense of herbage
Indirect government policies • Failed population planning policies • Irrigation subsidies • Settlement policies/land tenure • Improved infrastructure (e.g. roads, large-scale dams, canals, boreholes) • Promotion of cash crops & push towards nation/international markets • Price increases on agricultural produce • War • High interest rates	Drives overexploitation land-use practices • Increases need for food cultivation, hence overexploitation • Exacerbates flooding and salinization • Forces settlement of nomads, promotes concentrated use of land which often exceeds the carrying capacity • Although beneficial, can exacerbate the problem by attracting increased livestock and human populations or increasing risk from salinization, possible lowering of groundwater table below dams, problems of silting up reservoirs, water-logging; promotes large-scale commercial activity with little local benefit, flooding may displace people and perpetuate cycles of poverty • Displaces subsistence cropping, pushes locals into marginal areas to survive, promotes less resilient monocultures, & promotes expansion and intensification of land use • Incentive to crop on marginal lands • Valuable resources, both human and financial, are expended on war at the expense of environmental management and the needs of the people, large-scale migration with resultant increased pressure on receiving areas • Forcing grazing or cultivation to levels beyond land capacity
Natural • Extreme drought • Ecological fragility	• Decreased vegetation cover and increases land vulnerability for soil erosion. Creates an environment which exacerbates overexploitation • Impact of land-use practices – impact also depends on resilience of environment

Source: Williams (2000: table 2).

Figure 2.23 Deforestation for charcoal production and for firewood is a major cause of environmental change in the dry savanna woodlands of Swaziland (ASG).

Figure 2.24 In the drylands of north-west India, the use of buffalo dung as fuel rather than as fertilizer may have a deleterious effect on soil fertility (ASG).

possibly post-medieval creation (see Allchin et al., 1977, for a critique of such views), while Ehrlich and Ehrlich (1970) wrote: 'The vast Sahara desert itself is largely man-made, the result of over-grazing, faulty irrigation, deforestation, perhaps combined with a shift in the course of a jet stream.' Nothing could be further from the truth. The Sahara, while it has fluctuated greatly in extent, is many millions of years old, pre-dates human life, and is the product of the nature of the general atmospheric circulation, occupying an area of dry descending air.

One of the fascinating developments in the study of desertification in recent years has been the realization that there has been an increase in the greenness of the Sahel and some other areas. This 'recovery' may partially be due to some increase in rainfall, but is also possible that some of the greening is due to improved land management (including the protection of trees), and human migration from marginal areas (Rasmussen et al., 2001; Olsson et al., 2005). Repeat photography in Northern Ethiopia (Nyssen et al., 2009) has demonstrated that over the last 140 years, in spite of a tenfold increase in rural populations, there has been some regeneration of natural vegetation, the spread of new eucalypt woodlands, and improved soil and water husbandry. Land degradation in drylands is not irreversible and there is increasing evidence that the whole desertification concept needs re-evaluation (Behnke and Mortimore, 2016).

2.14   The Maquis of the Mediterranean Lands

Around much of the Mediterranean basin there is a plant formation called maquis (alternative names include *phrygana, matorral, macchia,* and *garrigue*). This consists of a stand of xerophilous non-deciduous bushes and shrubs which are evergreen and thick, and whose trunks are normally obscured by low-level branches. It includes such plants as holm oak (*Quercus ilex*), kermes oak (*Quercus coccifera*), tree heath (*Erica arborea*), broom heath (*Erica scoparia*), and strawberry trees (*Arbutus unedo*).

Holocene pollen analyses indicate that some maquis pre-dates substantial human impact (Collins et al., 2012), and some may represent a stage in the evolution towards true forest in places where the climax has not yet been reached; but in large areas it may represent the degeneration of forest caused by intensive land-use over millennia (Noti et al., 2009). Considerable concern has been expressed about the speed with which degeneration to, and degeneration beyond, maquis is taking place as a result of human influences (Tomaselli, 1977), of which cutting, grazing, and fire are probably the most

important and long continued. Charcoal burners, goats, and frequent outbreaks of fires among the resinous plants in the dry Mediterranean summer have all taken their toll. Such aspects of degradation in Mediterranean environments are discussed in Conacher and Sala (1998).

On the other hand, in some areas, particularly marginal mountainous and semi-arid portions of the Mediterranean basin, agricultural uses of the land have declined in recent decades, as local people have sought easier and more remunerative employment (Puddu et al., 2012). In such areas scrubland, sometimes termed 'post-cultural shrub formations', may start to invade areas of former cultivation (May, 1991), while maquis has developed to become true woodland. Mediterranean vegetation appears to be very resilient (Grove and Rackham, 2001).

There is considerable evidence that maquis vegetation is in part adapted to, and in part a response to, fire (Malkisnon et al., 2011). One effect of fire is to reduce the frequency of standard trees and to favour species which, after burning, send up a series of suckers from ground level. Both *Quercus ilex* and *Quercus coccifera* seem to respond in this way. Similarly, a number of species (for example, *Cistus albidus, Erica arborea,* and *Pinus halepensis*) seem to be distinctly advantaged by fire, perhaps because it suppresses competition or perhaps because a short burst of heat encourages germination (Wright and Wanstall, 1977).

2.15   The Prairies and Other Mid-latitude and High-altitude Grasslands

In mid-latitudes there are extensive grasslands. Those in Western Europe are for the most part secondary, and have been caused by forest clearance, but the large grasslands of the Eurasian steppes, the Prairies of North America, and the Pampas of Argentina are generally regarded as primary features that are a response to particular climatic conditions (Bredenkamp et al., 2002). They generally occupy areas where mean annual rainfall is about 300–1000 mm and where the length of the dry season ranges from 0 to 8 months.

The human role in the development of the North American prairies is the subject of controversy (Whitney, 1994). It was once fairly widely believed that the prairies were essentially a climatically related phenomenon (see Changnon et al., 2003, for a historical review). Workers like Weaver (1954) argued that under the prevailing conditions of soil and climate the invasion and establishment of trees was significantly hindered by the presence of a dense sod. High evapotranspiration levels combined with low precipitation were thought to give a competitive advantage to herbaceous plants with shallow, densely ramifying root systems, capable of completing their life cycles rapidly under conditions of pervasive drought. There is ample evidence that grasslands pre-date humans, with, for example, a great expansion of grasslands during the Miocene–Pliocene transition, 8 to 6 million years ago (Anderson, 2006).

An alternative view was, however, put forward by Stewart (1956: 128): 'The fact that throughout the tall-grass prairie planted groves of many species have flourished and have reproduced seedlings during moist years and, furthermore, have survived the most severe and prolonged period of drought in the 1930s suggests that there is no climatic barrier to forests in the area.'

Other arguments along the same lines have been advanced. Wells (1965), for example, pointed out that in the Great Plains a number of woodland species, notably the junipers, are remarkably drought-resistant, and that their present range extends into the Chihuahua Desert where they often grow in association with one of the most xerophytic shrubs of the American deserts, the creosote bush (*Larrea divaricata*). He remarked (p. 247): 'There is no range of climate in the vast grassland climate of the central plains of North America which can be described as too arid for all species of trees native to the region.' Moreover, confirming Stewart, he pointed out that numerous plantations and shelterbelts have indicated that trees can survive for at least 50 years in a 'grassland' climate. One of his most persuasive arguments was that, in the distribution of vegetation types in the plains, a particularly striking vegetational feature is the widespread but local occurrence of woodlands along escarpments and other abrupt breaks in topography remote from fluvial irrigation. A probable explanation for this is the fact that fire effects are greatest on flat, level surfaces, where there are high wind speeds and no interruptions to the course of fire. It has also been noted that where burning has been restricted there has been extension of woodland into grassland.

The reasons why fire tends to promote the establishment of grassland were summarized by Cooper (1961: 150–151).

> In open country fire favours grass over shrubs. Grasses are better adapted to withstand fire than are woody plants. The growing point of dormant grasses from which issues the following years growth, lies near or beneath the ground, protected from all but the severest heat. A grass fire removes only one year's growth, and usually much of this is dried and dead. The living tissue of shrubs, on the other hand, stands well above the ground, fully exposed to fire. When it is burned, the growth of several years is destroyed. Even though many shrubs sprout vigorously after burning, repeated loss of their top growth keeps them small. Perennial grasses, moreover, produce seeds in abundance one or two years after germination; most woody plants require several years to reach seed-bearing age. Fires that are frequent enough to inhibit seed production in woody plants usually restrict the shrubs to a relatively minor part of the grassland area.

Thus, as with savanna, anthropogenic fires may be a factor which maintains, and possibly forms, the prairies and there is now some palaeoecological information to support this view (Boyd, 2002). Though again, following the analogy with savanna, it is possible that some of the American prairies may have developed in a post-glacial dry phase, and that with a later increase in rainfall re-establishment of forest cover was impeded by humans through their use of fire and by grazing animals. The grazing animals concerned were not necessarily domesticated, however, for Larson (1940) has suggested that some of the short-grass plains were maintained by wild bison. These, he believed, stocked the plains to capacity so that the introduction of domestic livestock, such as cattle, after the destruction of the wild game was merely a substitution so far as the effect of grazing on plants is concerned. There is indeed pollen analytical evidence that shows the presence of prairie in the western mid-west over 11,000 years ago, prior to the arrival of human settlers (Bernabo and Webb, 1977). Therefore some of it, at least, may be natural.

Comparable arguments have attended the origins of the great Pampa grassland of Argentina. The first Europeans who penetrated the landscape were much impressed by the treeless open country and it was always taken for granted, and indeed became dogma, that the grassland was a primary climax unit. However, this interpretation was challenged, notably by Schmieder (1927a, b), who pointed out that planted trees thrived, that precipitation levels were quite adequate to maintain tree growth and that, in topographically favourable locations such as the steep gullies (*barrancas*) near Buenos Aires, there were numerous endemic representatives of the former forest cover (*monte*). Schmieder believed that Pampa grasslands were produced by a pre-Spanish aboriginal hunting and pastoral population, the density of which had been underestimated, but whose efficiency in the use of fire was proven. On the other hand, pollen analysis has shown that pampas grassland was present in the Late Pleistocene and probably prior to the arrival of substantial human populations. Moreover, severe seasonal drought and the presence of fine-textured soils favour grassland over trees in the region (Bredenkamp et al., 2002). Some of the grassland may also be derived from the formerly drier conditions of the Late Pleistocene and the drier phases of the Holocene, when dune, dust, and deflation activity were greater than today.

In addition to its lowland savannas, Africa has a series of high-altitude grasslands called 'Afromontane grasslands'. They extend as a series of 'islands' from the mountains of Ethiopia to those of the Cape area of South Africa. Are they the result mainly of forest clearance by humans in the recent past? Or are they a long-standing and probably natural component of the pattern of vegetation (Meadows and Linder, 1993)? Are they caused by frost, seasonal aridity, excessively poor soils, or an intensive fire regime? This is one of the great controversies of African vegetation studies. Almost certainly a combination of factors has given rise to these grasslands. On the one hand current land management practices, including the use of fire, prevent forest from expanding. There has undoubtedly been extensive deforestation in recent centuries. On the other hand, pollen analysis from various sites in southern Africa suggests that grassland was present in the area as long ago as 12,000 BP. This would mean that much grassland is not derived from forest through very recent human activities.

In recent centuries mid-latitude grasslands have been especially rapidly modified by human activities. Notable has been the role of excessive grazing in the western USA in causing grasslands to be invaded by dense covers of shrubs, such as creosote bush (*Larrea tridentata*) and mesquite (*Prosopis glandulosa*) (Eldridge et al., 2011). As Whitney (1994: 257) pointed out, these grasslands have been altered in ways that can be summarized in three phrases: 'ploughed out', 'grazed out', and 'worn out'. Very

few areas of natural North America prairies remain. The destruction of 'these masterpieces of nature' took less than a century. The preservation of remaining areas of North American grasslands is a major challenge for the conservation movement (Joern and Keeler, 1995).

Palaearctic steppes are primary grasslands dominating the landscape of the temperate Eurasian grassland belt from Central and Eastern Europe to Northern China. As a result of the high rate of anthropogenic conversion and their widespread degradation, these steppes have become one of the most endangered terrestrial biomes of the world. This is especially true in Eastern Europe, where more than 90% of original steppes have been destroyed due to conversion into croplands, afforestation, and other human activities. Currently, steppe vegetation is often restricted to places unsuitable for ploughing, such as ancient burial mounds called 'kurgans' (Deák et al., 2016). Across the Siberian and Central Asian steppes, the Virgin Lands Campaign of the Soviet Union led to large-scale conversion after the Second World War. Conversely, in Mongolia hardly any steppe has been converted to cropland, and in Chinese Inner Mongolia approximately 70% of natural steppes remains (Török et al., 2016).

On a global basis, Graetz (1994) estimated that grasslands have been reduced by about 20% from their pre-agricultural extent, but a more recent study by Boakes et al. (2010) suggests that about half the world's grasslands have been converted to agriculture since 1700, a greater decline than that experienced by the world's forests (Figure 2.25).

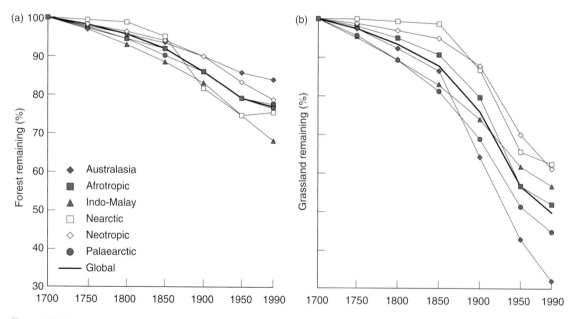

Figure 2.25 Percentage losses of (a) forest and (b) grassland, both globally and by biological realm, over the period 1700–1990. *Source:* adapted from Boakes et al. (2010: figure 1).

2.16 Post-glacial Vegetational Change in Britain and Europe

The classic interpretation of the vegetational changes of post-glacial (Holocene) times – that is, over the past 11,000 or so years – has been in terms of climate. That changes in the vegetation of Britain and other parts of Western Europe took place was identified by pollen analysts and palaeo-botanists, and these changes were used to construct a model of climatic change – the Blytt–Sernander model. There was thus something of a chicken-and-egg situation: vegetational evidence was used to reconstruct past climates, and past climates were used to explain vegetational change. The importance of humanly induced vegetation changes in the Holocene, associated primarily with farming and pastoralism means that, as Behre (1986: vii) pointed out, 'Human impact has been the most important factor affecting vegetation change, at least in Europe, during the last 7,000 years'.

Recent palaeo-ecological research has indicated that certain features of the post-glacial pollen record in Europe and Britain can perhaps be attributed to the action of Mesolithic and, especially, Neolithic peoples (Innes et al., 2010). It is, for example, possible that the expansion of the alder (*Alnus glutinosa*) was not so much a consequence of supposed wetness in the Atlantic period as a result of Mesolithic colonizers. Their removal of natural forest cover helped the spread of alder by reducing competition, as possibly did the burning of reed swamp. It may also have been assisted in its spread by the increased runoff of surface waters occasioned by deforestation and the burning of catchment areas. Furthermore, the felling of alder itself promotes vegetative sprouting and cloning, which could result in its rapid spread in swamp forest areas (Moore, 1986).

In the Yorkshire Wolds of northern England pollen analysis suggests that Mesolithic peoples may have caused forest disturbance as early as 8900 BP. They may even have so suppressed forest growth that they permitted the relatively open landscapes of the early post-glacial to persist as grasslands even when climatic conditions favoured forest growth (Bush, 1988). Also, late Mesolithic hunter-gatherers made extensive use of fire in the North York Moors (Innes et al., 2010) and in the Pennines (Ryan and Blackford, 2010).

One vegetational change which has occasioned particular interest is the fall in *Ulmus* pollen – the so-called elm decline – which appears in all pollen diagrams from north-west Europe, though not from North America. A very considerable number of radiocarbon dates have shown that this decline was approximately synchronous over wide areas and took place at about 5000 BP. It is now recognized that various hypotheses can be advanced to explain this major event in vegetation history: the original climatic interpretation; progressive soil deterioration; the spread of disease; or the role of people.

The climatic interpretation of the elm decline as being caused by cold, wet conditions has been criticized on various grounds (Rackham, 1980: 265):

> A deterioration of climate is inadequate to explain so sudden, universal and specific a change. Had the climate become less favourable for elm, this would not have caused a general decline in elm and elm alone; it would have wiped out elm in areas where the climate had been marginal for it, but would not have affected elm at the middle of its climatic range unless the change was so great as to affect other species also. A climatic change universal in Europe ought to have some effect on North American elms.

Humans may have contributed to soil deterioration and affected elms thereby. Troels-Smith (1956), however, postulated that around 5000 years ago a new technique of keeping stalled domestic animals was introduced by Neolithic peoples, and that these animals were fed by repeated gathering of heavy branches from those trees known to be nutritious – elms. This, it was held, reduced enormously the pollen production of the elms. In Denmark it was found that the first appearance of the pollen of a weed, Ribwort plantain (*Plantago lanceolata*), always coincided with the fall in elm pollen levels, confirming the association with human settlements.

Experiments have also shown that Neolithic peoples, equipped with polished stone axes, could cut down mature trees and clear by burning a fair-sized patch of established forest within about a week. Such clearings were used for cereal cultivation. In Denmark a genuine chert Neolithic axe was fitted into an ash-wood shaft. Three men managed to clear about 600 m^2 of birch forest in four hours. Remarkably, more than 100 trees were felled with one axe head, which had not been sharpened for about 4000 years (Cole, 1970: 38). Rackham, however, doubted whether humans alone could have achieved the sheer extent of change in such a short period (see also Peglar and Birks, 1993), and postulated that epidemics of elm disease may have played a role, aided by the fact that the cause of the disease, a fungus called *Ceratocystis*, is particularly attracted to pollarded elms (Rackham, 1980: 266). In reality the elm decline may have resulted from a complex cocktail of causes relating to climate change, soil deterioration, disease, and human activity. A model of the interacting factors that could be involved (Parker et al., 2002) is shown in Figure 2.26.

Figure 2.26 Relationships between factors influencing the mid-Holocene elm decline *Source:* after Parker et al. (2002: figure 9). Reproduced courtesy of Sage Publications.

The elm was not the only tree to show a decline in lowland Britain during the mid- Holocene. The lime (*Tilia*) was affected by clearance activity in the Late Neolithic to the Late Bronze Age (Grant et al., 2011).

2.17 Lowland Heaths

Heathland is characteristic of temperate, oceanic conditions on acidic substrates, and is composed of low shrubs, which form a closed canopy at heights which are usually less than 2 m. Dominant species are heathers (*Calluna*, *Erica*, etc.), woody legumes such as gorse (*Ulex*), broom (*Genista*), and various grasses (Loidi et al., 2010). Trees and tall shrubs are absent or scattered. Some heathlands are natural: for example, communities at altitudes above the forest limit on mountains and those on exposed coasts. There are also well-documented examples of heath communities which appear naturally in the course of plant succession as, for example, where *Calluna vulgaris* (heather) colonizes *Ammophila arenaria* (marram grass) and *Carex arenaria* (sand sedge) on coastal dunes.

However, at low and medium altitudes on the western fringes of Europe and North Africa between Morocco, Iberia, and Scandinavia (Figure 2.27), extensive areas of

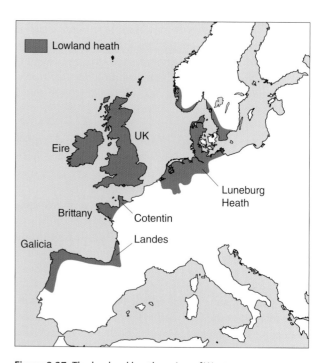

Figure 2.27 The lowland heath region of Western Europe. *Source:* adapted from Gimingham and de Smidt (1983: figure 2).

heathland occur. The origin of these is strongly disputed (Gimingham and de Smidt, 1983). Some areas were once thought to have developed where there were appropriate edaphic conditions (for example, well-drained loess or very sandy, poor soils), but pollen analysis showed that most heathlands occupy areas which were formerly tree covered. This evidence alone, however, did not settle the question whether the change from forest to heath might have been caused by Holocene climatic change. However, the presence of human artefacts and buried charcoal, and the fact that the replacement of forest by heath has occurred at many different points in time between the Neolithic and the late nineteenth century, suggest that human actions established, and then maintained, most of the heathland areas. In particular, fire is an important management tool for heather in locations such as upland Britain, since the value of *Calluna* (heather) as a source of food for grazing animals increases if it is periodically burned.

The area covered by heathland in Western Europe reached a peak around 1860, but since then there has been a very rapid decline. For example, by 1960 there had been a 60–70% reduction in Sweden and Denmark (Gimingham, 1981). In England, the Dorset heathlands that were such a feature of Thomas Hardy's Wessex novels are now a fraction of their former extent. Reductions in Britain as a whole averaged 40% between 1950 and 1984, and this was a continuation of a more long-term trend which saw a decline of 3.6 times between 1830 and 1980 in southern England (Nature Conservancy Council, 1984). The reasons for this fall are many, and include unsatisfactory burning practices, peat removal, drainage, fertilization, replacement by improved grassland, conversion to forest, and sand and gravel abstraction. The nature of lowland heaths is also currently being modified by the effects of increasing levels of nitrate additions from the atmosphere, which effects the growth of lichens and *Calluna* (Southon et al., 2012).

2.18 Introduction, Invasion, and Explosion

Thus far we have considered the human impact on general assemblages of vegetation over broad zones. However, in turning to questions such as the range of individual plant species, the human role is no less significant. People are important agents in the spread of plants and other organisms (Kleunen et al., 2015), and translocation of species has been going on since prehistoric times (Hofman and Rick, 2017). Some plants are introduced deliberately by humans to new areas; these include crops, ornamental and miscellaneous landscape modifiers (trees for reafforestation, cover plants for erosion control, etc.). Indeed, some plants, such as bananas and breadfruit, have become completely dependent on people for reproduction and dispersal, and in some cases they have lost the capacity for producing viable seeds and depend on human-controlled vegetation propagation. Most cultigens are not able to survive without human attention, partly because of this low capacity for self-propagation, but also because they cannot usually compete with the better-adapted native vegetation.

However, some domesticated plants have, when left to their own devices, shown that they are capable of at least ephemeral colonization, and a small number have successfully naturalized themselves in areas other than their supposed region of origin (Gade, 1976). Examples of such plants include several umbelliferous annual garden crops (fennel, parsnip, and celery) which, though native to Mediterranean Europe, have colonized wastelands in California. The Irish potato, which is native to South America, grows unaided in the mountains of Lesotho. The peach (in New Zealand), the guava (in the Philippines), coffee (in Haiti), and the coconut palm (on Indian Ocean island strands) are perennials that have established themselves as wild-growing populations, though the last-named is probably within the hearth region of its probable domestication. In Paraguay, orange trees (originating in South-East Asia and the East Indies) have demonstrated their ability to survive in direct competition with natural vegetation.

Plants that have been introduced deliberately because they have recognized virtues (Jarvis, 1979) can be usefully divided into an economic group (for example, crops, timber trees, etc.), and an ornamental or amenity one. In the British Isles, Jarvis believed that the great bulk of deliberate introductions before the sixteenth century had some sort of economic merit, but that only a handful of the species introduced thereafter were brought in because of their utility. Instead, plants were introduced increasingly out of curiosity or for decorative value.

A major role in such deliberate introductions was played by European botanic gardens (Figure 2.28) and those in the colonial territories from the sixteenth century onwards. Many of the 'tropical' gardens (such as those in Calcutta, Mauritius, and Singapore) were often more like staging posts or introduction centres than botanic gardens in the modern sense (Heywood, 1989).

Many plants, however, have been dispersed accidentally as a result of human activity: some by adhesion to moving objects, such as individuals themselves or their vehicles; some among crop seed; some among other plants (like fodder or packing materials); some among minerals (such as ballast or road metal); and some by the carriage of seeds for purposes other than planting

Figure 2.28 A monument in the botanic gardens in Mauritius, drawing attention to the value of introduced plants (ASG).

(as with drug plants). As illustrated in Figure 2.29, based on California, the establishment of alien species has proceeded rapidly over the last 150 years. In the Pampa of Argentina, Schmieder (1927b) estimated that the invasion of the country by European plants has taken place on such a large scale that at present only one-tenth of the plants growing wild in the Pampa are native.

Many trees have invaded, particularly along roads (Ghersa et al., 2002), and introduced conifers are a menace in many Southern Hemisphere countries (Simberloff et al., 2010). The differences in the nature and causes of plant invasions in different regions and environments is discussed by Heberling et al. (2017) and Kleunen et al. (2015).

The accidental dispersal of plants and organisms can have serious ecological consequences (see Williamson, 1996, and Henderson et al., 2006) and can lead to loss of biodiversity. In Britain, for instance, many elm trees died in the 1970s because of the accidental introduction of the Dutch elm disease fungus which arrived on imported timber at certain ports, notably Avonmouth and the Thames Estuary ports (Sarre, 1978). There are also other examples of the dramatic impact of some introduced plant pathogens (von Broembsen, 1989). The American chestnut (*Castanea dentata*) was, following the introduction of the chestnut blight fungus (*Cryphonectria parasitica*) in ornamental nursery material from Asia late in the 1890s, almost eliminated throughout its natural range in less than 50 years. Two North American hemlock species, *Tsuga Canadensis* and *Tsuga caroliniana*, have been threatened by another accidental Asian invader, a small sap-sucking insect, *Adelges tsugae* (Nuckolls et al., 2009). In Western Australia the great jarrah forests have been invaded and decimated by a root fungus, *Phytophthora cinnamomi*. This was probably introduced on diseased nursery material from eastern Australia, and the spread of the disease within the forests was facilitated by road building, logging, and mining activities that involved movement of soil or gravel containing the fungus. More than three million hectares of forest have been affected. In South Africa (Figure 2.30), the unique *fynbos* heathland, with its remarkable biodiversity (Allsop et al., 2014), has been

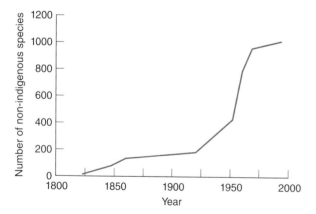

Figure 2.29 Number of non-indigenous plant species by date as reported for California. *Source:* Schwartz et al. (1996: figure 47.1, https://pubs.usgs.gov/dds/dds-43/VOL_II/VII_C47.PDF, accessed January 2018).

Figure 2.30 The invasion of Australian acacia (background) is a major threat to the Fynbos (foreground) of the Cape region of South Africa (ASG).

threatened by the spread of introduced pines and various types of Australian acacia. Significant declines have taken place in native species richness (Gaertner et al., 2009).

In the USA, Kudzu (*Pueraria montana*) has been a particularly difficult invader. It was introduced into the USA from Japan in 1876 and was promoted as an ornamental and forage crop plant. From 1935 to the mid-1950s it was recommended as a good means of reducing soil erosion. Unfortunately this large vine, with massive tap roots and the ability to spread at c. 30 cm per day, now smothers large expanses of the south-eastern USA. It is fiendishly difficult to eradicate because of the nature of its root system. No less difficult has been *Imperata cylindrica*. Originating from East Asia, it was introduced to the Mobile Bay area of Alabama in the mid-1900s, as a forage crop and soil stabilizer. It has since spread throughout much of the outer coastal plain region of the south-eastern USA and because of its fire resistance has the power to dominate natural ecosystems such as the long leaf pine (*Pinus palustris*) savanna (Brewer, 2008). It has invaded nearly 500,000 ha within the USA and over 500 million ha worldwide (Holzmueller and Jose, 2010). Another fiendishly bad invading weed in many parts of the world is the Spanish flag (*Lantana camara* L.). A native of the American tropics, it was introduced as an ornamental garden plant to Africa, Asia, and Oceania in

the mid-nineteenth century. It has invaded more than 13 million ha in India, 5 million ha in Australia, and 2 million ha in South Africa (Bhagwat et al., 2012).

The invasibility (vulnerability of a habitat and associated biological community to invasion) of particular types of environment is still an imperfectly understood area of study (Catford et al., 2012; Moles et al., 2012). However, ocean islands have often been particularly vulnerable to plant invasions (Sax and Gaines, 2008; Kleunen et al., 2015; Hofman and Rick, 2017) and other forms of degradation (Braje et al., 2017) (Figure 2.31). Dawson et al. (2017) found that the hotspot regions for established alien species richness, were the Hawaiian Islands, New Zealand's North Island, and the Lesser Sunda Islands (Indonesia). The simplicity of island ecosystems inevitably leads to diminished stability, and introduced species often find that the relative lack of competition enables them to broaden their ecological range more easily than on the continents. Moreover, because the natural species inhabiting remote islands have been selected primarily for their dispersal capacity, they have not necessarily been dominant or even highly successful in their original continental setting. Therefore, introduced species may prove more vigorous and effective. There may also be a lack of indigenous species to adapt to conditions such as bare ground caused by humans. Many successful invasive plants have escaped

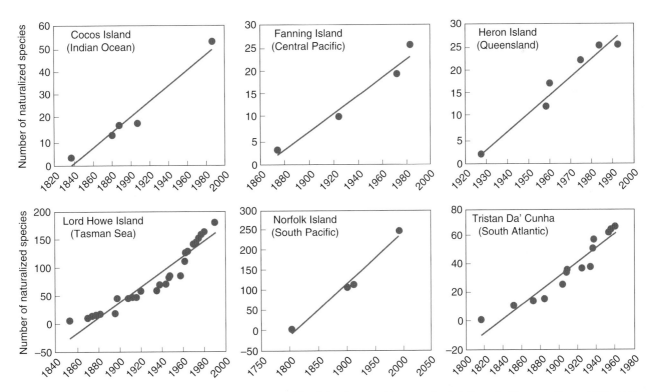

Figure 2.31 Naturalized plant richness on these six oceanic islands has increased in approximately linear fashion over the past 200 years. *Source:* adapted from Sax and Gaines (2008: figure 3).

Table 2.7 Alien plant species on oceanic islands.

Island	Number of native species	Number of alien species	% of alien species in flora
New Zealand	1200	1700	58.6
Campbell Island	128	81	39.0
South Georgia	26	54	67.5
Kerguelen	29	33	53.2
Tristan da Cunha	70	97	58.6
Falklands	160	89	35.7
Tierra del Fuego	430	128	23.0

Source: from data in Moore (1983).

the natural enemies that hold them in check, freeing them to utilize their full competitive potential (Callaway and Aschehoug, 2000). Thus introduced weeds may catch on.

Table 2.7 illustrates clearly the extent to which the floras of selected islands now contain alien species, with the percentage varying between about one-quarter and two-thirds of the total number of species present. Figure 2.31 shows the trends in the spread of naturalized species of plants for six oceanic islands over the last two hundred years.

There are a number of major threats that invasive plants pose to natural ecosystems (Levine et al., 2003). These have been discussed by Cronk and Fuller (1995) and Holzmueller and Jose (2010):

1) Replacement of diverse systems with single species stands of aliens, leading to a reduction in biodiversity, as for example where Australian acacias have invaded the fynbos heathlands of South Africa (Le Maitre et al., 2000).
2) Direct threats to native faunas by producing a change of habitat - the invasional meltdown hypothesis.
3) Alteration of soil chemistry. For example, the African *Mesembryanthemum crystallinum* (ice plant) accumulates large quantities of salt. In this way it salinizes invaded areas in Australia and may prevent the native vegetation from establishment. Some plants exude allelopathic chemicals (weapons) that are inhibitory to native species.
4) Alteration of geomorphological processes, especially rates of sedimentation and movement of mobile land forms (e.g. dunes and salt marshes).
5) Plant extinction by competition for light, nutrients, etc.

6) Alteration of fire regime. For example, in Florida, USA, the introduction of the Australasian myrtle (*Melaleuca quinquenervia*) has increased the frequency of fires because of its flammability, and has damaged the native vegetation which is less well adapted to fire.
7) Alteration of hydrological conditions (e.g. reduction in groundwater levels caused by some species having high rates of transpiration).

The introduction of new animals can have an adverse effect on plant species. A clear demonstration of this comes from the atoll of Laysan in the Hawaii group, where rabbits and hares were introduced in 1903 in the hope of establishing a meat cannery. The number of native species of plants at this time was 25; by 1923 it had fallen to four (Stoddart, 1968). Pigs are another animal that have been introduced extensively to the islands of the Pacific. Long-established feral populations are known on many islands. Like rabbits they have caused considerable damage, not least because of their non-fastidious eating habits and their propensity for rooting into the soil. This is a theme that is reviewed by Nunn (1991).

It has often been proposed that the introduction of exotic terrestrial mammals has had a particularly profound effect on the flora of New Zealand. Among the reasons that have been put forward for this belief are that the absence of native terrestrial mammalian herbivores permitted the evolution of a flora highly vulnerable to damage from browsing and grazing, and that the populations of wild animals (including deer and opossums) that were introduced in the nineteenth century grew explosively because of the lack of competitors and predators. It has, however, proved difficult to determine the magnitude of the effects which the introduced mammals had on the native forests (Veblen and Steward, 1982).

Overall, invasive species may be one of the prime causes of loss of biodiversity because of their role in competition, predation, and hybridization, though this is a view that has been challenged by Theodoropoulos (2003). They also have enormous economic costs. On a global basis plant and animal invaders may cost as much as $1.4 trillion a year, representing 5% of the world economy (Pimentel, 2003).

There are many other examples of ecological explosions – bioinvasions – caused by humans creating new habitats. Some of the most striking are associated with the establishment of artificial lakes in place of rivers. Riverine species which cannot cope with the changed conditions tend to disappear, while others that can exploit the new sources of food, and reproduce themselves under the new conditions, multiply rapidly in the absence of competition (Lowe-McConnell, 1975). Vegetation on land flooded as the lake waters rise decomposes to provide a rich supply of nutrients which allow explosive outgrowth of organisms as the new lake fills. In particular, floating plants may form dense mats of vegetation, which in turn support large populations of invertebrate animals, may cause fish deaths by deoxygenating the water, and can create a serious nuisance for turbines, navigators, and fishermen. On Lake Kariba in Central Africa there were dramatic growths in the communities of the South American water fern (*Salvinia molesta*), bladder-wort (*Utricularia*), and the African water lettuce (*Pistia stratiotes*); on the Nile behind the Jebel Aulia Dam there was a huge increase in the number of water hyacinths (*Eichhornia crassipes*); and in the Tennessee Valley lakes there was a massive outbreak of the Eurasian water-millfoil (*Myriophyllum*).

Roads have been of major importance in the spread of plants. As Frenkel (1970) has pointed out in a valuable survey of this aspect of anthropogenic biogeography:

> By providing a route for the bearers of plant propagules – man, animal and vehicle – and by furnishing, along their margins, a highly specialized habitat for plant establishment, roads may facilitate the entry of plants into a new area. In this manner roads supply a cohesive directional component, cutting across physical barriers, linking suitable habitat to suitable habitat.

Roadsides tend to possess a distinctive flora in comparison with the natural vegetation of an area. As Frenkel (1970: 1) has again written:

> Roadsides are characterized by numerous ecological modifications including: treading, soil compaction, confined drainage, increased runoff, removal of organic matter and sometimes additions of litter or waste material of frequently high nitrogen content (including urine and faeces), mowing or crushing of tall vegetation but occasionally the addition of wood chips or straw, substrate maintained in an ecologically open condition by blading, intensified frost action, rill and sheetwash erosion, snow deposition (together with accumulated dirt, gravel, salt and cinder associated with winter maintenance), soil and rock additions related to slumping and rock-falls, and altered microclimatic conditions associated with pavement and right-of-way structures. Furthermore, road rights-of-way may be used for driving stock in which case unselective, hurried but often close grazing may constitute an additional modification. Where highway landscaping or stability of cuts and fills is a concern, exotic or native plants may be planted and nurtured.

The speed with which plants can invade roadsides is impressive. A study by Helliwell (1974) demonstrated that the M1 motorway in England, less than twelve years after its construction, had on its cuttings and embankments not only the thirty species which had been deliberately sown or planted, but more than 350 species that had not been introduced there.

Railways have also played their role in plant dispersal. The classic example of this is provided by the Oxford ragwort, *Senecio squalidus*, a species native to southern Italy. It spread from the Oxford Botanical Garden (where it had been established since at least 1690) and colonized the walls of Oxford. Much of its dispersal to the rest of Britain (Usher, 1973) was achieved by the Great Western Railway, in the vortices of whose trains and in whose cargoes of ballast and iron ore the plumed fruits were carried. The distribution of the plant was very much associated with railway lines, railway towns, and waste ground.

Indeed, by clearing forest, cultivating, depositing rubbish, and many other activities, humans have opened up a whole series of environments which are favourable to colonization by a particular group of plants. Such plants are generally thought of as weeds. One weed which has caused especially severe problems in upland Britain is bracken (*Pteridium aquilinum*), although the problems it poses through rapid encroachment are of wider geographical significance (Pakeman et al., 1996). Indeed, Taylor (1985: 53) maintained that it 'may justifiably be dubbed as the most successful international weed of the twentieth century', for 'it is found, and is mostly expanding, in all of the continents'. This tolerant, aggressive opportunist follows characteristically in the wake of evacuated settlement, deforestation, or reduced grazing pressure. This encroachment results from reduced use of bracken as a resource (e.g. for roofing), and from changes in grazing practices in marginal areas. As bracken is hostile to many other plants and animals, and generates toxins, including some carcinogens, this is a serious issue.

2.19 Air Pollution and Its Effects on Plants

Air pollutants exist in gaseous or particulate forms. The gaseous pollutants may be separated into primary and secondary forms. The primary pollutants, such as sulphur dioxide, most oxides of nitrogen, and carbon monoxide, are those directly emitted into the air from, for example, industrial sources. Secondary air pollutants, like ozone and products of photochemical reactions, are formed as a consequence of subsequent chemical processes in the atmosphere, involving the primary pollutants and other agents such as sunlight. Particulate pollutants consist of very small solid – or liquid-suspended – droplets (for example, dust, smoke, and aerosolic salts), and contain a wide range of insoluble components (for example, quartz) and of soluble components (for example, various common cations, together with chloride, sulphate, and nitrate).

Some of the air pollutants humans have released into the atmosphere have had detrimental impacts on plants (Yunus and Iqbal, 1996): sulphur dioxide, for example, is toxic to them. Increasing levels of atmospheric nitrogen deposition appear to have had a marked effect on the biodiversity of grasslands in Britain (Maskell et al., 2010) and Europe (Stevens et al., 2010, 2011). Some species become crowded out by more robust plants which benefit from the fertilizing effect of this pollutant.

Lichens are also sensitive to air pollution and have been found to be rare in central areas of cities such as Bonn, Helsinki, Stockholm, Paris, and London. Overall it was calculated by Hawksworth and Rose (1976) that more than one-third of England and Wales, extending in a belt from the London area to Birmingham, broadening out to include the industrial Midlands and most of Lancashire and West Yorkshire, and reaching up to Tyneside, lost nearly all its epiphytic lichen flora, largely because of sulphur dioxide pollution (see Section 7.15). By 1970 there were very few lichens present on trees in central London. Hawksworth (1990: 50), indeed, believed 'the evidence that sulphur dioxide is the major pollutant responsible for impoverishment of lichen communities over wide areas of Europe is now overwhelming', but he also pointed out that sulphur dioxide is not necessarily always the cause of impoverishment. Nitrate pollution also can have an adverse effect (van Herk et al., 2003). Some lichens were, however, tolerant of sulphur dioxide (e.g. *Lecanora conizaeoides*) or of nitrate and so survived or flourished (Fenn et al., 2003). With the lower atmospheric sulphate levels of recent years, various cities have seen a dramatic recovery in the diversity of lichen species, as is the case in Tampere, Finland (Ranta, 2001) and in London (Larsen et al., 2007).

Local concentrations of industrial fumes also kill vegetation (Freedman, 1995), as with the smelters of the Sudbury mining district of Canada (Figure 2.32). However, the provincial government of Ontario imposed limits on smelter emissions in 1969 and 1970, and the release of atmospheric pollutants from the Sudbury smelters have been reduced by >95% since then. This has enabled a variety of organisms to recolonize the neighbouring aquatic systems, and the landscape has largely been re-vegetated (Gunn, 2012; Barrett and Watmough, 2015). In Norway a number of the larger Norwegian aluminium smelters built immediately after the Second World War were sited in deep, narrow, steep-sided

Figure 2.32 The great smelter at Sudbury in Canada. Pollution derived from the fumes from such sources can have many deleterious impacts on vegetation in their neighbourhood (ASG).

valleys at the heads of fjords. The relief has not proved conductive to the rapid dispersal of fumes, particularly of fluoride. In one valley a smelter with a production of 1,110,000 tonnes per year caused the death of Scots pines (*Pinus sylveststris*) for over 13 km in each direction up and down the valley. To about 6 km from the source all pines died. Birch, however, seems to be able to withstand these conditions, and to grow vigorously right up to the factory fence (Gilbert, 1975). Likewise in the Kola Peninsula of Russia, the impact of a copper–nickel smelter involves chlorosis and necrosis of boreal forest vegetation, which stretches as far as 55–60 km from the site, while the geochemical analysis of samples of plants and soils shows some impact even at distances of 80–90 km (Rees, 2012).

Photochemical smog is also known to have adverse effects on plants both within cities and on their outskirts. In California, Ponderosa pines (*Pinus ponderosa*) in the San Bernadino Mountains as much as 129 km to the east of Los Angeles have been extensively damaged by smog and ozone (Diem, 2003). Fumigation experiments in the USA show that plant injury can occur at levels only marginally above the natural maximum and well within the summertime levels now known to be present in Britain and the USA. Tropospheric ozone has a number of impacts on forests (Karnosky et al., 2007), including leaf damage, needle damage to conifers, decreasing photosynthesis, reduced productivity, and increasing susceptibility to pest attack. Vegetation will also be adversely affected by excessive quantities of suspended particulate matter in the atmosphere. The particles, by covering leaves and plugging plant stomata, reduce both the absorption of carbon dioxide from the atmosphere and the intensity of sunlight reaching the interior of the leaf. Both tendencies may suppress the growth of some plants.

The adverse effects of pollution on plants are not restricted to air pollution: water and soil pollution can also be serious. Excessive amounts of heavy metals may prove toxic to them and, as a consequence, distinctive patterns of plant species may occur in areas contaminated with the waste from copper, lead, zinc, and nickel mines (Cole and Smith, 1984). Heavy metals in soils may also be toxic to microbes, and especially to fungi which may in turn change the environment by reducing rates of leaf-litter decomposition. In many areas it has proved extremely difficult to undertake effective re-establishment of plant communities on mining spoil tips, though toxicity is only one of the problems (Kent, 1982).

Other types of industrial effluents may smother and poison some species. Salt marshes, mangrove swamps, and other kinds of wetlands are particularly sensitive to oil spills, for they tend to be anaerobic environments in which the plants must ventilate their root systems through pores or openings that are prone to coating and clogging (Lugo et al., 1981). The situation is especially serious if the system is not subjected to flushing by, for example, frequent tidal inundation.

2.20 Forest Decline

Forest decline, often called *Waldsterben* or *Waldschäden* (the German words for 'forest death' and 'forest decline'), was an environmental issue that attained considerable prominence in the 1980s. The common symptoms of this phenomenon (modified from World Resources Institute, 1986: table 12.9) are:

1) *Growth-decreasing symptoms*:
   discolouration and loss of needles and leaves;
   loss of feeder-root biomass (especially in conifers);
   decreased annual increment (width of growth rings);
   premature ageing of older needles in conifers;
   increased susceptibility to secondary root and foliar pathogens;
   death of herbaceous vegetation beneath affected trees;
   prodigious production of lichens on affected trees;
   death of affected trees.

2) *Abnormal growth symptoms*:
   active shedding of needles and leaves while still green, with no indication of disease;
   shedding of whole green shoots, especially in spruce;
   altered branching habit;
   altered morphology of leaves.
3) *Water-stress symptoms*:
   altered water balance;
   increased incidence of wet wood disease.

The decline appeared to be widespread in much of Europe and to be particularly severe in Poland (Figure 2.33) and the Czech Republic (see Table 2.8). The process was also thought to be undermining the health of North America's high-elevation eastern coniferous forests (World Resources Institute, 1986: chapter 12). In Germany it was the white fir, *Abies alba*, which was afflicted initially, but since then the symptoms have spread to at least ten other species in Europe, including Norway spruce (*Picea abies*), Scotch pine (*Pinus sylvestris*), European larch (*Larix decidua*), and seven broad-leaved species.

In south-western Europe and in north-west Africa, extensive dieback of the cork oak (*Quercus suber*) has occurred. Mediterranean cork oak savannas are ecosystems of high socio-economic and conservation value. Characterized by sparse tree cover and a diversity of understory vegetation – ranging from shrub formations to grasslands – they support high levels of biodiversity. They require active management and use by humans to ensure their continued existence. Cork oak has been under stress because management has declined, and this has allowed the spread of shrubs into pastures with cork oaks. Field abandonment has occurred because of a reduced demand for cork in the era of screw-top wine bottles (Costa et al., 2009; Bugalho et al., 2011). However, the decline of the cork oak has also been triggered by increasing drought, and subsequent attack by pathogens,

Figure 2.33 Dead conifer trees resulting from acid precipitation in the Stołowe Mountains, south-west Poland (ASG).

ASKHAM BRYAN
COLLEGE
LEARNING RESOURCES

Table 2.8 Results from forest damage surveys in Europe: percentage of trees with >25% defoliation (all species).

	Mean of 1993/94
Austria	8
Belarus	33
Belgium	16
Bulgaria	26
Croatia	24
Czech Republic	56
Denmark	35
Estonia	18
Finland	14
France	8
Germany	24
Greece	22
Hungary	21
Italy	19
Latvia	33
Lithuania	26
Luxembourg	29
Netherlands	22
Norway	26
Poland	52
Portugal	7
Romania	21
Slovak Republic	40
Slovenia	18
Spain	16
Switzerland	20
UK	15

Source: from FAO (2001).

including the fungus, *Phytophthora cinnamomi* (Costa et al., 2010; Tiberi et al., 2016). The holm oak (*Quercus ilex*) has also shown severe declines in Spain, and this has been attributed to increasing drought stress (Natalini et al., 2016).

Trees in North America were also adversely affected, probably because of acid rain. Likens (2010) reported that since the 1960s more than half of large-canopy red spruce in the Adirondack Mountains of New York and the Green Mountains of Vermont and approximately one-quarter of large-canopy red spruce in the White Mountains of New Hampshire have died. Extensive mortality among sugar maples in Pennsylvania has also occurred. In the mountains of the north-west USA and Canada, *Pinus albicaulis*, the whitebark, has suffered from a range of possible factors: fire suppression policies, blister rust, mountain pine beetle infestation, and warmer temperatures (Larson and Kipfmueller, 2012). Wong and Daniels (2017) examined the links between climate fluctuations and the impact of infestation in the Canadian Rockies, and found that climatic variation during a cool Pacific Decadal Oscillation phase (1947–1976) caused drought stress that may have predisposed trees to the blister rust pathogen (*Cronartium ribicola*). A subsequent decline in snowpack and warming temperatures probably then incited further climatic stress and with blister rust this reduced tree resistance to bark beetles (*Dendroctonus ponderosae*). Ultimately, bark beetles and blister rust contributed to tree death. Their findings pointed to the complexity of whitebark pine decline and the importance of considering multi-way drought–disease–insect interactions over various timescales when interpreting this decline.

Indeed, many hypotheses have been put forward to explain forest dieback (Wellburn, 1988): poor forest management practices, ageing of stands, climatic change, severe climatic events (such as the severe droughts in Britain during 1976), nutrient deficiency, viruses, fungal pathogens, and pest infestation (Hicke et al., 2012). The last of these has been accelerated by the introduction of invasive pests in plant imports (Liebhold et al., 2012). However, particular attention is being paid to the role of pollution, either by gaseous pollutants (sulphur dioxide, nitrous oxide, or ozone), acid deposition on leaves and needles, soil acidification and associated aluminium toxicity problems, excess leaching of nutrients (for example, magnesium), over-fertilization by deposited nitrogen, and trace metal or synthetic organic compound (e.g. pesticide, herbicide) accumulation as a result of atmospheric deposition. The arguments for and against each of these possible factors were expertly reviewed by Innes (1987), who believes that in all probability most cases of forest decline are the result of the cumulative effects of a number of stresses. He drew a distinction between predisposing, inciting, and contributing stresses (p. 25):

> Predisposing stresses are those that operate over long time scales, such as climatic change and changes in soil properties. They place the tree under permanent stress and may weaken its ability to resist other forms of stress. Inciting stresses are those such as drought, frost and short-term pollution episodes that operate over short time scales. A fully healthy tree would probably have been able to cope with these, but the presence of predisposing stresses interferes with the tree's mechanisms of natural recovery. Contributing stresses appear in weakened plants and are frequently classed as

secondary factors. They include attack by some insect pests and root fungi. It is probable that all three types of stress are involved in the decline of trees.

An alternative categorization of the stresses leading to forest decline was proposed by Nihlgård (1997). He also had three classes of stress that have a temporal dimension: predisposing factors (related primarily to pollution and long-term climatic change); triggering factors (including droughts, frosts, and inappropriate management or choice of trees); and mortal factors such as pests, pathogenic fungi, and extreme weather events, which can lead to plant death (Figure 2.34).

As with many environmental problems, interpretation of forest decline is bedevilled by a paucity of long-term data and detailed surveys. Given that forest condition oscillates from year to year in response to variability in climatic stress (e.g. drought, frost, wind throw) it is dangerous to infer long-term trends from short-term data. There may also be differences in causation in different areas. Thus while widespread forest death in Eastern Europe may result from high concentrations of sulphur dioxide combined with extreme winter stress, this is a much less likely explanation in Britain, where sulphur dioxide concentrations have shown a marked decrease in recent years (see Section 7.15). Indeed, in Britain Innes and Boswell (1990: 46) suggest that the direct effects of gaseous pollutants appear to be very limited.

It is also important to recognize that some stresses may be particularly significant for a particular tree species. Thus, in 1987 a survey of ash trees (*Fraxinus excelsior*) in Great Britain showed extensive dieback over large areas of the country. Almost one-fifth of all ash trees sampled showed evidence of this phenomenon. Hull and Gibbs (1991) indicated that there was an association between dieback and the way the land is managed around the tree, with particularly high levels of damage being evident in trees adjacent to arable land.

Uncontrolled stubble burning, the effects of drifting herbicides, and the consequences of excessive nitrate fertilizer applications to adjacent fields were seen as possible mechanisms. However, the prime cause of dieback was seen to be root disturbance and soil compaction by large agricultural machinery. Ash has shallow roots and if these are damaged repeatedly the tree's uptake of water and nutrients might be seriously reduced, while broken root surfaces would be prone to infection by pathogenic fungi. Ash dieback disease, caused by the fungal pathogen *Hymenoscyphus fraxineus* is a current epidemic in Europe (Gross et al., 2014; Needham et al., 2016). This introduced pathogen was previously called *Chalara fraxinea*. Trees now believed to have been infected with it were reported dying in large numbers in Poland in 1992 and by the mid-1990s it was also found in the Baltic States. By 2008 the disease was also discovered in Scandinavia, the Czech Republic (Czechia), Slovenia, Germany, Austria, and Switzerland. By 2012 it had spread to Belgium, France, Hungary, Italy, Luxembourg, the Netherlands, Romania, Russia, and the British Isles. Concerns are also being expressed that European ash trees could be severely damaged in the future by the eastward spread of the Emerald Ash Borer beetle (*Agrilus planipennis*). This same beetle has already entered North America from Asia and has caused the death of millions of ash trees (Herms and McCullough, 2014). The entry of exotic insect invaders and pathogens via the importation of live plants and wood packing material, such as pallets and crates, poses a major threat to the health of US forests. Already, introduced insects and diseases occur in forests, gardens, and parks throughout the United States, and the problem is particularly severe in the North-East and Upper Mid-West (Lovett et al., 2016). For example, the introduction of the hemlock woolly adelgid (*Adelges tsugae*) in the eastern United States from Japan has caused extensive damage to and extirpation of eastern hemlock (*Tsuga canadensis*) stands (Gómez et al., 2015).

Predisposing factors	Triggering factors	Mortal factors
Acid rain	Drought	Pathogenic fungi (on roots and stems)
Nitrogen deposition	Frost	Insect pests (on stems)
Gases (e.g. SO$_2$, O$_2$)	Strong precipitation (waterlogging)	Extreme weather perturbations
Heavy metals	Storm	
Climate change (causing physiological stress)	Wrong type of tree	

Figure 2.34 Some of the different stress variables used to explain forest decline. *Source:* adapted from Nihlgård (1997: figure 24-1).

Innes (1992: 51) suggested that there had been some modification in views about the seriousness of the European forest dieback problem since the mid-1980s:

> The extent and magnitude of the forest decline is much less than initially believed. The use of crown density as an index of tree health has resulted in very inflated figures for forest 'damage' which cannot now be justified ... If early surveys are discounted on the basis of inconsistent methodology ... then there is very little evidence for a large-scale decline of tree health in Europe.
>
> ... the term 'forest decline' is rather misleading in that there are relatively few cases where entire forest ecosystems are declining. Forest ecosystems are dynamic and may change through natural processes.

Removal of some stresses, such as reduction in atmospheric sulphur dioxide levels in recent decades, has enabled some forests to show signs of marked recovery (e.g. Elling et al., 2009; Hauck et al., 2012), though longer term nutrient imbalances may limit the amount of recovery that occurs (Jonard et al., 2012).

2.21 Miscellaneous Causes of Plant Decline

Some of the main causes of plant decline have already been referred to: deforestation, grazing, fire, and pollution. However, there are many records of species being affected by other forms of human interference. For example, casual flower-picking has resulted in local elimination of previously common species, and has been held responsible for decreases in species such as the primrose (*Primula vulgaris*) on a national scale in England. In addition, serious naturalists or plant collectors using their botanical knowledge to seek out rare, local, and unusual species can cause the eradication of rare plants in an area. More significantly, agricultural 'improvements' mean that many types of habitat are disappearing or that the range of such habitats is diminishing. Plants associated with distinctive habitats suffer a comparable reduction in their range. Other plants have suffered a reduction in range because of drainage activities.

The introduction of pests, either deliberately or accidentally, can also lead to a decrease in the range and numbers of a particular species (Liebhold et al., 2012). Reference has already been made to the decline in the fortunes of the elm in Britain, because of the unintentional establishment of Dutch Elm Disease, and to the current problem of ash dieback. Another example is that of *Opuntia* (prickly pear). This is a spiny perennial succulent shrub which is native to south-east USA, eastern Mexico, and some Caribbean Islands. This species has been recorded as naturalized and/or invasive in several African countries, India and Sri Lanka, Yemen and Saudi Arabia, France, Italy and Spain, and on the Galápagos Islands, Cuba, Madagascar, and Australia (Shackleton et al., 2017). It was initially introduced to many of these regions for ornamental and hedging purposes, but has escaped cultivation and has spread, including into conservation zones, rangelands, and agricultural areas (Figure 2.35). It was introduced into Australia some time before 1839, and spread dramatically. By 1900, it covered 4 million ha, and by 1925 more than 24 million. Of the latter figure approximately one-half was occupied by dense growth (1200–2000 tonnes per ha) and other more useful plants were excluded. To combat this menace one of *Opuntia's* natural enemies, a South American moth, *Cactoblastus*, was introduced to remarkable effect. By the year 1940 not less than 95% of the former area of prickly pear in Queensland had been wiped out (Dodd, 1959).

Figure 2.35 The prickly pear (*Opuntia*) is a plant that has been introduced from the Americas to Africa and Australia. It has often spread explosively. Recently it has been controlled by the introduction of moths and beetles, an example of biological control (ASG).

Finally, the growth of leisure activities is placing greater pressure on increasingly fragile communities, notably in tundra and high-altitude areas. These areas tend to recover slowly from disturbance, and both the trampling of human feet and the actions of vehicles can be severe.

2.22 The Change in Genetic and Species Diversity

The application of modern science, technology, and industry to agriculture has led to some spectacular progress in recent decades through such developments as the use of fertilizers and the selective breeding of plants and animals. The latter has caused some concern, for in the process of evolution domesticated plants have become strikingly different from their wild progenitors. Plant species that have been cultivated for a very long time and are widely distributed demonstrate this particularly clearly. Crop evolution through the millennia has been shaped by complex interactions reflecting the pressures of both artificial and natural selection. Alternate isolation of stocks followed by migration and seed exchanges brought distinctive stocks into new environments and permitted new hybridizations and the recombination of characteristics. Great genetic diversity resulted.

There are fears, however, that since the Second World War the situation has begun to change (Harlan, 1975). Modern plant-breeding programmes have been established in many parts of the developing world in the midst of genetically rich centres of diversity. Some of these programmes, associated with the so-called Green Revolution, have been successful, and new, uniform high-yielding varieties have begun to replace the wide range of old, local strains that have evolved over the millennia. This may lead to a serious decline in the genetic resources which could potentially serve as reservoirs of variability.

New, high-yielding crop varieties need continuous development if they are to avoid the effects of crop pests, and Ehrlich and Ehrlich (1982: 65) summarized the situation thus:

> The life of a new cultivated wheat variety in the American Northwest is about five years. The rusts (fungi) adapt to the strain, and a new resistant one must be developed. That development is done through artificial selection: the plant breeder carefully combines genetic types that show promise of giving resistance.

The impact of human activities on species diversity, while clearly negative on a global scale (as evidenced by extinction rates), is not so cut-and-dried on the local scale. Under certain conditions chronic stress caused by humans can lead to extremely high numbers of coexisting species within small areas. By contrast, site enrichment or fertilization can result in a decline of species density (Peet et al., 1983). Grassland enrichment experiments employing fertilizers have suggested that in many cases high growth rates result in the competitive exclusion of many plants. Thus the tremendous increase in fertilizer use in agriculture has had in retrospect the predictable result of a widespread decrease in the species diversity of grasslands.

Certain low productivity grasslands, which have been grazed for long periods, have high species densities in Japan, the UK, and the Netherlands. The same applies to Mediterranean scrub vegetation in Israel, and to savanna in Sri Lanka and North Carolina (United States). Studies have confirmed that species densities may increase in areas subject to chronic mowing, burning, domestic grazing, rabbit grazing, or trampling. It is likely that in such ecosystems humans encourage a high diversity of plant growth by acting as a 'keystone predator', a species which prevents competitive exclusion by a few dominant species.

One other area in which major developments will take place in the coming years, which will have implications for plant life, is the field of genetic engineering. This involves the manipulation of DNA, the basic chromosomal unit that exists in all cells and contains genetic information that is passed on to subsequent generations. Recombinant DNA technology (also known as *in vitro* genetic manipulation and gene cloning) enables the insertion of foreign DNA (containing the genetic information necessary to confer a particular target characteristic) into a vector. The advent of modern techniques of genetic modification (GM) enables the removal of individual genes from one species and their insertion into another, without the need for sexual compatibility. Once the new gene has been inserted, offspring that will contain copies of that new gene can be produced in the traditional manner. For example, a bacterial gene can be inserted into maize to give it resistance to certain insect pests. Indeed, genetic engineering is vastly different from conventional plant breeding methods because it allows scientists to insert a gene or genes from virtually any organism into any other organism. Fears have been expressed that this technology could produce pathogens that might interact detrimentally with naturally occurring species (see e.g. Beringer, 2000; Letourneau and Burrows, 2001).

It has also been feared that GM could make a plant more invasive, leading to a new threat from super-weeds. Equally, some genetically modified crops might be highly effective at controlling or eliminating weeds, thereby disrupting essential food sources for a wide range of organisms. Conversely, genetically modified herbicide-tolerant crops would bring greater economy and feasibility in weed control, so that fewer environmentally damaging chemical herbicides would be used than in conventional farming (Squire et al., 2003). Other beneficial traits from GM technology include resistance to insects or pathogens, drought resistance and salt tolerance, the ability to fix nitrogen, and so forth (Jones, 2011). There is an urgent need to evaluate the costs and benefits of this new technology, for already GM crops are being widely grown. The number of hectares planted to them in the USA increased from 1.4 million ha in 1996 to around 40 million ha in 2003. An estimated 38 trillion GM plants have now been grown in American soil! Globally, between 1997 and 2010 the total surface area of land cultivated with GM crops had increased from 17,000 km^2 to 1,480,000 km^2, though since then there has been some reduction in the rate of increase (Figure 2.36).

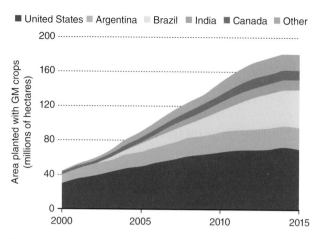

Figure 2.36 The area planted with GM crops in different parts of the world between 2000 and 2015. The rate has evened out in recent years. *Source:* Ledford, Heidi G.M. crop planting declines for the first time: Total area sown with genetically modified plants fell 1% in 2015, NATURE | TREND WATCH, April 2016.

2.23 Conclusion: Threats to Plant Life

Humans have transformed the biosphere and particularly over the last century have transformed the majority of the terrestrial biosphere into intensively used 'anthromes' with predominantly novel anthropogenic processes (Ellis, 2011). Land-use changes have impacted strongly on biodiversity (Newbold et al., 2015) and there is little evidence that despite some local successes and increasing responses (including extent and biodiversity coverage of protected areas, sustainable forest management, policy responses to invasive alien species, and biodiversity-related aid), the rate of biodiversity loss does not appear to be slowing (Butchart et al., 2010). There

have been few known global extinctions so far, but many additional species have not been recorded recently and may be extinct. Perhaps a third of all land plants are at risk of extinction (Corlett, 2016). Habitat loss and associated fragmentation is the biggest single threat to plant diversity, particularly in the tropics. Collection for the horticultural trade and for private collections is the biggest single threat to the cacti and, in many areas, orchids as well as cycads and ornamental species. Invasive alien species are another potential threat to native plant diversity, and every plant on Earth today is exposed to an atmosphere that differs significantly in composition from any that its ancestors would have experienced. However, more optimistically, there is some evidence that ecosystems can recover quite rapidly from many human impacts if sustainable practices are introduced (Jones and Schmitz, 2009).

Guide to Reading

Crutzen, P.J. and Goldammer, J.G. (1993) *Fire in the Environment*. Chichester: Wiley. A particularly useful study of fire's importance.

Douglas, I., Goode, D., Houck, C. and Wang, R. (eds) (2011) *The Routledge Handbook of Urban Ecology*. London: Routledge. A large edited compendium on the environment of cities.

Grove, A.T. and Rackham, O. (2002) *The Nature of Mediterranean Europe: An Ecological History*. New Haven, CT, and London: Yale University Press. A well-illustrated account of natural and human changes in the Mediterranean lands.

Holzner, W., Werger, M.J.A., Werger, I. and Ikusima, I. (eds) (1983) *Man's Impact on Vegetation*. The Hague: Junk. A wide-ranging edited work with examples from many parts of the world.

Imeson, A. (2012) *Desertification, Land Degradation and Sustainability*. Chichester: Wiley Blackwell. A review of research on desertification and on landscape degradation more generally.

Manning, R. (1995) *Grassland: The History, Biology, Politics and Promise of the American Prairie*. New York: Viking Books. A 'popular' discussion of the great grasslands of North America.

Meyer, W.B. and Turner, B.L. (eds) (1994) *Changes in Land Use and Land Cover: A Global Perspective.* Cambridge: Cambridge University Press. An excellent edited survey of human transformation of the biosphere.

Pimentel, D. (ed.) (2003) *Biological Invasions.* Washington, DC: CRC Press. An edited, international account of invasive species.

Stewart, C.N. (2004) *Genetically Modified Planet: Environmental Impacts of Genetically Engineered Plants.* Oxford: Oxford University Press. A readable review of the costs and benefits of GM plants.

Williams, M. (2003) *Deforesting the Earth: From Prehistory to Global Crisis.* Chicago: University of Chicago Press. A magisterial and scholarly overview of the global history of deforestation.

3

The Human Impact on Animals

CHAPTER OVERVIEW

Humans now have the greatest biomass or anthropomass of any species and it is an order of magnitude greater than the mass of all terrestrial mammals alive today. The impact that they have had on animals can be grouped conveniently into five main categories: domestication, dispersal, extinction, expansion, and contraction. Humans have domesticated many animals, to the extent that, as with many plants, those animals depend on humans for their survival and, in some cases, for their reproduction. As with plants, people have helped to disperse animals deliberately, though many have also been dispersed accidentally, for the numbers of animals that accompany people without their leave is enormous, especially if we include the clouds of micro-organisms that infest their land, food, clothes, shelter, domestic animals, and their own bodies. The extinction of animals by human predators has been extensive over the past 20,000 years, and in spite of recent interest in conservation continues at a high rate. In addition, the presence of humans has led to the contraction in the distribution and welfare of many animals (because of factors like pollution), though in other cases human alteration of the environment and modification of competition has favoured the expansion of some species, both numerically and spatially.

3.1 Domestication of Animals

We have already referred in Section 1.5 to one of the great themes in the study of human influence on nature: domestication. This has been one of the most profound ways in which humans have affected animals, for during the ten or eleven millennia that have passed since this process was initiated the animals that human societies have selected as useful to them have undergone major changes. The most important centre of animal domestication, shown in Figure 1.11, was South-West Asia (Diamond, 1997) (cattle, sheep, goat and pig), but other centres were important (e.g. the chicken in South-East Asia, the turkey in the Andes, and the horse in the Ukraine). Curiously, in spite of its large number of mammals, Africa was not a major centre of animal domestication (Beja-Pereira et al., 2004). Relatively few animal species have been domesticated in comparison with plant species, but for those that have been the consequences are so substantial that the differences between breeds of animals of the same species often exceed those between different species under natural conditions (Figure 3.1). A cursory and superficial comparison of the tremendous range of shapes and sizes of modern dog breeds (as, for example, between a wolfhound and a chihuahua) is sufficient to establish the extent of alteration brought about by domestication, and the speed at which domestication has accelerated the process of evolution. In particular, humans have changed and enhanced the characteristics for which they originally chose to domesticate animals. For example, the wild ancestors of cattle gave no more than a few hundred millilitres of milk; today the best milk cow can yield up to 15,000 litres of milk during its lactation period.

The wild ancestors of domesticated sheep had several characteristics, such as a relative lack of aggression, a manageable size, early sexual maturity, a social nature, and high reproduction rates, which made them particularly suitable candidates for domestication. As a result of domestication, sheep have changed enormously (Ryder, 1966). Wild sheep have short tails, while modern domestic sheep have long tails which may have arisen during human selection of a fat tail. Wild sheep also have an overall brown colour, whereas domestic sheep tend to be mainly white. Moreover, the woolly undercoats of wild sheep have developed at the expense of bristly outer

Human Impact on the Natural Environment: Past, Present and Future, Eighth Edition. Andrew S. Goudie.
© 2019 John Wiley & Sons Ltd. Published 2019 by John Wiley & Sons Ltd.
Companion website: www.wiley.com/go/goudie/human-impact-natural-environment

Figure 3.1 The consequences of domestication for the form of animals is dramatically illustrated by this large-horned but dwarf cow being displayed in a circus in Chamonix, France (ASG).

coats. With the ancestors of domestic sheep, wool (which served as protection for the skin and as insulation) consisted mainly of thick rough hairs and a small amount of down; the total weight of wool grown per year probably never reached 1 kilogram. Wild sheep were more hairy than woolly. The wool of present-day fine-fleeced sheep consists of uniform, thin down fibres and the total yearly weight may now reach 20 kilograms. Wild sheep also undergo a complete spring moult, while domestic sheep rarely shed wool. Indeed, one of the most important consequences or manifestations of the domestication of animals consists of a sharp change in their seasonal biology. Whereas wild ancestors of domesticated beasts are often characterized by relatively strict seasonal reproduction and moulting rhythms, most domesticated species can reproduce at almost any season of the year and tend not to moult to a seasonal pattern.

3.2 Dispersal and Invasions of Animals

Zoogeographers have devoted much time to dividing the world into regions with distinctive animal life – the great 'faunal realms' of Wallace and subsequent workers. This pattern of wildlife distribution evolved slowly over geological time. The most striking dividing line between such realms is probably that between Australasia and Asia – Wallace's Line. Because of its isolation from the Asian land mass, Australasia developed a distinctive fauna characterized by its relative absence of placental mammals, its well-developed marsupials, and the egg-laying monotremes (echidna and the platypus).

Modern societies, by moving wildlife from place to place, consciously or otherwise, are breaking down these classic distinct faunal realms. The human-assisted movement of plants, animals, and microbes around the world

has increased hugely over recent centuries, breaking down geographic barriers between species that exhibit incomplete genetic barriers to reproduction and, hence, setting the scene for a massive increase in levels of hybridization (Thomas, 2015). They are also facilitating what are called ecological or biological invasions (Davis, 2009), which are causing biotic homogenization (Olden et al., 2011). In terms of the number of countries where they are considered to be invasive, the Global Invasive Species Information Network (2011) (http:www.gisin.org?cwis438/Websites/GISNDirectory/SpeciesStatus_Topoinvasives.php?, accessed December 2017) listed rats (*Rattus rattus* and *Rattus norvegicus*), cats (*Felis catus*), goats (*Capra hircus*), American mink (*Mustela vison*), and the house mouse (*Mus musculus*) as the most widespread invasive animals. Highly adaptable and dispersive forms are spreading, perhaps at the expense of more specialized organisms. Humans have introduced a new order of magnitude into distances over which dispersal takes place, and through the transport by design or accident of seeds or other propagules, through the disturbance of native plant and animal communities and of their habitat, and by the creation of new habitats and niches, the invasion and colonization by adventive species is facilitated. The effective management of invasive alien species is a major concern for biological conservation worldwide (Clout and Williams, 2009), for invasive species are the major threat, for example, to seabird populations, including penguins, albatrosses, and petrels (Croxall et al., 2012).

Di Castri (1989) identified three main stages in the process of biological invasions stimulated by human actions. In the first stage, covering several millennia up to about AD 1500, human historical events favoured invasions and migrations primarily within the Old World. The second stage commenced about AD 1500, with the discovery, exploration, and colonization of new territories, and the initiation of 'the globalization of exchanges'. It was characterized by flows of invaders from, to, and within the Old World. The third stage, which only covers the last 100 to 150 years, sees an even more extensive 'multifocal globalization' and an increasing rate of exchanges. The Eurocentric focus has diminished.

Deliberate introductions of new animals to new areas have been carried out for many reasons: for food, sport, revenue, sentiment, control of other pests, and for aesthetic purposes. Such *deliberate* actions probably account, for instance, for the widespread distribution of brown trout (*Salmo trutta*) (Elliott, 1989) (see Figure 3.2). This was originally an essentially European species but has now been deliberately introduced for commercial and sport fishing to at least twenty-four countries outside Europe. Likewise the rainbow trout

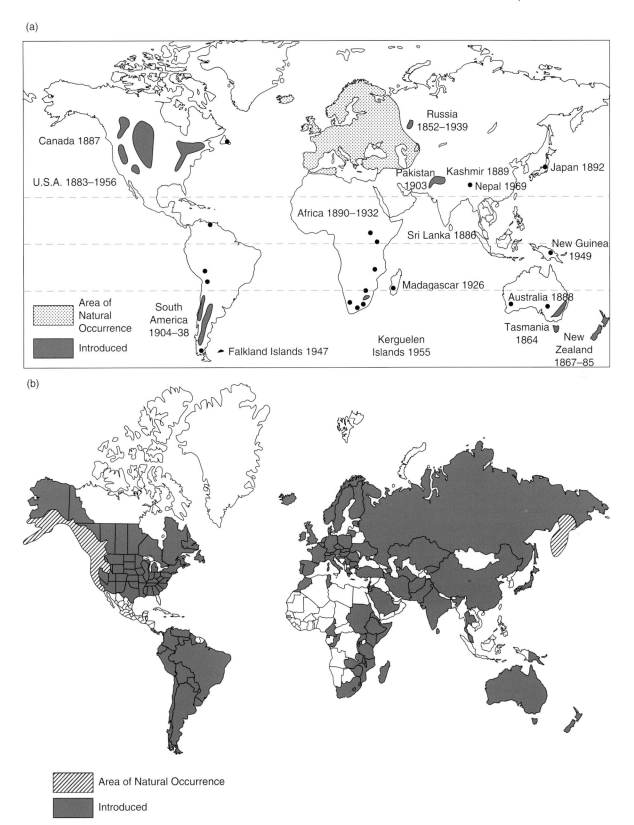

Figure 3.2 (a) The original area of distribution of the brown trout, *Salmo trutta*, areas where it has been artificially naturalized and the dates when first introduced. *Source:* adapted from MacCrimmon in Illies (1974: figure 3.2) and Elliott (1989: figure 2). (b) Native distribution of rainbow trout, *Oncorhynchus mykiss*, and the countries, states or provinces into which this species has been introduced. *Source:* adapted from Crawford and Muir (2008: figure 7).

(*Oncorhynchus mykiss*) has spread from its natural habitats on the Pacific margins of North America and Russia to much of the rest of the world (Crawford and Muir, 2008).

There have, however, been many *accidental* introductions, especially since the development of sea-going ships. This includes rats. These have been introduced to many islands, and the most intensive studies have been on the Pacific rat (*Rattus exulans*), a small South-East Asian species spread by Polynesians throughout the Pacific. These and the more recently introduced Norway rat (*R. norvegicus*) and ship (roof) rat (*R. rattus*) suppress some forest plants, and are associated with extinctions or declines of flightless invertebrates, ground-dwelling reptiles, land birds, and burrowing seabirds (Towns et al., 2006; Harper and Bunbury, 2015).

The rate of introductions is increasing, for whereas in the eighteenth century there were few ocean-going vessels of more than 300 tonnes, today there are thousands. Sea-borne trade exceeded 8.4 billion tonnes per year in 2010, with much of it carried in millions of containers. Many vessels dump ballast containing potentially invasive exotic species. The spread of the highly invasive fish, the goby (*Neoglobius melanostomus*) into the Great Lakes region of North America from the Black Sea is due to this cause (Kornis et al., 2012). Because of this, in the words of Elton (1958: 31), 'we are seeing one of the great historical convulsions in the world's fauna and flora'. Indeed, many animals are introduced with vegetable products, for 'just as trade followed the flag, so animals have followed the plants'. One of the most striking examples of the accidental introduction of animals given by Elton is the arrival of some chafer beetles, *Popillia japonica* (the Japanese beetle), in New Jersey in a consignment of plants from Japan. Despite concerted federal and state efforts to eradicate it, and then to limit its spread, this beetle progressively extended its range. It now is the most widespread and destructive insect pest of turf and landscape plants in the eastern United States. From an initial population of about one dozen beetles in 1916, the centre of population grew rapidly outwards to cover many thousands of square kilometres in only a few decades. By 1998, it was established in all states east of the Mississippi River except for Florida, as well as parts of Wisconsin, Minnesota, Iowa, and Nebraska, and into southern Ontario and Quebec, Canada (Potter and Held 2002).

A more recent example of the spread of an introduced insect in the Americas is provided by the Africanized honey bee which is popularly known as the 'killer bee' (Rinderer et al., 1993). A number of these were brought to Brazil from South Africa in 1957 as an experiment and some escaped. Since then (Figure 3.3) they have moved northwards to Central America and Texas, spreading at a rate of 300–500 km per year, and competing with established populations of European honey bees. In 1998 they reached as far north as Nevada and in 2009 as far north as southern Utah. Goulson (2003) reviews some of the adverse environmental effects of introduced bees, including their pollination of exotic weeds.

While domesticated plants have, in most cases, been unable to survive without human help, the same is not so true of domesticated animals. There are a great many examples of cattle, horses (see e.g. McKnight, 1959), donkeys, and goats which have effectively adapted to new environments and have virtually become wild (feral). Frequently feral animals have both ousted native animals and, particularly in the case of goats on ocean islands, caused desertification. Indeed, animal invaders have had tragic consequences for the native Australian fauna and flora. Among the worst offenders are the rabbit, the fox, feral pigs and goats, dogs, cats, mice, buffalo, horses, camels, rats, cane toads, and various birds (Bomford and Hart, 2002). In neighbouring New Zealand, Australian brushtail possums (*Trichosaurus vulpecula*) have become major pests, and their population is estimated to be around 30 million.

In northern Australia, water buffalo (*Bubalus bubalis*) were introduced (McKnight, 1971) between 1824 and 1849 into the Northern Territory from Timor and other islands in the Indonesian archipelago. In 1886, a few milking types were brought from India to Darwin. In 2008 there were estimated to be 150,000 animals across northern Australia. Prior to extensive culling in the 1980s, as part of the Brucellosis and Tuberculosis Eradication Campaign, there were as many as 350,000. The feral buffalo has been a major environmental disaster in the wetlands of the top end of the Northern Territory:

> When the population was at its highest, from the 1960s to the 1980s, the feral buffalo grossly altered the character of the northern floodplains. With its wallows, trails, dung, trampling and disturbance, it caused soil erosion, channelling of floodwaters, increased intrusion of saltwater into freshwater habitats and destruction of wetland vegetation. Many native wetland flora and fauna failed to thrive in the muddied or salt-polluted water. They also suffered from the disturbance and loss of cover. Crocodiles, barramundi, freshwater turtles and other native species declined, and many waterbirds, including magpie geese, lost their habitat. Feral buffalo eat large volumes of grasses and other plants, removing this food source for native wildlife, and they can damage the trees they regularly rub against. Their trampling and soil disturbance also promotes the spread of weeds across the landscape.

Figure 3.3 The spread of the Africanized honey bee in the Americas between 1957 (when it was introduced to Brazil) and 1990. *Source:* adapted from Texas Agricultural Experiment Station in *Christian Science Monitor*, September 1991.

(https://www.environment.gov.au/biodiversity/invasive-species/publications/factsheet-feral-water-buffalo-bubalus-bubalis, accessed December 2017)

The story of the feral camel in Australia is especially striking. The one-humped dromedary (*Camelus dromadarius*) was introduced in 1840 and between 1880 and 1907 some 20,000 were imported. However, with the advent of motor transport they became largely redundant, and between 1920 and 1941 between 5000 and 10,000 were released into the wild. There are now probably around one million feral camels spread over 3.3 million km² (Saalfield and Edwards, 2010). They have a wide range of adverse environmental effects (Edwards et al., 2010). The numbers of other feral animals are even greater, with 2.6 million goats, 5 million donkeys, and between 13 and 23 million pigs. In addition there are over 7 million red foxes, and more than 200 million rabbits.

A dreadful import into Australia is the cane toad. These have a major impact on other organisms, because they are highly poisonous – something Australians call 'toxic tucker'. They were originally introduced into Queensland from Hawaii in 1935 as a potential means of controlling beetles that were damaging sugar plantations. They have now spread as far as the north of Western Australia (Phillips et al., 2007).

The European rabbit (*Oryctolagus cuniculus*) was introduced into Britain in early medieval times and, originally an inhabitant of the western Mediterranean lands, it was kept for food and fur in carefully tended warrens. Agricultural improvements, especially to grassland, together with the increasing decline in the numbers of predators such as hawks and foxes, brought about by game-guarding landlords (Sheail, 1971), enabled the rabbit to become one of the most numerous of mammals in the British countryside. By the early 1950s there were 60–100 million of them. Frequently, as many contemporary reports demonstrated, they grazed the land so close that in areas of light soil, like the Breckland of East Anglia or in coastal dune areas, wind erosion became a serious problem. There are now probably around 37 million rabbits in the UK. Similarly, the rabbit flourished in Australia, especially after the introduction of the merino sheep which created favourable pasture-lands. Rabbits were introduced to Australia by the First Fleet and the first feral populations were established in Tasmania by 1827. The Victorian Acclimatisation Society released 24 rabbits on Christmas Day 1859 to hunt for sport and to help settlers feel more 'at home'. By 1886, rabbits had spread as far as the Queensland–New South Wales border and by 1900 they had reached Western Australia and the Northern Territory. In the 60 years following 1886, rabbits invaded 4 million square kilometres of Australia. By 1920 it is thought there were 10 billion rabbits in Australia. Erosion in susceptible lands like the Mallee was severe. Both in England and Australia an effective strategy developed to control the rabbit was the introduction of a South American virus, *Myxoma*. The current population of rabbits in Australia is currently estimated to be 200 million, a great reduction from that of the 1920s.

Deer are a British mammal, the recent expansion of which has had diverse ecological consequences. There are six species of them living wild in Great Britain: the red deer, roe deer, fallow deer, sika deer, Reeves's muntjac, and the Chinese water deer. Of those, red and roe deer are native and have lived in Britain throughout the Holocene. Fallow deer have been reintroduced twice, by the Romans and the Normans, after they died out in the last ice age. The other three are escaped or released alien species. The rapid increase in deer numbers occurring in Britain in recent decades (Ward, 2005) is due to several possible factors, including: increased woodland cover; milder winters leading to improved deer fecundity,

changes to agriculture, such as an increased area of winter crops, escape from parks and farms, greater connectivity between green space in urban areas, and a lack of natural predators, following, for example, the extirpation of the wolf. The British deer population is believed to be at its highest level for 1000 years, with some 1.5–2 million red, roe, fallow, sika, muntjac, and Chinese water deer in the countryside and in semi-urban areas. Numbers may have doubled since 1999. This has an impact on the status of other animals (Perrins and Overall, 2001) and the state of woodland trees and vegetation (Gill and Fuller, 2007).

One non-indigenous species that has spread dramatically in recent years is the Quagga Mussel (*Dreissena rostriformis bugensis*). Until the 1940s, the quagga mussel only occurred in the mouth of two rivers discharging into the Black Sea: the Southern Bug and the Dnieper in the Ukraine. The quagga mussel was first recorded in North America in Lake Erie in 1989, possibly via ballast water discharge. Subsequently it has spread to all the Great Lakes, to the St. Lawrence River in Canada, and to various lakes and rivers of the south-west USA. It has also spread into Western Europe and Britain, where the calculated average quagga invasion rate was 120 km per year. This spread has been facilitated by the construction of canals which have linked different river systems (Matthews et al., 2014). Quagga mussels will affect invaded ecosystems in a number of ways. Clearer waters resulting from their massive filtration capacity will, for example, lead to changes in algal diversity and abundance (Aldridge et al., 2014).

Invasive flatworms are another current menace (Hendrix, 2006). Dispersal of these invasive species occurs through the exchange and purchase of plants from nurseries, botanical gardens, garden centres, and gardeners. They are carnivores, and feed upon a variety of soil organisms such as earthworms, isopods, insects, and snails, and some may pose a threat to local biodiversity. Non-indigenous terrestrial flatworms have been recorded in thirteen European countries (Justine et al., 2014). The Obama flatworm (*Obama nungara*), which is native to South America, has recently arrived in the UK, as has the New Zealand flatworm (*Artioposthia triangulata*), while the voracious *Platydemus manokwari*, also known as the New Guinea flatworm, has arrived in Florida.

Another recent example of a detrimental invasion is that of the North American signal crayfish, *Pacifastacus leniusculus* (Dana). This is not native to Europe and was introduced to Britain in the 1970s (Freeman et al., 2010). The white-clawed crayfish, *Austropotamobius pallipes* (Lereboullet), is the only freshwater crayfish indigenous to Great Britain and Ireland. The exotic signal crayfish out-competes the native white-clawed crayfish. This is because it is larger and more aggressive. It is also responsible for the introduction and spread of crayfish plague, which has devastated white-clawed crayfish populations both in Britain and in Europe. Signal crayfish populations are causing significant changes to native flora and fauna through increased grazing and predation pressures; they also contribute to habitat degradation through burrowing.

Sometimes, however, introduced animals have spread so thoroughly and rapidly, and have led to such a change in the environment to which they were introduced, that they have sown the seeds of their own demise. Reindeer (*Rangifer tarandus*), for example, were brought from Lapland to Alaska in 1891–1902 to provide a new resource for the Eskimos, and the herds increased and spread to 640,000 animals in 1932. By the 1950s, however, there was less than a twentieth of that number left, since the reindeer had been allowed to eat the lichen supplies that are essential to winter survival; as lichen grows very slowly their food supply was drastically reduced (Elton, 1958: 129). Now there may be only around c. 18,000 reindeer in Alaska.

The accidental dispersal of animals can be facilitated by means other than transport on ships or introduction with plants. This applies particularly to aquatic life which can be spread through human alteration of waterways by methods such as canalization. The opening of the Suez Canal in 1869 enabled the exchange of animals between the Red Sea and the eastern Mediterranean. Initially, the high salinity of the Great Bitter Lake acted to prevent movement, but the infusion of progressively fresher waters (Figure 3.4) through the Suez Canal has meant that this barrier has gradually become less effective. Some 63 Red Sea fish immigrants have now been identified in the Mediterranean, and they are especially important in the Levant basin (Mavruk and Avsar, 2008). They have been less successful in invading the western Mediterranean but now are regularly encountered off Sicily. Menacing jellyfish (*Rhopilema nomadica*) have invaded Levantine beaches (Spanier and Galil, 1991). This type of movement has been termed 'Lessepsian migration' (Por, 2012).

Similarly, the construction of the Welland Canal, linking the Atlantic with the Great Lakes of North America, has permitted similar movements with disastrous consequences. Much of the native fish fauna has been displaced by alewife (*Alosa pseudoharengus*) through competition for food, and by the sea-lamprey (*Petromyzon marinum*) as a predator, so that once common Atlantic salmon (*Salmo salar*), lake trout (*Salvelinus namaycush*), and lake herring (*Leucichtys artedi*) have been nearly exterminated (Aron and Smith, 1971). The whole question of the presence and effects of exotic species in large lakes is reviewed by Hall and Mills (2000).

Can one make any generalizations about the circumstances that enable successful invasion by some exotic vertebrates and less successful invasion by others (Duncan et al. 2003)? Brown (1989) suggests that there may by 'five rules of biological invasions':

> *Rule 1*
> 'Isolated environments with a low diversity of native species tend to be differentially susceptible to invasion.'
>
> *Rule 2*
> 'Species that are successful invaders tend to be native to continents and to extensive, non-isolated habitats within continents.'
>
> *Rule 3*
> 'Successful invasion is enhanced by similarity in the physical environment between the source and target areas.'
>
> *Rule 4*
> 'Invading exotics tend to be more successful when native species do not occupy similar niches.'
>
> *Rule 5*
> 'Species that inhabit disturbed environments and those with a history of close association with humans tend to be successful in invading man-modified habitats.'

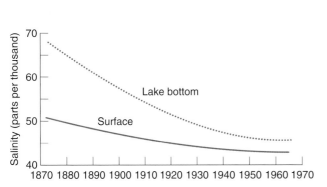

Figure 3.4 Decrease in the salinity of the Great Bitter Lake, Egypt, resulting from the intrusion of fresher water by way of the Suez Canal. *Source:* adapted from Wooster (1969), with subsequent modification.

3.3 Human Influence on the Expansion of Animal Populations

Although most attention tends to be directed towards the decline in animal numbers and distribution brought about by human agency, there are many circumstances where alterations of the environment and modification of competition has favoured the expansion of some species. Such expansion is not always welcome or expected.

Human actions, however, are not invariably detrimental, and even great cities may have effects on animal life which can be considered desirable or tolerable (Faeth et al., 2011). This has been shown in the studies of bird populations in several urban areas (Gil and Brumm, 2014). For example, Nuorteva (in Jacobs, 1975) examined the bird fauna in the city of Helsinki (Finland), in agricultural areas near rural houses, and in uninhabited forests (see Table 3.1). The city supported by far the highest biomass and the highest number of birds, but exhibited the lowest number of species and the lowest diversity. In the artificially created rural areas the number of species, and hence diversity, were much higher than in the uninhabited forest, and so was biomass. Altogether, human civilization appeared to have brought about a very significant increase of diversity in the whole area: there were 37 species in city and rural areas that were not found in the forest. Similarly, after a detailed study of suburban neighbourhoods in west-central California, Vale and Vale (1976) found that in suburban areas the number of bird species and the number of individuals increased with time. Moreover, when compared to the pre-suburban habitats adjacent to the suburbs, the residential areas were found to support a larger number of both species and individuals. Horticultural activities appear to provide more luxuriant and more diverse habitats than do pre-suburban environments. However, a later review of 51 bird studies found that 61% showed lower species richness compared with more natural rural areas (McKinney, 2002).

Table 3.1 Dependence of bird biomass and diversity on urbanization.

	City (Helsinki)	Near rural houses	Uninhabited forest
Biomass (kg km^{-2})	213	30	22
No. of birds (km^{-2})	1,089	371	297
Number of species	21	80	54
Diversity	1.13	3.40	3.19

Source: data from Nuorteva (1971) modified after Jacobs (1975: table 2).

In the UK, Tratalos et al. (2007) noted that species richness of birds in cities varied according to building density. This richness increased from low to moderate household densities and then declined at greater household densities. Although traffic-related mortality and the predations of domestic cats may be disadvantageous, urban environments support more stable and predictable food sources (Tryjanowski et al., 2015). In addition, horticultural activities appear to provide more luxuriant and more diverse habitats than do pre-suburban environments. In North America, species that were widespread in urban areas but not in non-urban areas included ducks and other aquatic species. This is probably because cities are generally near to natural or artificial water bodies, such as lakes, ponds, rivers, and ditches (Murthy et al., 2016).

In general, however, cities worldwide contain substantially lower densities of species compared with non-urban levels, but of the 10,052 recognized bird species worldwide, 2041 (20%) occur in our cities. These include a few cosmopolitan species. Four occur in more than 80% of cities: *Columba livia* (rock pigeon, 51 cities); *Passer domesticus* (house sparrow, 48 cities); *Sturnus vulgaris* (European starling, 44 cities); and *Hirundo rustica* (barn swallow, 43 cities) (Aronson et al., 2014). The behaviour of birds, including their singing activity and dates of migration, are also affected by the urban environment (Møller et al., 2015).

Some other types of beast are also favoured by urban expansion. Animals that can tolerate disturbance, have a high reproduction potential, are adaptable, utilize patches of open or woodland-edge habitat, creep about inside buildings, tap people's food supply surreptitiously, avoid recognizable competition with humans, or attract human appreciation and esteem, may increase in the urban milieu. For these sorts of reasons the north-east megalopolis of the United States hosts thriving populations of squirrels, rabbits, racoons, skunks, and opossums. Coyotes (*Canis latrans*) are also common in American cities, especially in the south-west, and may have greater densities than in rural areas, while some African cities are now frequently blessed with the scavenging attention of hyenas (*Crocuta crocuta*). In Britain and many other parts of the world, the red fox (*Vulpes vulpes*) has become common in many cities (Scott et al., 2014). The characteristics of such carnivores, often termed 'urban exploiters', are reviewed by Bateman and Fleming (2012).

There is, of course, considerable variability in the diversity of species and richness of populations in different parts of cities. Most central urban areas, heavily covered by pavements and buildings, have low biodiversity, but suburban areas with many gardens may be rich in wildlife, though not invariably richer than neighbouring rural areas (McKinney, 2002). However, urban wildlife may be composed of many exotic species rather than native ones (Kühn and Klotz, 2006) and a big question is whether the addition of non-native species associated with urbanization exceeds the loss of native species to produce a net gain in species richness with urbanization. McKinney (2008), in a review of a large number of previous studies in many parts of the world, found that whereas 65% of studies showed increasing species richness with moderate urbanization, only a minority of invertebrate studies (about 30%) and a very small minority of non-avian vertebrate studies (about 12%) showed increasing species-richness.

Human economic activities may lead to a rise in the number of examples of a particular habitat which can lead to an expansion in the distribution of certain species, though often humans have prompted a contraction in the range of a particular species because of the removal or modification of its preferred habitat. In Britain the range of the little ringed plover (*Charadrius dubius*), a species virtually dependent on anthropogenic habitats, principally wet gravel and sand pits, greatly expanded as mineral extraction accelerated (see Figure 3.5). Indeed, it needs to be stressed that the changes of habitat brought about by urbanization, industry (Ratcliffe, 1974), and mining need not be detrimental.

Some of the familiar British birds have benefitted from agricultural expansion. Formerly, when Britain was an extensively wooded country, the starling (*Sturnus vulgaris*) was a rare bird. The lapwing (*Vanellus vanellus*) is yet another component of the grassland fauna of Central Europe which has benefited from agriculture and the creation of open country with relatively sparse vegetation (Murton, 1971). There is also a large class of beasts which profit so much from the environmental conditions wrought by humans that they become very closely linked to them. These animals are often referred to as synanthropes. Pigeons and sparrows now form permanent and numerous populations in almost all the large cities of the world; human food supplies support many synanthropic rodents (rats and mice); a once shy forest-bird, the blackbird (*Turdus merula*), has in the course of a few generations become a regular and bold inhabitant of many gardens in the UK; and the squirrel (*Sciurus vulgaris*) in many places now occurs more frequently in parks than in forests (Illies, 1974: 101). The marked increase in many species of gulls over recent decades is largely attributable to their growing utilization of food scraps on refuse tips (Croxall et al., 2012). This is, however, something of a mixed blessing, for most of the gull species which feed on urban rubbish dumps breed in coastal areas, and

there is now good evidence to show that their greatly increased numbers are threatening other less common species, especially the terns (*Sterna* spp.). It may seem incongruous that the niches for scavenging birds which exploit rubbish tips should have been filled by seabirds, but the gulls have proved ideal replacements for the kites which humans had removed, as they have the same ability to watch out for likely food sources from aloft and then to hover and plunge when they spy a suitable meal. The English house sparrow (*Passer domesticus*), a familiar bird in towns and cities, currently exists over approximately one-quarter of Earth's surface, and over the past one hundred years it has doubled the area that it inhabits as settlers, immigrants, and others have carried it from one continent to another (Figure 3.6). It is found around settlements both in Amazonia and the Arctic Circle (Doughty, 1978). However, recently in Britain and Europe, it has suffered a decline in numbers, particularly in cities. Possible explanations include increased predation by cats, sparrow hawks, and magpies, loss of nesting opportunities, increased use of pesticides and herbicides, nitrogen pollution from vehicles, and increased road traffic (Summers-Smith, 2003).

Most of the examples given so far to illustrate how human actions can lead to expansion in the numbers and distributions of certain animal species, and have been used to make the point that such expansion frequently occurs as an incidental consequence of human activities. There are, of course, many ways in which people have intentionally and effectively promoted the expansion of particular species (Table 3.2 presents data for some introduced mammals in Britain). This may sometimes be done deliberately to reduce the numbers of a species which has expanded as an unwanted consequence of human actions. Perhaps the best-known example of this is biological control using introduced predators and parasites. Thus an Australian insect, the cottony-cushion scale, *Icerya purchasi*, was found in California in 1868. By the mid-1880s it was effectively destroying the citrus industry, but its ravages were quickly controlled by deliberately importing a parasitic fly and a predatory beetle (the Australian ladybird) from Australia. Because of the uncertain ecological effects of synthetic pesticides, such biological control has its attractions but the importation of natural enemies is not without its own risks. For example, the introduction into Jamaica of mongooses to control rats led to the undesirable decimation of many native birds and small land mammals.

From the mid-1800s to the early 1900s it was fashionable for owners of country estates in Great Britain to populate their grounds with specimens of exotic fauna

Figure 3.5 The changing range of the little ringed plover (*Charadrius dubius*): (a) The increase in the number summering in Britain. *Source:* adapted from Murton (1971: figure 6). (b) The increase in the range, related to habitat change, especially as a result of the increasing number of gravel pits. *Source:* adapted from Nature Conservancy Council (1977: figure 11). (c) The range of *Charadrius dubius* in 2004. *Source:* data courtesy of the National Biodiversity Network Gateway with thanks to all the data contributors.

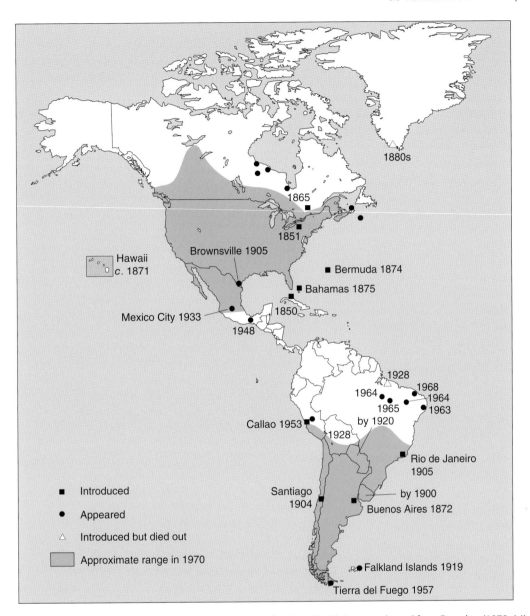

Figure 3.6 The spread of the English house sparrow in the New World. *Source:* adapted from Doughty (1978: 14).

(Mayle and Broome, 2013). The grey squirrel, *Sciurus carolinensis*, was one such species. It was introduced from the United States into approximately 30 sites in England and Wales between 1876 and 1929, into three sites in Scotland between 1892 and 1920 from Canada, and in 1911 into one site in Ireland from England. In spite of concerted efforts to control grey squirrels between the 1930s and 1960s they have spread throughout much of England and Wales and a significant area of Scotland.

One further calculated method of increasing the numbers of wild animals, of conserving them, and of gaining an economic return from them, is game cropping or ranching. There are now huge numbers of game ranches and communal conservancies in, for example, southern Africa, and these both protect wild species but also underpin a profitable tourism industry.

In some circumstances, because they are better adapted to, and utilize more components of, the environment, wild ungulates provide an alternative means of land use to domestic stock. The global warming of recent decades, which may be anthropogenic in origin, has also facilitated the expansion of some species. One example of this is the southward expansion of a sea urchin, *Centrostephanus rodgersii*, along the coast of Tasmania (Ling, 2008). Its grazing activities have had a massive and deleterious impact on the macro-algal beds of the region, causing what are termed 'sea urchin barrens'. In the UK there has been a great expansion in the distributions and populations of some marine species, including squid and anchovies.

ASKHAM BRYAN
COLLEGE
LEARNING RESOURCES

Table 3.2 Introduced mammals in Britain.

Species	Date of introduction of present stock	Reason for introduction
House mouse *Mus musculus*	Neolithic?	Accidental
Wild goat *Capra hircus*	Neolithic?	Food
Fallow deer *Dama dama*	Roman or earlier	Food, sport
Domestic cat *Felis catus*	Early Middle Ages	Ornament, pest control
Rabbit *Oryctolagus cuniculus*	Mid- to late twelfth century	Food, sport
Black rat *Rattus rattus*	Thirteenth century?	Accidental
Brown rat *Rattus norvegicus*	Early eighteenth century (1728–1729)	Accidental
Sika deer *Cervus nippon*	1860	Ornament
Grey squirrel *Sciurus carolinensis*	1876	Ornament
Indian muntjak *Muntiacus muntjak*	1890	Ornament
Chinese muntjak *Muntiacus reevesi*	1900	Ornament
Chinese water deer *Hydropetes inermis*	1900	Ornament
Edible dormouse *Glis glis*	1902	Ornament
Musk rat *Ondatra zibethica*	1929–1937	Fur
Coypu *Myocastor coypus*	1929	Fur
Mink *Mustela vison*	1929	Fur
Bennett's wallaby *Macropus rufogriseus bennetti*	1939 or 1940	Ornament
Reindeer *Rangifer tarandus*	1952	Herding, ornament
Himalayan (Hodgson's) porcupine *Hystrix hodgsoni*	1969	Ornament
Crested porcupine *Hystrix cristata*	1972	Ornament
Mongolian gerbil *Meriones unguiculatus*	1973	Ornament

Source: from Jarvis (1979: 188, table 1). Reproduced with permission of Sage Publishers.

3.4 Causes of Animal Contractions and Decline: Pollution

The extreme effect of human interference with animals is extinction, but before that point is reached humans may cause major contractions in both animal numbers and animal distribution. This decline may be brought about partly by intentional killings for subsistence and commercial purposes, but much wildlife decline occurs indirectly, for example, through pollution, habitat change or loss, and competition from invaders. The latest version of the *Living Planet Report* (WWF, 2016), produced by the Zoological Society of London and WWF (http://awsassets.panda.org/downloads/lpr_living_planet_report_2016.pdf, accessed January 2018), has indicated that global populations of fish, birds, mammals, amphibians and reptiles have already declined by 58% on average since 1970.

Concern has been expressed about the role of veterinary drugs and certain chemical pesticides in creating undesirable and unexpected changes (Mitra et al., 2011). Recently, for example, it has been noted that there has been a catastrophic decline in the numbers of Gyps vultures in both Africa and India, and this has been attributed to the fact that the diclofenac given to cattle for treating inflammation, pain, and fevers, is toxic to the vultures so that when they eat cattle carcases they are in effect poisoned (Naidoo et al. 2009). There has also been a catastrophic decline in bumble and honey bees in some parts of the world and this has been attributed to the use of neonicotinoid pesticides, which are often used as a seed dressing for crops (Henry et al., 2012; Whitehorn et al., 2012; Woodcock et al., 2016; Tsvetkov et al., 2017). This could have highly detrimental effects on pollination of crops and of wild plants. In Europe, some bees are also under threat because of the spread the invasive Asian hornet (*Vespo velutina*) (Monceau et al., 2014). Neonicotinoid use is also implicated in the decline of butterflies in California (Forister et al., 2016).

The classic case, however, is that of DDT and related substances (see Section 5.6). These were introduced on a worldwide basis after the Second World War and proved highly effective in the control of insects such as malarial mosquitoes. However, evidence accumulated that DDT was persistent, capable of wide dispersal, and reached high levels of concentration in certain animals at the top trophic levels. The tendency for DDT to become more concentrated as one moves up the food chain is illustrated further by the data in Table 3.3(c). DDT levels in river and estuary waters may be low, but the zooplankton and shrimps contain higher levels, the fish that feed on them higher levels still, while fish-eating birds have the highest levels of all.

DDT had a major effect on sea-birds. Their egg shells become thinned to the extent that reproduction fails in fish-eating birds. Similar correlations between eggshell thinning and DDT residue concentrations have been demonstrated for various raptorial land-birds. The bald eagle (*Haliaeetus leucocephalus*), peregrine falcon (*Falco peregrinus*), and osprey (*Pandion haliaetus*) all showed decreases in eggshell thickness and population decline from 1947 to 1967, a decline which correlated with DDT usage and subsequent reproductive and metabolic effects upon the birds (Johnston, 1974).

However, appreciation of the undesirable side-effects of DDD and DDT brought about by ecological concentration led to severe controls of their use. For example, DDT reached a peak in terms of utilization in the USA in

Table 3.3 Examples of biological magnification.

(a) Enrichment factors for the trace element compositions of shellfish compared with the marine environment.

Element	Enrichment factor		
	Scallops	Oysters	Mussels
Ag	23,002	18,700	330
Cd	260,000	318,000	100,000
Cr	200,000	60,000	320,000
Cu	3,000	13,700	3,000
Fe	291,500	68,200	196,000
Mn	55,000	4,000	13,500
Mo	90	30	60
Ni	12,000	4,000	14,000
Pb	5,300	3,300	4,000
V	4,500	1,500	2,500
Zn	28,000	110,300	9,100

Source: Merlini (1971) in King (1975: 303, table 8.8).

(b) Mean methyl mercury concentrations in organisms from a contaminated salt marsh.

Organism	Parts per million
Sediments	<0.001
Spartina	<0.001–0.002
Echinoderms	0.01
Annelids	0.13
Bivalves	0.15–0.26
Gastropods	0.25
Crustaceans	0.28
Fish muscle	1.04
Fish liver	1.57
Mammal muscle	2.2
Bird muscle	3.0
Mammal liver	4.3
Bird liver	8.2

Source: King (1975: 301, table 8.7).

(c) The concentration of DDT in the food chain.

Source	Parts per million
River water	0.000003
Estuary water	0.00005
Zooplankton	0.04
Shrimps	0.16
Insects – Diptera	0.30
Minnows	0.50
Fundulus	1.24
Needlefish	2.00
Tern	2.80–5.17
Cormorant	26.40
Immature gull	75.50

Source: Gardner et al. (1978) in Bryan (1979).

1959 (35×10^6 kg) and by 1971 was down to 8.1×10^6 kg. It was banned for general use in the USA in 1972. Although the populations of birds such as the skua and the osprey have shown dramatic recoveries in recent years (see, for example, Lazarus et al., 2015; Hammer et al., 2016), some areas still have high legacy concentrations of DDT, while in other areas (e.g. KwaZulu Natal in South Africa) DDT is still being used for malaria control and so continues to cause eggshell thinning and reduced breeding success (Humphries, 2013).

Other substances are also capable of concentration. For example, heavy metals and methyl mercury may build up in marine organisms, and filter feeders like shellfish have a strong tendency to concentrate the metals from very dilute solutions, as is clear in Table 3.3(a) and (b).

It is possible, however, that the importance of biological accumulation and magnification has been overstated in some textbooks. Bryan (1979) reviewed the situation and noted that, although the absorption of pollutants from foods is often the most important route for bioaccumulation and that transfer along food chains certainly occurs, this does not automatically mean that predators at high trophic levels will always contain the highest levels. He wrote (p. 497):

> Although, for a number of contaminants, concentrations in individual predators sometimes exceed those of their prey, when the situation overall is considered only the more persistent organochlorine pesticides, such as DDT and its metabolites and methyl mercury, show appreciable signs of being biologically magnified as a result of food-chain transfer.

Oil pollution is a serious, though declining, problem (Figure 5.37) for marine and coastal fauna and flora, although some of it derives from natural seeps. Sea-birds are especially vulnerable since oil clogs their feathers; while the ingestion of oil when birds attempt to preen themselves leads to enteritis and other complaints. Local bird populations may be seriously diminished (Guitart et al., 2010). Fortunately, though oil is toxic it becomes less so with time, and the oil spilt from the *Torrey Canyon* in March 1967 was almost biologically inert when it was stranded on the Cornish beaches (Cowell, 1976). Much of the damage caused to marine life as a result of this particular disaster was caused not by the oil itself but by the use of 2.5 million gallons of detergents to disperse it (Smith, 1968). There are 'natural' oil-degrading organisms in nature, so that recovery from oil spills can be rapid, and in most cases is complete within 2–10 years (Kingston, 2002).

It is possible that oil spills pose a particular risk in cold areas, for biodegradation processes achieved by microbes appear to be slow. This is probably because of a combination of low temperatures and limited availability of nitrogen, phosphorus, and oxygen. The last of these is a constraint because compared to temperate ecosystems arctic tundra and coastal ecosystems are relatively stagnant – ice dampens re-aeration due to wave action in marine ecosystems, while standing water in tundra soils limits inputs of oxygen to them. Detailed reviews are provided in Engelhardt (1985) and an authoritative discussion of the consequences and remediation of Arctic oil spills is provided by the National Research Council (2014).

There is far less information available on the effects of oil spills in freshwater environments, though they undoubtedly occur. Freshwater bodies have certain characteristics which, compared with marine environments, tend to modify the effects of oil spills. The most important of these are the smaller and shallower dimensions of most rivers, streams, and lakes, which means that dilution and spreading effects are not as vigorous and significant in reducing surface slicks as would be the case at sea. In addition, the confining dimensions of ponds and lakes are likely to cause organisms to be subjected to prolonged exposure to dissolved and dispersed hydro-carbons. Information on this problem is summarized in Green and Trett (2012).

One particular type of aquatic ecosystem where pollution is an increasingly serious problem, particularly in areas with a dense human population, is the coral reef (Sheppard et al., 2009; Tkachenko, 2017). They are affected by a number of stresses (Figure 3.7). Coral reefs are important because they are among the most diverse, productive, and beautiful communities in the world. Although they only cover an area of less than 0.2% of the world's ocean beds, up to one-quarter of all marine species and one-fifth of known marine fish species live in coral reef ecosystems (World Resources Institute, 1998: 253). They also provide coastal protection, opportunities for recreation, and potential sources of substances like drugs. Accelerated sedimentation resulting from poor land management (Nowlis et al., 1997; Fabricius, 2005), together with dredging, is probably responsible for more damage to reef communities than all the other forms of human insult combined, for suspended sediments create

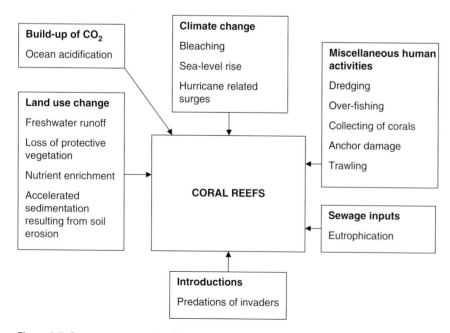

Figure 3.7 Stresses upon coral reefs.

turbidity which restricts the light penetration necessary for coral growth. Also, the soft, shifting sediments may not favour colonization by reef organisms. Sewage is the second worst form of stress to which coral reefs are exposed, for oxygen-consuming substances in sewage result in reduced levels of oxygen in the water of lagoons. The detrimental effects of oxygen starvation are compounded by the fact that sewage may cause nutrient enrichment to stimulate algal growth and feed various predators, which in turn can overwhelm coral.

Runoff from the land can also cause nutrient enrichment, because it may contain nitrates and other nutrients derived from fertilizers. Equally, poor land management can also cause salinity levels to be reduced below the level of tolerance of reef communities as a consequence of accelerated runoff of fresh water from catchments draining into lagoons. An interesting example of the role of sedimentation in damaging reef health is provided by geochemical studies of long-lived corals from Australia's Great Barrier Reef (McCulloch et al., 2003). These showed that since 1870 and the start of European settlement in its catchment, the Burdekin River has carried five to ten times more sediment to the reef than it did previously. Reefs may also be threatened by accelerated coral bleaching associated with recent global warming (Sweet and Brown, 2016). One of the reasons why all these stresses may be especially serious for reefs is that corals live and grow for several decades or more, so that it can take a long time for them to recover from damage. Whatever may be the causes, severe declines in coral cover on reefs have been identified in recent decades, though there are debates as to just how serious the degradation has been, not least in the context of the Great Barrier Reef (GBR) of Australia. On the one hand Hughes et al. (2011) have suggested that there has been a close to 40% loss of coral cover on the inner reefs of the GBR, whereas Sweatman et al. (2011) believe that losses of GBR corals over the last 40 years have probably been exaggerated. In the Indo-Pacific region coral cover declined from 42.5% in the early 1980s to only 22.1% by 2003, an average annual rate of 1%. In the Caribbean between 1977 and 2001 the annual rate was even higher – 1.5% (Bruno and Selig, 2007), and over the last 25 to 30 years coral cover in that region has fallen from an average of roughly 50% to only 10% (Hughes et al., 2013). Heavily degraded reefs are now little more than a mix of rubble, seaweed, and slime (Pandolfi et al., 2005).

Industrial air pollution has had an adverse effect on wild animals (Newman, 1979). Arsenic emissions from silver foundries are known to have killed deer and rabbits in Germany; sulphur emissions from a pulp mill in Canada are known to have killed many song-birds; industrial fluorosis has been found in deer living in the USA and Canada; asbestosis has been found in baboons and rodents in the vicinity of asbestos mines in South Africa; and oxidants from air pollution are recognized causes of blindness in bighorn sheep (*Ovis canadensis*) in the San Bernadino Mountains near Los Angeles in California.

In many parts of the world considerable concern has arisen over the effects of lead poisoning on wildlife, particularly on wildfowl. Poisoning occurs particularly in raptors, pigeons, partridge, and waterfowl, for example, when they feed and seek grit, since they ingest spent shotgun pellets or discarded anglers' weights in the process. Such pellets are eroded in the bird's gizzard and the absorbed lead causes a variety of adverse physiological effects that can result in death: damage to the nervous system, muscular paralysis, anaemia, and liver and kidney damage (Fisher et al., 2006; Guitart et al., 2010).

Soil erosion (see Section 4.19), by increasing stream turbidity (another type of pollution), may adversely affect fish habitats (Henley et al., 2000). The reduction of light penetration inhibits photosynthesis, which in turn leads to a decline in food and a decline in carrying capacity. Decomposition of the organic matter, which is frequently deposited with sediment, uses dissolved oxygen, thereby reducing the oxygen supply around the fish; sediment restricts the emergence of fry from eggs; and turbidity reduces the ability of fish to find food (though conversely it may also allow young fish to escape predators).

Turbidity has also been increased by mining waste, construction, and dredging. In the case of some of the Cornish rivers in china-clay mining areas, river turbidities reach 5000 mg per litre and trout are not present in streams so affected. Indeed, the non-toxic turbidity tolerances of river fish are much less than this figure. Alabaster (1972), reviewing data from a wide range of sources, believed that in the absence of other pollution, fisheries are unlikely to be harmed at chemically inert suspended sediment concentrations of less than 25 mg per litre, that there should be good or moderate fisheries at 25–80 mg per litre, that good fisheries are unlikely at 80–400 mg per litre, and that at best only poor fisheries would exist at more than 400 mg per litre.

Two other types of pollution deserve brief mention. Light pollution can attract insects and birds and disorientate various organisms such as bats, while sound pollution, caused, for example, by ships' propellers, can harm cetacea such as whales and dolphins (Dolman and Jasny, 2015).

3.5 Habitat Change and Animal Decline

Land-use and land-cover changes, including the conversion of natural ecosystems to cropland (Ramankutty and Foley, 1999), have so modified habitats that animal declines have ensued. Elsewhere ancient and diverse anthropogenic landscapes have themselves been modified by modern agricultural intensification. Good reviews of changes in biodiversity are provided by Heywood and Watson (1995) and Chapin et al. (2001). Certainly, many species have lost a very large part of their natural ranges as a result of human activities, and a study of historical and present distributions of 173 declining mammal species from six continents has indicated that these species have collectively lost over 50% of their historic range area (Ceballos and Ehrlich, 2002). A particularly stark example of a species whose range is shrinking, because of habitat loss and intense poaching, is the wild tiger, *Panthera tigris*. Its historical range was from the Caspian to southern China, but now, in less than a century, it occupies only 7% of this range (Dinerstein et al., 2007) (Figure 3.8). Now there may only be just under four thousand individuals left in the wild. In Britain, currently declining species include red squirrels, Scottish wildcats, mountain hares, harvest mice, dormice, and, in rural areas, hedgehogs (Macdonald and Burnham, 2011).

One of the most important habitat changes in Britain has been the removal of many of the hedgerows that form the patchwork quilt so characteristic of large tracts of the countryside (Sturrock and Cathie, 1980) and which provide a rich larder and refuge for many species. Their removal has taken place for a variety of reasons: to create larger fields, so that larger machinery can be employed and so that it spends less time turning; because as farms are amalgamated boundary hedges may become redundant; because as farms become more specialized (for example, just arable) hedges may not be needed to control stock or to provide areas for lambing and calving; and because drainage improvements may be more efficiently executed if hedges are absent. In 1962 there were almost 1 million km of hedge in Britain, probably covering the order of 180,000 ha, an area greater than that of the National Nature Reserves. Currently the figure is much lower, perhaps around 450,000 km (http://www.wildlifetrusts.org/wildlife/habitats/hedgerows, accessed December 2017). Bird numbers and diversity are likely to

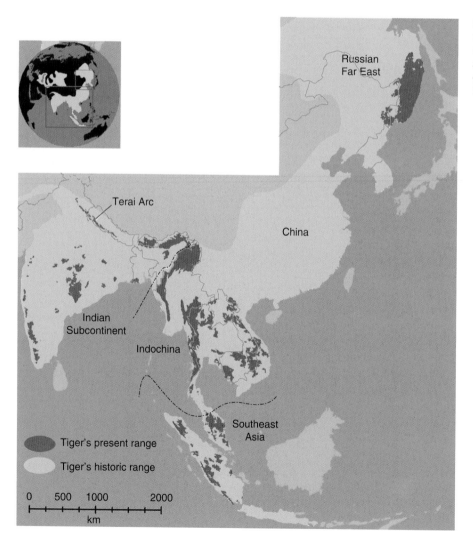

Figure 3.8 The historic and present distribution of tigers. They once occupied portions of central Asia around the Caspian Sea (see inset globe). *Source:* adapted from Dinenstein et al. (2007: figure 1).

be severely reduced if the removal of hedgerows continues, for most British birds are essentially of woodland type and, since woods only cover a small percentage of the land surface of Britain, depend very much on hedgerows (Moore et al., 1967).

Other types of British habitat have disappeared at a quick rate with agricultural changes (Nature Conservancy Council, 1977). For example, the botanical diversity of old grasslands is often reduced by replacing the lands with grass leys or by treating them with selective herbicides and fertilizers; this can mean that the habitat does not contain some of the basic requirements essential for many species. One can illustrate this by reference to the larva of the common blue butterfly (*Polyommatus icarus*) which feeds upon bird-foot trefoil (*Lotus corniculatus*). This plant disappears when pasture is ploughed

and converted into a ley, or when it is treated with a selective herbicide. Once the plant has gone the butterfly vanishes too because it is not adapted to feeding on the plants grown in the ley of improved pasture. Overall, in the UK, since 1976, the populations of butterflies associated strongly with semi-natural habitats (specialists) show a 70% decline, and those found in the wider countryside (generalists) show a 45% decline (Figure 3.9). However, it is not only countryside butterflies that have declined – the decline of urban butterflies has been even greater (Dennis et al., 2017), and has resulted from climate change and altered horticultural practices.

Over large parts of Western Europe the number of brown hares (*Lepus europaeus*) has declined sharply since the 1960s (Edwards et al., 2000). While this may have been partially due to hunting, to poisoning by pesticides such as

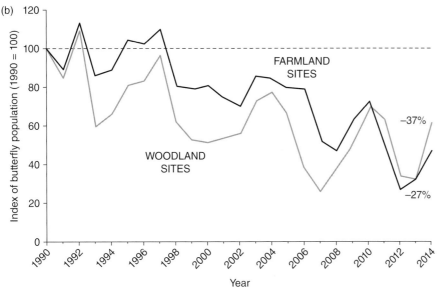

Figure 3.9 Changes in the butterfly population in the UK. (a) UK butterfly indicators for habitat specialists and wider countryside specialists, showing the percentage overall decline trend between 1976 and 2014. (b) Butterfly indicators for English woodland and farmland sites, showing the percentage overall decline trend between 1990 and 2014. *Source:* data in http://butterfly-conservation.org/files/soukb-2015.pdf, in https://www.gov.uk/government/uploads/system/uploads/attachment_data/file/389401/agindicator-de6-18dec14.pdf and in https://www.gov.uk/government/uploads/system/uploads/attachment_data/file/492540/6__Woodland_species_2015_FINAL.pdf (accessed January 2018).

Table 3.4 Decline in farmland birds in Britain between 1970 and 2013.

Species	% decline
Corn bunting	90
Grey partridge	92
Tree sparrow	90
Lapwing	65
Bullfinch	41
Song thrush	56
Turtle dove	97
Linnet	60
Skylark	60
Spotted flycatcher	87
Blackbird	16

Source: https://www.rspb.org.uk/Images/sukb2015_tcm9-409524.pdf (accessed December 2017).

paraquat, or to diseases such as European Brown Hare Syndrome, the prime cause appears to have been loss of crop and landscape diversity, which in turn has reduced the nutrition available to hares at certain times of year.

Agricultural intensification on British farms also appears to have had a deleterious effect on species of farmland birds, many of which have shown a precipitous downward trend in numbers over the last four decades (Table 3.4) (Gregory et al., 2004a). Four farmland birds, the grey partridge (*Perdix perdix*), the turtle dove (*Streptopelia turtur*), the tree sparrow (*Passer montanus*), and the corn bunting (*Milaria calandra*) had by 2013 declined by over 90% relative to 1970 (DEFRA, 2011).

This is because of habitat changes – lack of fallows, less mixed farming, new crops, modern farm management, biocide use, hedgerow removal, etc. (Fuller et al., 1991). However, in Europe, both farmland and woodland specialist birds have shown a decline since the 1980s (Gregory et al., 2007) whereas some more generalist species have flourished. In the USA the greatest declines over the last 40 years have been in grassland and arid land birds. This results from habitat loss from urban development, overgrazing, and the spread of invasive plants (State of the Birds, United States of America, 2009).

The replacement of natural oak-dominated woodlands in Britain by conifer plantations, another major land-use change of recent decades, also has its implications for wildlife. It has been estimated that where this change has taken place the number of species of birds found has been approximately halved (Figure 3.10). Likewise the replacement of upland sheep walks with conifer plantations led to a sharp decline in raven numbers in southern Scotland and northern England. The raven (*Corvus corax*) obtains much of its carrion from open sheep country (Marquiss et al., 1978). Other birds that have suffered from planting moorland areas with forest plantations are miscellaneous types of wader, golden eagles, peregrine falcons, and buzzards (Grove, 1983).

On a global basis the loss of wetland habitats (marshes, bogs, swamps, fens, mires, etc.) is a cause of considerable concern (Williams, 1990). In all, wetlands cover about 6–9% of the earth's surface (not far short of the total under tropical rain forest), and so they are far from being trivial, even though they tend to occur in relatively small patches. However, they also account for about one-quarter of the earth's total net primary productivity,

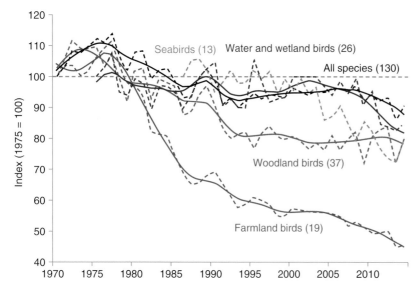

Figure 3.10 Population of wild birds in the UK by habitat, 1970–2014. Figures in brackets show the number of species. The graph shows unsmoothed trends (dashed lines) and smoothed trends (solid lines). *Source:* based on data from UK BTO, Defra, JNCC, and RSPB in https://www.bto.org/science/monitoring/developing-bird-indicators (accessed January 2018). Reproduced with permission of British Trust for Ornithology.

have a very diverse fauna and flora, sequester carbon, help to abate floods, and provide crucial wintering, breeding, and refuge areas for wildlife. According to some sources, the world may have lost half of its wetlands since 1900 (Zedler and Kercher, 2005), and the USA alone lost 53% of its original wetland area by the 1980s, primarily because of agricultural developments. There are, however, other threats, including drainage, dredging, filling, peat removal, urbanization, pollution, and channelization (see Section 6.8). In Europe and the USA 90% of riverine flood plains have been gravely and extensively modified as habitats and in ecological terms have been described as 'functionally extinct' (Tockner and Stanford, 2002). The rate of wetland loss in the USA is now somewhat lower than it was, partly because of a growing awareness of their value, the range of ecological services they provide, and also because of an important international treaty, the Ramsar Convention of 1971. Mangrove swamps are another wetland type that is under great pressure (see Section 6.15), and along the Atlantic and Pacific coasts of Central America as many as 40% of mangrove species are threatened with extinction (Polidoro et al., 2010). Techniques for wetland restoration are discussed by Zedler and Kercher (2005).

3.6 Other Causes of Animal Decline

One could list many other indirect causes of wildlife decline. For example, hunting and poaching of the African black rhino (*Diceros bicornis*), particularly for its horn, has caused a crash in numbers, from several hundreds of thousands in the early 1900s, to 70,000 in the late 1960s, and to a mere 2410 in 2004. Likewise, African elephant (*Loxondonta africana*) numbers were 3–5 million in the 1930s and 1940s, but are now only 415,000 (http://wwf.panda.org/what_we_do/endangered_species/elephants/african_elephants/, accessed December 2017) (Figure 3.11a). The giraffe (*Giraffa camelopardalis*), the tallest land mammal, has shown a dramatic 36–40% decline from approximately 151,702–163,452 individuals in 1985 to 97,562 in 2015. This is due to illegal hunting, habitat loss, and changes through expanding agriculture and mining, increasing human–wildlife conflict, and civil unrest (https://www.iucn.org/news/new-bird-species-and-giraffe-under-threat-%E2%80%93-iucn-red-list, accessed December 2017). The cheetah (*Acinonyx jubatus*) (Figure 3.11b) is also under threat. Only 7100 cheetahs remain globally, and it has been driven out of 91% of its historic range. Asiatic cheetah populations have been hit hardest, with fewer than 50 individuals remaining in one isolated pocket of Iran. Largely due to pressures on wildlife and their habitat outside protected areas, Zimbabwe's cheetah population

(a)

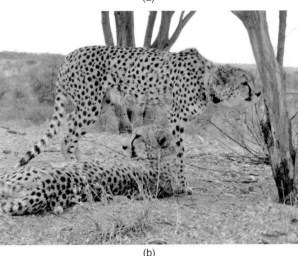

(b)

Figure 3.11 (a) An African elephant in the Etosha National Park, Namibia. In many African countries there has been a sharp decline in elephant numbers, though this is less true of southern Africa (ASG). (b) A pair of cheetahs in a protected area, Okonjima, Namibia (ASG).

has plummeted from 1200 to a maximum of 170 animals in just 16 years, representing a loss of 85% (Durant et al., 2017).

Purposeful hunting, particularly when it involves modern firearms and snares, means that the distribution of many animal species has become smaller very rapidly (Figure 3.12). This clearly illustrated by a study of the North American bison (*Bison bison*), which on the eve of European colonization still had a population of some 60 million in spite of the presence of a small Indian population. By 1850 only a few dozen examples of bison still survived, though conscious protective and conservation measures have saved it from extinction (Figure 3.13). By the late 1990s the total number of bison in North America had crept up to 250,000.

Figure 3.12 A major cause of animal decline is trapping. Here we see a sample of the many snares that have been found in a game reserve in Swaziland, southern Africa (ASG).

Figure 3.13 North American bison have been saved from extinction, as witnessed by these specimens from near Zion Canyon, Utah, USA (ASG).

Our domesticated animals can also have hugely deleterious effects on other animal populations. Cats have contributed to about 10 percent of the bird, mammal, and reptile extinctions and threaten many critically endangered species. In Britain about 10 million cats kill up to 100 million vertebrates a year, including about 30 million birds, while in the USA cats may kill over a billion vertebrates each year (Hambler and Canney, 2013: 76).

Animals native to remote ocean islands have been especially vulnerable to hunters since many have no flight instinct. They also provided a convenient source of provisions for seafarers. Thus the last example of the dodo (*Raphus cucullatus*) was slaughtered on Mauritius in 1681 and the last Steller's sea-cow (*Hydrodamalis gigas*) was killed on Bering Island in 1768 (Illies, 1974: 96). The land-birds, which are such a feature of coral

atoll ecosystems, rapidly become extinct when cats, dogs, and rats are introduced. The endemic flightless rail of Wake Island, *Rallus wakensis*, became extinct during the prolonged siege of the island in the Second World War, and the flightless rail of Laysan, *Porzanula palmeri*, is also now extinct. Sea-birds are more numerous on the atolls, but many colonies of terns, noddies, and boobies have been drastically reduced by vegetation clearance and by introduced rats and cats in recent times (Stoddart, 1968; Sax and Gaines, 2008). Other atoll birds, including the albatross, have been culled because of the threat they pose to aircraft using military airfields on the islands. Some birds have declined because they are large, vulnerable, and edible.

The fish resources of the oceans are still exploited by hunting and gathering techniques, and over 90 million tonnes of fish are caught in the world each year, a more than five-fold increase since 1950. The world catch may have peaked, however, with only modest expansion since 1990 (Food and Agriculture Organization, 2009) (Figure 3.14) for some major fisheries have collapsed as a result of unsustainable exploitation (Hilborn et al., 2003). Unfortunately, the data are subject to debate, and Pauly and Zeller (2016) believe that at its peak in 1996 the catch may have been very much higher than reported by FAO, reaching 130 million tonnes a year, and with a sharp decline since.

A dramatic illustration of a collapse in fish stocks is provided by the Atlantic cod (*Gadhus morhua*) off Newfoundland, Canada (Figure 3.15). Catches of this fish plummeted catastrophically after c. 1970. Chronic over-fishing is a particular problem in shallow marginal seas (e.g. the North Sea) and in the vicinity of coral reefs, where the removal of herbivorous fish can enable algal bloom to develop catastrophically (Hughes, 1994). Marine mammals are also at risk of extinction (Davidson et al., 2012). For instance, populations of the large varieties of whales, those that have been most heavily exploited, have been cut to a tiny fraction of their former sizes, and the hunting, especially by the Russians and the Japanese, still goes on, though since the 1980s most nations have banned whaling. It is extremely difficult to estimate whale stocks before whaling began and therefore to quantify the magnitude of hunting effects that have taken place. However, genetic techniques have recently been used to establish pre-whaling stocks (Rowman and Palumbi, 2003). These techniques have indicated that previous estimates of natural stocking levels were too low and that current populations are a fraction of past numbers. Pre-whaling populations in the North Atlantic of humpback, fin, and minke whales were perhaps 865,000 in total, whereas current populations are 215,000. With bans on whaling that now exist, a number of large whale species have shown signs of

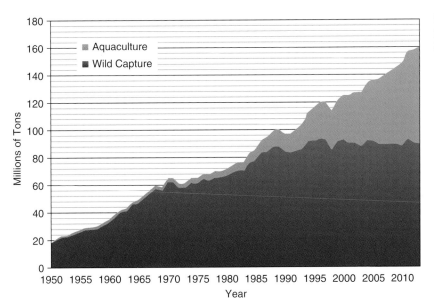

Figure 3.14 Global fish capture and production via aquaculture from 1950 to 2013. *Source:* data from FAO.

Figure 3.15 Catch history of Atlantic cod off Newfoundland since 1850. *Source:* adapted from Millennium Ecosystem Assessment (2005).

recovery, though the status of some baleen whale populations continues to cause concern. In addition even if commercial whaling was banned in perpetuity, whales would face other threats of mankind's making, including acoustic disturbance from seismic exploration, sonar, and motor-vessel traffic.

Dredging can be a particular threat to marine wildlife. The following are among the consequences that have been identified (Todd et al., 2015): Collision with dredging vessels is a known cause of injury and mortality in marine mammals; marine mammals, particularly cetaceans, are acoustically reliant animals that utilize sound for detecting prey, navigating, and communicating, and dredging can be a noisy operation; seabed disturbance

through extraction, disposal, and outwash of excess materials can result in increased turbidity and creation of sediment plumes; marine organisms associated with the seabed can suffer from entrainment (the unintentional removal of organisms by the suction field created by hydraulic dredgers); and habitats such as seagrass beds and coral reefs are at high risk from dredging, particularly because of physical removal, smothering, and a decrease in light intensity; over time, sediments accumulate toxins and pollutants such as hydrocarbons and heavy metals, and dredging disturbance of sediments can release contaminants into the water column. In addition to changing community structure, sediment deposition smothers or buries organisms associated with the seabed. Non-mobile organisms and those at early life stages that are unable to move out of the path of dredgers are susceptible to this effect.

Vehicles and roads threaten wildlife. Vehicle speed, noise, and mobility upset remote and sensitive wildlife populations, and this problem has intensified with the rapid development in the use of off-road recreation vehicles. The effects of roads are becoming ever more pervasive as a result of increasing traffic levels, vehicle speed, and road width and a new sub-discipline of road ecology has emerged (Sherwood et al., 2002; Forman, 2003). Roads affect the abiotic components of neighbouring ecosystems through pollution (e.g. by de-icing salts), by altering local hydrological conditions (e.g. through ponding), and by causing localized erosion and sedimentation. They also act as barriers to movement, as cause of death (roadkill), as corridors and conduits for migration, as facilitators for the movement of invasive species, as creators of noise disturbance, and as causes of habitat fragmentation (Coffin, 2007). A fine-meshed road network is a highly effective cause of habitat isolation, acting as a series of barriers to movement, particularly of small, cover-loving animals. As Oxley et al. (1974) have put it, 'a four-lane divided highway is as effective a barrier to the dispersal of small forest mammals as a body of fresh water twice as wide'. This barrier effect results from a variety of causes (Mader, 1984): roads interrupt microclimatic conditions; they are a broad band of emissions and disturbances; they are zones of instability due to cutting and spraying, etc.; they provide little cover against predators; and they subject animals to death and injury by moving wheels. Roads can also prevent animal migrations, and a proposed highway across the Serengeti in Tanzania has been opposed on the grounds that the area's huge herds of wildebeest (*Connochaetes*) would suffer a severe population collapse as a consequence (Dobson et al., 2010).

Dams across rivers cause fragmentation of river basins and alterations to flow, and these can adversely affect fish populations (Cooper at al., 2017). The construction of fences also poses a threat to aggregated migrations of large terrestrial mammals (Harris et al., 2009). Fencing has been used world-wide for a variety of purposes, including protecting remnant wildlife populations from overhunting, poaching, or invasive species and reducing human–wildlife conflict and human encroachment (Durant et al., 2015). In southern Africa, thousands of kilometres of veterinary fences criss-cross the area, dividing habitat and blocking the movement of animals (Gadd, 2012). Although the primary targets of these fences are livestock and wild ungulates carrying diseases that could threaten domestic livestock, the fences are not selective and create substantial physical barriers. They have adverse effects on wild mammals at the individual, population, and species levels, and alter community structure and ecosystem productivity. They disrupt individual daily movements and may lead to death by starvation, dehydration, or entanglement. They may prevent access to dry season wetland refuges. Fencing can also divide populations, prevent re-colonization, and render sub-populations prone to the risks faced by small populations. In addition, fencing also restricts the ranging of keystone species, such as elephants, which significantly influence ecosystem structure and function (see Section 2.12). The potentially damaging habitat impacts arising from 'compressing' elephants within protected areas are well known. Other new types of construction can also pose threats. As Doughty (1974) remarked '"wirescapes", tall buildings, and towers can become to birds what dams, locks, canals and irrigation ditches are to the passage of fish'. Pipelines and powerlines also have powerful effects, while the accelerating construction of wind turbines is regarded by many as a threat to birds, not least

in estuaries and shallow coastal waters (Powlesland, 2009). The construction of canals can cause changes in aquatic communities. Likewise turbines associated with hydroelectric schemes can cause numerous fish deaths, either directly through ingesting them, or through gas-bubble disease. This resembles the 'bends' in divers and is produced if a fish takes in water supersaturated with gases. The excess gas may come out of solution as bubbles which can lodge in various parts of the fish's body, causing injury or death. Supersaturation of water with gas can be produced in turbines or when a spillway plunges into a deep basin (Baxter, 1977).

Noise pollution generated by human activities has increased dramatically over recent decades as a result of the development of noisy forms of transportation (e.g. jet engines, outboard motors, roadway noise) and expansion of resource extraction (e.g. drilling noise) (Shannon et al., 2016). It can have a detrimental effect on animals, increasing the risk of death by changing the delicate balance in predator or prey detection and avoidance, and interfering with the use of sounds in communication, especially in relation to reproduction and in navigation.

Leisure activities in general may create problems for some species (Speight, 1973). A survey of the breeding status of the little tern (*Sterna albifrons*) in Britain gave a number of instances of breeding failure by the species, apparently caused by the presence of fishermen and bathers on nesting beaches. The presence of even a few people inhibited the birds from returning to their nests. In like manner, species building floating nests on inland waters, such as great crested grebes (*Podiceps cristatus*), are very prone to disturbance by water-skiers and power-boats. Dog walking, trampling, off-road recreation vehicles, and ski installations are also known to have adverse effects.

It might also be thought that human use of fire could be directly detrimental to animals, though the evidence is not conclusive. Many forest animals appear to be able to adapt to fire, and fire also tends to maintain habitat diversity. Thus, after a general review of the available ecological literature Bendell (1974) found that fires did not seem to produce as much change in birds or small mammals as one might have expected. Some of his data are presented in Table 3.5. The amount of change is fairly small, though some increase in species diversities and animal densities is evident. Indeed Vogl (1977) has pointed to the diversity of fauna associated with fire-affected ecosystems (p. 281):

> Birds and mammals usually do not panic or show fear in the presence of fire, and are even attracted to fires and smoking or burned landscapes … The greatest arrays of higher animal species, and the

Table 3.5 Environmental effects of burning.

(a) Change in number of species of breeding birds and small mammals after fire.

	Foraging zone	Before fire	After fire	Gained (%)	Lost (%)
Birds	Grassland and shrub	48	62	38	8
	Tree trunk	25	26	20	16
	Tree	63	58	10	17
	Totals	136	146	21	14
Small mammals	Grassland and shrub	42	45	17	10
	Forest	16	14	13	25
	Totals	58	59	16	14

(b) Change in density and trend of population of breeding birds and small mammals after fire.

		Density (%)			Trend (%)		
	Foraging zone	Increase	Decrease	No change	Increase	Decrease	No change
Birds	Grassland and shrub	50	9	41	24	10	66
	Tree trunk	28	16	56	4	8	88
	Tree	24	19	57	6	6	88
	Totals	35	15	50	12	8	80
Small mammals	Grassland and shrub	24	13	63	20	5	75
	Forest	23	42	35	0	11	89
	Totals	23	25	52	14	1	80

largest numbers per unit area, are associated with fire-dependent, fire-maintained, and fire-initiated ecosystems.

The introduction of a new animal species can cause the decline of another, whether by predation, competition, the introduction of disease, or by hybridization. The British native red squirrel (*Sciurus vulgaris*), which used to be widespread throughout Britain, has contracted in range very greatly since the introduction of the North American grey squirrel (*Sciurus carolinensis*) at the turn of the twentieth century and is now largely restricted to parts of Scotland. One cause of this is that red squirrels have been killed by a disease that was introduced with the grey squirrels, squirrel parapoxvirus (Tomkins et al., 2003) (see also Section 3.3). Hybridization has been found to be a major problem with fish in California, where many species have been introduced by humans. This results when fish are transferred from one basin to a neighbouring basin, since closely related species of the type likely to hybridize usually exist in adjacent basins. One species can eliminate another closely related to it through genetic swamping (Moyle, 1976).

Many species that have suffered serious contraction in numbers and range have done so for a variety of reasons, rather than in response to just one pressure. This was the case of the European otter, *Lutra lutra*, which in Britain had by the mid-1970s been reduced to such an extent that it only survived in Scotland, parts of Wales, and western England, with a few remnant populations in parts of England. This was caused by a combination of hunting, a general decline in water quality which reduced fish stocks upon which otter populations depended, and the introduction of the persistent organochlorine pesticides dieldrin and aldrin. Since the 1970s, however, because of new controls on water quality, restrictions on the use of organochlorine pesticides, legal protection of the species, and active re-introduction programmes, the otter has now returned to most of England (Environment Agency, 2010; Macdonald and Burnham, 2011).

The complexity of possible causes of decline and the difficulty of establishing the precise causes of such decline is exemplified by the case of the house sparrow (*Passer domesticus*). This bird, which used to be a prominent and cheeky inhabitant of cities in the UK and Western Europe, has suffered from near catastrophic crashes in numbers in the last few decades (Shaw et al., 2008). The possible explanations include:

1) Changes in the urban habitat because of the conversion of front gardens into parking spaces, the fashion of replacing lawns and flower beds with decking, infill between houses, the building of modern houses at high densities, a reduction in the rearing of chickens in gardens, and the demise of horse-drawn transport, and thus of seed-rich dung. All these factors have reduced the food supply.
2) The use of pesticides in gardens and parks has led to a decline in the availability of insects and other food sources.
3) Pollution from growth in the numbers of cars and from electromagnetic sources.
4) Reduction in nesting spaces as new houses have less nooks and crannies than old ones.
5) Increased predation by cats and sparrow hawks.
6) Increased competition for food from magpies, gulls, and feral pigeons.

Another example of the complex causes of animal decline is provided by the hedgehog (*Erinaceus europaeus*) in the United Kingdom. Its numbers have declined by a half over the last quarter of a century. Possible reasons include:

1) Loss of hedgerows.
2) Presence of less rough field edges.
3) Pesticide use.
4) Fragmented habitats.
5) Predation by badgers.

3.7 Animal Extinctions in Prehistoric Times

Between fifty and ten thousand years ago, most large mammals became extinct everywhere except Africa, and a range of hypotheses can be erected to account for this phenomenon (Table 3.6). Some workers, notably Martin (1967, 1974), believed that the human role in these late Quaternary extinctions was crucial. Martin (1982) argued that the global pattern of extinctions of the large land mammals follows the footsteps of Palaeolithic settlements. He suggested that Africa and parts of Southern Asia were affected first, with substantial losses at the end of the Acheulean, around 200,000 years ago. He believed that extinction closely followed the chronology of the spread of prehistoric civilization and the development of big-game hunting, and maintained that there are no known continents or islands in which accelerated extinction in the Pleistocene definitely pre-dates the arrival of human settlements.

Table 3.6 Hypotheses to explain the late Quaternary extinctions.

Type or name	Description
Environmental hypotheses	
Catastrophes	Mega-drought, rapid cooling, bolide impact?
Habitat loss	Preferred habitat types lost or too fragmented
Mosaic-nutrient hypothesis	Loss of floras with high local diversity
Co-evolutionary disequilibrium	Disruption of coevolved plant–animal interactions due to flora rearrangements
Self-organized instability	Collapse of systems due to intrinsic dynamics
Human impacts other than hunting	
Habitat alteration	Loss or fragmentation of viable habitat due to human impacts, including fires
Introduced predators	Direct predation by dogs, rats, cats, pigs, etc.
Hyper-disease	Introduction of virulent diseases
Overkill hypotheses	
Blitzkrieg	Rapid loss of prey due to overhunting
Protracted overkill	Loss of prey after prolonged interaction with predator
Combined hypotheses	
Keystone mega-herbivores	Ecosystem collapse due to loss of landscape altering mega-herbivores, perhaps with increase in fire
Prey-switching	Non-human carnivores switch prey as human usurp preferred prey
Predator avoidance	Herbivores restricted to inviable refugia

Source: modified from Koch and Barnosky (2006: table 1).

An alternative interpretation, however, is that the Late Pleistocene extinctions of big mammals were caused by the rapid and substantial changes of climate at the termination of the last glacial (Martin and Klein, 1984). Europe and northern Asia were affected between 20,000 and 10,000 years ago, but they were staggered over many millennia. In contrast, North and South America were stripped of large herbivores in a short phase between 12,000 and 10,000 years ago. Late Quaternary megafaunal extinction in South America appears to have been more extensive than on any other continent. Approximately 80% became extinct. The severity of the extinctions is strikingly illustrated by the fact that today the largest native South American mammals are Baird's tapir (*Tapirus bairdii*) and the lowland tapir (*Tapirus terrestris*), which average only about 350 and 250 kg in weight, respectively. Megafaunal extinctions in Australia may have occurred around 41,000 years ago, shortly after human arrivals (Roberts et al., 2001). Van der Kaars et al. (2017), working in Australia, utilized the number of spores from the dung fungus *Sporormiella* as a proxy for herbivore biomass. They recorded high levels of *Sporormiella* from 150 to 45 kyr ago, indicating that megafaunal populations were present under a range of climatic conditions from the warm, wet, interglacials to the hyper-aridity of the penultimate glacial. Importantly, however, they showed that *Sporormiella* underwent a marked and irreversible decline from 45 to 43.1 kyr ago, indicating megafaunal population collapse, with extinction apparently complete within 4000 years of human occupation of the continent. Conversely there is recent evidence that points to the loss of most species before the peopling of Sahul (circa 50–45 ka) (Stuart, 2015). Alternatively, Saltré et al. (2016) have argued that humans and megafauna coexisted for around 13,500 years.

Extinctions continued into the Holocene on oceanic islands (Turvey, 2009) and in the Galapagos Islands, for example, virtually all extinctions took place after the first human contact in AD 1535 (Steadman et al., 1991). Likewise the complete deforestation of Easter Island in the Pacific between 1200 and 800 years BP was an ecological disaster that led to the demise of much of the native flora and fauna and also precipitated the decline of the megalithic civilization that had erected the famous statues on the islands (Flenley et al., 1991). As Burney (1993: 536) has written:

> For millennia after the late-Pleistocene extinctions, these seemingly fragile and ungainly ecosystems apparently thrived throughout the world. This is one of the soundest pieces of evidence against purely climatic explanations for the passing of Pleistocene faunas. In Europe, for instance, the last members of the elephant family survived climatic warming not on the vast Eurasian land mass, but on small islands in the Mediterranean.

The dates of the major episodes of Pleistocene extinction are crucial to the discussion. Martin (1967: 111–115) wrote:

> Radiocarbon dates, pollen profiles associated with extinct animal remains, and new stratigraphic and archaeological evidence show that, depending on the region involved, late-Pleistocene extinction occurred either after, during or somewhat before worldwide climatic cooling of the last maximum … of glaciation … Outside continental Africa and

South East Asia, massive extinction is unknown before the earliest known arrival of prehistoric man. In the case of Africa, massive extinction coincides with the final development of Acheulean hunting cultures which are widespread throughout the continent … The thought that prehistoric hunters ten to fifteen thousand years ago (and in Africa over forty thousand years ago) exterminated far more large animals than has modern man with modern weapons and advanced technology is certainly provocative and perhaps even deeply disturbing.

The nature of the human impact on animal extinctions can conveniently be classified into three types (Marshall, 1984): the 'blitzkrieg effect', which involves rapid deployment of human populations with big-game hunting technology so that there is very rapid demise of animal populations (Faith and Surovell, 2009); the 'innovation effect', where-by long-established human population groups adopt new hunting technologies and erase fauna that have already been stressed by climatic changes; and the 'attrition effect', whereby extinction takes place relatively slowly after a long history of human activity because of loss of habitat and competition for resources. This may have been the case in Australia (Saltré et al, 2016). The effects of habitat loss, fire usage, and of introduced predators may be applicable in some circumstances (Koch and Barnosky, 2006).

The arguments that have been used in favour of an anthropogenic interpretation can be summarized as follows. First, massive extinction in North America seems to coincide in time with the arrival of humans in sufficient quantity and with sufficient technological skill in making suitable artefacts (the bifacial Clovis blades) to be able to kill large numbers of animals around 13,800–11,400 years ago (Faith and Surovell, 2009) (Figure 3.16). Second, in Europe the efficiency of Upper Palaeolithic hunters is attested by such sites as Solutré in France, where a late-Perigordian level is estimated to contain the remains of over 100,000 horses. Third, many beasts unfamiliar with people are remarkably tame and stupid in their presence, and it would have taken them a considerable time to learn to flee or hide at the sight or scent of human life. Moreover, some, such as birds on oceanic islands, may have lost the ability to fly away from predators. Fourth, humans, in addition to hunting animals to death, may also have competed with them for particular food or water supplies or may have introduced predators, much as the dingo in Australia, which then competed with native fauna (Johnson and Wroe, 2003). Fifth, Coe (1981, 1982) suggested that the supposed preferential extinction of the larger mammals (as in South America) could also lend support to the role of

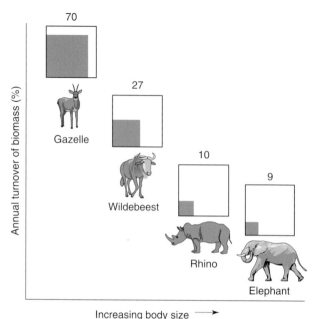

Figure 3.17 Decreasing rate of population biomass turnover with increasing body size in warm- and cold-blooded vertebrates. *Source:* adapted from Coe (1982).

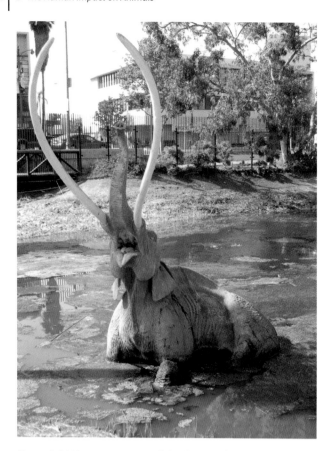

Figure 3.16 A reconstruction of the demise of one member of the mega-fauna, a mastodon, at the La Brea Tar Pits, Los Angeles (ASG).

human actions. He argued that while large body size has certain definite advantages, especially in terms of avoiding predation and being able to cover vast areas of savanna in search of food, large body size also means that these herbivores are required to feed almost continuously to sustain a large body mass. Furthermore, as the size and generation time of a mammal increases, the rate at which they turn over their biomass decreases (Figure 3.17). Hence a population of Thompson's gazelle (*Eudorcas thomsonii*) will turn over up to 70% of their biomass each year, a wildebeest over 27%, but a rhino only 10% and the elephant just 9%. The significance of this is that, since large mammals can only turn over a small percentage of their population biomass each year, the rate of slaughter that such a population can sustain in the face of even a primitive hunter is very low indeed.

Certain objections have been levelled against the climatic change model and these tend to support the anthropogenic model. It has been suggested, for instance, that changes in climatic zones are generally sufficiently gradual for beasts to be able to follow the shifting vegetation and climatic zones of their choice. Similar environments are available in North America today as were

present, in different locations and in different proportions, during Late Pleistocene times. It can also be argued that the climatic changes associated with the multiple glaciations, interglacials, pluvials, and interpluvials do not seem to have caused the same striking degree of elimination as those in the Late Pleistocene. The last glacial–interglacial transition was not so different from previous ones. A third difficulty with the climatic-cause theory is that animals like the mammoth occupied a broad range of habitats from arctic to tropical latitudes, so that it is unlikely all would perish as a result of a climatic change (Martin, 1982).

This is not to say, however, that the climatic hypothesis is without foundation or support (Haynes, 2012; Boulanger et al., 2014). The migration of animals in response to rapid climatic change could be halted by geographical barriers such as high mountain ranges or seas. The relatively rich state of the African big mammalian fauna is due, according to this point of view, to the fact that the African biota is not, or was not, greatly restricted by an insuperable geographical barrier. Another way in which climatic change could cause extinction is through its influence on disease transmission. It has been suggested that during glacials animals would be split into discrete groups cut off by ice sheets but that, as the ice melted (before 11,000 BP in many areas), contacts between groups would once again be made enabling diseases to which immunity might have been lost during isolation to spread rapidly. Large mammals, because of their low reproduction rates, would recover their numbers only slowly, and it was large mammals (according to Martin) that were the main sufferers in the Late Pleistocene extinctions.

The detailed dating of the European megafauna's demise lends further credence to the climatic model (Reed, 1970). The Eurasiatic boreal mammals, such as mammoth, woolly rhinoceros, musk ox, and steppe bison, were associated with and adapted to the cold steppe which was the dominant environment in northern Europe during the glacial phases of the last glaciation. Each of these forms, especially the mammoth and the steppe bison, had been hunted by humans for tens of thousands of years, yet managed to survive through the last glacial. They appear to have disappeared, according to Reed, within the space of a few hundred years when warm conditions associated with the Allerød interstadial led to the restriction and near disappearance of their habitat. Late Pleistocene climate change has also been implicated in the demise of the Siberian and Japanese mammoths (Nikolskiy et al., 2011; Iwase et al., 2012). In Australia, by dating palaeo-shorelines and river deposits in the Lake Eyre basin, Cohen et al. (2015) showed that major hydrological change caused previously overflowing megalakes to enter a final and catastrophic drying phase at 48 ± 2 ka just as the giant bird, *Genyornis newtoni*, went extinct (50–45 ka). They suggest a climate-driven hydrological transformation in the critical window of human arrival and megafaunal extinction. Moreover, as the radiocarbon dates for early societies in countries like Australia are pushed back, it becomes increasingly clear that humans and several species of megafauna were living together for quite long periods, thereby undermining the notion of rapid overkill (Wroe and Field, 2006). Grayson (1977) added to the doubts expressed about the anthropogenic overkill hypothesis. He suggested that the overkill theory, because it states that the end of the North American Pleistocene was marked by extraordinary high rates of extinction of mammalian genera, required terminal Pleistocene mammalian generic extinctions to have been relatively greater than generic extinctions within other classes of vertebrates at this time. When he examined the extinction of birds he found that an almost exactly comparable proportion became extinct at the end of the Pleistocene as one finds for the megafauna. Further arguments can be marshalled against the view that humans as predators played a critical role in the Late Pleistocene extinctions in North America (Butzer, 1972: 509–510). There are, for example, relatively few Palaeo-Indian sites over an immense area, and the majority of these have a very limited cultural inventory. In addition there is no clear evidence that Palaeo-Indian subsistence was necessarily based, in the main part, on big-game hunting; if it was, only two genera were hunted intensively: mammoth and bison. A final point that militates against the argument that humans were primarily responsible for the waves of extinction is the survival of many big-game species well into the Holocene (Johnson, 2005) and even to the nineteenth century, despite much larger and more efficient human populations.

Thus the human role in the great Late Pleistocene extinction is still a matter of debate (Field and Wroe, 2012). The problem is complicated because certain major cultural changes in human societies may have occurred in response to climatic change. The cultural changes may have assisted in the extinction process (Koch and Barnosky, 2006), and increasing numbers of technologically competent humans may have delivered the final *coup de grâce* to isolated remnants already doomed by rapid post-glacial environmental changes. In this context it is worth noting that Haynes (1991) suggested that at around 11,000 years ago conditions were dry in the interior of the USA and that Clovis hunters may as a result have found large game animals easier prey when concentrated around waterholes and under stress. Humans may have been assisted in their hunting efficiency as a result of their early domestication of hunting dogs (Fiedel, 2005). Humans may also inadvertently have caused animal declines because of the introduction of diseases (sometimes called 'hyperdiseases') to new environments (Lyons et al., 2004).

Actual extinction may have occurred after or concurrently with a dwarfing in the size of animals, and this too is a subject of controversy (Guthrie, 2003). On the one hand, there are those who believe that the dwarfing could result from a reduction in food availability brought about by climatic deterioration. On the other, it can be maintained that this phenomenon derives from the fact that small animals, being more adept at hiding and being a less attractive target for a hunter, are more likely to survive human predators, so that a genetic selection towards reduced body size takes place (Marshall, 1984).

Although the debate about the cause of this extinction spasm has now persisted for a long time, there are still great uncertainties. This is particularly true with regard to the chronologies of extinction and of human colonization (Brook and Bowman, 2002). It may well be that in many cases it was a combination of technological and climate changes that caused the extinctions to occur (Pushkina and Raia, 2008; Yule, 2009).

It is probable that the Late Pleistocene extinctions themselves had major ecological consequences (Birks, 1986: 49). This is a theme that has been reviewed by Johnson (2009) and Haynes (2012), who argue that the extermination of herbivores would have had profound influences on the structure of vegetation, by reducing the amount of heavy grazing, track generation, and trampling. Vegetation may have become less open, habitat mosaics may have become less varied, and with accumulation of uncropped plant material and increased vegetation density, fire may have increased. This has been indicated as having occurred in Australia by Rule et al. (2012). The extinction of large herbivores such as elephants will also have affected nutrient cycling. It may also have had an impact on global climates because of the changes in vegetation cover that ensued (Doughty et al., 2010).

A reasonable summary of causation is provided by Araujo et al. (2015: 6):

> The extinction of hundreds of species across the whole planet is such a complex process that one could hardly expect a single factor to completely explain every aspect of it. It is highly likely that causal factors like human impacts and climate changes both acted, in different ways in different places, to produce the final outcome … However, as recent analyses are making increasingly clear, this does not necessarily mean that both factors had equal importance. Many Late Quaternary megafaunal extinctions occurred in the absence of any relevant climatic change, but seldom, if ever, they occurred independently from human arrival.

3.8   Modern-day Extinctions

There are various types of extinction (Riddle et al., 2011). *Linnean extinction* is the extinction of undiscovered species inferred from the species-area relationship and diversity for a given ecosystem or region. *Wallacean extinction* is that of species that have not been documented for many years but in which extinction is uncertain because populations might survive in areas that have not been surveyed within the potential distributional range. *Phoenix extinction* is that of species that are extinct in the wild but genetic material is available for possible re-introduction. *Ecological extinction* relates to species which are extinct in the wild but with extant captive-bred population. *Local extinction* means that species are extinct in the wild within a clearly defined geographical area but with extant free-living populations outside that area. *Contemporary extinction* is extinction that has taken place since the international conservation movement (mid-nineteenth century), with the last-known population having been monitored and surveyed, and for which no captive-bred population or genetic material is available. *Historical extinction* is extinction prior to the international conservation movement and for which there is no authenticated record of an extant population, and for which no captive-bred

population or genetic material is available. These last two types are termed *true extinction*. Another term that is used in the literature is *extirpation* – this applies to species, which although not yet extinct, have disappeared from large areas of their original, natural habitat and range.

As the size of human populations has increased and technology has developed, humans have been responsible for the extinction of many species of animals and a reduction in biodiversity – 'the only truly irreversible global environmental change the Earth faces today' (Dirzo and Raven, 2003). As Lynas (2011: 30) put it, 'We have poisoned, outcompeted or simply eaten so many other species that the Earth is currently in the throes of its most severe mass extinction event for 65 million years …' That said, it is very difficult to estimate current rates of extinction (Stork, 2010), not least because we have a very imperfect idea of how many species exist. Nonetheless, it has often been maintained that there has been a close correlation between the curve of population growth since the mid-seventeenth century and the curve of the number of species that have become extinct. However, although it is likely that European expansion overseas during that time has led to many extinctions, the dramatic increase in the rate of extinctions over the last few centuries that is shown in Figure 3.18 may in part be a consequence of a dramatic increase in the documentation of natural phenomena.

Some modern extinctions of species are natural. Extinction is a biological reality: it is part of the process of evolution. In any period, including the present, there are naturally doomed species, which are bound to disappear, either through over-specialization or an incapacity to adapt themselves to climatic change and the competition of others, or because of natural cataclysms such as earthquakes, eruptions, and floods. Fisher et al. (1969) believed that probably one-quarter of the species of birds and mammals that have become extinct since 1600 died out naturally. In spite of this, however, the rate of animal extinctions brought about by humans in the last 400 years is of a very high order when compared to the norm of geological time. In 1600 there were approximately 4226 living species of mammals: since then 36 (0.85%) have become extinct; and at least 120 of them (2.84%) are presently believed to be in some (or great) danger of extinction. A similar picture applies to birds. In 1600 there were about 8684 living species; since then 94 (1.09%) have become extinct; and at least 187 of them (2.16%) are presently, or have very lately been, in danger of extinction (Fisher et al., 1969). At the present time, at least one-fifth are at risk of extinction in the wild (Hoffmann et al., 2011). Pimm et al. (2014) estimated that current rates of extinction are about 1000 times the likely background rate of extinction, while De Vos et al.

(2015) intimated that this could climb to 10,000 higher if the various threats, including climate change, develop. Ceballos et al. (2017) refer to the current phase of extinctions and population declines as 'biological annihilation'. Some trends in extinction are shown in Figure 3.18. They are discussed further by Ceballos et al. (2015) and Johnson et al. (2017).

Some beasts appear to be more prone to extinction than others, and a distinction is now often drawn between *r*-selected species and *k*-selected species. These are two ends of a spectrum. The former have a high rate of increase, short gestation periods, quick maturation, and the advantage that they have the ability either to react quickly to new environmental opportunities or to make use of transient habitats (such as seasonal ponds). The life duration of individuals tends to be short, populations tend to be unstable, and the species may over-exploit their environment to their eventual detriment. Many pests come into this category. The other end of the spectrum, the *k*-selection species, are those which tend to be endangered or to become extinct. Their prime characteristics are that they are better adapted to physical changes in their environment (such as seasonal fluctuations in temperature and moisture) and live in a relatively stable environment (Miller and Botkin, 1974). These species tend to have much greater longevity, longer generation times, fewer offspring, but a higher probability of survival of young and adults. They have traded a high rate of increase and the ability to exploit transient environments for the ability to maintain more stable populations with low rates of increase, but correspondingly low rates of mortality and a closer adjustment to the long-term

capacity of the environment to support their population. They also tend to be conspicuous, and so may easily be over-hunted, and because of their large size they may be useful as food. Because many of them require relatively stable habitats, including primary forest, they may be sensitive to disturbance such as logging.

Table 3.7, which is modified after Ehrenfeld (1972), attempts to bring together some of the characteristics of species which affect their survival in the human world. There are at least nine ecological or life history traits that have been proposed as factors which determine the sensitivity of an animal species to a reduction and fragmentation in habitat (World Conservation Monitoring Centre, 1992: 193):

Rarity
Several studies have found that the abundance of a species prior to habitat fragmentation is a significant predictor of extinction ... This is only to be expected, since fewer individuals of a rare species than a common species are likely to occur in habitat fragments, and the mechanisms of extinction mean that small populations are inherently more likely to become extinct than large.

Dispersal ability
If animals are capable of migrating between fragments or between 'mainland' areas and fragments, the effects of small population size may be partly or even greatly mitigated by the arrival of 'rescuers'. Species that are good dispersers may therefore be less prone to extinction in fragmented habitats than poor dispersers.

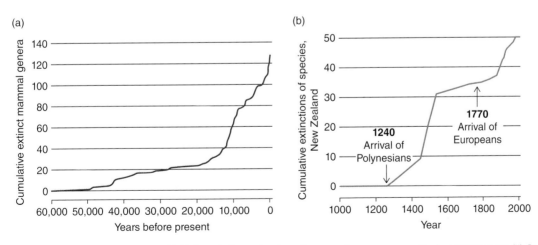

Figure 3.18 Trends in extinction. (a) (i) Cumulative extinction of mammalian genera over the last 60000 years. (ii) Cumulative extinctions of vertebrate species in New Zealand over the past 1000 years. *Source:* adapted from Johnson et al. (2017: figure 1). (b) Graphs, based on IUCN data, showing the cumulative vertebrate species recorded as extinct, possibly extinct or extinct in the wild between c. 1500 and the present. (i) Highly conservative estimate. (ii) Conservative estimate. Dashed black line represents the background rate. *Source:* adapted from Ceballos et al. (2015: figure 1).

(i)

(ii)

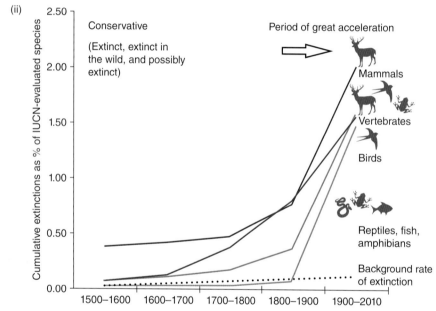

Figure 3.18 (*Continued*)

Degree of specialization

Ecological specialists often exploit resources which are patchily distributed in space and time, and therefore tend to be rare. Specialists may also be vulnerable to successional changes in fragments and to the collapse of coevolved mutualisms or food webs.

Niche location

Species adapted to, or able to tolerate, conditions at the interface between different types of habitats may be less affected by fragmentation than others.

For example, forest edge species may actually benefit from habitat fragmentation.

Population variability

Species with relatively stable populations are less vulnerable than species with pronounced population fluctuations, since they are less likely to decline below some critical threshold from which recovery becomes unlikely.

Trophic status

Animals occupying high trophic levels usually have small populations: e.g. insectivores are far

Table 3.7 Characteristics of species affecting survival.

Endangered	Safe
Large size	Small size
Predator	Grazer, scavenger, insectivore
Narrow habitat tolerance	Wide habitat tolerance
Valuable fur, oil, hide, etc.	Not a source of natural products
Restricted distribution	Broad distribution
Lives largely in international waters	
Migrates across international boundaries	Lives largely in one country
Reproduction in one or two vast aggregates	Reproduction by solitary pairs or in many small aggregates
Long gestation period	Short gestation period
Small litters	Big litters and quick maturation
Behavioural idiosyncracies that are non-adaptive today	Adaptive
Intolerance to the presence of humans	Tolerance of humans
Dangerous to humans, livestock, etc.	Perceived as harmless

fewer in number than their insect prey and, as noted above, rarer species are more vulnerable to extinction.

Adult survival rate

Species with naturally low adult survival rates may be more likely to become extinct.

Longevity

Long-lived animals are less vulnerable to extinction than short-lived.

Intrinsic rate of population increase

Populations which can expand rapidly are more likely to recover after population declines than those which cannot.

In addition, there seems to be a strong positive association between body size and extinction risk for mammals (Ripple et al., 2015). The most threatened families are dominated by large species, such as primates and ungulates, whereas the least threatened include small mammals such as rodents and bats. The explanation for this is that larger species tend to have lower population densities, slower life histories, larger home ranges, and a greater risk of being hunted (Schipper et al., 2008), not least for body parts. Organized crime is facilitating a dramatic decline of elephants and rhinoceros in parts of Africa and southern Asia.

Possibly one of the most fundamental ways in which humans are causing extinction is by reducing the area of natural habitat available to a species (Turner, 1996) and by fragmenting it (Fahrig, 2003). Habitat fragmentation divides once continuous, large populations into many smaller ones, which can be more or less isolated. Small population size and strong isolation of populations is associated with various negative consequences, which include susceptibility to natural disasters, genetic drift, and inbreeding (Lienert, 2004). Even wildlife reserves tend to be small 'islands' in an inhospitable sea of artificially modified vegetation or urban sprawl.

We know from many of the classic studies in true island biogeography that the number of species living at a particular location is related to area; islands support fewer species than do similar areas of mainland, and small islands have fewer species than do large ones. Thus it may well follow that if humans destroy the greater part of a vast belt of natural forest, leaving just a small reserve, initially it will be 'supersaturated' with species, containing more than is appropriate to its area when at equilibrium (Gorman, 1979). Since the population sizes of the species living in the forest will now be greatly reduced, the extinction rate will increase and the number of species will decline towards equilibrium. For this reason it may be a sound principle to make reserves as large as possible; a larger reserve will support more species at equilibrium by allowing the existence of larger populations with lower extinction rates. Several small reserves will plainly be better than no reserves at all, but they will tend to hold fewer species at equilibrium than will a single reserve of the same area. If it is necessary to have several small reserves, they should be placed as close to each other as possible so that each may act as a source area for the others. Connectivity of reserves is an important issue, and if it can be achieved their equilibrial number of species will be raised due to increased immigration rates.

There are situations when small reserves may have advantages over a single large reserve: they will be less prone to total decimation by some natural catastrophe such as fire; they may allow the preservation of a range of rare and scattered habitats; and they may allow the survival of a group of competitors one of which would exclude the others from a single reserve.

Reduction in area leads to reduction in numbers, and this in turn can lead to genetic impoverishment through inbreeding (Frankel, 1984). The effect on reproductive performance appears to be particularly marked. Inbreeding degeneration is, however, not the only effect of small population size for, in the longer term the depletion of genetic variance is more serious since it reduces the capacity for adaptive change. Space is therefore an important consideration, especially for those animals that require large expanses of territory. For example, the population density of the wolf (*Canis lupus*) is about one adult per 20 km^2, and it has been calculated that for a viable population to exist, one might need 600 individuals ranging over an area of 12,000 km². The significance of this is apparent when one realizes that most nature reserves are small: 93% of the world's national parks and reserves have an area less than 5,000 km², and 78% less than 1,000 km².

Equally, range loss, the shrinking of the geographical area in which a given species is found, often marks the start of a downward spiral towards extinction. Such a contraction in range may result from habitat loss or from such processes as hunting and capture. Particular concern has been expressed in this context about the pressures on primates. Figure 3.19 shows the fragmentation and reduction in area of rainforest within three locations: Sumatra, Costa Rica, and Borneo.

Although habitat change and destruction is clearly a major cause of extinction in the modern era, a remarkably important cause is the introduction of competitive species (Figure 3.20). When new species are deliberately or accidentally introduced to an area, they can cause the extermination of local fauna by preying on them or out-competing them for food and space. As we have seen elsewhere island species have proved to be especially subject to faunal extinctions. Since 1500, 95% of extinctions of birds and terrestrial mammals have been on islands, and on a per unit basis the extinction rate was 177 times higher for mammals and 187 times higher for birds than on continents (Loehle and Eschenbach, 2012).

The World Conservation Monitoring Centre, in its analysis of the known causes of animal extinctions since 1600 AD, believed that 39% were caused by species introduction, 36% by habitat destruction, 23% by hunting, and 2% for other reasons (*World Resources*, 1996: 149). With respect to land mammals, Schipper et al. (2008) suggested that habitat loss and degradation is the prime threat (affecting 40% of the species assessed), followed by harvesting (i.e. hunting or gathering for food, medicine, materials, etc.), which is the threat to 17% of land mammals. Among marine mammals the threats are very different. Here the dominant threat is accidental mortality, which affects 78% of species and is caused by fishing and shipping. Pollution is the second most prevalent threat to marine mammals. The main threat to seabirds is competition from invasive species (Croxall et al., 2012). Ripple et al. (2016) found that 301 terrestrial mammal species are threatened with extinction due to hunting by humans. All of these species occur in developing countries. Orders with the most species threatened by hunting include primates, even-toed ungulates, bats, diprotodont marsupials, rodents, and carnivores. The primary reason for hunting and trapping these mammals is to acquire meat for human consumption, medicinal products, ornamental use, and

the pet trade. The regions with the most species threatened by hunting include Asia (especially SE Asia) and Africa.

There are certainly some particularly important environments in terms of their species diversity (Myers, 1990; Myers et al., 2000) and such biodiversity 'hotspots' need to be made priorities for conservation. They include coral reefs, tropical forests (which support well over half the planet's species on only about 6% of its land area), and some of the Mediterranean climate ecosystems (including the extraordinarily diverse Fynbos shrublands of the Cape region of South Africa). Some environments are crucial because of their high levels of species diversity or endemic species, others are crucial because their loss would have consequences elsewhere. This applies for example, to wetlands which provide habitats for migratory birds and produce the nutrients for many fisheries. Myers et al. (2000) have argued that as many as 44% of all species of vascular plants and

(a) 1932

About 1980

Mid-1980s

Strait of Malacca

National Parks

Indian Ocean

Palembang

400 km

Figure 3.19 Progressive habitat fragmentation in the rain-forest environments of (a) Sumatra, (b) Costa Rica, (c) Borneo.
Source: adapted from Whitten et al. (1987) and Terborgh (1992) and with data from UNEP, and in http://costaricasrainforest.blogspot.co.uk (accessed January 2018).

(b)

(c)

Figure 3.19 (Continued)

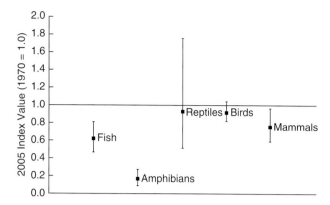

Figure 3.20 Population trends in fish, amphibians, reptiles, birds, and mammals since 1970. The change in the size of these populations relative to 1970 (1970 = 1.0) is plotted over time. Squares are index values in 2005, and bars are 95% confidence limits. *Source:* adapted from Baillie et al. (Baillie et al. 2010).

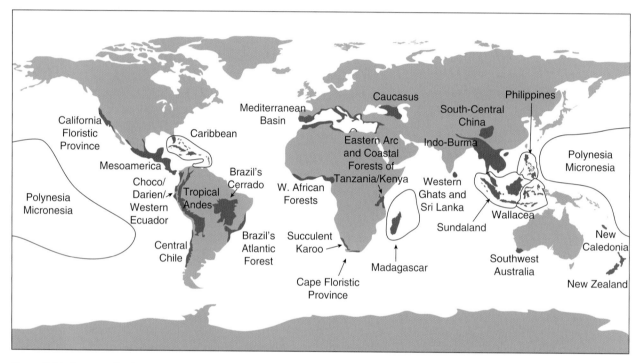

Figure 3.21 Conservation hot spot areas. Hot spots are habitats with many species found nowhere else and in greatest danger of extinction from human activity. *Source:* after Myers et al. (2000: figure 1). Reproduced with permission from *Nature*, 403, 853–858, © Nature Publishing Group.

35% of all species in four groups of vertebrate animals are confined to just 25 hotspots (Figure 3.21), which comprise a mere 1.4% of Earth's land surface. These are major locations for conservation.

Finally, future climate change could act as a major cause of extinctions in the coming decades and could be a major threat to biodiversity (Thomas et al., 2004). Climate disruption will undoubtedly cause species extinctions, but the range of estimates is large (Pimm et al., 2014). As we will see in Chapters 8 to 13, many habitats will change markedly, and as a result many nature reserves will be in the wrong place for the species they are meant to protect. For instance, high altitude habitats at the tops of mountains may simply disappear, and ice-dependent species like the polar bear (*Ursus maritimus*) may be particularly at risk (Stirling and Derocher, 2012).

Guide to Reading

Baillie, J.E.M., Griffiths, J., Turvey, S.T., Loh, J. and Collen, B. (2010) *Evolution Lost: Status and Trends of the World's Vertebrates*. London: Zoological Society of London. An authoritative and well-illustrated discussion of the current threats to the world's mammals, fish, birds, amphibians, and reptiles.

Clout, M.N. and Williams, P.A. (eds) (2009) *Invasive Species Management*. New York: Oxford University Press. An edited review of how to try and counter the threat of invasive species.

Davis, M.A. (2009) *Invasion Biology*. Oxford: Oxford University Press. A concise, comprehensive and controversial account of all aspects of biological invasions.

Forman, R.T.T. (2014) *Urban Ecology: Science of Cities*. Cambridge: Cambridge University Press. A discussion of how wildlife is affected by cities.

Gil, D. and Brumm, H. (eds) (2014) *Avian Urban Ecology: Behavioural and Physiological Adaption*. Oxford: Oxford University Press. An up-to-date consideration of how birds react to urbanization.

Martin, P.S. and Klein, R.G. (1984) *Pleistocene Extinctions*. Tucson: University of Arizona Press. An enormous survey of whether or not late Pleistocene extinctions were caused by humans.

Sodhi, N.S. and Ehrlich, P.R. (eds) (2010) *Conservation Biology for All*. Oxford: Oxford University Press. An edited collection of papers on threats to habitats and ways of conserving them.

Turvey, S.T. (ed.) (2009) *Holocene Extinctions*. Oxford: Oxford University Press. A wide-ranging survey of extinctions over the last 11,500 years.

Wilson, E.O. (1992) *The Diversity of Life*. Cambridge, MA: Belknap Press. A beautifully written and highly readable discussion of biodiversity.

4

The Human Impact on the Soil

CHAPTER OVERVIEW

Humans modify soils in many ways. Among the most important changes are those involving accelerated salinization, lateritization, podzolization, and acidification. Humans also affect soils by such processes as land drainage and the addition of fertilizers. Some soils owe so much of their character to human activities that they are termed 'anthrosols'. Of very great importance is accelerated erosion by water and wind brought about primarily by land-cover changes. Finally, humans may be altering another important component of soils – the microbiota – and this may have an impact on ecological services and on the whole Earth System.

4.1   Introduction

Humans live close to and depend on the soil. It is one of the thinnest and most vulnerable human resources and is one upon which, both deliberately and inadvertently, humans have had major impacts (Richter, 2007; Capra et al., 2015; Dazzi and Papa, 2015; Smith et al., 2016). Moreover, such impacts can occur with great rapidity in response to land-use change, new technologies, or waves of colonization. Soils modified by human activities are called anthrosols or anthropogenic soils (Howard, 2017).

Natural soil is the product of a whole range of factors and the classic expression of this is that of Jenny (1941):

$$s = f\left(cl, o, r, p, t \ldots\right)$$

where s denotes any soil property, cl is the regional climate, o the biota, r the topography, p the parent material, t the time (or period of soil formation), and the dots represent additional, unspecified factors. In reality soils are the product of highly complex interactions of many interdependent variables, and the soils themselves are not merely a passive and dependent factor in the environment. Nonetheless, following Jenny's subdivision of the classic factors of soil formation, one can see more clearly the effects humans have had on soil, be they detrimental or beneficial. These can be summarized as follows (adapted from the work of Bidwell and Hole, 1965):

1) *Parent material*
   Beneficial: adding mineral fertilizers; accumulating shells and bones; accumulating ash locally; removing excess amounts of substances such as salts.
   Detrimental: removing through harvest more plants and animal nutrients than are replaced; adding materials in amounts toxic to plants or animals; altering soil constituents in a way to depress plant growth.
2) *Topography*
   Beneficial: checking erosion through surface roughening, land forming and structure building; raising land level by accumulation of material; land levelling.
   Detrimental: causing subsidence by drainage of wetlands and by mining; accelerating erosion; excavating.
3) *Climate*
   Beneficial: adding water by irrigation; rainmaking by seeding clouds; removing water by drainage; diverting winds, etc.
   Detrimental: subjecting soil to excessive insolation, to extended frost action, to wind, etc.
4) *Organisms*
   Beneficial: introducing and controlling populations of plants and animals; adding organic matter including 'night-soil'; loosening soil by ploughing to admit more oxygen; fallowing; removing pathogenic organisms, e.g. by controlled burning.
   Detrimental: removing plants and animals; reducing organic content of soil through burning, ploughing, over-grazing, harvesting, etc.; adding or fostering pathogenic organisms; adding radioactive substances.

Human Impact on the Natural Environment: Past, Present and Future, Eighth Edition. Andrew S. Goudie.
© 2019 John Wiley & Sons Ltd. Published 2019 by John Wiley & Sons Ltd.
Companion website: www.wiley.com/go/goudie/human-impact-natural-environment

5) *Time*

Beneficial: rejuvenating the soil by adding fresh parent material or through exposure of local parent material by soil erosion; reclaiming land from under water.

Detrimental: degrading the soil by accelerated removal of nutrients from soil and vegetation cover; burying soil under solid fill or water.

Space precludes, however, that we can follow all these aspects of anthropogenic soil modification or, to use the terminology of Yaalon and Yaron (1966), of *metapedogenesis*. We will therefore concentrate on certain highly important changes which humans have brought about, especially chemical changes (such as salinization and lateritization), various structural changes (such as compaction), some hydrological changes (including the effects of drainage and the factors leading to peat-bog development), and, perhaps most important of all, soil erosion.

4.2   Salinity: Natural Sources

Increasing salinity has a whole series of consequences that include a reduction in the availability of potable water (for humans and/or their stock), deterioration in soil structure, reduction in crop yields, and decay of engineering structures and cultural treasures. It is, therefore, a major environmental issue.

Many semi-arid and arid areas are, however, naturally salty. These are zones of 'primary salinity', where there is a substantial water deficit because evapo-transpiration exceeds precipitation. Thus, whereas in humid areas there is sufficient water to percolate through the soil and to leach soluble materials from the soil and the rocks into the rivers and hence into the sea, in drylands this is not the case. Salts therefore tend to accumulate. This tendency is exacerbated by the fact that many desert areas are characterized by closed drainage basins or pans which act as terminal evaporative sumps for rivers.

The amount of natural salinity varies according to numerous factors, one of which is the source of salts. Some of the salts are brought in to the deserts by rivers. A second source of salts is the atmosphere – a source which in the past has often been accorded insufficient importance. Rainfall, coastal fogs, and dust storms all transport significant quantities of soluble salts. Further soluble salts may be derived from the weathering and solution of bedrock. In the Middle East, for example, there are extensive salt domes and evaporite beds within the bedrock which create locally high groundwater and surface-water salinity levels. In other areas, such as the Rift Valley of East Africa, volcanic rocks may provide a large source of sodium carbonate to groundwater, while elsewhere the rocks in which groundwater occurs may contain salt because they are themselves ancient desert sediments. Even in the absence of such localized sources of highly saline ground water it needs to be remembered that over a period of time most rocks will provide soluble products to groundwater, and in a closed hydrological system such salts will eventually accumulate to significant levels.

A further source of salinity may be marine transgressions. At times of higher sea-levels, it has sometimes been proposed that salts would have been laid down by the sea. Likewise in coastal areas, groundwater aquifers may be contaminated by contact with sea water.

4.3   Human Agency and Increased Salinity

Human activities cause enhanced or secondary salinization in drylands in a variety of ways (Goudie and Viles, 1997; Daliakopoulos et al., 2016). In Figure 4.1 and Table 4.1 these mechanisms are grouped into five main classes: irrigation

Figure 4.1 The causes of accelerated or enhanced salinization.

Table 4.1 Enhanced salinization.

1) Irrigation salinity
   a) Rise in groundwater
   b) Evaporation of water from fields
   c) Evaporation of water from canals & reservoirs
   d) Waterlogging produced by seepage losses
2) Dryland salinity
   a) Vegetation clearance
3) Urban salinity
   a) Water importation and irrigation
   b) Faulty drains & sewers
4) Inter-basin water transfers
   a) Mineralization of lake waters
   b) Deflation of salts from desiccating lakes
5) Coastal zone salinity
   a) Over-pumping
   b) Reduced freshwater recharge
   c) Sea-level rise
   d) Ground subsidence

salinity; dryland salinity; urban salinity; salinity brought about by inter-basin water transfers; and coastal zone salinity. In addition, mining activity can lead to salination.

Anthropogenic increases in salinity are not new. Jacobsen and Adams (1958) have shown that they were a problem for Mesopotamian irrigated agriculture after about 2400 BC. Individual fields, which in 2400 BC were registered as salt-free, can be seen in the records of ancient temple surveyors to have developed conditions of sporadic salinity by 2100 BC. Further evidence is provided by crop choice, for the onset of salinization strongly favours the adoption of crops which are most salt-tolerant. Counts of grain impressions in excavated pottery from sites in southern Iraq dated at about 3500 BC suggest that at that time the proportions of wheat and barley were nearly equal. A little more than 1000 years later the less salt-tolerant wheat accounted for less than 20% of the crop, while by about 2100 BC it accounted for less than 2% of the crop. By 1700 BC the cultivation of wheat had been abandoned completely in the southern part of the alluvial

plain. These changes in crop choice were accompanied by serious declines in yield which can also probably be attributed to salinity. At 2400 BC the yield was 2537 litres per ha, by 2100 BC it was 1460, and by 1700 BC it was down to 897. It seems likely that this played an important part in the break-up of Sumerian civilization, though the evidence is not conclusive. Moreover, the Sumarians appear to have understood the problem and to have had coping strategies (Powell, 1985).

Human-induced salinization affects about 77 million ha on a global basis, of which 48 million ha are in susceptible drylands (Middleton and Thomas, 1997) (Table 4.2). These include quite large tracts of southern Europe (Daliakopoulos et al., 2016). The salinization of Mesopotamia, noted above, goes on to this day. As Rahi and Halihan (2010) have found, the water salinity of the Euphrates River as it enters Iraq, expressed as total dissolved solids (TDS), has more than doubled compared to that of 1973. Downstream of Baghdad, the annual average TDS at Al Nassiriah, in the lower reaches of the Euphrates, increased from 1080 ppm (parts per million) in 1979 to more than 4500 ppm in 2001. This was due to the decreased flow that is entering Iraq because of upstream reservoirs and irrigation-return flow.

4.4 Irrigation Salinity

In recent decades there has been a rapid and substantial spread of irrigation across the world (Table 4.3). The irrigated area in 1900 amounted to less than 50 million ha. By 2000 the total area amounted to five times that figure. During the 1950s the irrigated area was increasing at over 4% annually, though this figure has now dropped to only about 1%. This spread of irrigation has brought about a great deal of salinization and waterlogging (Figure 4.2).

The amount of salinized irrigated land varies from area to area (Table 4.4), but in general ranges between 10 and 50% of the total. This is the case, for example, in Central Asia, where more than 50% of irrigated soils are salt affected and/

Table 4.2 Global extent of human-induced salinization in the susceptible drylands (million ha).

Continent	Light	Moderate	Strong	Extreme	Total	%
Africa	3.3	1.9	0.6	-	5.8	12.10
Asia	10.7	8.1	16.2	0.4	35.4	73.90
South America	0.9	0.1	-	-	1.0	2.08
North America	0.3	1.2	0.3	-	1.8	3.75
Europe	0.8	1.7	0.5	-	3.0	6.26
Australasia	-	0.5	-	0.4	0.9	1.87
Global total	16.0	13.5	17.6	0.8	47.9	100

Source: GLASOD; Middleton and Thomas (1997: table 4.17).

Table 4.3 Estimates of the increasing area of irrigated land on a global basis.

Year	Irrigated area (10^6 ha)
1900	44–48
1930	80
1950	94
1955	120
1960	168
1980	211
1990	245
2000	276
2012	324

Source: United Nations, World Population Prospects, the 2004 Revision and CIA World Factbook, https://www.cia.gov/library/publications/the-world-factbook/fields/2146.html#129 (accessed December 2017).

Table 4.4 Salinization of irrigated cropland.

Country	Percentage of irrigated lands affected by salinization
Algeria	10–15
Australia	15–20
China	15
Colombia	20
Cyprus	25
Egypt	30–40
Greece	7
India	27
Iran	<30
Iraq	50
Israel	13
Jordan	16
Pakistan	<40
Peru	12
Portugal	10–15
Senegal	10–15
Sri Lanka	13
Spain	10-15
Sudan	<20
Syria	30–35
USA	20–25

Source: FAO data as summarized in *World Resources* (1987: table 19.3).

Figure 4.2 The extension of irrigation in the Indus Valley of Pakistan by means of large canals has caused widespread salinization of the soils. Waterlogging is also prevalent. The white efflorescence of salt in the fields has been termed 'a satanic mockery of snow' (ASG).

or waterlogged (Qadir et al., 2009). However, there is a considerable range in these values according to the source of the data (compare Table 4.5) and this may in part reflect differences in the definition of the terms 'salinization' and 'waterlogging' (see Thomas and Middleton, 1993).

Irrigation causes secondary salinization in a variety of ways (Rhoades, 1990). Firstly, the application of irrigation water to the soil leads to a rise in the water table so that it may become near enough to the ground surface for capillary rise and subsequent evaporative concentration to take place. When groundwater comes within 3 m of the surface in clay soils, and even less for silty and sandy ones, capillary forces bring moisture to the surface where evaporation occurs. There is plenty of evidence that irrigation does indeed lead to rapid and substantial rises in the position of the water table. Rates typically range between 0.2 and 3 m per year.

Secondly, many irrigation schemes, being in areas of high temperatures and rates of evaporation, suffer from the fact that the water applied over the soil surface is readily concentrated in terms of any dissolved salts it may contain. This is especially true for crops with a high water demand (e.g. rice) or in areas where, for one reason or another, farmers are profligate in their application of water.

Thirdly, the construction of large dams and barrages creates extensive water bodies from which further evaporation can take place, once again leading to the concentration of dissolved solutes.

Fourthly, notably in sandy soils with high permeability, water seeps both laterally and downwards from irrigation canals so that waterlogging may occur. Many irrigation canals are not lined, with the consequence that substantial water losses can result.

4.5 Dryland Salinity

A prime cause of dryland salinity extension is vegetation clearance (Peck and Halton, 2003). The removal of native forest, by reducing interception and evapotranspirational

Table 4.5 Global estimate of secondary salinization in the world's irrigated lands.

Country	Cropped area (Mha)	Irrigated area (Mha)	Share of irrigated to cropped area (%)	Salt-affected land in irrigated area (%)	Share of salt-affected to irrigated land (%)
China	96.97	44.83	46.2	6.70	15.0
India	168.99	42.10	24.9	7.00	16.6
CIS	232.57	20.48	8.8	3.70	18.1
USA	189.91	18.10	9.5	4.16	23.0
Pakistan	20.76	16.08	77.5	4.22	26.2
Iran	14.83	5.74	38.7	1.72	30.0
Thailand	20.05	4.00	19.9	0.40	10.0
Egypt	2.69	2.69	100.00	0.88	33.0
Australia	47.11	1.83	3.9	0.16	8.7
Argentina	35.75	1.72	4.8	0.58	33.7
South Africa	13.17	1.13	8.6	0.10	8.9
Subtotal	852.80	158.70	18.8	29.62	20.0
World	1,473.70	227.11	15.4	45.4	20.0

Source: Ghassemi et al. (1995: table 18). Reproduced by permission of CAB International and the University of New South Wales Press.

losses, allows a greater penetration of rainfall into deeper soil layers which causes groundwater levels to rise, thereby creating conditions for the seepage of sometimes saline water into low-lying areas. This is a particularly serious problem in the wheatbelt of Western Australia and in some of the prairies of North America. In the former case it is the clearance of *Eucalyptus* forest that has led to the increased rate of groundwater recharge and to the spreading salinity of streams and bottomlands. Salt 'scalds' have developed. The speed and extent of groundwater rise following such forest clearance is shown in Figure 4.3. Until late 1976 both the Wights and Salmon catchments were forested. Then the Wights catchment was cleared. Before 1976 both catchments showed a

similar pattern of groundwater fluctuation, but after that date there was a marked divergence of 5.7 m (Peck, 1983). The process can be reversed by afforestation (Bari and Schofield, 1992). Re-vegetation policies could also provide increased carbon sinks and so could provide synergistic value (Pittock and Wratt, 2001: 603).

Groundwater levels have increased some tens of metres since clearance of the natural vegetation began: by up to 30 m since the 1880s in south-eastern Australia and by about 20 m in parts of south-west Australia. In some of the upland areas of New South Wales, groundwater levels have increased by up to 60 m over the last 70 to 80 years. In New South Wales, the area of land affected by dryland salinity in currently reported to be about 120,000 ha. However, if current land-use trends and groundwater rise continues, this figure has the potential to increase to as much as 7.5 million ha by 2050 (http://www.abs.gov.au/ausstats/abs@.nsf/Lookup/by%20Subject/1370.0~2010~Chapter~Salinity%20(6.2.4.4, accessed December 2017). In Western Australia there is already an estimated 1.8 million ha of farmland that is salt-affected. This area could double in the next 15 to 20 years and in all some 6.1 million ha have the potential to be affected by dryland salinity. Dryland salinity is also a major problem on the Canadian prairies. In Alberta, approximately 0.65 million ha are affected by secondary salinity, with an average crop yield reduction of 25%. In Saskatchewan 1.3 million ha are affected, and in Manitoba 0.24 million ha.

Rising water tables resulting from land-use changes are now being identified in other areas. For example, there has been a marked rise in the water table of the

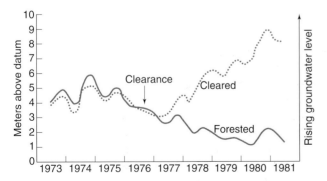

Figure 4.3 Comparison of hydrographs recorded from the boreholes in Wights (———) and Salmon (------) catchments in Western Australia. Both catchments were forested until late in 1976 when Wights was cleared. *Source:* adapted from Peck (1983: figure 1).

Continental Terminal in south-west Niger (Leduc et al., 2001). The rates have been between 0.01 and 0.45 m per year. The reason for this is the replacement of natural woodland savanna with millet fields and associated fallows. This has promoted increased surface runoff which concentrates in temporary endoreic ponds and then infiltrates to the water table.

4.6 Urban Salinity

Drylands have seen rapid rates of urbanization and there are now some enormous urban agglomerations. As Table 4.6 suggests, the average size of major dryland cities expanded 7.9 times between 1950 and 2000. Urbanization can cause a rise in groundwater levels by affecting the amount of moisture lost by evapotranspiration. Many elements of urbanization, and in particular the spread of

Table 4.6 Population of selected dryland cities in 1950 and 2010 (millions).

City and country	1950	2010
Cairo, Egypt	2.41	12.66
Ouagadougou, Burkina Faso	0.03	2.55
Ndjamena, Chad	0.04	1.58
Lanzhou, China	0.32	2.10
Alexandria, Egypt	1.04	5.53
Jodhpur, India	0.18	1.22
Tehran, Iran	1.04	8.71
Esfahan, Iran	0.18	3.92
Alma Ata, Kazakhstan	0.32	1.29
Kuwait City, Kuwait	0.09	1.51
Bamako, Mali	0.06	2.13
Karachi, Pakistan	1.03	16.61
Lima, Peru	0.97	8.84
Riyadh, Saudi Arabia	0.11	4.59
Jeddah, Saudi Arabia	0.12	2.75
Damascus, Syria	0.37	3.10
Las Vegas, USA	0.04	1.12
Phoenix, USA	0.22	2.86
Los Angeles, USA	4.05	13.86
Dubai, UAE	0.02	1.70
Abu Dhabi, UAE	0.01	1.09
Baghdad, Iraq	0.58	5.44
Windhoek, Namibia	0.02	0.23
Total	**13.37**	**105.38**

Source: UN data processed by author.

impermeable surfaces (roads, buildings, car parks, etc.) interrupt the soil evaporation process so that groundwater levels in *sabkha* (salt plain) areas along the coast of the Arabian Gulf have risen (Shehata and Lotfi, 1993).

Urbanization can lead to other changes in groundwater conditions that can aggravate salinization. In some large desert cities the importation of water, its usage, wastage, and leakage, can produce the ingredients to feed this phenomenon. This has, for example, been identified as a problem in Cairo and its immediate environs (Hawass, 1993). The very rapid expansion of Cairo's population has outstripped the development of an adequate municipal infrastructure. In particular, leakage losses from water pipes and sewers have led to a substantial rise in the groundwater level and have subjected many buildings to attack by sulphate- and chloride-rich water. There are other sites in Egypt, such as those of Luxor, where urbanization and associated changes in ground water levels have been regarded as a major cause of accelerated salt weathering of important monuments.

4.7 Inter-basin Water Transfers

A further reason for increases in levels of salinity is the changing state of water bodies caused by inter-basin water transfers. The most famous example of this is the shrinkage of the Aral Sea, the increase in its mineralization, and the deflation of saline materials from its surface and their subsequent deposition downwind (Saiko and Zonn, 2000; Kravtsova and Tarasenko, 2010) (Figure 4.4). The sea itself has had its mineral content increased more than threefold since 1960. Another illustration of the effects of inter-basin water transfers is the desiccation of the Owens Lake in California. Diversion of water to feed the insatiable demands of Los Angeles caused the lake to dry out, so that highly saline dust storms have become increasingly serious (Gill, 1996; Tyler et al., 1997). Data on recent salinity enhancement in lakes from the USA, Asia, and Australia is provided by Williams (1999) (Table 4.7).

4.8 Coastal Zone Salinity

Another prime cause of the spread of saline conditions is the incursion of sea water brought about by the over-pumping of groundwater (Ferguson and Gleeson, 2012). Salt water displaces less saline groundwater through a mechanism called the Ghyben-Herzberg principle. The Ghyben-Herzberg relationship (Figure 4.5) is based on the fact that fresh water has a lower density than salt water, such that a column of sea water can support a column of fresh water approximately 2.5% higher than itself (or a ratio of about 40:41). So where a body of fresh water has accumulated in a reservoir rock or sediment which is also open

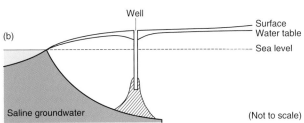

Figure 4.5 (a) The Ghyben-Herzberg relationship between fresh and saline groundwater. (b) The effect of excessive pumping from the well. The diagonal hatching represents the increasing incursion of saline water. *Source:* adapted from Goudie and Wilkinson (1977: figure 63).

Figure 4.4 Dust plumes caused by the deflation of salty sediments from the drying floor of the Aral Sea as revealed by a satellite image (153/Metero-Priroda, 18 May 1975). *Source:* adapted from Mainguet (1995: figure 4).

to penetration from the sea, it does not simply lie flat on top of the salt water but forms a lens, whose thickness is approximately 41 times the elevation of the piezometric surface above sea-level. The corollary of this rule is that if the hydrostatic pressure of the fresh water falls as a result of over-pumping in a well, then the underlying salt water will rise by 40 units for every unit by which the fresh-water table is lowered. A rise in sea-level can cause a comparably dramatic alteration in the balance between fresh and salt water bodies, a process which may be exacerbated by increasing inundation by cyclones and surges. This is especially serious on low islands and atolls (Figure 4.6) (Broadus, 1990; Terry and Chui, 2012) and on deltas, such as that of the Nile (Sušnik et al., 2015). An example of concern about

Table 4.7 Enhanced salinity of lake basins.

Lake	Period	Change (g l^{-1})
Mono (California)	1941–1992	48 to 90
Pyramid Lake (Nevada)	1933–1980	3.75 to 5.5
Dead Sea	1910–1990s	200 to 300
Aral Sea	1960–1991	10 to 30
Qinghai (China)	1950s–1990s	-6 to 12
Corangamite (Australia)	1960–1990s	35 to 50

Source: data in Williams (1999).

salinization following on from sea-level rise is the Shanghai area of China (Chen and Zong, 1999). The area is suffering subsidence as a result of delta sedimentation (at 3 mm per year) and groundwater extraction (now less than 10 mm per year). It is very low-lying and in some counties the groundwater table is at 1.0–1.2 m. Thus a rise in sea-level will raise the groundwater level, prolong waterlogging, and cause a greater dominance of saline water in the deltaic area.

The problem of salt water incursion presents itself on the coastal plain of Israel, on the island of Bahrain, and on some of the coastal aquifers of the United Arab Emirates. It is also a widespread phenomenon in the coastal regions of North America (Barlow and Reichard, 2010). Figure 4.7 shows the spread of salt water into the Biscayne aquifer in Miami-Dade County in Florida between 1904 and 1995. A comparable situation has also arisen in the Nile Delta (Kotb et al., 2000), though here the cause is not necessarily solely groundwater over-pumping, but may also be due to changes in water levels and freshwater recharge caused by the construction of the Aswan High Dam. Figure 4.8 shows the way in which chloride concentrations have increased and spread in the Llobregat Delta of eastern Spain because of the incursion of sea water.

In any one location the causes of incursion may be complex. A good exemplification of this is provided by the coastal plains of northern Australia. Here Mulrennan and Woodroffe (1998) have assessed the potential role of such factors as sea-level change, rainfall variability, boat erosion of creeks, the activities of feral water buffalo, and sediment compaction.

Figure 4.6 Impact of sea level rise on an island water table. Note: The freshwater table extends below sea level 40 cm for every 1 cm by which it extends above sea level. (a) For islands with substantial elevation a 1-m rise in sea level simply shifts the entire water table up 1 m, and the only problem is that a few wells will have to be replaced with shallower wells. (b) However, for very low islands the water table cannot rise due to runoff, evaporation, and transpiration. A rise in sea level would thus narrow the water table by 40 cm for every 1 cm that the sea level rises, (c) effectively eliminating groundwater supplies for the lowest islands. *Source:* adapted from Broadus (1990).

Commonly, groundwaters associated with mineral resources (e.g. coal, oil, and gas) exhibit high salinity. Although the volume of water used by mining is typically small relative to other users, such as agriculture and the environment, cumulative volumes of groundwater that may require disposal can be large and so can pose a salination threat (Greene et al., 2016).

4.9 Consequences of Salinity

One consequence of the evaporative concentration of salts, and the pumping of saline waters back into rivers and irrigation canals from tubewells and other sources, is that river waters leading from irrigation areas show higher levels of dissolved salts. These, particularly when they contain nitrates, can make the water undesirable for human consumption.

A further problem is that, as irrigation water is concentrated by evapotranspiration, calcium and magnesium components tend to precipitate as carbonates, leaving sodium ions dominant in the soil solution. The sodium ions tend to be absorbed by colloidal clay particles, deflocculating them and leaving the resultant structureless soil almost impermeable to water and unfavourable to root development.

The death of vegetation in areas of saline patches, due both to poor soil structure and toxicity, creates bare ground which becomes a focal point for erosion by wind and water. Likewise, deflation from the desiccating surface of the Aral Sea (see Section 4.7) causes large amounts of salt to be blown away in dust storms and to be deposited downwind.

Probably the most serious impact of salination is on plant growth (Läuchli and Grattan, 2007). This takes place partly through its effect on soil structure, but more significantly through its effects on osmotic pressures and through direct toxicity. When a water solution containing large quantities of dissolved salts comes into contact with a plant cell it causes a shrinkage of the protoplasmic lining. The phenomenon is due to the osmotic movement of the water, which passes from the cell towards the more concentrated soil solution. The cell collapses and the plant succumbs. Crop yields fall.

The toxicity effect varies with different plants and different salts. Sodium carbonate, by creating highly alkaline soil conditions, may damage plants by a direct caustic effect, while high nitrate levels may promote undesirable vegetative growth in grapes or sugar beets at the expense of sugar content. Boron is injurious to many crop plants at solution concentrations of more than 1 or 2 ppm.

4.10 Reclamation of Salt-affected Lands

Because of the extent and seriousness of salinity, be the causes natural or anthropogenic, various reclamation techniques have been initiated. These can be divided into three main types: eradication, conversion, and control.

Eradication predominantly involves the removal of salt either by improved drainage or by the addition of quantities of fresh water to leach the salt out of the soil. These both involve considerable expense and pose severe technological problems in areas of low relief and limited fresh-water availability. Improved drainage can either be provided by open drains or by the use of tubewells (as at Mohenjo Daro, Pakistan) to reduce groundwater levels

Figure 4.7 Saltwater intrusion in the Biscayne aquifer near Miami, Florida, between 1904 and 1995. *Source:* adapted from Barlow and Reichard (2010: figure 5).

and associated salinity and waterlogging. A minor eradication measure, which may have some potential, is the biotic treatment of salinity through the harvesting of salt-accumulating plants such as *Suaeda fruticosa* (shrubby seablite), or through bioremediation with crops such as licorice (*Glycyrrhiza glabra*) (Qadir et al., 2009). Dryland salinity can be reduced or reversed if replanting schemes are introduced (Dagar and Minhas, 2016).

Conversion involves the use of chemical methods to convert harmful salts into less harmful ones. For example, gypsum is frequently added to sodic soils to convert caustic alkali carbonates to soluble sodium sulphate and relatively harmless calcium carbonate:

$$Na_2CO_3 + CaSO_4 \leftrightarrow CaCO_3 + Na_2SO_4 \downarrow \text{leachable}$$

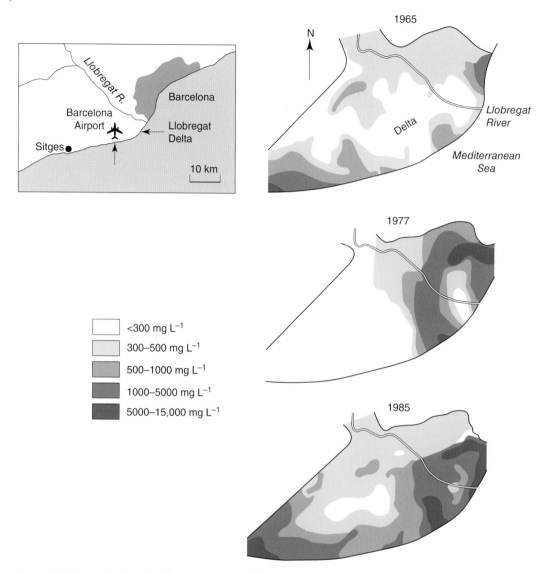

Figure 4.8 Changes in the chloride concentration of the Llobregat delta aquifer, Barcelona, Spain as a result of sea-water incursion caused by the over-pumping of groundwater. *Source:* adapted from Custodio et al. (1986).

Some of the most effective ways of reducing the salinity hazard involve miscellaneous control measures, such as less wasteful and lavish application of water through the use of sprinklers rather than traditional irrigation methods; the lining of canals to reduce seepage (Figure 4.9); the realignment of canals through less permeable soils; and the use of more salt-tolerant plants. As salinity is a particularly serious threat at the time of germination and for seedlings, various strategies can be adopted during this critical phase of plant growth: plots can be irrigated lightly each day after seeding to prevent salt build-up; major leaching can be carried out just before planting; and areas to be seeded can be bedded in such a way that salts accumulate at the ridge tops with the seed planted on the slope between the furrow bottom and the ridge top. Useful general reviews of methods for controlling soil salinity are given by Rhoades (1990), and Qadir et al. (2000).

4.11 Lateritization

In some parts of the tropics there are extensive sheets of laterite, an iron and/or aluminium-rich duricrust (see Macfarlane, 1976). These sheets result naturally, either because of a preferential removal of silica during the course of extensive weathering (leading to a *relative* accumulation of the sesquioxides of iron and aluminium), or because of an *absolute* accumulation of these compounds. In some parts of West Africa, lateritization is termed 'bowalization' (Padonou et al., 2015).

Figure 4.9 A lined irrigation canal in Haryana, India. Such lining is an important way in which to reduce waterlogging and salinization (ASG).

One of the properties of laterites is that they harden on exposure to air and through desiccation. Once hardened they are not favourable to plant growth. One way in which exposure may take place is by accelerated erosion, while forest removal may so cause a change in microclimate that desiccation of the laterite surface can take place. Indeed, one of the main problems with the removal of humid tropical rain forest is that soil hardening may occur in some, but by no means in all so-called tropical soils (Richter and Babbar, 1991). Should hardening occur, it tends to limit the extent of successful soil utilization and severely retards the re-establishment of forest. Although Vine (1968: 90) and Sanchez and Buol (1975) have rightly warned against exaggerating this difficulty in agricultural land use, there are records from many parts of the tropics of accelerated induration brought about by forest removal (Goudie, 1973). In the Cameroons, for example, around 2 m of complete induration can take place in less than a century. In India, foresters have for a long time been worried by the role that plantations of teak (*Tectona grandis*) can play in lateritization. Teak is deciduous, demands light, likes to be well spaced (to avoid crown friction), dislikes competition from undergrowth, and is shallow-rooted. These characteristics mean that teak plantations expose the soil surface to erosive and desiccative forces more than does the native vegetation cover.

One of the main exponents of the role that human agency has played in lateritization in the tropical world has been Gourou (1961: 21–22). Although he may be guilty of exaggerating the extent and significance of laterite, a material he termed a 'pedological laprosy', Gourou gives many examples from low latitudes of falling agricultural productivity resulting from the onset of lateritization.

4.12 Accelerated Podzolization and Acidification

There is an increasing amount of evidence that the introduction of agriculture, deforestation, and pastoralism to parts of upland Western Europe promoted some major changes in soil character: notably an increase in the development of acidic and podzolized conditions, associated with the development of peat bogs. Climatic changes may have played a role, as could progressive leaching of last glacial drifts during the passage of the Holocene. But the association in time and space of human activities with soil deterioration has become increasingly clear.

By replacing the natural forest vegetation with cultivated land and pasture, human societies set in train various related processes, especially on base-poor materials. First, the destruction of deep-rooting trees curtailed the enrichment of the surface of the soil by bases brought up from the deeper layers. Second, the use of fire to clear forest may have released nutrients in the form of readily soluble salts, some of which were inevitably lost in drainage, especially in soils poor in colloids (Dimbleby, 1974). Third, the taking of crops and animal products depleted the soil reserves to an extent probably greater than that arising from any of the manuring practices of prehistoric settlements. Fourth, as the soil degraded, the vegetation which invaded – especially bracken and heather – itself tended to produce a more acidic humus type of soil than the original mixed deciduous forest, and so continued the process.

The development of podzols and their associated iron-pans (Cunningham et al., 2001), by impeding downward percolating waters, may have accelerated the formation of peats, which tend to develop where there is waterlogging through impeded drainage. Another fact which would have contributed to their development is that when a forest canopy is removed (as by deforestation) the transpiration demand of the vegetation is reduced, less rainfall is intercepted, so that the supply of groundwater is increased, aggravating any waterlogging. It has been argued that many peat bogs in highland Britain coincide broadly in age with the first major land-clearance episodes (Moore, 1973), but this has been disputed by Tipping (2008) who argued that peat development was essentially controlled by climatic conditions, that it was widespread in highland Scotland very early in the Holocene, and that there is very little evidence that it is the result of anthropogenic activities.

One serious type of soil acidification is that which produces acid sulphate soils. As Dent and Pons (1995: 263) wrote:

> Acid sulphate soils are the nastiest soils in the world. They generate sulphuric acid that brings their pH as low as 2 and leaks into drainage and

floodwaters. In this acid environment, aluminium and other toxic elements kill vegetation and aquatic life or, in sub-lethal doses, render many species stunted and sickly. Generations of people depending on these soils have been impoverished and, probably, poisoned by their drinking water.

The reason for the development of such extremely acid soils is that originally they accumulated as sediments under severely reducing conditions in environments like tidal (e.g. mangrove) swamps, or brackish lakes. Large amounts of sulphitic mud accumulated. When such materials are drained reduction is replaced by oxidation, and sulphuric acid is produced. Infamous examples are known from the drained polders of the Netherlands and from the drained coastal swamps of South-East Asia.

Some soils are currently being acidified by air pollution and the deposition of acid precipitation (Grieve, 2001) (see also Section 7.15). Many soils have a resistance to acidification because of their buffering capacity, which enables them to neutralize acidity. However, this resistance very much depends on soil type and situation, and soils which have a low buffering capacity because of their low calcium content (as, for example, on granite), and which are subjected to high levels of precipitation, may build up high levels of acidity. The concept of critical loads has been developed. They are defined as exposures below which significant harmful effects on sensitive elements of the environment do not occur according to currently available knowledge. The critical load for sensitive forest soils on gneiss, granite, or other slow-weathering rocks is often less than 3 kg of sulphur per ha per year. In some of the more polluted parts of central Europe, the rates of sulphur deposition may have been between 20 and 100 kg per ha per year (Ågren and Elvingson, 1996). Areas where crucial loads are being exceeded include the heavily industrialized regions of the eastern USA, Europe, Russia, and large parts of Asia, but risks are increasing in parts of Brazil, Argentina, and South Africa (Bouwman et al., 2002).

The immediate impact of high levels of acid input to soils is to increase the exchange between hydrogen (H+) ions and the nutrient cations, such as potassium (K+), magnesium (Mg++), and calcium (Ca++). As a result of this exchange, such cations can be quickly leached from the soil, along with the sulphate from the acid input. This leaching leads to nutrient deficiency. Acidification also leads to a change in the rate at which dead organic matter is broken down by soil microbes. It can also render some ions, such as aluminium, more mobile and this has been implicated in the phenomenon of forest decline (see Section 2.20).

On the other hand, the recent reduction in acid rain in some areas as a result of pollution controls and a reduction in the burning of sulphur-rich fossil fuels has seen some reversal of soil acidity (RoTap, 2012). There has, for example, been an increase in soil pH in UK forested areas in recent years (Vanguelova et al., 2010).

Changing levels of acid precipitation are not, however, the sole reason for acidity trends in soils. A recent study in China (Guo et al., 2010) has indeed shown widespread acidification of agricultural soils since the 1980s, and this has been attributed to high nitrogen fertilizer application rates, together with the uptake and removal of base cations by plants.

4.13 Soil Carbon

One important consequence of land-use and land-cover modification is changes in the carbon content of soils. Soil organic carbon includes plant, animal, and microbial residues. This has potential significance in terms of carbon release to the atmosphere and hence for the enhanced greenhouse effect, though there are still debates about whether or not soil erosion is a source or sink for carbon (Chappell et al., 2016; Dialynas et al., 2016).

Under prolonged cultivation there is strong evidence for loss of soil carbon. Agricultural practices that contribute to this are deforestation and biomass burning, drainage of wetlands, ploughing and other forms of soil disturbance, and removal of crop residues. Soil carbon is depleted by oxidation or mineralization due to breakdown of aggregates leading to exposure of carbon, leaching and translocation of dissolved organic carbon or particulate organic carbon, and accelerated erosion by runoff or wind (Lal, 2002). Losses of soil organic carbon of as much as 50% in surface soils (20 cm) have been observed after cultivation for 30–50 years. Reductions average around 30% of the original amount in the top 100 cm (Post and Kwon, 2000). Soil carbon loss may also be caused by intensive logging, though the literature is full of different opinions on this matter (see, Dean et al., 2017). Soil salinization is another process that may have an effect on soil carbon stocks. The stock of soil organic carbon (SOC) reflects the balance between carbon (C) inputs from plants, and losses through decomposition, leaching, and erosion. Soil salinity decreases plant productivity and hence C inputs to the soil, but also microbial activity and therefore SOC decomposition rates (Setia et al., 2013).

Much depends, however, on the nature of land management and tillage operations (Nath and Lal, 2017). In recent decades, for example, the carbon stock in agricultural land in the USA may have increased because of the adoption of conservation tillage practices on cropland and a reduction in the use of bare fallow (Eve et al., 2002). The use of nitrogenous fertilizers may also explain some of the increase (Buyanovsky and Wagner, 1998).

Conversely, re-afforestation and conversion of cropland to grassland can cause substantial gains in soil organic carbon. In general, after afforestation there may be a period when soil organic carbon declines, because of low rates of litter fall and continuing decomposition of residues from the preceding agricultural phase. As the forest cover develops, inputs of carbon exceed outputs. The rates of building of carbon vary, and tend to be greater in cool and humid regions and under hardwoods and softwoods rather than under *Eucalyptus* or *Pinus radiata* (Paul et al., 2002).

Much work is currently being done on the addition of biochar (charcoal produced by pyrolysis of biomass) to soils as a means of mitigating the effects of increasing atmospheric carbon dioxide levels (i.e. it is one approach to geo-engineering) (see Section 7.13) (Lehmann and Joseph, 2015). Its climate mitigation potential results from its highly recalcitrant nature, which slows the rate at which photosynthetically produced carbon is returned to the atmosphere (Woolf et al., 2010).

4.14 Soil Structure Alteration

One of the most important features of a soil, in terms of both its suitability for plant growth and its inherent erodibility, is its structure. There are many ways in which humans can alter this, especially by compacting it with agricultural machinery (Horn et al., 2000), forestry operations (Goutal et al., 2013), the use of recreation vehicles, skiing (de Jong et al., 2015), changing its chemical character through irrigation, and trampling (Grieve, 2001; Batey, 2009). Soil compaction, which involves the compression of a mass of soil into a smaller volume, tends to increase the resistance of soil to penetration by roots and emerging seedlings, and limits oxygen and carbon dioxide exchange between the root zone and the atmosphere. Moreover, it reduces the rate of water infiltration into the soil, which may change the soil moisture status and accelerate surface runoff and soil erosion (Nawaz et al., 2012).

For example, the effects of the passage of vehicles on some soil structural properties are shown in Table 4.8. Excessive use of heavy agricultural machinery is perhaps the major cause of soil compaction, and most procedures in the cropping cycle, from tillage and seedbed preparation, through drilling, weeding, and agrochemical application to harvesting, are now largely mechanized, particularly in the developed world. Most notable of all is the reduction that is caused in soil infiltration capacity, which may explain why vehicle movements can often lead to gully development.

Grazing is another activity that can damage soil structure through trampling and compaction. Heavily grazed lands tend to have considerably lower infiltration capacities than those found in ungrazed ones. Particular fears have been expressed that the replacement of Amazonian rainforest to cattle-trampled pasture could lead to great increases in the frequency and volume of stormflow. One study showed that the frequency of storm flow in such grazed areas increased twofold, while its volume increased seventeenfold (Germer et al., 2010). The removal of vegetation cover and associated litter also changes infiltration capacity, since cover protects the soil from packing by raindrops and provides organic matter for binding soil particles together in open aggregates. Soil fauna that live on the organic matter assist this process by churning together the organic material and mineral particles.

An interesting study of the effect of grazing on soil infiltration capacities has been undertaken in the Nama-Karoo rangelands of South Africa (du Toit et al., 2009). There no simple linear relationship was found between grazing pressure and soil infiltration rates. Ungrazed areas had biological crusts which meant that infiltration rates were low. Moderately grazed areas had their crusts disrupted by trampling and so had higher infiltration rates. Heavily grazed areas became compacted and so had lower infiltration capacities.

In general, experiments show that re-afforestation improves soil structure, especially the pore volume of the soils. Ploughing is also known to produce a compacted layer at the base of the zone of ploughing. This layer has been termed the 'plough sole'. The normal action of the plough is to leave behind a loose surface layer and a dense subsoil where the soil aggregates have been pressed together by the sole of the plough. The compacting action can be especially injurious when the depth of ploughing is both constant and long term, and when heavy machinery is used on wet ground (Greenland and Lal, 1977).

Attempts have been made to reduce soil crusting by applying municipal and animal wastes to farm land, by adding chemicals such as phosphoric acid, and by adopting a cultivation system of the no-tillage type. The last practice is based on the idea that the use of herbicides has eliminated much of the need for tillage and cultivation in row crops; seeds are planted directly into the soil without ploughing, and weeds are controlled by the herbicides. With this method less bare soil is exposed and heavy farm machinery is less likely to create soil compaction problems.

Soil structures may also be modified to increase water runoff, particularly in arid zones where the runoff obtained can augment the meagre water supply for crops, livestock, industrial and urban reservoirs, and groundwater recharge projects. In the Negev farming was practised in this way, especially in the Nabatean and the Romano-Byzantine periods (about 300 BC to AD 630), and attempts were made to induce runoff by clearing the surface gravel of the soil

Table 4.8 Change to soil properties resulting from the passage of 100 motorcycles in New Zealand.

Soil property	Total no. of sites	No. of sites with significant change*	Mean percentage at significant sites	No. of sites with significant increase	No. of sites with significant decrease	Main direction of change	Mean percentage change in direction
Infiltration capacity	16	16 (100%)	84.3	3	13	Decrease	78.1
Bearing capacity	21	10 (48%)	22.8	2	8	Decrease	18.6
Soil moisture	20	14 (70%)	15.5	5	9	Decrease	16.7
Dry bulk density	19	11 (58%)	13.6	9	2	Decrease	13.3

*Change is significant when greater than: 10% for infiltration capacity; 10% for bearing capacity; 5% for soil moisture; 5% for bulk density.
Source: Crozier et al. (1978: table 1).

and heaping it into thousands of mounds. This exposed the finer silty soil beneath, facilitating soil crust formation by raindrop impact, decreasing infiltration capacity, and reducing surface roughness, so that runoff increased (Evenari et al., 1971).

4.15 Soil Drainage and its Impact

Soil drainage 'has been a gradual process and the environmental changes to which it has led have, by reason of that gradualness, often passed unnoticed' (Green, 1978: 171). To be sure, the most spectacular feats of drainage – arterial drainage – involving the construction of veritable rivers and large dike systems, as seen in the Netherlands and the Fenlands of eastern England, have received attention. However, more widespread than arterial drainage, and sometimes independent of it, is the drainage of individual fields, either by surface ditching or by underdrainage with tile pipes and the like. Green (1978) mapped the areas of drained agricultural land in Europe, and found that in Finland, Denmark, Great Britain, the Netherlands, and Hungary the majority of agricultural land is drained. Such drainage is also widespread in the US Corn Belt and so, for example, nearly a half of Indiana was artificially drained by the 1960s (Kumar et al., 2009).

In Britain underdrainage was promoted by government grants and reached a peak of about one million ha per year in the 1970s in England and Wales. More recently government subsidies have been cut and the uncertain economic future of farming has led to a reduction in farm expenditure. Both tendencies have led to a reduction in the rate of field drainage, which by 1990 was down to only 40,000 ha per year (Robinson, 1990).

The drainage conditions of the soil have also frequently been altered by the development of ridge and furrow patterns created by ploughing. Such patterns are a characteristic feature of many of the heavy soils of lowland England where large areas, especially of the Midland lowlands, are striped by long, narrow ridges of soil, lying more or less parallel to each other and usually arranged in blocks of approximately rectangular shape. They were formed by ploughing with heavy ploughs pulled by teams of oxen; the precise mechanism has been described by Coones and Patten (1986: 154).

Soil drainage has been one of the most successful ways in which communities have striven to increase agricultural productivity; it was practised by Etruscans, Greeks, and Romans (Smith, 1976). Large areas of marshland and floodplain have been drained to human advantage. By leading water away, the water table is lowered and stabilized, providing greater depth for the root zone. Moreover, well-drained soils warm up earlier in the spring and thus permit earlier planting and germination of crops. Farming is easier if the soil is not too wet, since the damage to crops by winter freezing may be minimized, undesirable salts carried away, trafficability of farm equipment improved, and the general physical condition of the soil ameliorated. In addition, drained land may have certain inherent virtues: tending to be flat it is less prone to erosion and more amenable to mechanical cultivation. It will also be less prone to drought risk than certain other types of land. Paradoxically, by reducing the area of saturated ground, drainage can alleviate flood risk in some situations by limiting the extent of a drainage basin that generates saturation excess overland flow.

Conversely, soil drainage can have quite undesirable or unplanned effects. For example, some drainage systems, by raising drainage densities, can increase flood risk by reducing the distance over which unconcentrated overland flow (which is relatively slow) has to travel before reaching a channel (where flow is relatively fast). In central Wales, for instance, the establishment of drainage ditches in peaty areas to enable afforestation increased flood peaks in the rivers Wye and Severn (Howe et al., 1966) and this has also been a problem in northern England (Holden et al., 2006). Stream flow trends have also been influenced by subsoil drainage in Indiana (Kumar et al., 2009) and Minnesota (Schottler et al., 2014) in the USA. In addition, the quality of stream flow may be impacted by drainage, leading to the export of dissolved organic matter (Dalzell et al., 2011), nitrates (Cuadra and Vidon, 2011), and phosphates (Gardner et al., 2002). Drainage of organic soils causes large-scale oxidation, which releases large quantities of carbon dioxide (CO_2) and nitrous dioxide (N_2O) into the atmosphere (Tubiello et al., 2016).

Drainage can also cause long-term damage to soil quality. A fall in water level in organic soils can lead to the oxidation and eventual disappearance of peaty materials (Leifeld et al., 2011), which in the early stages of post-drainage use may be highly productive. This has occurred, for instance, in the English Fenland (Dawson et al., 2010), the Sacramento-San Joaquin Delta of California (Drexler et al., 2009; Deverel et al., 2016), and the Everglades of Florida, where drainage of peat soils has led to a subsidence in the soil of 32 mm per year (Stephens, 1956). The drainage of the northernmost one-fourth of the Everglades, one of the largest deposits of organic soils in North America, began in the 1880s. The estimated peat volume was originally about 7×10^9 m^3 and is currently about 3×10^9 m^3 (Aich et al., 2013). In another study in the area, Hohner and Dreschel (2015) estimated that the current Everglades covers approximately half its original area (50.9%), has less than a quarter of its pre-drainage peat volume (23.5%), mass (17.3%), and carbon (19.1%). The issue of land subsidence is discussed further in Section 6.4.

Soil moisture content can also determine the degree to which soils are subjected to expansion and contraction effects, which in turn may affect engineering structures in areas with expansive soils. Soils containing sodium montmorillonite type clays, when drained or planted with large trees, may dry out and cause foundation problems (Driscoll, 1983).

4.16 Soil Fertilization

Attempts to maintain or increase soil fertility have a long history, and Bogaard et al. (2013) presented stable isotope determinations of charred cereals and pulses from Neolithic sites across Europe (dating c. 5900–2400 cal BC), which showed that early farmers used livestock manure and water management to enhance crop yields. More recently, however, the chemistry of soils has been changed deliberately by the introduction of chemical fertilizers. Their employment on a large scale is little more than 150 years old. In the early nineteenth century nitrates were first imported from Chile, and sulphate of ammonia was produced only after the 1820s as a by-product of coal gas manufacture. In 1843 the first fertilizer factory was established at Deptford Creek (London), but for a long time superphosphates were the only manufactured fertilizers in use. In the twentieth century synthetic fertilizers, particularly nitrates, were developed, notably by Scandinavian countries which used their vast resources of water power. Potassic fertilizers came into use much later than the phosphatic and nitrogenous; nineteenth-century farmers hardly knew them. The rise in nitrogen fertilizer consumption for the world as a whole in recent decades is shown in Figure 4.10. Global

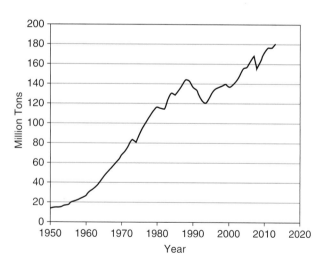

Figure 4.10 Global consumption of fertilizer, 1950–2013. *Source:* based on data from International Fertilizer Association, Earth Resources Institute and others.

fertilizer consumption in 2015 was around 191 million tonnes of nutrient of which around 115 were nitrogen, 43 were phosphate and 32 were potash (http://www.fao.org/3/a-i4324e.pdf, accessed January 2018). The use of synthetic fertilizers has greatly increased agricultural productivity in many parts of the world, and remarkable increases in yields have been achieved. It is also true that in some circumstances proper fertilizer use can help minimize erosion by ensuring an ample supply of roots and plant residues, particularly on infertile or partially degraded soils.

On the other hand, the increasing use of synthetic fertilizers can create environmental problems such as water pollution, while their substitution for more traditional fertilizers may accelerate soil structure deterioration and soil erosion. One effect has been the increase in the water repellency of some surface soil materials. This in turn can reduce soil infiltration rates and cause an increase in erosion by overland flow (Conacher and Conacher, 1995: 39). Fertilizers can also promote soil acidity and may lead to deficiencies or toxic excesses of major nutrients and trace elements. They may also contain impurities, such as fluoride, lead, cadmium, zinc, and uranium, some of which can inhibit water uptake and plant growth. They may also become concentrated in food crops, which can have important implications for human health.

4.17 Fires and Soil Quality

The importance and antiquity of fire as an agency through which the environment is transformed (see Section 2.3) requires that some attention be given to the effects of fire on soil characteristics (Santín and Doerr, 2016).

Fire has often been used intentionally to change soil properties, and both the release of nutrients by fire and the value of ash have long been recognized, notably by those involved in shifting agriculture based on slash-and-burn techniques. Following cultivation, the loss of nutrients by leaching and erosion is very rapid, and this why after only a few years the shifting cultivators have to move on to new plots. Depending on the fire intensity and duration, fire rapidly alters the amount, form, and distribution of plant nutrients in ecosystems, and, compared to normal biological decay of plant remains, burning rapidly releases some nutrients into a plant-available form. Indeed, the amounts of P, Mg, K, and Ca released by burning forest and scrub vegetation are high in relation to both the total and available quantities of these elements in soils (Raison, 1979). In particular phosphate loss can be very detrimental to soil fertility (Thomas et al., 2000). In forests, burning often causes the pH of the soil to rise by three units or more, creating alkaline conditions where formerly there was acidity. Soil organic matter may be reduced (Miesel et al., 2015). Burning also leads to some direct nutrient loss by volatilization and convective transfer of ash, or by loss of ash to water erosion or wind deflation. The effects of fires on soil erosion rates are discussed in Section 4.25. The removal of the forest causes soil temperatures to increase because of the absence of shade, so that humus is often lost at a faster rate than it is formed.

4.18 Some Anthrosols Resulting from Agriculture and Urbanization

As have seen, an anthrosol is a type of soil that has been formed or heavily modified due to long-term human activity. Traditional agricultural systems have often employed laborious techniques to augment soil fertility and to reduce such properties as undesirable acidity. In Britain, for example, the addition of chalk to light sandy land goes back at least to Roman times and the marl pits from which the chalk was dug are a striking feature of the Norfolk landscape, where Prince (1962) has identified at least 27,000 hollows. Similarly, in the sandy lowlands of the Netherlands, Germany, Belgium, and western Russia there are soils which for centuries have been built up (often over 50 cm) and fertilized with a mixture of manure, animal bedding, sods, litter, or sand. Such humiferous soils are called *plaggen soils* (Blume and Leinweber, 2004; Giani et al., 2014). Plaggen soils also occur in Ireland and Scotland, where the addition of sea-sand to peat was carried out in pre-Christian times. Around the Baltic Sea, chernozem soils have been much modified since the Bronze Age by fire residues and the addition of seaweed (Acksel et al., 2017). Likewise, before European settlement in New Zealand, the Maoris used thousands of tonnes of gravel and sand, carried in flax baskets, to improve soil structure (Cumberland, 1961). In West Africa there has been an indigenous soil management system in which targeted waste deposition transforms highly weathered, nutrient-, and carbon-poor tropical soils into enduringly fertile, carbon-rich black soils, called 'African Dark Earths' (Solomon et al., 2016b).

Likewise, in Amazonia, recent studies have revealed the existence of some distinctive *Amazonian Dark Earths* under what was previously thought to be pristine rain forest. In pre-European times, before their numbers were decimated, there appear to have been shifting cultivator communities in the region who over a few hundreds or thousands of years deliberately or non-deliberately modified soils with various types of rubbish such as food remains, ash, human excrement, and collapsed houses (Neves et al., 2003).

Another type of soil showing evidence of human influence is the *paddy soil*. Long-continued irrigation, levelling, and manuring of terraced land in China and elsewhere have changed the nature of the pre-existing soils in the area. Among the most important modifications that have been recognized (Zhang and Gong, 2003) are an increase in organic matter, an increase in base saturation, and the translocation and reduction of iron and manganese.

Irragric anthrosols form as a result of prolonged deposition of fine sediments from irrigation water. Ancient irragric soils centuries to millennia old occur in several world regions, especially in the arid environments of Central Asia, Mesopotamia, Egypt, Peru, and the American southwest (Woodson et al., 2015).

Many soils in urban areas have distinctive characteristics, and some pedologists now talk about *urban soils* (Jim, 1998). Soils in cities, because of the limited vegetation cover, may suffer from a decline in organic content through time. In addition they may be compacted by traffic, churned up and eroded during construction, contaminated with large amount of rubble, and polluted with heavy metals such as cadmium, lead, and mercury.

Anthrosols are often characterized by high phosphorous contents. The anthropogenic sources of this element include human and animal waste, refuse derived from bone, meat, fish, and plants, burials, and manure used as fertilizer (Holliday, 2017).

4.19 Soil Erosion: General Considerations

Soils take a long time to form, but only a short time to erode. Soil erosion is a major and serious aspect of the human role in environmental change (Sauer, 1938). Montgomery (2007: 3) has referred to it as 'the skinning of our planet', while in parts of China soil erosion has been so severe that the bedrock surface has been exposed, a process that Chinese workers call 'rocky desertification' (e.g. Jiang et al., 2014). There is a long history of weighty publications on soil erosion (see e.g. Marsh, 1864; Bennett, 1938; Jacks and Whyte, 1939; Morgan, 1995; Imeson, 2012), and Dotterweich (2013) provides a good global review of its history. As we shall see later in Section 4.30, although many techniques have been developed to reduce the intensity of the problem, it appears to remain intractable.

One serious consequence of accelerated erosion is the sedimentation that takes place in reservoirs, shortening their lives and reducing their capacity. Many small reservoirs, especially in semi-arid areas and in areas with erodible sediments in their catchments such as the loess lands of China, appear to have an expected life of only thirty years or even less (see Rapp et al., 1972). Soil erosion also has serious implications for soil productivity. A reduction in soil thickness reduces available water capacity and the depth through which root development can occur. Loss of soil humus, whether as a result of fire,

Table 4.9 The beneficial properties of humus.

Property	Explanation	Effect
(a) Chemical properties		
Mineralization	Decomposition of humus yields CO_2, NH^{+4}, NO^{-3}, PO^{3-4}, and SO^{2-4}	A source of nutrient elements for plant growth
Cation exchange	Humus has negatively charged surfaces which bind cations such as Ca^+ and K^+	Improved cation exchange capacity (CEC) of soil. From 20 to 70 per cent of the CEC of some soils (e.g. Mollisols) is attributable to humus
Buffer action	Humus exhibits buffering in slightly acid, neutral and alkaline ranges	Helps to maintain a uniform pH in the soil
Acts as matrix for biochemical action in soil	Binds other organic molecules electrostatically or by covalent bonds	Affects bioactivity persistence and biodegradability of pesticides
Chelation	Forms stable complexes with Cu^{2+}, Mn^{2+}, Zn^{2+}, and other polyvalent cations	May enhance the availability of micronutrients to higher plants
(b) Physical properties		
Water retention	Organic matter can hold up to 20 times its weight in water	Helps prevent drying and shrinking. May significantly improve moisture-retaining properties of sandy soils
Combination with clay	Cements soil particles into structural units called aggregates	Improves aeration. Stabilizes structure. Increases permeability
Colour	The typical dark colour of many soils is caused by organic matter	May facilitate warming

Source: Swift and Sanchez (1984: table 2).

drainage, deforestation, or ploughing, is an especially serious manifestation of human alteration of soil. As Table 4.9 indicates, humus has many beneficial effects on both the chemical and the physical properties of soil. Its removal by human activity can be a potent contributory cause of soil erosion.

The water-holding properties of the soil may be lessened as a result of the preferential removal of organic material and fine sediment. Hardpans and duricrusts, including laterites, may become exposed at the surface, and provide a barrier to root penetration (Section 4.11). Furthermore, splash erosion may cause soil compaction and crusting, both of which may be unfavourable to germination and seedling establishment. Erosion also removes nutrients, fertilizers, and seeds from the soil. Some damage may be caused by associated excessive sedimentation.

4.20 The Causes of Soil Erosion

Although construction, urbanization, war, mining, and other such activities are often significant in magnifying the problem, the prime causes of accelerated soil erosion are deforestation and farming (Figure 4.11). Land with a permanent vegetation cover is characterized by soil losses which are more than an order of magnitude lower than those on agricultural land (Cerdan et al., 2010). Pimentel

Figure 4.11 Soil erosion near Baringo in Kenya has exposed the roots of a tree, thereby indicating the speed at which soil can be lost (ASG).

(1976) estimated that in the USA soil erosion on agricultural land operates at an average rate of about 30 tonnes per ha per year, which is approximately eight times quicker than topsoil is formed. He calculated that water runoff delivers around 4 billion tonnes of soil each year to the rivers of the forty-eight contiguous states, and that three-quarters of this comes from agricultural land. More recently, Pimentel et al. (1995) have argued that about 90% of US cropland is losing soil above the sustainable rate, and that about 54% of US pasture land is overgrazed and subject to high rates of erosion. However, as Trimble and Crosson (2000) and Boardman (1998) point out, determination of general rates of soil erosion is fraught with uncertainties.

4.21 Forest Removal

Forests protect the underlying soil from the direct effects of rainfall, generating what is generally an environment in which erosion rates tend to be low. The canopy plays an important role by shortening the fall of raindrops, decreasing their velocity, and thus reducing kinetic energy. There are some examples of certain types (e.g. beech) in certain environments (e.g. maritime temperate) creating large raindrops, but in general most canopies reduce the erosion effects of storms. Possibly more important than the canopy in reducing erosion rates in forest is the presence of humus in forest soils (Trimble, 1988), for this both absorbs the impact of raindrops and has an extremely high permeability. Thus forest soils have high infiltration capacities. Another reason that forest soils have an ability to transmit large quantities of water through their fabrics is that they have many macropores produced by roots and their rich soil fauna. Forest soils are also well aggregated, making them resistant to both wetting and water drop impact. This superior degree of aggregation is a result of the presence of considerable organic material, which is an important cementing agent in the formation of large water-stable aggregates. Furthermore, earthworms also help to produce large aggregates. Finally, deep-rooted trees help to stabilize steep slopes by increasing the total shear strength of the regolith.

It is therefore to be expected that with the removal of forest, rates of soil loss will rise (Figure 4.12), rock will be

Figure 4.12 The removal of vegetation in Swaziland creates spectacular gully systems, which in southern Africa are called *dongas*. The smelting of local iron ores in the early nineteenth century required the use of a great deal of firewood which may have contributed to the formation of this example (ASG). Reproduced with permission of Cranfield University.

exposed to create 'rocky desertification' (Yang et al., 2011b), and mass movements will increase in magnitude and frequency. This has been the case in New Zealand, where the clearance of indigenous forest caused actively eroding gullies to develop, particularly from the 1880s to the 1920s (Marden et al., 2012). The rates of erosion that result will be particularly high if the ground is left bare; under crops the increase will be less marked. Furthermore, the method of ploughing, the time of planting, the nature of the crop, and size of the fields will all have an influence on the severity of erosion.

Table 4.10, which is based on data from tropical Africa, shows the comparative rates of erosion for three main types of land use: trees, crops, and barren soil. It is very evident from these data that under crops, but more especially when ground is left bare or under fallow, soil erosion rates are greatly magnified. At the same time, and causally related, the percentage of rainfall that becomes runoff is increased. Labrière et al. (2015) compiled and analyzed more than 3600 measurements of soil loss from 21 countries in the humid tropics. They established that the erosion rate in forests was c. one-tenth and one-150th that of croplands and bare soils, respectively, while mean soil loss values for grasslands and shrublands were about half that of croplands.

The replacement of savanna woodland with cultivation may cause a jump in both runoff and erosion rates. This was demonstrated in the *cerrado* of Brazil by Oliveira et al. (2015), where on average the runoff coefficient was ~20% for the plots under bare soil and less than 1% under native *cerrado* vegetation. The mean annual soil losses in the plots under bare soil and *cerrado* were 1240 t km^{-2} yr^{-1} and 1.0 t km^{-2} yr^{-1}, respectively.

One issue is the impact that temporary deforestation associated with shifting cultivation (*swidden*) in the tropics has on erosion rates. This ancient form of agriculture is currently practised by 200 to 500 million people around the world. It has two key features: the use of fire to prepare fields for cultivation and the subsequent abandonment of those fields as productivity declines as a result of the depletion of soil nutrients and the invasion of pests and weeds (Cornell and Miller, 2007). Once abandoned, however, fields are allowed to return to a more natural state as native plant and tree species reclaim them. If long intervals occur between clearance phases, slash and burn agriculture appears to cause less soil erosion than more intensive forms of agriculture (Ziegler et al., 2009). Douglas (1996) reported that in Borneo shifting cultivation does not increase sediment yields significantly, largely because so much organic debris is left on the ground.

The replacement of forest with perennial plantation crops, such as oil palm, rubber, tea, cocoa, and coffee may be associated with low rates of erosion, but this depends on the nature of the cover crop under the canopy, its

Table 4.10 Runoff and erosion under various covers of vegetation in parts of Africa.

Locality	Average annual rainfall (mm)	Slope (%)	Annual runoff (%)			Erosion (t ha^{-1} yr^{-1})		
			A	B	C	A	B	C
Ouagadougou (Burkina Faso)	850	0.5	2.5	2–32	40–60	0.1	0.6–0.8	10–20
Sefa (Senegal)	1,300	1.2	1.0	21.2	39.5	0.2	7.3	21.3
Bouake (Ivory Coast)	1,200	4.0	0.3	0.1–26	15–30	0.1	1–26	18–30
Abidjan (Ivory Coast)	2,100	7.0	0.1	0.5–20	38	0.03	0.1–90	108–170
Mpwapwa* (Tanzania)	c. 570	6.0	0.4	26.0	50.4	0	78	146

Note: A = forest or ungrazed thicket

B = crop

C = barren soil

*From Rapp et al. (1972: 259, figure 5).

Source: after Charreau (table 5.5, p. 153) in Greenland and Lal (1977).

management and maintenance, the density of planting, the exposure of access routes, and the time taken for a full canopy to develop (Hartemink, 2006).

Erosion can be exacerbated by the construction of logging roads (Table 4.11). High rates of sediment production occur after their construction (Clarke and Walsh, 2006; Walsh et al., 2006), especially when they are used for frequent transport of logs or when no upkeep is carried out. It is indeed probable that a large proportion of the erosion associated with forestry operations is caused by road construction. The alteration of hillside profiles, with consequent disruption of surface and subsurface flows, the construction of cut slopes with steep gradients (Luce and Black, 1999), the lack of plant cover to protect the soil, the highly compacted surface of the roadbed (Croke et al., 2001), and the low infiltration capacities of unpaved road surfaces (Ziegler and Giambelluca, 1997), largely explain the variety and intensity of erosion processes related to logging roads.

It would be wrong to think that all accelerated erosion associated with roads and paths is related to forestry. In southern England, especially in areas with sandy bedrock, sunken lanes have developed over the centuries (Boardman, 2013). Similar 'hollow ways' are common in the Middle East around Bronze Age and Chalcolithic mounds (tells) (Wilkinson et al., 2010). Footpaths used for recreation in highland areas are also a source of erosion. Not surprisingly, the rates of this tend to increase with greater visitor pressures, but long-term studies of rates are few (Rodway-Dyer and Walling, 2010). The digging of drainage ditches in upland pastures and peat moors to permit tree-planting in central Wales has also been found to cause accelerated erosion (Clarke and McCulloch, 1979) and reservoir pollution with sediment (Burt et al., 1983).

García-Ruiz (2010) has provided a full analysis of how land-use changes in Spain have affected soil erosion rates. One recent change is the abandonment of farmland because of rural depopulation and the problems of mechanization on small packets of land on steep slopes. On the one hand one would expect vegetation recolonization to cause erosion rates to be reduced, but on the other the lack of maintenance of field terraces on steep slopes can cause gully erosion to occur. Overall, however, the effects of farmland abandonment and reductions in grazing pressures appear to have been to reduce overland flow and sediment yield from hillslopes (Nadal-Romero et al., 2013). Studies of lake cores in the Iberian Range (Barreiro-Lostres et al., 2017) showed that the most significant periods of increased sediment delivery (26–483 T km yr^{-1}) took place during the fifteenth–sixteenth and eighteenth–nineteenth centuries as a result of large land-use changes and land clearing. In addition, positive synergies between increasing human population and more humid periods led to peaks in sediment delivery during some portions of the Little Ice Age. Land abandonment during the mid-twentieth century caused decreased sediment delivery to the lakes due to the re-vegetation of the landscape (6–200 T km yr^{-1}).

Nonetheless, in some parts of Spain and other Mediterranean countries, soil erosion has become severe in some vineyards because their soils are often left bare for much of the year, and many vineyards are on steep slopes. Olive and almond cultivation, some of which has been encouraged because of European Union subsidies, can also be a major cause of accelerated erosion on susceptible soils (see Goudie and Viles, 2016, section 6.6).

Soil erosion resulting from deforestation and agricultural practice is often thought to be especially serious in tropical or semi-arid areas (see Moore, 1979), but it is also a problem in some humid parts of Europe (Fullen, 2003), Russia (Sidorchuk and Golosov, 2003), and the UK.

Table 4.11 Debris-avalanche erosion in forest, clear-cut and roaded areas.

Site	Period of records (years)	Area (%)	Area (km²)	No. of slides	Debris-avalanche erosion (m³ km⁻² yr⁻¹)	Rate of debris-avalanche erosion relative to forested areas
Stequaleho Creek, Olympic Peninsula						
Forest	84	79	19.3	25	71.8	x 1.0
Clear-cut	6	18	4.4	0	0	0
Road	6	3	0.7	83	11,825	x 165
TOTAL	-	-	24.4	108	-	-
Alder Creek, western Cascade Range, Oregon						
Forest	25	70.5	12.3	7	45.3	x 1.0
Clear-cut	15	26.0	4.5	18	117.1	x 2.6
Road	15	3.5	0.6	75	15,565	x 344
TOTAL	-	-	17.4	100	-	-
Selected drainages, Coast Mountains, south-west British Columbia						
Forest	32	88.9	246.1	29	11.2	x 1.0
Clear-cut	32	9.5	26.4	18	24.5	x 2.2
Road	32	1.5	4.2	11	282.5	x 25.2
TOTAL	-	-	276.7	58	-	-
H.J. Andrews Experimental Forest, western Cascade Range, Oregon						
Forest	25	77.5	49.8	31	35.9	x 1.0
Clear-cut	25	19.3	12.4	30	132.2	x 3.7
Road	25	3.2	2.0	69	1,772	x 49
TOTAL	-	-	64.2	130	-	-

Source: after Swanston and Swanson (1976: table 4).

Measurements by Morgan (1977) on sandy soils in the English East Midlands near Bedford indicate that rates of soil loss under bare soil on steep slopes can reach 17.7 tonnes per hectare per year, compared with 2.4 under grass and nothing under woodland (Table 4.12), and subsequent studies have demonstrated that water-induced soil erosion is a substantial problem, in spite of the relatively low erosivity of British rainfall. Walling and Quine (1991: 123) identified the following farming practices as contributing to this developing problem:

1) Ploughing up of steep slopes that were formerly under grass, in order to increase the area of arable cultivation.
2) Use of larger and heavier agricultural machinery which has a tendency to increase soil compaction.
3) Removal of hedgerows and the associated increase in field size. Larger fields cause an increase in slope length with a concomitant increase in erosion risk.
4) Declining levels of organic matter resulting from intensive cultivation and reliance on chemical fertilizers, which in turn lead to reduced aggregate stability.

5) Availability of more powerful machinery which permits cultivation in the direction of maximum slope rather than along the contour. Rills often develop along tractor and implement wheelings and along drill lines.
6) Use of powered harrows in seedbed preparation and the rolling of fields after drilling.
7) Widespread introduction of autumn-sown cereals to replace spring-sown cereals. Because of their longer growing season, winter cereals produce greater yields and are therefore more profitable. The change means that seedbeds are exposed with little vegetation cover throughout the period of winter rainfall.

One type of erosion associated with agriculture is called 'tillage erosion'. Tillage is responsible for the movement of soil material, particularly on slopes, and leads to a net soil loss from convex landscape positions and a net soil gain in concave landscape positions. Erosion rates for mechanized agriculture are often of the order of 400–800 kg m⁻¹ yr⁻¹ and are of the same order of magnitude or larger than water erosion rates (Van Oost et al., 2006).

Table 4.12 Annual rates of soil loss (tonnes per hectare) under different land-use types in eastern England.

Plot	Splash	Overland flow	Rill	Total
1. Bare soil				
Top slope	0.33	6.67	0.10	7.10
Mid-slope	0.82	16.48	0.39	17.69
Lower slope	0.62	14.34	0.06	15.02
2. Bare soil				
Top slope	0.60	1.11	-	1.71
Mid-slope	0.43	7.78	-	8.21
Lower slope	0.37	3.01	-	3.38
3. Grass				
Top slope	0.09	0.09	-	0.18
Mid-slope	0.09	0.57	-	0.68
Lower slope	0.12	0.05	-	0.17
4. Woodland				
Top slope	-	-	-	0.00
Mid-slope	-	0.012	-	0.012
Lower slope	-	0.008	-	0.008

Source: from Morgan (1977). Reproduced with permission of Cranfield University.

4.22 Soil Erosion Associated with Grazing

Severe grazing by domestic stock causes compaction of soil surfaces, removal of vegetation (not least along the banks of rivers), the breakdown of protective biological crusts by trampling, the physical dislodgement of particles downslope (Ries et al., 2014), and reduction in soil infiltration capacities. These processes in turn increase rates of soil erosion by water (du Toit et al., 2009; Boardman et al., 2017) (Figure 4.13) and by wind (Aubault et al., 2015). The situation is severe because, for example, world cattle numbers have tripled since 1890. Cattle, as Trimble and Mendel (1995) have argued, are a particularly serious cause of soil compaction because of their large mass and their small hoof area relative to that mass. In northern Australia, large numbers of feral water buffaloes have, according to Skeat et al. (2012), compacted soils, damaged stream banks, and increased erosion rates. In a review and analysis of the literature for semi-arid to sub-humid rangelands van Oudenhoven et al. (2015) found that erosion rates had a clear relationship to the intensity of grazing. Mean annual soil loss values in the '*natural ungrazed*', '*low intensity grazed*', '*high intensity grazed rangelands*', and '*man-made pastures*' regimes were, respectively, 717, 1370, 4048, and 4249 kg ha^{-1} yr^{-1}. Mean surface runoff values for the same regimes were 98, 170, 505, and 919 m^3 ha^{-1} yr^{-1}, respectively.

Figure 4.13 Linear erosion furrows along domestic animal tracks developed in vertisols in the highlands of Ethiopia (ASG).

4.23 Irrigation and Erosion

Although research has been sparse, there is some evidence that irrigation can lead to soil erosion. One reason for this is that irrigation water may cause the dispersion of clay minerals in soils, which changes their structure so that they become erodible and susceptible to piping (García-Ruiz et al., 1997). Another reason is that erosion may occur along irrigation furrows (Berg and Carter, 1980).

4.24 Replacement of Grassland by Shrubland in Drylands

The nature of vegetation cover controls the infiltration capacities of dryland surfaces (see Section 5.3.2). Thus the replacement of grassland to shrubland, which humans have caused in the western USA (Bhark and Small, 2003), may affect runoff rates, overland flow velocities, and rill formation (Parsons, et al., 1996; Ravi et al., 2009). As Turnbull et al. (2010: 410) explain on the basis of their erosion and runoff plot studies in New Mexico:

> Over the grassland to shrubland transition, the connectivity of bare areas where runoff tends to be preferentially generated increases. Therefore, from the grass, grass-shrub, shrub-grass to shrub plots, flow lines become increasingly well connected, which increases the capacity for flow to entrain and transport sediment, leading to the greater sediment yields monitored over shrubland.

4.25 Soil Erosion Produced by Fire

Humans start many fires, either deliberately or non-deliberately (see Section 2.4), and because fires remove vegetation and expose the ground they tend to increase rates of erosion (see Table 4.13). Fire causes a loss of vegetation and leaf litter cover which reduces the interception of rainfall. Overland flow is increased in volume and speed as a result of the increased percentage of rainfall available and the reduction in surface roughness caused

Table 4.13 Recent examples of fire-induced soil erosion.

Source	Location
Wilson (1999)	Tasmania
Cerda (1998); Shakesby (2011)	Mediterranean region
Moody and Martin (2001)	Colorado Front Range, USA
Dragovich and Morris (2002)	Eastern Australia
Pierson et al. (2002)	Idaho, USA
Martin et al. (2011)	Canadian Rockies
Kean et al. (2011); Warrick et al. (2012)	California
Neris et al. (2013)	Canary Islands
Inbar et al. (2014)	Israel
Shakesby et al. (2015)	Portugal

by the removal of the vegetation and litter. The resulting exposure of the soil leaves it prone to rainsplash detachment (Shakesby et al., 2007). Most, though not all, studies indicate that fires can lead to a decrease in soil resistance because of a reduction in soil organic content and in aggregate stability. If the fire does not succeed in destroying the organic-rich surface layer (sometimes called 'duff'), then the effect of burning on soil erosion may be limited, as in parts of the Canadian Rockies (Martin et al., 2011).

However, in general, the burning of forests can, especially in the first years after the fire event, lead to high rates of soil loss. Burnt forests often have rates a whole order of magnitude higher than those of protected areas. Large changes in soil erosion rates have resulted from the burning of heather (*Calluna*) in the Yorkshire moors in northern England (Table 4.14), and the effects of burning may be felt for the six years or more that may be required to regenerate the heather.

Likewise, watershed experiments in the chaparral of the south-west USA have shown marked increases in runoff and erosion after burning (Warrick et al., 2013). The causes of this are particularly interesting. There is normally a distinctive 'non-wettable' layer in the soils supporting chaparral. This layer, composed of soil particles coated by hydrophobic substances leached from the shrubs or their litter, is normally associated with the upper part of the soil profile, and builds up through time in the unburned chaparral. The high temperatures which accompany chaparral fires cause these hydrophobic substances to be distilled so that they condense on lower soil layers. This process results in a shallow layer of wettable soil overlying a non-wettable layer. Such a condition, especially on steep slopes, can result in severe surface erosion (Ravi et al., 2009; Shakesby, 2011). However, the importance of fire-induced water repellency varies between different vegetation types and observations made in chaparral may not necessarily apply to Australian eucalyptus forest (Shakesby et al., 2007). Similarly, the time taken for forests to recover from a severe burn also varies between different plant types, and eucalypts, for example, may quickly re-sprout whereas conifers may rely upon seed germination to recover.

Nonetheless, in chaparral terrain it is possible to envisage a fire-induced sediment cycle (Graf, 1988: 243), which starts with a fire that destroys the scrub and the root net, and changes surface soil properties in the way already discussed. After the fire, a precipitation event of low magnitude (with a return interval of around one or two years) is sufficient to induce extensive sheet and rill erosion, which removes enough soil to retard vegetation recovery. Eventually, a larger precipitation event occurs (with a return interval of around five to ten years) and, because of limited vegetation

Table 4.14 Soil erosion associated with *Calluna* (heather) burning on the North Yorkshire moors.

Condition of *Calluna* or ground surface	Mean rate of litter accumulation (+) or erosion (-) (mm/year)	No. of observations
(a) *Calluna* 30–40 cm high. Complete canopy	+3.81	60
(b) *Calluna* 20–30 cm high. Complete canopy	+0.25	20
(c) *Calluna* 15–20 cm high. 40–100% cover	−0.74	20
(d) *Calluna* 5–15 cm high. 10–100% cover	−6.4	20
(e) Bare ground. Surface of burnt *Calluna*	−9.5	19
(f) Bare ground. Surface of peaty or mineral subsoil	−45.3	25

Source: data in Imeson (1971).

cover, produces severe debris slides (Kean et al., 2011). Slowly the vegetation cover re-establishes itself, and erosion rates diminish. However, in due course enough vegetation grows to create a fire hazard, and the whole process starts again.

4.26 Soil Erosion Associated with Construction and Urbanization

There are now a number of studies which illustrate clearly that urbanization can create significant changes in erosion rates and sediment production. The highest rates of erosion are produced during the construction phase, when there is a large amount of exposed ground and much disturbance produced by vehicle movements and excavations. Pioneer studies by Wolman and Schick (1967) and Wolman (1967) showed that the equivalent of many decades of natural or even agricultural erosion may take place during a single year in areas cleared for construction. In Maryland, USA, they found that sediment yields during construction reached 55,000 tonnes per km^2 per year, while in the same area rates under forest were around 80–200 tonnes per km^2 per year and those under farm 400 tonnes per km^2 per year. New road cuttings in Georgia were found to have sediment yields up to 20,000–50,000 tonnes per km^2 per year. In Virginia, Vice et al. (1969) noted equally high rates of erosion during construction and reported that they were ten times those from agricultural land, 200 times those from grassland, and 2000 times those from forest in the same area. Likewise, in Devon, England, Walling and Gregory (1970) found that suspended sediment concentrations in streams draining construction areas were two to ten times (occasionally up to 100 times) higher than those in undisturbed areas. Rates of sediment production may be especially high in humid tropical cities, where there is highly intense rainfall (Chin, 2006).

However, construction does not go on for ever and, once the disturbance ceases, roads are surfaced and gardens and lawns are cultivated. Thus rates of erosion fall dramatically and may be of the same order as those under natural or pre-agricultural conditions (Table 4.15). Moreover, even during the construction phase several techniques can be used to reduce sediment removal, including the excavation of settling ponds, the seeding and mulching of bare surfaces, and the erection of rock dams and straw bales (Reed, 1980).

Even small rural villages can produce substantial amounts of erosion, especially in the tropics. For example, De Meyer et al. (2011) have shown that in Uganda village compounds and associated unpaved footpaths and roads generate sediment that is a significant source of pollution in neighbouring Lake Victoria. Indeed, a scarcity of paved roads, especially in areas with communal land and easily motorable terrain, encourages motorists to make multiple tracks, and this can accelerate land erosion and other forms of degradation (Keshkamat et al., 2012).

4.27 Long-term Studies of Rates of Erosion

It is seldom that we have reliable records of rates of erosion over a sufficiently long time-span to show just how much human activities have accelerated these effects, and it is important to try and isolate the role of human impacts from climatic changes (Wilby et al., 1997). There are plainly huge difficulties in estimating erosion rates in pre-human times, but in an analysis McLennan (1993) has estimated that the pre-human suspended sediment discharge from the continents was about 12.6×10^{15} g per year, which is about 60% of the present figure.

Techniques have now been developed which enable rates of erosion on slopes to be gauged over a lengthy time-span by means of dendrochronological techniques that date the time of root exposure for suitable species of tree. In Colorado, USA, Carrara and Carroll (1979) found that rates over the last 100 years have been about 1.8 mm per year, whereas in the previous 300 years rates were

Table 4.15 Rates of erosion associated with construction and urbanization.

Location	Land use	Source	Rate (t km^{-2} yr^{-1})
1. Maryland, USA	Forest	Wolman (1967)	39
	Agriculture		116–309
	Construction		38,610
	Urban		19–39
2. Virginia, USA	Forest	Vice et al. (1969)	9
	Grassland		94
	Cultivation		1,876
	Construction		18,764
3. Detroit, USA	General non-urban	Thompson (1970)	642
	Construction		17,000
	Urban		741
4. Maryland, USA	Rural	Fox (1976)	22
	Construction		37
	Urban		337
5. Maryland, USA	Forest and grassland	Yorke and Herb (1978)	7–45
	Cultivated land		150–960
	Construction		1,600–22,400
	Urban		830
6. Wisconsin, USA	Agricultural	Daniel et al. (1979)	<1
	Construction		19.2
7. Tama New Town, Japan	Construction	Kadomura (1983)	c. 40,000
8. Okinawa, Japan	Construction	Kadomura (1983)	25,000–125,000

between 0.2 and 0.5 mm per year, indicating an acceleration of about sixfold. This great jump was attributed to the introduction of large numbers of cattle to the area about a century ago.

Another way of obtaining long-term rates of soil erosion is to estimate rates of sedimentation on continental shelves and on lake floors. The former method was employed by Milliman et al. (1987) to evaluate sediment removal down the Yellow River in China. They found that, because of accelerated erosion, rates of sediment accumulation on the shelf over the last 2300 years have been ten times higher than those for the rest of the Holocene (i.e. since around 10,000 BP). Lu et al. (2017a) obtained cores from the floor of the Dead Sea. They found that during the last ~11.5 kyr the average detrital accumulation rate was ~3–4 times that during the last two glacial cycles (MIS 7c-2), and that the average thickness of detritus laminae in the last ~11.6 kyr was ~4.5 times that between ~21.7 and 11.6 ka, implying an increased erosion rate on the surrounding slopes during the Holocene. They suggested that the beginning of the period of intensified erosion overlaps with the onset of Neolithic settlement in the southern Levant and the drastic depletion of vegetation during the establishment of permanent large villages and the domestication of plants and animals.

A further example of using long-term sedimentation rates to infer long-term rates of erosion is provided by Hughes et al.'s (1991) study of the Kuk Swamp in Papua New Guinea (Figure 4.14). They identified low rates of erosion until 9000 BP, when, with the onset of the first phase of forest clearance, erosion rates increased from 0.15 cm per thousand years to about 1.2 cm per thousand years. Rates remained relatively stable until the last few decades when, following European contact, the extension of anthropogenic grasslands, subsistence gardens, and coffee plantations has produced a rate that is very markedly higher: 34 cm per thousand years.

Another good long-term study of the response rates of erosion to land-use changes is provided by a study undertaken on the North Island of New Zealand by Page and Trustrum (1997). During the last 2000 years of human settlement their catchment has undergone a change from indigenous forest to fern/scrub following Polynesian settlement (c. 560 BP) and then a change to pasture following European settlement (AD 1878). Sedimentation

Figure 4.14 Rates of erosion in Papua New Guinea in the Holocene derived from rates of sedimentation in Kuk Swamp. *Source:* adapted from Hughes et al. (1991: figure 5).

rates under European pastoral land use are between five and six times the rates that occurred under fern/scrub and between eight and seventeen times the rate under indigenous forest. In a broadly comparable study, Sheffield et al. (1995) looked at rates of infilling of an estuary fed by a steepland catchment in another part of New Zealand. In pre-Polynesian times rates of sedimentation were 0.1 mm per year, during Polynesian times the rate climbed to 0.3 mm per year, while since European land clearance in the 1880s the rate has shot up to 11. Other examples of such trends in New Zealand are provided by Nichol et al. (2000) and Glade (2003).

The introduction of sheep grazing by Europeans in South Africa caused gully formation and soil erosion (Boardman et al., 2017). Similarly, the arrival of Europeans in Australia caused major changes in land use. For instance, savanna catchments across northern Australia underwent changes from traditional Aboriginal management to widespread cattle grazing on unimproved rangelands. There were major alterations in grass cover, woodland thickening, introduction of exotic vegetation species, and changed fire regimes. Gully development resulted from this modification of the environment (Shellberg et al., 2016) and 'post-European settlement alluvium' accumulated on floodplains in the south-eastern Australian Tablelands (Portenga et al., 2016).

A convincing case study of the effect of European settlement on soil erosion rates in Australia was given by Olley and Wasson (2003). They found that since European settlement began 180 years ago, the sediment flux in the upper Murrumbidgee River has changed as a result of grazing, climate variations, and dam closures. They believed that of these, the introduction of grazing stock, which triggered widespread gully erosion, had the largest effect, increasing the sediment flux by a factor of more than 150. The sediment flux out of this 10,500 km² catch-

ment prior to settlement was estimated to have been ~2400 t yr⁻¹. Degradation of the vegetated valley bottoms by introduced stock in the 1840s and 1850s triggered a massive phase of gully erosion, so that over the next 40 to 50 years the erosion rates in the headwater areas increased by a factor of nearly 245, and ~43 000 000 t of sediment was generated per year. However, as the gully networks reached maximum extension, sediment yield from the headwater areas declined by a factor of ~40 and are now estimated to be about six times the pre-European rates.

There have been a number of studies of the history of erosion in the Holocene in Europe and Britain (Foulds and Macklin, 2006; Notebaert and Verstraeten, 2010; Dusar et al., 2011), of accelerated sedimentation in fluvial systems (Verstraeten et al., 2017) and spasms of colluvium accumulation (Henkner et al., 2017; Kühn et al., 2017). For example, Macklin et al. (2010) have shown that in British catchments there was a very marked increase in erosion and associated floodplain sediment accumulation after c. 1000 years ago, which can be related to the agricultural revolution of the Middle Ages. Similarly, Heine et al. (2005), working in Bavaria, showed how agricultural intensification led to both slope colluviation and floodplain sedimentation. Also working in Germany, Dreibrodt et al. (2010) suggested that erosion was at a maximum in the late Bronze Age and pre-Roman Iron Age (c. 1600 BC–1000 AD), high and late Medieval times (c. 1000–1350 AD) and late modern times (from c. 1500 until today). The combination of slope clearance for agriculture with times of intense storms would be an especially powerful stimulus to soil erosion and colluviation (Henkner et al., 2017), and catastrophic soil erosion in Central Europe was identified for the first half of the fourteenth century and in the mid-eighteenth to the early nineteenth century by Dotterweich (2008). Some of the sediment produced by accelerated erosion accumulates as colluvium downslope, some on floodplains (Knox, 2002), and some in lake basins (Section 6.6).

Nearing et al. (2017: 77) have attempted a broad-scale analysis of soil erosion rates under natural and human conditions. They have argued that:

> Average rates of soil erosion under natural, non-cropped conditions have been documented to be less than 2 Mg ha⁻¹ yr⁻¹. On-site rates of erosion of lands under cultivation over large cropland areas, such as in the United States, have been documented to be on the order of 6 Mg ha⁻¹ yr⁻¹ or more. In northeastern China, lands that were brought into production during the last century are thought to have average rates of erosion over this large area of as much as 15 Mg ha⁻¹ yr⁻¹ or more. Broadly applied soil conservation practices, and in particular conservation tillage and no-till cropping, have been

found to be effective in reducing rates of erosion, as was seen in the United States when the average rates of erosion on cropped lands decreased from on the order of $9\,Mg\,ha^{-1}\,yr^{-1}$ to 6 or $7\,Mg\,ha^{-1}\,yr^{-1}$ between 1982 and 2002, coincident with the widespread adoption of new conservation tillage and residue management practices.

4.28 Peat Bog Erosion

Another example of drainage incision that demonstrates the problem of disentangling the human from the natural causes of erosion is provided by the eroding peat bogs of highland Britain (Evans and Warburton, 2007). Over many areas, including the Pennines (Figure 4.15) and the Brecon Beacons, blanket peats are being severely eroded to produce pool and hummock topography, areas of bare peat and incised gullies (*haggs*). Many rivers draining such areas are discoloured by the presence of eroded peat particles, and sediment yields of organic material are appreciable (Labadz et al., 1991; Clay et al., 2012).

Some of the observed peat erosion may be an essentially natural process, for the high water content and low cohesion of undrained peat masses make them inherently unstable. Moreover, the instability must normally become more pronounced as peat continues to accumulate, leading to bog slides and bursts round margins of expanded peat blankets. Conway (1954) suggested that an inevitable end-point of peat build-up on high-altitude flat or convex surfaces is that a considerable depth of

unconsolidated and poorly humidified peat overlies denser and well-humidified peat, so adding to the instability. Once a bog burst or slide occurs, this leads to the formation of drainage gullies which extend back into the peat mass, slumping-off marginal peat downslope, and leading to the drawing off of water from the pools of the hummock and hollow topography of the watershed.

Tallis (1985) believed that there have been two main phases of erosion in the Pennines. The first, initiated 1000–1200 years ago, may have been caused by natural instability of the type outlined above. However, there was a second stage of erosion, initiated 200–300 years ago, in which miscellaneous human activities appear to have been important. Radley (1962) suggested that among the pressures that had caused erosion were heavy sheep grazing, regular burning, peat cutting, the digging of boundary ditches, the incision of packhorse tracks, and military manoeuvres during the First World War. Other causes may include footpath erosion (Wishart and Warlenston, 2001) and severe air pollution (Tallis, 1965), the latter causing the loss of a very important peat forming moss, *Sphagnum*. In South Wales, there is evidence that the blanket peats have degenerated as a result of contamination by particulate pollution (soot, etc.) during the Industrial Revolution (Chambers et al., 1979). On the other hand, in Scotland lake core studies indicate that severe peat erosion was initiated between AD 1500 and 1700, prior to air pollution associated with industrial growth, and Stevenson et al. (1990) suggested that this erosion initiation may have been caused either by the adverse climatic conditions of the Little Ice Age or by an

Figure 4.15 A satellite image of severe pear erosion and drainage incision from the Peak District in northern England. *Source:* ©2016 Google, ©2016 Infoterra and Bluesky.

increasing intensity of burning as land-use pressures increased.

In the future it is possible that peat bog erosion may be accelerated by a combination of worsening summer droughts and increasingly erosive winter rainstorms (Evans et al., 2006). Globally, Gallego-Sala and Prentice (2012) have argued that blanket bog regions are at risk of progressive erosion and vegetation changes as a direct consequence of climatic change.

4.29 Accelerated Wind Erosion

Human activities have had an important effect on soil erosion by wind, and a good review of its effect of agricultural land is provided by Warren (2002). The fundamentals of soil erosion and the use of modelling in its study are discussed by Shao (2008) and Webb and McGowan (2009), while a review of current techniques for its study by scientists in the USA is given by Webb et al. (2016). It is an important facet of desertification (Section 2.13), leading to a loss of fertile top-soil, a reduction in soil depth, and the abrasion of crops.

Dust storms are a major manifestation of wind erosion of surface materials. Changes in their frequency may be due to human activities. Von Suchodoletz et al. (2010) have even speculated that humans intensified dust storm activity in the north-west Sahara as early as 7–8 ka ago. The situation becomes less speculative as we move towards the present, and Neff et al. (2008), for instance, used analyses of lake cores in the San Juan Mountains of Colorado, USA, to show that dust levels increased by 500% above the late Holocene average during the nineteenth and early twentieth centuries following the increased western settlement and livestock grazing. These results have been confirmed by Routson et al. (2016). A dust core from the Antarctic Peninsula (McConnell et al., 2007) showed a doubling in dust deposition in the twentieth century, and this was explained by increasing temperatures, decreasing relative humidity, and widespread desertification in the source region – Patagonia and northern Argentina. In the Tibetan Plateau, Wan et al. (2016a) estimated dust accumulation rates from a core from Lake Qinghai and found that whereas from the 1730s to the 1950s the rate averaged $169 \, g/m^2/yr$, between the 1950s and 2011 the rate averaged $259 \, g/m^2/yr$. This resulted from a great migration of people into north-west China following 'The Great Leap Forward'. Finally, analysis of a 3200-year-long ocean core off West Africa showed a marked increase in dust activity at the beginning of the nineteenth century, at the time when there was the advent of commercial activity (including groundnut production) in the Sahel (Mulitza et al., 2010). Ginoux et al. (2012) have calculated that around one quarter of global dust emissions come from anthropogenic

sources (primarily agricultural land), while Mahowald et al. (2010) estimated that global dust loads doubled in the twentieth century due to anthropogenic activities. However, meteorological records have indicated that not all drylands have shown increasing dust storm trends in recent decades (Goudie, 2013: chapter 3). Some areas have shown increasing trends (e.g. the Sahel zone of Africa and the eastern Mediterranean in the late twentieth century), while others have shown declining trends in the late twentieth century (e.g. China and Australia), followed by a spike of activity in the early years of the present century (Mitchell et al., 2010). An apparent upward trend in dust activity in the Middle East between 2001 and 2012, as revealed by the monitoring of aerosol optical depth, seems to owe little to local anthropogenic factors and to be a result of increasing temperatures and decreasing relative humidity (Klingmüller et al., 2016), though in some areas, such as parts of Iraq and Syria, recent humanly caused desertification has been implicated (Moridnejad et al., 2015).

The Dust Bowl of the 1930s in the plains of the USA (Figure 4.16) was in part caused by a series of hot, dry years which depleted the vegetation cover and made the soils dry enough to be susceptible to wind erosion. Increased dust loadings in the atmosphere may have had a feedback effect on the drought itself (Cook et al., 2009). The effects of this drought were gravely exacerbated by years of over-grazing, unsatisfactory farming techniques, and the rapid expansion of wheat cultivation. The number of cultivated hectares doubled during the First World War as tractors and combine harvesters (for the first time) rolled out on to the Great Plains by the thousands. The farmer, busy sowing wheat and reaping gold, could foresee no end to his land of milk and honey, but the years of favourable climate were not to last, and over large areas the tough sod which had exasperated the earlier homesteaders had given way to friable soils of high erosion potential. Drought, acting on damaged soils, created 'black blizzards'.

Dust storms remain a serious problem in various parts of the United States; the Dust Bowl was not solely a feature of the 1930s. Thus, for example, in the San Joaquin Valley of California in 1977 a dust storm caused extensive damage and erosion over an area of about $2000 \, km^2$. More than 25 million tonnes of soil were stripped from grazing land within a 24-hour period. While the combination of drought and a very high wind provided the predisposing natural conditions for the stripping to occur, over-grazing and the general lack of windbreaks played a more significant role. In addition, areas of land had recently been stripped of vegetation, levelled, or ploughed up prior to planting. Other quantitatively less important factors included stripping of vegetation for urban expansion, extensive denudation of land in the vicinity of oilfields, and local denudation of land by vehicular recreation

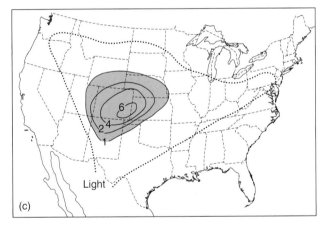

Figure 4.16 The concentration of dust storms (number of days per month) in the USA in 1939, illustrating the extreme localization over the High Plains of Texas, Colorado, Oklahoma and Kansas. a) March. b) April. c) May. *Source:* adapted from Goudie (1983).

A comparable acceleration of dust storm activity occurred in the former Soviet Union. After the 'Virgin Lands' programme of agricultural expansion in the 1950s, dust storm frequencies in the southern Omsk region of Russia increased on average by a factor of 2.5 and locally by factors of 5 to 6. Archival studies by Cattle (2016) confirm the role that land-cover changes (including those brought about by the cropping of marginal lands and by rabbit grazing), combined with drought phases, played in creating a dust bowl in south-eastern Australia between 1895 and 1945. Data on trends elsewhere are evaluated by Goudie (1983) and Goudie and Middleton (1992).

What has emerged is that dust storm frequencies may well have been increased by human activities but that in some parts of the world climatic factors have played the prime role. In southern Africa fluctuations in the emission of dust from the Mkgadikgadi Pans of Botswana over the period 1980–2000 suggest that dust loadings are intermittently influenced by the extent and frequency of lake inundation, sediment inflows, and surface wind-speed variability. The variability of these is in turn influenced by the El Niño-Southern Oscillation (ENSO) and Indian Ocean sea-surface temperature anomalies (Bryant et al., 2007). Variability in Sahel and Saharan dust emissions may be related not only to droughts, but also to changes in wind velocities (Evan et al., 2016; Kim et al., 2016). It also seems to be related to fluctuations in the North Atlantic Oscillation (NAO) (Engelstaedter et al., 2006; Wong et al., 2008) and the Atlantic Multidecadal Oscillation (Jilbert et al., 2010). In China, dust activity in the Tarim Basin is high during the negative phase of the Arctic Oscillation (AO) Index (Gao and Washington, 2010), while in the south-west USA the Pacific Decadal Oscillation (PDO) is a major control of windiness and drought (Hand et al., 2016).

Figure 4.17 Surface degradation on a stone pavement caused by thoughtless off-road driving in the Libyan Desert, Egypt (ASG).

(Wilshire et al., 1981). Elsewhere in California dust yield has been considerably increased by mining operations in dry lake beds (Wilshire, 1980) and by disturbance of playas (Gill, 1996). In many drylands, vehicles can disturb desert pavement surfaces, exposing the fine material under the surface lag to wind deflation (Figure 4.17).

4.30 Soil Conservation

Because of the adverse effects of accelerated erosion by water a whole array of techniques has now been widely adopted to conserve soil resources (Hudson, 1987; Morgan, 2005) (Table 4.16) (Figure 4.18). Some of the techniques, such as hill-slope terracing, may be of some antiquity, and traditional techniques have both a wide range of types and have many virtues (see Critchley et al., 1994; Reij et al., 1996). The following are some of the main ways in which soil cover may be conserved:

1) *Revegetation*:
   a) Deliberate planting;
   b) Suppression of fire, grazing, etc., to allow regeneration.

Table 4.16 Examples of the evaluation of methods to control water erosion on slopes in drylands.

Techniques	Source
Soil compaction	Poesen et al. (2003).
Hedges	Poesen et al. (2003), Kiepe (1996), Smolikowski et al. (2001).
Control of trampling by sheep	Eldridge (1998)
Fallow cropping	Valentin et al. (2004)
Plant strips	Martinéz Raya et al. (2006)
Geotextiles	Rickson (2006)
Trash and stone lines	Wakindiki and Ben Hur (2002), Quinton et al. (1997)
Vegetation cover	Durán Zuazo et al. (2004), Rogers and Schumm (1991), Snelder and Bryan (1995)
Engineering trenches	Marston and Dolan (1999)
Bench terracing	Ternan et al. (1996)
Matorral species	Bochet et al. (1998)
Mulching	Bautista et al. (1996), Smith et al. (1992a)
Juniper control	Belsky (1996)
Blade ploughing and exclosure	Eldridge and Robson (1997)
Rock mulches	Poesen et al. (1994)
Crop residue management	Unger et al. (1991)
Addition of fertilizer	Lasanta et al. (2000)
No tillage	Kabakci et al. (1993)
Afforestation	Cao et al (2010), Romero-Diaz et al. (2010)
Synthetic polymers and biopolymers	Orts et al. (2007)

Figure 4.18 Soil conservation banks across a small ephemeral channel (wadi) in the Matmata area of Tunisia (ASG).

2) *Measures to stop stream-bank erosion.*
3) *Measures to stop gully enlargement*:
   a) Planting of trailing plants, etc.
   b) Weirs, dams, gabions, etc.
4) *Crop management*:
   a) Maintaining cover at critical times of year;
   b) Rotation;
   c) Cover crops.
5) *Slope runoff control*:
   a) Terracing;
   b) Deep tillage and application of humus;
   c) Transverse hillside ditches to interrupt runoff;
   d) Contour ploughing;
   e) Preservation of vegetation strips (to limit field width).
6) *Prevention of erosion from point sources like roads, feedlots*:
   a) Intelligent geomorphic location;
   b) Channelling of drainage water to non-susceptible areas;
   c) Covering of banks, cuttings, etc., with vegetation.
7) *Suppression of wind erosion*:
   a) Soil moisture preservation;
   b) Increase in surface roughness through ploughing up clods or by planting windbreaks.

Morgan (1995) provided an alternative way of classifying soil conservation. He identified three main types of measure: agronomic, soil management, and mechanical. The effect of these in relation to the main detachment and transport phases of erosion are shown in Table 4.17.

There are some parts of the world where terraces (a mechanical measure) are one of the most prominent components of the landscape. This applies to many wine-growing areas (Figure 4.19a), to some arid-zone regions (such as southwest USA, Yemen (Figure 4.19b), western Saudi Arabia,

Table 4.17 Effect of various soil conservation practices on the detachment (D) and transport (T) phases of erosion.

	Rainsplash		Runoff		Wind	
Practice	D	T	D	T	D	T
Agronomic measures						
Covering soil surface	*	*	*	*	*	*
Increasing surface roughness	–	–	*	*	*	*
Increasing surface depression storage	+	+	*	*	–	–
Increasing infiltration	–	–	+	*	–	–
Soil management						
Fertilizers, manures	+	+	+	*	+	*
Subsoiling, drainage	–	–	+	*	–	–
Mechanical measures						
Contouring, ridging	–	+	+	*	+	*
Terraces	–	+	+	*	–	–
Shelterbelts	–	–	–	–	*	*
Waterways	–	–	–	–	*	–

– no control; + moderate control; * strong control
D = detachment, T = transport
Source: Morgan (1995: table 7.1). Reproduced with permission of Pr. R. P. C Morgan.

and Peru), and to a wide selection of localities in the more humid tropics (Luzon, Java, Sumatra, Assam, Ceylon, Uganda, Cameroons, the Andes, etc.). However, much traditional terracing only had soil erosion control as a secondary motive. More often these were constructed to provide level planting surfaces, to provide deeper soil, and to manage the flow of water (Doolittle, 2000).

Some attempts at soil conservation have been particularly successful. In New Zealand, gully systems produced by the removal of indigenous forest in the 1880s–1920s have been stabilized as a result of replanting with exotic plantations (Marden, 2012). In Wisconsin, USA, a study by Trimble and Lund (1982) showed that in the Coon Creek Basin, erosion rates declined fourfold between the 1930s and the 1970s. One of the main reasons for this was the progressive adoption of contour-strip ploughing.

Since the Dust Bowl of the 1930s, the modern concept of no-till farming – now generally known as Conservation Agriculture (CA) – has developed. This involves the simultaneous application of three inter-linked principles (Kassam et al., 2014): (i) permanently minimizing or avoiding mechanical soil disturbance (no-till seeding); (ii) maintaining a continuous soil cover of organic mulch with plants (crop residue, stubble and green manure/cover crops including legumes); and (iii) growing diverse plant species in associations, sequences, or rotations.

However, it is important to stress that soil conservation techniques are sometimes unsuccessful. For example, in

semi-arid Tunisia, where approximately 1 million ha of agricultural land have been installed with anti-erosive contour benches, the life of the benches has proved to be limited (Baccari et al., 2008). It was also found that soil conservation was in part achieved at the cost of reduced runoff and thus a reduction in available water resources for irrigation. Indeed, soil erosion counter-measures can be counter-productive, as has been made evident by reviews of large-scale afforestation schemes in China (Cao et al., 2010, 2011) and Spain (Romero-Diaz et al., 2010). This latter study showed that aggressive land sculpting and the subsequent planting of inappropriate trees on scrublands actually accelerated rates of erosion on marl slopes by between one and two orders of magnitude. Bulldozing can be a curse in Mediterranean environments. One also needs to be aware that some species of exotic plant that have been introduced for control of water erosion can prove to be highly invasive, as with mesquite in Kenya (Muturi et al., 2009) (see Section 2.12).

Moreover, attempts at soil conservation can have drawbacks. For example, the establishment of ground cover in dry areas to limit erosion may greatly reduce soil moisture because of accelerated evapotranspiration. On a wider scale, major afforestation schemes can cause substantial runoff depletion in river catchments. Likewise, the provision of mulching is sometimes detrimental: in cool climates, reduced soil temperature shortens the growing season, whilst in wet areas, higher soil

(a)

(b)

Figure 4.19 Terraces to conserve soil. (a) The vine growing area of the Douro Valley, Portugal. (b) South-west Yemen. *Source:* © 2016 CNES/Astrum and © 2016 Google. Scale bar 470 m.

moisture may induce gleying and anaerobic conditions. Similarly strip cropping, because it involves the farming of small areas, is incompatible with highly mechanized agricultural systems, and insect infestation and weed control are additional problems which it has posed.

Various attempts have been made to control the occurrence of wind erosion, dune movement (Figure 4.20), and dust storms (Sterk, 2003; Nordstrom and Hotta, 2004; Ravi et al., 2011). These techniques are normally classified into three categories: (i) crop management practices,

Figure 4.20 Palm frond fences to reduce sand movement and dune migration in Erfoud, Morocco (ASG).

(ii) mechanical tillage operations, and (iii) vegetative barriers. All of these aim to decrease wind speed at the soil surface by increasing surface roughness and/or increasing the threshold velocity that is required to initiate particle movement by wind. The numerous crop management practices, also commonly referred to as agronomic measures, can influence both the detachment and transport phases of soil particle movement, particularly when combined with good soil management. They use living vegetation and crop residues to protect the soil and to absorb the wind's shear stress. Mechanical methods are designed to be effective in preventing soil transport (Morgan, 2005). They include barriers such as fences, windbreaks, and shelterbelts (Gardner, 2009) (Figures 4.21a, b). Soil management requires the reduction in the intensity of tillage and the provision of soils which, because of their structure, are resistant to wind attack. Since soil only blows when it is dry, anything which conserves soil moisture is beneficial.

It is undoubtedly true that soil degradation is one of the most significant ways in which humans change the environment, and one in which they have had some of the most detrimental effects. Lowdermilk (1935: 409) wrote:

> The great enemy of the human race is soil erosion which has been associated with the habitations of man since before the dawn of history. It is no new land disease, but has only recently been diagnosed and named for what it is. The removal of vegetation … exposes soils to the dash of rain or the blast of wind, against which they had been protected for thousands of years. Topsoils blow away or wash away, or both. Unprotected sloping lands are usually bared to hard and tight subsoils, which drain off the water as from a tiled roof.

The overall situation is still at least as bleak as it was in the post-Dust Bowl years when Jacks commented:

(a)

(b)

Figure 4.21 Various methods to control dune encroachment and wind erosion in the Dunhuang area of north-west China. (a) Sand fences, vegetation planting, and irrigation. (b) A network of plastic squares to restrict sand and dust movement across a major highway (ASG).

'The organization of civilized societies is founded upon the measures taken to wrest control of the soil from wild Nature, and not until complete control has passed into human hands can a stable super-structure of what we call civilization be erected on the land' (Jacks and Whyte, 1939: 17).

4.31 Soils, Microbiology, and the Earth System

To conclude this chapter let us consider the ways in which humans may be altering the nature of soil microbiota, and how these may have significance for ecosystem services and the whole Earth System. Soil microbes consist of bacteria, archaea, viruses, fungi, parasites, and protozoa. These comprise the vast majority of the biological diversity on Earth. Various human activities can affect them. Agricultural intensification and land-use change is a major driver because it alters plant communities and soil properties. Above ground, plant communities significantly alter microbial community composition and functions through such mechanisms as rooting patterns, water use, litter chemistry, canopy structure, and subsequent influences on soil properties and microclimate. In addition to land-use change, one process that reduces the diversity of soil microbiota is pollution by heavy metals (Singh et al., 2014). Others are the application of pesticides (Imfeld and Vuilleumier, 2012) and of fertilizers (O'Donnell et al., 2001). Soil erosion is also an important control (Park et al., 2014). Future climate changes also need to be considered (Sayer et al., 2017), because, for example, Maestre et al. (2015) found that increases in aridity reduce the diversity and abundance of soil bacteria and fungi.

Soil microbes play a crucial role in providing ecosystem services (Aislabie and Deslippe, 2013; Fichtner et al., 2014) (see Section 13.3). For example, by mineralizing soil carbon and nutrients, microbes are major determinants of the carbon storage capacity of soils and thus of global carbon budgets. Denitrifying bacteria and fungi and methane-producing and consuming bacteria regulate nitrous oxide (N_2O) and methane (CH_4) emissions from soils, thereby influencing greenhouse gas budgets. Soil microbes mobilize nutrients from insoluble minerals to support plant growth, and they contribute to soil formation through nutrient cycling and organic matter production. Microbial products are critical to soil aggregation, improved soil structure, and making soil more habitable for plants. Further, they are the foundation of soil food webs thereby underpinning the diversity of higher trophic levels. Interactions among soil microbes and plants often determine plant biodiversity.

Guide to Reading

Conacher, A.J. and Sala, M. (eds) (1998) *Land Degradation in Mediterranean Environments of the World.* Chichester: Wiley. An edited discussion of land degradation processes in Mediterranean environments.

Fullen, M.A. and Catt, J.A. (2004) *Soil Management: Problems and Solutions.* London: Arnold. A review of some of the problems involved in the management of soils in the face of human impacts.

Holliday, V.T. (2004) *Soils in Archaeological Research.* New York: Oxford University Press. This book includes a treatment of long-term human impacts on soils.

Howard, J. (2017) *Anthropogenic Soils.* New York: Springer International Publishing. A wide-ranging discussion of the history and nature of soils that have been modified by humans.

McTainsh, G. and Boughton, W.C. (1993) *Land Degradation Processes in Australia.* Melbourne: Longman Cheshire. An Australian perspective on soil modification.

Morgan, R.P.C. (2005) *Soil Erosion and Conservation* (3rd edn). Oxford: Blackwell. A revised edition of a fundamental work.

Wall, D.H. and Bardgett, R.D. (eds) (2012) *Soil Ecology and Ecosystem Services.* Oxford: Oxford University Press. This multi-author work assesses the importance of soils and also some of the changes that have taken place as a result of human activities.

5

The Human Impact on the Waters

CHAPTER OVERVIEW

The chapter starts with a consideration of the various ways in which humans have deliberately modified river systems, by the creation of dams, reservoirs, embankments, and through channelization. It then considers how stream flows and lake levels have been transformed by land-cover changes, and how groundwater levels have been modified by water abstraction. The second part of the chapter concentrates on changes in water quality, whether caused by pollution or by changes in river catchment conditions. Finally, there is a consideration of the ways in which our oceans and seas are being modified by pollution.

5.1 Introduction

Because water is so important to them, humans have sought to control water resources in a whole variety of ways (Carpenter et al., 2011). They have done this since prehistoric times (see Section 1.5) (Angelakis and Zheng, 2015). During the Minoan Era (c. 3200–1100 BC), for example, aqueducts were constructed to provide settlements in Greece with water (De Feo et al., 2013; Nikolaou et al., 2016) and this was a practise developed by the Romans. Lifting devices, such as the *shaduf*, were used in Mesopotamia at around 3000 BC and appeared in Upper Egypt sometime after 2000 BC, during the 18th Dynasty (c. 1570 BC) (Yannopoulos et al., 2015). Rainfall harvesting has also been practised since Minoan times (Sazakli et al., 2015), and cisterns were developed to store and harvest water (Mays, 2014). Mithen (2012) provides a masterful review of water use in the ancient world, with particular reference to the Sumerians and to the civilizations of the Americas.

Because water is such an important part of so many natural and human systems its quantity and quality have undergone major changes as a consequence of human activities. As Lynas (2011: 139) has graphically remarked:

> Whole natural drainage basins, which once responded to the grand seasonal cycles of winter flood and summer drought, now react meekly to the whims of water managers seated in the control rooms that govern sluice gates in tens of thousands of large dams. The Colorado River may have gouged out the most spectacular cutting in the world – the Grand Canyon – but today the flow of this powerful torrent is as much a product of human hydrological engineering as it is of any natural force.

In recent decades human demand for fresh water has increased rapidly. Global water use has more than tripled since 1950, and annual irretrievable water losses increased about sevenfold in the twentieth century (Table 5.1a). Trends in the interception of runoff and in the capacity of reservoirs are shown in Figure 5.1. Many rivers now have highly modified flow regimes as a result of a variety of human interventions (Table 5.2). Because of a whole range of factors, including the drying up of water bodies such as the Aral Sea and the creation of great reservoirs, planetary-scale changes in the occurrence of water and land have taken place. Using remote sensing, Donchyts et al. (2016) estimated that globally, between 1985 and 2015, an area of about 173,000 km^2 – about the size of Washington State – has been converted to land, and an area of 115,000 km^2 has been converted into water. Anthropogenic changes to hydrological systems may have very wide implications both for biodiversity and for Earth's carbon budgets (Sutfin et al., 2016; Wohl et al., 2017a).

Human Impact on the Natural Environment: Past, Present and Future, Eighth Edition. Andrew S. Goudie.
© 2019 John Wiley & Sons Ltd. Published 2019 by John Wiley & Sons Ltd.
Companion website: www.wiley.com/go/goudie/human-impact-natural-environment

Table 5.1 Major changes in the hydrological environment.

(a) Irretrievable water losses (km³/yr).

Users	1900	1940	1950	1960	1970	1980	1990	2000
Agriculture	409	679	859	1,180	1,400	1,730	2,050	2,500
Industry	3.5	9.7	14.5	24.9	38.0	61.9	88.5	117
Municipal supply	4.0	9.0	14	20.3	29.2	41.1	52.4	64.5
Reservoirs	0.3	3.7	6.5	23.0	66.0	120	170	220
TOTAL	417	701	894	1,250	1,540	1,950	2,360	2,900

(b) Number of large dams (>15m high) constructed or under construction, 1950–1986.

Continent	1950	1982	1986	Under construction 31.12.86
Africa	133	665	763	58
Asia	1,562	22,789	22,389	613
Australasia/Oceania	151	448	492	25
Europe	1,323	3,961	4,114	222
North and Central America	2,099	7,303	6,595	39
South America			884	69
TOTAL	5,268	35,166	36,327*	1,036

*The figure by the end of the twentieth century was c. 45,000.
Source: data provided by UNEP and World Commission on Dams.

5.2 Deliberate Modification of River Systems Connectivity

There are a great variety of methods of direct river channel manipulation and many of them have a long history. Perhaps the most widespread of these is the construction of dams and reservoirs (Figure 5.2). The first recorded dam was one built in Egypt some 5000 years ago, but since that time the adoption of this technique has spread, variously to improve agriculture, prevent floods, generate power, or to provide a reliable source of water. Other early dams and reservoirs were developed *inter alia* in Jordan, the Nile Valley, Sri Lanka, Cambodia, and China (Scarborough and Tankersley, 2017). Some dams – impoundment dams – are of immense size, but others are much smaller – 'run-of-river dams' (Csiki and Rhoads, 2010) – and the implications of these two types may be very different. Cumulatively, however, the presence of many small dams in an area may have a great effect on river flow and on sediment retention (Boardman and Foster, 2011). Although there is now a growing number of multipurpose dams, most dams are single-purpose dams. Among the single purpose dams, 48% are for irrigation, 17% for hydropower (production of electricity), 13% for water supply, 10% for flood control, 5% for recreation, and less than 1% for navigation and fish farming (http://www.icold-cigb.org/GB/world_register/general_synthesis.asp, accessed January 2018).

There are some 75,000 dams in the USA. Most are small, but the bulk of the storage of water is associated with a relatively limited number of structures. Those dams creating reservoirs of more than 1.2×10^9 cubic metres account for only 3% of the total number of structures, but they account for 63% of the total storage. In all the dams are capable of storing a volume of water almost equalling one year's runoff and they store around 5000 cubic metres of water per person. The decade of the 1960s saw the greatest spate of dam construction in American history (18,833 dams were built then). Since the 1980s, however, there have been only relatively minor increases

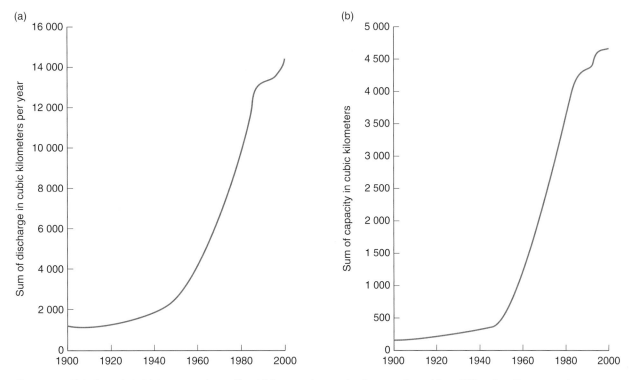

Figure 5.1 Global trends in (a) intercepted runoff and (b) reservoir capacity. *Source:* adapted from Millennium Ecosystem Assessment (2005).

Table 5.2 Human impacts on river flow characteristics.

Engineering
    Dams, ponds, reservoirs
    Swamp drainage
    Land drainage
    Inter-basin water transfers
    Groundwater abstraction
    Channelization, embankments, etc.
    Log jam removal

Land changes
    Urbanization
    Afforestation and deforestation
    Removal or introduction of riparian vegetation

Anthropogenic climate change
    (see Chapter 10)

in storage. The dam building era is over, but the environmental effects remain and the physical integrity of many rivers has been damaged (Graf, 2001).

The construction of large dams increased markedly, especially between 1945 and the early 1970s. Engineers have now built more than 45,000 large dams (i.e. more than 15 m high) around the world (Table 5.1b). Indeed, one of the most striking features of dams and reservoirs is that they have become increasingly large. Thus in the 1930s the Hoover or Boulder Dam in the USA (221 m high) was by far the tallest in the world and it impounded the biggest

reservoir, Lake Mead, which contained just under 38 billion cubic metres of water. By the 2000s it was exceeded in height by at least 29 others, and four of these impounded reservoirs (Kariba, Bratsk, Nasser, and Volta) with more than four times the volume of Lake Mead. The tallest dam, which is 335 m high, is the Rogun Dam in Tajikistan.

Most dams achieve their aim: to regulate river discharge. They are also highly successful in fulfilling the needs of surrounding communities: millions of people depend upon them for survival, welfare, and employment. However, dams have a whole series of environmental consequences that may or may not have been anticipated (Figure 5.3) (World Commission on Dams, 2000). Several of these may in turn affect the viability of the scheme for which the dam was created. Some of these are dealt with in greater detail elsewhere, such as subsidence (Section 6.4), earthquake triggering (Section 6.5), the transmission and expansion in the range of organisms, inhibition of fish migration, the build-up of soil salinity (Section 4.3), changes in groundwater levels creating slope instability (Section 6.11), and water-logging (Section 4.4). Regulation of river flows may also affect aeolian landscapes by modifying sources of sediment and sand transport paths, as has happened on the Colorado River (Draut, 2012).

The construction of dams causes river fragmentation and this, along with other human modifications, changes the natural connectivity within and among river systems (Grill et al., 2015; Poeppl et al., 2017). Currently, more than

(a)   (b)

Figure 5.2 (a) The Kariba Dam on the Zambezi River between Zambia and Zimbabwe. (b) The Hoover Dam and Lake Mead on the Colorado River between Nevada and Arizona, USA. Such large dams can provide protection against floods and water shortages, and generate a great deal of electricity. However, they can have a whole suite of environmental consequences (ASG).

50% of the world's river flow crosses one or more dams before reaching the oceans. This fraction could climb up to 90% by 2030. Connectivity has (i) a longitudinal aspect that connects upstream and downstream ecosystems, (ii) a lateral dimension by linking riverine systems with wetlands and floodplains, and (iii) a vertical component that connects surface water with groundwater flows. The first of these aspects is particularly important ecologically because

Figure 5.3 Generalized representation of the possible effects of dam construction on human life and various components of the environment.

of its relation to species migration and dispersal as well as its role in community structure and biodiversity patterns in channels and riparian zones. Longitudinal and lateral connectivity also function as transport pathways for organic and inorganic matter downstream, into riparian zones and into floodplains, and thus have a major impact on nutrient fluxes (Van Cappellen and Maavara, 2016) and carbon budgets (Wohl et al., 2017a).

Sediment deposition in reservoirs has various possible consequences, including a reduction in flood-deposited nutrients on fields, less nutrients for fish in the south-east Mediterranean Sea, accelerated erosion of the Delta, and accelerated riverbed erosion since less sediment is available to cause bed aggradation. The last process is called 'clear-water erosion', and in the case of the Hoover Dam it caused channel incision in the bed of the Colorado for 150 km downstream. In turn, such channel incision may initiate headward erosion in tributaries and may cause the lowering of groundwater tables and the undermining of bridge piers and other structures downstream of the dam. On the other hand, in regions such as northern China, where modern dams trap silt, the incision of the river channel downstream may alleviate the strain on levées and lessen the expense of levée strengthening or heightening.

However, clear-water erosion does not always follow from silt retention in reservoirs. There are examples of rivers where, before impoundment, floods carried away the sediment brought into the main stream by steep tributaries. Reduction of the peak discharge after the completion of the dam leaves some rivers unable to scour away the sediment that accumulates as large fans of sand or gravel below each tributary mouth (Dunne and Leopold, 1978). The bed of the main stream is raised and if water-intakes or other structures lie alongside the river they can be threatened by flooding or channel shifting across the accumulating wedge of sediment. Rates of aggradation of a metre a year have been observed, and tens of kilometres of channel have been affected by sedimentation. One of the best-documented cases of aggradation concerns the Colorado River below Glen Canyon Dam in the USA. Since dam closure, the extremes of river flow have been largely eliminated so that the ten years' recurrence interval flow has been reduced to less than one-third. The main channel flow is no longer capable of removing sediment provided by flash-flooding tributaries (Petts, 1985: 133). In the Rio Grande, vertical channel accretion of 2.75–3.0 m occurred between 1991 and 2008 (Dean and Schmidt, 2011). The reduction in peak floods below dams can also permit the expansion of riparian vegetation, such as Tamarisk (see Section 6.9), which may trap sediment (Birken and Cooper, 2006) and so add to the amount of accretion that occurs. Rapid aggradation has also been noted in the channel of the Yellow River in China, partly because inputs of aeolian sands are no longer so effectively flushed out (Ta et al., 2008).

Some river landscapes in the world are dominated by dams, canals, and reservoirs (Figure 5.4 a and b). Probably the most striking example of this is the 'tank' landscape of south-east India where myriads of little streams and areas of overland flow have been dammed by small earth structures to give what Spate (Spate and Learmonth, 1967: 778) likened to 'a surface of vast overlapping fish-scales'. In the northern part of the subcontinent, in Sind, the landscape changes wrought by hydrology are no less striking, with the mighty snow-fed Indus being controlled by large embankments (*bunds*) and interrupted by great barrages. Its waters are distributed over thousands of square kilometres by a canal network that has evolved over the past 4000 years (Figure 5.5). No less impressive is the wholesale transformation of the Netherlands that has taken place (Hoeksema, 2007).

The establishment of water meadows was an important cause of landscape change in some parts of Europe. This is an area of grassland subject to controlled irrigation by a system of artificial channels (leats) and sluices to increase agricultural productivity on floodplains. They were mainly used from the sixteenth to the early twentieth centuries, but have now largely been abandoned. However, the field patterns and water channels of derelict water-meadows remain common in areas where they were used, such as parts of Northern Italy, Switzerland, and England (see Figure 5.6). Water meadows were adopted because irrigation in early spring kept frosts off the ground and so allowed grass to grow several weeks earlier than otherwise, and in dry summer weather irrigation kept the grass growing (Cook et al., 2003).

Another direct means of river manipulation is channelization (Figure 5.7). This involves the construction of embankments, dikes, levées, and floodwalls to confine floodwaters, and improving the ability of channels to transmit floods by enlarging their capacity through straightening, widening, deepening, or smoothing (Table 5.3).

Some of the great rivers of the world are lined by extensive embankment systems such as those that run for more than 1000 km alongside the Nile, 700 km along the Hwang Ho, 1400 km by the Red River in Vietnam, and over 4500 km in the Mississippi Valley. Like dams, embankments and related structures often fulfil their purpose, but they may also create some environmental problems and have some disadvantages. For example, they reduce natural storage for floodwaters, both by preventing water from spilling on to much of the floodplain, and by stopping bank storage in cases where impermeable floodwalls are used. Likewise the flow of water in tributaries may be constrained. In addition, embankments may occasionally exacerbate the flood problem they were designed to reduce by preventing floodwaters downstream of a breach from draining back into the channel once the peak has passed.

(a)

(b)

Figure 5.4 Complex drainage systems associated with irrigation in (a) Gezira, Sudan (scale bar 5.59 km) and (b) Mesopotamia, Iraq (scale bar 2.68 km). *Sources:* (a) © 2016 CNES/Astrium; (b) © 2016 CNES/Spot Image and © 2016 Google.

Channel improvement, designed to improve water flow, may also have unforeseen or undesirable effects. For example, the more rapid movement of water along improved channel sections can aggravate flood peaks further downstream and cause excessive erosion. On the other hand, the lower reaches of a channelized system can see accumulation of the eroded sediment from the upper reaches, so that plugs of sediment accumulate. These sediment plugs can block channels and cause water and sediment to be forced onto the neighbouring floodplain even at times of low flow, so creating swamp conditions along, for example, the rivers

of Tennessee and elsewhere in the US coastal plain (Shankman and Smith, 2004; Hupp et al., 2009). In addition, lined channels may obstruct soil water movement (interflow) and shallow ground water flow, and so cause surface saturation. The diversity of habitats in natural meandering channels means that straitening may lead to a reduction in the diversity of organisms (Garcia et al., 2012).

Channelization may also have miscellaneous effects on fauna through the increased velocities of water flow, reductions in the extent of shelter in the channel bed, and by reduced nutrient inputs due to the destruction of

Figure 5.5 An irrigation canal in the plains of Haryana, India (ASG).

overhanging bank vegetation (see Keller, 1976). In the case of large swamps, like those of the Sudd in Sudan or the Okavango in Botswana, the channelization of rivers could completely transform the whole character of the swamp environment. Figure 5.8 illustrates some of the differences between natural and artificial channels. Brookes (1985) and Gregory (1985) provide useful reviews of the impact of channelization.

Deliberate modification of a river regime can be achieved by long-distance inter-basin water transfers (Shiklomanov, 1985). The total volume of water in the various transfer systems in operation and under construction on a global scale is about 300 km^3 a year, with the largest countries in terms of volume of transfers being Canada, the former Soviet Union, the USA, and India. China's South–North Water Transfer (SNWT) Project is now the world's largest inter-

Figure 5.6 Traces of channels created to make water meadows in the Frome Valley, just to the east of Dorchester in Dorset, southern England. *Source:* ©2016 Infoterra Ltd and BlueSky. Scale bar = 151 m.

Figure 5.7 A channelized river in Dunhuang, north-west China, designed to offer protection from flooding and erosion of the Mogao grottoes (ASG).

basin transfer scheme, connecting four major river basins. Its purpose is to address the imbalance in the distribution of 'China's water resources, by transferring water from the wetter south to the drier north via the Yangtze River to the Hai, Huai, and Yellow river basins (Pohlner, 2016; Rogers et al., 2016) (Figure 5.9a). In future decades it is likely that many even greater schemes will be constructed (Figure 5.9 b, c, and d), route lengths of some hundreds of kilometres will be common, and the water balances of many rivers and lakes will be transformed. This has already happened in the former Soviet Union (Figure 5.10), where the operation of various anthropogenic activities of this type have caused runoff in the most intensely cultivated central and southern areas to decrease by 30–50% compared to normal natural

Table 5.3 Selected terminologies for the methods of river channelization in the USA and UK.

American term	British equivalent	Method involved
Widening	Resectioning	Increase of channel capacity by manipulating width and/or depth variable
Deepening	Resectioning	
Straightening	Realigning	Increasing velocity of flow by steepening the gradient
Diking	Embanking	Raising of channel banks to confine floodwaters
Bank stabilization	Bank protection	Methods to control bank erosion e.g. gabions and concrete structures
Clearing and snagging	Pioneer tree clearance Control of aquatic plants Dredging of sediments Urban clearing	Removal of obstructions from a watercourse, thereby decreasing the resistance and increasing the velocity of flow

Source: Brookes (1985: table 1).

Natural channel

Artificial channel

Suitable water temperatures:

  adequate shading; good cover for fish life; minimal variation in temperatures; abundant leaf material input

Increased water temperatures:

  no shading; no cover for fish life; rapid daily and seasonal fluctuations in temperatures; reduced leaf material input

Pool (silt, sand and fine gravel)   Pool –riffle sequence   Riffle (coarse gravel)

Mostly riffle

Sorted gravels provide diversified habitats for many stream organisms

Unsorted gravels:
  reduction in habitats; few organisms

Pool environment

High flow

High flow

Diversity of water velocities: high in pools, lower in riffles. Resting areas abundant beneath undercut banks or behind large rocks, etc.

May have stream velocity higher than some aquatic life can withstand. Few or no resting places

Low flow

Low flow

Suffient water depth to support fish and other aquatic life during dry season

Insufficient depth of flow during dry seasons to support diversity of fish and aquatic life. Few if any pools (all riffle)

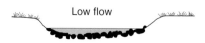

Figure 5.8 Comparison of the natural channel morphology and hydrology with that of a channelized stream, suggesting some possible ecological consequences. *Source:* adapted from Keller (1976: figure 4).

Figure 5.9 Some major schemes proposed for large-scale inter-basin water transfers. (a) The North–South Water Transfer Project in China. *Source:* adapted from Pohlner (2016: figure 1). (b) Projected water transfer systems in the CIS: 1. From the Onega River and in future from Onega Bay. 2. From the Sukhona and Northern Dvina Rivers. 3. From the Svir River and Lake Onega. 4. From the Pechora River. 5. From the Ob River. 6. From the Danube Delta. (c) Projected systems for water transfers in India: 1. Scheme of the national water network. 2. Scheme of the Grand Water Garland. (d) Some major projects for water transfers in North America: 1. NAWAPA. 2. Grand Canal. 3. Texas River Basins. *Source:* after Shiklomanov (1985: figures 12.6, 12.9 and 12.11, in Facets of Hydrology II, ed. J.C. Rodda). By permission of John Wiley & Sons Ltd.

runoff. At the same time, inflows into the Caspian and Aral Seas have declined sharply. The Aral has shrivelled (see Section 5.4). The various negative and positive effects of major schemes has been reviewed by Zhuang (2016).

When one turns to the coastal portions of rivers, to estuaries, the possible effects of another human impact, dredging, can be as complex as the effects of dams and reservoirs upstream. Dredging and filling are certainly widespread and often desirable. Dredging may be performed to create and maintain canals, navigation channels, turning basins, harbours, and marinas; to lay pipelines; and to obtain a source of material for fill or construction. Filling is the deposition of dredged materials to create new land. There are miscellaneous ecological

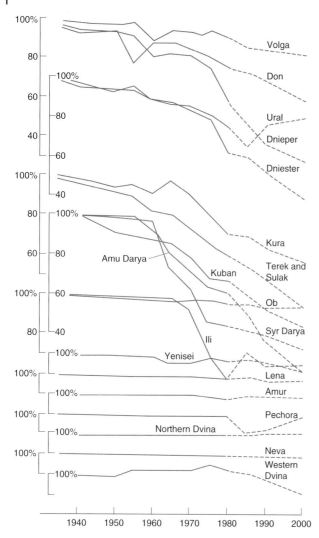

Figure 5.10 Changes in annual runoff in the Commonwealth of Independent States (former Soviet Union) due to human activity during 1936–2000. *Source:* from Shiklomanov (1985: figure 12.7, in *Facets of Hydrology II*, ed. J.C. Rodda). By permission of John Wiley & Sons Ltd).

effects of such actions. In the first place, filling directly disrupts habitats. Second, the generation of large quantities of suspended silt tends physically to smother bottom-dwelling plants and animals; tends to smother fish by clogging their gills; reduces photosynthesis through the effects of turbidity; and tends to lead to eutrophication by an increased nutrient release. Likewise, the destruction of marshes, mangroves, and sea grasses by dredge and fill can result in the loss of these natural purifying systems. The removal of vegetation may also cause erosion. Moreover, as silt deposits stirred up by dredging accumulate elsewhere in the estuary they tend to create a 'false bottom'. Characterized by shifting, unstable sediments, the dredged bottom, fill deposits, or spoil areas are slowly – if at all – recolonized by fauna and flora.

Furthermore, dredging tends to change the configuration of currents and the rate of fresh-water drainage and may provide avenues for salt-water intrusion.

5.3 Changes in River Flow

All over the world, humans have inadvertently caused changes in river flows as a result of land-cover and land-use changes, urbanization, land drainage, and the like. Many rivers across the world have experienced significant changes in flow over the last decades (Salmoral et al., 2015), and drivers of this change are multiple, and include many of the factors shown in Figure 5.11. However, many of these drivers interact simultaneously, sometimes making it difficult to establish the impact of each driver individually and Dadson et al. (2017) provide a wide-ranging analysis of the possible controls – natural and anthropogenic – on flood magnitudes in the UK.

5.3.1 The Effects of Dams

Large dams are capable of causing almost total regulation of the streams they impound but, in general, the degree to which peak flows are reduced depends on the size of the dam and the impounded lake in relation to catchment characteristics. In Britain, as Table 5.4 shows, peak flow reduction downstream from selected reservoirs varies considerably, with some tendency for the greatest degree of reduction to occur in those catchments where the reservoirs cover the largest percentage of the area. In the USA, Fitzhugh and Vogel (2011) have mapped the impacts of dams on flood flows. Across the country as a whole the estimated reduction in median annual flood for large rivers averages 29%, for medium rivers 15%, and for small rivers 7%. The greatest reductions have taken place to the west of the Mississippi and especially in the Great Plains, the deserts of the south-west and in northern California.

When considering the magnitude of floods of different recurrence intervals before and after dam construction, it is clear that dams have much less effect on rare events of high magnitude (Petts and Lewin, 1979), and this is brought out in Table 5.5.

5.3.2 Vegetation Modification and its Effect on River Flow

As we have already noted in Section 1.1, one of the first major indications that humans could inadvertently adversely affect the environment was the observation that deforestation, produced by felling and/or fire (Scott, 1997), could create torrents and floods. Whether or not deforestation promotes serious flooding is, however,

Figure 5.11 Factors that affect river flows.

Table 5.4 Peak flow reduction downstream from selected British reservoirs.

Reservoir	% of catchment inundated	% of peak flow reduction
Avon, Dartmoor	1.38	16
Fernworth, Dartmoor	2.80	28
Meldon, Dartmoor	1.30	9
Vyrnwy, mid-Wales	6.13	69
Sutton Bingham, Somerset	1.90	35
Blagdon, Mendip	6.84	51
Stocks, Forest of Bowland	3.70	70
Daer, Southern Uplands	4.33	56
Camps, Southern Uplands	3.13	41
Catcleugh, Cheviots	2.72	71
Ladybower, Peak District	1.60	42
Chew Magna, Mendips	8.33	73

Source: after Petts and Lewin (1979: 82, table 1).

Table 5.5 The ratios of post- to pre-dam discharges for flood magnitudes of selected frequency.

	Recurrence interval (years)			
Reservoir	**1.5**	**2.3**	**5.0**	**10.0**
Avon, R. Avon	0.90	0.89	0.93	1.02
Stocks, R. Hodder	0.83	0.86	0.84	0.95
Sutton Bingham, R. Yeo	0.52	0.61	0.69	0.79

Source: after Petts and Lewin (1979: 84, table 2). Reproduced with permission of SAGE Publications.

the subject of continuing investigation and debate (Bradshaw et al., 2007), and whether or not afforestation can reduce major floods in large catchments is not entirely clear, and it may have an impact on small floods but not on larger ones (Dadson et al., 2017).

The reasons why the removal of a forest cover and its replacement with pasture, crops, or bare ground has important effects on stream flow are many. First, forests greatly modify the accumulation and ablation of snow. Second, a mature forest probably has a higher rainfall interception rate, a tendency to reduce rates of overland flow, and probably generates soils with a higher infiltration capacity and better general structure. All these factors will tend to produce both a reduction in overall runoff levels and less extreme flood peaks.

The first experimental study, in which a planned land-use change was executed to enable observation of the effects of stream flow, began in 1910 at Wagon Wheel Gap, Colorado. Here stream flows from two similar watersheds of about 80 hectares each were compared for eight years. One valley was then clear-felled and the records were continued. After the clear-felling the annual water yield was 17% above that predicted from the flows of the unchanged control valley. Peak flows also increased.

A comprehensive analysis of the effects of land-use change on stream flows was conducted in the Andes of South America by Ochoa-Tocachi et al. (2016). They found that cultivated catchments respond to rainfall events with higher and more rapid peak flows, while the recession curves drop faster sustaining lower baseflows. The flow regime also drastically changes under afforestation, reducing the entire flow distribution but increasing the steepness of the flow duration curves. They reported that high and mean daily flows in afforested catchments are approximately four times lower, whilst low flows are seven times lower than under natural conditions. Grazing with high-density livestock produced much faster and higher peaks as well as more rapid flow recessions. This flashy response of grazed catchments was mainly attributed to severe soil compaction.

Experiments with tropical catchments have shown typical maximum and mean annual stream-flow increases of 400–450 mm per year on clearance with increases in water yield of up to 6 mm per year for each percentage reduction in forest area above a 15% change in cover characteristics (Anderson and Spencer, 1991: 49). Additional data for the effects of land-use change on annual runoff levels are presented for tropical areas in Table 4.9. In central Queensland, Australia, Siriwardena et al. (2006) investigated the effects that clearance of Brigalow (*Acacia harpophylla*) forest in the 1960s and its replacement with grass and cropland had had on runoff. They found that runoff in the post-clearing period was greater by 58% than if clearing had not occurred.

As vegetation regenerates after a forest has been cut or burned, so stream flow tends to revert to normal, though the process may take some decades. This is illustrated in Figure 5.12 which shows the dramatic effects produced

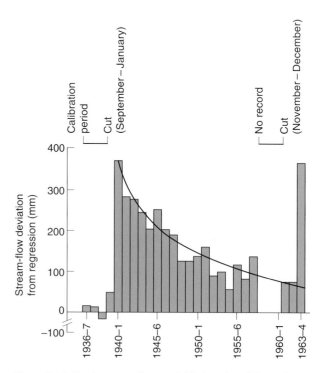

Figure 5.12 The increase of water yield after clear-felling a forest: a unique confirmation from the Coweeta catchment in North Carolina, USA. *Source:* adapted from Pereira (1973: figure 8).

on the Coweeta catchments in North Carolina by two spasms of clear-felling, together with the gradual return to normality in between.

The substitution of one forest type for another may also affect stream flow. This can again be exemplified from the Coweeta, where two experimental catchments were converted from a mature deciduous hardwood forest cover to a cover of white pine (*Pinus strobus*). Fifteen years after the conversion, annual stream flow was found to be reduced by about 20% (Swank and Douglass, 1974). The reason for this notable change is that the interception and subsequent evaporation of rainfall is greater for pine than it is for hardwoods during the dormant season. Another example of the effects of different types of tree cover was provided for South-East Asia by Lacombe et al. (2016). They demonstrated that afforestation by tree planting or by natural forest regeneration induced opposite hydrological changes. The conversion of rice-based shifting cultivation to teak plantations in Laos led to increased seasonal stream flow, whereas the conversion of annual crops and mixed-trees plantations to naturally re-growing forest in Vietnam led to decreased seasonal stream flow. Soil infiltrability controlled by surface crusting was the predominant process explaining why the two modes of afforestation (natural regeneration vs. planting) led to opposite changes in stream-flow regime.

Fears have also been expressed that the replacement of tall natural forests by eucalyptus will produce a decline in streamflow. However, most current research does not support this contention, for transpiration rates from eucalyptus are similar to those from other tree species (except in situations with a shallow groundwater table) while their interception losses are if anything generally rather less than those from other tree species of similar height and planting density (Bruijnzeel, 1990).

Afforestation and reforestation tend to reverse the effects of deforestation. For example, the work of López-Moreno et al. (2006) in the Ebro basin of Spain and of Buendia et al. (2016) in the Pyrenees, showed a general negative trend in flood intensity in recent decades, together with an increase in the importance of low flows in the total annual contribution. This they attributed to the increase in vegetation cover resulting from the farmland abandonment and reforestation that occurred during the twentieth century. Increasing forest cover in Uruguay has had a similar set of consequences (Silveira and Alonso, 2009). Farley et al. (2005) analyzed available global data and found that annual runoff was reduced on average by 44% and 31% when grasslands and shrublands were afforested, respectively.

In northern England, Birkinshaw et al. (2014) analyzed data from the Coalburn catchment (1.5 km^2). Their site was instrumented in 1967, ploughed and planted in 1972/73, and the trees have now reached maturity. Their results show that after ploughing there was an increase of around 50–100 mm in annual stream flow compared with the original upland grassland vegetation. However, the mature trees now show a decrease of around 250–300 mm in the annual stream flow compared with the original vegetation and a decrease of around 350 mm compared with when the site was ploughed.

In many studies the runoff from clean-tilled land tends to be greater than that from areas under a dense crop cover. In the Upper Mississippi river basin in the USA, the tendency for the discharge of the river since the 1940s to increase more than can be explained by increasing precipitation alone has been attributed to the great spread in soybean cultivation (Schilling et al., 2010).

However, tilling the soil surface does not always increase runoff (Gregory and Walling, 1973: 345). There were reports from the former Soviet Union suggesting that the reverse may be the case, and that autumn ploughing can decrease surface runoff, presumably because of its effect on surface detention and on soil structure. Indeed, with careful management the replacement of forest by other land-use types need not be detrimental in terms of either sediment loss or flood generation. In Kenya, for example, the tea plantations with shade trees, protective grass covers, and carefully designed culverts were found to be 'a hydrologically effective substitute for natural forest' (Pereira, 1973: 127).

In mountain and piedmont areas in Europe there has been a remarkable expansion of riparian forest cover over the last century (Stoffel et al., 2016). One of the effects of riparian forest development was the intensification of large wood recruitment and increased flood hazard resulting from wood transport and deposition during flood events. This created an increased frequency of clogging by wood in critical river sections such as those with bridges. Another process affecting floods in such environments was channel incision caused by land-use changes. Channel incision decreases local frequencies of overbank flows and – as a result of increased channel conveyance – affects downstream flow patterns. The increase in flood peaks recorded downstream was attributed to the increased concentration of flood flows in the deepened channel that reduced floodplain storage of floodwater and increased relative channel smoothness.

Fires affects soils (see Section 4.17) and this in turn impacts upon runoff. This is because wildfires combust live plant canopy cover and leaf litter and increase the severity of soil water repellency (hydrophobicity). Moreover, canopy removal in fires tends to increase throughfall, which – after combustion of the leaf litter layer – promotes surface sealing, and reduces infiltration. Fire also may reduce transpiration. These factors combine to cause burned areas to have a higher water yield than unburned areas (Wine and Cadol, 2016).

Infiltration capacities, which are so important in determining the nature of stream runoff, may be modified by various human activities that cause soil compaction, including livestock grazing and trampling (Trimble and Mendel, 1995), off-road vehicular movements (Webb, 1982), and the replacement of grasslands by shrublands (Bhark and Small, 2003). The relationships between grazing pressures and soil infiltration capacities are complex. On the one hand, moderate stocking levels may increase infiltration capacities by breaking down surface biological or rainbeat crusts, while on the other high stocking levels may remove all vegetation cover, cause breakdown of soil aggregates, and produce severe trampling and soil compaction, thereby decreasing soil infiltration rates (du Toit et al., 2009).

The infiltration capacities of desert surfaces are highly variable; one cause of such variability is the nature of vegetation cover, and humans have often in areas like the western USA caused grassland to be replaced by shrubland (Figure 5.13). The differences between grass and shrub surfaces have been the subject of an extensive literature. Ravi et al. (2009) and Parsons et al. (1996), for example, found that as a result of rainfall simulation experiments, compared to grasslands, the inter-rill portions of shrubland hillslopes had higher runoff rates, higher overland flow velocities, and greater rates of erosion. In general, it can be argued that under a shrub canopy infiltration capacities will be relatively high because the addition of organic matter and the activity of roots increase soil porosity. On the other hand, the decreased infiltration capacity in inter-canopy areas may more than offset higher infiltration capacities under the shrub canopies, with the net result that runoff from shrub-dominated hillslopes may be many times greater than those dominated by grassland. Furthermore, as Turnbull et al. (2010: 410) explain on the basis of their erosion and runoff plot studies in New Mexico:

> Over the grassland to shrubland transition, the connectivity of bare areas where runoff tends to be preferentially generated increases. Therefore, from the grass, grass-shrub, shrub-grass to shrub plots, flow lines become increasingly well connected, which increases the capacity for flow to entrain and transport sediment, leading to the greater sediment yields monitored over shrubland.

Human encroachment on papyrus swamps has been shown to be an influence on streams flowing into Lake Victoria (Ryken et al., 2015). Sub-catchments with papyrus wetlands still intact, due to their strong buffering capacity, had a slower rainfall-runoff response, smaller peak runoff discharges, and lower rainfall-runoff ratios.

Figure 5.13 *Larrea tridentata* (creosote bush) is a shrub that has expanded in its range in parts of California, USA (ASG).

5.3.3 The Role of Invasive Plants

In some parts of the world, such as southern Africa, the spread of invasive exotic plants (Section 2.18) may cause greater loss of water than the native vegetation and so cause reduction in streamflow. Some calculations of this are presented in Table 5.6. The incremental water use of alien plants is estimated to be 3300 million m^3 per year, equivalent to a 190-mm reduction in rainfall, and equivalent to almost three-quarters of the virgin mean annual runoff of the huge Vaal River (Le Maitre et al., 2000).

In the south-west USA many streams are lined by the salt cedar (*Tamarix pentandra*). With roots either in the water table or freely supplied by the capillary fringe, these shrubs have full potential transpiration opportunity. The removal of such vegetation can cause large increases in stream flow. It is interesting to note that the salt cedar itself is an alien, native to Eurasia, which was introduced by humans (Chew, 2009). It has spread explosively in the south-west USA, increasing from about 4000 ha in 1920 to almost 400,000 ha in the early 1960s (Harris, 1966). In the Upper Rio Grande Valley in New Mexico, the salt cedar was introduced to try and combat anthropogenic soil erosion, but it spread so explosively that it came to consume approximately 45% of the area's total available water (Hay, 1973). Some recent studies, however, suggest that the hydrological impact of non-native riparian vegetation may not be as serious as has sometimes been proposed (e.g. Hultine and Bush, 2011).

5.3.4 Land Drainage

The drainage of soil by such means as ditches and underground pipes impacts upon stream flows. Considerable interest has been attached to the impact of peat drainage

Table 5.6 Impact of water use by invading alien plants on the mean annual runoff (MAR) in primary catchment areas of South Africa and Lesotho.

River system	Mean annual runoff (millions of m^3)	Condensed invaded area (ha)	Incremental water use (millions of m^3)	Water use (% of MAR)	Reduction in rainfall equivalents (mm)
Limpopo	2,381.82	122,457	190.38	7.99	155
Olifants	2,904.10	217,855	290.44	10.00	133
Vaal	4,567.37	64,632	190.53	4.17	295
Orange	7,147.76	141,012	141.40	1.98	100
Olifants, Sout, & Doring	1,008.35	37,623	35.52	3.52	94
Namaqualand coast	25.01	46,618	22.76	91.00	49
W. Cape & Agulhas coast	2,056.75	384,636	646.50	31.43	168
Breede & Riversdale coast	2,088.35	84,398	181.63	8.70	215
Gouritz	670.63	59,399	74.79	11.15	126
S. Cape coast	1,297.30	52,993	134.46	10.36	254
Gamtoos	494.71	34,289	96.53	19.51	282
PE Coast, Swartkops & Coega	150.04	11,358	40.18	26.78	354
Sundays	279.89	3,964	8.34	2.98	210
Bushmans & Alexandria coast	172.92	22,894	73.08	42.26	319
Gt Fish	520.72	6,980	21.12	4.06	303
Border Coast	578.91	12,483	55.58	9.60	445
Great Kei	1,042.35	30,694	138.22	13.26	450
Former Transkei	7,383.76	68,493	217.38	2.94	317
S. KwaZulu-Natal	3,121.20	46,442	126.37	4.05	272
Tugela	3,990.88	62,151	104.67	2.62	168
N. KwaZulu-Natal	4,741.74	100,574	229.86	4.85	229
Komati to Nwanedzi	2,871.4	124,494	283.26	9.86	228
RSA	**49,495.96**	**1,736,438**	**3,303.00**	**6.67**	**190**

Source: Le Maitre et al. (2000). Reproduced with permission of Water Research Commission.

associated with the desire for afforestation. The hydrological effects of this are the subject of controversy, since there are cases of both increased and decreased flood peaks after drainage (Holden et al., 2004). It has been suggested that differences in peat type alone might account for the different effects. Thus it is conceivable that the drainage of a *Sphagnum* moss catchment would lead to increased flooding since *Sphagnum* compacts with drainage, reducing its storage volume and its permeability. On the other hand, in the case of non-*Sphagnum* peat there would be relatively less change in structure, but there would be a reduction in moisture content and an increase

in storage capacity, thereby tending to reduce flood flows. The nature of the peat is, however, but one feature to consider (Robinson, 1979). The intensity of the drainage works (depth, spacing, etc.) may also be important. In any case, there may be two (sometimes conflicting) processes operating as a result of peat drainage: the increased drainage network will facilitate rapid runoff, and the drier soil conditions will provide greater storage for rainfall. Which of these two tendencies is dominant will depend on local catchment conditions.

However, the impact of land drainage upon downstream flood incidence has long been a source of controversy.

Much depends on the scale of study, the nature of land management, and the character of the soil that has been drained. After a detailed review of experience in the UK, Robinson (1990) found that the drainage of heavy clay soils that are prone to prolonged surface saturation in their undrained state generally led to a reduction of large and medium flow peaks. He attributed this to the fact that their natural response is 'flashy' (with limited soil water storage available), whereas their drainage of permeable soils, which are less prone to such surface saturation, improves the speed of subsurface flow, thereby tending to increase peak flow levels.

In the USA, Frans et al. (2013) found that drainage had caused an increase in flows in the basin of the Mississippi. Also working in the USA, Schottler et al. (2014) compared changes in hydrology for 21 southern Minnesota catchments and showed that artificial drainage was a major driver of increased river flow over the last 70 years, exceeding the effects of precipitation changes and crop conversion. The majority of the increase in flow was attributed to changes in water residence time on the landscape and subsequent reductions in evapotranspiration resulting from installation of artificial drainage networks. Studies of tile drains in Iowa have shown that they may also impact upon flood flows (Sloan et al., 2016), though the nature of this impact depends upon such factors as the size and spacing of the drains, the hydraulic conductivity of the soils in which they are installed, and the magnitude of the flood event.

5.3.5 Groundwater Exploitation

In many parts of the world humans obtain water by pumping from underground aquifers (Wada et al., 2010) (see also Section 5.5). Global groundwater abstraction increased from c. 312 km^3 per year in 1960, to c. 734 km^3 per year in 2000, and this abstraction exceeded recharge, so that over the same period groundwater reserves became depleted. Moreover, the rate of global groundwater depletion has probably more than doubled since the period 1960–2000 (Aeschbach-Hertig and Gleeson, 2012). The trends of groundwater depletion, globally and in the USA, are shown in Figure 5.14. Flows, especially in streams in sedimentary rocks where groundwater makes a major contribution to stream discharges, may be reduced as a result of this drawdown (Hiscock et al., 2001; Kirk and Herbert, 2002; Weber and Perry, 2006). Zektser et al. (2005) and Wen and Chen (2006) established that extensive irrigational pumping has caused stream-flow depletion in the High Plains of the USA (Figure 5.15). Rugel et al. (2012) found that karstic groundwater exploitation in Georgia had also led to flow declines.

5.3.6 Urbanization and its Effects on River Flow

The process of urbanization has a considerable hydrological impact, in terms of controlling rates of erosion and the delivery of pollutants to rivers, and in terms of influencing the nature of runoff and other hydrological characteristics (Hollis, 1988; Chin, 2006). A pioneer attempt to generalize some of these impacts using a historical model of urbanization was summarized usefully by Savini and Kammerer (1961) and is reproduced here in Table 5.7. Chen et al. (2016) estimated that for the contiguous USA about 1.9 billion m^3 of average annual runoff were generated due to urbanization from 2001 to 2006 and about 1.4 billion m^3 of average annual runoff were gained from urbanization from 2006 to 2011. This means that 3.3 billion m^3 of average annual runoff was gained due to urbanization for the decade from 2001 to 2011, which is about 10% of the total amount of urban runoff in 2001.

Research both in the United States and in Britain has shown that, because urbanization produces extended impermeable surfaces of bitumen, tarmac, tiles, and concrete, there is a tendency for flood runoff to increase in comparison with rural sites (Hupp et al., 2013; Hopkins et al., 2015; Remondi et al., 2016). Sheng and Wilson (2009) provided an analysis of how urbanization in the Los Angeles metropolitan region has increased flood hazard.

It has been estimated that c. 9% of the terrestrial surface in Europe is now covered with an impermeable layer, while in Beijing, China, the average cover of impermeable surface reached over 67% in the city centre, falling to around 9% in the outer parts of the urban area (Parris, 2016: 22). However, the infiltration capacities of impermeable surfaces are highly variable and, for example, whilst small samples of new road surface materials studied in laboratory conditions are highly impermeable, actual *in situ* roads that have been in place for a number of years are shown to allow considerable infiltration (Redfern et al., 2016). Another very important control of the response of urban streams to rainfall inputs is the nature of the drains, culverts, and pipe networks of a particular urban area (Walsh et al., 2016b). Sometimes this is referred to as 'urban karst' (Bonneau et al., 2017). Equally, in some cities, as they expand in extent and population density, existing streams are systematically modified and buried, leaving extensive watershed areas devoid of stream channels. Such areas are called 'urban stream deserts' (Napieralski and Carvalhaes, 2016).

City drainage densities may be greater than those in natural landscapes and the installation of sewers and storm

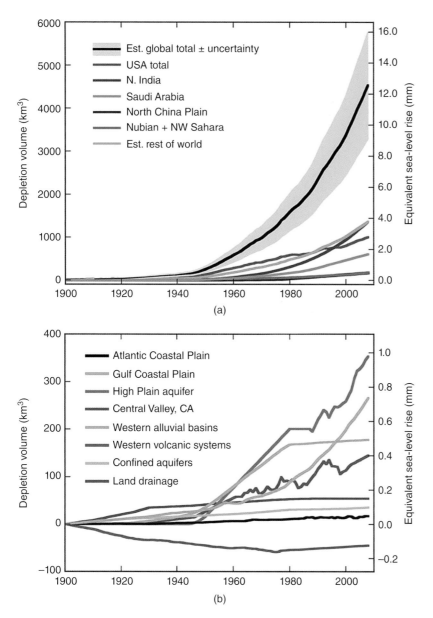

Figure 5.14 (a) Estimated cumulative global groundwater depletion, 1900–2008. (b) Cumulative new groundwater depletion in major aquifer systems or groups in the United States, 1900–2008. *Source:* Kornikow (2011: figures 1 and 2). Reproduced with permission of American Geophysical Union.

drains accelerates runoff, as illustrated in Figure 5.16a. The greater the area that is underlain by sewers, the greater is the discharge for a particular recurrence level (Figure 5.16b). Peak discharges are higher and occur sooner after runoff starts in basins that have been affected by urbanization and the installation of sewers. Some runoff may be generated in urban areas because low vegetation densities mean that evapotranspiration is limited.

However, in many cases the effect of urbanization is greater on small floods; as the size of the flood and its recurrence interval increase, so the effect of urbanization diminishes (Hollis, 1975). A probable explanation for this is that, during a severe and prolonged storm event, a non-urbanized catchment may become so saturated and its channel network so extended that it begins to behave hydrologically as if it were an impervious catchment with a dense surface-water drain network. Under these conditions, a rural catchment produces floods of a type and size similar to those of its urban counterpart. Moreover, a further mechanism probably

Figure 5.15 Circular fields created by irrigation with centre pivot schemes, High Plains, West Texas, USA. *Source:* © 2016 GoogleEarth. They are c. 1 mile and 0.5 mile in diameter. Scale bar 2.26 km.

operates in the same direction, for in an urban catchment it seems probable that some throttling of flow occurs in surface-water drains during intense storms, tending to attenuate the very highest discharges. Thus, Hollis believed, whilst the size of small frequent floods is increased many times by urbanization, large, rare floods (the ones likely to cause extreme damage) are not significantly affected by the construction of suburban areas within a catchment area (Figure 5.16c). Hollis's findings may not be universally applicable. For example, Wilson (1967) working in Jackson, Mississippi, found that the fifty-year flood for an urbanized catchment was three times higher than that of a rural one, and Sheng and Wilson (2009), working in Los Angeles, found that both frequent and rare floods were sensitive to urbanization.

In semi-arid southern California, which relies heavily on imported water for domestic use, a synthesis of river discharge data has revealed that summer (June, July, and August) river discharge in catchments that have at least 50% urban, suburban, and/or commercial land cover has increased by 250% or more over the past half-century, without any substantial precipitation change occurring during these months. Total annual discharge in the Los Angeles River has also increased by up to several hundred percent. According to Townsend-Small et al. (2013), three factors probably account for these trends: (1) increased groundwater recharge rates from leaking water pipelines, (2) inputs of treated wastewater into streams and rivers, and (3) increased runoff or recharge due to over-irrigation of ornamental landscaping.

A whole series of techniques have been developed in an attempt to reduce and delay urban storm runoff (Table 5.8). Of particular current interest are Sustainable Urban Drainage Systems (SUDS). These tackle urban surface runoff problems at source using features such as soakaways or infiltration basins (Brander et al., 2004), permeable pavements (Brattebo and Booth, 2003), grassed swales or vegetated filter strips, infiltration trenches, ponds (detention and retention basins), and wetlands to attenuate flood peak flows.

5.4 The Human Impact on Lake Levels

One of the results of human modification of river regimes is that lake levels have suffered some change, though it is not always possible to distinguish between the part played by humans and that played by natural climatic changes.

A lake basin for which there are particularly long records of change is the Valencia Basin in Venezuela (Böckh, 1973). It was the declining level of the waters in this lake which so struck the great German geographer von Humboldt in 1800 (Section 1.1). He recorded its level as being about 422 m above sea level, and some previous observations on its level were made by Manzano in 1727, which established it as being at 426 m. The 1968 level was about 405 m, representing a fall of no less than 21 m in about 240 years (Figure 5.17). Humboldt believed that the cause of the declining level was the deforestation

Table 5.7 Stages of urban growth and their miscellaneous hydrological impacts.

Stage	Impact
1). *Transition from pre-urban stage:* a) Removal of trees or vegetation b) Construction of scattered houses with limited sewerage and water facilities c) Drilling of wells d) Construction of septic tanks, etc.	Decrease in transpiration and increase in storm flow Some lowering of water table Some increase in soil moisture and perhaps some contamination
2.) *Transition from early-urban to middle-urban stage:* a) Bulldozing of land b) Mass construction of houses, etc. c) Discontinued use and abandonment of some shallower wells d) Diversion of nearby streams for public supply e) Untreated or inadequately treated sewerage into streams and wells	Accelerated land erosion Decreased infiltration Rise in water table Decrease in runoff between points of diversion of disposal Pollution of streams and wells
3.) *Transition from middle-urban to late-urban stage:* a) Urbanization of area completed by addition of more buildings b) Larger quantities of untreated waste into local streams c) Abandonment of remaining shallow wells because of pollution d) Increase in population requiring establishment of new water supply and distribution systems e) Channels of streams restricted at least in part to artificial channels and tunnels f) Construction of sanitary drainage system and treatment plant for sewerage g) Improvement of storm drainage system h) Drilling of deeper, large-capacity industrial wells i) Increased use of water for air-conditioning j) Drilling of recharge wells k) Waste-water reclamation and utilization	 Reduced infiltration and lowered water table, higher flood peaks and lower low flows Increased pollution Rise in water table Increase in local stream flow if supply is from outside basin Higher stage for a given flow (therefore increased flood damage) changes in channel geometry and sediment load Removal of additional water from area Lowered water pressure, some subsidence, salt-water encroachment Overloading of sewers and other drainage facilities Raising of water pressure surface Recharge of groundwater aquifers: more efficient use of water resources

Source: modified after Savini and Kammerer (1961).

brought about by humans, and this has been supported by Böckh (1973), who pointed also to the abstraction of water for irrigation. This remarkable fall in level meant that the lake ceased to have an overflow into the River Orinoco. It has as a consequence become subject to a build-up in salinity, and is now eight times more saline than it was 250 years ago.

In the south-west USA, water abstraction for municipal supply and irrigation has led to catastrophic falls in the levels of both Mono and Owens lakes (Gill, 1996). In the case of the former, since the first diversions of its tributaries to quench the thirst of growing Los Angeles in 1941, its water level has dropped by 11 m. Water abstraction for irrigation has led to declines in lake levels in the Great Basin, where, beginning in the mid-nineteenth century, the introduction of agriculture upstream of Walker Lake resulted in the water from inflowing rivers being diverted. As a result,

its level dropped approximately 40 m between 1882 and 1994.

Even the world's largest lake, the Caspian, has been modified by human activities. The most important change was the fall of 3 m in its level between 1929 and the late 1970s (Figure 5.18). This decline was undoubtedly partly the product of climatic change (Micklin, 1972), for winter precipitation in the northern Volga Basin, the chief flow-generating area of the Caspian, was generally below normal for that period because of a reduction in the number of moist cyclones penetrating into the Volga Basin from the Atlantic. Nonetheless, human actions have contributed to this fall, particularly since the 1950s, because of reservoir formation, irrigation, municipal and industrial withdrawals, and agricultural practices. In addition to the fall in level, salinity in the northern Caspian has increased by 30% since the early 1930s. A secondary effect of the changes in level

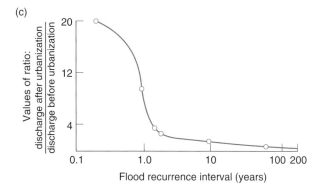

Figure 5.16 Some hydrological consequences of urbanization. (a) Effect of urban development on flood hydrographs. Peak discharges (Q) are higher and occur sooner after runoff starts (T) in basins that have been developed or sewered. *Source:* adapted from Fox (1979: figure 3). (b) Flood frequency curves for a 1-square-mile basin in various states of urbanization. *Source:* adapted from US Geological Survey in Viessman et al. (1977: figure 11.33). (c) Effects of flood magnitude of paving 20% of a basin. *Source:* adapted from Hollis (1975).

has been a decline in fish numbers due to the disappearance of the shallows. These are biologically the most productive zones of the lake, providing a food base for the more valuable types of fish and also serving as spawning grounds for some species. There are plans to divert some water from northward-flowing rivers in Siberia towards the Volga to correct the decline in Caspian levels, but the possible climatic impacts of such action have caused some concern. In any event, an amelioration of climate since the late 1970s has caused some two metres of recovery in the level of the lake (Sapozhnikov et al., 2010).

Perhaps the most severe change to a major inland sea is that taking place in the Aral Sea (Figure 5.19) (Saiko and Zonn, 2000). Between 1960 and 1990, largely because of diversions of river flow, it had lost more than 40% of its area and about 60% of its volume, and its level had fallen by more than 14 m. By 2002 its level had dropped another 6 m. By 2008, the area of the Aral Sea was just 15.7% of that in 1961 (Kravtsova and Tarasenko, 2010) and it had become separated into four water bodies. This has lowered the artesian water table over a band 80–170 km in width, has exposed 24,000 km^2 of former lake bed to desiccation, and has created salty surfaces from which salts are deflated to be transported in dust storms, to the detriment of soil quality downwind. The mineral content of the Aral has increased by more than twentyfold (Micklin, 2010). However, efforts have been and are being undertaken to partially restore the sea's hydrology. Its northern part has been separated from the southern part by a dike and dam, leading to a rise or stabilization in the level of the former (Micklin, 2016).

Water abstraction from the Jordan River has caused a decline in the level of the Dead Sea (Figure 5.20). During the last four decades increasing amounts of water have been diverted from surface and groundwater sources in its catchment. Under current conditions on average the annual inflow from all sources to the Dead Sea has been one-half to one-quarter that of the inflow prior to development. The water level has fallen about 20 metres over that period. Since the late 1990s its level has been decreasing by approximately 1 m per year (Filin et al., 2014), reaching 426 m below mean sea level in 2013 (Figure 5.21).

Another lake in the Middle East that has shown a recent catastrophic reduction in size is Urmia in Iran (Figure 5.22). According to Tourian et al. (2015) it was the largest inland body of salt water in the Middle East and the largest permanent hypersaline lake in the world with an area varying from 5200 to 6000 km^2 in the twentieth century. The lake has lost about 70% of its surface area over the last 14 years, partly because of drought but also because of an increase in groundwater exploitation that has caused a fall in the water-table. It is likely to become a major dust source as it dries up (Sotoudeheian et al., 2016).

Table 5.8 Measures for reducing and delaying urban storm runoff, including various types of Sustainable Urban Drainage Systems.

Surface type	Reduction in runoff	Delaying of runoff
Flat roof	Storage in cisterns Cultivation of rooftop gardens Pool and/or fountain storage Growing of sod roof (green) cover	Ponding on roof by constricted drainpipes Increasing roof roughness by means of rippled or gravel roofs
Car parks	Porous pavement by means of gravel, and/or porous or punctured asphalt Concrete vaults and cisterns beneath car parks Vegetated ponding areas Gravel trenches	Grassy strips Grassed waterways draining car parks Ponding and detention measures for impervious areas (e.g. rippled pavements, depressions and basins)
Residential areas	Cisterns Porous gravel drives Contoured landscapes Groundwater recharge by means of perforated and porous pipes, sand or gravel areas, trenches, dry wells, and vegetated depressions	Reservoir or detention basins Planting of grass with a high roughness Grassy gutters or channels Increased length of travel of runoff by means of gutters, diversions, etc.

Source: modified after US Department of Agriculture, Soil Conservation Service (1972) in Viessman et al. (1977: 569).

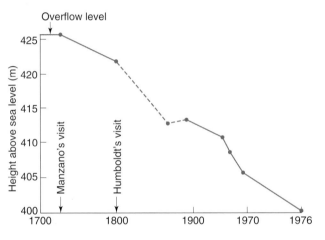

Figure 5.17 Variations in the level of Lake Valencia, Venezuela, to 1976. *Source:* adapted from Bockh (1973: figure 18.2), and other sources.

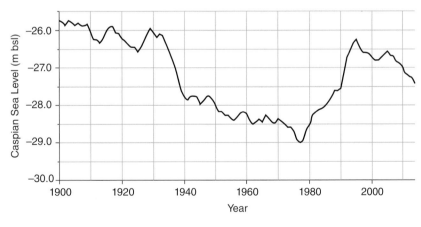

Figure 5.18 Annual fluctuations in the level of the Caspian Sea since 1900. Sources: World Meteorological Organization (1995: figure 15.3); Sapozhnikov et al. (2010: figure 1); and Haghani et al. (2016: figure 1).

The levels of lakes in East Africa have also been responding to a range of pressures. For example, abstraction of water to supply the cut-flower industry has led to a fall in the level of Lake Naivasha in Kenya (Mekonnen et al., 2012), while in Ethiopia two lakes, Haromaya and Adele, have dried up completely because of changes in land use in their catchments, water abstraction for irrigation and municipal supply, and siltation (Alemayehu et al., 2007). South of Addis Ababa, the level of Lake Abiyata has fallen some metres because of water

(a)

(b)

(c)

Figure 5.19 Changes in the Aral Sea: (a) level from 1950–2010. *Source:* Micklin (2016: figure 5); (b) extent from 1960–2014. *Source:* Micklin (2016: figure 3); and (c) inflows from 1920–2010. *Source:* Micklin (2016: figure 4). Reproduced with permission from Springer.

Figure 5.20 Recessional shorelines caused by the ongoing decline in the level of the Dead Sea, Jordan (ASG).

abstraction connected with the potash industry (Ayenew and Legesse, 2007; Seyoum et al., 2015).

A case study of the combined effects of climate change and anthropogenic pressures is Bosten Lake (Guo et al., 2015), the largest inland freshwater lake in China. This has shown three dramatic fluctuations of lake level over the past 50 years, with the causes being different in each period. In the first period (from 1958–1987) the lake level showed a continuously declining trend due to an increase in lake evaporation. In the second period (from 1988 to 2002), the lake level rose rapidly by 4.6 m because outflow was controlled by humans and the water inflow to the lake increased at the same time. In the third period from 2003 to 2010, the emergency project of transferring water to the Tarim River led to increased lake outflow, while inflow decreased at the same time due to a reduction in precipitation, and these factors combined to cause the lake level to decrease sharply by 3.8 m.

From time to time there have been proposals for major augmentation of lake volumes, either by means of river diversions or by allowing the ingress of sea water through tunnels or canals. Among such plans have been those to flood the salt lakes of the Kalahari by transferring water from the rivers of central Africa such as the Zambezi; the scheme to transfer Mediterranean water to the Dead Sea and to the Quattara Depression in the eastern Sahara; and the Zaire–Chad scheme. Perhaps the most ambitious idea has been the so-called 'Atlantropa' project, whereby the Mediterranean would be empoldered, a

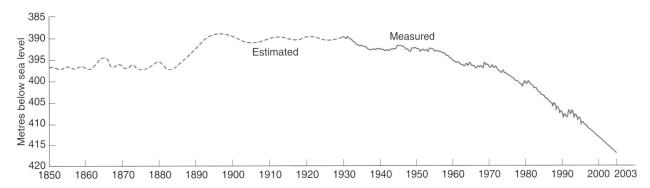

Figure 5.21 The level of the Dead Sea since 1850. Notice the 20-metre fall since the 1960s.

(a)   (b)

Figure 5.22 The state of Lake Urmia in Iran in 1999 and 2011. *Source:* courtesy of NASA Earth Observatory.

dam built at the Straits of Gibraltar, and water fed into the new lake from the Zaire River (Cathcart, 1983). There have also been proposals that the level of the Aral Sea could be restored by transferring water from the Black Sea into the Caspian and then into the Aral (Badescu and Cathcart, 2011).

5.5 Changes in Groundwater Conditions

In many parts of the world humans obtain water supplies by pumping from groundwater (Wada et al., 2010, 2012a and b). Now about 38% of the world's irrigated areas are groundwater-based and about 43% of irrigation water is derived from underground aquifers (Siebert et al., 2010). Groundwater is also important as a source of water for municipal consumption. Increasing population levels and the adoption of new exploitation techniques (for example, the replacement of irrigation methods involving animal or human power by electric and diesel pumps) has increased these problems.

Global groundwater abstraction increased from c. 312 km³ per year in 1960, to c. 734 km³ per year in 2000, and this abstraction exceeded recharge, so that over the same period groundwater reserves became depleted (Figure 5.23). This had two main effects: the reduction in the levels of water tables and the replacement, in coastal areas, of fresh water by salt water (Barlow and Reichard, 2010). Environmental consequences of these two phenomena include ground subsidence and soil salinization.

Some of the reductions in groundwater levels that have been caused by abstraction are considerable. Figure 5.24a

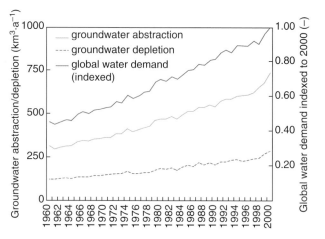

Figure 5.23 1960–2000 trends in total global water demand (right axis indexed for the year 2000), global groundwater abstraction and depletion (left axis). *Source:* adapted from Wada et al. (2010: figure 3).

shows the rapid increase in the number of wells tapping groundwater in the London area from 1850 until after the Second World War, while Figure 5.24b illustrates the substantial changes in groundwater conditions that resulted. The piezometric surface in the confined chalk aquifer has fallen by more than 60 m over hundreds of square kilometres. Likewise, beneath Chicago, Illinois, pumping since the late nineteenth century has lowered the piezometric head by some 200 m. The drawdown that has taken place in the Great Artesian Basin of Australia locally exceeds 80–100 m (Lloyd, 1986).

The reductions in water levels that are taking place in the High Plains from Nebraska to Texas are some of the

(a)

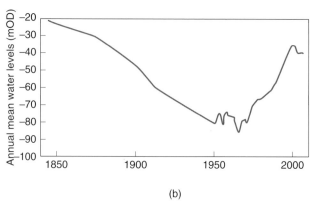

(b)

Figure 5.24 (a) Construction of wells tapping the confined aquifer below London, 1850–1965. (b) Changing groundwater levels beneath Trafalgar Square, Central London, from 1845 to 2005, showing the sharp decline until the 1950s and the 1960s, and the substantial rise since then. *Source:* data from Centre for Ecology and Hydrology, Wallingford.

Figure 5.25 In the High Plains of the USA, fields are irrigated by centre-pivot irrigation schemes which use groundwater. Groundwater levels have fallen rapidly in many areas because of the adoption of this type of irrigation technology (ASG).

most serious (Sophocleous, 2010; Scanlon et al., 2012) and threaten the long-term viability of irrigated agriculture in that area. Before irrigation development started in the 1930s, the High Plains groundwater system, one of the largest in the world and covering some 450,000 km^2, was in a state of dynamic equilibrium, with long-term recharge equal to long-term discharge. Then everything was changed through 'the perfect triad' of electricity, the centrifugal pump, and centre-pivot irrigation (Alley and Alley, 2017). The groundwater is now being mined at a rapid rate to supply centre-pivot schemes (Figure 5.25). In a matter of only 50 years or less, the water level declined by 30 to 60 m, particularly in a large area to the north of Lubbock. This decline is ongoing (Figure 5.26). One consequence of this is that streams in the area now receive less groundwater input, so that their flows have declined (Kustu et al., 2010).

Another example of excessive 'mining' of a finite resource is the exploitation of groundwater resources in the oil-rich kingdom of Saudi Arabia. Most of that country is desert, so climatic conditions are not favourable for rapid large-scale recharge of aquifers. Also, much of the groundwater that lies beneath the desert is a fossil resource, created during more humid conditions – pluvials – that existed in the Late Pleistocene, between 15,000 and 30,000 years ago. In spite of these inherently unfavourable circumstances, Saudi Arabia's demand for water is growing inexorably as its economy develops. In 1980 the annual demand was 2.4 billion m^3. By 1990 it had reached 12 billion m^3 (a fivefold increase in just a decade), and by 2009 it had reached 18.7 billion m^3. Only a very small part of the demand can be met by runoff; over three-quarters of the supply is obtained from predominantly non-renewable groundwater resources. The drawdown on its aquifers is thus enormous. Much of the water is used ineffectively and inefficiently in the agricultural

sector (Al-Ibrahim, 1991), to irrigate crops that could easily be grown in more humid regions and then imported.

The North China Plain aquifer is another example of over exploitation. A significant proportion of this shallow aquifer has seen water levels fall by 20 m since 1960, and in some parts the decline is over 40 m. Similarly severe depletion is also occurring in the Indus River Plains aquifer on the border between India and Pakistan (Rodell et al., 2009), and according to Tiwari et al. (2009: 1) this area has 'probably the largest rate of groundwater loss in any comparable-sized region on Earth'.

However, there are situations where humans deliberately endeavour to increase the natural supply of groundwater by attempting artificial recharge of groundwater basins (Peters, 1998). This has been practised, for example, in south-eastern Florida (Barlow and Reichard, 2010). Where the materials containing the aquifer are permeable (as in some alluvial fans, coastal sand dunes, or glacial deposits) the technique of water-spreading is much used. In relatively flat areas river water may be diverted to spread evenly over the ground so that infiltration takes place. Alternative water-spreading methods may involve releasing water into basins which are formed either by natural processes (like the playas of the High Plains in the USA), or by excavation, or by the construction of dikes or small dams. On alluvial plains water can also be encouraged to percolate down to the water table by distributing it to a series of ditches or furrows. In some situations natural channel infiltration can be promoted by building small check dams down a stream course. In irrigated areas surplus water can be spread by irrigating with excess water during the dormant season. When artificial groundwater recharge is required in sediments with impermeable layers such water-spreading techniques are not effective and the appropriate method may then be to pump water into deep pits or into wells. This last technique is used on the coastal plain of Israel, both to replenish the groundwater reservoirs when surplus irrigation water is available, and to attempt to diminish the problems associated with salt-water intrusion.

In some industrial areas, reductions in industrial activity have caused a recent reduction in groundwater abstraction, and as a consequence groundwater levels have begun to rise – a trend that is exacerbated by considerable leakage losses from ancient, deteriorating pipe and sewer systems. In cities like London, Liverpool, and Birmingham an upward trend has already been identified (Brassington and Rushton, 1987; Price and Reed, 1989). In London, because of a 46% reduction in groundwater abstraction, the water table in the Chalk and Tertiary beds has risen by as much as 20 m. Such a rise has numerous implications, which are listed in Table 5.9. The trend in groundwater levels beneath Trafalgar Square is shown in Figure 5.24b.

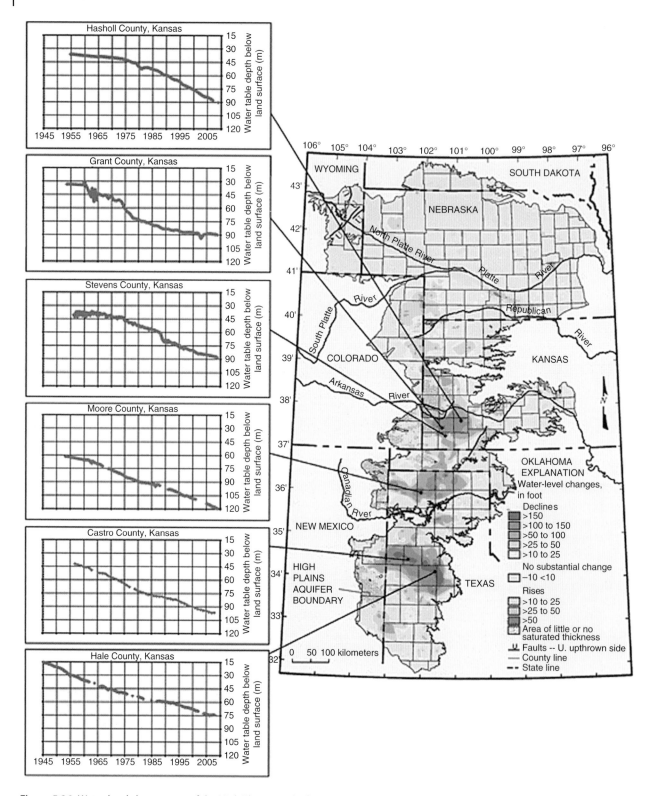

Figure 5.26 Water-level change map of the High Plains aquifer from predevelopment to 2007 and selected water level hydrographs from predevelopment to 2008–2009. *Source:* modified from Sophocleous (2010: figure 2). Reproduced with permission from Springer.

Table 5.9 Possible effects of a rising groundwater level.

Increase in spring and river flows

Re-emergence of 'dry springs'

Surface water flooding

Pollution of surface waters and spread of underground pollution

Flooding of basements

Increased leakage into tunnels

Reduction of slope and retaining wall stability

Reduction in bearing capacity of foundations and piles

Increased hydrostatic uplift and swelling pressures on foundations and structures

Swelling of clays

Chemical attack on foundations

Source: modified after Wilkinson and Brassington (1991: table 4.3, 42).

There is, finally, a series of ways in which unintentional changes in groundwater conditions can occur in urban areas. As we have clearly seen, in cities surface runoff is increased by the presence of impermeable surfaces. One consequence of this would be that less water went to recharge groundwater. However, there is an alternative point of view, namely that groundwater recharge can be accelerated in urban areas because of leaking water mains, sewers, septic tanks, and soakaways (Figure 5.27). In cities in arid areas there is often no adequate provision for storm runoff, and the (rare) increased runoff from impermeable surfaces will infiltrate into the permeable surroundings. In some cities recharge may result from over-irrigation of parks and gardens. Indeed, where the climate is dry, or where large supplies of water are imported, or where pipes and drains are poorly maintained, groundwater recharge in urban areas is likely to exceed that in rural areas.

In addition to causing changes in groundwater levels, humans have had major impacts on groundwater quality, as is the case with accelerated salinization (see, for example, Section 4.5) and as a result of the various processes discussed in the next section.

5.6 Water Pollution

Water pollution is not new, but is frequently undesirable: it causes disease transmission through infection; it may poison humans and animals; it may create objectionable odours and unsightliness; it may be the cause of the unsatisfactory quality even of treated water; it may cause the eutrophication of water bodies, and it may affect economic activities like shellfish culture.

Many human activities can contribute to changes in water quality, including land-use and land-cover changes, agriculture, fertilizer application, irrigation, leaching from

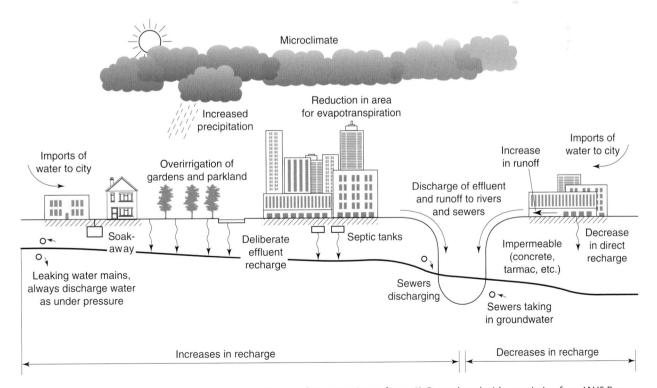

Figure 5.27 Urban effects on groundwater recharge. *Source:* after Lerner (1990: figure 2). Reproduced with permission from IAHS Press.

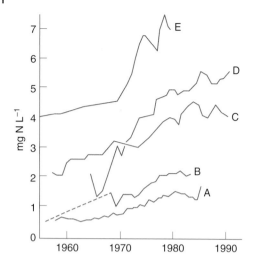

Figure 5.28 Recent trends of nitrate concentrations in some rivers. A: Mississippi at mouth; B: Danube at Budapest; C: Rhine at the Dutch/German border; D: Seine at mouth; E: Thames at mouth. *Source:* Meybeck (2001b: figure 17.6). Reproduced with permission from the Freie Universität Berlin.

landfill, seawater incursion promoted by over-pumping of groundwater, sewage discharges, leakage from septic tanks, urbanization, industrial processes, mining, and many others. Of these, agriculture is probably the most important. Some pollutants merely have local effects, while others, such as acid rain or DDT, may have continental or even planetary implications.

It is also possible to categorize water pollutants according to whether or not they are derived from 'point' or 'non-point' (also called 'diffuse') sources. Municipal and industrial wastes tend to fall into the former category because they are emitted from one specific and identifiable place (e.g. a sewage pipe or industrial outfall). Pollutants from non-point sources include agricultural wastes, many of which enter rivers in a diffuse manner as chemicals percolate into groundwater or are washed off into fields, as well as some mining pollutants, uncollected sewage, and some urban storm-water runoff.

It is plainly not a simple matter to try to estimate the global figure for the extent of water pollution caused by humans. For one thing we know too little about the natural long-term levels of dissolved materials in the world's rivers. Nonetheless, Meybeck (1979) calculated that about 500 million tonnes of dissolved salts reach the oceans each year as a result of human activity. These inputs have increased by more than 30% the natural values for sodium, chloride, and sulphate, and have created an overall global augmentation of river mineralization by about 12%. Likewise, Peierls et al. (1991) demonstrated that the quantity of nitrates in the world's rivers now appears to be closely correlated to human population density. Using published data for 42 major world rivers

they found a highly significant correlation between annual nitrate concentration and human population density that explained 76% of the variation in nitrate concentration for the 42 rivers. They maintained that 'human activity clearly dominates nitrate export from land'. Meybeck (2001a) argued that, on a global scale, nutrient inputs to the oceans by rivers have already increased 2.2 times for nitrate and four times for ammonia.

There are three main classes of chemical pollutant that deserve particular attention: nitrates and phosphates; metals; and synthetic and industrial organic pollutants. Nitrates and phosphates, trends in the concentration of which are reviewed by Heathwaite et al. (1996), are an important cause of a process called eutrophication. Anthropogenic sources include synthetic fertilizers, sewage, and animal wastes from feedlots. Land-use changes (e.g. logging) can also increase nitrate inputs to streams. Global trends in nitrate loadings of rivers are discussed by Green et al. (2004). Nitrate trends in most rivers in Europe and North America reveal a marked increase since the 1950s. This can be attributed to the growth in use of nitrate fertilizers (Meybeck, 2001b). Trends for the Mississippi, Danube, Rhine, Seine, and Thames are shown in Figure 5.28. Trends in nitrogen concentrations in lowland regions of North America are not as great as those reported in lowland regions of Britain. This probably reflects the higher population density and greater intensity of land use in Britain (Heathwaite et al., 1996).

The River Thames in southern England provides a notable and unique long record of nitrogen pollution (Howden et al., 2013) (Figure 5.29). The historical record of mean monthly nitrate concentrations shows an overall increase over the period from 1868 to 2008. This pattern of long-term change is very typical of lowland rivers in the United Kingdom and in other parts of Western Europe. The increase in the Thames was predominantly due to two step changes in mean concentration, one during the 1940s and another in the early 1970s associated with wartime ploughing of permanent pastures and post-war agricultural intensification. Between 1867 and 1940 there was a gradual decline in arable production (with a consequent increase in the area of permanent grassland) and a decline in animal numbers; this was due to the availability of cheap imports from Canada and other British dominions and colonies. The second major change came at the start of World War II due to the need for an increase in domestic food production as imports became curtailed. This resulted in large areas of permanent grassland being ploughed and brought back into arable production. The third change reflects modernization of agriculture through mechanization and

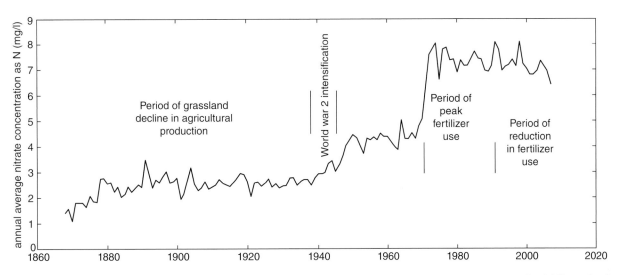

Figure 5.29 Time series of nitrate concentrations for the River Thames, England, from 1868–2008, showing periods of different land management. *Source:* adapted from Howden et al. (2013). Reproduced with permission from Taylor and Francis Group.

the use of inorganic fertilizers. Fertilizer inputs to arable land were relatively stable at about 20 kg/ha/year prior to 1940 and rose to around 90 kg/ha/year by the mid-1960s. During the late 1970s to the mid-1980s, these inputs rose to a peak of 160 kg/ha/year and have remained around 150 kg/ha/year ever since. Fertilizer inputs to permanent grassland were around 4 kg/ha/year prior to 1940 and rose exponentially to around 80 kg/ha/year by 1970. Thereafter, N use continued to rise, albeit at a slower rate, to the mid-1980s, when inputs peaked at 130 kg/ha/year. Since then, inputs have fallen to around 65 kg/ha/year. The decline in inorganic fertilizer inputs has been occurring since 1984, driven by rising cost, improvements in agronomic precision, and schemes to limit application rates, such as Nitrate Vulnerable Zones (NVZ). However, it may take years for reductions to occur in nitrate levels in rivers associated with fertilizer application reductions (Burt et al., 2008; Burt et al., 2010), especially in groundwater-fed streams. This is also the case with many European rivers (Bouraouni and Grizzetti, 2011).

There has also been some anxiety in Britain over a possible decline in the amount of organic matter present in the soil, which could limit its ability to assimilate nitrogen. Moreover, the pattern of tillage may have affected the liberation of nitrogen via mineralization of organic matter. The increased area and depth of modern ploughing accelerates the decay of residues and may change the pattern of water movement in the soil. Finally, tile drainage has also been used extensively in England. This has affected the movement of water through the soil and hence the degree of leaching of nitrates and other materials (Burt and Haycock, 1992).

The trend in nitrate concentrations in British groundwaters is still a matter for concern. Investigations have revealed a large quantity of nitrate in the unsaturated zone of the principal aquifers (mainly Chalk and Triassic sandstone), and this is slowly moving down towards the main groundwater body. The slow transit time means that in many water supply wells increased nitrate concentrations will not occur for 20 to 30 years, but they will then be above acceptable levels for human health.

Phosphate levels are also rising in some parts of the world. Major sources include detergents, fertilizers, and human wastes (Jarvie et al., 2006; Naden et al. 2016). On the other hand, in the United Kingdom, due to phosphorous stripping at sewage plants, phosphate concentrations in river waters appear to have gone down (Bowes et al., 2011), though in Europe more generally, in spite of EC regulations, nutrient concentrations have not shown any very great decline (Bouraouni and Grizzetti, 2011). Powers et al. (2016) pointed out on the basis of their studies of the Thames (England), the Yangtse (China), and the Maumee (USA) that human-dominated river basins may undergo a prolonged but finite accumulation phase when phosphorus inputs (e.g. from sewage and fertilizers) exceed agricultural demand, and that this accumulated phosphorus may continue to mobilize and enter rivers long after inputs decline.

Metals occur naturally in soil and water. However, as the human use of metals has burgeoned, so has the amount of water pollution that they cause. In addition, some metal ions reach river waters because they become more quickly mobilized as a result of acid rain (see Section 7.15). Aluminium is a notable example of this. From a human point of view, the metals of greatest concern are probably lead, mercury, arsenic, and cadmium, all of which have adverse health effects. Other metals can be toxic to aquatic life, and these include copper, silver, selenium, zinc, and chromium.

The anthropogenic sources of metal pollution include the industrial processing of ores and minerals, the use of metals, the leaching of metals from garbage and solid waste dumps, and animal and human excretions. Nriagu and Pacyna (1988) estimated the global anthropogenic inputs of trace metals into aquatic systems (including the oceans), and concluded that the sources producing the greatest quantities were, in descending order, the following (the metals produced by each source are listed in parentheses):

- domestic wastewater effluents (arsenic, chromium, copper, manganese, nickel);
- coal-burning power stations (arsenic, mercury, selenium);
- non-ferrous metal smelters (cadmium, nickel, lead, selenium);
- iron and steel plants (chromium, molybdenum, antimony, zinc);
- the dumping of sewage sludge (arsenic, manganese, lead).

However, in some parts of the world metal pollution may be derived from other sources. There is increasing evidence, for example, that in the western USA water derived from the drainage of irrigated lands may contain high concentrations of toxic or potentially toxic trace elements such as arsenic, boron, chromium, molybdenum, and selenium. Application of phosphate fertilizer, derived from mined phosphate rock, can be a significant contributor of some of these potentially hazardous trace elements in croplands and in water (Jiao et al., 2012). These can cause human health problems and poison fish and wildlife in desert wetlands (Lently, 1994). The tanning of leather often involves the use of large quantities of chromium and is guilty of causing severe pollution of the Ganges and many other water bodies (Belay, 2010).

Mining can also create serious chemical pollution by creating what is known as acid mine drainage (AMD) or acid rock drainage (ARD). In Britain, coal seams and mudstones in the coal measures contain pyrite and marcasite (ferrous sulphide). In the course of mining the water table is lowered, air gains access to these minerals, and they are oxidized. Sulphuric acid may be produced. Should mining cease, as is the situation in the coalfields of Britain, pumping may stop, groundwater may rise through the worked mine, and acid derived from it may discharge into more and more surface waters. Acidity may also be produced by the mining of other minerals that contain sulphide, including zinc and gold, as in South Africa (McCarthy, 2011).

As a consequence, mine drainage waters may be very acid and have pH values as low as 1 or even less (Romero et al., 2011; Tao et al., 2012). They have high sulphate and iron concentrations, they may contain toxic metals such as arsenic and cadmium and because of the reaction of the acid on clay and silicates in the rocks they may also contain appreciable amounts of calcium, magnesium, aluminium, and manganese. Following reactions with sediments or mixing with alkaline river waters, or when chemical or bacterial oxidation of ferrous compounds occurs, the iron may precipitate as ferric hydroxide. This may discolour the water and leave unsightly deposits.

The nature of acid drainage from mines and the remedial measures, such as lime neutralization and the use of aerobic wetlands, that can be adopted to deal with it are discussed by Robb and Robinson (1995) and Johnson and Hallberg (2005), while the adverse effects on stream organisms are discussed by Hogsden and Harding (2012). Affected soils may prevent growth of vegetation, thereby creating 'AMD barrens' (Lupton et al., 2013).

Rock salt (sodium chloride) has been used in increasing quantities since the Second World War for minimizing the dangers to motorists and pedestrians from icy road and pavements. With the rise in the number of vehicles there has been a tendency throughout Europe and North America for a corresponding increase in the use of salt for de-icing purposes. Data for the UK between 1960 and 1991 are shown in Figure 5.30 and demonstrate that while there is considerable inter-annual variability (related to weather severity), there has also been a general upward trend so that in the mid-1970s to end-1980s more than two million tonnes of de-icing salt were being purchased each year (Dobson, 1991). Data on de-icing salt application in North America are given by Jackson and Jobbágy (2005). The total use of de-icing salts in the USA increased at a nearly exponential rate between the 1940s and the 1970s, increasing from about 200,000 metric tonnes in 1940 to approximately 9,000,000 tonnes in 1970. This represented a doubling time of about five years. By the early 2000s the annual rate exceeded 18 million tonnes (Figure 5.31). Runoff from salted roads can cause ponds and lakes (Novotny et al., 2008) to become salinized, concrete to decay, and susceptible trees to die. It has also caused a considerable increase in the salinity of streams in the north-eastern United States. Kaushal et al. (2005) found that some streams in Maryland, New Hampshire, and New York had winter chloride concentrations of up to 25% of the concentration of sea water, and that summer chloride concentrations remained up to 100 times greater than un-impacted forest streams. Many animals can be adversely affected, including amphibians. With their permeable skin and eggs they are a particularly vulnerable group. Sodium chloride in particular has been shown to

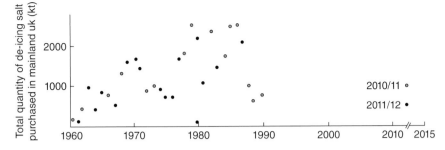

Figure 5.30 Estimates of the total quantity of de-icing salt purchased annually in mainland Britain during the period 1960–1991 and in 2010/11 and 2011/12. *Source:* data provided by ICI in Dobson (1991: figure 1.1) and in http://www.local.gov.uk/community-safety/-/journal_content/56/10180/3510492/ARTICLE (accessed January 2017).

negatively affect survival of all life-stages of frogs and toads (Hopkins et al., 2013b).

Similarly, storm-water runoff from urban areas may contain large amounts of contaminants, derived from litter, garbage, car-washings, horticultural treatments, vehicle drippings, industry, construction, animal droppings, and the chemicals used for snow and ice clearance. Comparison of contaminant profiles for urban runoff and raw domestic sewage, based on surveys throughout the USA, indicates the importance of pollution from urban runoff sources (Table 5.10). In New York City, within a short distance of Trump Tower, some half million discerning dogs leave up to 20,000 tonnes of pollutant faeces and up to 3.8 million litres of urine in the city streets each year, all of which is flushed by gutters to storm-water sewers. Taking Britain as a whole, dogs deposit 1000 tonnes of excrement and three million gallons of urine on the streets every day (Ponting, 1991).

Synthetic and industrial organic pollutants have been manufactured and released in very large quantities since the 1960s. The dispersal of these substances into water-

courses has resulted in widespread environmental contamination. There are many tens of thousands of synthetic organic compounds currently in use, and many are thought to be hazardous to life, even at quite low concentrations. Among these pollutants are synthetic organic pesticides, including chlorinated hydrocarbon insecticides. Some of these can reach harmful concentrations as a result of biological magnification in the food chain. Pesticides can have adverse effects on fish populations (Scholz et al., 2012). There is now a tremendous range of pesticides and they differ greatly in their mode of action, in the length of time they remain in the biosphere, and in their toxicity. Much of the most adverse criticism of pesticides has been directed against the chlorinated hydrocarbon group of insecticides, which includes DDT and Dieldrin. These insecticides are toxic not only to the target organism but to other insects too (that is, they are non-specific). They are also highly persistent. Appreciable quantities of the original application may survive in the environment in unaltered form for years, and so sometimes they are referred to as 'legacy

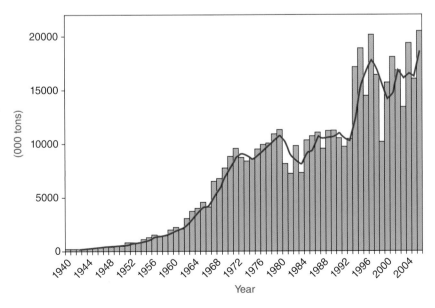

Figure 5.31 Sales of rock salt for highway use in the USA from 1940 to 2004. *Source:* adapted from Jackson and Jobbágy (2005: figure 1).

Table 5.10 Comparison of contaminant profiles for urban surface runoff and raw domestic sewage, based on surveys throughout the USA.

Constituent[*]	Urban surface runoff	Raw domestic sewage
Suspended solids	250–300	150–250
BOD[†]	10–250	300–350
Nutrients		
a) Total nitrogen	0.5–5.0	25–85
b) Total phosphorus	0.5–5.0	2–15
Coliform bacteria (MPN/100 ml)	10^4–10^6	10^6 or greater
Chlorides	20–200	15–75
Miscellaneous substances		
a) Oil and grease	yes	yes
b) Heavy metals	(10–100) times sewage concentration	traces
c) Pesticides	yes	seldom
d) Other toxins	potential exists	seldom

[*]All concentrations are expressed in mg l^{-1} unless stated otherwise.
[†]Biochemical oxygen demand.
MPN – Most probable number.
Source: Burke (1972: table 7.36.1).

chemicals'. They can have two rather severe effects: global dispersal and the 'biological magnification' of these substances in food chains. This last problem is well illustrated for DDT in Figure 5.32, traces of which can persist in fish and sediments long after its use has been banned (Jürgens et al., 2016).

Similarly, due to their persistence, bioaccumulation potential and toxicity, many Persistent Organic Pollutants (POPs) remain of concern. These compounds include organochlorine pesticides (OCPs), polychlorinated biphenyls (PCBs), and polybrominated diphenyl ethers (PBDEs) (Lu et al., 2017b). PCBs have been used extensively in the electrical industry as di-electrics in large transformers and capacitors. Other POPs include: PAHs (Polycylic Aromatic Hydrocarbons), which result from the incomplete burning of fossil fuels; various organic solvents used in industrial and domestic processes; phthalates, which are plasticizers used, for example, in the production of polyvinyl chloride resins; and DBPs (Disinfection By-Products). Like DDT they have the potential to cause harm decades after their production and use was stopped. The long-term health effects of cumulative exposure to such substances are difficult to quantify. However, some work suggests that they may be implicated in the development of birth defects and certain types of cancer.

Nonetheless, it would be misleading to create the impression that water pollution is either a totally insoluble problem or that levels of pollution must inevitably rise. It is true that some components of the hydrological system – for example, lakes, because they may act as sumps – will prove relatively intractable to improvement, but in many rivers and estuaries striking developments have occurred in water quality in recent decades.

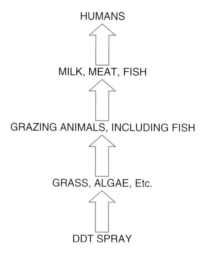

Figure 5.32 Biological concentration occurs when relatively indestructible substances (DDT, for example) are ingested by lesser organisms at the base of the food pyramid. An estimated 1000 kg of plant plankton are needed to produce 100 kg of animal plankton. These in turn are consumed by 10 kg of fish, the amount needed by one person to gain 1 kg. The ultimate consumer (man or woman) then takes in the DDT taken in by the 1000 kg of the lesser creatures at the base of the food pyramid, when he or she ingests enough fish to gain 1 kg.

This is clear in the case of the River Thames, which suffered a serious decline in its quality and in its fish as London's pollution and industries expanded. However, after about 1950, because of more stringent controls on effluent discharge, the downward trend in quality was reversed (see Figure 5.33), and many fish, long absent from the Thames, returned (Gameson and Wheeler, 1977). Stringent controls on phosphorus pollution have been highly effective in improving the quality of lake waters in parts of the UK (May et al., 2012). There also appears to have been some improvement in pollution levels in the North American Great Lakes since the mid-1970s as indicated by phosphorus loadings, and DDT and PCB levels (Figure 5.34). One very important way of reducing the input of pollutants to stream courses is to provide a buffer zone of vegetation between them and the fields from which the pollution comes. Alternatively, bans can be instituted to prevent fertilizer applications in particularly sensitive zones with respect to pollutants such as nitrates.

5.7 Eutrophication

Eutrophication is the enrichment of waters by nutrients. The process occurs naturally during, for example, the slow ageing of lakes, but it can be accelerated both by runoff from fertilized agricultural land and by the discharge of domestic sewage and industrial effluents. This process, often called 'cultural eutrophication', commonly leads to

excessive growths of algae followed in some cases by a serious depletion of dissolved oxygen as the algae decay after death. Oxygen levels may become too low to support fish life, resulting in fish kills. Changes in diatom assemblages can also occur (see Battarbee, 1977). The nature of these changes is summarized in Table 5.11. Trends in the eutrophication of lakes in the Anthropocene have been analyzed by Keatley et al. (2011). Analyzing data from Europe and North America since 1945 they have demonstrated that European lakes have undergone greater cultural eutrophication as indicated from diatom-inferred total phosphorus levels than North American ones. They attributed this to Europe's relatively longer history of intensive agriculture as well as to its higher current and historical population density. However, eutrophication of lakes is becoming evident in many parts of the world, and is even detectable in such large water bodies as Lake Malawi (Otu et al., 2010) and Lake Victoria (Sitoki et al., 2010) in Africa.

In addition to the influence of nitrate fertilizers, the confining of animals on feedlots (also called *concentrated animal feeding operations* (CAFOs)) results in tremendously concentrated sources of nutrients and pollutants. Animal wastes in the USA are estimated to be as much as 1.6 billion tonnes per year, with 50% of this amount originating from feedlots. The overwhelming majority of beef cattle spend their last months with hundreds if not thousands of other cows in feedlots, where they are fattened before being slaughtered. US animal feedlots produce 100,000 metric tonnes of manure per minute (Clay,

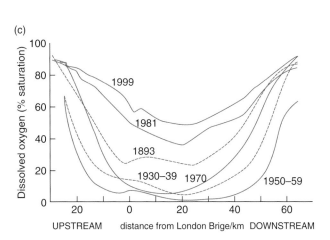

Figure 5.33 The average dissolved oxygen content of the River Thames at half-tide in the July–September quarter since 1890: (a) 79 km below Teddington Weir. (b) 95 km below Teddington Weir. *Source:* adapted from Gameson and Wheeler (1977: figure 4). (c) The pattern from 1893 to 1999.

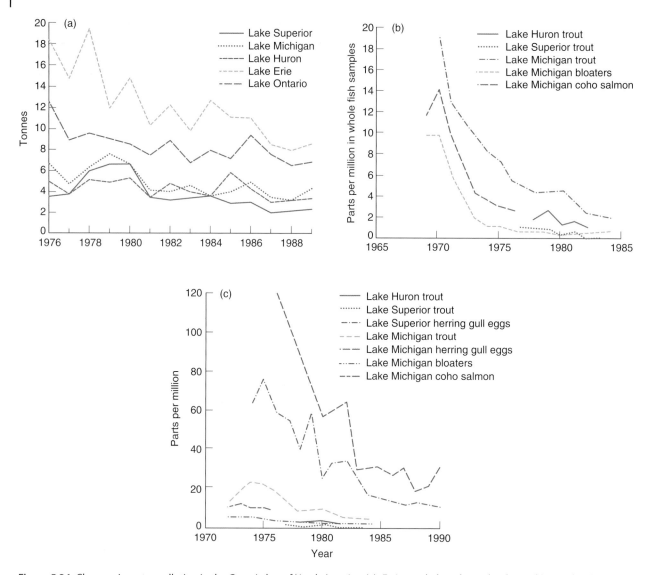

Figure 5.34 Changes in water pollution in the Great Lakes of North America: (a) Estimated phosphorus loadings. (b) DDT levels. (c) PCB levels. *Source:* after Council on Environmental Quality, 17th (1986) and 22nd (1992) Annual Reports.

2004). It needs to be remembered that 1000 head of beef produce the equivalent organic load of 6000 people (Sanders, 1972) and that the amount of solid manure produced by US farm animals is 130 times the amount produced by the human population. Cattle feedlot runoff is a high-strength organic waste, high in oxygen-demanding material, and polluted with antibiotics and hormones, and has caused many fish kills in rivers in states such as Kansas. In North Carolina and Virginia industrial style hog and poultry operations have caused large waste spills, especially during severe storms, and these too have caused massive fish kills.

5.8 Pollution by Acid Rain

Changes in surface-water chemistry may be produced by the washing out of acids that pollute the air in precipitation. This is particularly clear in the heavily industrialized area of north-western Europe, where there is a marked zonation of acid rain with pH values that often fall below 4 or 5. A broadly comparable situation exists in North America (Johnson, 1979). Very considerable fears have been expressed about the possible effects that acid deposition may have on aquatic ecosystems, and particularly on fish populations. It is now generally accepted that decades of increasing lake and river acidification

Table 5.11 Characteristics of lakes experiencing 'cultural eutrophication'.

Biological factors

a) *Primary productivity*: usually much higher than in unpolluted water and is manifest as extensive algal blooms

b) *Diversity of primary producers*: initially green algae increase, but blue-green algae rapidly become dominant and produce toxins. Similarly, macrophytes (e.g. reed maces) respond well initially but due to increased turbidity and anoxia (see below) they decline in diversity as eutrophication proceeds

c) *Higher trophic level productivity*: overall decrease in response to factors given in this table

d) *Higher trophic level diversity*: decreases due to factors given in this table. The species of macro- and micro-invertebrates which tolerate more extreme conditions increase in numbers. Fish are also adversely affected and populations are dominated by surface dwelling coarse fish such as pike and perch

Physical factors

a) *Mean depth of water body*: as infill occurs the depth decreases

b) *Volume of hypolimnion*: varies

c) *Turbidity*: this increases as sediment input increases and restricts the depth of light penetration which can become a limiting factor for photosynthesis. It is also increased if boating is a significant activity

Source: modified after Mannion (1992: table 11.4).

caused fish kills and stock depletion. Fishless lakes now occur in areas like the Adirondacks in the north-east USA. Species of fish vary in their tolerance to low pH, with rainbow trout being largely intolerant to values of pH below 6.0, while salmon, brown and brook trout are somewhat less sensitive. Values of 4.0–3.5 are lethal to salmonids, while values of 3.5 or less are lethal to most fish. Numerous lacustrine molluscs and crustaceans are not found even at weakly acid pH values of 5.8–6.0, and crayfish rapidly lose their ability to re-calcify after moulting as the pH drops from 6.0 to 5.5.

Fish declines and deaths in areas afflicted by acid rain are not solely caused by water acidity *per se*. It has become evident that under conditions of high acidity certain metal ions, including aluminium, are readily mobilized, leading to their increasing concentration in fresh waters. Some of these metal ions are highly toxic and many mass mortalities of fish have been attributed to aluminium poisoning rather than high acidity alone. The aluminium adversely affects the operation of fish gills, causing mucus to collect in large quantities; this eventually inhibits the ability of the fish to take in necessary oxygen and salts. In addition, aluminium's presence in water can reduce the amount of available phosphates, an essential food for phytoplankton and other aquatic plants. This decreases the available food for fish higher in the food chain, leading to population decline (Park, 1987).

Fortunately, however, during the 1980s and 1990s rates of acid deposition decreased over large portions of North America (Figure 5.35) and Europe (Stoddart et al., 1999; Cooper and Jenkins, 2003), and some recovery in streams and lakes has resulted. Reversal of acidification, while not

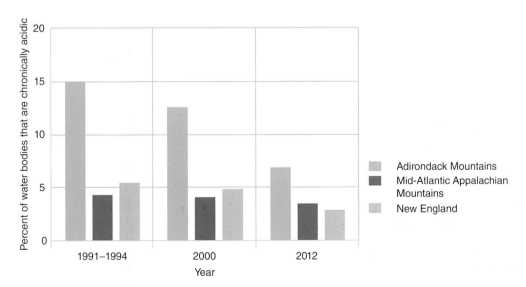

Figure 5.35 Lake and stream acidity in selected acid-sensitive regions in the USA, 1991–2012. *Source:* http://www.epa.gov/roe/lale-stream-acidity_exhibit-1USEPA (accessed January 2018).

universal, has been noted, for example, in the English Lake District (Tipping et al., 2000), in Scandinavia (Fölster and Wilander, 2002), in Finland (Vuorenmaa and Forsius, 2008), in Central Europe (Vesely et al., 2002), and in the English Pennines (Evans and Jenkins, 2000). In Europe, recovery has been strongest in the Czech Republic and Slovakia, moderate in Scandinavia and the UK, and weakest in Germany (Evans et al., 2001). The period required for recovery may in some areas be considerable. In the Adirondacks of the eastern USA recovery may take many decades because, on the one hand, they have been exposed to acid deposition for long periods of time so that they have been relatively depleted of substances that can neutralize acids, and on the other their soils are thin and so can offer less material to neutralize the acid from precipitation (US General Accounting Office, 2000).

5.9 Deforestation and its Effects on Water Quality

The removal of a tree cover not only may affect river flow (Section 5.3.2) and stream-water temperature (Section 5.10), it may also cause changes in stream-water chemistry. The reason for this is that in many forests large quantities of nutrients are cycled through the vegetation, and in some cases (notably in humid tropical rain forest) the trees are a great store of the nutrients. If the trees are destroyed the cycle of nutrients is broken and a major store is disrupted. The nutrients thus released may become available for crops, and shifting cultivators, for example, may utilize this fact and gain good crop yields in the first year after burning and felling forest. Some of the

nutrients may, however, be leached out of the soils, and appear as dissolved load in streams. Large increases in dissolved load may have undesirable effects, including eutrophication, soil salinization, and a deterioration in public water supply.

A classic but, it must be added, extreme exemplification of this is the experiment that was carried out in the Hubbard Brook catchments in New Hampshire, USA (Bormann et al., 1968). These workers monitored the effects of 'savage' treatment of the forest on the chemical budgets of the streams. The treatment was to fell the trees, leave them in place, kill lesser vegetation, and prevent re-growth by the application of herbicide. The effects were dramatic: the total dissolved inorganic material exported from the basin was about fifteen times larger after treatment, and, in particular, there was a very substantial increase (on average fifty times) in stream nitrate concentrations.

It has been argued, however, that the Hubbard Brook results are atypical (Sopper, 1975) because of the severity of the treatment. Most other forest clear-cutting experiments in the US (Table 5.12) indicate that nitrate–nitrogen additions to stream water are not so greatly increased. Under conventional clear-cutting the trees are harvested rather than left, all saleable material is removed, and encouragement is given to the establishment of a new stand of trees. Aubertin and Patric (1974), using such conventional clear-cutting methods rather than the drastic measures employed in Hubbard Brook, found that clear-cutting in their catchments in West Virginia had a negligible effect on stream temperatures (they left a forest strip along the stream), pH, and the concentration of most dissolved solids.

Table 5.12 Nitrate–nitrogen losses from control and disturbed forest ecosystems.

Site	Nature of disturbance	Nitrate-nitrogen loss ($kg\ ha^{-1}\ y^{-1}$)	
		Control	Disturbed
Hubbard Brook	Clear-cutting without vegetation removal, herbicide inhibition of re-growth	2.0	97
Gale River (New Hampshire)	Commercial clear-cutting	2.0	38
Fernow (West Virginia)	Commercial clear-cutting	0.6	3.0
Coweeta (North Carolina)	Complex	0.05	7.3[*]
H.J. Andrews Forest (Oregon)	Clear-cutting with slash-burning	0.08	0.26
Alsea River (Oregon)	Clear-cutting with slash-burning	3.9	15.4
MEAN		1.44	26.83

[*] This value represents the second year of recovery after a long-term disturbance. All other results for disturbed ecosystems reflect the first year after disturbance.

Source: modified after Vitousek et al. (1979).

Even if clear-cutting is practised, there is some evidence of a rapid return to steady-state nutrient cycling because of quick regeneration. Hewlett et al. (1984) found no evidence in the Piedmont region of the USA that clear-cutting would create such extreme nitrate loss that soil fertility would be impaired or water eutrophication caused. They pointed out that rapid growth of vegetation minimizes nutrient losses from the ecosystem by three main mechanisms. It channels water from runoff to evapotranspiration, thereby reducing erosion and nutrient loss; it reduces the rates of decomposition of organic matter through moderation of the microclimate so that the supply of soluble ions for loss in drainage water is reduced; and it causes the simultaneous incorporation of nutrients into the rapidly developing biomass so that they are not lost from the system.

5.10 Thermal Pollution

The pollution of water by increasing its temperature is called thermal pollution. Many organisms are affected by temperature, so this environmental impact has some significance for metabolic rates, physiology, life history traits, nutrient cycling, productivity, and habitat suitability (Langford, 1990; Poole and Berman, 2001). An increase in water temperature causes a decrease in the solubility of oxygen which is needed for the oxidation of biodegradable wastes. At the same time, the rate of oxidation is accelerated, imposing a faster oxygen demand on the smaller supply and thereby depleting the oxygen content of the water still further. Temperature also affects the lower organisms, such as plankton and crustaceans. In general, the more elevated the temperature is, the less desirable the types of algae in water. In cooler waters diatoms are the predominant phytoplankton in water that is not heavily eutrophic; with the same nutrient levels, green algae begin to become dominant at higher temperatures and diatoms decline; at the highest water temperatures, blue-green algae thrive and often develop into heavy blooms. One further ecological consequence of thermal pollution is that the spawning and migration of many fish are triggered by temperature and this behaviour can be disrupted by thermal change, while the temporary shutdown of power plants may create severe cold-shock kills of fish in discharge-receiving waters in winter (Clark, 1977).

In industrial countries probably the main source of thermal pollution is from condenser cooling water released from electricity generating stations. Water discharged from power stations has been heated some 6–9°C, but usually has a temperature of less than 30°C. The extent to which water affects river temperature depends very much on the state of flow. For example, below the Ironbridge power station in England, the Severn River undergoes a temperature increase of only 0.5°C during floods, compared with an 8°C increase at times of low flow (Rodda et al., 1976).

Over the past few decades both the increase in the capacity of individual electricity power-generating units and the improvements in their thermal efficiency have led to a diminution in the heat rejected in relation to the amount of cooling water per unit of production. Economic optimization of the generating plant has cut down the flow of cooling water per unit of electricity, though it has raised its temperature. This increased temperature rise of the cooling water is more than offset by the reduction achieved in the volume of water utilized. Nonetheless, the expansion of generating capacity has meant that the total quantity of heat discharged has increased, even though it is much less than would be expected on a simple proportional basis.

An attempt to assess the global pattern of thermal pollution by power plants has been made by Raptis et al. (2016). They found that of the rivers they analyzed, the Mississippi receives the highest total amount of heat emissions (90% of which come from coal-fuelled and nuclear power plants) and presents the highest number of instances where the commonly set limit of a 3°C temperature increase above natural background levels is equalled or exceeded. The Rhine receives 20% of the thermal emissions compared to the Mississippi, but is the thermally most polluted basin in relation to the total flow per watershed, with one third of its total flow experiencing a temperature increase of >5°C on average over the year. In other smaller basins in Europe, such as the Weser and the Po, the share of the total stream flow with a temperature increase >3°C goes up to 49% and 81% respectively, during July–September.

Thermal pollution of streams may also follow from urbanization (Kinouchi et al., 2007; Hathaway et al., 2016). This results from various sources: wastewater from municipal treatment plants; changes in the temperature regime of streams brought about by reservoirs according to their size, their depth, and the season; changes produced by the urban heat island effect (see Section 7.11) and the spread of paved surfaces (Herb et al., 2008); changes in the configuration of urban channels (for example, their width–depth ratio); changes in the degree of shading of the channel, either by covering it over or by removing natural vegetation cover (Hester and Doyle, 2011); changes in the volume of storm runoff; reduction in flow because of water withdrawals; and changes in the ground-water contribution. Impervious surfaces with high sun exposure draining directly via overland flow to surface waters may be the most detrimental to stream ecology in terms of acute exposure prior to in-stream mixing (Jones et al., 2012; Somers et al., 2013). Pluhowski (1970) found that the basic effects of cities on river-water temperatures on Long Island, New York, was to raise temperatures in summer (by as much as 5–8°C) and to lower then in winter (by as much as 1.5–3.9°C).

In rural areas human activities can also cause significant modifications in river-water temperature. Deforestation is especially important (Lynch et al., 1984). Swift and Messer (1971), for example, examined stream temperature measurements during six forest-cutting experiments on small basins in the southern Appalachians, USA. They found that with complete cutting, because of shade removal, the maximum stream temperatures in summer went up from 19 to 23°C. Likewise, in Wales Stott and Marks (2000) found that after clear felling summer temperatures in a catchment were as much as 7°C higher than they had been under plantation forest.

Reservoir construction can also affect stream-water temperatures. Crisp (1977) established, for example, that as a result of the construction of a reservoir at Cow Green (Upper Teesdale, northern England) the temperature of the river downstream was modified. He noted a reduction in the amplitude of annual water-temperature fluctuations, and a delay in the spring rise of water temperature by 20–50 days, and in the autumn fall by up to 20 days. In the Ebro valley of Spain, Prats et al. (2010) found that as a result of reservoir construction and emissions of warm water from a nuclear plant, an increase in mean annual water temperature of 2.3°C occurred.

5.11 Pollution with Suspended Sediments

Probably the most important effect that humans have had on water quality is the contribution to levels of suspended sediments in streams (Section 6.7). This is a theme which is intimately tied up with that of soil erosion, on the one hand, and with channel manipulation by activities such as reservoir construction, on the other. The clearance of forest, the introduction of ploughing and grazing by domestic animals, the construction of buildings, and the introduction of spoil materials into rivers by mineral extraction industries, have all led to very substantial increases in levels of stream turbidity. Frequently sediment levels are a whole order of magnitude higher than they would have been under natural conditions. However, the introduction of soil conservation measures, or a reduction in the intensity of land use, or the construction of reservoirs, can cause a relative (and sometimes absolute) reduction in sediment loads.

5.12 Marine Pollution

The subject of marine pollution has been well reviewed by Clark (2001) and Weis (2015). At first sight, as Jickells et al. (1991: 313) pointed out, two contradictory thoughts may cross our minds on this issue:

> The first is the observation of ocean explorers, such as Thor Heyerdahl, of lumps of tar, flotsam and jetsam, and other products of human society thousands of kilometres from inhabited land. An alternative, vaguer feeling is that given the vastness of the oceans (more than 1,000 billion billion litres of water!), how can man have significantly polluted them?

What is the answer to this conundrum? Jickells et al. (1991: 330) drew a clear distinction between the open oceans and regional seas and in part come up with an answer:

> The physical and chemical environment of the open oceans has not been greatly affected by events over the past 300 years, principally because of their large diluting capacity … Material that floats and is therefore not diluted, such as tar balls and litter, can be shown to have increased in amount and to have changed in character over the past 300 years.

In contrast to the open oceans, coastal areas (including estuaries) in close proximity to large concentrations of people show evidence of increasing concentrations of various substances that are almost certainly linked to human activities (Howarth et al., 2011). This has produced what have been termed 'dead zones' (Diaz and Rosenberg, 2008). Thus the partially enclosed North Sea and Baltic (Conley et al., 2011) show increases in phosphate concentrations as a result of discharges of sewage and agriculture. The same is true of the more enclosed Black Sea (Mee, 1992). The Mediterranean also suffers from many threats, including over-fishing, species invasion, aquaculture, increased sedimentation, and pollution from growing urban centres and from intensive agriculture (Claudet and Fraschetti, 2010). Chesapeake Bay (Kemp et al., 2005) and the Gulf of Mexico are other examples (Kemp et al., 2005).

On a global basis, organic point source pollution has been identified as one of the greatest threats (Halpern et al., 2007). This can cause accelerated eutrophication – often called 'cultural eutrophication' – which can lead to excessive growths of algae and to hypoxia (Selman et al., 2008; Zhang et al., 2010d). Coastal and estuary water are sometimes affected by algal foam and scum, often called 'red tides'. Some of these blooms are so toxic that consumers of seafood that have been exposed to them can be affected by diarrhoea, sometimes fatally. A thorough analysis of eutrophication in Europe's coastal waters is provided by the European Environment Agency (2001). The nature of red tides has been discussed by Anderson (1994), who points out that these blooms, produced by certain types of phytoplankton (tiny pigmented plants), can grow in such abundance that they change the colour of the sea water not only red but also brown or even green. They may be sufficiently toxic to kill marine animals such as fish and seals. Long-term studies at the local and regional level in many parts of the world suggest that these so-called red tides are increasing in extent and frequency as coastal pollution worsens and nutrient enrichment occurs more often. For example, Figure 5.36 shows the trend in the number of harmful algal blooms that have occurred in the East China Sea. There were 10 in 1993 and 86 in 2003. This is largely a consequence of a huge increase in the application of fertilizer in the catchments that drain into the sea.

Eutrophication also has adverse effects on coral reefs, as explained by Weber (1993: 49):

> Initially, coral productivity increases with rising nutrient supplies. At the same time, however, corals are losing their key advantage over other organisms: their symbiotic self-sufficiency in nutrient poor seas. As eutrophication progresses, algae start to win out over corals for newly opened spaces on the reef because they grow more rapidly than corals when fertilized. The normally clear waters cloud as phytoplankton begin to multiply, reducing the intensity of the sunlight reaching the corals, further lowering their ability to compete. At a certain point, nutrients in the surrounding waters begin to overfertilize the corals' own zooxanthellae, which multiply to toxic levels inside the polyps.

Eutrophication may also lead to black band and white band disease, two deadly coral disorders thought to be caused by algal infections. Through these stages of eutrophication, the health and diversity of reefs declines, potentially leading to death.

Hypoxia in tropical waters may be an under-reported but severe threat to coral reefs (Altieri et al., 2017).

Likewise it is clear that pollution in the open ocean is, as yet, of limited biological significance. GESAMP (1990), an authoritative review of the state of the marine environment for the United Nations Environment Programme, reported (p. 1):

> The open sea is still relatively clean. Low levels of lead, synthetic organic compounds and artificial radionuclides, though widely detectable, are biologically insignificant. Oil slicks and litter are common along sea lanes, but are, at present, of minor consequence to communities of organisms living in open-ocean waters.

On coastal waters it reported (p. 1):

> The rate of introduction of nutrients, chiefly nitrates but sometimes also phosphates, is increasing, and areas of eutrophication are expanding, along with enhanced frequency and scale of unusual plankton blooms and excessive seaweed growth. The two major sources of nutrients to coastal waters are sewage disposal and agricultural run-off from fertilizer-treated fields and from intensive stock raising.

Attention is also drawn to the presence of synthetic organic compounds – chlorinated hydrocarbons – which build up in the fatty tissues of top predators such as seals

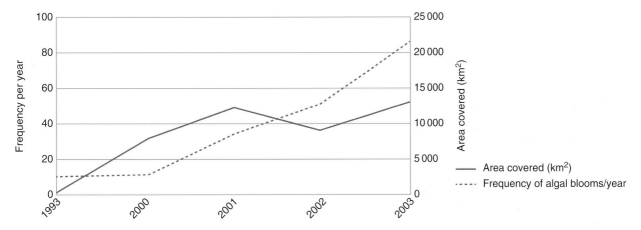

Figure 5.36 The number of harmful algal blooms in the East China Sea. *Source:* adapted from Geo4, UNEP (2007: figure 4.9).

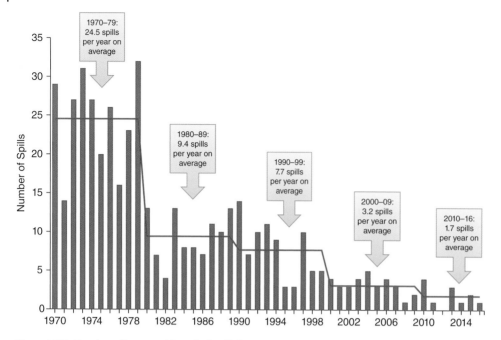

Figure 5.37 Number of large accidental oil spills from tankers, combined carriers and barges (over 700 tonnes) from 1970 to 2016. *Source:* http://www.itopf.com/knowledge-resources/data-statistics/statistics/) (accessed January 2018). Reproduced with permission from International Tanker Owners Pollution Federation.

which dwell in coastal waters. Levels of contamination are decreasing in northern temperate areas but rising in tropical and subtropical areas due to continued use of chlorinated pesticides there.

The world's oceans have been greatly contaminated by oil. The effects of this pollution on animals have been widely studied. The sources of pollution include tanker collisions with other ships, the explosion of individual tankers because of the build-up of gas levels, the wrecking of tankers on coasts through navigational or mechanical failure, seepage from offshore oil installations, the flushing of tanker holds, and explosive releases from offshore drilling rigs. There is no doubt that the great bulk of the oil and related materials polluting the oceans results from human action, though humans should not be attributed with all the blame, for natural seepages are reasonably common. Paradoxically, human actions mean that many natural seepages have diminished as wells have drawn down the levels of hydrocarbons in the oil-bearing rocks. Likewise, the flow of asphalt that once poured from the Trinidad Pitch Lake into the Gulf of Paria has also ceased because mining of the asphalt has lowered the lake below its outlet.

Of the various serious causes of oil pollution, a more important mechanism than the much-publicized role of tanker accidents is the discharge of the ballast water taken into empty tankers to provide stability on the return voyage to the loading terminal. It is in this field, however, that technical developments have led to most amelioration. For example, the quantity of oil in tanker ballast water has been drastically reduced by the LOT (load on top) system, in which the ballast water is allowed to settle so that the oil rises to the surface. The tank is then drained until only the surface oil in the tank remains, and this forms part of the new cargo. In the future large tankers will be fitted with separate ballast tanks not used for oil cargoes, called segregated or clean ballast systems. Given such advances it appears likely than an increasing proportion of oil pollution will be derived from accidents involving tankers of ever-increasing size. The spills from the *Atlantic Empress* (1979, off Tobago), the *ABT Summer* (1991, off Angola), the *Castilo de Bellver* (1983, off South Africa), and the *Amoco Cadiz* (1978, off Brittany) all exceeded 200,000 tonnes of oil. Even here, however, some progress has been made. Since 1980 there has been a reduction in the number of major oil spills, partly as a consequence of diminished long-distance oil transport to Western Europe (Figure 5.37).

The increasing exploitation of offshore oil reserves, some of them located in deep waters, has created a new dimension with regard to oil pollution. This was brought out very clearly in April, 2010, when a rig, the *Deepwater Horizon*, exploded in the Gulf of Mexico and released huge amounts of oil, some of which reached the coastlines of Louisiana, Florida, and other states bordering the Gulf. This, however, was not a unique event (Jernelöv, 2010).

There are various reasons for a concern about some emerging issues relating to marine pollution. Weis (2015) lists accumulation of pharmaceuticals and personal care products (PPCPs), flame retardants called polybrominated diphenyl ethers (PBDEs), fluorinated compounds that are produced to resist heat, oil, stains, grease, and water, alkylphenols used in the production of detergents and other cleaning products, mineral nanoparticles, noise, and light. A further threat that is attracting increasing attention is the pollution of the marine environment by plastic debris (Derraik, 2002; Moore, 2008; Barnes et al., 2009; Goldstein et al., 2012). Even on the most remote islands, like Henderson Island in the mid-Pacific, plastic debris is present in unpleasantly large quantities. This threatens marine life due to ingestion and due to entanglement (especially in discarded fishing gear). Some plastics contain polychlorinated biphenyls (PCBs), which can lead, *inter alia*, to reproductive disorders and death. Drift plastics can also provide a platform for invasive species. Another topic of current debate is the extent to which new technologies and pressures, including ocean acidification (see Section 9.9), may begin to impact on the 'Last Great Wilderness', the deep recesses of the oceans (Ramirez-Llodra et al., 2011).

To conclude, Rice et al. (2016) recognized the following as some of the main types of human impacts on the world's oceans (http://www.un.org/depts/los/global_reporting/WOA_RPROC/Chapter_54.pdf, accessed January 2018):

(a) Climate change (and ocean acidification, including the resulting changes in salinity, sea-level, ocean heat content and sea-ice coverage, reduction in oxygen content, changes in ultra-violet radiation); (b) Human-induced mortality and physical disturbance of marine biota (such as capture fisheries, including by-catch), other forms of harvesting, accidental deaths such as through collisions and entanglement in discarded nets, disturbance of critical habitat, including breeding and nursery areas); (c) Inputs to the ocean (these can be broken down according to the nature of their effects: toxic substances and endocrine disruptors, waterborne pathogens, radioactive substances, plastics, explosives, excessive nutrient loads, hydrocarbons). Remobilization of past inputs also needs to be considered; (d) Demand for ocean space and alteration, or increase in use, of coasts and seabed (conflicting demands lead to both changes in human use of the ocean and changes to marine habitats); (e) Underwater noise (from shipping, sonar, and seismic surveys); (f) Interference with migration from structures in the sea or other changes in routes along coasts or between parts of the sea and/or inland waters (for example, wind-farms, causeways, barrages, major canals, coast reinforcement, etc.); and (g) Introduction of non-native species.

Guide to Reading

Alley, W.M. and Alley, R. (2017) *High and Dry: Meeting the Challenges of the World's Growing Dependence on Groundwater.* New Haven, CT: Yale University Press. A very readable account of how groundwater is being depleted around the world.

Clark, R.B. (2001) *Marine Pollution* (5th edn). Oxford: Oxford University Press. The standard work on this important topic.

Downs, P.W. and Gregory, K.J. (2004) *River Channel Management.* London: Arnold. A comprehensive treatment of river channels, human impacts, and river system management techniques.

Gleick, P.H. (ed.) (1993) *Water in Crisis: A Guide to the World's Freshwater Resources.* New York: Oxford University Press. A compendium of information on trends in water quality and consumption.

Kabat, P. and 9 others (eds) (2004) *Vegetation, Water, Humans and Climate.* Berlin: Springer. A high-level research collection that investigates in particular the effects of vegetation change on climate and hydrological processes.

Laffoley, D. and Baxter, J.M. (eds) (2016) *Explaining Ocean Warming: Causes, Scale, Effects and Consequences.* Gland, Switzerland: IUCN. A major discussion of the various threats facing the world's oceans, including climate change.

Petts, G.E. (1985) *Impounded Rivers: Perspectives for Ecological Management.* Chichester: Wiley. A treatment of the many consequences of dam construction.

Weis, J.S. (2015) *Marine Pollution: What Everyone Needs to Know.* Oxford: Oxford University Press. A highly accessible treatment of all aspects of marine pollution.

6

Human Agency in Geomorphology

CHAPTER OVERVIEW

Humans create a whole suite of landforms deliberately through excavation, construction, and dumping. However, there are also the many incidental consequences of human activities, including ground subsidence, earthquake activity, accelerated erosion and sedimentation, river channel changes, changes in the weathering environment, acceleration and triggering of mass movements, and coastal erosion and deposition.

6.1   Introduction

The human role in creating landforms and modifying the operation of geomorphological processes such as weathering, erosion, and deposition is a theme of great importance though one that, particularly in the Western world, has not received the attention it deserves.

The range of the human impacts on both forms and processes is considerable (Nir, 1983; Syvitski and Kettner, 2011; Goudie and Viles, 2016). In Table 6.1 there is a list of some anthropogenic landforms together with some of the causes of their creation. There are very few spheres of human activity which do not, even indirectly, create landforms (Szabó et al. 2010), and landform changes in the Anthropocene in the UK have, for instance, been considerable (Zalasiewicz et al., 2018). It is, however, useful to recognize that some features are produced by *direct* anthropogenic processes (Table 6.2). These tend to be more obvious in their form and origin and are frequently created deliberately and knowingly. They include landforms produced by constructional activity (such as tipping), excavation (Figure 6.1), travel, hydrological interference, and farming. Hillsides have been terraced in many parts of the world for many centuries to enable cultivation on steep slopes, notably in the arid and semi-arid highlands of the New World (Donkin, 1979; Denevan, 2001), but examples are also known from southern England, where in Roman and Medieval times *strip lynchets* have been produced by ploughing on steep slopes (Figure 6.2). Some terrace features have been built since the Neolithic for the control and harvesting of flood waters, as in the Near East (Bruins, 2012; Beckers et al., 2013). At the present time, some traditional systems are being abandoned as people move to the cities, as in Peru (Inbar and Llerena, 2000) and around the Mediterranean (Tarolli et al., 2014). A very special type of terrace occurs along the Pacific Northwest coast of North America, where rock-walled beach terraces locally known as 'clam gardens' are evidence of an ancient system of cultivation of clams and other marine resources. Coastal First Nations constructed rock walls in the lowest intertidal zone to trap loose sediments, thus creating or expanding clam habitat and increasing bivalve production (Neudorf et al., 2017).

Landforms produced by *indirect* anthropogenic processes are often less easy to recognize, not least because they tend to involve, not the operation of a new process or processes, but the acceleration of natural processes. They are the result of environmental changes brought about inadvertently by human technology. Nonetheless, it is probably this indirect and inadvertent modification of process and form which is the most crucial aspect of anthropogeomorphology (a term introduced by Golomb and Eder, 1964). By removing natural vegetation cover – through the agency of cutting, burning, and grazing (see Trimble and Mendel, 1995) – humans have accelerated erosion and sedimentation. Sometimes the results will be obvious, for example when major gully systems rapidly develop; other results may have less immediate effect on landforms but are, nevertheless, of great importance.

Human Impact on the Natural Environment: Past, Present and Future, Eighth Edition. Andrew S. Goudie.
© 2019 John Wiley & Sons Ltd. Published 2019 by John Wiley & Sons Ltd.
Companion website: www.wiley.com/go/goudie/human-impact-natural-environment

Table 6.1 Some anthropogenic landforms.

Feature	Cause
Banks along roads	Noise abatement
Canals	Transport, irrigation
City mounds (*tells*)	Human occupation
Craters	War, *qanat* construction
Cuttings and sunken lanes	Transport
Dikes, polders	River and coast management
Embankments	Transport, river, and coast management
Moats	Defence
Mounds	Defence, memorials
Norfolk Broads	Peat extraction
Pits and ponds	Mining, marling, cattle pens (*sirikwa*), clam ponds
Plains	Mountaintop removal
Reservoirs	Water management, cooling basins
Ridge and furrow	Agriculture
Spoil heaps	Mining, waste disposal
Subsidence depressions	Mineral and water extraction
Terracing, lynchets	Agriculture

Table 6.2 Major anthropogeomorphic processes.

Direct anthropogenic processes

Constructional
  Tipping, molding, plowing, terracing, reclamation, land creation
Excavational
  digging, cutting, mining, blasting of cohesive or non-cohesive materials, cratering, tramping, churning, trawling of sea bed
Hydrological interference
  flooding, damming, canal construction, dredging, channel modification, draining, coastal protection

Indirect anthropogenic processes

Acceleration of erosion and sedimentation
  agricultural activity and clearance of vegetation, engineering, especially road construction and urbanization
  incidental modifications of hydrological regime
Subsidence: collapse, settling
  mining (e.g. of coal and salt)
  hydraulic (e.g. groundwater and hydrocarbon pumping)
  thermokarst (melting of permafrost)
  changes in organic soils
Slope failure: landslides, flows, accelerated creep
  loading
  undercutting
  shaking
  lubrication

Table 6.2 (Continued)

Earthquake generation
  loading (reservoirs)
  lubrication (fault plane)
  fracking
Weathering
  acidification of precipitation
  accelerated salinization
  lateritization
  podzolization

Figure 6.1 The Rössing uranium mine near Swakopmund in Namibia, southern Africa. The excavation of such mines involves the movement of prodigious amounts of material (ASG).

By other indirect means humans may create subsidence features and hazards, trigger off mass movements like landslides, and even influence the operation of phenomena like earthquakes.

Finally there are situations where, through a lack of understanding of the operation of processes and the links between different processes and phenomena, humans may deliberately and directly alter landforms and processes and thereby set in train a series of events which were not anticipated or desired. There are, for example, many records of attempts to reduce coast erosion by expensive engineering solutions, which, far from solving erosion problems, only exacerbated them (Section 6.14).

6.2 Landforms Produced by Excavation

Of the landforms produced by direct anthropogenic processes those resulting from excavation are widespread, and may have some antiquity. Canals have been dug for irrigation and other purposes in areas like Mesopotamia, since six thousand years ago, and more recently, canals have been used to link up seaways. Neolithic peoples in the Breckland of East Anglia in

Figure 6.2 Strip lynchets in south Dorset, England. *Source:* © 2016 Google.

England used antler picks and other means to dig a remarkable cluster of deep pits in the chalk. The purpose of this was to obtain good-quality non-frost-shattered flint to make stone tools. In many parts of Britain chalk has also been excavated to provide marl for improving acidic, light, sandy soils, and Prince (1962, 1964) made a study of the 27,000 pits and ponds in Norfolk that have resulted mainly from this activity – an activity particularly prevalent in the eighteenth century. Very large numbers of marl pits, dating to the Iron Age and the Roman period, are also found in north-eastern France (Etienne et al., 2011).

It is often difficult in individual cases to decide whether the depressions are the results of human intervention, for solutional and periglacial depressions are often evident in the same area, but pits caused by human action do tend to have some distinctive features: irregular shape, a track leading into them, proximity to roads, etc. (see the debate between Prince, 1979, and Sperling et al., 1979). Difficulties of identifying the true origin of excavational features were also encountered in explaining the Broads, a group of twenty-five fresh-water lakes in the county of Norfolk in eastern England. They are of sufficient area and depth for early workers to have precluded a human origin. Later it was proposed instead that they were natural features caused by uneven alluviation and siltation of river valleys which were flooded by the rapidly rising sea-level of the Holocene (Flandrian) transgression. It was postulated by Jennings (1952) that the Broads were initiated as a series of discontinuous natural lakes, formed beyond the limits of a thick estuarine clay wedge laid down in Romano-British times by a transgression of the sea over earlier valley peats. The waters of the Broads were thought to have been impounded in natural peaty hollows between the flanges of the clay and the marginal valley slopes, or in tributary valleys whose mouths were blocked by the clay.

It is now clear, however, that the Broads are the result of human work (Lambert et al., 1970). Some of them have rectilinear and steep boundaries, most of them are not mentioned in early topographic books, and archival records indicate that peat-cutting (*turbary*) was widely practised in the area. On these and other grounds it is believed that peat-diggers, before AD 1300, excavated 25.5 million m^3 of peat and so created the depressions in which the lakes have formed. The flooding may have been aided by sea-level change. Comparably extensive peat excavation was also carried on in the Netherlands, notably in the fifteenth century.

Other excavational features result from war, especially craters caused by bomb or shell impact. Regrettably, human power to create such forms is increasing. It has been calculated (Westing and Pfeiffer, 1972) that between 1965 and 1971, 26 million craters, covering an area of 171,000 ha, were produced by bombing in Indo-China. This represents a total displacement of no less than 2.6 billion m^3 of earth, a figure much greater than calculated as being involved in the peaceable creation of the Netherlands. Hupy and Schaetzl (2006) and Hupy and Koehler (2012) have coined the term 'bombturbation' to describe the process of land disturbance caused by explosive munitions.

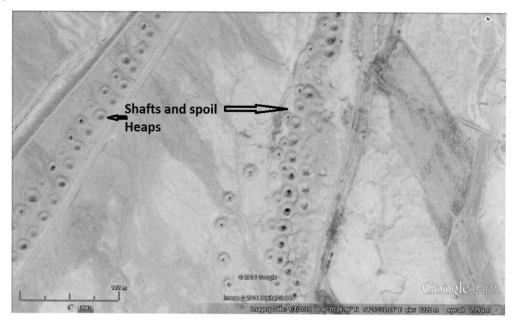

Figure 6.3 Qanat in Iran. *Source:* © 2016 Google, © 2016 DigitalGlobe. Scale bar 122m.

In drylands in various parts of the world, large tunnels and shafts have been constructed since as early as 2700 years ago to capture groundwater for irrigation (Wilkinson, 1977). In Iran some shafts are 100–120 m deep and the tunnels may run as far as 40–50 km. These remarkable structures are called *falaj* in Oman and *foggara* in North Africa (Figure 6.3). In some locations, because of the lowering of the water table by modern systems of pumping they are in decline (Remini et al., 2011).

Some excavation is undertaken on a large scale for purely aesthetic reasons, when nature offends the eye (Prince, 1959), while in many countries where land is scarce whole hills are levelled and extensive areas stripped to provide fill for harbour reclamation. One of the most spectacular examples of this kind was the deliberate removal of steep-sided hills in the centre of Brazil's Rio de Janeiro, for housing development. A more specialized excavational activity is the removal of limestone pavements – areas of exposed limestone in northern England which were stripped by glaciers and then moulded into bizarre shapes by solutional activity – for ornamental rock gardens (Ward, 1979). In East Africa there are some large depressions that were created as cattle pens – the *sirikwa* (Sutton, 1965).

One of the most important causes of excavation is mineral extraction (Figure 6.4), producing open-pit mines, strip mines, quarries for structural materials, borrow pits along roads, and similar features. Of these, the environmental devastation produced by strip mining is exceptional, especially in Pennsylvania, Ohio, West

Virginia, Kentucky, and Illinois (Miller, et al., 2014) and can lead to changes in water quality and river channel forms (Jaeger, 2015). Oil shales, a potential source of oil that at present is relatively untapped, can be exploited by open-pit mining, by traditional room and pillar mining, and by underground *in situ* pyrolysis. Vast reserves exist (as in Alberta, Canada) but the amount of excavation required will probably be about three times the amount of oil produced (on a volume basis), suggesting that the extent of both the excavation and subsequent dumping of overburden and waste will be considerable. Huge pits

Figure 6.4 The mining of sand from large linear sand dunes to provide material for the construction industry in Dubai, United Arab Emirates (ASG).

are associated with some mines. The Bingham Canyon mine in Utah, USA, is more than 1.2 km deep and 4 km wide.

Dredging to improve harbours and navigation is another type of excavation. It has a long history, particularly in the Mediterranean, where at locations like Naples and Marseille it dates back to Romano-Byzantine times (Marriner et al., 2017).

An early attempt to provide a general picture of the importance of excavation in the creation of the landscape of Britain was given by Sherlock (1922). He estimated (Table 6.3) that up until the time in which he wrote, human society had excavated around 31 billion m³ of material in the pursuit of its economic activities. That figure must now be a gross underestimate, partly because Sherlock himself was not in a position to appreciate the anthropogenic role in creating features like the Norfolk Broads, and partly because, since his time, the rate of excavation has greatly accelerated. Sherlock's 1922 study covers a period when earth-moving equipment was still ill-developed. Nonetheless, on the basis of his calculations, he was able to state that 'at the present time, in a densely peopled country like England, Man is many times more powerful, as an agent of denudation, than all the atmospheric denuding forces combined' (p. 333). The most notable change since Sherlock wrote has taken place in the production of aggregates for concrete. Demand for these materials in the UK grew from 20 million tonnes per annum in 1900 to 202 million tonnes in 2001, a tenfold increase. Douglas and Lawson (2001) estimated that in Britain the total deliberate shift of earth-surface materials is between 688 and 972 million tonnes per year, depending on whether or not the replacement of overburden in opencast mining is taken into account.

Hooke (1994) produced some data on the significance of deliberate human earthmoving actions in the United States and globally and these are shown in Table 6.4. In all he calculates that deliberate human earth moving causes 30 billion metric tonnes to be moved per year on a global basis. Douglas and Lawson (2001) gave a rather larger figure – 57 Gt per year. It has been estimated that the amount of sediment carried into the ocean by the world's rivers each year amounts to between 8.3 and 51.1 Gt per year (Walling, 2006). Thus the amount of material moved by humans is rather greater than that moved by the world's rivers to the oceans. Price et al. (2011: 1056) remarked that over the last 200 years, people in Britain 'have excavated, moved and built up the equivalent of at least six times the volume of Ben Nevis'. As technology changes, this ability increases still further (Haff, 2010). Furthermore, land-use change, and in particular the development of agriculture, has caused a leap in the amount of erosion of the world's land surfaces. Wilkinson and McElroy (2007) calculated that 'natural' sediment fluxes to the world's rivers are about 21 Gt/yr, and that 'anthropogenic' losses may be around 75Gt/yr.

Table 6.3 Total excavation of material in Great Britain until 1922.

Activity	Approximate volume (m³)
Docks and harbours	77,000,000
Foundations of buildings and street excavation	385,000,000
Manchester Ship Canal	41,154,000
Mines	15,147,000,000
Other canals	153,800,000
Quarries and pits	11,920,000000
Railways	2,331,000,000
Road cuttings	480,000,000
TOTAL	30,534,954,000

Source: Sherlock (1922: 86).

Table 6.4 Humans as earthmovers.

Omitting the indirect effects of actions such as deforestation and cultivation, the following are the magnitudes of deliberate human earthmoving actions in the United States.

	Billion metric tonnes per year
Excavation for housing and other construction	0.8
Mining	3.8
Road work	3.0
Total United States	7.6
World total (roughly four times the US total)	30.0

For comparison, the following figures represent estimated world totals due to natural earthmoving processes.

River transport	
• to oceans and lakes	14
• short-distance transport within river basins	40
Tectonic forces lifting continents	14
Volcanic activity elevating sea floor	30
Glacial transport	4.3
Wind transport	1.0

Source: Hooke (1994). Reproduced with permission of USA Today.

6.3 Landforms Produced by Construction and Dumping

The construction of mounds and embankments and the creation of dry land where none previously existed is longstanding. In the Middle East and other areas where human urban settlement dates back a long way, including Bulgaria, Hungary, Greece, Turkey, the Middle East, North Africa, and South Asia, the accumulated debris of life has gradually raised the level of the land surface, and occupation mounds (*tells*) (Menze and Ur, 2012). In many coastal areas (and to a lesser extent along some lakes and rivers) shell or kitchen middens occur as mounds consisting of discarded seafood waste (Erlandson, 2013). Accumulation of waste means that the land surface may build up over time. Price et al. (2011) suggested that in north-west England, in industrial Salford and Manchester, as much as 10 m of artificial ground had been produced, while in Italy the city of Pisa is built on a debris mound that is some 4 m high (Bini et al., 2017).

In southern England the 37-metre-high mound at Silbury Hill dates back to the Neolithic, while the pyramids of Central America, Egypt, and the Far East are even more spectacular early feats of landform creation. Likewise in the Americas Native Indians, prior to the arrival of Europeans, created large numbers of mounds of different shapes and sizes for temples, burials, settlement, and effigies (Denevan, 1992: 377). Burial mounds (tumuli and barrows) and hill forts, of which there are more than 4000 in the UK, are other prominent landscape features that date back to prehistoric times. In the same way, hydrological management has involved, over many centuries, the construction of massive banks and walls – the ultimate result being the landscape of the present-day Netherlands. Transport developments have also required the creation of large constructional landmarks, but probably the most important features are those resulting from the dumping of waste materials, especially those derived from mining. It has been calculated that there are at least 2000 million tonnes of shale lying in pit heaps in the coalfields of Britain (Richardson, 1976). Today, with the technical ability to build that humans have, even estuaries may be converted from ecologically productive environments into suburban sprawl by the processes of dredging and filling. Indeed, one of the striking features of the distribution of the world's population is the tendency for large human concentrations to occur near vast expanses of water. Many of these cities have extended out on to land that has been reclaimed from the sea (for example, Hong Kong, Figure 6.5a, and Bahrain, Figure 6.5b), thereby providing valuable sites for development, but sometimes causing the loss of rich fishing grounds and ecologically valuable wetlands. In the Middle East, large artificial islands have been built (i.e. off Dubai, Ras Al Khaimah, Bahrain, and Qatar), and artificial reefs, which are submerged structures constructed on the seabed to help fisheries, protect coasts, and provide improved conditions for divers and surfers, are proliferating (Baine, 2001; Perkol-Finkel et al., 2006). Embankments and levées have been constructed along many rivers, often for flood protection, and some, as in the Indus Valley, date back to the Harappan Civilization c. 4600 years ago.

At the present time, large quantities of waste are sent to landfill sites. In 1995, member states of the European Union (EU) landfilled more than 80% of their waste, but under the EU Landfill Directive this figure has been reduced substantially to around 37% in 2010. Germany, Austria, Sweden, and Belgium send less than 1% of their waste to landfill, but Latvia, Lithuania, Bulgaria, and Romania still send over 90%.

Many of the features created by excavation in one generation are filled in by another, since phenomena like water-filled hollows produced by mineral extraction are often both wasteful of land and also suitable locations for the receipt of waste. Watson (1976), for example, mapped the distribution of hollows, which were largely created by marl diggers in the lowlands of south-west Lancashire and north-west Cheshire, as they were represented on mid-nineteenth-century topographic maps (Figure 6.6a). When this distribution is compared with the present-day distribution for the same area (Figure 6.6b), it is evident that a very substantial proportion of the holes have been filled in and obliterated by humans, with only 2114 out of 5380 remaining. The densities of holes have fallen from 121 to 47 per km^2. The loss of ponds in Great Britain has been a fairly general phenomenon, with their numbers falling from c. 800,000 in the late nineteenth century to only c. 200,000 by the mid-1980s (Jeffries, 2012). Since that time, partly because their biodiversity value is now being appreciated, the number of ponds in Great Britain has shown a modest increase (Williams et al., 2010).

6.4 Ground Subsidence

Not all ground subsidence is caused by humans. For example, limestone solution can, in the absence of humankind, create a situation where a cavern collapses to produce a surface depression or sinkhole, and permafrost will sometimes melt to produce a thermokarst depression without human intervention. Similarly, deltaic subsidence can be caused by a whole range of natural processes. In the case of the Mississippi Delta of the USA, for instance, six categories of process have been identified (Yuill et al., 2009) that can cause subsidence, four of

Figure 6.5 (a) Map of Hong Kong showing main urban reclamation areas. (b) The coastline of northern Bahrain in 2005 (top) and 2016 (bottom). *Source:* © 2016 Google. Scale bar 8.85 km.

which are natural, including tectonics (faulting and halokinesis), Holocene sediment compaction (Törnquist et al., 2008), sediment loading by the delta, and glacial isostatic adjustment. Fluid removal and surface water drainage and management are the two anthropogenic

processes. Indeed, ground subsidence can be caused or accelerated by humans in a variety of ways (Figure 6.7): by the transfer of subterranean fluids (such as oil, gas, and water); by the removal of solids through underground mining (Bell et al., 2000) or by dissolving solids

Figure 6.6 The distribution of pits and ponds in a portion of north-western England (a) in the mid-nineteenth century, (b) in the mid-twentieth century. *Source:* adapted from Watson (1976).

and removing them in solution (for example, sulphur and salt); by the disruption of permafrost; and by the compaction or reduction of sediments because of drainage and irrigation (Johnson, 1991; Barends et al., 1995).

Some of the most dangerous and dramatic collapses have occurred in limestone areas because of the dewatering of the rock mass by mining activities or groundwater abstraction (Gutiérrez et al., 2014). In the Far West Rand of South Africa, gold mining has required the abstraction of water to such a degree that the local water table has been lowered by more than 300 m. The fall of the water table caused miscellaneous clays and other materials filling the roofs of large caves to dry out and

shrink so that they collapsed into the underlying void. One collapse created a depression 30 m deep and 55 m across, killing 29 people. In Alabama in the southern United States, water-level decline consequent upon pumping has had equally serious consequences in a limestone terrain; and Newton (1976) estimated that since 1900 about 4000 induced sinkholes or related features have been formed, while fewer than 50 natural sinkholes have been reported over the same interval. Sinkholes that may result from such human activity are also found in Georgia, Florida, Tennessee, Pennsylvania, and Missouri. In some limestone areas, however, a reverse process can operate. The application of water to

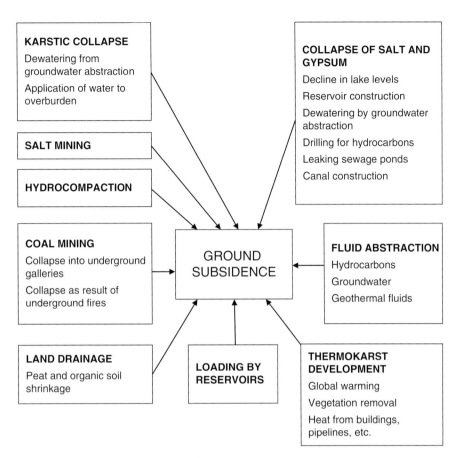

Figure 6.7 The causes of ground subsidence.

overburden above the limestone may render it more plastic so that the likelihood of collapse is increased. Williams (1993) provides a survey of the diverse effects of human activities on limestone terrains.

In areas where thick salt deposits have accumulated as a result of their precipitation in saline lake basins, solution may cause sinkhole development. This is the case in the Dead Sea basin, where the recent decline in level caused by water abstraction has promoted their formation. More than a thousand potentially dangerous sinkholes have opened up along its shorelines since the early 1980s as a result of the flow of under-saturated groundwater dissolving the evaporites (Yechieli et al., 2006). Similar problems have been encountered on the Jordanian side of the Dead Sea, with karstic collapse creating major problems for the chemical plants on the Lisan Peninsula (Closson et al., 2007). Subsidence can be accelerated by the direct solution of susceptible rocks. For example, collapses have occurred in gypsum bedrock because of solution brought about by the construction of a reservoir (Johnson, 2008).

Subsidence produced by oil abstraction is a problem in some parts of the world. The classic area is Los Angeles, where 9.3 m of subsidence occurred as a result of exploitation of the Wilmington oilfield between 1928 and 1971. Likewise, the Inglewood oilfield displayed 2.9 m of subsidence between 1917 and 1963. Some coastal flooding problems occurred at Long Beach because of this process. Similar subsidence has been recorded from the Lake Maracaibo field in Venezuela (Prokopovich, 1972) and from some Russian fields (Nikonov, 1977). Subsidence in the Mississippi Delta and elsewhere in the Gulf Coast region of the USA may be in part the result of hydrocarbon extraction (Morton et al., 2005, 2006). Gas abstraction can also lead to subsidence, as in northeast Italy (Gambolati et al., 1991).

Groundwater abstraction for industrial, domestic, and agricultural purposes is a widespread cause of subsidence. Table 6.5 presents some data from various parts of the world. The ratios of subsidence to water level decline are strongly dependent on the nature of the sediment composing the aquifer. Ratios range from 1:7 for Mexico City, to 1:80 for the Pecos in Texas, and to less than 1:400 for London, England (Rosepiler and Reilinger, 1977; Chi and Reilinger, 1984). In Japan subsidence has also emerged as a major problem (Nakano and Matsuda, 1976). In 1960 only

Table 6.5 Ground subsidence.

Location	Amount (m)	Date	Rate (mm/y)
(a) Ground subsidence produced by oil and gas abstraction			
Azerbaydzhan, USSR	2.5	1912–1962	50
Atravopol, USSR	1.5	1956–1962	125
Wilmington, USA	9.3	1928–1971	216
Inglewood, USA	2.9	1917–1963	63
Maracaibo, Venezuela	5.03	1929–1990	84
(b) Ground subsidence produced by groundwater abstraction			
London, England	0.06–0.08	1865–1931	0.91–1.21
Savannah, Georgia (USA)	0.1	1918–1955	2.7
Mexico City	7.5	–	250–300
Houston, Galveston, Texas	1.52	1943–1964	60–76
Central Valley, California	8.53	–	–
Tokyo, Japan	4	1892–1972	500
Osaka, Japan	>2.8	1935–1972	76
Niigata, Japan	>1.5	–	–
Pecos, Texas	0.2	1935–1966	6.5
South-central Arizona	2.9	1934–1977	96
Bangkok, Thailand	2.05	1933–2002	Up to 120
Shanghai, China	2.62	1921–1965	60

Source: data in Cooke and Doornkamp (1990); Prokopovich (1972); Rosepiler and Reilinger (1977); Holzer (1979); Nutalaya and Rau (1981); Johnson (1991); Phien-wej (2006).

35.2 km^2 of the Tokyo lowland was below sea-level, but continuing subsidence meant that by 1974 this had increased to 67.6 km^2, exposing a total of 1.5 million people to major flood hazard. Shanghai and neighbouring parts of the Yangtze Delta region in China is another low-lying area that has suffered from subsidence, with as much as 2 to 3 m since 1921 (Chai et al., 2004). Similar amounts of subsidence are also known from Tianjin and Xi'an (Xue et al., 2005), but as China develops the amount of subsidence that is occurring is becoming more widespread and over 50 Chinese cities are threatened (Hu, 2006). In Bangkok, subsidence in the early 1980s was proceeding at a rate of as much as 120 mm per year and by 2002 2.05 m of subsidence had occurred (Phien-wej et al., 2006), causing flooding and building damage. Subsidence caused by groundwater and gas abstraction has also been a problem in Venice, where it has greatly increased flood risk, but the rate has fallen since c. 1970 because of controls on this abstraction (Carbognin et al., 2010).

The subsidence caused by mining is perhaps the most familiar, though its importance varies according to such factors as the thickness of seam removed, its depth, the width of working, the degree of filling with solid waste after extraction, the geological structure, and the method of working adopted (Wallwork, 1974). In general terms, however, the vertical displacement by subsidence is less than the thickness of the seam being worked, and decreases with an increase in the depth of mining. This is because the overlying strata collapse, fragment, and fracture, so that the mass of rock fills a greater space than it did when naturally compacted. Consequently the surface expression of deep-seated subsidence may be equal to little more than one-third of the thickness of the material removed. Studies in the Ruhr district of Germany indicate values that can be as high as 5.16 m, though the mean value is 1.6 m (Harnischmacher et al., 2010), while in Polish Silesia up to 30 m of subsidence has occurred (Machowski et al., 2016). Subsidence associated with coal mining may disrupt surface drainage (Sidle et al., 2c000) and the resultant depressions then become permanently flooded. In the Ruhr, a lake, Lake Lanstrop, formed between 1963 and 1967 in response to up to 9 m of subsidence (Bell et al., 2000).

Rock salt extraction also causes serious subsidence. In Cheshire, north-west England, rock salt is extracted from two major seams in the Triassic Mercia Mudstone Group, each about 30 m in thickness (Cooper and Saunders, 2002). Moreover, these seams occur at no great depth – the uppermost being at about 70 m below the surface. A further factor to be considered is that the rock salt is highly soluble in water, so the flooding of mines may cause additional collapse. These three conditions – thick seams, shallow depth, and high solubility – have produced optimum conditions for subsidence and many subsidence lakes called 'flashes' have developed (Wallwork, 1956). In the Perm district of Russia huge sinkholes (up to 200 m deep) have developed in association with phosphate mines.

In some volcanic regions, geothermal water is abstracted for power generation, and associated subsidence has been encountered in New Zealand (Allis et al., 2009), California (Massonnet et al., 1997) and Mexico (Carnec and Fabriol, 1999).

Some subsidence is created by a process called hydro-compaction (Houston et al., 2001), which is explained thus. Moisture-deficient, unconsolidated, low-density sediments tend to have sufficient dry strength to support considerable effective stresses without compacting. However, when such sediments, which may include alluvial fans or loess, are thoroughly wetted for the first time (for example, by percolating irrigation water) the inter-granular strength of the deposits is diminished, rapid compaction takes place, and ground surface subsidence follows. Unequal subsidence can create problems for irrigation schemes.

Land drainage can promote subsidence of a different type, notably in areas of organic soils (see Section 4.15). The lowering of the water table makes peat susceptible to oxidation and deflation so that its volume decreases. A record of this process, and one of the clearest demonstrations of its efficacy, has been provided by the measurements at Holme Fen Post in the English Fenlands (Dawson et al., 2010). Approximately 3.8 m of subsidence occurred between 1848 and 1957 (Fillenham, 1963), with the fastest rate occurring soon after drainage had been initiated (Figure 6.8). At its maximum natural extent the peat covered around 1750 km^2. Now only about one-quarter (430 km^2) remains. Subsidence following drainage of organic soils has also occurred in the Netherlands (Hoogland et al., 2012; Brouns et al., 2015), the Venice region of Italy (Zanello et al., 2011), and in South-East Asia (Hooijer et al., 2012).

A further type of subsidence, sometimes associated with earthquake activity, results from the effects on Earth's crust of large masses of water impounded behind reservoirs. As we shall see later in Section 6.5, seismic effects can be generated in areas with susceptible fault systems and this may account for earthquakes. This process whereby a mass of water causes crustal depression is called hydro-isostasy.

In tundra regions subsidence is associated with thermokarst development, this being irregular, hummocky terrain produced by the melting of ground ice, permafrost (Figure 6.9). The development of thermokarst is due primarily to the disruption of the thermal equilibrium of the permafrost and an increase in the depth of the active layer. This is illustrated in Figure 6.10. The key process involved in thermokarst subsidence is the state of the active layer and its thermal relationships. When, for example, vegetation is cleared for agricultural or constructional purposes the depth of thaw will tend to increase. The clearance of vegetation for seismic lines has also created widespread degradation in Canada and Alaska (Braverman and Quin-

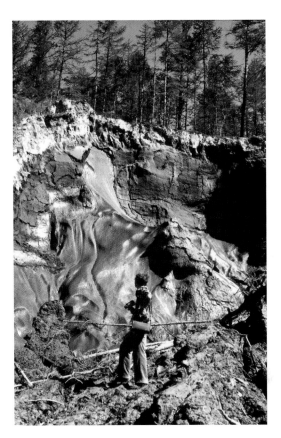

Figure 6.9 Permafrost in Siberia. *Source:* courtesy of the late M.M. Sweeting.

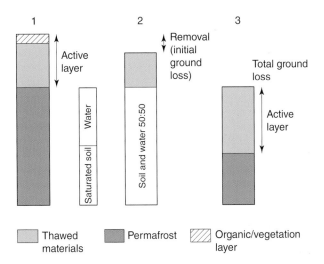

Thawed materials   Permafrost   Organic/vegetation layer

Figure 6.10 Diagram illustrating how the disturbance of high ice content terrain can lead to permanent ground subsidence. 1–3 indicate stages before, immediately after, and subsequent to disturbance. *Source:* after Mackay in French (1976: figure 6.1). Reproduced with permission by Hugh French.

Figure 6.8 The subsidence of the English Fenlands peat in Holme Fen Post from 1842 to 1960 following drainage. *Source:* from data in Fillenham (1963).

ton, 2015). The movement of tracked vehicles has been particularly harmful to surface vegetation and deep channels may soon result from permafrost degradation.

Figure 6.11 The city of Mexico has subsided by many metres as a result of groundwater abstraction. Many of the ancient buildings in the city centre have been severely damaged, and have been cracked and deformed (ASG).

Similar effects may be produced by the siting of heated buildings on permafrost, and by the laying of oil, sewer, and water pipes in or on the active layer.

Thus subsidence is a diverse but significant aspect of the part humans play as geomorphological agents. Among the effects are broken dams, cracked buildings (Figure 6.11), offset roads and railways, fractured well casings, ground fissure development, deformed canals and ditches, bridges that need re-levelling, saline encroachment, and increased flood damage.

6.5 The Human Impact on Seismicity and Volcanoes

The seismic and tectonic forces which mould the relief of the earth and cause such hazards to human civilization are one of the fields in which efforts to control natural events have had least success and where least has been attempted. Nonetheless, the fact that humans have been able, inadvertently, to trigger off small earthquakes by nuclear blasts, as in Nevada, by injecting water into deep wells, as in Colorado, by mining, by building reservoirs, and by

fluid extraction, suggests that in due course it may be possible to 'defuse' earthquakes by relieving tectonic strains gradually in a series of non-destructive, low-intensity earthquakes. One problem, however, is that there is no assurance that an earthquake purposefully triggered by human action will be a small one, or that it will be restricted to a small area. The legal implications are immense.

Perhaps the most important anthropogenically induced seismicity results from the creation of large reservoirs (Guha, 2000; Gupta, 2002; Durá-Gómez and Talwani, 2010). These impose stresses of significant magnitude on crustal rocks at depths rarely equalled by any other human construction. With the ever-increasing number and size of reservoirs the threat rises. There are at least six cases (Koyna, Kremasta, Hsinfengkiang, Kariba, Oroville (California), Hoover, and Marathon) where earthquakes of a magnitude greater than 5, accompanied by a long series of foreshocks and aftershocks, have been related to reservoir impounding. In China there is ongoing debate as to whether the magnitude 7.9 Wenchuan earthquake of 2008, which killed 80,000 people, was triggered by the reservoir behind the 156-metre-high Zipingpu Dam (Qiu, 2012).

As Figure 6.12 shows, there are many more locations where the filling of reservoirs behind dams has led to appreciable levels of seismic activity, though this is often minor. Detailed monitoring has shown that earthquake clusters occur in the vicinity of some dams after their reservoirs have been filled, whereas before construction activity was less clustered and less frequent. Similarly, there is evidence from Vaiont (Italy), Lake Mead (USA), Kariba (Central Africa), Koyna (India), and Kremasta (Greece) of a linear correlation between the storage level in the reservoir and the logarithm of the frequency of shocks.

One reason why dams induce earthquakes is the hydro-isostatic pressure exerted by the mass of the water impounded in the reservoir, together with changing water pressures across the contact surfaces of faults (Qiu and Fenton, 2015). Given that the deepest reservoirs provide surface loads of only 20 bars or so, direct activation by the mass of the impounded water seems an unlikely cause (Bell and Nur, 1978) and the role of changing pore pressure assumes greater importance. Paradoxically, there are some possible examples of reduced seismic activity induced by reservoirs (Milne, 1976). One possible explanation of this is the increased incidence of stable sliding (fault creep) brought about by higher pore-water pressure in the vicinity of the reservoir.

However, the ability to prove an absolutely concrete cause-and-effect relationship between reservoir activity and earthquakes is severely limited by our inability to measure stress below depths of several kilometres, and

Figure 6.12 Worldwide distribution of reservoir-triggered changes in seismicity. *Source:* after Gupta (2002: figure 1). Reproduced with permission from Elsevier.

some examples of induced seismicity may have been built on the false assumption that because an earthquake occurs in proximity to a reservoir it has to be induced by that reservoir (Meade, 1991).

The demonstration that increasing water pressures could initiate small-scale faulting and seismic activity was unintentionally demonstrated near Denver (Evans, 1966), where nerve-gas waste was being disposed of at a great depth in a well in the hope of avoiding contamination of groundwater supplies. The waste was pumped in at high pressures and triggered off a series of earthquakes, the timing of which corresponded very closely to the timing of waste disposal in the well. It is also now thought that the pumping of fluids into the Inglewood oil field, Los Angeles, to raise the hydrostatic pressure and increase oil recovery, may have been responsible for triggering the 1963 earthquake which fractured a wall of the Baldwin Hills Reservoir. It appears that increased fluid pressure reduces the frictional force across the contact surface of a fault, allows slippage to occur, thereby causing an earthquake.

In general earthquake triggering has been related to fluid injection, but for reasons that are still obscure there are many cases where increased seismicity has resulted from fluid abstraction (Segall, 1989). Cases where seismicity and faulting can be attributed to fluid extraction come, for example, from the oilfields of Texas and California and the gas fields of the Po Valley in Italy and of Uzbekistan (Donnely, 2009; Suckale, 2010).

Hough and Page (2016) presented evidence for an association between the initial oil boom in the greater Los Angeles area and earthquakes between 1915 and 1932, including the damaging 22 June 1920 Inglewood and 8 July 1929 Whittier earthquakes. Frohlich et al. (2016) have undertaken an historical analysis of the links between petroleum exploitation and seismic activity in Texas.

Some recent seismic activity may be related to a process called 'hydrofracturing' or 'fracking', whereby water is injected into the rock to create distinct fractures that increase permeability and thus facilitate the extraction of fluids and the production of geothermal energy (Majer et al., 2007). In 2011, test drilling for gas exploitation by fracking in the Blackpool area of north-west England caused some small earthquakes. Seismicity related to fracking is also known from Canada (Atkinson et al., 2015).

Miscellaneous other human activities appear to affect seismic levels. In Johannesburg, South Africa, for example, gold mining and associated blasting activity have produced tens of thousands of small tremors, and there is a notable reduction in the number that occurs on Sundays, a day of rest. In Staffordshire, England, coal mining has caused increased seismic activity and up to a quarter of all earthquakes recorded by the British Geological Survey may be related to coal mining. Seismicity induced by coal mining is also a feature of the Ruhr coalfield in Germany (Bischoff et al., 2009). In the future, seismicity might be induced by underground carbon sequestration projects.

As a result of these various mechanisms, it is now becoming apparent that there is a significantly increased incidence of earthquakes. Ellsworth (2013) reports that the earthquake count in the central and eastern USA has increased dramatically over the last few years and McGarr et al. (2015) have gone so far as to refer to a 'seismic surge'.

When looking at the human impact on volcanic activity human impotence becomes apparent, though some success has been achieved in the control of lava flows. Thus in 1937 and 1947 the US Army attempted to divert lava from the city of Hilo, Hawaii, by bombing threatening flows, while elsewhere, where lava rises in the crater, breaching of the crater wall to direct lava towards uninhabited ground may be possible. In 1973 an attempt was made to halt advance of lava with cold water during the Icelandic eruption of Krikjufell. Using up to 4 million litres of pumped waste per hour, the lava was cooled sufficiently to decrease its velocity at the flow front so that the chilled front acted as a dam to divert the still fluid lava behind (Williams and Moore, 1973). There has also been some success in controlling lava flows from Mount Etna in Sicily using earthen barriers (Barberi et al., 2003).

Both tectonic activity, volcanic eruptions, and tsunami generation may conceivably be affected by anthropogenic climate change (McGuire, 2012). Torrential storms may stimulate earthquake occurrence and the melting of ice caps may stimulate volcanic activity and fault movements as crustal pressures are modified (Tuffen, 2013).

6.6 Accelerated Sedimentation

Land-use changes have a range of impacts on slopes and valleys, though it is not always easy to separate the effects of such changes from those produced by climate change. Among the consequences of land-use change that have been identified in Holocene Britain are slope instability, which leads to gullying and deposition of debris cones and alluvial fans in upland catchments, and colluviation in the lowlands; valley floor sedimentation; increased runoff leading to incision (mainly in upland catchments); and high water tables and flooding (mainly in lowland catchments) (Foulds and Macklin, 2006). That said, one inevitable consequence of the accelerated erosion produced by human activities has been accelerated sedimentation (see, for example, Komar et al.'s 2004 study of sedimentation in Tillamook Bay, Oregon). Some of the eroded material accumulates downslope as colluvium (Verstraeten et al., 2009)

(Figure 6.13a), some on floodplains, some in lakes, and some in estuaries. Ecologically important wetlands can also be threatened by accelerated sedimentation, which causes them to shrink or disappear, as is the case with many small depressions or playas in the Great Plains of the USA (Skagen et al., 2016; Bowen and Johnson, 2017). In some parts of the world, sedimentation has been increased by the deliberate addition of sediments to stream channels as a result of the need to dispose of mining and other wastes.

Before European colonization, there is, according to James (2011) rather sparse evidence of any substantial human geomorphological impacts on erosion and sedimentation in North America, though Wohl et al. (2017b) have made the case that river systems and sediment movement were affected by pre-European inhabitants, through the use of fire and their agricultural activities. However, the situation changed dramatically after European contact. For example, serious sedimentation of bays and estuaries caused by human activity occurred on the eastern coast of America (Gottschalk, 1945). He calculated that at the head of the Chesapeake Bay 65 million m^3 of sediment were deposited between 1846 and 1938. The average depth of water over an area of 83 km^2 was reduced by 0.76 m. New land comprising 318 ha was added to the state of Maryland and, as Gottschalk remarked, 'the Susquehanna River is repeating the history of the Tigris and Euphrates'. The trend in sedimentation rate (Pasternack et al., 2001) over the last three centuries is shown in Figure 6.13b and demonstrates the low rate in pre-European settlement times, the high rates in the mid-nineteenth century at a time of peak deforestation and of intensive agriculture, and the decline that took place in the twentieth century. Salt marshes expanded rapidly as a result of rapid rates of sediment delivery (Kirwan et al., 2011).

Much of the material entrained by erosive processes on upper slopes as a result of agriculture in Maryland, however, was not evacuated as far as the coast. Costa (1975) suggested that only about one-third of it left the river valleys. The remainder accumulated on floodplains as alluvium and colluvium at rates of up to 1.6 cm per year. Similarly, Happ (1944), working in Wisconsin, carried out an intensive augering survey of floodplain soils and established that, since the development of agriculture, floodplain aggradation had proceeded at a rate of approximately 0.85 cm per year. He noted that channel and floodplain aggradation had caused the flooding of low alluvial terraces to be more frequent, more extensive, and deeper. The rate of sedimentation has since declined (Trimble, 1976, 2008a, 2011), because of less intensive land use and the institution of effective erosion control measures on farmland.

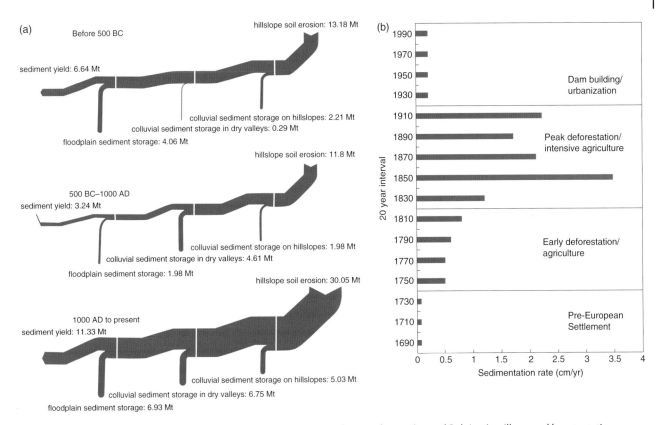

Figure 6.13 (a) Changing sediment dynamics through time in the Nethen catchment (central Belgium) as illustrated by a tentative sediment budget for three different time periods. *Source:* modified from Verstraeten et al. (2009: figure 7). Reproduced with permission from Elsevier. (b) Sedimentation chronology for Chesapeake Bay, USA, for three centuries. *Source:* modified after Pasternack et al. (2001: figure 10). Reproduced with permission from John Wiley & Sons.

Such valley sedimentation is not restricted to the newly settled terrains of North America. There is increasing evidence to suggest that silty valley fills in Germany, France, and Britain, many of them dating back to the Bronze and Iron ages, result from accelerated slope erosion produced by the activities of early farmers (Bell, 1982). Macklin et al. (2014) have used the term 'Anthropocene Alluvium' to describe floodplain sediments that have been generated by human activities. Indeed, in recent years, various studies have been undertaken with a view to assessing the importance of changes in sedimentation rate caused by humans at different times in the Holocene in Britain (e.g. Chiverrell et al., 2009; Foster et al., 2009). Among the formative events that have been identified are initial land clearance by Mesolithic and Neolithic peoples; agricultural intensification and sedentarization in the late Bronze Age; the widespread adoption of the iron plough in the early Iron Age; settlement by the Vikings and the introduction of sheep farming (Table 6.6). In British and Irish catchments, Foulds and Macklin (2006) suggest that geomorphic instability linked with Holocene land-use changes was especially intense in the Bronze Age and

the Iron Age. Rates of sedimentation on British floodplains appear to have accelerated greatly in the last thousand or so years (Figure 6.14) (Macklin et al., 2010).

A core from Llangorse Lake in the Brecon Beacons of Wales (Jones et al., 1985) provides excellent long-term data on changing sedimentation rates:

Period (years BP)	Sedimentation rate (cm 100 y^{-1})
9000–7500	3.5
7500–5000	1.0
5000–2800	13.2
2800–AD 1840	14.1
c. AD 1840–1980s	59.0

The thirteenfold increase in rates after 5000 BP seems to have occurred rapidly and is attributed to initial forest clearance. The second dramatic increase of more than fourfold took place in the last 150 years and is a result of agricultural intensification.

In the last two centuries rates of sedimentation in lake basins have changed in different ways in different basins according to the differing nature of economic activities

Table 6.6 Accelerated sedimentation in Britain in prehistorical and historical times.

Location	Source	Evidence and date
Howgill Fells	Harvey et al. (1981)	Debris cone production following tenth-century AD introduction of sheep farming
Upper Thames Basin	Robinson and Lambrick (1984)	River alluviation in late Bronze Age and early Iron Age
Lake District	Pennington (1981)	Accelerated lake sedimentation at 5000 BP as a result of Neolithic agriculture
Mid-Wales	Macklin and Lewin (1986)	Floodplain sedimentation (Capel Bangor unit) on Breidol as a result of early Iron Age sedentary agriculture
Brecon Beacons	Jones et al. (1985)	Lake sedimentation increase after 5000 BP at Llangorse due to forest clearance
Weald	Burrin (1985)	Valley alluviation from Neolithic onwards until early Iron Age
Bowland Fells	Harvey and Renwick (1987)	Valley terraces at 5000–2000 BP (Bronze or Iron Age settlement) and after 1000 BP (Viking settlement)
Southern England	Bell (1982)	Fills in dry valleys: Bronze and Iron Age
Callaly Moor (Northumberland)	Macklin et al. (1991)	Valley fill sediments of late Neolithic to Bronze Age
Ribble, north-west England	Foster et al. (2009)	Iron Age/Roman and Medieval.
Semer Water and Raydale, North Yorkshire	Chiverrell et al. (2008)	Bronze Age

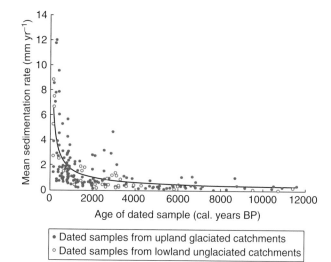

Figure 6.14 Holocene floodplain sedimentation rates in Great Britain plotted for upland (glaciated) and lowland (unglaciated) catchments. *Source:* Adapted from Macklin et al. (2010: figure 18). Reproduced with permission from Elsevier.

Table 6.7 Data on rates of erosion and sedimentation in two English lakes in the last two centuries.

Dates	Activity	Rates of erosion in catchment (R. Cober) as determined from lake sedimentation rates (t km^{-2} y^{-1})
(a) Loe Pool (Cornwall) (from O'Sullivan et al., 1982)		
1860–1920	Mining and agriculture	174
1930–1936	Intensive mining and agriculture	421
1937–1938	Intensive mining and agriculture	361
1938–1981	Agriculture	12
(b) Seeswood Pool (Warwickshire) (from Foster et al., 1986)		
1765–1853		7.0
1854–1880		12.2
1881–1902		8.1
1903–1919		9.6
1920–1925		21.6
1926–1933		16.1
1934–1947		12.7
1948–1964		12.0
1965–1972		13.9
1973–1977		18.3
1978–1982		36.2

in catchments. Some data from various sources are listed for comparison in Table 6.7. In the case of the Loe Pool in Cornwall (south-west England) rates of sedimentation were high while the mining industry was active, but fell dramatically when mining was curtailed. In the case of Seeswood Pool in Warwickshire, a dominantly agricultural catchment area in central England, the highest rates have occurred since 1978 in response to various land management changes, such as larger fields, continuous cropping, and increased dairy herd size. In other catchments, pre-afforestation ploughing may have caused sufficient disturbance to cause accelerated sedimentation. For example, Battarbee et al. (1985b) investigated sediment cores in the Galloway area of south-west Scotland and found that in Loch Grannoch the introduction of ploughing in the catchment caused an increase in sedimentation from 0.2 cm per year to 2.2 cm per year.

Work by Binford et al. (1987) on the lakes of the Peten region of northern Guatemala (Central America), an area of tropical lowland dry forest, is also instructive with respect to early agricultural colonization. By combining studies of lake stratigraphy and archaeology, they reconstructed the diverse environmental consequences of the growth of Mayan civilization (Figure 6.15). This civilization showed a dramatic growth after 3000 years BP, but collapsed in the ninth century AD. The hypotheses put forward to explain this collapse include warfare, disease, earthquakes, and soil degradation. The population has remained relatively low ever since, and after the first European contact (AD 1525) the region

was virtually depopulated. The period of Mayan success saw a marked reduction in vegetation cover, an increase in lake sedimentation rates and in catchment soil erosion, an increased supply of inorganic silts and clays to the lakes, a pulse of phosphorus derived from human wastes, and a decrease in lacustrine productivity caused by high levels of turbidity. In parts of Guatemala, a spasm of soil erosion occurred during the Maya Late Classic phase (AD 550–830), and here depressions record 1–3 m of aggradation in two centuries (Beach et al., 2006).

In a classic study, G.K. Gilbert (1917) demonstrated that hydraulic gold mining in the Sierra Nevada Mountains of California led to the addition of vast quantities of sediments into the river valleys draining the range (James et al., 2017). Much of this sediment remains to this day (James, 1989), and some of it may be contaminated with the mercury that was used as part of the process of collecting the gold (Lecce et al., 2008). This legacy sediment in itself raised channel bed levels, changed their channel configurations, and caused the flooding of lands that had previously been immune. Of even greater significance was the fact that the rivers transported vast quantities of debris into the estuarine bays of the San Francisco system, and caused extensive shoaling which in turn diminished the tidal prism of the bay. Gilbert calculated the volume of shoaling produced by hydraulic mining since the discovery of gold to be 846 million m^3. Mining waste being dumped in channels has also caused rapid aggradation in Tasmania (Knighton, 1991). Conversely, channel sediments may themselves be mined to provide aggregate for the construction industry (Rinaldi et al., 2005).

Sedimentation has severe economic implications because of the role it plays in reducing the effective lifetime of reservoirs. In the tropics capacity depletion through sedimentation is commonly around 2% per annum (Myers, 1988: 14), so that the expected useful life of some dams is just a matter of decades.

6.7 Sediment Transport by Rivers

Sediment transport by rivers has been modified by humans in two main ways (Wasson, 2012). On the one hand, the construction of dams (see Chapter 5) has caused much sediment to be trapped in reservoirs. On the other, sediment delivery to rivers has been increased as a result of accelerated rates of soil erosion. In the south-east USA, the results of these two tendencies have been analyzed by McCarney-Castle et al. (2010). Under pre-European conditions (1680–1700) the mean annual suspended sediment load transfer rate was 6.2 Mt per year, under pre-dam (1905–1925) conditions the rate

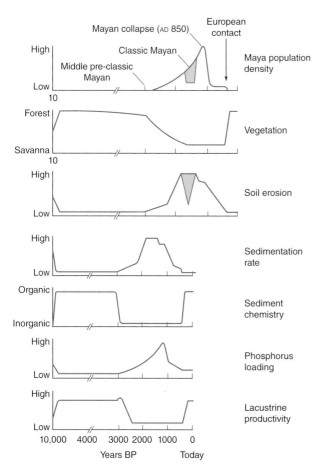

Figure 6.15 The human and environmental history of the Peten Lakes, Guatemala. The hatched areas indicate a phase of local population decline. *Source:* Adapted from Binford et al. (1987: figure 5). Reproduced with permission from Elsevier.

Table 6.8 Silt concentrations (in parts per million) in the Nile at Gaafra before and after the construction of the Aswan High Dam.

BEFORE (averages for the period 1958–1963)

Jan.											**Dec.**
64	50	45	42	43	85	674	2702	2422	925	124	71

AFTER

| 44 | 47 | 45 | 50 | 51 | 49 | 48 | 45 | 41 | 43 | 48 | 47 |

RATIO

| 1.5 | 1.1 | 1.0 | 0.8 | 0.8 | 1.7 | 14.0 | 60.0 | 59.1 | 21.5 | 2.58 | 1.63 |

Source: Abul-Atta (1978: 199).

was 15.04 Mt per year, whereas now, following dam construction, the rate is 5.2 Mt per year.

Sediment retention is well illustrated by the Nile (Table 6.8), both before and after the construction of the great Aswan High Dam. Until its construction the late summer and autumn period of high flow was characterized by high silt concentrations, but since it has been finished the silt load is rendered lower throughout the year and the seasonal peak is removed. Petts (1985: table XVIII) indicated that the Nile now only transports 8% of its natural load below the Aswan High Dam, although this figure seems to be exceptionally low. Other rivers for which data are available carry between 8 and 50% of their natural suspended loads below dams.

A similarly clear demonstration of sediment retention has been given for the South Saskatchewan River in Canada (Table 6.9) by Rasid (1979). During the pre-dam period, typified by 1962, the total annual suspended loads at Saskatoon and Lemsford Ferry were remarkably similar. As soon as the reservoir began to fill late in 1963, however, some of the suspended sediment began to be trapped, and the transitional period was marked by a progressive reduction in the proportion of sediment which reached Saskatoon. In the four years after the dam was fully operational the mean annual sediment load at Saskatoon was only 9% that at Lemsford Ferry.

Even more dramatic are the data for the Colorado River in the USA (Figure 6.16). Prior to 1930 it carried around 125–150 million tonnes of suspended sediment per year to its delta at the head of the Gulf of California. Following the construction of a series of dams the Colorado now discharges neither sediment nor water to the sea (Schwarz et al., 1991). There have also been marked changes in the amount of sediment passing along the Missouri and Mississippi rivers (Figure 6.17a) (Tweel and Turner, 2012), and Meade (1996) attempted to compare the situation in the 1980s with that which existed before humans started to interfere with those rivers (c. AD 1700) (Figure 6.17b). Before 1900, the Missouri–Mississippi river system carried an estimated 400 million metric tonnes of sediment per year to coastal Louisiana.

Table 6.9 Total yearly suspended load (thousand imperial tons) of the South Saskatchewan River at Lemsford Ferry and Saskatoon, 1962–1970.

Period of record	Lemsford Ferry	Saskatoon	Difference at Saskatoon (%)
Pre-dam 1962			
1962	1813	1873	+3
Transitional			
1963	4892	447	−8
1964	7711	4146	−46
1965	9732	2721	−72
1966	5228	1675	−68
MEAN	6891	3255	−53
Post-dam			
1967	12,619	446	−96
1968	2661	101	−96
1969	10,562	2146	−80
1970	5643	118	−98
MEAN	7871	703	−91

Source: Rasid (1979: table 1).

By 1987 to 2006 this figure had dropped to an average of 145 million metric tonnes per year. About half of this decline was accounted for by sediment trapping behind dams, and the rest by such actions as bank revetments and soil erosion management (Meade and Moody, 2010). Also in the USA, the Columbia River has seen a >50% reduction in total sediment transport since the mid-nineteenth century, largely because of flow regulation (Naik and Jay, 2011).

In India, dams on the Krishna and Godavari rivers have also caused major changes in discharges and sediment loads (Rao et al., 2010). The Krishna discharged 61.9 km^3 of water between 1951 and 1959, but this had reduced to 11.8 km^3 by 2000–2008. Its suspended sediment load was 9 million tonnes during 1966–1969 but was as low as 0.4 million tones by 2000–2005. This

Figure 6.16 Historical (a) sediment and (b) water discharge trends for the Colorado River, USA. *Source:* after the United States Geological Survey in Schwarz et al. (1991).

change has promoted accelerated recession of its delta. The Indus has also undergone a marked reduction in flow and sediment transport, especially since the completion of the Tarbela Dam in the early 1970s. Between 1931 and 1947, the river at Kotri had a flow of about 70–150 km³ per year, and a sediment discharge of 190–330 million tonnes per year. For the period from 1962 to 1986 the respective figures were 10–100 km³ per year and 10–130 million tonnes per year (Meadows and Meadows, 1999).

In the case of the Yangtze in China, in 2003–2005 sediment load in the upper river was only 17% of that in the 1950s–1960s (Xu et al., 2007). The Three Gorges Dam has had a particularly marked impact since it began to impound sediment and water in 2003 (Xu and Milliman, 2009). There have also been massive changes in the sediment load of the Yellow River associated with dam and reservoir construction (Ran et al., 2013).

On a global basis, Syvitski et al. (2005) calculated that sediment retention behind dams has reduced the net flux of sediment reaching the world's coasts by c. 1.4 billion metric tonnes per year, and that over 100 billion metric tonnes have been trapped within the last 50 years. Reservoirs impounded by dams now trap c. 26% of the global sediment delivery to the coastal ocean (Syvitski

and Milliman, 2007). Conversely, Syvitski et al. (2005) calculated that humans have simultaneously increased the sediment transport by global rivers through soil erosion by c. 2.3 billion metric tonnes per year. On balance, therefore, global river sediment loads have gone up more as a result of soil erosion than they have been reduced by dam retention. However, plainly there are great differences between rivers and between areas. In central Japan, for example, sediment loads were reduced in the last decades of the twentieth century because land that had formerly been cultivated intensively had become urbanized (Siakeu et al., 2004). In the case of Chinese rivers draining into the Pacific, recent declines in sediment load have been caused by a combination of factors (Chu et al., 2009): dam retention (56%), soil and water conservation (23%), water abstraction (15%), and in-channel sand mining (6%). The same is true of the Sacramento River in California. Its sediment load decreased by about one-half during the period between 1957 and 2001 because of a range of factors: a depletion in the amount of old hydraulic mining debris, trapping of sediment in reservoirs, riverbank protection, the construction of levees, and altered land use (e.g. urbanization replacing agriculture) (Wright and Schoellhamer, 2004). In Colombia, the Magdalena drainage basin has witnessed an increase in sediment transport of 33% since 1980, largely because of deforestation (Restrepo and Escobar, 2016).

6.8 Deliberate Modification of Channels

To improve navigation and flood control humans have deliberately straightened many river channels (Figure 6.18). Indeed, the elimination of meanders contributes to flood control in two ways. First, it eliminates some overbank floods on the outside of curves, against which the swiftest current is thrown and where the water surface rises highest. Second, and more importantly, the resultant shortened course increases both the gradient and the flow velocity, and the floodwaters erode and deepen the channel, thereby increasing its flood capacity. Some landscapes have become dominated by artificial channels, normally once again because of the need for flood alleviation and drainage. This is especially evident in an area like the English Fenlands where straight constructed channels contrast with the sinuous courses of original rivers such as the Great Ouse.

It was for flood control that a programme of channel cut-offs was initiated along the Mississippi in the early 1930s. By 1940 it had lowered flood stages by as much as 4 m at Arkansas City, Arkansas. By 1950 the length of the river between Memphis, Tennessee, and Baton Rouge,

Louisiana (600 km down the valley) had been reduced by no less than 270 km as a result of 16 cut-offs.

Many channels have been constrained by the emplacement of riprap (rock armour) (Reid and Church, 2015), while others, like the Los Angeles River in Los Angeles, have been put in a corset of concrete. Valleys often carry roads and railways. Blanton and Marcus (2013) have considered the effects of such transport corridors on channel forms and suggest that these can impede the natural meandering and migration of channels across their floodplains. This in turn disrupts the erosion and cut-and-fill alluviation that creates high habitat and biological diversity across the active channel and floodplain. Within the channel, confining structures concentrate

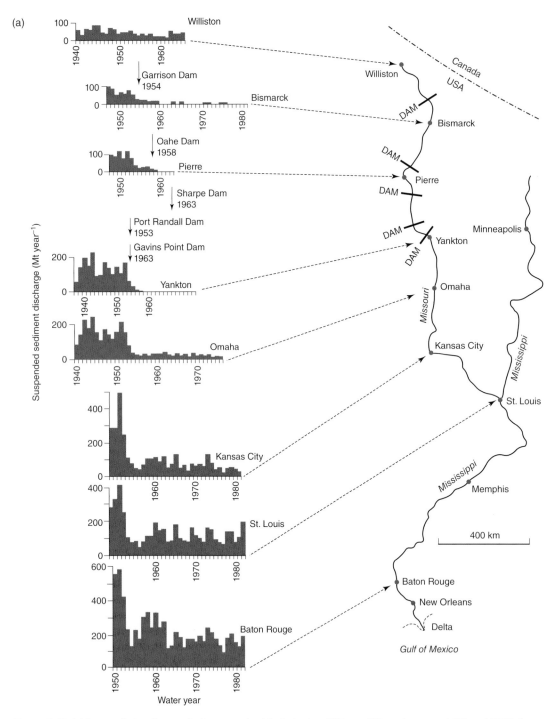

Figure 6.17 (a) Suspended sediment discharge on the Mississippi and Missouri Rivers between 1939 and 1982. *Source:* adapted from Meade and Parker (1985), with modifications. (b) Long-term average discharges of suspended sediment in the lower Mississippi River c. 1700 and c. 1980.

(b)

Figure 6.17 (Continued).

Figure 6.18 The strait, lined, channelized, Los Angeles River in California, USA (ASG).

Figure 6.19 Principal types of adjustment in straightened river changes. *Source:* after Brookes (1987: figure 4). Reproduced with permission of John Wiley & Sons. For an explanation of the different types see text.

energy, which leads to higher shear stress and stream power that can wash out riffles and degrade low-velocity habitats such as pools and alcoves.

Deliberate channel straightening causes various types of sequential channel adjustment both within and downstream from straightened reaches, and the types of adjustment vary according to such influences as stream gradient and sediment characteristics. Brookes (1987) recognized five types of change (Figure 6.19) *within* the straightened reaches (types W1 to W5) and two types of change *downstream* (types D1 and D2):

Type W1 is degradation of the channel bed, which results from the fact that straightening increases

the slope by providing a shorter channel path. This in turn increases its sediment transport capability.

ASKHAM BRYAN COLLEGE LEARNING RESOURCES

Type W2 is the development of an armoured layer on the channel bed by the more efficient removal of fine materials as a result of the increased sediment transport capability referred to above.

Type W3 is the development of a sinuous thalweg in streams which are not only straightened but which are also widened beyond the width of the natural channel.

Type W4 is the recovery of sinuosity as a result of bank erosion in channels with high slope gradients.

Type W5 is the development of a sinuous course by deposition in streams with a high sediment load and a relatively low valley gradient.

Types D1 and D2 result from deposition downstream as the stream tries to even out its gradient, the deposition occurring as a general raising of the bed level, or as a series of accentuated point bar deposits.

6.9   Non-deliberate River Channel Changes

The complexity and diversity of causes of stream channel change is brought out in the context of Australia (Table 6.10) (Rutherford, 2000), and more generally by Downs and Gregory (2004). Major changes in the configuration of channels can be achieved accidentally (Figure 6.20, Table 6.11) either because of human-induced changes in stream discharge or in their sediment

load: both parameters affect channel capacity. The causes of observed cases of riverbed degradation, including avulsion (Heyvaert and Walstra, 2016), are varied and complex and result from a variety of natural and human changes.

It is now widely recognized that the urbanization of a river basin results in an increase in peak flood flows (Bledsoe and Watson, 2001). It is also recognized that the morphology of stream channels is related to their discharge characteristics, and especially to the discharge at which bank full flow occurs. Navratil et al. (2013) and Hawley et al. (2013) discussed the role of urbanization in

Table 6.10 Human impacts on Australian stream channel morphology.

Acceleration of meander migration rates by removal of riparian vegetation

Channel avulsion because of clearing of floodplain vegetation

Channel contraction below dams

Channel enlargement by sand and gravel extraction

Channel incision by changes to resistance of valley flow (drains, cattle tracks)

Channel invasion and narrowing by exotic vegetation

Channelization and river training

Enlargement due to catchment clearing and grazing

Erosion by boats

Scour downstream from dams

Sedimentation resulting from mining

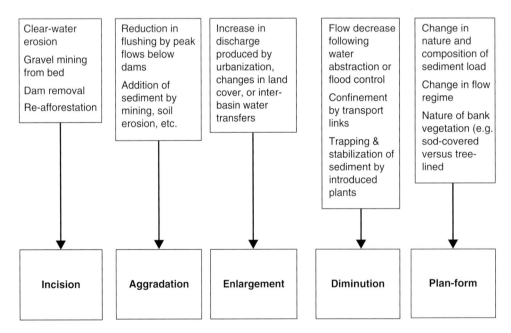

Figure 6.20 The causes of channel change.

Table 6.11 Accidental channel changes.

Phenomenon	Cause
Channel incision	Clear-water erosion below dams caused by sediment removal
Channel aggradation	Reduction in peak flows below dams Addition of sediment to streams by mining, agriculture, etc.
Channel enlargement	Increase in discharge level produced by urbanization
Channel diminution	Discharge decrease following water abstraction or flood control
	Trapping and stabilizing of sediment by artificially introduced plants
Channel plan-form	Change in nature of sediment load and its composition, together with flow regime

channel enlargement and incision, for urban development causes flashier, larger, more erosive discharges than occur with increased frequency and duration. In an analysis of the literature, Chin (2006) stressed how variable river channel response to urbanization could be, but found that enlargement was reported in ~75% of the studies recording morphological results with cross-sectional areas generally increasing 2–3 times and on occasion as much as 15 times. Other urban-induced channel changes include reductions in sinuosity which commonly result from artificial straitening, a tendency (not invariable) for bed material to coarsen from scouring of fines and increased competence because of higher peak flows, and an overall increase in drainage densities. As a result of urbanization, the frequency of discharges which fill the channel will increase, with the effect that the beds and banks of channels in erodible materials will be eroded so as to enlarge the channel (Trimble, 1997; Krhoda and Kwambuke, 2016). Data from humid and temperate environments around the world indicate that urbanization causes channels to enlarge to 2–3 times and as much as 15 times the original size (Chin, 2006). This in turn will lead to bank caving, possible undermining of structures, and increases in turbidity. Other changes include decreases in channel sinuosity and increases in bed material size (Grable and Harden, 2006). Trimble (2003) provides a good historical analysis of how the San Diego Creek in Orange County, California, has responded to flow and sediment yield changes related to the spread of both agriculture and urbanization.

Changes in channel morphology also result from discharge diminution and sediment load changes produced by flood-control works and diversions for irrigation (Brandt, 2000). This can be shown for the North Platte and the South Platte in America, where both peak discharge and mean annual discharge have declined to 10–30% of their pre-dam values. The North Platte, 762–1219 m wide in 1890 near the Wyoming–Nebraska border, has narrowed to about 60 m at present, while the South Platte River was about 792 m wide, 89 km above its junction with the North Platte in 1897, but had narrowed to about 60 m by 1959 (Schumm, 1977). The tendency of both rivers has been to form one narrow, well-defined channel in place of the previously wide, braided channels, and, in addition, the new channel is generally somewhat more sinuous than the old (Figure 6.21). River regulation structures have also had marked impacts on the form of Spain's Ebro River, which became much less sinuous and much narrower during the twentieth century (Magdaleno et al., 2012).

Similarly, the building of dams can lead to channel aggradation upstream from the reservoir and channel deepening downstream because of the changes brought about in sediment loads (Figure 6.22). Some data on observed rates of degradation below dams are presented in Table 6.12. They show that the average rate of degradation has been of the order of a few metres over a few decades following closure of the dams. However, over time the rate of degradation seems to become less or to cease altogether, and Leopold et al. (1964: 455) suggested that this can be brought about in several ways. First, because degradation results in a flattening of the channel slope in the vicinity of the dam, the slope may become so flat that the necessary force to transport the available materials is no longer provided by the flow. Second, the reduction of flood peaks by the dam reduces the competence of the transporting stream to carry some of the material on its bed. Thus if the bed contains a mixture of particle sizes the river may be able to transport the finer sizes but not the larger, and the gradual winnowing of the fine particles will leave an armour of coarser material that prevents further degradation.

The overall effect of the creation of reservoir by the construction of a dam is to lead to a reduction in downstream channel capacity (Petts, 1979). This seems to amount to between about 30 and 70% (Table 6.13).

In recent years, partly because some old dams have become unsafe or redundant, they have been demolished (Ibisate et al., 2016). Most of the dams involved have been just a few metres high (Table 6.14), though one example from Australia was 15 m high (Neave et al., 2009). Among the consequences of dam removal are incision into the sedimentary fill that had accumulated in the reservoir behind the dam, migration of a knickpoint upstream, deposition of liberated sediment, and the formation of bars and the like downstream (Major et al., 2012). However, the precise consequences vary greatly depending on the nature and erodibility of the fill

(a) Brule

(b) Brule

N

1 km

(c)

Figure 6.21 The configuration of the channel of the South Platte River at Brule, Nebraska, USA: (a) in 1897 and (b) in 1959. Such changes in channel form result from discharge diminution (c) caused by flood-control works and diversions for irrigation. *Source:* adapted from Schumm (1977: figure 5.32) and Williams (1978).

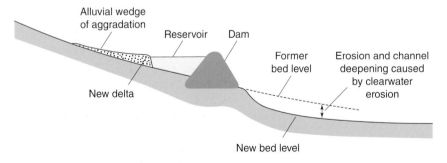

Figure 6.22 Diagrammatic long profile of a river showing the upstream aggradation and the downstream erosion caused by dam and reservoir construction.

and the regime of the river. Some rivers appear to remove their fill rapidly and almost entirely, while others do not.

Even more far-reaching changes in channel form are produced by land-use changes and the introduction of soil conservation measures. Figure 6.23 is an idealized

representation of how the river basins of Georgia in the United States have been modified through human agency between 1700 (the time of European settlement) and the present. Clearing of the land for cultivation (Figure 6.23b) caused massive slope erosion which

Table 6.12 Riverbed degradation below dams.

River	Dam	Amount (m)	Length (km)	Time (years)
South Canadian (USA)	Conchos	3.1	30	10
Middle Loup (USA)	Milburn	2.3	8	11
Colorado (USA)	Hoover	7.1	111	14
Colorado (USA)	Davis	6.1	52	30
Red (USA)	Denison	2.0	2.8	3
Cheyenne (USA)	Angostura	1.5	8	16
Saalach (Austria)	Reichenhall	3.1	9	21
South Saskatchewan (Canada)	Diefenbaker	2.4	8	12
Yellow (China)	Samenxia	4.0	68	4

Source: from data in Galay (1983).

Table 6.13 Channel capacity reduction below reservoirs.

River	Dam	% channel capacity loss
Republican, USA	Harlan County	66
Arkansas, USA	John Martin	50
Rio Grande, USA	Elephant Buttre	50
Tone, UK	Clatworthy	54
Meavy, UK	Burrator	73
Nidd, UK	Angram	60
Burn, UK	Burn	34
Derwent, UK	Ladybower	40

Source: modified after Petts (1979: table 1).

resulted in the transfer of large quantities of sediment into channels and floodplains. The phase of intense erosive land use persisted and was particularly strong during the nineteenth century and the first decades of the twentieth century, but thereafter (Figure 6.23c) conservation measures, reservoir construction, and a reduction in the intensity of agricultural land use led to further channel changes (Trimble, 1974). Streams ceased to carry such a heavy sediment load, they became much less turbid, and incision took place into the flood-plain sediments, lowering their beds by as much as 3–4 metres.

In south-west Wisconsin a broadly comparable picture of channel change was documented by Knox (1977). There, as in the Upper Mississippi Valley (Knox, 1987), it is possible to identify stages of channel modification associated with various stages of land use, culminating in

Table 6.14 Selected studies of the consequences geomorphological effects of dam removal in the USA.

Source	Location	Height(m)
Pearson et al., 2011	Merrimack, New Hampshire	4
Rapid incision and clearance of fill		
Kibler et al., 2011	Brownsville, Oregon	1.8–3.4
Release of gravel fill causing bars and pools and riffles downstream		
Burroughs et al., 2009	Pine River, Michigan	5
Big headcut, but only 12% of sediment fill eroded after 10 years		
Major et al., 2008, 2012	Marmot Dam, Oregon	14
Knickpoint migrates 1.5 km upstream, and creation of multiple thread channel over 2 km downstream		
Doyle et al., 2003	Koshonong, Wisconsin	3.3
Little downstream aggradation as limited erosion from dam area		
Doyle et al., 2003	Baraboo, Wisconsin	2
Channel incision upstream and temporary aggradation of point bar downstream		
Cheng and Granata, 2007	Sandusky, Ohio	2.2
Less than 1% of sediment stored in reservoir was transported downstream		
Wildman and MacBroom, 2005	Anaconda, Connecticut	3.35
Only c. one-third of sediment removed after 5 years. Channel widening		
upstream of dam but incision limited by original channel armouring		
Rumschlag and Peck, 2007	Muroe, Ohio	3.66
Vertical incision to pre-impoundment substrate within one month. 1 m of aggradation downstream		

decreased overbank sedimentation as a result of better land management in the last half century.

In Australia, dramatic channel incision occurred both on valley sides and on valley floors, often within a few decades of European settlement (Rutherford, 2000). Most of this historical incision was triggered by disturbances to the material making up valley floors. Drains, cattle tracks, roads, and other forms of flow concentration made the valley floors more susceptible to higher runoff from cleared and trampled catchments and from storms. Other causes of channel change identified by Rutherford included channel enlargement by sand and gravel extraction, changes in flow as a result of dam construction, channel invasion by exotic vegetation, removal of riparian vegetation, and bank erosion by boats.

Figure 6.23 Changes in the evolution of fluvial landscapes in the Piedmont of Georgia, USA, in response to land-use change between 1970. *Source:* after Trimble (1974: 117), in S.W. Trimble, *Man-induced Soil Erosion on the Southern Piedmont*, Soil Conservation Society of America. © Soil Conservation Society of America. Reproduced with permission.

Other significant changes produced in channels include those prompted by accelerated sedimentation associated with humanly induced changes in the vegetation communities growing along channels. Riparian vegetation is an important control of river bank stability and thus of channel form (Tickner et al., 2001; Teo and Marren, 2015; Zaimes and Schutz, 2015) whilst forms and flows in turn affect riparian vegetation (Hupp and Osterkamp, 1996). The establishment or re-establishment of riparian forest has been implicated with channel narrowing in south-eastern France during the twentieth century (Liébault and Piégay, 2002). The nature of arid zone channels may be particularly markedly affected by riparian vegetation. In fact, phreatophytes such as tamarisk, cottonwood, and willow, which draw their sustenance from groundwater at depth, can significantly influence channel geometry by increasing bank resistance to erosion, inducing deposition and increasing roughness, and by taking up so much water that discharge is reduced. Such vegetation can lead to significantly reduced channel width and, as a result, to increased overbank discharge (flooding) (Birken and Cooper, 2006). Thus, Graf (1978) showed that major river channels of the Colorado River and the plateau country in the USA had an average width reduction of 27% when tamarisk, a highly effective invasive species (Tickner et al., 2001), was established after 1930. Graf (1981) demonstrated that in the ephemeral Gila River channel, sinuosity was increased from 1.13 to 1.23 as phreatophyte density increased in the 1950s. Tamarisk, because of its root system, is capable of resisting the hydraulic stresses of flash-floods. It is also drought tolerant and has an ability to produce denser stands than native species, which gives it a competitive advantage.

There is, however, a major question about the ways in which different vegetation types affect channel form (Trimble, 2004). Are tree-lined banks more stable than those flowing through grassland? On the one hand tree roots stabilize banks and their removal might be expected to cause channels to become wider and shallower (Brooks and Brierly, 1997). On the other hand, forests produce log-jams which can cause aggradation or concentrate flow onto channel banks, thereby leading to their erosion. These issues are discussed in Trimble (1997) and Montgomery (1997).

Another organic factor which modifies channel form is the activity of grazing animals. These break the banks down directly by trampling and can reduce bank resistance by removing protective vegetation and loosening soil (Trimble and Mendel, 1995). The presence of wild animals has also influenced channels. As Butler (2006) has recounted, the extirpation of species can affect river forms and dynamics. In particular he has drawn attention to the role of beavers and the effects of their near-extirpation during the period following European contact and expansion across North America. In the pre-contact landscape beaver ponds entrapped hundreds of billions of cubic meters of sediment. Their widespread removal by fur trappers led to increased stream incision and attendant changes from relatively clear-flowing to sediment-laden streams.

The construction of water-powered mills has also been identified as a potent cause of historical channel change in the eastern United States. Walter and Merritts (2008), using old maps and archives, showed that whereas before European settlement the streams of the region were small anabranching channels within extensive vegetated wetlands, after the construction of tens of thousands of seventeenth- to nineteenth- century milldams, 1 to 5 m of slackwater sedimentation occurred and buried the pre-settlement wetlands with fine sediment.

Finally, the addition of sediments to stream channels by mining activity causes channel aggradation. Mine wastes can clog channel systems (Gilbert, 1917; Lewin et al., 1983), and cause them to aggrade (Knighton, 1991). Some of this mining waste is polluted with heavy metals and the like (Taylor and Little, 2013). Equally, the mining of aggregates from river beds themselves can lead to channel deepening (Bravard and Petts, 1996; Rinaldi et al., 2005).

6.10 Arroyo Trenching and Gullies

In the south-western United States many broad valleys and plains became deeply incised with valley-bottom gullies (arroyos) over a short period between 1865 and 1915, with the 1880s being especially important (Cooke and Reeves, 1976; Aby, 2017) (Figure 6.24). This cutting had a rapid and detrimental effect on the flat, fertile, and easily irrigated valley floors, which are the most desirable sites for settlement and economic activity in a harsh environment. The causes of the phenomenon have been the subject of prolonged debate (Elliott et al., 1999; Gonzalez, 2001).

Many students of this phenomenon have believed that thoughtless human actions caused the entrenchment, and the apparent coincidence of white settlement and arroyo development tended to give credence to this viewpoint. The range of actions that could have been culpable is large: timber-felling, overgrazing, cutting grass for hay in valley bottoms, compaction along well-travelled routes, channelling of runoff from trails and railways, disruption of valley-bottom sods by animals' feet, and the invasion of grasslands by miscellaneous types of scrub (Miller, 2017).

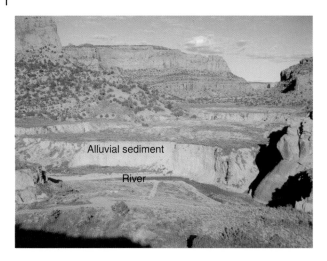

Figure 6.24 An arroyo in the south-west USA: Laguna Creek, Arizona (ASG).

On the other hand, study of the long-term history of the valley fills shows that there have been repeated phases of aggradation and incision and that some of these took place before the influence of humans could have been a significant factor (Waters and Haynes, 2001). This has prompted debate as to whether the arrival of white communities was in fact responsible for this particularly severe phase of environmental degradation. Huntington (1914), for example, argued that valley filling would be a consequence of a climatic shift to more arid conditions. These, he believed, would cause a reduction in vegetation which in turn would promote rapid removal of soil from devegetated mountain slopes during storms, and overload streams with sediment. With a return to humid conditions vegetation would be re-established, sediment yields would be reduced, and entrenchment of valley fills would take place. Bryan (1928) put forward a contradictory climatic explanation. He argued that a slight move towards drier conditions, by depleting vegetation cover and reducing soil infiltration capacity, would produce significant increases in storm runoff which would erode valleys. Another climatic interpretation was advanced by Leopold (1951), involving a change in rainfall intensity rather than quantity. He indicated that a reduced frequency of low-intensity rains would weaken the vegetation cover, while an increased frequency of heavy rains at the same time would increase the incidence of erosion. Support for this contention comes from the work of Balling and Wells (1990) in New Mexico. They attributed early twentieth-century arroyo trenching to a run of years with intense and erosive rainfall characteristics that succeeded a phase of drought conditions in which the productive ability of the vegetation had declined. It is also possible, as Schumm et al. (1984) have pointed out, that incision

could result from neither climatic change nor human influence. It could be the result of some natural geomorphological threshold being crossed. Under this argument, conditions of valley-floor stability decrease slowly over time until some triggering event initiates incision of the previously 'stable' reach.

It is therefore clear that the possible mechanisms that can lead to alternations of cut-and-fill of valley sediments are extremely complex, and that any attribution of all arroyos in all areas to human activities may be a serious oversimplification of the problem (Figure 6.25). In addition, it is possible that natural environmental changes, such as changes in rainfall characteristics, have operated at the same time and in the same direction as human actions.

In the Mediterranean lands there have also been controversies surrounding the age and causes of alternating phases of aggradation and erosion in valley bottoms. Vita-Finzi (1969) suggested that at some stage during historical times many of the steams in the Mediterranean area, which had hitherto been engaged primarily in downcutting, began to build up their beds. Renewed downcutting, still seemingly in operation today, has since incised the channels into the alluvial fill. He proposed that the reversal of the downcutting trend in the Middle Ages was both ubiquitous and confined in time, and that some universal and time-specific agency was required to explain it. He believed that vegetation removal by humans was not a medieval innovation and that some other mechanism was required. A solution he gave to account for the phenomenon was precipitation change during the climatic fluctuation known as the Little Ice Age (AD 1550–1850). This was not an interpretation which found favour with Butzer (1974). He reported that his investigations showed plenty of post-Classical and pre-1500 alluviation (which could not therefore be ascribed to the Little Ice Age), and he doubted whether Vita-Finzi's dating was precise enough to warrant a 1550–1850 date. Instead, he suggested that humans were responsible for multiple phases of accelerated erosion from slopes, and accelerated sedimentation in valley bottoms, from as early as the middle of the first millennium BC.

Butzer's interpretation was favoured by van Andel et al. (1990) who detected an intermittent and complex record of cut and fill episodes during the late Holocene in various parts of Greece. They believed that this evidence was compatible with a model of the control of timing and intensity of landscape destabilization by local economic and political conditions. This is a view shared in the context of the Algarve in Portugal by Chester and James (1991). In general recent work has suggested that alluvial sequences are more complex than was formerly thought, that some alluvial and incision sequences may

Figure 6.25 A model for the formation of arroyos (gullies) in the south-western USA. *Source:* after Cooke and Reeves (1976: figure 1.2). Reproduced with permission from Oxford University Press.

be associated with extreme events rather than with climatic change *per se* (see Macklin and Woodward, 2009: 338), and that multiple depositional phases may have occurred in the Holocene, as in Italy (Boenzi et al., 2008) and Spain (Carmona and Ruiz, 2011), some caused by land-use changes and some by climatic events.

In recent years some caution has been expressed as to the extent to which humans have been responsible for more general landscape degradation in the Mediterranean lands. Rackham and Moody (1996: 9) have paraphrased the traditional view thus:

> The persistent theory in Mediterranean studies is that of the Ruined Landscape or Lost Eden, which runs like this. Well into historic times, the land was covered with magnificent forests. Men cut

down the forests to make homes and ships, or burned them to make farmland; the trees failed to grow again, and multitudes of goats devoured the remains. Trees, unlike other vegetation, have a magic power of retaining soil. The trees gone, the soil washed away into the sea or the plains, the land became 'barren', and some say that the very climate got worse.

They then go on to question it (p. 10):

> Scholars play up the landscape of the past and play down the landscape of the present: they write about ancient forests when the original text mentioned only trees; they ignore modern forests or dismiss them as mere 'scrub' or 'maquis'.

Figure 6.26 *Lavaka* in Madagascar. *Source:* © 2016 DigitalGlobe. Scale bar 306 m.

This is a view that has been developed by Roberts (1998: 191):

> it would be wrong to assume that all Mediterranean hills are anthropogenic landscapes. A salutary lesson in this comes from the badlands of south-east Spain. Here integrated geo-archaeological studies have found in situ Bronze Age sites lying uneroded on vulnerable bare slopes. The badlands had already formed by *c.* 4500 years ago, and later agricultural clearances have done little to alter erosion rates. While giving the appearance of recent degradation, these and similar Mediterranean Badlands ... are ancient landscapes created by long-term geological instability rather than the ravages of the goat and the plough.

A further location with spectacular gullies, locally called *lavaka*, is Madagascar (Figure 6.26). Here too there have been debates about cultural versus natural causation. Proponents of cultural causes have argued that since humans arrived on the island in the last two thousand years there has been excessive cattle grazing, removal of forest for charcoal and for slash-and-burn cultivation, devastating winter (dry season) burning of grasslands, and erosion along tracks and trails. However, the situation is more complex than that and the *lavaka* are polygenetic. Tectonism and natural climatic aridification may be at least as important, and given the climatic and soil types of the island many

lavaka are a natural part of the landscape's evolution. Some of them also clearly pre-date both primary (i.e. uncut) rain forest and human settlement (Mietton et al., 2014). The many factors, natural and cultural, involved in *lavaka* development are well reviewed by Wells and Andriamihaja (1993), Zavada et al. (2009), and Cox et al. (2010).

6.11 Accelerated Mass Movements

There are many examples of mass movements being triggered by human actions (Jaboyedoff et al., 2016). It is very seldom, however, that humans deliberately accelerate mass movements; most are accidentally caused, the exception possibly being the deliberate triggering of threatening snow avalanches.

The forces producing slope instability and landsliding can usefully be divided into disturbing forces and resisting properties. The factors leading to an increase in shear stress (disturbing forces) can be listed as follows (modified after Cooke and Doornkamp, 1990: 113):

1) Removal of lateral or underlying support:
   undercutting by water (for example, river, waves), or glacier ice;
   weathering of weaker strata at the toe of the slope;
   washing out of granular material by seepage erosion;
   human cuts and excavations, drainage of lakes or reservoirs.

2) Increased disturbing forces:
   natural accumulations of water, snow, talus;
   pressure caused by human activity (for example, stockpiles of ore, tip-heaps, rubbish dumps, or buildings).
3) Transitory earth stresses:
   earthquakes;
   continual passing of heavy traffic.
4) Increased internal pressure:
   build-up of pore-water pressures (for example, in joints and cracks, especially in the tension crack zone at the rear or the slide);
   build-up of pore water pressure by addition of irrigation water.

Some of the factors are natural, while others (italicized) are affected by humans. Factors leading to a decrease in the shearing resistance of materials making up a slope can also be summarized (also modified after Cooke and Doornkamp, 1990: 113).

1) Materials:
   beds which decrease in shear strength if water content increases (clays, shale, mica, schist, talc, serpentine) (for example, *when local water-table is artificially increased in height by reservoir construction*), or as a result of stress release (vertical and/or horizontal) following slope formation;
   low internal cohesion (for example, consolidated clays, sands, porous organic matter);
   in bedrock: faults, bedding planes, joints, foliation in schists, cleavage, brecciated zones, and pre-existing shears.
2) Weathering changes:
   weathering reduces effective cohesion, and to a lesser extent the angle of shearing resistance;
   absorption of water leading to changes in the fabric of clays (for example, loss of bonds between particles or the formation of fissures).
3) Pore-water pressure increase:
   high groundwater table as a result of increased precipitation or *as a result of human interference* (for example, *dam construction, irrigation*) (see 1 above).

Once again the italics show that there are a variety of ways in which humans can play a role.

Jaboyedoff et al. (2016) created a sevenfold classification of the causes of human induced landslides:

1) Slope re-profiling: embankments; fill slopes; cut slopes; construction work; excavation work; tailing hills.
2) Groundwater flow perturbation and fast pore pressure changes: pipe leaks; dam reservoirs; leaks in old canalization networks; pipe bursting.
3) Surface water overland flow modifications: deficient drainage systems; diverting of rivers.
4) Land-use changes and land degradation: deforestation; forest fires; urbanization.
5) Inappropriate artificial structures: inappropriate retaining walls; infrastructure breaks.
6) Vibrations and explosives: blasting; heavy traffic.
7) Ageing and degradation of infrastructure: weakening of terrace walls; filling of check dams across torrents.

Let us consider a selection of these triggers and causes in more detail. Some mass movements are created by humans piling up waste soil and rock into unstable accumulations that fail spontaneously. At Aberfan, in South Wales, a major disaster occurred in 1966 when a coal-waste tip 180 m high began to move as an earth flow. The tip had been constructed not only as a steep slope but also upon a spring line. This made an unstable configuration which eventually destroyed a school and claimed over 150 lives. In Hong Kong, where a large proportion of the population is forced to occupy steep slopes developed on deeply weathered granites and other rocks, mass movements are a severe problem, and So (1971) has shown that many of the landslides and washouts, (70% of those in the great storm of June 1966, for example) were associated with road sections and slopes artificially modified through construction and cultivation. In south-eastern France humans have accelerated landslide activity by building excavations for roads and by loading slopes with construction material (Julian and Anthony, 1996). The undercutting and removal of the trees of slopes for the construction of roads and paths has also led to landsliding in many parts of South-East Asia (Sidle et al., 2006), and the Himalayas (Barnard et al., 2001). This is also the case in mountainous Nepal, where the number of fatal landslides shot up during the 1990s (Petley et al., 2007) (Figure 6.27). This increase seems to be correlated with the rapid development of the road network after about 1990. Similarly, landslides that were triggered by a great earthquake in Kashmir in 2005 occurred preferentially in areas where road construction had taken place (Owen et al., 2008). Many landslides in China appear to have been triggered by surface excavation and mining activity (Huang and Chan, 2004) and also by road construction (Sidle et al., 2011), though some, as at Heifangtai near Lanzhou in China, have resulted from the application of irrigation water to fields at the top of susceptible, steep slopes developed in loess (Figure 6.28) (Xu et al., 2012).

The construction of dams and the impoundment of reservoirs change groundwater conditions which can impact on slope stability. One of the most serious examples of this was the mass movement, partly caused by human activity, which led to the Vaiont Dam disaster in

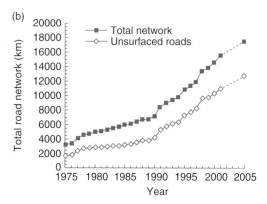

Figure 6.27 Landslides in Nepal. (a) Number of fatal landslides per year (smoothed by five-year running mean) and (b) the growth of the road network. *Source:* adapted from Petley et al. (2007: figures 12b and 13b).

Figure 6.28 The effects of a landslide in loess terrain at Heifangtai, near Lanzhou, China. The slide was triggered by irrigation of fields on the plateau surface (ASG).

Italy in 1963, in which 2600 people were killed (Genevois and Ghirotti, 2005). Heavy antecedent rainfall and the presence of young, highly folded sedimentary rocks provided the necessary conditions for a slip to take place, but it was the construction of the Vaiont Dam itself

which changed the local groundwater conditions sufficiently to affect the stability of a rock mass on the margins of the reservoir: 240 million m^3 of ground slipped, causing a rise in water level which overtopped the dam and caused flooding and loss of life downstream. There have also been fears that slope failures could occur around the reservoir impounded by the Three Gorges Dam in China (Wang et al., 2008).

Although the examples of accelerated mass movements that have been given here are essentially associated with the effects of modern construction projects, more long-established activities, including deforestation and agriculture, are also highly important.

Forests help to prevent shallow landslides by modifying the soil moisture regime via evapotranspiration, by providing root reinforcement within the soil mantle or regolith. In shallow soils, tree roots may penetrate the entire soil mantle and anchor the soil into a more stable substrate. Dense lateral root systems in the upper horizons stabilize the soil, while larger tree roots provide reinforcement across planes of weakness along the flanks of potential slope failures. Although woody roots significantly reduce shallow (<1 to 2 m deep) landslide potential on steep slopes, deeper soil mantles (>5 m) benefit much less from such reinforcement, as root density decreases dramatically with depth and few large roots are able to anchor across the basal failure plane. The only benefit of root strength to the stabilization of deep-seated landslides is when very large lateral woody roots cross planes of weakness along the flanks of potential failures (Stokes et al., 2009). Forests are also important in controlling rock-falls. In some cases initiation of rock-falls is increased by roots as they may promote detachment while penetrating cracks and fissures in the rock. Rocks may be slowly forced apart by root growth thereby forming a pathway for water to further enter the rock mass. Conversely, however, roots have also been found to reduce rock-fall activity by binding slope materials together (Sakals et al., 2006).

Innes (1983) demonstrated, on the basis of lichenometric dating of debris-flow deposits in the Scottish Highlands, that most of the flows have developed in the last 250 years, and he suggested that intensive burning and grazing may be responsible. In north-west England, Chiverrell et al. (2007) were able to relate phases of gullying, alluvial fan deformation, and valley slope deposition to land-use pressures in Iron Age/Roman and medieval times. The arrival of European settlers in New Zealand, particularly since the 1840s, had a profound effect on landslide activity and slope gullying, as they cleared the forest and converted it to pasture (Glade, 2003; Marden et al., 2012). The runout of rockfalls in New Zealand increased in size compared to those of pre-Anthropocene times (Borella et al., 2016). Similarly, in the Italian Alps grazing and deforestation have reduced the retention of debris by vegetation and has resulted in thicker debris flow layers within lake sediments (Schneider et al., 2010). In northern Spain, changes in landslide occurrence in the Upper Pleistocene and Holocene can partly be attributed to periods of intense precipitation or seismic activity, but the sharp increase in landslide numbers since the early 1980s appears to be related to increasing human pressures (Remondo et al., 2005). In an alpine area in Switzerland, where the area affected by landslides increased by 92% from 1959 to 2004, the causes were a combination of an increase in the occurrence of torrential rain events and an increase in cattle stocking (Meusberger and Alewell, 2008). However, on a longer time span of 3600 years, pulses of increased landslide activity in the Swiss Alps have been linked to phases of deforestation (Dapples et al., 2002). The mountains of Japan are another area where clear-felling of trees has caused a surge in landslide activity (Saito et al., 2017. Phases of intense precipitation can be implicated in some phases of slope instability, as indicated by the work of Remondo et al. (2005) in northern Spain and of Meusberger and Alewell (2008) in Switzerland.

Fire, whether natural or man-induced, can be a major cause of slope instability and debris flow generation by removing or reducing protective vegetation, by increasing peak stream flows, and by leading to larger soil moisture contents and soil-water pore pressures (because of reduced interception of rainfall and decreased moisture loss by transpiration) (Kinoshita et al., 2016). Examples of fire-related debris flow generation are known from many sites in the USA, including Colorado (Cannon et al., 2001b), New Mexico (Cannon et al., 2001a), the Rocky Mountains, and the Pacific North-West (Wondzell and King, 2003). Some detailed data on debris-avalanche production in North American catchments as a result of deforestation and forest road construction are presented in Table 4.11.

Because of the hazards presented by both natural and accelerated mass movements, humans have developed a whole series of techniques to attempt to control them. Techniques for landslide mitigation can be classified into three main types: (1) geometric methods, in which the slope of the hillside is changed; (2) hydrogeological methods, in which an attempt is made to lower the groundwater level or to reduce the water content of the material; and (3) chemical and mechanical methods to increase the shear strength of the unstable mass, and to counter destabilizing forces (e.g. anchors, rock or ground nailing, structural wells, piles, geotextiles, and application of shotcrete).

Such methods are listed in Table 6.15. These techniques are increasingly necessary, as human capacity to change a hillside and to make it more prone to slope

Table 6.15 Methods used to control mass movements on slopes.

Type of movement	Method of control
Falls	Benching the slope
	Covering of walls with steel mesh
	Drainage
	Flattening the slope
	Reinforcement of rock walls by grouting with cement, anchor bolts
Slides and flows	Drainage of surface water with ditches
	Grading or benching to flatten slope
	Pilings through the potential slide mass Retaining walls at foot
	Rock and earth buttresses at foot
	Sealing surface cracks to prevent infiltration
	Sub-surface drainage

Source: after R.F. Baker and H.E. Marshall, in Dunne and Leopold (1978: table 15.16).

failure has been transformed by engineering development. Excavations are going deeper, buildings and other structures are larger, and many sites which are at best marginally suitable for engineering projects are now being used because of increasing pressure on land. This applies especially to some of the expanding urban areas in the humid parts of low latitudes – Hong Kong, Kuala Lumpur, Rio de Janeiro, and many others.

6.12 Accelerated Weathering and the Tufa Decline

There is some evidence that human activities have produced changes in the nature and rate of weathering (Winkler, 1970). The prime cause of this is probably air pollution. As a result of increased emissions of sulphur dioxide through the burning of fossil fuels, there are higher levels of sulphuric acid in rain over many industrial areas. This reacts with stones and causes their decay. Acid rain has been implicated in the weathering of the limestone of St Paul's Cathedral in London, though there are signs that emission controls have led to a reduction in the rate of weathering in the last few decades (Inkpen et al., 2012). Because acid precipitation causes accelerated dissolution of carbonate rocks, it can lead to increasing calcium loads in streams, as has been observed in the north-eastern USA (Kaushal et al., 2013). Chemical reactions involving sulphur dioxide also generate calcium sulphate and magnesium sulphate, which may be effective in causing the physical breakdown of rock through the mechanism of salt weathering. They also create crusts on buildings and natural stone outcrops (Marszałek et al., 2014). Coatings of rock varnish associated with rock art in north-west Australia, have also been dissolved by acid pollution (Black et al., 2017).

Similarly, atmospheric carbon dioxide levels have been rising because of the burning of fossil fuels, and deforestation. Carbon dioxide may combine with water to produce weak carbonic acid which can dissolve limestone, marbles, and dolomites. Weathering can also be accelerated by changes in groundwater levels resulting from irrigation. This can be illustrated by considering the Indus Plain in Pakistan (Goudie, 1977), where irrigation has caused the water table to be raised by about 6 m since 1922. This has produced increased evaporation and salinization. The salts that are precipitated by evaporation above the capillary fringe include sodium sulphate, a very effective cause of stone decay. Indeed buildings, such as the great archaeological site of Mohenjo-Daro are decaying at a catastrophic rate.

In other cases accelerated weathering has been achieved by moving stone from one environment to another. Cleopatra's Needle, an Egyptian obelisk in New York City, is an example of rapid weathering of stone in an inhospitable environment (Winkler, 1965). Originally erected on the Nile opposite Cairo about 1500 BC, in 1880 it was moved to New York. It immediately began to suffer from scaling and the inscriptions were largely obliterated within ten years because of the penetration of moisture which enabled frost-wedging and hydration of salts to occur.

Accelerated weathering and transport of dissolve materials may occur in association with urban development (Kaushal et al., 2017). A growing number of studies suggest that dissolved inorganic carbon (DIC) and base cations can be significantly elevated in streams and rivers draining urban watersheds compared with forested ones. Among the abiotic and biotic processes which can contribute to this are chemical weathering, road salts, sewage inputs, and decreased biological uptake by vegetation. Disturbance of soils during the urban construction phase can bring bedrock materials to the surface, where they are available for chemical weathering reactions and alkalinization of water chemistry, releasing base cations in the process. Chemical weathering of carbonate-rich urban infrastructure can also be a potential source of DIC, Ca^{2+}, Mg^{2+}, and other major ions to streams and contributes to a distinct urban lithology known as the 'urban karst'. Road salts (see Section 5.6) can also be direct sources of base cations and other anions including sulphates⁻ in streams. In addition, ion exchange reactions in response to salinization from road

salts can also be an important component of chemical weathering in soils.

Humans may create a variety of small pits and related forms on bedrock outcrops, particularly on sandstones and granites, which have many morphological similarities to natural weathering features, such as alveoles and small tafones. These are often called cupules or kettles (Soukopova, 2017), and were a feature of many prehistoric cultures from the Lower Palaeolithic onwards. There are many possible reasons for their creation, including sharpening of weapons, rock art, and the collection of material for religious purposes.

During the 1970s and 1980s an increasing body of isotopic dates became available for deposits of tufa (secondary freshwater deposits of limestone, also known as travertine). Some of these dates suggest that over large parts of Europe, from Britain to the Mediterranean basin and from Spain to Poland, rates of tufa formation were high in the early and mid-Holocene, but declined markedly thereafter (Weisrock, 1986: 165–167). Vaudour (1986) maintains that since around 3000 BP 'the impact of man on the environment has liberated their disappearance', but he gives no clear indication of either the basis of this point of view or of the precise mechanism(s) that might be involved. If the late Holocene reduction in tufa deposition is a reality (which is contested by, for example, Baker and Sims, 1998), then it is necessary to consider a whole range of possible mechanisms, both natural and anthropogenic (Nicod, 1986: 71–80) (Table 6.16). As yet the case for an anthropogenic role is not proven (Goudie et al., 1993) and it is possible that climate changes were a more important determinant of the tufa decline (Wehrli et al., 2010). More recent degradation of tufa landscapes may be caused by pollution, and in the case of a subalpine to alpine region of Sichuan Province, China, research indicates that wet deposition (including rain and snow) polluted by anthropogenic SO_2, NO_x, and NH_3 emissions dissolves exposed tufa and may considerably reduce tufa deposition rate and cause tufa dissolution (Qiao et al., 2016).

6.13 Reactivation and Stabilization of Sand Dunes

To George Perkins Marsh (see Section 1.1) the reactivation and stabilization of sand dunes, especially coastal dunes, was a theme of great importance in his analysis of human transformation of nature. He devoted 54 pages to it. He was fascinated by 'the warfare man wages with the sand hills' and asked (1965: 410) 'in what degree the naked condition of most dunes is to be ascribed to the improvidence and indiscretion of man'. His analysis

Table 6.16 Some possible mechanisms to account for the alleged Holocene tufa decline.

Climatic/natural	Anthropogenic
Discharge reduction following rainfall decline leading to less turbulence	Discharge reduction due to overpumping, diversions, etc.
Degassing leads to less deposition	Increased flood scour and runoff variability of channels due to deforestation, urbanization, ditching, etc.
Increased rainfall causing more flood scour	Channel shifting due to deforestation of floodplains leads to tufa erosion
Decreasing temperature leads to less evaporation and more CO_2 solubility	Reduced CO_2 flux in system after deforestation
Progressive Holocene peat development and soil podzol development through time leads to more acidic surface waters	Introduction of domestic stock causes breakdown of fragile tufa structures
	Deforestation = fewer fallen trees to act as foci for tufa barrages
	Increased stream turbidity following deforestation reduces algal productivity

showed quite clearly that most of the coastal dunes of Europe and North America had been rendered mobile, and hence a threat to agriculture and settlement, through human action, especially because of grazing and clearing. In Britain the cropping of dune warrens by rabbits was a severe problem, and a most significant event in their long history was the myxomatosis outbreak of the 1950s, which severely reduced the rabbit population and led to dramatic increases in vegetative cover and stability (Doody, 1989).

Appreciation of the problem of dune reactivation on mid-latitude shorelines, and attempts to overcome it, go back a long way (Kittredge, 1948). For example, the menace of shifting sand following denudation is recognized in a decree of 1539 in Denmark which imposed a fine on those who destroyed certain species of sand plants on the coast of Jutland. The fixation of coastal sand dunes by planting vegetation was initiated in Japan in the seventeenth century, while attempts at the re-afforestation of the spectacular Landes dunes in south-west France began as early as 1717, and came to fruition in the nineteenth century: 81,000 hectares of moving sand had been fixed in the Landes by 1865. In Britain possibly the most impressive example of sand control is provided by the re-afforestation of the Culbin Sands in north-east Scotland with conifer plantations (Edlin, 1976).

Along coastlines, dunes have been modified by a whole range of human activities, not least around the Mediterranean (Feola et al., 2011; Ciccarelli, 2014):

Land-use change: afforestation, deforestation, agriculture, grazing, golf courses, plantations

Hydrological and geomorphological change: aggregate, sand, and mineral extraction, beach raking, fluvial flow and sediment supply interruption, littoral drift interruption by jetties, etc., inundation and eutrophication by waste water, shoreline stabilization, training wall construction and dredge spoil dumping which change bathymetry and erosion attack

Disturbance: trampling, military activity and warfare, pipeline landfalls, introduction of rabbits, sewage outfall construction, urbanization, vehicular disturbance, recreation and tourism

Miscellaneous: fire, hunting, introduction of invasive plants, nutrient enrichment

There are numerous examples of dune systems being transformed quite early in the Holocene. However, it has not always been easy to discriminate between phases of increased dune activity caused by changes in climate (including windiness) and those caused by human activities (Clarke and Rendell 2009; Roskin et al., 2013). In inland areas of Europe, clearing, fire, and grazing have affected some of the late Pleistocene dune fields that were created on the arid steppe margins of the great ice sheets. In Germany dunes may have been destabilized as early as the Mesolithic (Nicolay et al., 2014) and showed reactivation due to land-use changes later in the Holocene (Küster et al., 2014). The inland dunes of Hungary (Kiss et al., 2012) were also modified by phases of human activity during the Subatlantic and some changes in the European sand belt may date back to the Neolithic (Tolksdorf and Kaiser, 2012). Indeed, phases of dune instability may occur when both appropriate climatic conditions and human pressures coincide (Beerten et al., 2014). In Europe the tempo of change in coastal dunes probably increased in medieval times (Provoost et al., 2011) and into the nineteenth century (Buynevich et al., 2007), but in some areas has been further accelerated in recent decades because of vehicular disturbance, tourism, the spread of accidentally introduced plants such as marram (*Ammophila*), animal introductions, eutrophication by nitrates in waste water or polluted air, groundwater pumping, and urbanization. On the eastern seaboard of the USA a suite of human activities, including the depredations of voracious hogs, caused large-scale dune mobilization in the nineteenth century (Senter, 2003). Polynesian migrants appear to have modified dune systems in New Zealand (Horrocks et al., 2007) and aboriginal peoples induced dune activity in the Great Plains of Canada (Wolfe et al., 2007) and on the Channel Islands of California (Erlandson et al., 2005).

However, it is possibly on the margins of the great subtropical and tropical deserts that some of the strongest fears are being expressed about sand-dune reactivation. This is one of the facets of desertification (see Section 2.13). Increasing numbers of both humans and their domestic animals, brought about respectively by improvements in health and by the provision of boreholes, has led to an excessive pressure on the limited vegetation resources. As ground cover has been reduced, so dune instability has increased. The problem is not so much that dunes in the desert cores are relentlessly marching on to moister areas, but that the fossil dunes, laid down during the more arid phase peaking around 20,000 years ago, or during dry phases of the Holocene, have been reactivated *in situ*. Not all such dunes will, however, necessarily become reactivated, for decimation of buffalo herds, the extension of irrigation, and the suppression of prairie fires could lead to their stability (Forman et al., 2001).

A wide range of methods (Figure 6.29) is available to attempt to control drifting sand and moving dunes as follows:

1) Drifting sand:
   enhancement of deposition of sand by the creation of large ditches, vegetation belts and barriers and fences;
   enhancement of transport of sand by aerodynamic stream-lining of the surface, change of surface materials or panelling to direct flow;
   reduction of sand supply, by surface treatment, improved vegetation cover or erection of fences;
   deflection of moving sand, by fences, barriers, tree belts, etc.

2) Moving dunes:
   removal by mechanical excavation;
   destruction by reshaping, trenching through dune axis or surface stabilization of barchan arms;

In practice most solutions to the problem of dune instability and sand blowing have involved the establishment of a vegetation cover. This is not always easy. Species used to control sand dunes must be able to endure undermining of their roots, burning, abrasion, and often severe deficiencies of soil moisture. Thus the species selected need to have the ability to recover after partial growth in the seedling stages, to promote rapid litter development, and to add nitrogen to the soil through root nodules. During the early stages of growth they may need to be protected by fences, sand traps, and surface mulches. Growth can also be stimulated by the addition of synthetic fertilizers.

In hearts of deserts sand dunes are naturally mobile because of the sparse vegetation cover. Even here, however, humans sometimes attempt to stabilize sand surfaces to protect settlements, pipelines, industrial plant, and agricultural land. The use of relatively porous barriers to prevent or divert sand movement has proved comparatively successful, and palm fronds or chicken wire have made adequate stabilizers. Elsewhere surfaces have been strengthened by the application of high-gravity oil or by salt-saturated water (which promotes the development of wind-resistant surface crusts). Frequently these techniques are not particularly successful and very often the best solution is to site and design engineering structures to allow free movement of sand across them. Alternatively, by mapping different dune types and knowing their direction and rate of movement, structures should be located out of harm's way. Avoidance may be better than defence.

Studies of the comparative effectiveness of different stabilization techniques have been undertaken in recent years. For example, Zhang et al. (2004) found that the best means of stabilizing moving dunes in Inner Mongolia, China, were wheat straw checkerboards and the planting of *Artemisia halodendron*. This finding was confirmed by a study in the Kerqin Sandy Land of northern China (Li et al., 2009). Along a major highway in the Taklamakan Desert, checkerboards, reed fences, and nylon nets were found to be effective (Dong et al., 2004). In north-west Nigeria, Raji et al. (2004) found that shelterbelts were the most effective technique, and were superior to mechanical fencing. Some success has also been claimed for chemical stabilizers (Han et al., 2007) and for geotextiles (Escalente and Pimentel, 2008). Some devices are prohibitively expensive (e.g. chemical fixers) (Dong et al., 2004), while others, such as checkerboards, are not.

Figure 6.29 A sand fence on a dune that threatens part of the town of Walvis Bay in Namibia (ASG).

In temperate areas coastal dunes have been effectively stabilized by the use of various trees and other plants (Ranwell and Boar, 1986). In Japan *Pinus thumbergii* has been successful, while in the great Culbin Sands plantations of Scotland *P. nigra* and *P. laricio* have been used initially, followed by *P. sylvestris*. Of the smaller shrubs, *Hippophae* has proved highly efficient, sometimes too efficient, at spreading. Its clearance from areas where it is not welcome is difficult precisely because of some of the properties that make it such an efficient sand stabilizer: vigorous suckering growth and the rapid regrowth of cut stems (Boorman, 1977). Different types of grass have also been employed, especially in the early stages of stabilization. These include two grasses which are moderately tolerant of salt: *Elymus farctus* (sand twitch) and *Leymus arenarius* (lime grass). Another grass which is much used, not least because of its rapid and favourable response to burial by drifting sand, is *Ammophila arenaria* (marram).

Further stabilization of coastal dunes has been achieved by setting up sand fences. These generally consist of slats about 1.0–1.5 m high, and have a porosity of 25–50%. They have proved to be effective in building incipient dunes in most coastal areas. By installing new fences regularly, large dunes can be created with some rapidity (Figure 6.30). Alternative methods, such as using junk cars on the beaches at Galveston, Texas, have been attempted with little success. Larger dunes may also be created by the bulldozing of beach sediments, a process termed scraping, but such material may be easily eroded and cause downdrift accretion (Kratzmann and Hapke, 2012).

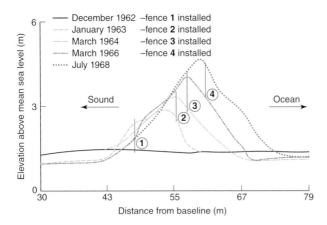

Figure 6.30 Sand accumulation using the method of multiple fences in North Carolina, USA. This raised the dune height approximately 4 metres over a period of 6 years. *Source:* Savage, R. P., and Woodhouse, W. W. Jr., 1969. Creation and stabilization of coastal barrier dunes. Proc. 11th Conf. on Coastal Engineering. A.S.C.E., pp. 671-700.

6.14 Accelerated Coastal Erosion

Coastal dunes are not the only parts of our seashores that are being affected by human activities. Human impacts on coasts are legion. General treatments of coastal problems and their management are provided by French (1997 and 2001) and by Viles and Spencer (1995), while Reeve et al. (2012) give an account of coastal engineering from an engineering viewpoint.

Because of the high concentration of settlements, industries, transport facilities, and recreational developments on coastlines, the pressures placed on coastal landforms are often acute (Nordstrom, 1994; Evans, 2008), and the consequences of excessive erosion serious. Active erosion is a pervasive feature of many beaches, and, for instance, over two-thirds of the coastline of New England and the mid-Atlantic region of the USA has suffered from erosion in recent decades (Hapke et al., 2013). A recent acceleration in the rate of sea-level rise has been linked to this (Hinkel et al., 2013). While most areas are subject to some degree of natural erosion and accretion, the balance can be upset by human activity in a whole range of ways (Table 6.17). However, humans seldom attempt to accelerate coastal

Table 6.17 Causes of beach erosion (possible human interventions in brackets).

Beach sediment wastage through long-term attrition

Change in wave incidence and energy

Degradation of backing dunes (e.g. by urbanization, deforestation, trampling)

Interception of sediment delivery by longshore drift (e.g. by pier and breakwater)

Lack of protective vegetation (e.g. by deforestation)

Loss of beach sediment by drift along shore

Loss of permafrost and of sea ice protection against wave attack (e.g. by warming)

Reduction in sediment supply from eroding cliffs (e.g. by sea wall construction)

Reduction in sediment supply from inland dunes (e.g. by dune stabilization)

Reduction in sediment supply from the sea floor (e.g. by dredging)

Reduction of fluvial sediment supply to coast (e.g. by dam and reservoir construction)

Removal of beach sediment (e.g. by mining)

Removal of beach sediment by runoff

Rise in the beach water-table (e.g. by irrigation)

Submergence and increased wave attack (e.g. as result of rising sea levels or subsidence)

Wave reflection (e.g. from sea walls)

erosion deliberately. More usually, it is an unexpected or unwelcome result of various economic projects. Frequently coast erosion has been accelerated as a result of human efforts to reduce it. Sea walls, for example, can be a barrier which interrupts exchange and supply of sediment between the beach and its hinterland (Hanley et al., 2014).

A good beach is one of the best forms of coastal protection. If material is removed from a beach, accelerated cliff retreat may take place. Removal of beach materials may be necessary to secure valuable minerals, including heavy minerals, or to provide aggregates for construction. The classic example of the latter was the mining of 660,000 tonnes of shingle from the beach at Hallsands in Devon, England, in 1887 to provide material for the construction of dockyards at Plymouth. The shingle proved to be undergoing little or no natural replenishment and in consequence the shore level was reduced by about 4 m. The loss of the protective shingle soon resulted in cliff erosion to the extent of 6 m between 1907 and 1957. The village of Hallsands was cruelly attacked by waves and is now in ruins.

Another common cause of beach and cliff erosion at one point is coast protection at another (Figure 6.31). As already stated, a broad beach serves to protect the cliffs behind, and beach formation is often encouraged by the construction of a range of 'hard engineering' structures (Figure 6.32). These include groynes, bulkheads, sea walls and revetments, breakwaters and sills, artificial headlands, and sand fences (Nordstrom, 2014; Williams et al., 2016). However, these structures sometimes merely displace the erosion (possibly in an even more marked form) further along the coast. This is illustrated in Figure 6.33.

Figure 6.31 Coastal defence in Weymouth, southern England. The piecemeal emplacement of expensive sea walls and cliff protection structures is often only of short-term effectiveness and can cause accelerated erosion downdrift (ASG).

Piers or breakwaters can have similar effects to groynes. Figure 6.34 shows the coast at West Bay in Dorset, southern England, following the construction of a jetty. The beach in the foreground appears to have been built outwards, while the cliff behind the jetty has retreated and so needs to be protected with a sea-wall and with large imported rock armour. Likewise, the construction of some sea-walls (Figure 6.35a & b), erected to reduce coastal erosion and flooding, has had the opposite effect to the one intended (Figure 6.36). Given the extent to which artificial structures have spread along the coastlines of the world, this is a serious matter (Walker, 1988).

Problems of coastal erosion are exacerbated because there is now abundant evidence to suggest that much of the reservoir of sand and shingle that creates beaches is in some respects a relict feature. Much of it was deposited on continental shelves during the maximum of the last glaciation (around 20,000 year BP), when sea-level was about 120 m below its present level. It was transported shoreward and incorporated in present-day beaches during the phase of rapidly rising post-glacial sea-levels that characterized the Flandrian (Holocene) transgression until about 6000 years BP. Since then, with the exception of minor oscillations of the order of a few metres, world sea-levels have been stable and much less material is, as a consequence, being added to beaches and shingle complexes (Hails, 1977). It is because of these problems that many erosion prevention schemes now involve beach nourishment (by the artificial addition of appropriate sediments to build up the beach) (Hanley et al., 2014), or employ miscellaneous sand bypassing techniques (including pumping and dredging) whereby sediments are transferred from the accumulation side of an artificial barrier to the erosional side. Such methods of beach nourishment are reviewed by Bird (1996). In recent years there has been an increasing trend towards so-called 'soft engineering' as a means of coastal protection (Temmerman et al., 2013), rather than using hard engineering structures such as sea walls or groynes. In addition to beach nourishment, the encouragement of dune formation and promotion of salt marsh accretion are becoming recognized as being aesthetically pleasing, effective, and economically advantageous.

In some areas, however, rivers bring material into the coastal zone which becomes incorporated into beaches through the mechanism of longshore drift. Thus any change in the sediment load of such rivers may result in a change in the sediment budget of neighbouring beaches. When accelerated soil erosion occurs in a river basin the increased sediment load may cause coastal accretion and siltation. But where the sediment load is reduced through the construction of large reservoirs, behind which sediments accumulate, coastal erosion

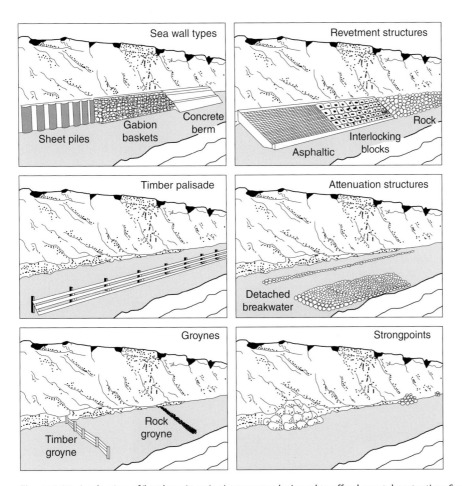

Figure 6.32 A selection of 'hard engineering' structures designed to afford coastal protection. *Source:* adapted from A.H. Brampton, 'Cliff Conservation and Protection: Methods and Practices to Resolve Conflicts', in Hooke (1998: figures 3.1, 3.2, 3.4, 3.5, 3.6 and 3.7).

may result. In China the construction of around 50,000 dams in the Yangtze basin of China has caused sediment starvation and severe erosion of its delta (Yang et al., 2011a).

The construction of the Aswan and other dams on the Nile has caused accelerated recession of the Nile Delta. Formerly, sediments, on reaching the sea, generated sand bars and dunes which contributed to delta accretion, but over a century ago an inverse process was initiated and the delta began to retreat. For example, the Rosetta mouth of the Nile lost about 1.6 km of its length from 1898 to 1954. The imbalance between sedimentation and erosion appears to have started with the Delta Barrages (1861) and culminated with the High Dam itself a century later. In addition, large amounts of sediment are retained in an extremely dense network of irrigation channels and drains that has been developed in the Nile Delta itself (Stanley, 1996). Much of the Egyptian coast is now 'undernourished' with sediment.

Delta erosion is a pervasive and developing problem, not least in south and south-east Asia. This is partly because they sink under their own weight of sediment, may

suffer from compaction of organic sediments, may be subsiding because of the removal of fluids, and are subjected to on-going sea-level rise. Deltas also suffer from a reduction in the number of distributary channels as a consequence of a need to support navigation in a limited number of larger channels (Syvitski and Saito, 2007; Svyitski et al., 2009). Indeed, such actions have already been implicated in the changes that have taken place in the morphology of the Nile Delta and its lagoons over the last half century (El Banna and Frihy, 2009). Anthony (2015) argued that the present-day tendency for significant reductions in fluvial sediment supply to deltas may signify the demise of many of them in the coming decades through a process of delta shoreline straitening by waves.

In Texas, where over the last century four times as much coastal land has been lost as has been gained, one of the main reasons for this change is believed to be the reduction in the suspended loads of some of the rivers discharging into the Gulf of Mexico (Table 6.18). The four rivers listed carried in 1961–1970 on average only about one-fifth of what they carried in 1931–1940.

(a)

(b)

Figure 6.33 (a) Diagrammatic illustration of the effects of groyne construction on sedimentation on a beach. (b) Groynes on Cape Cod, north-east USA. *Source:* © 2016 Google. Scale bar 262m.

Comparably marked falls in sediment loadings occurred elsewhere in the eastern United States (Figure 6.37). In California, where the rivers provide between 75 and 90% of beach material, the reduction in sediment supply caused by dams and reservoirs has been a major cause of erosion of the recreational beaches of southern California (Willis and Griggs, 2003). Likewise, in France the once mighty Rhône only carries about 5% of the load it did in the nineteenth century; and in Asia, the Indus discharges less than 20% of the load it did before construction of large barrages over the last half century (Milliman, 1990). On a global basis, large dams may retain 25–30% of the global flux of river sediment (Vörösmarty et al., 2003) (see also Section 5.3.1).

Construction of great levées on the lower Mississippi River since 1717 has affected the Gulf of Mexico coast. The channelization of the river has increased its velocity, reduced overbank deposition of silt onto swamps, marshes, and estuaries, and changed the salinity conditions of marshland plants. As a result, the coastal marshes and islands have suffered from increased erosion or a reduced rate of development. The changes between 1956 and 1990 are shown in Figure 6.38. However, as with so many examples of environmental change, it is unlikely that just one

Figure 6.34 In the nineteenth century a jetty was built at West Bay, Dorset, southern England to facilitate entry to the harbour. By the twenty-first century accretion has taken place in the foreground and erosion in the background (ASG).

Figure 6.35 (a) Coastal protection measures at Arica, northern Chile. (b) A sea wall on Portland, Dorset, southern England (ASG).

Figure 6.36 Sea walls and erosion: (a) a broad, high beach prevents storm waves breaking against a sea wall and will persist, or erode only slowly; but where the waves are reflected by the wall (b) scour is accelerated, and the beach is quickly removed and lowered (c). *Source:* adapted from Bird (1979: figure 6.3).

Table 6.18 Suspended loads of Texas rivers discharging into the Gulf of Mexico.

	Suspended load (million tonnes)		
River	**1931–1940**	**1961–1970**	**%***
Brazos	350	120	30
San Bernard	1	1	100
Colorado	100	11	10
Rio Grande	180	6	3
TOTAL	631	138	20

* 1961–1970 loads as % 1931–1940 loads.
Source: modified from Hails (1977: table 9.1) after data from Stout et al. and Curtis et al.

factor, in this case channelization, is the sole cause of the observed trend. In their study of erosion loss in the Mississippi Delta and neighbouring parts of the Louisiana Coast, Walker et al. (1987) suggested that this loss is the result of a variety of complex interactions among a number of physical, chemical, biological, and cultural processes. These processes include, in addition to channelization, worldwide sea-level changes, subsidence resulting from sediment loading by the delta of the underlying crust, changes in the sites of deltaic sedimentation as the delta evolves, catastrophic storm surges, and subsidence resulting from subsurface fluid withdrawal. Tweel

Figure 6.37 The decline in suspended sediment discharge to the eastern seaboard of the USA between 1910 and 1970 as a result of soil conservation measures, dam construction, and land-use changes. *Source:* adapted from Meade and Trimble (1974).

and Turner (2012) suggested that an important factor has been changes in the amount of sediment carried by the Mississippi in response to land-use changes and river engineering. Plainly, however, as seen from space (Figure 6.39), the birdfoot delta is a very fragile structure.

In some areas anthropogenic vegetation modification creates increased erosion potential. This was illustrated for the hurricane-afflicted coast of Belize, Central America, by Stoddart (1971). He showed that natural, dense vegetation thickets on low, sand islands (cays) acted as a baffle against waves and served as a massive sediment trap for coral blocks, shingle, and sand transported during extreme storms. However, on many islands the natural vegetation had been replaced by coconut plantations. These had an open structure easily penetrated by sea water, they tended to have little or no ground vegetation (thus exposing the cay surface to stripping and channelling), and they had a dense but shallow root net easily undermined by marginal sapping.

Other examples of markedly accelerated coastal erosion and flooding result from anthropogenic degradation of dune ridges. Frontal dunes are a natural defence against erosion (Saye et al., 2005), and coastal changes may be long-lasting once they are breached. Many of those areas in eastern England which most effectively resisted the great storm and surge of 1952 were those where humans had not intervened to weaken the coastal dune belt.

Estuaries are another type of shoreline that has been subjected to human pressures (Irabien et al., 2015). Embankments, training walls, dredging, and reclamation have resulted in the loss of many estuarine mudflats and wetlands (Pye and Blott, 2014). On the other hand, elsewhere, deforestation and subsequent erosion of catchments draining into estuaries has led to their active sedimentation (Poirier et al., 2011), as in Chesapeake Bay (Maryland), Roanoke Bay (North Carolina) (Pasternack et al., 2001), and San Pablo Bay (California) (Jalowska et al., 2015). Figure 6.40 shows a heavily affected estuary in north-west Madagascar. In many estuaries oyster reefs have been lost (Beck et al., 2011b). Deltas in the Mediterranean lands show the large amounts of accretion associated with accelerated catchment soil erosion in Hellenistic/Roman to Byzantine times (Stock et al., 2016).

Coral reefs are also undergoing profound change at the present time. Many are being heavily degraded. As Pandolfi et al. (2005: 1275) remarked, 'Large animals, like turtles, sharks and groupers, were once abundant on all coral reefs, and large long-lived corals created a complex architecture supporting diverse fish and invertebrates. Today the most degraded reefs are little more than rubble, seaweed, and slime.' This is a theme that is discussed in more detail in Section 3.4.

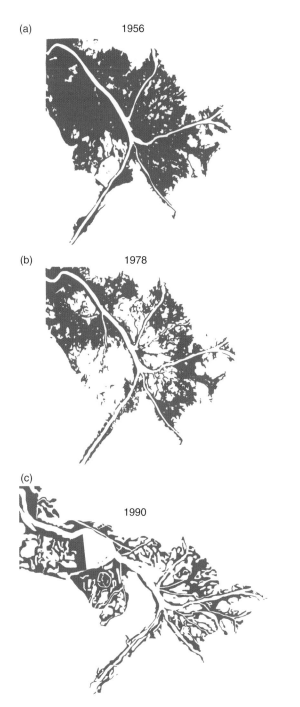

(a) 1956

(b) 1978

(c) 1990

Figure 6.38 Comparison of the outlines of the Mississippi Birdsfoot Delta from the 1930s to 1990 gives a clear indication of the transformation from marsh to open water. Artificial controls upriver have decreased the amount of sediment carried by the river; artificial levées along much of the lower course have kept flood-borne sediment from replenishing the wetlands; and in the active delta itself rock barriers installed across breaks similarly confine the river. The Gulf of Mexico is intruding as the marshland sinks or is washed away.

Figure 6.39 A satellite image of the present day Mississippi Birdsfoot Delta. *Source:* NASA.

6.15 Changing Rates of Salt Marsh Accretion

Salt marshes are important habitats for wildlife and also help in coastal protection. However, in Britain, the nature of some salt marshes, and the rate at which they accrete, has been transformed by a major vegetational change, namely the introduction of a salt marsh plant, *Spartina alterniflora*. This cord-grass appears to have been introduced to Southampton Water in southern England by accident from the east coast of North America, possibly in shipping ballast. The crossing of this species with the native *Spartina maritima*, produced an invasive cordgrass of which there were two forms: *Spartina townsendii* and *Spartina anglica*, the latter of which is now the main species. It appeared first at Hythe on Southampton Water in 1870 and then spread rapidly to other salt marshes in Britain, partly because of natural spread and partly because of deliberate planning. *Spartina* now reaches as far north as the Island of Harris in the west of Scotland and to the Cromarty Firth in the east (Doody, 1984). The plant has often been effective at excluding other species and also at trapping sediment. Rates of accretion can therefore become very high. Ranwell (1964) gives rates as high as 8–10 cm per year. There is evidence that this has caused progressive silting of estuaries such as those of the Dee. *Spartina* invasion has also occurred in other parts of the world including the Netherlands, Australia, New Zealand, California, and China (Gedan et al., 2009; Strong and Ayres, 2009).

However, for reasons that are not fully understood, *Spartina* marshes have frequently suffered dieback, which has sometimes led to marsh recession (Hughes and Paramor, 2004). In the case of Poole Harbour and Beaulieu Estuary in southern England, this may date

Figure 6.40 Estuarine infilling in north-west Madagascar. *Source:* © 2016 Google. Scale bar 19.9 km.

back to the 1920s, but elsewhere on the south coast it has generally been rapid and extensive since about 1960. Among the hypotheses that have been put forward to explain dieback in various parts of the world are the role of rising sea-level, pathogenic fungi, increased wave attack, competition from and bioturbation by the polychaete, *Nereis diversicolor*, grazing by the crab *Sesarma reticulatum* (Bertness and Silliman, 2008), and the onset of waterlogging and anaerobic conditions on mature marsh (Hübner et al., 2010).

However, *Spartina* invasion is not the sole cause of changes in accretion rates on marshes (Gedan et al., 2011). Other important factors include runoff and sediment erosion from the land as a result of land-cover changes (Mattheus et al., 2010), the construction of dykes and levees, the digging of canals, the throwing up of spoil banks, land reclamation schemes, grid ditches to help control mosquitoes, tidal restriction by bridges and berms, and subsidence resulting from fluid abstraction (Kennish, 2001; Gedan et al., 2009). It seems that some of the salt marshes along the coast of North America expanded rapidly during the eighteenth and nineteenth centuries due to increased rates of sediment delivery following deforestation associated with European settlement (Kirwan et al., 2011). Salt marshes are in some case threatened by eutrophication, for many estuaries are affected by nutrient loading from human land uses in the surrounding watersheds. One consequence of increased nutrient levels is proliferation of opportunistic macroalgae. Wasson et al. (2017) found that algal addition to a

Californian marsh decreased salt marsh cover, flowering, and canopy height, increased retreat rate, and caused conversion of marsh habitat to mudflat through bank erosion.

In some parts of the world, including north-west Europe and the USA, the growth of marshes is being deliberately encouraged by the removal of coastal defence structures and the allowing of natural sediment to accumulate to construct a new marsh on what was agricultural land. This 'managed re-alignment' has been described by Esteves (2014) and Friess et al. (2014). As Boorman and Hazelden (2017: explained, this is defined as:

'the adoption of a new, generally landwards situated, sea defence line, usually a sea wall but which may be on rising ground or upland. Where a sea defence line is in the form of a sea wall, and is to be relocated landwards, then there are two options for the old sea wall. Most commonly the wall is breached giving the sea access through one or more openings in the wall; but a more expensive option is to remove the old wall completely. Either way, this increases the inter-tidal area and facilitates new inter-tidal habitat development, most desirably salt marsh, seaward of this wall as an ecological buffer. Using salt marsh vegetation as a buffer affords the sea wall additional protection from erosion and thus saves on building and maintenance costs.'

Guide to Reading

Downs, P.W. and Gregory, K.J. (2004) *River Channel Management.* London: Arnold. A comprehensive review of river channels and their management.

Goudie, A.S. and Viles, H.A. (2016) *Geomorphology in the Anthropocene.* Cambridge: Cambridge University Press. A lengthy treatment of anthropogeomorphology and of the geomorphological changes wrought by humans in the Anthropocene.

James, L.A. and Marcus, W.A. (eds) (2006) 37th Binghamton Geomorphology Symposium: The Human Role in Changing Fluvial Systems. Geomorphology 79, 1–506. A special issue of a major journal that includes some excellent reviews of the ways in which humans have modified rivers.

Szabó, J., Dávid, L. and Lóczy, D. (eds) (2010) *Anthropogenic Geomorphology.* Dordrecht: Springer. A largely Hungarian view of the human impact on landforms.

7

The Human Impact on Climate and the Atmosphere

CHAPTER OVERVIEW

This chapter considers the various ways in which humans can change climate, at a global scale, concentrating on such factors as greenhouse gas loadings in the atmosphere, surface albedo changes brought about by land cover change, and the presence of aerosol particles in the atmosphere. It then considers changes at the more local scale, including the climates of urban areas and the possible means and consequences of deliberate climate modification, including geoengineering. The second part of the chapter looks at issues relating to air quality, urban pollution, photochemical smogs, acidification of precipitation, and stratospheric ozone depletion.

7.1 World Climates

The climate of the world has fluctuated frequently and extensively in the three or so million years during which humans have inhabited the earth. The bulk of these changes have nothing to do with human intervention. Climate has changed, and is currently changing, because of a wide range of different natural factors which operate over a variety of time scales (Figure 7.1) (Anderson et al., 2013).

While humans are at present incapable of modifying some of these natural mechanisms of climate change – the output of solar radiation, the presence of fine interstellar matter, the earth's orbital variations, volcanic eruptions, mountain building, and the overall pattern of land masses and oceans – there are some key areas where humans may be capable of making significant changes to global climates (Figure 7.2). The most important categories of influence are in terms of the chemical composition of the atmosphere and the albedo of Earth's surface, though, as the following list shows, there are some others that also need to be considered:

Gas emissions
    carbon dioxide
    methane
    chlorofluorocarbons (CFCs)
    nitrous oxide
    water vapour

    miscellaneous trace gases
    stratospheric ozone depletion
Aerosol generation
    dust, smoke, black carbon, etc.
Thermal pollution
Albedo change
    dust and black carbon addition to ice caps
    deforestation and afforestation
    overgrazing
Extension of irrigation
Alteration of ocean currents by constricting straits
Diversion of fresh waters into oceans, affecting thermo-
    haline circulation system
Impoundment of large reservoirs

Figure 7.2, based on an Intergovernmental Panel on Climate Change report (IPCC, 2007a and b), shows the relative importance of different human factors in forcing climate between 1750 (the start of the industrial revolution) and 2005. That warming of Earth's climate has taken place over the last four to five decades is unequivocal, and the IPCC (2013: 17) asserts that 'Human influence has been detected in warming of the atmosphere and the ocean, in changes in the global water cycle, in reductions in snow and ice, in global mean sea level rise, and in changes in some climate extremes … It is extremely likely that human influence has been the dominant cause of the observed warming since the mid-20th century.'

Human Impact on the Natural Environment: Past, Present and Future, Eighth Edition. Andrew S. Goudie.
© 2019 John Wiley & Sons Ltd. Published 2019 by John Wiley & Sons Ltd.
Companion website: www.wiley.com/go/goudie/human-impact-natural-environment

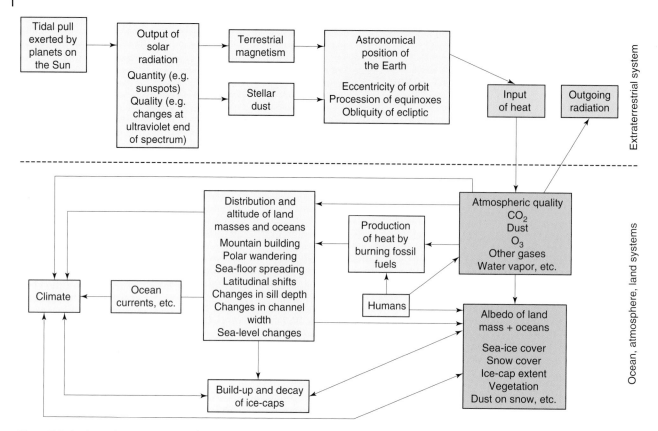

Figure 7.1 A schematic representation of some of the possible influences causing climatic change. *Source:* adapted from Goudie (1992: figure 1).

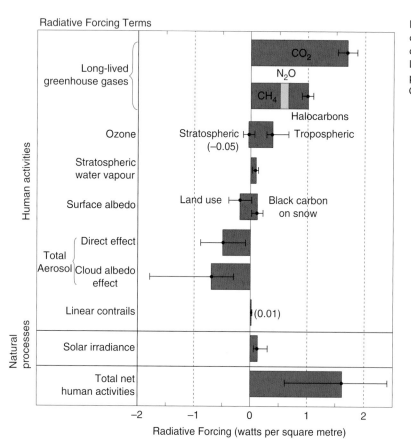

Figure 7.2 Summary diagram of the principal components of the radiative forcing of climate change between 1750 and 2005. *Source:* after IPCC (2007a: FAQ 2.1, figure 2). Reproduced with permission of Intergovernmental Panel on Climate Change.

7.2 The Greenhouse Gases – Carbon Dioxide

The greenhouse effect occurs in the atmosphere because of the presence of certain gases that absorb infrared radiation (Figure 7.3). Light and ultra-violet radiation from the sun are able to penetrate the atmosphere and warm Earth's surface. This energy is re-radiated as infrared radiation, which, because of its longer wavelength, is absorbed by certain substances such as water vapour, carbon dioxide, and other trace gases. This causes the average temperature of the earth's surface and atmosphere to increase. Should the quantities of each substance in the atmosphere be increased, then the greenhouse effect will become enhanced (Hansen et al., 1981).

Humans have been enhancing the greenhouse effect, most significantly by increasing carbon dioxide levels in the atmosphere. This may have started with deforestation in the Holocene (Boyle et al., 2011) and with the spread of rice cultivation (Ruddiman et al., 2011) but has accelerated in recent centuries. Since the beginning of the industrial revolution humans have been taking stored carbon out of the earth in the form of coal, oil, and natural gas, and burning it to make carbon dioxide (CO_2), heat, water vapour, and smaller amounts of sulphur dioxide (SO_2) and other gases. The pre-industrial level of carbon dioxide is a matter of some debate, but may have been as low as 260–270 parts per million by volume (ppmv). The 2016 level was around 400 ppmv, and the upward trend is evident in records from various parts of the world (Figure 7.4). At the present rate it would reach 500 ppmv by the end of the twenty-first century. The prime cause of increased carbon dioxide emissions is fossil fuel combustion and cement production (c. 5.5 GtC/yr in the 1980s and now approaching 9 GtC/yr). Some countries are achieving reductions in their CO_2 emissions, and in 2016 UK emissions were at their lowest level since the 1890s. In addition, the release of carbon dioxide by changes in tropical land use (primarily deforestation) is a significant factor (c. 1.6GtC/yr) in terms of global emissions. The amount of carbon derived from deforestation has increased greatly from about 0.4 GtC/yr in 1850 (Figure 7.5) (Woodwell, 1992) and now contributes between 6 and 17% of global anthropogenic CO_2 emissions (Baccini et al., 2012). A recent analysis of global and regional carbon fluxes related to land-cover

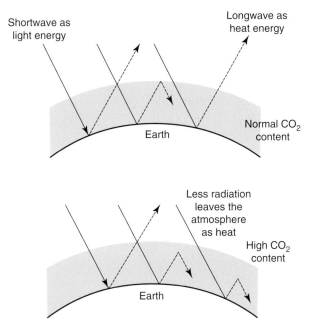

Figure 7.3 The greenhouse effect: short-wave radiation from the sun is absorbed by the earth's surface which, in turn, radiates heat at far longer wavelengths because of its temperature of around 280°K, compared with 6,000°K for the sun.

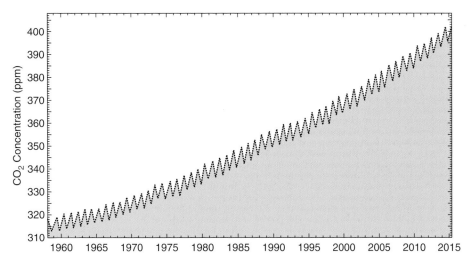

Figure 7.4 Atmospheric carbon dioxide concentrations at Mauna Loa, Hawaii (parts per million by volume) from 1960 to 2015. *Source:* data from NOAA.

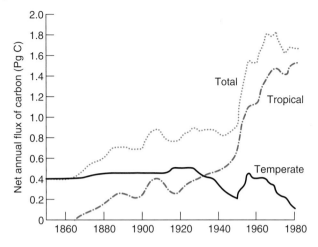

Figure 7.5 The net annual flux of carbon from deforestation in tropical and temperate zones globally, 1850–1980. *Source:* derived from data in Houghton and Skole (1990: figure 23.2), and Woodwell (1992: figure 5.2).

and land-use changes since the mid-nineteenth century has been provided by Houghton and Nassikas (2017), but huge uncertainties still exist.

7.3 Other Gases

In addition to carbon dioxide, it is probable that other gases will contribute to the greenhouse effect (Table 7.1). Individually their effects may be minor, but as a group they may be major. Indeed, molecule for molecule some of them may be much more effective as greenhouse gases than CO_2, as the data in Table 7.2 show.

One of the more important of the trace gases is methane (CH_4), which has a strong infrared absorption band at 7.66 μm. This gas is produced from a number of sources (Table 7.3) (Karakurt et al., 2012). Saunois et al. (2016) classified these sources in the atmosphere according to the emitting process (thermogenic, biogenic, or pyrogenic) and by whether or not they were natural. Biogenic methane is the final product of the decomposition of organic matter in anaerobic environments, such as water-saturated soils, swamps, paddy fields, marine sediments, landfills, waste-water facilities, or inside animal intestines. Thermogenic methane is formed on long geological timescales by the breakdown of buried organic matter due to heat and pressure deep in the Earth's crust. It reaches the atmosphere through gas seeps and during the exploitation and distribution of fossil fuels. Pyrogenic methane is produced by the incomplete combustion of biomass and peat fires. Biomass burning in deforested or degraded areas and biofuel usage are the largest sources of pyrogenic methane. Methane hydrates, ice-like cages of methane trapped in continental shelves and below

Table 7.1 Sources of four principal greenhouse gases.[1]

Gas	Natural sources	Human-derived sources
Carbon dioxide	Terrestrial biosphere Oceans	Fossil fuel combustion Cement production Land-use modification
Methane	Natural wetlands Termites Oceans and freshwater lakes	Fossil fuels (natural gas production, coal mines, petroleum industry, coal combustion) Enteric fermentation (e.g. cattle) Rice paddies Biomass burning Landfills Animal waste Domestic sewage
Nitrous oxide	Oceans Tropical soils (wet forests, dry savannas) Temperate soils (forests, grassland)	Nitrogenous fertilizers Industrial sources Land-use modification (biomass burning, forest clearing) Cattle and feed lots
Chlorofluoro-carbons[2]	Nil	Rigid and flexible foam Aerosol propellants Teflon polymers Industrial solvents

1) Sources listed in order of decreasing magnitude of emission except where otherwise indicated.
2) Sources of chlorofluorocarbons not in order of decreasing magnitudes of emission.

sub-sea and land permafrost, can be of biogenic or thermogenic origin.

Ice core studies and recent direct observations (Figure 7.6b) suggest that until the beginning of the industrial revolution in the eighteenth century background levels were relatively stable at around 600 parts per billion by volume (ppbv) although they may have been increased prior to that by rice farming and other

Table 7.2 Radiative forcing relative to CO_2 per unit molecule change in the atmosphere.

Gas	Relative radiative forcing	Residence time in atmosphere (years)
CO_2	1	100
CH_4 (methane)	21	10
N_2O (nitrous oxide)	206	100–200
CFC-11	12,400	65
CFC-12	15,800	130

Source: extracted from Houghton et al. (1990: 53, table 2.3).

Table 7.3a Estimated sources and sinks of methane in millions of tonnes per year.

Sources	Best estimate
Natural	
Wetlands	150
Termites	20
Ocean	15
Other (including hydrates)	15
Human-generated	
Coal mining, natural gas, petroleum industry	100
Rice paddies	60
Enteric fermentation	90
Waste treatment	25
Landfills	40
Biomass burning	40
Sinks	
Atmospheric removal	545
Removal by soils	30
Atmospheric increase	22

Source: after Houghton (2009: table 3.2).

Table 7.3b Estimates of nitrous oxide (N_2O) source strengths and sinks.

Sources/sinks	Range (10^6 t a^{-1})
Sources	
Oceans	1.4–2.6
Soils (tropical forests)	2.2–3.7
Soils (temperate forests)	0.7–1.5
Fossil fuel combustion	0.1–0.3
Biomass burning	0.02–0.2
Fertilizer (including groundwater)	0.01–2.2
Sinks	
Removal by soils	Unknown
Photolysis in the stratosphere	7–13
Atmospheric increase	3–4.5

Source: data in UNEP (1991).

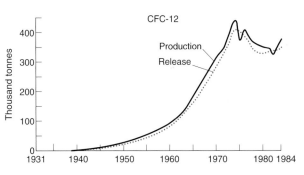

Figure 7.6 The changing concentrations of accessory greenhouse gases in the atmosphere: (a) Nitrous oxide. Note these remained fairly constant between 23,000 years ago and AD 1850 at approximately 285 parts per billion. *Source:* after Khalil and Rasmussen (1987). Reproduced with permission of Elsevier. (b) Methane. *Source:* after Khalil and Rasmussen (1987). Reproduced with permission of Elsevier. (c) The changing production and release of two CFC gases (CFC-11 and CFC-12) between 1931 and 1992.

agricultural activities (Ruddiman and Thomson, 2001). They rose steadily between AD 1700 and 1900, and then increased still more rapidly, attaining levels that averaged 1300 ppbv in the early 1950s and 1600 ppbv by the mid-1980s (Khalil and Rasmussen, 1987). Kirschke et al. (2013) found that there was a sustained increase in atmospheric CH_4 levels in the 1980s (by an average of 12 ± 6 ppbv yr^{-1}), a slowdown in growth in the 1990s (6 ± 8 ppbv yr^{-1}), and a general stabilization from 1999 to 2006 to 1773 ± 3 ppbv. Since 2007, CH_4 levels have been rising again, and exceeded 1803 ppbv in 2011 (Figure 7.6a). This increase of three times over background levels resulted primarily from increased rice cultivation in waterlogged paddy fields, the enteric fermentation produced in the growing numbers of flatulent and belching domestic cattle, and the burning of fossil fuels (Crutzen et al., 1986). In some countries, including the UK, emissions have recently declined because of a reduction in coal burning, and reductions in emissions from rice cultivation in Asia also occurred in the last years of the twentieth century (Kai et al., 2011) as a result of increases in fertilizer application and reductions in water use.

Chlorofluorocarbons (CFCs) are non-toxic, non-flammable chemicals containing atoms of carbon, chlorine, and fluorine. They have been used in the manufacture of aerosol sprays, blowing agents for foams and packing materials, as solvents, and as refrigerants. CFCs are classified as halocarbons, a class of compounds that contain atoms of carbon and halogen atoms. They occur as relatively trace amounts in the atmosphere, but emissions increased very markedly in the second half of the twentieth century (Figure 7.7). CFCs have a very strong greenhouse effect even in relatively small amounts. On the other hand, the ozone depletion they have caused in the stratosphere may to some limited extent counteract this effect, for stratospheric ozone depletion results in a decrease in radiative forcing (Houghton et al., 1992). Conversely, the build-up of lower-level tropospheric ozone can contribute to the greenhouse effect. As a consequence of the Montreal Protocol, which came into force in 1989, CFC concentrations in the atmosphere are now starting to decline.

Nitrous oxide (N_2O) is also no laughing matter, for it can contribute to the greenhouse effect, primarily by absorption of infrared at the 7.8 and 17 μm bands. Combustion of hydrocarbon fuels, the use of ammonia-based fertilizers, deforestation, and biomass burning are among the processes that could lead to an increase in atmospheric N_2O levels (Figures 7.6a and 7.7 and Table 7.3b). In 2011 the concentration of nitrous oxide was 324 ppb, and exceeded the pre-industrial levels by about 20%. Other trace gases that could play a greenhouse role include bromide compounds, carbon tetraflouride, carbon tetrachloride, and methyl chloride.

The continued role of greenhouse gases other than CO_2 in changing the climate is already not greatly less important than that of CO_2. If present trends continue, the combined concentrations of atmospheric CO_2 and other greenhouse gases would be radiatively equivalent to a doubling of CO_2 from pre-industrial levels possibly as early as the 2030s. The relative amounts of radiative forcing for different greenhouse gases since pre-indus-

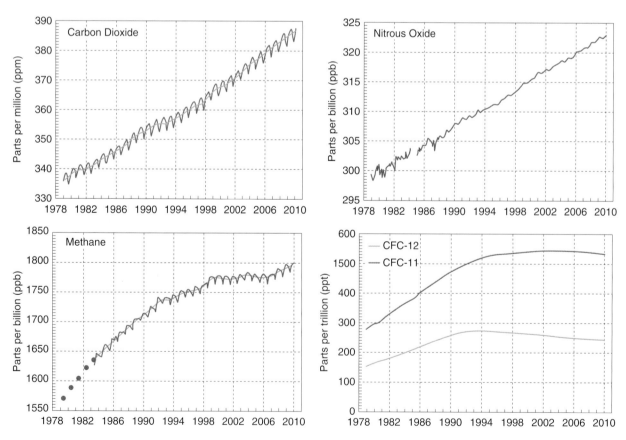

Figure 7.7 Changes in concentrations of some greenhouse gases from 1978 to 2010. *Source:* NOAA.

trial times are, according to the Intergovernmental Panel on Climate Change (2013), as follows:

CO_2	1.68 Wm^{-2}
CH_4	0.97 Wm^{-2}
N_2O	0.17 Wm^{-2}
Halocarbons	0.18 Wm^{-2}

Another important feature of the various greenhouse gases is their residence time in the atmosphere. CH_4 has a residence time of about 10 years, the shortest of all the major greenhouse gases. This means that if we could stop the enhanced emissions of that gas, its concentration in the atmosphere should fall to its natural level in a decade. By contrast, CFCs (44–180 years), N_2O (100–200 years) and CO_2 (c. 100 years) have much longer residence times, so that even if we could control their sources immediately it would still take a very long time for them to fall to their natural levels.

Global temperatures have been climbing since the end of the nineteenth century (Figure 7.8) and it is now regarded as highly probable that increased greenhouse gas loadings in the atmosphere have contributed to this.

7.4 Ozone Depletion and Climate Change

The decline in stratospheric ozone concentrations (Section 7.16) and the development of an ozone hole over Antarctica is now recognized as having potential climatic significance, especially in the Southern Hemisphere. The ozone depletion causes cooling over Antarctica which in turn causes the Hadley Cell to shift poleward which alters precipitation patterns in the subtropics (Kang et al., 2011)

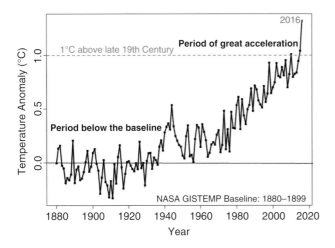

Figure 7.8 Global average temperature at Earth's surface, 1880–2016. *Source:* NASA data in http:data.giss.nasa.gov/gistemp/graphs_v3/ (accessed January 2018).

and cause a southward expansion of the subtropical dry zones (Son et al., 2009; Feldstein, 2011; Polvani et al., 2011; Purich and Son, 2012).

7.5 Aerosols

Aerosols are finely divided solid or liquid particles dispersed in the atmosphere. In general terms it is believed that they affect climate because they intercept and scatter a small portion of incoming radiation from the sun, thus reducing the energy reaching the ground. This is called the 'direct effect' of aerosols. The direct effect increases with both the number and size of aerosols in the atmosphere. Aerosols also have an 'indirect effect'. This is because they are key elements in cloud formation. The number of cloud droplets that a cloud possesses is determined by the number of aerosol particles available onto which water vapour can condense. Clouds with large numbers of droplets reflect more sunlight back into space and so can also contribute to cooling. Aerosols do not, however, inevitably cause cooling. So, for example, and Brazel and Idso (1979) point to the two contrasting tendencies of dust: the backscattering effect producing cooling, and the thermal-blanketing effect causing warming. The second of these absorbs some of the earth's thermal radiation that would otherwise escape to space, and then re-radiates a portion of this back to the land surface, raising surface temperatures. They believe that natural dust from volcanic emissions tends to enter the stratosphere (where backscattering and cooling are the prime consequences), while anthropogenic dust more frequently occurs in the lower levels of the atmosphere, causing thermal blanketing and warming.

There is a variety of ways in which human activities have increased atmospheric aerosol loadings. These include biomass burning and industrial emissions of smoke and dust particles. In addition, intensive agricultural exploitation of desert margins could create a dust pall in the atmosphere by exposing larger areas of surface materials to deflation in dust storms and there is evidence that humans have caused desert dust loadings in the atmosphere to increase (Section 4.29) (Mahowald et al., 2010; Ginoux et al., 2012) (Figure 7.9). Dust palls could so change atmospheric temperature that convection, and thus rainfall, would be reduced. There is thus the possibility that human-induced desertification generates dust which could in turn increase the degree of desertification by its effect on rainfall levels. Studies of the links between dust in the atmosphere and temperatures, precipitation and clouds has been a major area of current research (see e.g. Tegen et al., 1996; Miller and Tegen, 1998). Much of the current interest in dust storms relates to their possible role in the Earth System

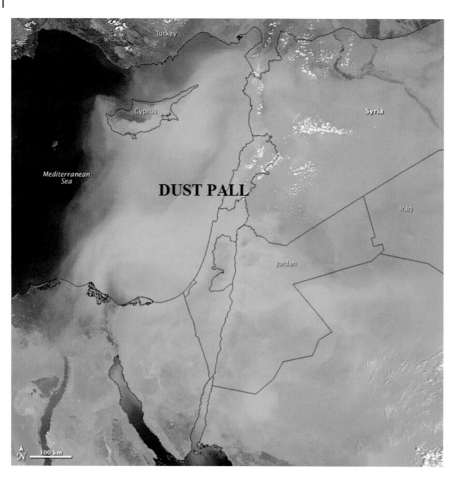

Figure 7.9 Dust storm over the Levant on 8 September 2015. *Source:* NASA Earth Observatory.

(see Goudie and Middleton, 2006: table 1:1). Dust loadings may affect air temperatures through the absorption and scattering of solar radiation (Durant et al., 2009), modify cloud formation (Toon, 2003) and convectional activity, influence sulphur dioxide levels in the atmosphere, either by physical absorption or by heterogeneous reactions (Adams et al., 2005), and influence marine primary productivity and thus atmospheric carbon dioxide levels (Ridgwell, 2003). Wong et al. (2008) has linked the strength of African dust outbreaks in the Saharan air layer to changes in hurricane intensity in the North Atlantic Region (see also Evan et al., 2006). There are still huge uncertainties about the relationship between atmospheric mineral dust aerosol levels and radiative forcing, and an increasing number of observational and modelling studies are investigating this issue (see, for example, Zhu et al., 2007). Dust particle size is a major control on whether elevated dust loadings cause cooling or warming (Kok et al., 2017). It remains a major research priority, not least because of the possibility that dust aerosols could be an accelerant of aridity trends (Cook et al., 2013).

There is also some evidence that other types of aerosol, caused by air pollution, may affect precipitation levels. For example, midweek increases in summer rainfall and storm heights in the south-east USA have been detected and are correlated with higher particulate concentrations compared to that which occurs at weekends, when industrial emissions are less (Bell et al., 2008), while in south-west China intense pollution may have so affected precipitation that enhanced flood activity occurred (Fan et al., 2015).

In recent years, there has been a growing interest in the role of black carbon (soot) in the atmosphere (Allen et al., 2012). This is derived from a variety of sources. Fossil fuel combustion is an important one, and current estimates show that the dominant black carbon emissions within the Arctic today are caused by flaring related to the oil and gas fields in north-western Russia (Sand et al., 2013). Also important are biomass burning (associated with deforestation and crop residue burning) and cooking with biofuels (Ramanathan and Carmichael, 2008). For example, three billion of the poorest people of the world rely on cooking with solid fuels and this is the largest source of anthropogenic black carbon emissions. Making up a significant part of what has been called an 'atmospheric brown cloud' over Asia, black carbon absorbs and scatters solar radiation and may contribute to global warming, not least in the Arctic (Shindell and Faluvegi, 2009). It absorbs solar radiation and exerts a positive forcing over white surfaces, both in the atmosphere and when deposited on snow. This makes the forcing and the potential impact of black carbon particularly high in the Arctic during spring, when there are large amounts of sunlight available, most of the surfaces are still covered with snow and sea ice, and the black carbon concentrations are at a maximum (Sand et al., 2013). When deposited on ice or snow it darkens the surface, significantly enhances heat absorption and so accelerates melting of glaciers (Yasunari et al., 2013; Li et al., 2016b) and sea ice. It can also contribute to a weakening of the South Asian summer monsoon and a reduction in precipitation, especially in the tropics (Meehl et al., 2008; Bollasina et al., 2011; Ganguly et al., 2012).

The most catastrophic effects of anthropogenic aerosols in the atmosphere could be those resulting from a nuclear exchange between the great powers (Dörries, 2011). Explosion, fire, and wind might generate a great pall of smoke and dust in the atmosphere which would make the world dark and cold (Westing, 2013). It has been estimated that if the exchange reached a level of several thousand megatons, a 'nuclear winter' would be as low as -15° to -25°C (Turco et al., 1983), though simulations by Schneider and Thompson (1988) suggested that some previous estimates may have been exaggerated. They suggested that in the Northern Hemisphere maximum average land surface summertime temperature depressions might be of the order of 5–15°C. The concept is discussed by Cotton and Pielke (2007: chapter 10).

Fears were also expressed that as a result of the severe smoke palls generated by the Gulf War in 1991 there might have been severe climate impacts. Studies have suggested that because most of the smoke generated by the oil well fires stayed in the lower troposphere and only had a short residence time in the air, the effects were local (some cooling) rather than global, and that the operation of the monsoon was not affected to any significant degree (Bakan et al., 1991; Browning et al., 1991). Furthermore, in the event the emissions of smoke particles were less than some forecasters had predicted, and they were also rather less black (Hobbs and Radke, 1992).

Aircraft, both civil and military, discharge some water vapour into the atmosphere as contrails. Contrails form in the wake of planes if the air is cold and moist enough. Their ice crystals scatter incoming shortwave radiation and this leads to a reduction in solar radiation at the surface (shortwave cooling). On the other hand, absorption and emission of longwave radiation reduce the out-

going terrestrial radiation, because absorbed infrared radiation is emitted from the cloud tops at significantly lower temperatures than from the Earth surface (longwave warming). On average, for contrail cirrus, the warming effect dominates (Bock and Burkhardt, 2016). At present, the water content of the stratosphere is very low, as is the exchange of air between the lower stratosphere and other regions. Consequently, comparatively modest amounts of water vapour discharge by aircraft could have a significant effect on the natural balance. It is possible that contrails and the development of thin cirrus clouds could lead to warming of the Earth's surface and future radiative forcing by aircraft could triple by 2050. Observations of cirrus cloud cover over the last 50 years near to major USA flight corridors show a clear upward trend that seems to correlate with US domestic jet fuel trends over the same period (Yang et al. 2010a). However, the Intergovernmental Panel on Climate Change (IPCC, 2007a: 30) concluded 'No best estimates are available for the net forcing from spreading contrails. Their effects on cirrus cloudiness and the global effect of aviation aerosol on background cloudiness remain unknown'. The whole role of aircraft impacts on the atmosphere and climate is discussed by Lee et al. (2010).

Over the world's oceans a major source of aerosols is dimethylsulphide (DMS). This is produced by planktonic algae in sea water and then oxidized in the atmosphere to form sulphate aerosols. Because the albedo of clouds (and thus the Earth's radiation budget) is sensitive to cloud-condensation nuclei density, any factor that controls planktonic algae may have an important impact on climate. The production of such plankton could be affected by water pollution in coastal areas or by global warming (Charlson et al., 1987). The role of DMS in driving climate change, however, is still far from certain (Land et al., 2014; Tesdal et al., 2016). An even more important source of sulphate aerosols is the burning of fossil fuels and the subsequent emission of sulphur dioxide (SO_2), and these types of sulphate aerosol are concentrated over and downwind of major industrial regions. They have probably served to reduce the rate of global warming that has taken place in recent decades and may help to explain the cessation in global warming that took place in some regions between the 1940s and 1970s (Taylor and Penner, 1994).

7.6 Global Dimming and Global Brightening

There is some evidence that the amount of solar radiation that reached the Earth's surface declined by c 0.2–0.3% per year between c. 1960 and c. 1990 – a phenomenon called 'Global Dimming' (Stanhill and Cohen, 2001; Wild, 2009). Possible causes could include changes in clouds, increasing amounts of anthropogenic aerosols and reduced atmospheric transparency after explosive volcanic eruptions (Pinker et al., 2005). Air pollution may have worked in two ways – by reflecting sunlight back into space, and by making clouds more reflective. Global dimming may to a certain degree have masked the greenhouse effect. Since about 1990, the trend has been reversed and is referred to as 'Global Brightening' (Wild et al., 2005; Wild, 2012; Sanchez-Lorenzo et al., 2015). This may have enabled the effects of rising greenhouse gas loadings to have become more evident during the 1990s (Wild et al., 2007). The reason for this change may be that in some respects levels of atmospheric pollutants, particularly sulphur dioxide and black carbon, have declined in many regions (e.g. over Eastern Europe) (Streets et al., 2006). Elsewhere, however, as in China, sunshine hours have decreased appreciably in many areas in response to increased atmospheric pollution (Wang et al., 2012; Yang et al., 2012).

7.7 Vegetation and Albedo Change

Incoming radiation of all wavelengths is partly absorbed and partly reflected. Albedo is the term used to describe the proportion of energy reflected and hence is a measure of the ability of the surface to reflect radiation. Land-use changes create differences in albedo which have important effects on the energy balance, and hence on the water balance, of an area. Tall rain forest may have an albedo as low as 9%, while the albedo of a desert may be as high as 37% (Table 7.4).

There has been growing interest recently in the possible consequences of afforestation and deforestation on climate through their effect on albedo (Li et al., 2016a). Ground deprived of a vegetation cover as a result of deforestation and overgrazing has a very much higher albedo than ground covered in plants. This could affect temperature levels. Satellite imagery of the Sinai–Negev region of the Middle East shows an enormous difference in image between the relatively dark Negev and the very bright Sinai–Gaza strip area. This line coincides with the 1948–1949 armistice line between Israel and Egypt and results from different land-use and population pressures. Otterman (1974) suggested that this albedo change has produced temperature changes of the order of 5°C. Charney and others (1975) also argued that the increase in surface albedo, resulting from a decrease in plant cover, would lead to a decrease in the net incoming radiation, and an increase in the radiative cooling of the air. Consequently, they argue, the air would sink to maintain thermal equilibrium by adiabatic compression, and cumulus convection and its associated rainfall would be suppressed. A positive feedback mechanism would

Table 7.4 Albedo values for different land-use types.

Surface type	Location	Albedo (%)
Agricultural grassland	England and Wales	24
Bamboo forest	Kenya	16
Citrus orchard	Israel	16.8
Conifer plantation	England and Wales	16
Deciduous woodland	England and Wales	18
Desert	Israel	37.3
Evergreen scrub (maquis)	Israel	15.9
Heather moorland	England and Wales	15
Lake	Israel	11.3
Open oak forest	Israel	17.6
Peat and moss	England and Wales	12
Pine forest	Israel	12.3
Rough grass hillside	Israel	20.3
Tall rain forest	Kenya	9
Tea bushes	Kenya	20
Towns	England and Wales	17

Source: from miscellaneous data in Pereira (1973) collated by author.

appear at this stage, for the lower rainfall would in turn adversely affect plants and lead to a further decrease in plant cover. However, this view was disputed by Ripley (1976) who suggested that Charney and his colleagues, while considering the impact of vegetation changes on albedo, had completely ignored the effect of vegetation on evapotranspiration. He pointed out that vegetated surfaces are usually cooler than bare ground since much of the absorbed solar energy is used to evaporate water, and concludes from this that protection from over-grazing and deforestation might, in contrast to Charney's views, be expected to lower surface temperatures and thereby reduce, rather than increase, convection and precipitation.

Removal of humid tropical rain forests has also been seen as a possible mechanism of anthropogenic climatic change through its effect on albedo. Potter et al. (1975) proposed the following model for such change:

Reduced evaporation and sensible heat flux from the surface

|

Reduced convective activity and rainfall

|

Reduced release of latent heat, weakened Hadley circulation and cooling in the mid- and upper troposphere

|

Increased tropical lapse rates

|

Increased precipitation in the latitude bands 5–25°N and 5–25°S, and a decrease in the Equator–pole temperature gradient

|

Reduced meridional transport of heat and moisture out of equatorial regions

|

Global cooling and decrease in precipitation between 45–85°N and 40–60°S

However, some studies (e.g. Potter et al., 1981) have suggested that globally over the past few thousand years the climatic effects of albedo changes wrought by humans have been small and probably undetectable. Similarly, Henderson-Sellers and Gornitz (1984) sought to model the possible future effects of albedo changes produced by humans and also predicted that there would be but little alteration brought about by current levels of tropical deforestation. On the other hand, Lean and Warrilow (1989) used a general circulation model (GCM) which showed greater changes than previous models and suggested that Amazon basin deforestation would, through the effects of changes in surface roughness and albedo, lead to reductions in both precipitation and evaporation. Likewise a UK Meteorological Office GCM indicated that the deforestation of both Amazonia and Zaire would, by changing surface albedo, cause a decrease in precipitation levels (Mylne and Rowntree, 1992). There are now an increasing number of modelling experiments that suggest vegetation removal can have important regional and even global effects (Table 7.5), though there are considerable divergences between different models (Nobre et al., 2004). Nonetheless, most show *decreases* in mean evapotranspiration of from 25.5 to 985.0 mm per year, *increases* in mean surface temperatures of 0.1–3.8°C and *reductions* in regional precipitation (Sampaio et al., 2007; Tölle et al., 2017). It is even possible that the effects of Amazonian deforestation on precipitation could extend some distance away from there, to the Dakotas and the Midwest Triangle in the USA, as modelling by

Table 7.5 Some studies of climatic effects of vegetation removal.

Source	Location	Subject
Fuller and Ottka (2002)	West Africa	Albedo and desertification
Fu (2003)	East Asia	Reduced atmospheric and soil moisture in East Asian monsoon region
Chase et al. (2000)	Global	Effects on main circulation features
Werth and Avissar (2002)	Amazonia	Reduction of local precipitation, evapotranspiration, and cloudiness, and also global effects
Berbet and Costa (2003)	Amazonia	Precipitation variability
Reale and Dirmeyer (2000)	Mediterranean Basin	Increased precipitation prior to deforestation in Roman times
Taylor et al. (2002)	Sahel	Rainfall decrease
Sampaio et al. (2007)	Amazonia	Rainfall decrease
Doughty et al. (2012)	South America	Rainfall decrease

Werth and Avissar (2002) has shown, while deforestation and afforestation in monsoon Asia could influence precipitation in the Sahara and Arabia (Dallmeyer and Claussen, 2011).

Albedo effects may be significant in higher latitudes as well. As Betts (2000) has pointed out, in a snowy environment, forests are generally darker than open land, because trees generally remain exposed when cultivated land can become entirely snow-covered. Snow-free foliage is darker than snow. This means that forest has a smaller surface albedo and so may exert a warming influence. Thus land-cover changes in the boreal forest zone can have substantial climatic implications. Betts (2001) suggested that mid-latitude agricultural regions would be approximately 1–2 K cooler in winter and spring in comparison with their previously forested state, due to deforestation increasing the surface albedo during periods of snow cover. Conversely, mid-latitude afforestation, which has taken place in recent decades, by increasing surface temperatures, may have a widespread influence on the general atmospheric circulation, even in the tropics, and on amounts of precipitation (Swann et al, 2012). Similarly, Naik and Abiodun (2016) modelled the response of climate in South Africa to increasing vegetation cover caused by shrub encroachment (see Section 2.12) and afforestation.

They found that the darker forest (relative to pre-existing vegetation cover) decreases the surface albedo and increases the amount of solar radiation absorbed at the surface. This extra energy in the system increases the amount of sensible and latent heat, and increases the temperature and rainfall, respectively.

7.8 Forests, Irrigation, and Climate

The belief that forests can increase precipitation levels has a long history (Thornthwaite, 1956; Grove, 1997). The replacement of forest with crops, in addition to leading to a change in surface albedo of the type just discussed, also changes some other factors that may have climatic significance, including surface aerodynamic roughness, leaf and stem areas, and amount of evapotranspiration (Betts, 2001). In particular large amounts of moisture may be transpired by deep-rooting plants, which means that moisture is pumped back into the atmosphere, leading to increased levels of precipitation. Conversely, removal of such deep-rooting vegetation could exacerbate drought. Forests are far more effective than other vegetation types at trapping cloud, fog, and mist. Hence deforestation or afforestation can affect water budgets through the degree to which they intercept non-rainfall precipitation.

Bonan (1997) tried to model the climatic consequences of replacing the natural forests of the United States with crops and argued that it would cause cooling of up to 2°C in the summer months over a wide region of the central United States. He suggested (p. 484) that 'land use practices that resulted in extensive deforestation in the Eastern United States, replacing forests with crop, have resulted in a significant climate change that is comparable to other well-known anthropogenic climate forcings.' Similarly, the clearing of native vegetation in eastern Australia seems to have led to an increase in the number of dry and hot days, thereby intensifying drought conditions (Deo et al., 2009).

There is one other land-use change that may result in measurable changes in precipitation; namely large-scale crop irrigation in arid and semi-arid regions. The High Plains of the United States are normally covered with sparse grasses and have dry soils throughout the summer; evapotranspiration is then very low. In the last five decades irrigation has been developed throughout large parts of the area, greatly increasing summer evapotranspiration levels. Barnston and Schickdanz (1984) produced strong statistical evidence of warm-season rainfall enhancement through irrigation in two parts of this area: one extending through Kansas, Nebraska, and Colorado, and a second in the Texas Panhandle. The largest absolute increase was in the latter area and,

significantly, occurred in June, the wettest of the three heavily irrigated months. The effect appears to be especially important when stationary weather fronts occur, for this is a situation which allows for maximum interaction between the damp irrigated surface and the atmosphere. Hailstorms and tornados are also significantly more prevalent than over non-irrigated regions (Nicholson, 1988). However, Moore and Rojstaczer (2001) thought that overall the irrigation effect on precipitation is both difficult to quantify unambiguously and probably of minor significance. Irrigation may also lead to lower air surface temperatures compared to that found above natural desert surfaces, and this has been found in the northern Great Plains of the USA (Mahmood et al., 2006). Finally, Lee et al. (2011) have suggested that there is now so much irrigated land over Asia that not only does it lead to a decrease in surface temperatures, but it may also affect upper level pressure and wind conditions.

7.9 The Possible Effects of Water Diversion Schemes

The levels of the Aral and Caspian seas in Central Asia have fallen (Section 5.4), as have water tables all over the wide continental region. There have been proposals to divert some major rivers to help overcome these problems. However, this raises difficult questions 'because it appears to touch a peculiarly sensitive spot in the existing climatic regime of the northern hemisphere' (Lamb, 1977: 671). The low-salinity water which forms a 100–200 m upper layer to the Arctic Ocean is in part caused by the input of fresh water from the large Russian and Siberian rivers. This low-salinity water is the medium in which the pack ice at present covering the polar ocean is formed. The tapping of any large proportion of this river flow might augment the area of salt water in the Arctic Ocean and thereby reduce the area of pack ice correspondingly. Temperatures over large areas might rise, which in turn might change the position and alignment of the main thermal gradients in the Northern Hemisphere and, with them, the jet stream and the development and steering of cyclonic activity. However, assessment of this particular climatic impact is still very largely speculative, and some numerical models indicate that the climate of the Arctic will not be drastically affected by river diversions (Semtner, 1984). At the present time, because of climate change, the amount of fresh water entering the Arctic Sea is actually increasing (Haine et al., 2015), so that the potential influence of water diversion schemes is as yet minimal.

7.10 Lakes and Climate

It has often been implied that the presence of a large body of inland water must modify the climate around its shores, and therefore that artificial lakes have a significant effect on local or regional climates (Vendrov, 1965). Schemes have been put forward for augmenting desert rainfall by flooding desert basins in the Sahara, Kalahari, and Middle East (e.g. Schwarz, 1923). However, whether evaporation from lake surfaces can raise local precipitation levels is open to question, for precipitation depends more on atmospheric instability than upon the humidity content of the air. Moreover, most lakes are too small to affect the atmosphere materially in depth, so that their influence falls heavily under the sway of the regional circulation. In addition, one needs to remember that some of the world's driest deserts occur along coastlines. Thus a relatively small artificial lake would be even more impotent in creating rainfall. However, particularly in areas with Mediterranean and semi-arid climates, there is now some evidence that rainfall quantity and intensity is augmented in the vicinity of large dams (Hossain, 2009; Degu et al., 2011). Thunderstorm activity may also be modified (Haberlie et al., 2016). However, the climatic effect of artificial lakes is evident in other ways, notably in terms of a local reduction in frost hazard. In the case of the Rybinsk reservoir (c. 4,500 km^2) in the CIS, it has been calculated that the climatic influence extends 10 km from the lake and that the frost-free season has been extended by 5–15 days on average (D'Yakanov and Reteyum, 1965). The loss of a large body of water, such as the progressive desiccation of the Aral Sea (see Section 5.4) might exacerbate the climate changes associated with global warming (McDermid and Winter, 2017).

7.11 Urban Climates

With the increasing number of people living in big cities, there is an ever-increasing interest in how urban areas modify their climates (Landsberg, 1981; Souch and Grimmond, 2006). It has been said that 'the city is the quintessence of man's capacity to inaugurate and control changes in his habitat' (Detwyler and Marcus, 1972). Individual urban areas can at times, with respect to their weather, 'have similar impacts as a volcano, a desert, and as an irregular forest' (Changnon, 1973: 146). Some of the changes that can result are listed in Table 7.6.

There is particular interest in the production of heat by the burning of fossil fuels, which at the local scale produces the 'urban heat island' (Jones and Lister, 2009). Following an analysis of urban and rural temperature trends in 50 of the most populous cities in the USA

Table 7.6a Average changes in climatic elements caused by cities.

Element	Parameter	Urban compared with rural (−, less; +, more)
Radiation	On horizontal surface	−15%
	Ultraviolet	−30% (winter); −5% (summer)
Temperature	Annual mean	+0.7°C
	Winter maximum	+1.5°C
	Length of freeze-free season	+2 to 3 weeks (possible)
Wind speed	Annual mean	−20 to −30%
	Extreme gusts	−10 to −20%
	Frequency of calms	+5 to 20%
Relative humidity	Annual mean	−6%
	Seasonal mean	−2% (winter); −8% (summer)
Cloudiness	Cloud frequency + amount	+5 to 10%
	Fogs	+100% (winter); −30% (summer)
Precipitation	Amounts	+5% to 10%
	Days	+10%
	Snow days	−14%

Source: Reproduced with permission of Oxford University Press.

Table 7.6b Effect of city surfaces.

Phenomenon	Consequence
Heat production (the heat island)	Rainfall + Temperature +
Retention of reflected radiation by high walls and dark-coloured roofs	Temperature +
Surface roughness increase	Wind − Eddying +
Dust increase (the dust dome)	Fog + Rainfall + (?)

Source: H. Landsberg in Griffiths (1976: 108). Reproduced with permission of Oxford University Press.

between 1951 and 2000, Stone (2007) found a mean decadal difference in urban and rural temperatures of 0.05°C suggesting an amplification of background warming rates of 0.5°C per century in large US cities.

Compared with rural surfaces, city surfaces (Table 7.6b) absorb significantly more solar radiation, because a higher proportion of the reflected radiation is retained by the high walls and dark-coloured roofs of the city streets. The concreted city surfaces have both great thermal capacity and conductivity, so that heat is stored during the day and released by night. By contrast the plant cover of the countryside acts like an insulating blanket, so that rural areas tend to experience relatively lower temperatures by day and night, an effect enhanced by the evaporation and transpiration taking place. In addition, the energy partitioned for evapotranspiration is less in urban areas, leading to greater surface heating. Another thermal change in cities, contributing to the development of the 'urban heat island', is the large amount of artificial heat produced by industrial, commercial, and domestic users (Phelan et al., 2015).

In general the highest temperature anomalies are associated with the densely built-up area near the city centre, and decrease markedly at the city perimeter. Observations in Hamilton, Ontario, and Montreal, Quebec, suggested temperature changes of 3.8 and 4.0°C respectively per kilometre (Oke, 1978). Temperature differences also tend to be highest during the night. The form of the urban temperature effect has often been likened to an 'island' protruding distinctly out of the cool 'sea' of the surrounding landscape. The rural–urban boundary exhibits a steep temperature gradient or 'cliff' to the urban heat island. Much of the rest of the urban area appears as a 'plateau' of warm air with a steady but weaker horizontal gradient of increasing temperature towards the city centre. The urban core may be a 'peak' where the urban maximum temperature is found. The difference between this value and the background rural temperature defines the *urban heat island intensity (T_{u-r} (max))* (Oke, 1978: 225).

The heat island of New York City is of impressive size and impacts upon a large area. The difference in temperature between the urban core and the surrounding rural areas averages about 4°C on summer nights. Figure 7.10 shows the urban heat island that was evident on a warm, summer night on 14 August 2002. Surface air temperature readings showed that the city was several degrees warmer than the suburbs, and up to 8°C warmer than the rural areas within 100 km of the city (Rosenzweig et al., 2009). Data on the urban heat island for major cities in the USA is provided by Ramamurthy and Sangobanwo (2016). Seattle had the highest average urban heat island effect with a summer daytime peak of around 5°C, followed by Houston with 2.7°C. Most other cities experienced a peak between 2 and 2.5°C.

Table 7.7 lists the average annual urban–rural temperature differences for several large cities. Values range from 0.6 to 1.8°C. In their analysis of 419 cities with a population of over one million, Peng et al. (2012) found that the mean vales were 1.5°C by day and 1.1°C by night. The relationship between city size and urban–rural difference, however, is not necessarily linear; sizeable nocturnal temperature contrasts have been measured even in relatively small cities. Factors such as building density are at least as important as city size, and high wind velocities will tend to reduce the heat island effect

Figure 7.10 New York City's urban heat island (°C) at 0600 EST on 14 August 2002. *Source:* adapted from Rosenzweig et al. (2009: figure 1).

Table 7.7 Annual mean urban-rural temperature differences of cities.

City	Temperature differences (°C)
Berlin, Germany	1.0
Chicago, USA	0.6
London, UK	1.8
Los Angeles, USA	0.7
Moscow, Russia	0.7
New York, USA	1.1
Paris, France	0.7
Philadelphia, USA	0.8
Washington, DC, USA	0.6

Source: from data in Detwyler (1971) and Wilby (2003).

(Schlünzen et al., 2010). The presence or absence of urban vegetation is also significant (Peng et al., 2012), as are the moderating effects of wetlands (Cai et al., 2016).

Nonetheless, Oke (1978: 257) has found that there is some relation between heat-island intensity and city size. Using population as a surrogate of city size, T_{u-r} (max) is found to be proportional to the log of the population. Other interesting results of this study include the tendency for quite small centres to have a heat island, the observation that the maximum thermal modification is about 12°C, and the recognition of a difference in slope between the North American and the European relationships (Figure 7.11a). The explanation for this last result is not clear, but it may be related to the fact that population is a surrogate index of the central building density. Imhoff et al. (2010), working on a large number of American cities, and Benz et al. (2017) working in Germany, also found a strong correlation between city size and the size of the urban heat island, and this was confirmed on a global basis by Cui et al. (2016), who also found that heat island intensity increased with levels of GDP (Gross Domestic Product). The relationship between maximum heat island intensity and urban population, the sky-view factor (a measure of building height and density), and the impermeable surface coverage of cities are shown in Figure 7.11c. Heat island intensity increases with all three indices (Nakagawa, 1996).

In many older towns and cities in Western Europe and North America, the process of 'counter-urbanization' has in recent years led to a decline in population, and it is worth considering whether this is reflected in a decline in the intensity of urban heat islands. One attempt to do this, in the context of London (Lee, 1992), revealed the perplexing finding that the heat-island intensity has decreased by day, but increased by night. The explanation that has been tentatively advanced to explain this is

Figure 7.11 Relationships between the maximum heat island intensity and (a) urban population for Japanese, Korean, North American, and European cities; (b) the sky view factor for Japanese, Korean, North American, and European cities; (c) the ratio of impermeable surface coverage for Japanese and Korean cities. *Source:* after Nakagawa (1996: figures 2, 3, and 4). Reproduced with permission from Association of Japanese Geographers.

that there has been a decrease in the receipt of daytime solar radiation as a result of vehicular atmosphere pollution, whereas at night the presence of such pollution absorbs and re-emits significant amounts of out-going terrestrial radiation, maintaining higher urban nocturnal minimum temperatures. The urban heat island may also be more marked at night because reduced nocturnal turbulent mixing keeps the warmer air near the surface. In mid-latitude cities like London, urban heat-island effects are generally stronger in summer than in winter because of higher levels of solar radiation being absorbed by building materials during the day. In winter the urban–rural contrast is weaker because solar energy absorption is lower and hence there is less energy to radiate, despite higher levels of urban space heating (Wilby, 2003).

The urban–industrial effects on clouds, rain, snowfall, and associated weather hazards such as hail and thunder are harder to measure and explain than the temperature changes. The changes can be related to various influences (Changnon, 1973: 143): thermally induced upward movement of air; increased vertical motions from mechanically induced turbulence; increased cloud and raindrop nuclei; and industrial increases in water vapour. Table 7.8 illustrates the differences in summer rainfall, thunderstorms, and hailstorms between various rural and urban areas in the United States. These data indicate that in cities rainfall increased from 9 to 27%, the incidence of thunderstorms by 10 to 42%, and hailstorms by 67 to 430%. Such changes have been identified in Houston, Texas, where the average warm-season rainfall amount in the urban area increased by 25% from the pre- to the post-urban period, while the amount in the upwind control region declined by 8% (Burian and Shepherd, 2005). Urban effects on summer thunderstorm rainfall have also been identified in Atlanta, Georgia (Rose et al., 2008; Shem and Shepherd, 2009; Haberlie et al., 2015) and more generally in the south-east United States (Ashley et al., 2012). In Shanghai, China, urban warming accounts for the consistent increase in hourly heavy

precipitation over the whole Shanghai area during recent times in comparison with its rural surroundings (Liang and Ding, 2017). Convective storms have also been intensified over Sydney, Australia (Gero et al., 2006), and lightning activity seems to be affected by the metropolitan area of São Paulo, Brazil (Farias et al., 2009; Bourscheidt et al., 2016). Urban aerosols appear to play an important role both in terms of enhancing precipitation and enhancing lightning (Heever and Cotton, 2007; Kar et al., 2009).

An interesting example of the effects of major conurbations on precipitation levels is provided by the London area. In this case it seems that the mechanical effect of the city was dominant in creating localized maxima of precipitation both by being a mechanical obstacle to air flow, on the one hand, and by causing frictional convergence of flow, on the other (Atkinson, 1975). A long-term analysis of thunderstorm records for south-east England is highly suggestive – indicating the higher frequencies of thunderstorms over the conurbation compared to elsewhere (Atkinson, 1968). The similarity in the morphology of the thunderstorm isopleth and the urban area is striking (Figure 7.12a and b). Moreover, Brimblecombe (1977) shows a steadily increasing thunderstorm frequency as the city has grown (Figure 7.12c). Similarly the detailed Metromex investigation of St Louis in the United States (Changnon, 1978) showed that in the summer the city affects precipitation and other variables within a distance of 40 km. Increases were found in various thunderstorm characteristics (about +10 to +115%), hailstorm conditions (+3 to +330%), heavy rainfall characteristics (+35 to +100%), and strong gusts (+90 to +100%).

Table 7.8 Areas of maximum increases (urban-rural difference) in summer rainfall and severe weather events for eight American cities.

City	Rainfall		Thunderstorms		Hailstorms	
	%	Location*	%	Location*	%	Location*
Chicago	+17	C	+38	A, B, C	+246	C
Cleveland	+27	C	+42	A, B	+90	C
Houston	+9	A	+10	A, B	+430	B
Indianapolis	0	-	0	-	0	-
New Orleans	+10	A	+27	A	+350	A, B
St Louis	+15	B	+25	B	+276	C
Tulsa	0	-	0	-	0	-
Washington, DC	+9	C	+36	A	+67	B

* A = within city perimeter
B = 8–24 km downwind
C = 24–64 km downwind.
Source: after Changnon (1973: 144, figure 1.5).

Figure 7.12 Thunder in south-east England: (a) Total thunder rain in south-east England, 1951–1960, expressed in inches. *Source:* after Atkinson (1968: figure 6). Reproduced from *Transactions of the Institute of British Geographers*, 44, published by Taylor and Francis, 1968. Reproduced with permission. (b) Number of days with thunder overhead in south-east England, 1951–1960. *Source:* after Atkinson (1968: figure 5). Reproduced with permission. (c) Thunderstorms per year in London (decadal means for whole year). *Source:* after Brimblecombe (1977: figure 2). Reproduced with permission from Elsevier.

However, increases in precipitation are not universal over urban areas, and some studies show the reverse. Work in the Pearl River delta cities of south-east China (Kaufman et al., 2007) produced the concept of an 'urban precipitation deficit'. The reasons for this may have been a reduced flow of moisture into the air because of the replacement of rural vegetation with concrete surfaces, and also the effects of urban aerosol pollution on clouds and the precipitation from them. Precipitation suppression as a result of aerosol build up in cities has also been identified in Brisbane and the Gold Coast of Australia (Bigg, 2008) and in parts of Israel and California (Givati and Rosenfeld, 2004). The urban heat-island effect can also be seen as a cause of a reduction in dew frequency in comparison with rural areas (Beysens et al., 2017).

Cities also affect winds in their vicinity. Two main factors are involved in this: the rougher surface they present in comparison with rural areas; and the frequently higher temperatures of the city fabric. Buildings, especially those in cities with a highly differentiated skyline, exert a powerful frictional drag on air moving over and around them (Chandler, 1976). This creates turbulence, with characteristically rapid spatial and temporal changes in both direction and speed. The average speed of the winds is lower in built-up areas than over rural areas, but Chandler found that in London, when winds are light, speeds are greater in the inner city than outside, whereas the reverse relationship exists when winds are strong. The overall annual reduction of wind speed in central London is about 6%, but for the higher velocity winds (more than 1.5 metres per second) the reduction is more than doubled.

Studies in both Leicester and London (Chandler, 1976), England, have shown that on calm, clear nights, when the urban heat-island effect is at its maximum, there is a surface inflow of cool air towards the zones of highest temperatures. These so-called 'country breezes' have low velocities and become quickly decelerated by intense surface friction in the suburban areas. A practical implication of these breezes is that they transport pollution from the outer parts of an urban area into the city centre, accentuating the pollution problem during smogs.

The existence of the urban heat island has a number of implications; city plants bud and bloom earlier, some birds are attracted to the thermally more favourable urban habitat, humans find added warmth stressful if the city is already situated in a warm area, during summer heat-waves exacerbated temperatures may cause mortality among sensitive members of the population as has been proved in Shanghai, China (Tan et al. 2010), less winter space-heating is required, but, conversely, more summer air-conditioning is necessary.

Because of their environmental importance, various mitigation strategies can be attempted to try and reduce the heat-island effect. These can be roughly lumped into two categories: increased vegetation (trees, landscaping, and green spaces) and changes to building practices (materials for higher albedo and/or modified thermal properties, alternative pavements and paved surfaces designs, building types, and other materials selections). These are reviewed by Phelan et al. (2015).

7.12 Deliberate Climatic Modification

It has long been a human desire to modify weather and climate, but it is only since the Second World War and the development of high-altitude observations of clouds that serious attempts have been made to modify such phenomena as rainfall, hailstorms, and hurricanes (Cotton and Pielke, 2007). It was in 1946 that Irving Langmuir discovered that tiny particles of dry ice and silver iodide could stimulate the precipitation process by providing a nucleus to which cloud-borne moisture could cling. Both civilian and military interest arose and there was considerable US government support for work on deliberate climate modification, support which is now miniscule compared to that of the 1970s (Harper, 2008). Research continues in some other countries, however, including China (Guo and Zheng, 2009).

Following on from Langmuir's work, the most fruitful human attempts to augment natural precipitation have been through cloud seeding. Rainmaking experiments of this type are based on three main assumptions (Chorley and More, 1967: 159).

1) Either the presence of ice crystals in a supercooled cloud is necessary to release snow and rain, or the presence of comparatively large water droplets is necessary to initiate the coalescence process.
2) Some clouds precipitate inefficiently or not at all, because these components are naturally deficient.
3) The deficiency can be remedied by seeding the clouds artificially, either with solid carbon dioxide (dry ice) or silver iodide, to produce crystals, or by introducing water droplets or large hygroscopic nuclei (e.g. salt).

These methods of seeding are not universally productive and in many countries, expenditure on such procedures has been reduced. In the USA the glory days of weather modification were in the 1970s, and since then federal expenditure has declined (Cotton and Pielke, 2007). Under conditions of orographic lift and in thunderstorm cells, when nuclei are insufficient to generate rain by natural means, some augmentation may be attained, especially if cloud temperatures are of the order of –10 to –15°C. The increase of precipitation gained under favourable conditions may be of the order of 10–20% in any one storm. In lower latitudes, where cloud-top temperatures frequently remain above 0°C, silver-iodide or dry-ice seeding is not applicable. Therefore alternative methods have been introduced whereby small water droplets of 50 mm diameter are sprayed into the lower layers of deep clouds, so that the growth of cloud particles will be stimulated by coalescence. Other techniques of warm cloud seeding include the feeding of hygroscopic particles into the lower air layers near the updraught of a growing cumulus cloud (Breuer, 1980).

The results of the many experiments now carried out on cloud seeding are still controversial, very largely because we have an imperfect understanding of the physical processes involved. This means that the evidence has to be evaluated on a statistical rather than a scientific basis so, although precipitation may occur after many seeding trials, it is difficult to decide to what extent artificial stimulation and augmentation is responsible. It also needs to be remembered that this form of planned weather modification applies to small areas for short periods. As yet, no means exist to change precipitation appreciably over large areas on a sustained basis.

Other types of deliberate climatic modification have also been attempted. For example, it has been thought that the production of many more hailstone embryos by silver-iodide seeding will yield smaller hailstones which would both be less damaging and more likely to melt before reaching the ground. Some results in Russia were encouraging, but one cannot exclude the possibility that seeding may sometimes even increase hail damage (Atlas, 1977). Similar experiments have been conducted in lightning suppression. The concept here is to produce in a thundercloud, again by silver-iodide seeding, an abnormal abundance of ice crystals that would act as added corona points and thus relieve the electrical potential gradient by corona discharge before a lightning strike could develop (Panel on Weather and Climate Modification, 1966: 4–8).

Hurricane modification is perhaps the most desirable aim of those seeking to suppress severe storms, because of the extremely favourable benefit-to-cost ratio of the work (Cotton and Pielke, 2007: section 2.6). The principle once again is that of introducing freezing nuclei into the ring of clouds around the hurricane centre to trigger the release of the latent heat of fusion in the eye-wall cloud system which, in turn, diminishes the maximum horizontal temperature gradients in the storm, causing a hydrostatic lowering of the surface temperature. This eventually should lead to a weakening of the damaging winds (Smith, 1975: 212). A 15% reduction in maximum winds is theoretically possible, but as yet work is largely at an experimental stage. A 30% reduction in maximum winds was claimed following seeding of Hurricane Debbie in 1969 but US attempts to seed hurricanes were discontinued in the 1970s following the development of new computer models of the effects of seeding on hurricanes. The models suggested that although maximum winds might be reduced by 10–15% on average, seeding may increase the winds just outside the region of maximum winds by 10–15%, may either increase or decrease the maximum storm surge, and may or may not affect the direction of the storm (Sorkin, 1982). Seeding of hurricanes is unlikely to recommence until such uncertainties can be resolved.

Fog dispersal, vital for airport operation, is another aim of weather modification. Seeding experiments have shown that fog consisting of supercooled droplets can be cleared by using liquid propane or dry ice. In very cold fogs this seeding method causes rapid transformation of water droplets into ice particles. Warm fogs with temperatures above freezing point occur more frequently than supercooled fogs in mid-latitudes and are more difficult to disperse. Some success has been achieved using sodium chloride and other hygroscopic particles as seeding agents but the most effective method is to evaporate the fog. The French developed the 'turboclair' system in which jet engines are installed alongside the runway at major airports and the engines produce short bursts of heat to evaporate the fog and improve visibility as an aircraft approaches (Hess, 1974).

The planting of windbreaks is an even more important attempt by humans to modify local climate deliberately. Shelterbelts have been in use for centuries in many wind-swept areas of the globe, both to protect soils from blowing and to protect the plants from the direct effects of high-velocity winds. The size and effectiveness of the protection depends on their height, density, shape, and frequency. However, the belts may have consequences for microclimates beyond those for which they were planted. Evaporation rates are curtailed; snow is arrested, and its melting waters are available for the fields; but the temperatures may become more extreme in the stagnant space in the lee of the belt, creating an increase in frost danger.

Traditional farmers in many societies have been aware of the virtues of microclimatic management (Wilken, 1972). They manage shade by employing layered cropping systems or by covering the plant and soil with mulches; they may deliberately try to modify albedo conditions. Tibetan farmers, for example, reportedly throw dark rocks on to snow-covered fields to promote late spring melting; and in the Paris area of France some very dense stone walls were constructed to absorb and radiate heat.

7.13 Geoengineering

In coming decades it is possible that more ambitious attempts at global climatic modification may be attempted, to which the term geoengineering (or climate engineering) is often applied (Lovelock, 2008). In particular such techniques may be developed to combat global warming (Table 7.9). Geoengineering methods can be divided into two basic 'classes' (Royal Society, 2009). The first of these is a group of carbon dioxide removal (CDR) techniques which aim to address the root cause of climate change by removing greenhouse gases from the atmosphere: land-use management to protect or enhance land carbon sinks; the use of biomass for carbon sequestration as well as a carbon neutral energy source; enhancement of natural rock weathering processes to remove CO_2 from the atmosphere; direct engineered capture of CO_2 from ambient air; and the enhancement of oceanic uptake of CO_2 by fertilization of the oceans with naturally scarce nutrients, or by increasing upwelling of ocean water. The second class of techniques are called solar radiation management (SRM) techniques or, more colloquially 'sunshade geoengineering' (Irvine et al., 2016). These aim to offset the effects of increased greenhouse gas concentrations by causing the Earth to absorb less solar radiation. Among the methods put forward are: placing shields or reflectors in space to reduce the amount of solar energy reaching the Earth; brightening the surface of the Earth (e.g. by covering deserts with mirrors or other reflective material) so that more incoming radiation is reflected back to space; and injecting sulphate aerosols into the low stratosphere to mimic the cooling effect achieved by volcanic eruptions. The knock-on impacts that these technologies may have on the environment are themselves highly speculative but potentially very significant (McCormack et al., 2016).

7.14 Urban Air Pollution

The concentration of large numbers of people, factories, power stations, and cars mean that large amounts of pollutants may be emitted into urban atmospheres. If weather conditions permit, the level of pollution may build up. The nature of the pollutants (Table 7.10) has changed as technologies have changed. For example, in the early phases of the industrial revolution in Britain the prime cause of air pollution in cities may have been the burning of coal, whereas now it may be vehicular emissions. Different cities may have very different levels of pollution, depending on factors such as the level

Table 7.9 Geoengineering technologies to attempt to address climate change.

Solar reflection ('sunshade engineering'):	*Carbon dioxide removal:*
• Enhancing surface brightness (e.g. by painting roofs and other surfaces white)	• Afforestation, reforestation, and avoidance of deforestation so that trees can sequester carbon from the atmosphere
• Enhancing cloud brightness (e.g. by spraying them with sea-water droplets to increase their cooling effect)	• Algae-coated buildings (the algae absorb carbon dioxide through photosynthesis)
• Increasing stratospheric aerosols to mimic cooling effects of volcanic eruptions (e.g. injecting sulphur dioxide into the stratosphere to help form reflective clouds)	• Biochar (converting agricultural and forest waste by pyrolysis into a form of charcoal that holds carbon and retains nutrients and water in soils)
• Placing reflectors and mirrors in space	• Enhancing chemical weathering of carbonate or silicate rocks to remove CO_2 from the atmosphere as the rocks decompose
	• Ocean fertilization (supplying nutrients to enhance the growth of tiny plants that absorb CO_2)
	• Capture of CO_2 from ambient air

Table 7.10 Major urban pollutants.

Type	Some consequences
Carbon monoxide (CO)	Heart problems, headaches, fatigue, etc.
Oxides of nitrogen (NO_x)	Photochemical reactions, accelerated weathering of buildings, respiratory problems, production of acid rain and haze
Photochemical oxidants: ozone and peroxyacetyl nitrate (PAN)	Headaches, eye irritation, coughs, chest discomfort, damage to materials (e.g. rubber), damage to crops and natural vegetation, smog
Sulphur dioxide (SO_2)	Respiratory problems, can cause asthma attacks. Damage to plants and lichens, corrosion of buildings and materials, production of haze and acid rain
Suspended particulate matter (characteristically 0.1–25 μm in diameter)	Fog, respiratory problems, carcinogens, soiling of buildings
Toxic chemicals: dioxins, etc.	Poisoning, cancers, etc.
Toxic metals: lead	Poisoning, reduced educational attainments and increased behavioural difficulties in children

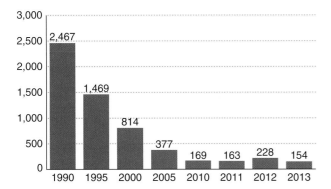

Figure 7.13 Trends in sulphur dioxide emissions from coal combustion in the UK from 1990–2013 in thousands of tonnes. *Source:* data from Office for National Statistics, UK.

of technology, size, wealth, and anti-pollution legislation. Differences may also arise because of local topographic and climatic conditions. Photochemical smogs, for example, are a more serious threat in areas subjected to intense sunlight.

Fenger (1999) argued that the development of urban air pollution shows certain general historical trends. At the earlier stages air pollution increases to high levels. There then follow various abatement measures that cause a stabilization of air quality to occur. Levels of pollution then fall as high-technology solutions are applied, though this may be countered to a certain extent by growth in vehicular traffic.

In some developed cities concentrations of pollutants have indeed tended to fall over recent decades. This can result from changes in industrial technology or from legislative changes (e.g. clean air legislation, restriction on car use, etc.). In many British cities, for example, legislation since the 1950s has reduced the burning of coal, either for domestic heating or for power generation (Figure 7.13). As a consequence, fogs have become less frequent and the amount of sunshine has increased. (Musk, 1991). Similarly lead concentrations in the air in British cities have declined sharply following the introduction of unleaded petrol (Kirby, 1995), as they have in Copenhagen (Figure 7.14c) (Fenger, 1999) and in the USA (Figure 7.15). The concentrations of various pollutants have also been reduced in the Los Angeles area of California (Figure 7.16). Here, carbon monoxide, non-methane hydrocarbon, nitrogen oxide, and ozone concentrations all fell steadily over the period since the late 1960s (Lents and Kelly, 1993). Urban air quality has also improved in New York State (Buckley and Mitchell, 2010) since the 1980s. Carbon monoxide, sulphur dioxide, nitrogen dioxide, ozone, lead, and particulate matter all showed statistically significant downward trends. A further clear

example of a recent decline in urban pollution is provided by New Jersey (Lioy and Georgopoulos, 2011) (Figure 7.17).

However, these examples of improving trends come from developed countries. In many cities in poorer countries, heavy reliance on coal, oil, and even wood for domestic cooking and heating means that their levels of sulphur dioxide and suspended particulate matter (SPM) are high and climbing. In addition, rapid economic development is bringing increased emissions from industry and motor vehicles, which are generating progressively more serious air-quality problems. NO_x emissions from vehicles have, for example, climbed dramatically in China (UNEP, 2007).

Particular attention is being paid at the present time to the chemical composition of SPMs, and particularly to those particles that are small enough to be breathed in (i.e. smaller than 10 μm, and thus often known as PM10s). Also of great concern in terms of human health are elemental carbon (for example, from diesel vehicles), polynuclear aromatic hydrocarbons (PAHs), and toxic base metals (e.g. arsenic, lead, cadmium, and mercury), in part because of their possible role as carcinogens.

A major cause of urban air pollution is the development of photochemical smog. The name originates from the fact that most of the less desirable properties of such fog result from the products of chemical reactions induced by sunlight. Unburned hydrocarbons play a major role in this type of smog formation and result from evaporation of solvents and fuels, as well as incomplete combustion of fossil fuels. In the presence of oxides of nitrogen, strong sunlight, and stable meteorological conditions, complex chemical reactions occur, forming a family of peroxyacyl nitrates (sometimes collectively abbreviated to PANs) (Table 7.10).

Photochemical smog appears 'cleaner' than other kinds of fog in the sense that it does not contain the very large particles of soot that are so characteristic of smog derived from coal burning. However, the eye irritation and damage to plant leaves it causes make it unpleasant. Its adverse properties also include a high lead content. Photochemical smog occurs particularly where there is large-scale combustion of petroleum products, as in car-dominated cities like Los Angeles, and is triggered by a series of chemical reactions involving sunlight. Because sunlight is a crucial factor in their development they are most common in the tropics or during seasons of strong sunshine. Their especial notoriety in Los Angeles is due to a meteorological setting dominated at times by subtropical anti-cyclones with weak winds, clear skies, and a subsidence inversion, combined with the general topographic situation and the high vehicle density. However, photochemical ozone pollution can, on certain summer

(a)

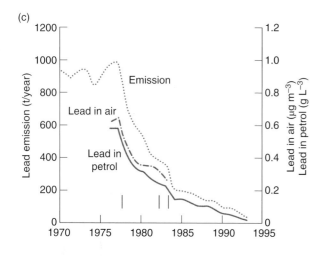

Figure 7.14 (a) Schematic presentation of a typical development of urban air pollution levels. *Source:* after Fenger (1999: figure 3). Reproduced with permission of Elsevier. (b) Lead concentration (annual means) in UK urban sites from 1980–2005 (Defra data). (c) Annual average values for the total Danish lead emissions 1969–1993, the lead pollution in Copenhagen since 1976, and the average lead content in petrol sold in Denmark. The dates of tightening of restrictions on lead content are indicated with bars. *Source:* after Fenger (1999: figure 12). Reproduced with permission of Elsevier.

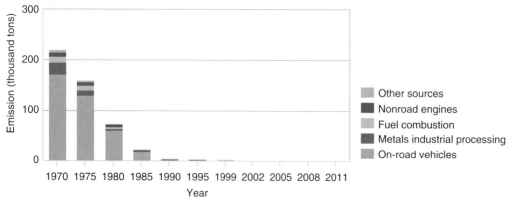

Figure 7.15 Anthropogenic lead emissions in the USA by source category, 1970–2011. *Source:* US EPA (2014).

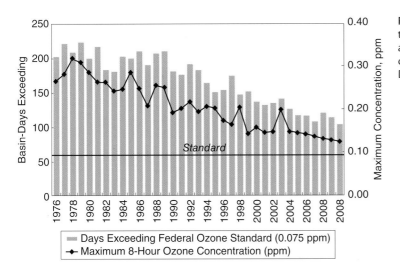

Figure 7.16 The decline in urban ozone pollution in the Los Angeles area, 1976 to 2010. *Source:* www. aqmd.gov/smog/o3trend/html. Reproduced by courtesy of South Coast Air Quality Management District (SCAQMD).

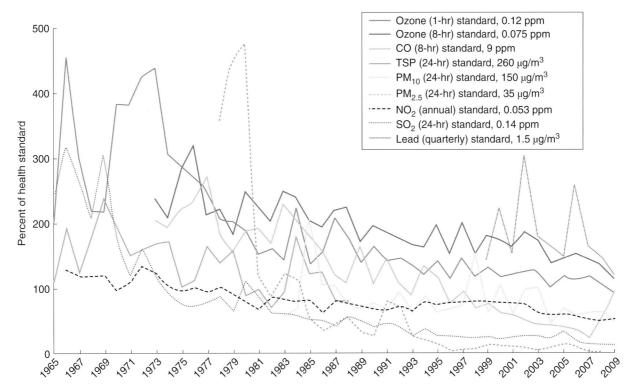

Figure 7.17 The decline in various atmospheric pollutants in New Jersey, USA, from 1965 to 2009. *Source:* from Lioy and Georgopoulos (2011). Reproduced with permission from *Environmental Health Perspectives*.

days, with anti-cyclonic conditions bringing air in from Europe, reach appreciable levels even in the UK (Jenkins et al., 2002), especially in large cities such as London.

Rigorous controls on vehicle emissions can greatly reduce the problem of high urban ozone concentrations and this has been a major cause of the reduction in ozone levels in Los Angeles since the 1970s, in spite of a growth in that city's population and vehicle numbers (Pollack et al., 2013). A full discussion of tropospheric ozone trends on a global basis is provided by Guicherit and Roewer (2000) and Oltmans et al. (2006). A report by the Royal Society (2008) suggests that under hot and sunny conditions, O_3 concentrations in polluted locations may peak at over 200 parts per billion by volume (ppb), but background concentrations of ground-level ozone have also climbed. Between the late nineteenth century and the present they have more than doubled to 35–40 ppb.

7.15 Air Pollution: Some Further Effects

This chapter has already made much reference to the ways in which humans have changed the turbidity of the atmosphere and the gases within it. However, the consequences of air pollution go further than either their direct impact on human health or their impact on local, regional, and global climates.

First of all, the atmosphere acts as a major channel for the transfer of pollutants from one place to another, so that some harmful substances have been transferred long distances from their sources of emission. DDT is one example; lead is another. Thus, from the start of the industrial revolution, the lead content of the Greenland ice cap, although far removed from the source of the pollutant (which is largely derived from either industrial or automobile emissions) rose very substantially (Figure 7.18a). The same applies to its sulphate content (Figure 7.18b). An analysis of pond sediments from a remote part of North America (Yosemite) indicates that lead levels were raised as a result of human activities, being more than 20 times the natural levels. The lead, which came in from atmospheric sources, showed a fivefold elevation in the plants of the area and a fiftyfold elevation in the animals compared with natural levels (Shirahata et al., 1980). A study of lead pollution history from a varved lake in Finland (Meriläinen et al., 2011) provides data back to Roman times on rates of lead deposition. During Roman times they were 0.2–0.3 mg m^2 per year, they then fell to less than this after the collapse of Rome, climbed to 2.6 mg m^2 per year between 1420 and 1895, and then attained values of 11–22 mg m^2 per year between 1926 and 1985.

Some workers have also compared the total quantities of heavy metals that humans are releasing into the atmosphere with emissions from natural sources (Nriagu, 1979). The increase was eighteenfold for lead, ninefold for cadmium, sevenfold for zinc, and threefold for copper.

As a result of pollution control regulations some of these trends are now being reversed. Boutron et al. (1991), for example, analyzed ice and snow that has accumulated over Greenland in the previous two decades and found that lead concentrations had decreased by a factor of 7.5 since 1970 (Figure 7.18c). They attribute this to a curbing of the use of lead additives in petrol. Likewise, in Sweden, lead deposition rates have fallen by more than 90% since 1970 (Bindler, 2011). Over the same period cadmium and zinc concentrations have decreased by a factor of 2.5. It is very clear that, since 1970, the emissions of cadmium, lead, and mercury have plummeted (Table 7.11). Again, the precipitous decline in lead emissions is due primarily to the prohibition of lead additives in vehicle fuel. This downward trend in lead in the UK is shown in Figure 7.18d.

A second example of the possible widespread and ramifying ecological consequences of atmospheric pollution is provided by 'acid rain' or other types of acid precipitation, including fog and cloud water (Likens and Bormann, 1974; Likens, 2010). Acid rain is rain which has a pH of less than 5.65, this being the pH which is produced by carbonic acid in equilibrium with atmospheric CO_2. In many parts of the world, rain may be markedly more acid than this normal, natural background level. Snow and rain in the north-east United States have been known to have pH values as low as 2.1, while in Scotland in one storm the rain was the acidic equivalent of vinegar (pH 2.4). In the eastern United States the average annual precipitation acidity values tend to be between pH 4 and 4.5 (Figure 7.19), and the degree of acidulation appears to have increased between the 1950s and 1970s. The acidity of the precipitation in turn leads to greater acidity in rivers and lakes. The causes of acid deposition are the quantities of sulphur oxides and nitrogen oxides emitted from fossil-fuel combustion. Figure 7.20 shows the trend in the global and regional emissions of sulphur dioxide from anthropogenic sources.

Sulphate levels increased in European precipitation between the 1950s and 1970s. Two main factors contributed to the increasing seriousness of the problem at the time. One was the replacement of coal by oil and natural gas. The second, paradoxically, was a result of the implementation of air pollution control measures (particularly increasing the height of smoke stacks and installing particle precipitators). These appear to have transformed a local 'soot problem' into a regional 'acid rain problem'. Coal burning produced a great deal of sulphate, but was largely neutralized by high calcium contents in the relatively unfiltered coal smoke emissions. Natural gas burning creates less sulphate but that which is produced is not neutralized. The new higher chimneys pump the smoke so high that it is dispersed over wide areas, whereas previously it returned to earth nearer the source.

Very long-term records of lake acidification provided dramatic evidence for the magnification of the acid deposition problem as a result of the industrial revolution. These were obtained by extracting cores from lake floors and analyzing their diatom assemblages at different levels. The diatom assemblages reflect water acidity levels at the time they were living. Two studies serve to illustrate the trend. In south-west Sweden (Renberg and Hellberg, 1982) for most of post-glacial time (that is, the last 12,500 years) the pH of the lakes appears to have decreased gradually from around 7.0 to about 6.0 as a result of natural ageing processes. However, especially since the 1950s, a marked decrease

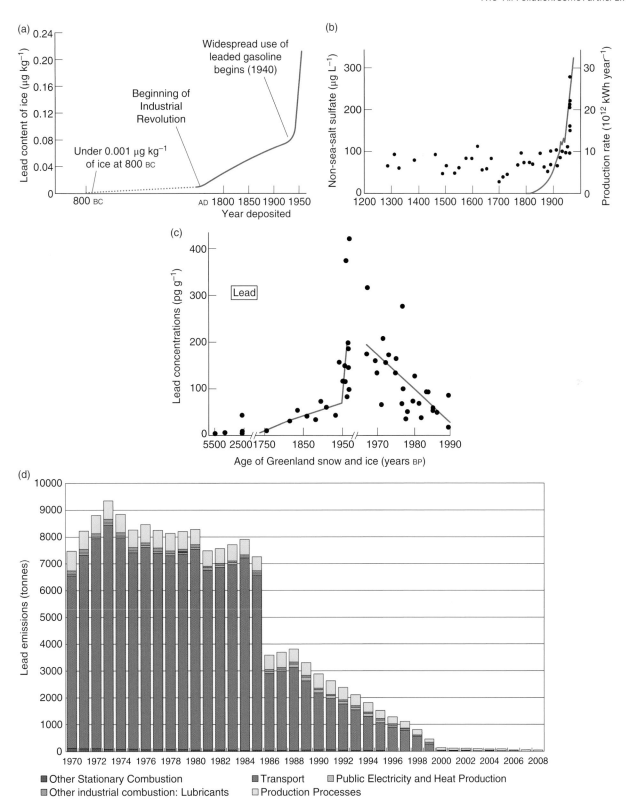

Figure 7.18 Trends in atmospheric quality: (a) Lead content of the Greenland ice cap due to atmospheric fallout of the mineral on the snow surface. A dramatic upturn in worldwide atmospheric levels of lead occurred at the beginning of the industrial revolution in the nineteenth century and again after the more recent spread of the automobile. *Source:* adapted from Murozumi et al. (1969: 1247). (b) The sulphate concentration on a sea-salt-free basis in north-west Greenland glacier ice samples as a function of year. The curve represents the world production of thermal energy from coal, lignite, and crude oil. *Source:* adapted from Koide and Goldberg (1971: figure 1). (c) Lead concentrations in Greenland snow. *Source:* Boutron et al. (1991). Reprinted with permission from *Nature*. Copyright © 1991, Macmillan Magazines Limited. (d) Time series of lead emissions in the UK from 1970 to 2008, showing major sources. *Source:* National Atmospheric Emissions Inventory, AEA (2010: figure 3.5).

Table 7.11 UK emissions of selected heavy metals (in tonnes per year) from 1970 to 2010.

	1970	2010	decrease(x)
Cadmium	34.996	3.0887	11.33.
Lead	7456.5	61.62	121.01
Mercury	61.16	6.503	9.40

Source: http://naei.defra.gov.uk/overview/pollutants?pollutant_id=12 (accessed January 2018).

occurred to present-day values of about 4.5. In Britain, the work of Battarbee and collaborators (1985a and b) showed that at sensitive sites pH values before around 1850 were close to 6.0 and that since then pH declines have varied between 0.5 and 1.5 units. More monitoring of lake acidity also demonstrated that significant changes were taking place. Studies by Beamish et al. (1975) demonstrated that between 1961 and 1975 pH had declined by 0.13 pH units per year in George Lake, Canada, and a comparable picture emerges from Sweden, where Almer et al. (1974) found that the pH in some lakes had decreased by as much as 1.8 pH units since the 1930s.

The effects of acid rain (Figure 7.21) are especially serious in areas underlain by highly siliceous types of bedrock (for example, granite, some gneisses, quartzite, and quartz sandstone), such as the old shield areas of the Fenno-Scandian shield in Scandinavia and the Laurentide

Figure 7.19 Isopleths showing average pH for precipitation in North America. Note the low values for eastern North America and the relatively higher values to the west of the Mississippi. *Source:* combined from Likens et al. (1979) and Graedel and Crutzen (1995), with modifications.

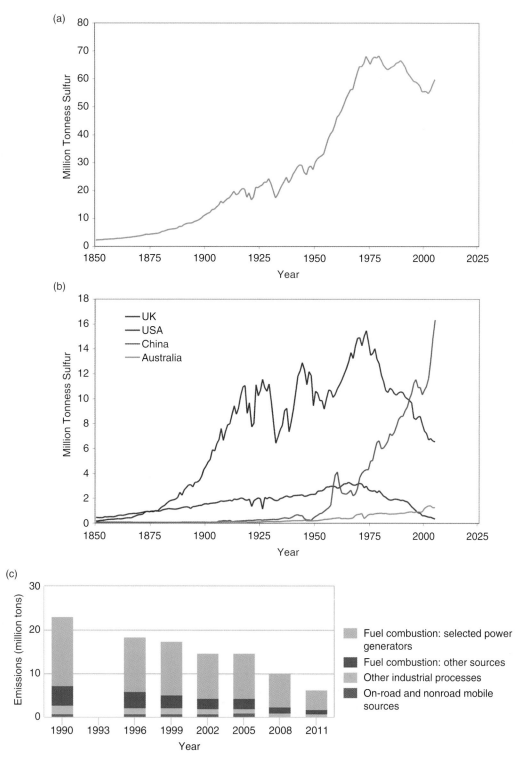

Figure 7.20 Trends in (a) world and (b) regional sulphur dioxide emissions from 1850–2005, and (c) in the USA from 1990–2011. *Source:* US EPA (2014).

shield in Canada (Likens et al., 1979). This is because of the lack of buffering by cations. Mobile anions are able to cause the leaching of basic cations (nutrients).

The ecological consequences of acid rain have been the subject of debate. Krug and Frink (1983) argued that acid rain only accelerates natural processes, and point

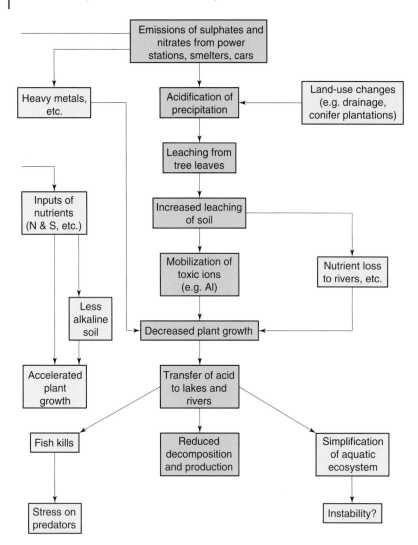

Figure 7.21 Pathways and effects of acid precipitation through different components of the ecosystem, showing some of the adverse and beneficial consequences.

out that the results of natural soil formation in humid climates include the leaching of nutrients, the release of aluminium ions, and the acidification of soil and water. They also note that acidification by acid rain may be superimposed on longer-term acidification induced by changes in land use. Thus the re-growth of coniferous forests in what are now marginal agriculture areas, such as New England and highland Western Europe, can increase acidification of soils and water. Similarly, it is possible, though in general unproven (see Battarbee et al., 1985a), that in areas like western Scotland a decline in upland agriculture and the regeneration of heathland could play a role in increasing soil and water acidification. Likewise Johnston et al. (1982) suggested that acid rain can cause either a decrease or an increase in forest productivity, depending on local factors. For example in soils where cation nutrients are abundant and sulphur or

nitrogen are deficient, moderate inputs of acid rain are very likely to stimulate forest growth.

In general, however, it is the negative consequences of acid rain that have been stressed. One harmful effect is a change in soil character. The high concentration of hydrogen ions in acid rain causes accelerated leaching of essential nutrients, making them less available for plant use. Furthermore, the solubility of aluminium and heavy metal ions increases and instead of being fixed in the soil's sorption complex, these toxic substances become available for plants or are transferred into lakes, where they become a major physiological stress for some aquatic organisms.

Fresh-water bodies with limited natural cations are poorly buffered and thus vulnerable to acid inputs. The acidification of thousands of lakes and rivers in southern Norway and Sweden during the late twentieth century has been attributed to acid rain, and this increased acidity resulted in the decline of various species of fish, particularly trout and salmon. But fish are not the only aquatic organisms that may be affected. Fungi and moss may proliferate, organic matter may start to decompose less rapidly, and the number of green algae may be reduced. Forest growth can also be affected by acid rain, though the evidence is not necessarily proven. Acid rain can damage foliage, increase susceptibility to pathogens, affect germination, and reduce nutrient availability. However, since acid precipitation is only one of many environmental stresses, its impact may enhance, be enhanced by, or be swamped by other factors. For example, Blank (1985), in considering the fact that an estimated one-half of the total forest area of the former West Germany was showing signs of damage, referred to the possible role of ozone or of a run of hot, dry summers on tree health and growth. The whole question of forest decline is addressed in Section 2.20.

The seriousness of acid rain caused by sulphur dioxide emissions in the western industrialized nations peaked in the mid-1970s or early 1980s. Changes in industrial technology, in the nature of economic activity, and in legislation caused the output of SO_2 in Britain to decrease by 35% between 1974 and 1990. In 2009, SO_2 emissions were 89% lower than 1990 levels (DEFRA, 2011). Nitrogen oxide emissions also fell in the UK (Figure 7.22a and b). There is now clear evidence that over the last two decades the rainfall and surface waters in the UK have become less acid (Kernan et al. 2010; Battarbee et al., 2014). This was also the case in many other industrialized countries, including the United States (Malm et al., 2002; Hidy and Blanchard,

2016). Figure 7.23 shows how power station emissions of sulphates and nitrates have declined in New England. However, there has been a shift in the geographical sources of sulphate emissions, so that whereas in 1980 60% of global emissions were from the US, Canada, and Europe, by 1995 only 38% of world emissions originated from this region (Smith et al., 2001). There are also increasing controls on the emission of NO_x in vehicle exhaust emissions, although emissions of nitrogen oxides in Europe have not declined (Table 7.12). A similar picture emerges from Japan (Seto et al., 2002), where sulphate emissions have fallen because of emission controls, whereas nitrate emissions have increased with an increase in vehicular traffic. This means that the geography of acid rain may change, with it becoming less serious in the developed world, but with it increasing in locations like China, where economic development will continue to be fuelled by the burning of low quality sulphur-rich coal in enormous quantities. From 2000–2006 sulphate emissions in China increased by 53%, an annual growth rate of 7.3% (Lu et al., 2010) and precipitation became increasingly acid (Tang et al., 2010).

Emissions from the diesel engines of large ships are, in spite of increasing controls, locally a serious issue, contributing to emissions not only of sulphates, but also of particulates and nitrates. Emissions are likely to continue in the future due to the increase of global-scale trade. They are serious in busy shipping areas, such as the North Sea (Viana et al., 2014), the port of Los Angeles, and various Chinese cities, including Hong Kong, and can affect cities and ecosystems away from coastal areas (Aulinger et al., 2016). Wan et al. (2016b) have reported

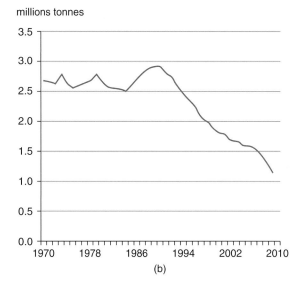

Figure 7.22 (a) Sulphur dioxide emissions and sources in the UK from 1970 to 2010 and (b) NO_x emissions and sources in the UK from 1970 to 2010. *Source:* data from AEA National Atmospheric Emissions Inventory (2010: figures 2.24 and 2.12).

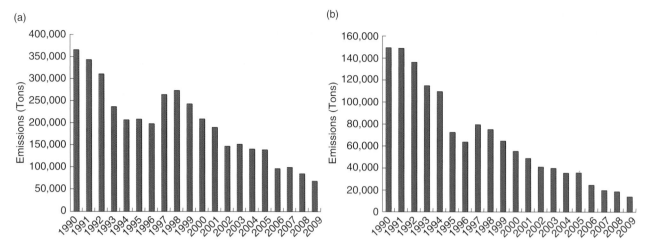

Figure 7.23 Trends in emissions of (a) SO_2 and (b) NO_x from power plants in New England since 1990. *Source:* based on data from USA Environmental Protection Agency.

that the seaborne container trade has grown from 100 million tonnes in 1980 to about 1.6 billion tonnes in 2014, and that low-grade marine fuel oil contains 3500 times more sulphur than road diesel. They stated that worldwide, from 2007 to 2012, shipping accounted for 15% of annual NO_x emissions from anthropogenic sources, 13% of SO_x, and 3% of CO_2. In Europe in 2013, ships contributed 18% of NO_x emissions, 18% of SO_x, and 11% of particles less than 2.5 micrometres in size

($PM_{2.5}$). For road transport, the figures were 33%, 0%, and 12%, respectively. Aviation, by contrast, accounted for only 6%, 1%, and 1%, respectively, and rail just 1%, 0%, and 0%.

In those countries where acid rain remains or is increasing as a problem there are various methods available to reduce its damaging effects. One of these is to add powdered limestone to lakes to increase their pH values. As Holmgren et al. (2016) have reported, thou-

Table 7.12a Emissions of sulphur and nitrogen oxides (as NO_2) in 1000 tonnes a year for selected European countries in 1980 and 1993.

Country	Sulphur			Nitrogen oxides		
	1980	1993	1993 as % of 1980	1980	1993	1993 as % of 1980
Czech Republic	1128	710	62.9	937	574	61.26
Denmark	226	78	34.51	274	264	96.35
Finland	292	60	20.55	264	253	95.83
France	1669	568	34.03	1823	1519	83.32
Germany	3743	1948	52.04	2440	2904	84.42
Ireland	111	78	70.27	73	122	167.12
Italy	1900	1126	59.26	1480	2053	138.72
Netherlands	244	84	34.43	582	561	96.39
Norway	70	18	25.71	185	225	120.96
Poland	2050	1362	66.44	1500	1140	76.00
Spain	1660	1158	69.76	950	1257	132.32
Sweden	254	50	19.69	424	399	94.10
UK	2454	1597	65.08	2395	2355	98.32
			47.28			103.47

Table 7.12b Percentage contributions for four regions to global sulphur dioxide emissions.

	Sulphur dioxide emissions by geographic region (%)				
	1980	1985	1990	1995	2000
US/Canada	21	18	18	16	15
Europe	39	36	31	22	19
Asia	26	31	35	43	46
Rest of world	14	15	16	18	20

Source: Smith et al. (2001).

sands of Swedish lakes and streams have been regularly treated with limestone to mitigate acidification. Such liming became a large-scale programme in the 1980s, and the number of local liming projects increased at the same time as large-scale measures were taken to decrease airborne emissions of sulphur and nitrogen compounds. The annual amount of limestone spread peaked at more than 200,000 tonnes during 1998–2002. As an adjustment to decreasing acidification, the amount of lime decreased and has recently stabilized at about 120,000 tonnes per year. The effects on fish has been noticeable. Stream fish occurrence, species richness, and abundance increased after liming.

However, the only really effective and practical long-term treatment is to curb the emission of the offending gases. This can be achieved in a variety of ways: by reducing the amount of fossil fuel combustion; by using less sulphur-rich fossil fuels; by using alternative energy sources that do not produce nitrate or sulphate gases (e.g. hydropower or nuclear power); and by removing the pollutants before they reach the atmosphere. For example, after combustion at a power station, sulphur can be removed ('scrubbed') from flue gases by a process known as flue gas desulphurization (FGD), in which a mixture of limestone and water is sprayed into the flue gas which converts the sulphur dioxide (SO_2) into gypsum (calcium sulphate). NO_x in flue gas can be reduced by adding ammonia and passing it over a catalyst to produce nitrogen and water (a process called selective catalytic reduction or SCR). NO_x produced by cars can be reduced by fitting catalytic converters.

The improving situation with regard to acid precipitation in such areas as the eastern USA and Western Europe does not mean that ecosystems will recover immediately. Curtis et al. (2014: 412) suggested that in the UK, 'while the threat from acid deposition has declined sharply since the 1980s, its legacy remains a major concern; recovery is taking place but even assuming a complete chemical and biological recovery to a pre-industrial baseline were possible, dynamic models suggest that this could take another 100 years'. Likens (2010) suggested that stream macro-invertebrates may recover relatively rapidly (i.e. within 3 years), while lake zooplankton may need a decade or more to fully re-establish. Fish populations in lakes and streams should recover in five to ten years following the recovery of the macro-invertebrates and zooplankton that act as their food sources. With regard to terrestrial ecosystems, given the relatively long life-span of trees and the long delay in the response of soils to decreases in acid deposition, decades may be required for affected trees on sensitive sites to recover.

7.16 Stratospheric Ozone Depletion

A very major area of concern in pollution studies has been the current status of stratospheric ozone levels. The atmosphere has a layer of relatively high concentration of ozone (O_3) at a height of about 16 and 18 km in the polar latitudes and of about 25 km in equatorial regions. This layer is important because it absorbs incoming solar ultraviolet radiation, thus warming the stratosphere and creating a steep inversion of temperature at heights between about 15 and 50 km. This in turn affects convective processes and atmospheric circulation, thereby influencing global weather and climate. However, the role of ozone in controlling receipts of ultraviolet radiation at the earth's surface has great ecological significance, because it modifies rates of photosynthesis. One class of organism that has been identified as being especially prone to the effects of increased ultraviolet radiation consequent upon ozone depletion are phytoplankton – aquatic plants that spend much of their time near the sea surface and are therefore exposed to such radiation. A reduction in their productivities would have potentially ramifying consequences, because these plants directly and indirectly provide the food for

Figure 7.24 World production of major chlorofluorocarbons (tonnes/year). World production of the three major CFCs peaked in about 1988 and has since declined to very low values.

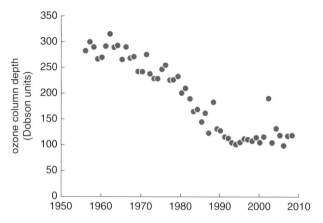

Figure 7.25 Ozone concentrations in Dobson Units (DUs) over Halley Bay, Antarctica. *Source:* based on data provided by the British Antarctic Survey.

almost all fish. Ozone also protects humans from adverse effects of ultraviolet radiation, which include damage to the eyes, suppression of the immune system, and higher rates of skin cancer.

Human activities appear to have caused ozone depletion in the stratosphere, most notably over the south polar regions, where an 'ozone hole' has been identified (Staehelin et al. 2001; Abbasi and Abbasi, 2017). Possible causes of ozone depletion are legion, and include various combustion products emitted from high-flying military and civil supersonic aircraft; nitrous oxide released from nitrogenous chemical fertilizers; and chlorofluorocarbons (CFCs) used in aerosol spray cans, refrigerant systems, and in the manufacture of foam fast-food containers. However, the greatest attention has been focused on the role of CFCs, the production of which climbed greatly in the decades after the Second World War (Figure 7.24). These CFCs may diffuse upwards into the stratosphere where solar radiation causes them to become dissociated to yield chlorine atoms which react with and destroy the ozone (Titus and Seidel, 1986). In addition there are some other ozone depleting substances. Several human-produced chlorocarbons not controlled by the Montreal Protocol are also present in Earth's atmosphere. Among the most abundant of these compounds is dichloromethane (CH_2Cl_2), an industrial solvent that is being increasingly emitted (Hossaini et al., 2017).

The Antarctic ozone hole was identified through satellite monitoring and by monitoring of atmospheric

chemistry on the ground. The decrease in ozone levels at Halley Bay is shown in Figure 7.25. The reasons why this zone of ozone depletion is so well developed over Antarctica include the very low temperatures of the polar winter, which seem to play a role in releasing chlorine atoms; the long sunlight hours of the polar summer, which promote photochemical processes; and the existence of a well-defined circulation vortex. This vortex is a region of very cold air surrounded by strong westerly winds, and air within this vortex is isolated from that at lower latitudes, permitting chemical reactions to be contained rather than more widely diffused. No such clearly defined vortex exists in the Northern Hemisphere, though ozone depletion does seem to have occurred in the Arctic as well (Proffitt et al., 1990), with a particularly severe ozone loss occurring in 2011 (Manney et al., 2011). Decreases in stratospheric ozone levels on a global basis were analyzed by Harris et al. (2003). The most negative trends occurred at mid- to high latitudes.

Global production of CFC gases (Section 7.4) increased from around 180 million kg per year in 1960 to nearly 1100 million kg per year in 1990. However, in response to the thinning of the ozone layer, many governments signed an international agreement called the Montreal Protocol in 1987. This pledged them to a rapid phasing out of CFCs and halons. Production has since dropped substantially. However, because of their stability, these gases will persist in the atmosphere for decades or even centuries to come. Even with the most stringent controls that are now being considered, it will be the middle of the twenty-first century before the chlorine content of the stratosphere falls below the level that triggered the formation of the Antarctic 'ozone hole' in the first place. In spite of controls on CFC production, it is likely that the Antarctic ozone hole 'will be

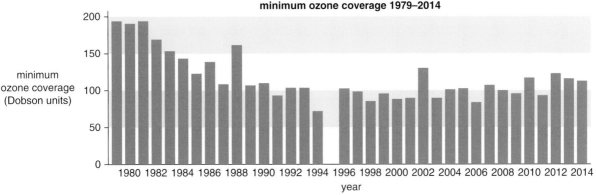

Figure 7.26 Size of the Antarctic ozone hole from 1979 to 2014. *Source:* NASA Ozone Watch.

present for the better part of the 21st century' (Salby et al., 2011). Using satellites, ground-based instruments, and ozone-measuring weather balloons, recent researches have shown that, since 2000, the September Antarctic ozone hole has shrunk by 4 million square kilometers – an area bigger than India. In other words, there is evidence that the hole is starting to heal (Solomon et al., 2016a; Kuttippurath and Nair, 2017). The changing extent area of the Antarctic Ozone hole is shown in (Figure 7.26).

7.17 Conclusions

Changes in the composition of Earth's atmosphere as a result of human emissions of trace gases, and changes in the nature of land cover, have caused great concern in recent years. Global warming, ozone depletion, and acid rain have become central issues in the study of environmental change. Although most attention is often paid to climatic change resulting from greenhouse gases, there is a whole series of other mechanisms which have the potential to cause climatic change. Most notably, this chapter has pointed to the importance of other changes in atmospheric composition and properties,

whether these are caused by aerosol generation or albedo change.

However, the greenhouse effect and global warming may prove to have great significance for the environment and for human activities. Huge uncertainties remain about the speed, degree, direction, and spatial patterning of potential change. Nonetheless, if the Earth warms up by a couple of degrees over the next hundred or so years, the impacts, some negative and some positive, are unlikely to be trivial. This is something that will form a focus of the following chapters.

For many people, especially in cities, the immediate climatic environment has already been changed. Urban climates are different in many ways from those of their rural surroundings. The quality of the air in many cities has been transformed by a range of pollutants, but under certain circumstances clean air legislation and other measures can cause rapid and often remarkable improvements in this area. The same is true of two major pollution issues – stratospheric ozone depletion and acid deposition. Both processes have serious environmental consequences and their effects may remain with us for many years, but both can be slowed down or even reversed by regulating the production and output of the offending substances.

Guide to Reading

Colls, J. and Tiwary, A. (2009) *Air Pollution: Measurement, Modelling and Mitigation* (3rd edn). London: Routledge. This much-used text covers the three major issues connected with the study of air pollution.

Cotton, W.R., and Pielke, R.A. (2007) *Human Impacts on Weather and Climate* (2nd edn). Cambridge: Cambridge University Press. A discussion of deliberate and non-deliberate attempts to modify weather and climate.

Harvey, L.D.D. (2001) *Global Warming: The Hard Science*. Harlow: Prentice Hall. A summary of the science behind global warming.

Houghton, J.T. (2009) *Global Warming: The Complete Briefing* (4th edn). Cambridge: Cambridge University Press. An introduction by a leading scientist.

IPCC (2013) *Climate Change 2013, the Physical Science Basis*. Cambridge: Cambridge University Press. A massive distillation of views on the causes and consequences of climate change.

Kemp, D.D. (2004) *Exploring Environmental Issues: An Integrated Approach*. London: Routledge. An introductory survey.

Metcalfe, S. and Derwent, D. (2005) *Atmospheric Pollution and Environmental Change*. London: Hodder Arnold. An introductory review that is comprehensive in scope.

Ruddiman, W.F. (2005) *Plows, Plagues and Petroleum: How Humans Took Control of Climate*. Princeton, NJ, and Oxford: Princeton University Press. A discussion of the ways in which humans may have altered global climates through time.

Weart, S.R. (2003) *The Discovery of Global Warming*. Cambridge, MA: Harvard University Press. A review of the development of the global warming theory.

Williams, M.A.J. and Balling, R.C. (1996) *Interactions of Desertification and Climate*. London: Arnold. A study of land-cover changes and their effects.

8

The Future: Introduction

CHAPTER OVERVIEW

The main focus of this chapter is on future climate change. Current views on the main types of change that may occur are outlined, and then the point is stressed that some environments will be especially sensitive to change. There is also discussion of the question of 'tipping points' that cause positive feedbacks to magnify changes in the environment. Finally, general consideration is given of likely changes in the biosphere and to landforms and geomorphological processes.

8.1 Introduction

Human induced global warming, or, to use, Lovelock's more frightening term, 'global heating' (Lovelock, 2008), produced by the emissions of a cocktail of greenhouse gases into the atmosphere, is now occurring and will continue to affect the global climate for decades and centuries. The Royal Society (2010: 13) believed that 'There is strong evidence that changes in greenhouse gas concentrations due to human activity are the dominant cause of the global warming that has taken place over the last half century'. Concentrations of carbon dioxide, methane, nitrous oxide, and the chlorofluorocarbons, all greenhouse gases, have increased. The international body charged with such matters, the Intergovernmental Panel on Climate Change (IPCC), set up in the 1980s, has considered these changes and their impacts in great detail (e.g. IPCC, 2013).

The atmospheric concentration of CO_2 has increased by 40% since 1750 and is currently over 400 ppm. This value has not been exceeded during the past 420,000 years and possibly during the past 20 million years. The atmospheric concentration of methane has more than doubled in the past 150 years, rising from c. 715 ppb in pre-industrial times to 1803 ppb in 2011 (IPCC, 2013). Compared to 1750, nitrous oxide concentrations have increased by 18%. The atmospheric concentrations of carbon dioxide, methane, and nitrous oxide have increased to levels unprecedented in at least the last 800,000 years. CFCs, which are entirely artificial, have

been emitted, and although the Montreal Protocol and its amendments have effectively curtailed emissions, they have a long residence time in the atmosphere.

The globally averaged combined land and ocean surface temperature data as calculated by a linear trend, show a warming of 0.85 °C, over the period 1880 to 2012 (IPCC, 2013). The years since have been the warmest on record. The 1990s were the warmest decade in the instrumental record and in the Northern Hemisphere the increase in temperature is likely to have been the largest of any century during the last 1000 years. The rate of change reduced from ~1998 and was used by some sceptics as evidence for a slowing down in global warming – a so-called 'global warming hiatus'. However, the rate has accelerated again and 2014 and 2015 had record temperatures. The decade 2000–2009 was, globally, around 0.15 °C warmer than the decade 1990–1999 and was characterized by heatwaves and precipitation extremes that may not bode well for the future (Coumou and Rahmstorf, 2012). In the Northern Hemisphere, 1983–2012 was likely the warmest 30-year period of the last 1400 years.

The IPCC (2013) suggested the global mean surface temperature change for the period 2016–2035 relative to 1986–2005 will likely be in the range of 0.3 °C to 0.7 °C. The increase of global mean surface temperatures for 2081–2100, relative to 1986–2005, is projected to probably be in the range of 1.7 °C to 4.8 °C. This represents a much larger rate of warming than that observed over the twentieth century and, based on palaeoclimatic data, is

---

Human Impact on the Natural Environment: Past, Present and Future, Eighth Edition. Andrew S. Goudie.
© 2019 John Wiley & Sons Ltd. Published 2019 by John Wiley & Sons Ltd.
Companion website: www.wiley.com/go/goudie/human-impact-natural-environment

very likely to surpass anything experienced over the last 10,000 years. In its turn, increased temperatures will transform the behaviour of the atmospheric heat engine that drives the general circulation of the air and the oceans, leading to changes in the nature, pattern, and amount of precipitation. Table 8.1, adapted from the IPCC (2007a: table SPM2), indicates some of the projections for future climate. In particular it is likely that northern high latitudes will warm more rapidly than the global average, probably by more than 40%. However, warming may not be constant or universal, depending on the time-scale under consideration. For example, melting of the ice caps could release large amounts of cold water into the oceans, which in turn, for a period, could lead to cooling of the Southern Ocean, slowing of the Southern Ocean overturning circulation, warming of the ice shelves, and growing ice sheet mass loss, slowdown and eventual shutdown of the Atlantic overturning circulation with cooling of the North Atlantic region and markedly reduced warming or even cooling in Europe (Hansen et al., 2016).

Marked changes in precipitation will occur, with a tendency for increases to occur globally, but particularly over northern mid- to high latitudes and Antarctica in winter. Figure 8.1 shows the predicted pattern of future precipitation change in North America, and shows that in general it will get wetter in the north and drier in the south. In lower latitudes some areas will see reductions in precipitation (which will exacerbate soil moisture losses caused by increased evapotranspiration), while others may become

wetter. In general climate models predict that precipitation will generally increase in areas with already high amounts of precipitation and generally decrease in areas with low amounts of precipitation (New et al., 2011). Monsoonal areas may become greater, be more intense, and have higher amounts of precipitation (Hsu et al., 2012).

If global warming and associated changes in rainfall and soil moisture amounts occur, then the effects may be substantial and rapid. Some environments will change more than others – 'geomorphological hotspots', especially when crucial thresholds are crossed. There are four types of reasons why some geomorphological processes, hazards, and landform assemblages will show particularly substantial modification as climate changes.

The first of these is threshold reliance. Some landforms and land-forming processes change across crucial climatic thresholds. For example, aeolian activity in drylands is dependent on wind energy, sand supply, and the nature and extent of vegetation cover. If the last falls below a certain level due to a reduction in moisture availability, wind action (e.g. deflation and dune movement) is sharply intensified. Another example of threshold dependence is the coral reef. These features of tropical coastlines are highly sensitive to any changes in cyclone activity but also to coral bleaching (Teneva et al., 2012) caused by elevated sea-surface temperatures (as has happened during recent El Niño years in the Caribbean and elsewhere) and to sea-level rise itself. Terminal lake basins, such as those of the African Rift valleys or Lake

Table 8.1 Recent trends, assessment of human influence on the trends, and projections for extreme weather events for which there is an observed late twentieth-century trend.

Phenomena and direction of trend	Likelihood that trend occurred in late 20th century (typically post 1960)	Likelihood of a human contribution to observed trend	Likelihood of future trends based on projections for 21st century
Warmer and fewer cold days and nights over most land areas	*Very likely*	*Likely*	*Virtually*
Warmer and more frequent hot days and nights over most land areas	*Very likely*	*Likely (nights)*	*Virtually certain*
Warm spells/heat waves. Frequently increases over most land areas	*Likely*	*More likely than not*	*Very likely*
Heavy precipitation events. Frequently (or proportion of total rainfall from heavy falls) increases over most areas	*Likely*	*More likely than not*	*Very likely*
Areas affected by droughts increases	*Likely in many regions since 1970s*	*More likely than not*	*Likely*
Intense tropical cyclone activity increases	*Likely in some regions since 1970*	*More likely than not*	*Likely*
Increased incidence of extreme high sea level (excludes tsunamis)	*Likely*	*More likely than not*	*Likely*

Source: modified after IPCC (2007a: table SPM 2).

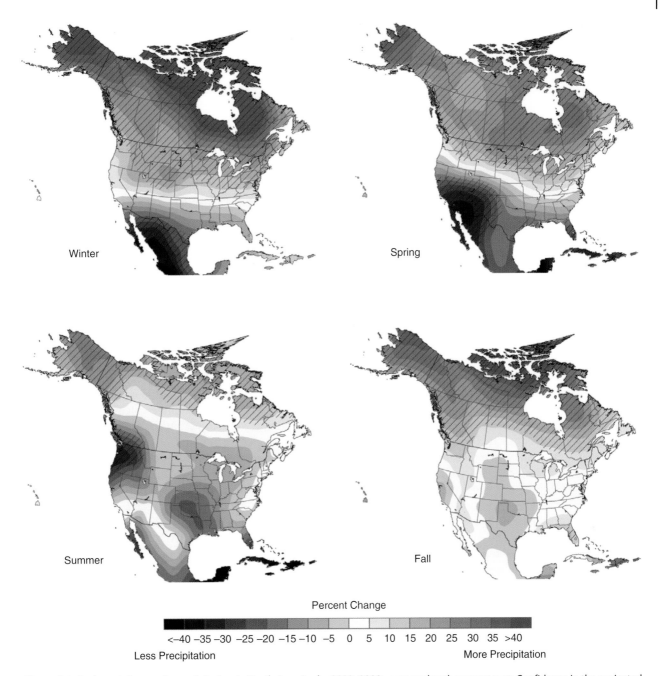

Figure 8.1 Projected changes in precipitation in North America by 2080–2099 compared to the recent past. Confidence in the projected changes is greatest in the hatched areas. *Source:* adapted from Karl et al. (2009: 31).

Chad, are other landforms that have shown very rapid and substantial variations in response to Holocene and twentieth-century changes in temperature, precipitation, and evapotranspiration.

Secondly, there are many examples of landform change being promoted by a combination of climate changes and other human pressures – the compound effect. Indeed, desertification is often most intense when climatic (drought) and human pressures (e.g. over-grazing, deforestation, or over-cultivation) coincide (Section 2.13). In coastal regions, the effects of rising global sea-levels are compounded by local geophysical changes (Sallenger et al., 2012) and by local subsidence caused by fluid (water, hydrocarbons) abstraction, while beaches, marshes, and deltas starved of sediment by the damming of rivers and the construction of coastal defences will be especially prone to erosion and inundation as sea levels rise (Blum and Roberts, 2009) (Section 6.14).

Thirdly, some landforms are robust, while others are less so. For example, *dongas* (erosion scars) in colluvial aprons in southern Africa (Figure 4.12) are gully systems that have a history of cut and fill in response to climate and land-cover changes. This is because they are developed in materials that have high exchangeable sodium percentages and thus are prone to severe erosion if the vegetation cover is changed. Likewise, once their protective vegetation cover is removed, sand dunes in semi-arid areas are easily reactivated. Similarly, muddy and sandy coastlines will plainly be more prone to erosion than hard-rock coastlines, and heavily lithified reefs will be more resistant than less lithified ones (Woodroffe, 2008).

Fourthly, the severity of climate change, and thus its likely impact, will vary spatially. Reductions in soil moisture and stream flows may be especially great in some areas that are currently relatively dry, so that stream networks will shrink (De Wit and Stanciewicz, 2006; Goudie, 2006). Warming will have an especially strong impact on river behaviour in areas where winter precipitation currently falls as snow, such as the mountains of South Asia or the Andes. Giorgi (2006) developed a Regional Climate Change Index (RCCI) based on four variables: changes in mean regional precipitation and inter-annual precipitation variability, and changes in regional surface air temperatures and their inter-annual variability. On this basis certain climate change hot-spots were identified, including the Mediterranean and north-eastern European regions, Central America, southern Equatorial Africa and the Sahara, and eastern North America. Similarly, Sheffield and Wood (2008) recognized some potential future long-term drought hot spots, including the Mediterranean, West Africa, Central Asia, and Central America. Markedly increased aridity in the Mediterranean lands was also proposed by Gao and Giorgi (2008), with the central and southern portions of the Iberian, Italian, Greek, and Turkish peninsulas among the areas that will be particularly vulnerable to water stress and desertification under global warming conditions.

There are, of course, considerable uncertainties built into any consideration of the future (Schiermeier, 2007). Our models are crude and relatively simple and it is difficult to build in all the complexities and feedbacks in the atmosphere, pedosphere, lithosphere, oceans, biosphere, and cryosphere. Different models often provide very different future scenarios, particularly with respect to future rainfall amounts. Other difficulties are presented by the existence of non-linearities and thresholds in natural systems. There may be complex responses to change and sometimes indeterminable time lags. There are also great uncertainties about how emissions of greenhouse gases will change in coming decades as a result of changes in the global economy, technological changes, and the adoption of mitigation strategies. Among the uncertainties identified by the Royal Society (2010) are (1) those produced by the inadequacies of some of our observations of change through time, (2) limited knowledge about the extent to which clouds and water vapour can be incorporated into global warming models, (3) a poor understanding of the future uptake of carbon dioxide by the land and oceans, (4) an inability to speak with confidence about changes in the Atlantic's ocean circulation, (5) a poor understanding of the future behaviour of the Greenland and West Antarctic ice sheets, and (6) our limited ability to make confident predictions at the regional scale. This is because many of our models have a coarse spatial resolution and are difficult to use at more local scales. It is also problematic to use past warm phases as analogues for the future, for the driving mechanisms may be different. Finally, changes brought about by enhanced greenhouse loadings cannot be seen in isolation. They will occur concurrently with other natural and anthropogenic climatic changes. In some cases other human activities could compound (or reverse) the effects of global warming.

There is also an increasing concern that there are some key tipping points in the climate system and that we may be crossing various thresholds or 'planetary boundaries' (Rockström et al., 2009). As Walker (2006: 802) has written, 'The idea that passing some hidden threshold will drastically worsen man-made change has been around for decades, normally couched in technical terms such as "nonlinearity," "positive feedback" and "hysteresis". Recently, the term tipping point has come into vogue to describe the moment at which internal dynamics start to propel change previously driven by external forces. It has become recognized that there are some specific locations or environments – 'tipping elements' (Lenton et al., 2008) – where a small change may make a big difference. Among the questions that are being asked are 'Is climatic change getting out of control?' and 'Are we at a point of no return?' For example does the melting of Arctic ice lead to such a change in albedo (surface reflectivity) that it is self-reinforcing? Studies by Flannery et al. (2011) and Lenton (2012) suggest that it is. Could increasing amounts of melting of Arctic sea ice and the Greenland ice cap cause the thermohaline circulation of the oceans to flip from one state to another? Could melting of organic-rich permafrost (*Yedoma*) release great amounts of carbon dioxide and methane, so adding to the greenhouse effect? (Schuur and Abbott, 2011; Kort et al., 2012)? Could a rise in temperature cause the Amazon rainforest to be replaced by scrub or desert, thereby causing the Earth to lose another cooling mechanism? (Lovelock, 2006: 51). These and other examples of potential non-linear climate changes are discussed by McNeall et al. (2011) and Drijfhout et al. (2015). Moreover, palaeoclimate records have shown that the Earth has a long history of undergoing rapid, abrupt transitions (Thomas, 2016).

As Flannery (2005: 83) has argued, global warming may change climate in jerks, during which patterns jump from one state to another. As he put it, 'The best analogy is perhaps that of a finger on a light switch. Nothing happens for a while, but if you slowly increase the pressure a certain point is reached, a sudden change occurs, and conditions swiftly alter from one state to another.' Flannery recognized three potential climatic tipping points: a slowing or collapse of the Gulf Stream, the demise of the Amazon rainforest, and the release of gas hydrates (methane) from the floor of the Arctic. However, there are doubtless more tipping points than these, including disintegration of the West Antarctic Ice Sheet or a shift to a more persistent El Niño regime (Kriegler et al., 2009), and a map of such locations is provided by Kemp (2004).

The causes, consequences, and controversies associated with global warming have been extensively treated elsewhere (e.g. Harvey, 2000). The purpose of the following chapters of this book is not to review and revisit this literature, but to examine the implications that global warming has for landscapes and habitats.

8.2 Changes in the Biosphere

Climate change and changes in the concentrations of carbon dioxide in the atmosphere are likely to have a whole suite of biological consequences (Gates, 1993; Joyce et al., 2001). The ranges and the productivity of organisms will change, particularly in the case of systems closer to critical thresholds, which will respond more sensitively to external perturbations caused by climate change (Seddon et al., 2016). Traits that commonly make a species vulnerable to climate change include limited dispersal abilities, slow reproductive rates, specialized habitat and dietary requirements, restricted distribution and rarity, and narrow physiological tolerances (Pacifici et al., 2015, 2017). Depending on the degree of future climate change, some species face the risk of extinction (Urban, 2015), and studies suggest that climate change could surpass habitat destruction as the greatest global threat to biodiversity over the next several decades. The velocity of climate change may present daunting challenges for terrestrial organisms and much of the world could experience climate change velocities greater than 1 km/year over the twenty-first century, and in some locations the velocities could be much higher. Diffenbaugh and Field (2013) believe that the combination of high velocities of climate change and multidimensional human fragmentation of habitat will present terrestrial ecosystems with an environment that is unprecedented in recent evolutionary history.

There are various ways in which climate change may impact upon plants and animals. Cahill et al. (2012) divided these into abiotic and biotic factors. With regard to the former, many effects of anthropogenic climate change follow from an increase in temperature. The most obvious proximate factor causing extinction is temperatures that exceed the physiological tolerance of the species. Similarly, increased temperatures may both decrease activity time and increase energy maintenance costs, leading faunal elements to die from starvation rather than from overheating. In addition, decreasing precipitation may lead directly to water stress, death, and local extinction for terrestrial species and loss of habitat for freshwater species. Climate change can also increase the frequency of fires, and these fires may themselves be proximate causes of extinction. Similarly, increases in temperature lead to melting of the cryosphere and rising sea-levels. These may eliminate coastal habitats and modify the salinity of freshwater habitats.

With regard to biotic factors, these can be placed into three general categories.

1) Negative impacts on beneficial species
   Climate change may cause local extinction of a given species by causing declines in a species upon which it depends. These may include prey for predators, hosts for parasites and specialized herbivores, species that create necessary microhabitats, and species that are essential for reproduction (e.g. pollinators).
2) Positive impacts on harmful species
   Climate change may cause extinction through positive effects on species that have negative interactions with a focal species, including competitors, predators, and pathogens. Warming can also benefit introduced species, exacerbating their negative effects on native flora and fauna.
3) Temporal mismatch between interacting species
   Climate change may also create incongruence between the activity times of interacting species.

Bellard et al. (2012) analyzed the various ways in which species can in theory respond to climate change, and proposed that this would take place along three distinct but non-exclusive axes: spatial, temporal, or self. First, species can track appropriate conditions in space and then follow them. This is typically done through long-distance dispersal, but shifts to a different habitat at the local or micro-habitat levels are also relevant. Second, in order to keep up with changing abiotic factors that show cyclic variation over time, such as temperature on a daily or yearly period, individuals can also respond to climate change through a shift in time. Phenology, i.e. the timing of life cycle events such as flowering, fruiting, and seasonal migrations, is one of the most ubiquitous responses to twentieth-century climate warming. Third, species can cope with changing climatic conditions by adapting themselves to the new conditions in their local range, rather than by tracking their current optimal conditions in space or time. These *in situ* changes they termed 'self'. Species can move along this self axis by physiological alterations that allow tolerance to warmer or drier conditions or by behavioural modifications of, for example, diet, activity, and energy budget.

Altitudinal changes in vegetation zones will be of considerable significance, and photographic evidence has indicated that these have already occurred in the mountainous and desert areas of the American southwest over the last half century (Brusca et al., 2013; Guida et al., 2014). In the twentieth century there is some evidence that warming affected the position of tree lines, and Kullman (2001), for example, found that in Sweden a 0.8 °C warming in the last 100 years caused the tree limit to migrate upwards by more than 100 m. In general, Peters (1988) believes that with a 3 °C temperature change vegetation belts will move about 500 m in altitude. One consequence of this would be the probable elimination of Douglas fir (*Pseudotsuga taxifolia*) from the lowlands of California and Oregon, because rising temperatures would preclude the seasonal chilling this species requires for seed germination and shoot growth. The retreat of agricultural activity in some highland areas, as in Austria, combined with warming, may lead to an upward movement of the tree line and a reduction in alpine grasslands (Tasser et al., 2017). In addition, changes in precipitation may have an influence on vegetation zonation in mountains (Engler et al., 2011). Particularly sensitive areas because of what can be called 'the altitudinal squeeze' include the European Alps (Dirnböck et al., 2011; Dullinger et al., 2012) and tropical alpine regions and cloud forests (Buytaert et al., 2011; Rojas-Soto et al., 2012), where important habitats for endemic species may be lost.

Vegetation will also change latitudinally and some models suggest that wholesale change will occur in the distribution of biomes (Hickler et al., 2012). Theoretically, a rise of 1 °C in mean temperature could cause a poleward shift of vegetation zones of about 200 km (Ozenda and Borel, 1990). However, uncertainties surround the question of how fast plant species would be able to move to and to settle new habitats suitable to the changed climatic conditions. Post-glacial vegetation migration rates appear to have been in the range of a few tens of km per century. For a warming of 2–3 °C forest bioclimates could shift northwards about 4–6 ° of latitude in a century, indicating the need for a migration rate of some tens of km per decade. Furthermore, migration could be hampered because of natural barriers, ecological fragmentation, zones of cultivation, etc.

Changes in forest composition or location could be slow, for mature trees tend to be long-lived and resilient. This means that they can survive long periods of marginal climate. However, it is during the stage of tree regeneration or seedling establishment that they are most vulnerable to climate change. Seedlings are highly sensitive to temperature and may not be able to grow under altered climatic conditions. This means that if climate zones do indeed shift at a faster rate than trees migrate, established adults of appropriate species and genotypes will be separated from the place where seedling establishment is needed in the future (Snover, 1997). It is probable that future climate change will not cause catastrophic dieback of forests, but that faster growing tree species will enter existing forests over extended time periods (Hanson and Weltzin, 2000).

An early attempt to model changes on a global basis was made by Emmanuel et al. (1985). Using the GCM developed by Manabe and Stouffer (1980) for a doubling of CO_2 levels and mapping the present distribution of ecosystem types in relation to contemporary temperature conditions, they found *inter alia* that the following changes would take place: boreal forests would contract from their present position of comprising 23% of total world forest cover to less than 15%; grasslands would increase from 17.7% of all world vegetation types to 28.9%; deserts would increase from 20.6 to 23.8%; and forests would decline from 58.4 to 47.4%.

Smith et al. (1992b) attempted to model the response of Holdridge's Life Zones to global warming and associated precipitation changes as predicted by a range of different GCMs. These are summarized for some major biomes in Table 8.2. All the GCMs predicted conditions that would lead to a very marked contraction in the tundra and desert biomes, and an increase in the areas of grassland and dry forests. There is, however, some disagreement as to what will happen to mesic forests as a whole, though within this broad class the humid tropical rainforest element will show an expansion.

Zabinski and Davis (1989) modelled the potential changes in the range of certain tree species in eastern North America, using a GISS GCM and a doubling of atmospheric carbon dioxide levels. The difference between their present ranges and their predicted ranges is very large (Figure 8.2). Melillo et al. (2001) have modelled shifts in major vegetation types for the whole of the United States, using the Hadley (HadCM2) and Canadian Centre for Climate Modelling and Analysis simulations and various biogeography models. The results of their simulations for 2099 are summarized in Table 8.3.

Vegetation will also probably be changed by variations in the role of certain extreme events that cause habitat

Table 8.2 Changes in areal coverage (km² x 10³) of major biomes as a result of climatic conditions predicted for a 2 x CO₂ world by various General Circulation Models.

Biome	Current	OSU	GFDL	GISS	UKMO
Tundra	939	−302	−5.5	−314	−573
Desert	3699	−619	−630	−962	−980
Grassland	1923	380	969	694	810
Dry forest	1816	4	608	487	1296
Mesic forest	5172	561	−402	120	−519

OSU = Oregon State University
GFDL = Geophysical Fluid Dynamic Laboratory
GISS = Goddard Institute for Space Studies
UKMO = UK Meteorological Office
Source: from Smith et al. (1992b: table 3).

Hemlock   Yellow Birch

Beech   Sugar Maple

Figure 8.2 Present and future range of four tree species in eastern North America: (a) present range; (b) range in AD 2090 under the GISS GCM 2 x CO₂ scenario. The black area is the projected occupied range considering a rate of migration of 100 km per century. The grey area is the potential projected range with climate change. *Source:* adapted from Zabinski and Davis (1989).

disturbance, including fire (O'Connor et al., 2011), heat stress (Allen et al., 2010), windstorms, hurricanes (Lugo, 2000), coastal flooding (Overpeck et al., 1990), and drought (Hanson and Weltzin, 2000). Warming temperatures in the future mean three things with respect to drought in forests: (1) droughts will become hotter, (2) the drying capacity of the air, measured as the vapour pressure deficit (VPD) will become greater, and (3) a smaller fraction of precipitation will fall as snow (Luce et al., 2016). Experimental and modelling studies by McDowell et al. (2016) on conifers in the south-west of the USA have suggested that increasing summer drought could cause widespread and massive mortality of needle-leaf evergreen trees such as piñon pine (*Pinus edulis*) and juniper (*Juniperus monosperma*). The iconic Joshua Tree (*Yucca brevifolia*) of the American south-west may also have its range greatly contracted as a result of increasing drought stress (Cole et al., 2011).

Table 8.3 Projected changes in major vegetation types in the United States (after Melillo et al., 2001).

North-east
Under both simulated climates, forests remain the dominant natural vegetation, but the mix of forest types changes. For example, winter-deciduous forests expand at the expense of mixed conifer-broadleaf forests.
Under the climate simulated by the Canadian model, there is a modest increase in savannas and woodlands.

South-east
Under the climate simulated by the Hadley model, forest remains the dominant natural vegetation, but once again the mix of forest types changes.
Under the climate simulated by the Canadian model, all three biogeography models show an expansion of savannas and grasslands at the expense of forests. For two of biogeography models, LPJ and MAPSS, the expansion of these non-forest ecosystems is dramatic by the end of the twenty-first century. Both drought and fire play an important role in the forest break-up.

Midwest
Under both simulated climates, forests remain the dominant natural vegetation, but the mix of forest types changes.
One biogeography model, LBJ, simulates a modest expansion of savannas and grasslands.

Great Plains
Under the climate simulated by the Hadley model, two biogeography models project an increase in woodiness in this region, while the third projects no change in woodiness.
Under the climate simulated by the Canadian model, the biogeography models project either no change in woodiness or a slight decrease.

West
Under the climate simulated by both the Hadley and Canadian models, the area of desert ecosystems shrinks and the area of forest ecosystem grows.

North-west
Under both simulated climates, the forest area grows slightly.

Other possible non-climatic effects of elevated CO_2 levels on vegetation include changes in photosynthesis, stomatal closure, and carbon fertilization, though these are still matters of controversy (Karnosky et al., 2001;

Wullschleger et al., 2002; Karnosky, 2003). However, especially at high altitudes, it is possible that elevated CO_2 levels would have potentially significant effects on tree growth, causing growth enhancement. Likewise, warm, drought-stressed ecosystems such as the chaparral in the south-west United States might be very responsive to elevated CO_2 levels (Oechel et al., 1995). Increased carbon dioxide levels have also been implicated in the increasing density of trees that has been observed in some savannas (Buitenwerf et al., 2012; Bond and Midgley, 2012).

Peterson (2000) investigated the potential impact of climate change on the role of catastrophic winds from tornadoes and downbursts in causing disturbance to forests in North America. It is feasible that with warmer air masses over middle latitude areas, the temperature contrast with polar air masses will be greater, providing more energy and thus more violent storms, but much more work needs to be undertaken before this can be said with any certainty. It is still far from clear whether tropical hurricane frequencies and intensities will increase in a warmer world. However, whether they increase or decrease, there are likely to be a number of possible ecosystem responses (Table 8.4).

The frequency and intensity of fires is an important factor in many biomes (Nitschke and Innes, 2013), and fires are highly dependent on weather and climate, being more likely to occur in drought years or when there are severe lightning strikes. Wind conditions are also a significant control of fire severity. Fire frequencies have grown substantially in the boreal forests of Russia, Canada, and the USA in recent warming decades (Soja et al., 2007) (Figure 8.3). For the Earth as a whole, Jolly et al. (2015) showed that from 1979–2013 there had been a significant increase in the length of the fire season and in the area burned. An analysis by Flannigan et al. (2000) suggested that future fire severity could ramp up over much of North America. They anticipated increases in the area burned in the United States of 25–50% by the middle of the twenty-first century, with most of this occurring in Alaska and the

Table 8.4 Potential response of ecosystems to changes in hurricane characteristics (modified after Lugo, 2000).

Response associated with increased hurricane frequency and intensity:
A larger fraction of the natural landscape will be set back in successional stage, i.e. there will be more secondary forests.
Forest aboveground biomass and height will decrease because vegetation growth will be interrupted more frequently or with greater intensity.
Familiar species combinations will change as species capable of thriving under disturbance conditions will increase in frequency at the expense of species that require long periods of disturbance-free conditions to mature.

Response associated with decreased hurricane frequency and intensity:
A larger fraction of the natural landscape will advance in successional stage, i.e. there will be more mature forests and fewer secondary forests.
Forest aboveground biomass and height will increase because the longer disturbance-free periods allow greater biomass accumulation and tree height.
Species combinations will change as species capable of thriving under disturbance conditions will decrease in frequency and species typical of disturbance-free conditions will increase.

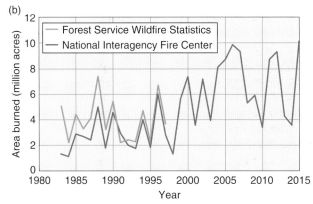

Figure 8.3 (a) Area burned annually in Canada since 1920. Note the increase in the number of extreme fire years over the last five decades. *Source:* after Soja et al. (2007: figure 6). Reproduced with permission from Elsevier. (b) Changing area of wildfires in USA since the 1980s. *Source:* EPA, *Climate Change Indicators* 2016, https://www.epa.gov/climate-indicators (accessed January 2018).

south-east United States. For Canada they forecast that the area burned could increase by 74–118% by the end of the century (Flannigan et al., 2005).

Other disturbances to vegetation communities could be brought about by changing patterns of insects and pathogens (Ayres and Lombardero, 2000; Pautasso et al., 2013). For example, in temperate and boreal forests, increases in summer temperatures could accelerate the development rate and reproductive potential of insects, whereas warmer winter temperatures could increase over-winter survival. In addition, it is possible that the ranges of introduced alien invasive species could change (Simberloff, 2000).

Let us now turn to a consideration of some particular biomes. First, the boreal forest (Figure 8.4; Table 8.5), which is dominated by such species as spruce (*Picea*), pine (*Pinus*), and larch (*Larix*), is the northernmost and coldest forested biome in the Northern Hemisphere (Chapin et al., 2010). The boreal forest encompasses ~30% of the global forest area, contains more surface freshwater than any other biome, is estimated to sequester ~20% of the total carbon sink generated by the world's forests, and provides more than 33% of the lumber and

Figure 8.4 Boreal forest in southern Sweden (ASG).

25% of the paper on the world export market (Gauthier et al., 2015). Its future health is therefore very important.

Over the course of the twenty-first century, the boreal biome is expected to experience the largest increase in temperatures of all forest biomes. It is thus not surprising that potential changes in the geographical extent of boreal forests in the Northern Hemisphere are especially striking. The southern boundary will move from the southern tip of Scandinavia to the northernmost portion. Basically, boreal forest will be lost to other biomes (such as temperate forest) on its southern margins but will expand into tundra on its northern margins (Figure 8.5) (Chapin and Danell, 2001). This biome will also be subject to increasing fire frequencies and insect infestations (Calef, 2010), for

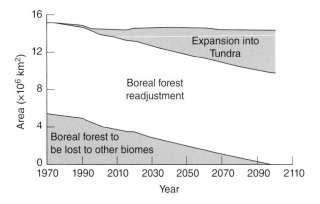

Figure 8.5 Changes in areas of boreal forest projected by the IMAGE model in response to scenarios of future change in climate and land use. Although the total area of boreal forest is projected to remain relatively constant, about one-third of the present boreal forest is projected to be converted to other biomes, and an additional third will be added as trees advance into tundra. *Source:* Chapin and Danell (2001: figure 6.1). Reproduced with permission from Springer.

Table 8.5 Potential drivers of future boreal forest composition and extent.

Primary climatic changes with effects on plant growth
    Temperature
    Evapotranspiration
    Precipitation
    Winds

Secondary climatic changes
    Droughts
    Floods
    Frost frequency and intensity
    Snowpack extent and duration

Environmental responses to climate change
    Invasive species
    Pests
    Disease
    Fire
    State of permafrost

Human responses to climate change
    Ease of access for logging, etc.
    Changes in land use and spread of agriculture with longer growing season
    Tree planting for carbon sequestration

---

there is evidence that these have been rising in recent decades (Soja et al., 2007). Within the forest, species composition may change because some species, such as white spruce and black spruce, appear to be highly influenced by temperature conditions and moisture availability (Beck et al., 2011a; Girardin et al., 2016). In Siberia deciduous larch (*Larix*) may be replaced by evergreen conifers (Shuman et al., 2011). In Canada, Boulanger et al. (2016) suggested that on the southern border of the forest, warmth-induced changes in the competitiveness of dominant tree species, and substantial intensification of the fire regime, appear likely to combine in driving major changes in boreal forest. They believed that resulting cumulative impacts would include (i) a strong decrease in the biomass of the dominant boreal species, especially mid- to late-successional conifers, (ii) increases in the abundance of some temperate species able to colonize disturbed areas in a warmer climate, (iii) increases in the proportions of pioneer and fire-adapted species in these landscapes, and (iv) an overall decrease in biomass. Biomass decreases have already been identified in the boreal forests of western Canada since the 1950s (Chen and Luo, 2015).

One biome that may suffer a particularly severe loss in area as a result of warming is arctic and alpine tundra, an environment where climatic impacts on vegetation have already been detected (Grabherr et al., 2010; Kapfer and Grytnes, 2017) and where changes in the cryosphere will be considerable (Chapter 11). As the tree line moves up mountains and migrates northwards in the Northern Hemisphere, the extent of tundra will be greatly reduced, perhaps by as much as 55% in total (Walker et al., 2001). The alpine tundra zone may disappear completely from some mountain tops. Moreover, recent Arctic warming has led to increases in tundra shrub cover (alder and willow) in the Eurasian Arctic and elsewhere (Macias-Fauria et al., 2012; Myers-Smith et al., 2015), a process somewhat inelegantly called 'shrubification'. In Alaska, tundra areas and the tundra-boreal forest boundary zone may be subjected to increased flammability (Young et al., 2016b), and with increasing air temperatures, permafrost thaw is also expected to drastically change boreal forest structure in the taiga (Helbig et al., 2016). Another mechanism by which climate change affects tundra vegetation is abrupt thaw resulting in local collapse of the permafrost (Kolk et al., 2016). Due to thaw pond (thermokarst) formation, changes in northern permafrost landscapes from dry birch forests or shrub-dominated vegetation towards ponds or wetlands dominated by graminoids may occur with climatic change.

The animals of the tundra may also be affected by warming. Forbes et al. (2016), for instance, have shown that sea ice loss is accelerating in the Barents and Kara Seas (BKS). At the same time, autumn/winter rain-on-snow (ROS) events have become more frequent and intense. They can be catastrophic for reindeer in the autumn when rain turns to an ice crust as plummeting normal temperatures return. This crust, often several centimetres thick, prevents the reindeer from feeding on fodder beneath the snow throughout the winter months. Two major ROS events during November 2006 and 2013 led to massive winter reindeer mortality episodes on the Yamal Peninsula. If future sea ice declines are linked with increased precipitation and higher temperatures in the BKS region, then it is logical to infer that ROS events will be more frequent in these situations and that more reindeer will starve.

A somewhat precarious biome, located as it is at the southernmost tip of Africa and so with little scope for displacement, is the very diverse Fynbos Biome. It is a predominantly sclerophyll shrubland, characterized by the pre-eminence of hard-leaved shrubs, many of which are proteas. In addition to being extraordinarily diverse, this biome contains many endemic species. Modelling, using the Hadley Centre CM2 GCM, indicates a likely contraction of the extent of Fynbos by c. 2050 (Figure 8.6) (Midgley et al., 2003). Climate in the Fynbos is predicted to get drier and hotter and is already experiencing an increase in extreme weather events. While fires are an important natural disturbance essential to the life-history strategies of many Fynbos plant species, there are also indications from several sources that climate changes are resulting in detrimental increases in fire frequency (Lee

Figure 8.6 Current mapped Fynbos Biome (upper panel, after Rutherford and Westfall, 1994) and the modelled extent of the biome under current (middle panel) and future (c. 2050) climate conditions (lower panel), the latter based on climate change projections for the region generated by the GCM HadCM2. *Source:* Midgley et al. (2003: figure 1). Reproduced with permission from Elsevier.

and Barnard, 2016). The neighbouring Succulent Karoo biome, with it great diversity of succulents, is likely to be impacted as well (Young et al., 2016a). Likewise, the highly specialized, diverse, and localized fauna and flora of Madagascar, including the iconic baobabs, could be under threat.

The vegetation in the Mediterranean region may also change substantially. With a decrease in precipitation and an increase in temperatures of 2 °C or more, the

vegetation will be unlike that witnessed over the last 10,000 years. Under one Representative Concentration Pathway (RCP)8.5 scenario, Guiot and Cramer (2016) predict that all of southern Spain turns into desert, deciduous forests invade most of the mountains, and Mediterranean vegetation replaces most of the deciduous forests in a large part of the Mediterranean basin. Because of aridification in the mountains of southern Europe, the geographical ranges of broadleaf forests will be reduced, and Euro-Siberian conifers at mid- and high elevations will be displaced by Mediterranean sclerophyllous species (Ruiz-Labourdette et al., 2012).

In the UK, the MONARCH programme (UK Climate Impacts Programme, 2001) has investigated potential changes in the distribution of organisms. Among the consequences of global warming they identify as being especially serious are the loss of montane heaths in the mountains of Scotland and the dieback of beach (*Fagus*) woodlands in southern Britain as summer droughts become more intense. However, it needs to be remembered that climate is not the only control on the distribution of species and that other factors such as biotic interactions and species' dispersal are also likely to be significant (Pearson and Dawson, 2003).

Mangroves, important components of coastlines in the warmer parts of the world, are also sensitive to temperature (see also Section 9.10). The best developed mangrove swamps are found near the Equator in Indonesia, New Guinea, and the Philippines, where the temperature in the coldest month does not fall below 20 °C. The number of species decreases with increasing latitude. Walter (1984) indicates that the last outposts of mangrove are to be found at 30 °N and 33 °S in Eastern Africa, 37–38 °S in Australia and New Zealand, 20 °S in Brazil, and 32 °N in the Bermudas. Mangroves in such areas might expand their poleward range under warmer conditions and with less prevalence of freezing. This has been proposed for the Gulf of Mexico (Armitage et al., 2015) and for Florida (Cavanaugh et al., 2014). There is evidence that over the past half century mangrove species have proliferated at or near their poleward limits on at least five continents, at the expense of ordinary salt marshes (Saintilan et al., 2014). The regional responses of mangroves to changes in temperature, precipitation, storminess, and other factors are expertly reviewed by Ward et al. (2016). Kelleway et al. (2017) suggest that encroachment of woody mangrove shrubs and trees into herbaceous salt marshes may represent a substantial change in ecosystem structure, enhance carbon storage, and increase the capacity of a wetland to increase surface elevation in response to sea-level rise. They theorize that mangrove encroachment may also increase nutrient storage and improve storm protection, but cause declines in habitat availability for fauna that require an open vegetation structure (such as migratory birds and foraging bats). Gabler et al. (2017) discuss the likely effects of climate changes on coastal wetlands more generally.

Seagrass communities are another type of marine habitat at risk (Short et al., 2011). These are composed of flowering plants that include the widely distributed genera *Zostera*, *Thalassia*, and *Posidonia*. They are highly productive ecosystems that support marine food webs and provide essential habitat for many coastal species. They are currently declining fast (Waycott et al., 2009), but in areas like the Mediterranean may decline further as sea water temperatures rise (Jordà et al., 2012).

Finally, great interest is emerging in the future of Amazonia. As we saw in Section 7.7, the replacement of rain forest with other forms of land use is likely in itself to cause a reduction in annual rainfall amounts over the area. However, in addition, the concern is that global warming will also modify climatic conditions in the area so that rainfall totals are reduced, droughts become more common, the forest starts to die back, and, as a consequence, more carbon is released into the atmosphere thereby accentuating the greenhouse effect, while increased temperatures may themselves have deleterious effects on some plants (Corlett, 2011). In other words, there is a worry that Amazonia could be at a tipping point (Nepstad et al., 2008; Nobre and Borma, 2009). The 2005 drought in Amazonia raised awareness of the potential threat of a more drought-prone Amazon (Betts et al., 2008) and the potential role that changes in sea surface conditions could have on rainfall amounts. One particularly grim modelling simulation by Cook and Vizy (2008) suggested that there could be a 70% reduction in the extent of the Amazon rain forest by the end of the century and a large eastward expansion of the drought resistant *caatinga* that is prominent in parts of north-east Brazil today. They concluded (p. 558):

> The coupled regional model simulation projects a 70% reduction in the extent of the Amazon rain forest … Rain forest vegetation disappears entirely from Bolivia, Paraguay, and Argentina, and most of Brazil and Peru. Rain forest in Columbia is largely maintained, as all of the surviving rain forest is concentrated close to the equator. Venezuela and French Guiana experience small reductions … North of about 15 °S the rain forest is primarily replaced by savanna vegetation.

Salazar et al. (2007) came up with a much lower figure for the reduction in tropical forest area in South America: c. 18% by the end of the century. Anadon et al. (2014) predicted that savanna would expand at the expense of tropical forest, with shifts reaching up to 600 km northward for the forest–savanna boundary in eastern Amazonia. However, what is predicted for South America does not necessarily apply to other parts of the tropical world, and forest expansion might, for example, occur in the Congo Basin (Zelazowski et al., 2011).

To recapitulate, the wholesale changes in the biomes discussed so far in this chapter, together with the changes that will take place in, for example, the Arctic and in coral reefs, will impact upon individual organisms and species and may mean that protected areas are in the wrong place (Gillson et al., 2013; Johnston et al., 2013; Feeley and Silman, 2016). In addition, climate changes will affect a whole raft of factors that may be important for individual species: disease incidence and distribution; the occurrence of fires, floods, droughts, or windstorms; the success of ecological invaders; habitat loss or gain due to sea-level change; changes in the timing and success of breeding, hibernation, or migration; the extinction of habitats at the tops of mountains; the sex determination of embryos; and changes in food availability. Some organisms may prove to be relatively resilient in the face of such changes, such as those that live in burrows, but those that are highly specialized, have restricted geographical distributions, have long gestation times, and only migrate slowly, may be more prone to contraction in their numbers and range. The potential effects of climate change on marine mammals is reviewed by Learmonth et al. (2006), while the vulnerability of one particular types of marine mammal – the marine turtle – is covered by Poloczanska et al. (2010). The vulnerability of land mammals in Africa is assessed by Thuiller et al. (2006), of birds by Crick (2004), and of fish by Rijnsdorp et al. (2009).

8.3 Climate and Geomorphology

Attempts to relate landforms and land-forming processes to climatic conditions have been long continued and climatic geomorphology has a long and distinguished history (Gutierrez-Elorza, 2001). Certainly, any change in climatic variability and extreme events would have considerable geomorphological significance (Viles and Goudie, 2003) (Table 8.6).

It is self-evident that some landforms and land-forming processes are intimately related to temperature. In general terms, for example, permafrost today only occurs in areas where the mean annual temperature is less than -2 °C and it is virtually ubiquitous north of the –6 to –8 °C isotherm in the Northern Hemisphere. Likewise, temperature is one of the major controls of ablation of glacier ice. At the other extreme, coral reefs have a restricted distribution in the world's oceans which reflects their levels of temperature tolerance. They do not thrive in cool waters (i.e. <20 °C mean annual sea surface temperature),

Table 8.6 Examples of geomorphological effects of decadal-to century-scale oscillations.

Environment affected	Impacts upon
Terrestrial hydrology	Glacier mass balance Lake levels Permafrost River flows Snow cover
Terrestrial geomorphology	Dune movements Effects of fire frequency with knock-on effects on weathering Floodplain sedimentation and erosion Geochemical sediment growth Runoff and slope instability Slope instability/mass movements Soil erosion
Coastal/marine ecology and geomorphology	Coastal dune activation Coastal erosion Coral bleaching Mangrove defoliation/land loss

Table 8.7 Factors affecting rates of evaporation and runoff.

Evaporation	Runoff
Temperature (daily means and seasonal range)	Ground temperature
Duration of ice cover	Precipitation frequency and seasonal distribution
Depth of water in lake and basin morphology (water volume)	Precipitation intensity (event magnitude and duration)
Humidity (vapour pressure gradient)	Precipitation type (rain, snow, etc.)
Salinity of lake water	Slope gradients (stream size and number)
Wind speed	Soil type (infiltration capacity)
Cloudiness and solar radiation receipts	Vegetation cover and type

Source: Bradley (1985).

but equally many coral species cannot tolerate temperatures greater than about 30 °C, and have been stressed by warm ENSO years.

Some relatively clear relationships have also been established between precipitation levels and geomorphic processes and forms. Large sand dunes only occur under dry conditions where rainfall levels are less than 150–200 mm per year, and dust storms appear to be a feature of hyper-arid areas where annual rainfall totals are around 0–150 mm per year. However, for other phenomena the climatic controls may be rather more complex. Take, for example, the case of lake basins. These, and particularly those with no outlets, can respond in a dramatic manner to changes in their hydrological balance. During times of positive water budgets (due to high rates of water input and/or low rates of evapotranspirational loss), lakes may develop and expand over large areas, only to recede and desiccate during times of negative water balance. Shoreline deposits and sediment cores extracted from lake floors can provide a detailed picture of lake fluctuations (e.g. Street and Grove, 1979). However, given the range of factors affecting rates of evaporation and runoff over a lake basin (Table 8.7) their precise climatological interpretation needs to be determined with care. A full review is provided by Mason et al. (1994).

Many of the studies of the links between climate and geomorphology have employed rather crude climatic parameters such as mean annual temperature or mean annual rainfall. It is, however, true that climatic extremes and climatic variability may be of even greater significance. Unfortunately, they are not very effectively dealt with in GCMs. We have imperfect knowledge of how extreme events and climate variability will change in a warmer world. It is, however, possible that climatic variability, such as the ENSO phenomenon, could be influenced by global warming (Latif and Keenlyside, 2009). The situation here is far from clear, for as An et al. (2008: 3) have put it 'dynamical understanding of ENSO responses to global warming is still in a toddling stage!' Some models suggest a weakening of ENSO activity under a global warming scenario, while others do not (Chand et al., 2017).

The impacts of climatic variability on ecological and geomorphic systems may be non-linear, as recently found for rainfall erosivity and ENSO in the south-west United States (D'Odorico et al., 2001). Indeed, Brunsden (2001) drew attention to the complex responses of landforms to environmental changes and events, while Knox (1993) showed how modest changes in climate can cause very large changes in the flood response of rivers. The complexity of future changes in the environment makes effective prediction and modelling extremely difficult (Blum and Törnqvist, 2000). As Bogaart et al. (2003) have pointed out, landscape response to climate change is highly non-linear and characterized by numerous feedbacks between different variables and by lead-lag phenomena. The example they give is of an increase in precipitation in an initially semi-arid area. This would by itself increase hillslope erosion and sediment transport capacity. However, over time, soil and vegetation conditions would adjust to the new environmental conditions, resulting in a better soil structure and more vegetation cover. As a result after a lag of time hillslope erosion and sediment yield might decrease.

Some ideas on the clustering of events and complex responses to them can be presented as conceptual diagrams. Figure 8.7a indicates in a general way how clusters of climatic events can produce variable overtopping of geomorphic thresholds, although it represents a simple linear view of geomorphic response which may be an oversimplification for many geomorphic systems. Figure 8.7b illustrates how complex chains of linkages

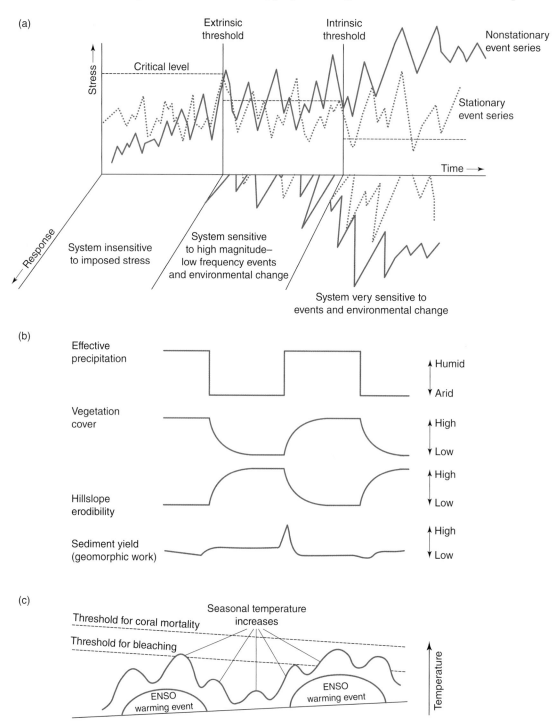

Figure 8.7 Representation of the impacts of climatic variability on geomorphic systems. (a) Stress-response sequences including thresholds under stable and changing climate conditions. *Source:* adapted from Brunsden (2001: figure 1). (b) A simplified view of the biogeomorphic response model. *Source:* adapted from Knox (1972) and Roberts and Barker (1993: figure 6.1). (c) A model of the possible interactions of different time scales of warming and their impact on coral bleaching. *Source:* adapted from Williams and Bunkley-Williams (1990) and Viles and Spencer (1995: figure 6.11).

between climatic, vegetation, and geomorphic processes produce a complex geomorphic response, and Figure 8.7c provides a simple conceptual model of the synergistic associations between different scales of warming producing coral bleaching.

The term 'climate change' involves changes in a whole package of climatic parameters, such as rainfall amounts, rainfall intensity, temperature amounts and variability, wind intensity, etc. This in itself means that the response of

land-forming processes to climate change will be complex. This is brought out in Table 8.8, which is based on the work of Crozier (2010) and provides a framework for understanding slope stability and how it might be impacted upon by diverse climatic parameters.

In the following chapters we shall consider some of the challenges that face some major types of environment in the face of global warming and other trends that have been discussed in this brief introduction.

Table 8.8 Direct changes and potential slope stability responses to climate change (modified after Crozier, 2010: table 1).

Climate change	Condition /process affected	Slope stability response
Increase in precipitation totals	Wetter antecedent conditions	Less rainfall in an event required to achieve critical water content Reduction in soil capillarity – reduction in cohesion Softened layers can act as lubricants Higher water tables – reduction in shear strength
	Increased weight (surcharge)	Increased bulk density, leading to decrease in shear strength/stress ratio in cohesive material
	Higher water tables for longer periods	More frequent attainment of critical water content during rainfall events
	Increased lubrication of contact surfaces between certain minerals	Reduction in friction (only occurs with certain platy minerals e.g. micas)
	Increase in river discharge	Increased bank scour and removal of lateral and basal support from slopes Higher lake levels, increase in bordering slope water tables Increase in rapid draw down events and higher drag forces, removal of lateral confining pressure plus perched groundwater levels on flood recession, increasing shear stress
Increase in rainfall intensity	Infiltration more likely to exceed subsurface drainage rates	Landslides triggering by reduction in effective normal stress leading to reduction in shear strength
	Rapid build-up of perched water tables	Increase in cleft water pressures
	Increased throughflow	Increase in seepage and drag forces, particle detachment and piping. Piping removes underlying structural support Enhanced drainage unless blockage occurs
Shift in cyclone tracks and other rain bearing weather systems	Areas previously unaffected, subject to high rainfall	Rapid adjustment of slopes to new climate regime
Increased variability in precipitation and temperature	More frequent wetting and drying cycles	Increase fissuring, widening of joint systems Reduction in cohesion and rock mass joint friction
Increased temperature	Reduction in antecedent water conditions through evapotranspiration Reduction in interstitial ice and permafrost Rapid snow melt-runoff and infiltration Reduction in glacier volume Increased sea level	Reduction in cohesion in jointed rock masses, debris, and soil Build up of porewater pressure and strength reduction Removal of lateral support to valley side slopes Enhanced basal erosion on coasts, increase in groundwater levels on costal slopes
Increased wind speed and duration	Enhanced evapotranspiration Enhanced root levering by trees Increased wave action on shorelines (enhanced by higher sea levels)	Reduction of soil moisture Enhanced drying and cracking Loosening and dislodging of joint blocks Removal of slope lateral support

Guide to Reading

Archer, D. (2007) *Global Warming: Understanding the Forecast.* Oxford: Blackwell. This book provides the scientific background required to understand global warming.

Arnell, N. (1996) *Global Warming, River Flows and Water Resources.* Chichester: Wiley. A study of potential future hydrological changes.

Chapin, F.S., Sala, O.E. and Huber-Sannwald, E. (eds) (2001) *Global Biodiversity in a Changing Environment.* Berlin: Springer Verlag. A wide-ranging assessment of how biodiversity may change in response to climate and land-use changes.

Flannery, T. (2005) *The Weather Makers.* London: Allen Lane. A hard-hitting 'popular' treatment of the consequences of future climate change.

IPCC (Intergovernmental Panel on Climate Change) (2013) *Climate Change 2013: The Physical Science Basis: Contribution of Working Group I to the Fifth Assessment Report of the Intergovernmental Panel on Climate Change*, ed. T.F. Stocker, D. Qin, G-K. Plattner, M. Tignor, S.K. Allen, J. Boschung, A. Nauels, Y. Xia, V. Bex, and P.M. Midgley. Cambridge: Cambridge University Press. The latest authoritative review by the international body charged with predicting future climate change.

Karl, T.R., Melillo, J.M. and Peterson, T.C. (2009) *Global Climate Change Impacts in the United States.* Cambridge: Cambridge University Press. An accessible and well-illustrated discussion of future climate change impacts in the USA.

Richardson, K., Steffen, W. and Liverman, D. (eds) (2011) *Climate Change: Global Risks, Challenges and Decisions.* Cambridge: Cambridge University Press. A synthesis of knowledge relevant to the climate change issue, this book ranges from the basic science documenting the need for policy action to the technologies, economic instruments, and political strategies that can be employed in response to climate change.

Romm, J. (2016) *Climate Change: What Everyone Needs to Know.* Cambridge: Cambridge University Press. A very accessible guide to the causes, consequences, and mitigation of climatic change.

9

The Future: Coastal Environments

CHAPTER OVERVIEW

One consequence of global warming is that sea levels will rise, partly in response to the thermal expansion of the oceans (the steric effect) and partly because of the melting of portions of the cryosphere. Sea level is presently rising, and the rate will accelerate in the future. It poses a particular threat to areas that are also subsiding. Among the coastal environments that may be sensitive to sea-level rise are coral reefs, mangrove swamps, salt marshes, deltas, estuaries, cliffed coasts, and sandy beaches. Some coastal environments will also be affected by changes in storm intensity, and coral reefs may be affected by increases in ocean acidity caused by the build-up of carbonic acid.

9.1 Introduction

If temperatures climb in coming decades, so will sea levels. Indeed, on a global basis, sea levels are rising at the present time, and always have in warmer periods in the past. The reasons why sea levels will rise include the thermal expansion of sea water (the steric effect), the melting of the cryosphere (glaciers, ice sheets, and permafrost), and miscellaneous anthropogenic impacts on the hydrological cycle (which will modify how much water is stored on land). Rising sea levels will have substantial geomorphological consequences for the world's coastlines. Moreover, as Viles and Spencer (1995) have pointed out, about 50% of the population in the industrialized world lives within 1 km of a coast, about 60% of the world's population live in the coastal zone (Figure 9.1), and two-thirds of the world's cities with populations of over 2.5 million people are near estuaries. Thirteen of the world's twenty largest cities are located on coasts. Rising sea levels will thus have an impact on a large proportion of the Earth's human population (Leatherman, 2001; FitzGerald et al. 2008). Areas at less than 10 m in altitude (the so-called Low Elevation Coastal Zone – the LECZ) account for c. 2% of the world's land area but contain 10% of the population. While only 13% of urban settlements with populations of less than 100,000 occur in the LECZ, the figure rises to over 65% among cities of 5 million or more. Many of the most severely impacted countries with respect to the effects of

sea-level rise and higher storm surges are in developing countries (Dasgupta et al. 2009; Brecht et al., 2012), including Vietnam, Pakistan, Philippines, Guyana, Suriname, Belize, Benin, Egypt, Jamaica, and Tunisia. Jakarta, in Indonesia, already has about 40% of its area below sea level, and because of subsidence caused by groundwater abstraction the threat of inundation is rising (Ward et al., 2011). Nicholls et al. (2011) suggest that were global temperatures to rise by 4 °C, then sea levels would rise by 0.5–2.0 m, causing the displacement of between 72 and 187 million people. There is a strong research need to identify particularly susceptible shorelines, as has, for example, been attempted for Scotland (Fitton et al., 2016).

Florida provides an excellent example of the threats posed to low-lying coastal areas. Approximately 10% of the state's land area is less than 1 m above present sea level. However, parts of it are especially vulnerable. A 0.6 m rise in sea level would inundate about 70% of the total land surface of the Florida Keys, 71% of the population, and 68% of property, while a 1.5 m rise would inundate 91% of the land surface, 71% of the population, and 68% of the property (Noss, 2011). Severe consequences have also been proposed as likely for California (Heberger et al., 2011; Revell et al., 2011).

However, it is not just the rise of sea levels that one needs to consider (Nicholls et al., 2007). Also important are the effects of high carbon dioxide levels on ocean acidification and the health of corals, the effects of higher sea-water temperatures on various marine organisms,

Human Impact on the Natural Environment: Past, Present and Future, Eighth Edition. Andrew S. Goudie.
© 2019 John Wiley & Sons Ltd. Published 2019 by John Wiley & Sons Ltd.
Companion website: www.wiley.com/go/goudie/human-impact-natural-environment

Figure 9.1 An informal coastal settlement in Kota Kinabalu, Sabah, Malaysia. Such settlements will be particularly at risk as a consequence of rising sea levels (ASG).

changes in the freshwater inputs to estuaries and lagoons, and changes in wave energy and storm surges. In addition, there are many other human influences on coastlines, including modification of the sediment budgets of rivers (Section 6.7) that nourish beaches, and accelerated ground subsidence brought about by fluid removal (Section 6.4). Many of these are discussed in Laffoley and Baxter (2016). The range of climate drivers for coastal systems listed by the IPCC (2007a) is shown in Table 9.1.

Table 9.1 Main climate drivers for coastal systems.

Climate driver	Effects
CO_2 concentration increase	Ocean acidification
Sea surface temperature increase	Change in ocean circulation, reduced sea ice in high latitudes, coral bleaching, stimulation of coral growth in cooler seas, poleward species migration, more algal blooms and red tides
Sea level	Inundation, flood and storm surge damage, beach erosion, saltwater intrusion up estuaries etc., rising water tables, impeded drainage, wetland loss
Storm intensity	Increased extreme water levels and wave heights
Storm frequency	Altered surges and storm waves
Wave climate	Changes in wave conditions, leading to altered patterns of erosion and accretion; re-orientation of beach plan form
Run-off	Altered flood risk in coastal lowlands, water quality/salinity, fluvial sediment supply, and circulation and nutrient supply

9.2 The Steric Effect

As the oceans warm up, their density decreases and their volume increases. This thermal expansion, the steric effect, causes sea levels to rise. Uncertainties arise as to the rate at which different parts of the oceans will warm up in response to increased atmospheric temperatures (Gregory et al., 2001). The steric effect over the twentieth century accounts for at least one-third of the observed eustatic change over that period, and from 1993–2010 it operated at a rate of c. 1.1 mm per year (out of a total of 3.2 mm of global sea-level rise per annum) (IPCC, 2013: Table 13.1). With regard to the future, sea-level rise caused by thermal expansion between 1990 and 2100 is thought likely to be around 0.28 m out of a total predicted sea-level rise due to climate change of 0.49 m (Church et al., 2001: table 11.14). The IPCC (2007a) suggested that thermal expansion is likely to account for 70–75% of sea-level rise by the end of the century, but in 2013 the IPCC suggested a somewhat lower contribution of about 30–55% (IPCC, 2013: 1180). However, this proportion might change if the contribution of the melting of the Greenland Ice Cap becomes a more important component of the total (Vermeer and Rahmstorf, 2009).

9.3 Anthropogenic Contributions to Sea-Level Change

Human activities have an impact upon the hydrological cycle in a wide range of ways (Chapter 5), so that changes in sea level could result from such processes as groundwater exploitation, drainage of lakes and wetlands, the construction of reservoirs behind dams, and modification of runoff and evapotranspiration rates from different types of land cover. Some of these processes could accelerate sea-level rise by adding more water to the oceans, whereas others would decelerate the rate of sea-level rise by impounding water on land. Unfortunately, quantitative data are sparse and sometimes contradictory and so it is difficult to assess the importance of anthropogenic contributions to sea-level change. The IPCC (Church et al., 2001: 658) came to three conclusions:

1) The effect of changes in terrestrial water storage on sea level might be considerable.
2) The net effect on sea level could be of either sign.
3) The rate of hydrological interference has increased over the last few decades.

9.3.1 Reduction in Lake-Water Volumes

Increased use of irrigation and inter-basin water transfers have contributed to reduced volumes of water being stored in some lake basins (Section 5.4). Classic examples of this include the Aral and Caspian seas of Central Asia and Owens Lake in the south-west United States. Unfortunately, as not all lake-level declines are due to human actions it is not always easy to disentangle these from the effects of natural decadal scale climate fluctuations. Equally it is difficult to calculate the proportion of the extracted water that reaches the world ocean by runoff and evapotranspiration. Some of it may enter groundwater stores, causing groundwater levels to rise and waterlogging of the land to occur. Controversy has thus arisen on this topic. On the one hand Sahagian (2000) has argued that this could be a process of some significance, perhaps contributing around 0.2 mm per year to sea-level rise, whereas Gornitz et al. (1997) believe that the net effect of the drying up of interior lakes is probably only small and indirect.

9.3.2 Water Impoundment in Reservoirs

Recent decades have seen the construction of large numbers of major dams and reservoirs. Today, nearly 500,000 km^2 of land worldwide are inundated by reservoirs that are capable of storing 6000 km^3 of water (Gleick, 2002). Newman and Fairbridge (1986) calculated that between 1957 and 1982 as much as 0.75 mm per year of sea-level rise potential was stored in reservoirs and irrigation projects. More recently, Gornitz et al. (1997) have estimated that 13.6 mm of sea-level rise potential has been impounded in reservoirs, equivalent since the 1950s to a potential average reduction in sea-level rise of 0.34 mm per year. The figure given even more recently by Pokhrel et al. (2012) is 0.39. However, as Sahagian (2000: 43) reported, 'the total amount of impounded water is not known because there have been no comprehensive inventories of the millions of small reservoirs such as farm ponds and rice paddies. As a result, the total contribution of impounded water to global hydrological balance has remained unclear and most likely severely underestimated'.

9.3.3 Groundwater Mining

Groundwater mining is the withdrawal of groundwater in excess of natural recharge. Many large groundwater aquifers are currently being heavily mined, leading to massive falls in aquifer levels and volumes (see Section 5.5). Examples include the Ogallala aquifer of the High Plains in the United States, the Nubian Sandstone aquifers of Libya and elsewhere in North Africa, and the great aquifers of the Arabian Peninsula. Estimates of the volumes of groundwater that are being removed from storage on a global basis are around 1000 to 1300 km^3, but not all of it is transferred to the oceans. Nonetheless, Church et al. (2001: 657) believed that it is probably the largest positive anthropogenic contributor to sea-level rise (apart from anthropogenic climatic change), amounting to perhaps 0.2 to 1.00 mm per year. This is a view that is largely confirmed by Wada et al. (2012b) and Pokhrel et al. (2012). This source may not continue indefinitely, however, because groundwater contributions may become exhausted in some regions. While groundwater depletion has elevated sea level during the past century and is currently contributing to sea-level rise, the rise rate is not uniform across the oceans, however, because the mass unloading associated with this depletion locally uplifts Earth's solid surface and depresses the geoid, leading to slower relative sea-level rise near areas of significant groundwater loss. The work of Veit and Conrad (2016) suggests that relative sea level is currently as much as 30 mm lower in California and 50 mm lower in India (both major areas of groundwater depletion) than it would be in the absence of such depletion.

9.3.4 Urbanization and Runoff

Urbanization leads to a net increase in total runoff from the land surface (see Section 5.3.6) due to the spread of areas of impermeable ground (e.g. concrete-, tile-, and tarmac-covered surfaces) which impede groundwater replenishment. In addition, water may be evacuated efficiently from urban areas in storm-water drains and sewers. Plausible rates of sea-level rise due to this mechanism are in the range of 0.35 to 0.41 mm per year.

9.3.5 Deforestation and Runoff

As discussed in Section 5.3.2, deforestation can lead to increases in runoff from land surfaces. For example, experiments with tropical catchments have shown typical increases in stream flow of 400–450 mm per year (Anderson and Spencer, 1991). The reasons for this include changes in rainfall interception, transpiration, and soil structure. Combining data on rates of tropical deforestation with average values for increases in runoff, Gornitz et al. (1997: 153) came up with an estimate that this could cause a rate of sea-level rise of 0.13 mm per year.

9.3.6 Wetland Losses

The reclamation or drainage of wetlands may release stored water that can then enter the oceans. Gornitz et al. (1997: 153) do not see this as a significant mechanism of sea-level change.

9.3.7 Irrigation

The area of irrigated land on earth has gone up dramatically (Section 5.4). Gornitz et al. (1997) estimated that evapotranspiration of water from irrigated surfaces would lead to an increase in the water content of the atmosphere and so to a fall in sea level of 0.14–0.15 mm per year. Irrigation water might also infiltrate into groundwater aquifers, removing 0.40–0.48 mm per year of sea-level equivalent.

9.3.8 Synthesis

As we have already noted, individual mechanisms can in some cases be significant in amount, with some augmenting sea-level rise and some reducing it. Gornitz et al. (1997: 158) summarized their analysis thus:

> Increased runoff from groundwater mining and impermeable urbanized surfaces are potentially important anthropogenic sources contributing to sea-level rise. Runoff from tropical deforestation and water released by oxidation of fossil fuel and biomass, including wetlands clearance, provide a smaller share of the total. Taken together, these processes could augment sea level by some 0.6–1.0 mm/year.
>
> On the other hand, storage of water behind dams, and losses of water due to infiltration beneath reservoirs and irrigated fields, along with evaporation from these surfaces could prevent the equivalent of 1.5–1.8 mm/year from reaching the ocean. The net effect of all of these anthropogenic processes is to withhold the equivalent of 0.8 ± 0.4 mm/year from the sea. This rate represents a significant fraction of the observed recent sea-level rise of 1–2 mm/year, but opposite in sign.

9.4 Permafrost Degradation, Melting of Glaciers, and Sea-Level Rise

Increases in temperatures in cold regions will lead to substantial reductions in the area of permanently frozen subsoil (permafrost). In effect, ground ice will be converted to liquid water which could in principle contribute to a rise in sea level (Section 11.6). However a proportion, unknown, of this water could be captured in ponds, thermokarst lakes, and marshes, rather than running off into the oceans. Another uncertainty relates to the volume of ground ice that will melt. Bearing these caveats in mind, Church et al. (2001: 658) suggested that

the contribution of permafrost to sea-level rise between 1990 and 2100 will be somewhere between 0 and 25 mm per year.

Many glaciers will be reduced in area and volume as global warming occurs (Section 11.3) and their meltwater will flow into the oceans, causing sea level to rise (Gregory and Oerlemans, 1998; Radić and Hock, 2011). In some situations, on the other hand, positive changes in precipitation may nourish glaciers, causing them to maintain themselves or to grow in spite of a warming tendency. Other uncertainties are produced by a lack of knowledge about how the mass balance of glaciers will respond to differing degrees of warming. The problems of mass balance estimations have been well summarized by Arendt et al. (2002: 382):

> Conventional mass balance programs are too costly and difficult to sample adequately the >160,000 glaciers on Earth. At present, there are only but 40 glaciers worldwide with continuous balance measurements spanning more than 20 years. High-latitude glaciers, which are particularly important because predicted climate warming may be greatest there, receive even less attention because of their remote locations. Glaciers that are monitored routinely are often chosen more for their ease of access and manageable size than for how well they represent a given region or how large a contribution they might make to changing sea level. As a result, global mass balance data are biased toward small glaciers (<20 km^2) rather than those that contain the most ice (>100 km^2). Also, large cumulative errors can result from using only a few point measurements to estimate glacier-wide mass balances on an individual glacier.

The IPCC (2013: 1163) suggested that during the present century, the melting of glaciers will contribute c. 0.06 to 0.15 m of sea-level change, second, therefore, only to steric effects.

9.5 Ice Sheets and Sea-Level Rise

The ice sheets of Greenland and Antarctica (Section 11.2) have proved pivotal in ideas about future sea-level changes. In the 1980s there were fears that these could decay at near catastrophic rates, causing sea levels to rise rapidly and substantially, perhaps by 3 m or more by 2100. Since that time this has become thought to be less likely and that far from suffering major decay, the ice sheets (particularly of Antarctica) might show some accumulation of mass as a result of increasing levels of nourishment by snow. However, considerable debates still exist on this and there remain major uncertainties about how the two great polar ice masses may respond in coming decades and whether the West Antarctic Ice Sheet (WAIS) is inherently and dangerously unstable (see e.g. Oppenheimer, 1998; Sabadini, 2002; van der Ween, 2002). These are issues that will be addressed in Chapter 11.

Were the WAIS to collapse into the ocean, the impacts of the resulting 5 m increase in sea level would be catastrophic for many coastal lowlands. The IPCC (2001) thought that it was very unlikely that this would occur in the twenty-first century. They believed that the contribution that the Antarctica and Greenland ice caps would make to sea-level change would be modest and less than those of glaciers or thermal expansion (the steric effect).

9.6   How Fast are Sea Levels Rising?

Observational estimates of sea-level change are based on the short (only a few decades or so) satellite record of sea-level height (Cabanes et al., 2001) and on the longer, but geographically sparse and uneven tide gauge network. Tide gauges are rare in mid-ocean locations and very inadequate for the ocean-dominated Southern Hemisphere. In addition, difficulties in determining global (eustatic) sea-level changes are bedevilled by the need to make allowances for land motion caused by post-glacial isostatic rebound and tectonic movements (Church, 2001). Between 1910 and 1960 annual rates of global sea-level rise ranged from 0.25 to 0.75 mm while those between 1960 and 1990 ranged from 0.60 and 1.09 mm. From 1993–2010, the rate accelerated to c. 3.2 mm per year. The steric effect over the period 1910 to 1990 accounts for about one-third of the observed eustatic change over that period (Cazenave and Llovel, 2010). The shrinkage of glaciers as warming occurs releases meltwater that flows into the oceans, also causing sea-level rise (Radić and Hock, 2011). Over the period 1993 to 2010, the IPCC (2013) suggests that global mean sea-level rise is, with high confidence, consistent with the sum of the observed contributions from ocean thermal expansion due to warming $(1.1\,[0.8\,\text{to}\,1.4]\,\text{mm}\,\text{yr}^{-1})$, from changes in glaciers $(0.76\,[0.39\,\text{to}\,1.13]\,\text{mm}\,\text{yr}^{-1})$, Greenland ice sheet $(0.33\,[0.25\,\text{to}\,0.41]\,\text{mm}\,\text{yr}^{-1})$, Antarctic ice sheet $(0.27\,[0.16\,\text{to}\,0.38]\,\text{mm}\,\text{yr}^{-1})$, and land water storage $(0.38\,[0.26\,\text{to}\,0.49]\,\text{mm}\,\text{yr}^{-1})$. The sum of these contributions is $2.8\,[2.3\,\text{to}\,3.4]\,\text{mm}\,\text{yr}^{-1}$. The record of sea-level change since 1880 is shown in Figure 9.2.

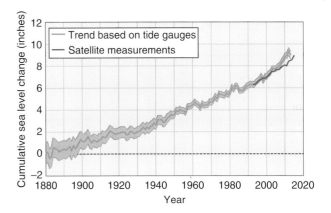

Figure 9.2 Sea level rise since 1880. *Source:* https://www.epa.gpv/climate-indicators/climate-change-indicators-sea-level (accessed January 2018).

9.7   The Amount of Sea-Level Rise By 2100

Over the years there has been a considerable diversity of views about how much sea-level rise is likely to occur by 2100. In general, however, estimates have tended to be revised downward through time (French et al., 1995; Pirazzoli, 1996) (Figure 9.3). Figure 9.4 shows the possible extent of sea-level rise by the end of the century, and the sources of such change. Researchers have now settled at best estimates of just under 50 cm by 2100. This implies rates of sea-level rise of around 5 mm per year, which compares with a rate of about 1.5 to 2.0 mm during the twentieth century (Miller and Douglas, 2004). However, with increasing evidence that polar ice sheets are melting rapidly (Rignot et al., 2011), there are those who believe that the rates should be revised upwards and that by the end of the century sea level might be 0.5–1.4 m above the 1990 level (Rahmstorf, 2007), or even 0.75–1.9 m (Vermeer and Rahmstorf, 2009). Nicholls et al. (2011) believed that, with a 4 °C or more rise in temperature, a credible upper bound for twenty-first-century sea-level rise is 2 m. The amount of sea-level rise will show regional differences (IPCC, 2013: 1148), due to such factors as climate-forced circulation changes and gravitational effects resulting from glacier and land ice mass changes, and one area where sea-level rise will be greater than the global norm is the heavily populated Atlantic coastline in the vicinity of New York, USA (Carson et al., 2016; Davis and Vinogradova, 2017).

9.8   Land Subsidence

The effects of global sea-level rise will be compounded in those areas that suffer from local subsidence as a result of tectonic movements, isostatic adjustments, and fluid

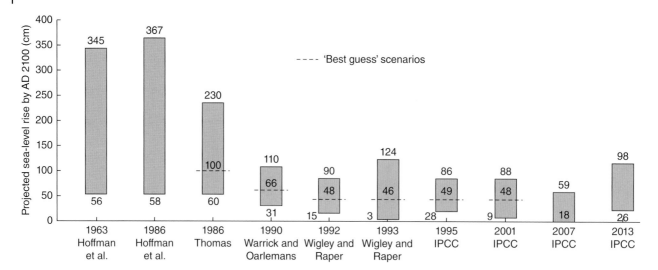

Figure 9.3 Revisions of anticipated sea level rise by 2100. *Source:* after French et al. (1995), with modifications to show the IPCC estimates since 1995.

abstraction (Section 6.4). Areas where land is rising because of isostasy (e.g. Fennoscandia or the Canadian Shield) or because of tectonic uplift (e.g. much of the Pacific coast of the Americas) will be less at risk than subsiding regions (Figure 9.5). In general those sectors of the world's coastline that have been subsiding in recent decades include a large tract of the eastern seaboard of the United States, south-eastern England, and some of the world's great river deltas (e.g. Indus, Ganges, Mekong, Tigris–Euphrates, and Zambezi). Loading of sediment on to the crust by the river causes delta subsidence to occur and sediment compaction occurs through time. So, for example, Fairbridge (1983) calculated subsidence of the Mississippi at a rate of c. 15 mm per year during the Holocene, while Stanley and Chen (1993) calculated Holocene subsidence rates for the Yangtze delta in China

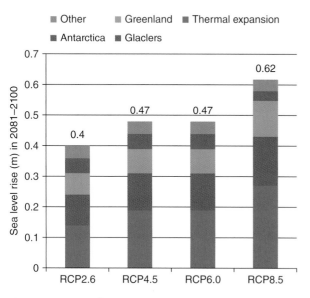

Figure 9.4 Twenty-first-century sea-level rise projections for four different scenarios of the IPCC (2013). *Source:* https://www.carbonbrief.org/what-the-new-ipcc-report-says-about-sea-level-rise. Accessed 29th August, 2016. Reproduced with permission of Carbon Brief Ltd.

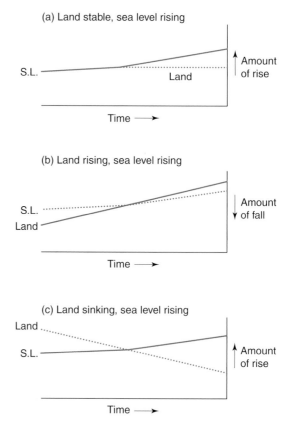

Figure 9.5 The effects of global sea-level rise will be either compounded or mitigated according to whether the local environment is one that is stable, rising, or sinking.

1.6–4.4 mm per year. The Rhone Delta has subsided at between 0.5 and 4.5 mm per year (L'Homer, 1992), while the Nile Delta is subsiding at c. 4.7 mm per year (Sherif and Singh, 1999).

Some areas are prone to subsidence because of on-going adjustment to the application and removal of ice loadings to the crust in the Pleistocene. During glacials, areas directly under the weight of ice caps were depressed, whereas areas adjacent to them bobbed up by way of compensation (the so-called 'peripheral bulge'). Conversely, during the Holocene, following removal of the ice load, the formerly glaciated areas have rebounded whereas the marginal areas have foundered. A good example of this is the Atlantic coast of North America (Engelhart et al., 2009). Areas of appreciable subsidence also include some ocean islands (see Lambeck, 1988: 506–509).

Elsewhere, human actions can promote subsidence (Section 6.4): the withdrawal of groundwater, oil, and gas (Table 6.6); the extraction of coal, salt, sulphur, and other solids, through mining; the hydro-compaction of sediments; the oxidation and shrinkage of organic deposits such as peats and humus-rich soils; the degradation of permafrost; and the catastrophic development of sinkholes in karstic terrain.

9.9 Coral Reefs

Future changes in sea level, and in other environmental factors, will have impacts on a range of sensitive coastal environments. Among these are coral reefs, which are landforms that are more or less restricted to the tropics (Figure 9.6). Coral reefs are extremely important habitats. Not only do they have an estimated area of 600,000 km^2 globally, they are also the hosts to a great diversity of species, especially in the warm waters of the Indian Ocean and the western Pacific. They have been called the marine version of the tropical rainforests, rivalling their terrestrial counterparts in both richness of species and biological productivity. They are also of aesthetic importance. As Norris (2001: 37) wrote:

> Clear blue sea, brightly coloured fish and amazing underwater structures built up over generations from the calcified remains of the tiny animals called coral polyps. It's a spectacular sight. No one who has ever visited one of the world's great coral reefs is ever likely to forget it. But it looks like we are one of the last generations who will have the opportunity to experience this spectacle. Reefs as we know them are on their way out.

The reason for Norris's pessimism is that coral reefs are under a whole series of direct anthropogenic threats (pollution, sedimentation, dynamiting, over-fishing, etc.), and that they face a suite of potential threats from climate change and sea-level rise (Hoegh-Guldberg, 2011; Kayanne, 2016; Hughes et al., 2017). Those corals stressed by temperature or pollution might well find it more difficult to cope with rapidly rising sea levels than would healthy coral. Moreover, it is possible that increased ultraviolet radiation because of ozone-layer depletion could aggravate bleaching and mortality caused by global warming. One potential change is that

Figure 9.6 Aldabra atoll in the Indian Ocean. *Source:* © 2016 DigitalGlobe. Scale bar 10.2 km.

of hurricane frequency, intensity, and distribution. They might build some coral islands up, erase others, and through high levels of runoff and sediment delivery they could change the turbidity and salinity of the water in which corals grow. If hurricane frequency, intensity, and geographical spread were to change, it would have significant implications. This is a matter that is discussed further in Section 10.3.

Increased sea surface temperature could have deleterious consequences for corals which are near their thermal maximum (Hoegh-Guldberg, 2001). Most coral species cannot tolerate temperature greater than about 30 °C and even a rise in sea water temperature of 1–2 °C could adversely affect many shallow-water coral species. Various studies suggest that coral bleaching was a widespread feature in the warm years of the 1980s and 1990s, and the Great Barrier Reef was severely affected by the warm conditions experienced in 2016. The frequency of thermal stress events is likely to increase with ocean warming, leading to declines in coral cover, shifts in the composition of corals and other reef-dwelling organisms, and stress on the human populations who rely upon these ecosystems for food, income, and shoreline protection (Donner, 2009).

Coral bleaching, which can produce mass mortality of corals in extreme cases, has been found to be strongly correlated with elevated water temperatures and high UV solar irradiance (e.g. Brown, 1997; Spencer et al., 2000). Although bleaching itself is a complex phenomenon to which corals can respond in a variety of ways (Brown et al., 2000; Fitt et al., 2001; Loya et al., 2001), ENSO-related heating, cooling, and migrations of ocean water masses have been found to be important controls of mass bleaching episodes (Spencer et al., 2000). For example, in 1998, sea surface temperatures in the tropical Indian Ocean were as much as 3–5 °C above normal, and this led to up to 90% coral mortality in shallow areas (Wilkinson et al., 1999; Edwards et al., 2001). McClanahan (2000) notes that warm conditions of between 25 and 29 °C favour coral growth, survival, and species richness, and that somewhere about 30 °C there are species-, environment-, or regionally specific thresholds above which many of the dominant coral species are lost. As Hoegh-Guldberg (1999), Souter and Linden (2000), Sheppard (2003), and Baker et al. (2008) have suggested, continued warming trends superimposed on interannual and decadal patterns of variability are likely to increase the incidence of bleaching and coral mortality unless significant adaptation to increased temperatures occurs. Donner (2009) has argued that the majority of the world's reefs may experience harmfully frequent thermal stress events before 2050, and Teneva et al. (2012) suggest that the most threatened reefs may be in the Central and Western Equatorial Pacific. On the other hand, some

corals appear to have some ability to acclimatize to elevated temperatures (Palumbi et al., 2014; Sweet and Brown, 2016) allowing them to inhabit reef areas with water temperatures far above their expected tolerances.

Goreau and Hayes (1994) produced maps of global coral bleaching episodes between 1983 and 1991 and related them to maps of sea surface temperatures over that period. They found that areas of severe bleaching are related to what they described as ocean 'hotspots' where marked positive temperature anomalies exist. They argued that coral reefs are ecosystems that may be uniquely prone to the effects of global warming (Goreau and Hayes, 1994: 179):

> If global warming continues, almost all ecosystems can be replaced by migration of species from lower latitudes, except for the warmest ecosystems. These have no source of immigrants already adapted to warmer conditions. Their species must evolve new environmental tolerances if their descendants are to survive, a much slower process than migrations.

However, Kinsey and Hopley (1991) believed that few of the reefs in the world are so close to the limits of temperature tolerance that they are likely to fail to adapt satisfactorily to an increase in ocean temperature of 1–2 °C, provided that there are not very many more short-term temperature deviations. Indeed in general they believed that reef growth will be stimulated by the rising sea levels of a warmer world, and they predict that reef productivity could double in the next 100 years from around 900 to 1800 million tonnes per year. They did, however, point to a range of subsidiary factors that could serve to diminish the increase in productivity: increased cloud cover in a warmer world could reduce calcification because of reduced rates of photosynthesis; increased rainfall levels and hurricane activity could cause storm damage and fresh water kills; and a drop in sea-water pH might adversely affect calcification. In cooler ocean regions, moreover, warming may lead to a rapid poleward expansion in the range of tropical reef corals, as appears to have taken place since the 1930s (Yamano et al., 2011).

In the 1980s there were widespread fears that if rates of sea-level rise were high (perhaps 2–3 m or more by 2100) then coral reefs would be unable to keep up and submergence of whole atolls might occur. Particular concern was expressed about the potential fate of Tokelau, the Marshall Islands, Tuvalu, the Line Islands, and Kiribati in the Pacific Ocean, and of the Maldives in the Indian Ocean. However, with the reduced expectations for the degree of sea-level rise that may occur, there has arisen a belief that coral reefs may survive and even prosper with moderate rates of sea-level rise. As is the case with coastal marshes and other wetlands, reefs are dynamic features that may be able to respond adequately to rises in sea level (Spencer, 1995). During the early Late Pleistocene and early Holocene, rates of sea-level rise were sometimes 30 to 50 mm yr^{-1}, which is markedly higher than those generally predicted for coming decades of c. 5–8 mm yr^{-1}. In spite of this coral reefs grew upwards. Current data on reef accretion suggest a modal rate of vertical growth of 6–7 mm yr^{-1}. The implication of this is that it is unlikely that existing coral reefs will be extensively 'drowned out' by any future sea-level rise (Kench et al., 2009). On the other hand, because of the effects of coral bleaching, etc., there is some evidence in the Caribbean that rates of coral accretion have declined in recent years (Perry et al., 2013). This makes keeping up with rising sea level more difficult.

An example of the pessimistic tone of opinion in the 1980s is provided by Buddemeier and Smith (1988). Employing 15 mm per year as the probable rise of sea level over the next century, they suggested that this would be (p. 51) 'five times the present modal rate of vertical accretion on coral reef flats and 50% greater than the maximum vertical accretion rates apparently attained by coral reefs'. Using a variety of techniques they believed (p. 53) 'the best overall estimate of the sustained maximum of reef growth to be 10 mm/year …'. They predicted (p. 54) that:

> Inundated reef flats in areas of heavy seas will be subjected to progressively more destructive wave activity as larger waves move across the deepening flats … Reef growth on the seaward portions of inundated, wave swept reef flats may therefore be negligible compared to sea-level rise over the next century, and such reef flats may become submerged by almost 1.5 m.

Reefs have a range of topographies, and low-lying reef islands on the rims of atolls may be especially vulnerable to the effects of sea-level rise (Woodroffe, 2008). In addition to the potential effects of submergence, there is the possibility that higher sea levels could promote accelerated erosion of reefs (Dickinson, 1999). Sea-level rise could also cause enhanced sedimentation and turbidity as tides ebb and flow over shallow, fringing reefs (Field et al., 2011).

Reefs may also suffer from increasing ocean acidification (Royal Society, 2005) for a proportion of the extra carbon dioxide being released into the atmosphere by the burning of fossil fuels and biomass is absorbed by sea water. This produces carbonic acid, an increase of which will cause that water to become more acidic (i.e. it will have a lower pH than now). The absorption of carbon dioxide has already caused the pH of modern sea surface waters to be about 0.1 lower (i.e. more acidic and less alkaline) than in pre-industrial times and the recent trends are shown in Figure 9.7. Ocean pH may fall an additional 0.3 by 2100 (Gattuso et al., 1998; Caldeira and Wickett, 2003), which means that the oceans may be more acidic than they have been for 25 million years. Several centuries from now, if we continue to add carbon dioxide to the atmosphere, ocean pH will be lower than at any time in the past 300 million years (Doney, 2006). It is also notable that the rate of change in acidity will be very rapid. This will be particularly harmful to those organisms (corals, molluscs, and plankton) that depend on the presence of carbonate ions to build their shells (or other hard parts) out of calcium bicarbonate (Orr et al., 2005a and b; Pelejero et al., 2010). A coral reef, as Kleypas et al. (1999) have pointed out, represents the net accumulation of calcium carbonate produced by corals and other calcifying organisms. Equally, Leclercq et al. (2000) have calculated that the calcification rate of scleractinian-dominated communities could decrease by 21% between the pre-industrial period (1880) and the year at which atmospheric carbon dioxide concentrations will double (2065). Thus were calcification to decline, then reef-building capacity would also decline. It is also possible that ocean acidification will accelerate coral bleaching (Anthony et al., 2008).

The future wave environments of coral reefs may be transformed (Quataert et al., 2015). Coral bleaching events, which are likely to become more numerous, kill off corals and result in a decrease in hydrodynamic roughness of coral reefs. Similarly, ocean acidification may reduce coral cover and, thus, hydrodynamic roughness. Together or independently, these processes will reduce bottom friction, which would increase wave heights, wave run-up, and wave-driven flooding. In addition, climate change may drive changes in extreme wave heights and their directions, which would further alter the resulting nearshore wave heights, water levels, and wave run-up. Coral reefs play an important role in coastal protection against storms so that 'we can anticipate that decreasing rates of reef accretion, increasing rates of bioerosion, rising sea levels, and intensifying storms may combine to jeopardize a wide range of coastal barriers' (Hoegh-Guldberg et al., 2007: 1742).

In some parts of the world, meadows of seagrass can over time trap sediment, build upwards, and create various forms of reef. This is the case with the *Posidonia oceanica* meadows of the Mediterranean (Bonhomme et al., 2015). These are highly vulnerable to human activities, (e.g. coastal development, reduced light penetration in coastal zones because of nutrient enrichment and an overall reduction in water quality, establishment of port facilities, small pleasure boats which unwittingly plough furrows at low tide to cross the reef, deliberate dredging

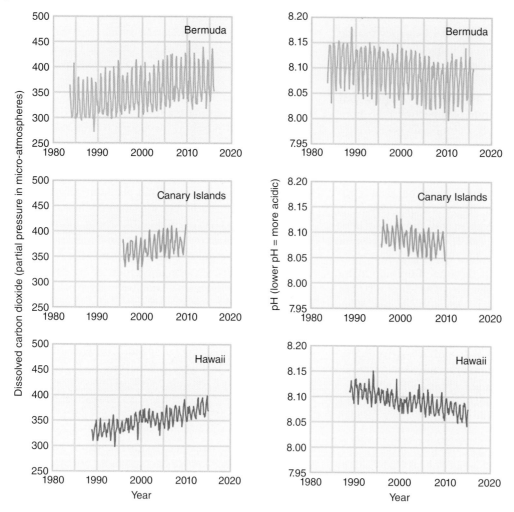

Figure 9.7 Trends in ocean acidification and in relation to dissolved carbon dioxide levels. *Source:* EPA, *Climate Change Indicators*, 2016, https://www.epa.gov/climate-indicators (accessed January 2018).

of channels to allow boats to moor within the lagoon, and artificial beaches). On a global basis, seagrass loss rates are comparable to those reported for mangroves, coral reefs, and tropical rainforests and place seagrass meadows among the most threatened ecosystems on Earth (Waycott et al., 2009). Rates of loss have accelerated from c. 1% per year before 1940 to c. 7% today (Laffoley and Baxter, 2016).

9.10 Salt Marshes and Mangrove Swamps

Coastal marshes (Figure 9.8) may be susceptible to the effects of increased CO_2, sea-level rise, storm frequency and intensity, changes in ambient temperature, and ocean physical changes, including elevated sea temperature, and acidification (Morzaria-Luna et al., 2014).

These wetland environments, including the mangrove swamps of the tropics, are extremely valuable ecosystems that are potentially highly vulnerable in the face of sea-level rise (Gedan et al., 2011; Woodroffe et al., 2016), particularly in those circumstances where sea defences and other barriers prevent the landward migration of marshes as sea level rises. In such locations what is termed 'coastal squeeze' occurs (Doody, 2013; Phan et al., 2015). Sediment supply, organic and inorganic, is a crucial issue (Reed, 2002). On coasts with limited sediment supply a rise in sea level will impede the normal process of marsh progradation, and increasing wave attack will start or accelerate erosion along their seaward margins. The tidal creeks that flow across the marsh will tend to become wider, deeper, and more extended headwards as the marsh is submerged. The marsh will attempt to move landwards, and where the hinterland is low lying the salt marsh vegetation will tend to take over from freshwater or terrigenous communities. Such landward

Figure 9.8 Salt marshes near Maldon, Essex, eastern England. They are heavily constrained by the presence of sea defences to landward. *Source:* © 2016 Google, © 2016 Infoterra and Bluesky. Scale bar 104 m.

movement is impossible where sea walls or embankments have been built at the inner margins of a marsh (Figure 9.9). Marshes would be further threatened if climate change increased the incidence of severe droughts (Thomson et al., 2002). Table 9.2 demonstrates the differences between marshes in terms of their sensitivity. However, salt marshes are highly dynamic features and in some situations may well be able to cope, even with quite rapid rises of sea level (Reed, 1995). Indeed, Kirwan et al. (2016) have argued that, in general, increased tidal inundation caused by rising sea level promotes more frequent and longer episodes of mineral sediment settling on the marsh platform, enhanced vegetation growth, and faster rates of organic matter accumulation. This feedback results in accretion rates that have accelerated in parallel with observed historical sea-level rise. For marshes that are dependent upon inorganic-sediment accretion, increased storm activity and beach erosion which might be associated with the greenhouse effect could conceivably mobilize sufficient sediments in coastal areas to increase their sediment supply.

Reed (1990) suggested that salt marshes in riverine settings may receive sufficient inputs of sediment that they are able to accrete rapidly enough to keep pace with projected rises of sea level. Areas of high tidal range, such as the marshes of the Severn Estuary in England/Wales, or the Tagus Estuary of Portugal, are also areas of high sediment-transport potential and may thus be less

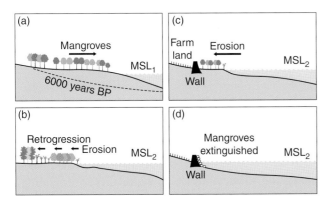

Figure 9.9 Changes on mangrove-fringed coasts as sea level rises (a) and (b) will be modified where they are backed by a wall built to protect farmland (c). The mangrove fringe will then be narrowed by erosion, and may eventually disappear (d), unless there is a sufficient sediment supply to maintain the substrate and enable the mangroves to persist. MSL is mean sea level. *Source:* adapted from Bird (1993: figure 45).

Table 9.2 Salt marsh vulnerability.

Less sensitive
Areas of high sediment input
Areas of high tidal range (high sediment transport potential)
Areas with effective organic accumulation
More sensitive
Areas of subsidence
Ares of low sediment input (e.g. cyclically abandoned delta areas)
Constraint by seawalls, etc. (nowhere to go)
Mangroves (longer life cycle, therefore slower response)
Micro-tidal areas (rise in sea-level represents a larger proportion of total tidal range)
Reef settings (lack of allogenic sediment)

vulnerable to sea-level rise (Simas et al., 2001). Likewise, some vegetation associations, e.g. *Spartina* swards, may be relatively more effective than others at encouraging accretion, and organic matter accumulation may itself be significant in promoting vertical build-up of some marsh surfaces. Marsh areas that may be highly prone to sea-level rise include areas of deltaic sedimentation where, because of sediment movement controls (e.g. reservoir construction) or because of cyclic changes in the location of centres of deposition, rates of sediment supply are low. Such areas may also be areas with high rates of subsidence. A classic example of this is portions of the Mississippi Delta. Micro-tidal marshes (<2-m tidal range) may also be peculiarly vulnerable (Kearney and Turner, 2016). Here mineral inputs may be low to negligible, for these marshes are characterized by average flood velocities too low to import appreciable mineral sediment into marsh interiors. Thus organic inputs play a dominant role in vertical accretion, but are subject to substantial losses from decomposition. Indeed, their reliance on organic accumulation makes them vulnerable to any factor that affects annual biomass inputs, whether by animal overgrazing, damage to physiological functioning (e.g. by substrate anoxia, excess hydrogen sulfide, and nutrient concentrations), or erosion from coastal storms. Kearney and Turner believed that recent changes in sea level are likely to be playing a role in the widely documented degradation and loss of micro-tidal marshes, though perhaps as much from the increasing decadal and inter-decadal variability as from the overall global rate of rise.

Ray et al. (1992) examined the past and future response of salt marshes in Virginia in the United States to changes in sea level, and were particularly interested in the response of mid-lagoon marshes. Between 6000 and 2000 years ago, when the rate of sea-level rise was about 3 mm per year, the lagoons were primarily open water environments with little evidence of mid-lagoon marshes. After AD 1200, land subsidence in the area slowed down, and sea-level rise was only about 1.3 mm per year. This permitted mid-lagoon marshes to expand and flourish. Such marshes in general lack an inorganic sediment supply so that their upwards growth rate approximates only about 1.5 mm per year. Present rates of sea-level rise exceed that figure (they are about 2 mm per year) and cartographic analysis shows a 16% loss of marsh between 1852 and 1968. As sea-level rise accelerates as a result of global warming, almost all mid-lagoon marsh will be lost. Working on the Gulf Coast of Florida in the USA, Raabe and Stumpf (2015) found that tidal wetland systems had shifted landward over the last 120 years. Loss of tidal marsh at the shoreline was −43 km², representing a 9% loss to open water. They documented 1.2 m yr⁻¹ of marsh shoreline erosion, and 2.3 m yr⁻¹

inland marsh expansion. 82 km² of forest converted to marsh and 66 km² of forest converted to forest-to-marsh transitional habitat. The result was a net regional gain of 105 km² of intertidal area, an increase of 23%, constituting a marine transgression of coastal lowland. Loss of salt marsh due to a combination of sea-level rise and the expansion of mangrove has also been identified in Texas (Armitage et al., 2015). In southern New England, Watson et al. (2017) reported that evidence is accruing that neither tidal sediment accretion nor subsurface accumulation of refractory peat material is allowing wetlands to grow vertically at rates approaching that of sea level in this region.

Rises in sea level will increase near shore water depths and thereby modify wave refraction patterns. This means that wave energy amounts will also change at different points along a particular shoreline. Pethick (1993) maintained that this could be significant for the classic Scolt Head Island salt marshes of Norfolk, eastern England, which are at present within a low to medium wave energy zone. After a 1.0 m rise in sea level these marshes will experience high wave energy because of the migration of wave foci. Pethick remarked (p. 166):

> The result will be to force the long shore migration of salt marsh and mudflat systems over distances of up to ten kilometres in 50 years – a yearly migration rate of 200 meters. It is doubtful whether salt marsh vegetation could survive in such a transitory environment – although intertidal mudflat organisms may be competent to do so – and a reduction of total loss of these open coast wetlands may result.

One particular type of marsh that may be affected by anthropogenically accelerated sea-level rise is the mangrove swamp (Figure 9.10) (Woodroffe et al., 2016). As with other types of marsh the exact response will depend on the local setting, sources and rates of sediment supply, and the rate of sea-level rise itself. As Ward et al. (2016) have pointed out, sea-level rise is regionally variable and is likely to have a lesser impact in those areas with high sediment availability, uplifting or stable coasts, high productivity, and large tidal ranges such as the Amazon estuary. However, where there is extensive coastal exploitation and development, such as in Asia, South and North America, or where there are very high rates of sea-level rise, such as in Indonesia and the Mississippi Delta, or on low islands such as in the Pacific, mangroves are likely to be substantially threatened. Mangroves in semi-arid areas with predicted decreases in future precipitation, such as in the Middle East and north-east Brazil, are likely to suffer from increases in salt stress and resultant decreases in pro-

Figure 9.10 Mangrove swamps on the Kimberley coastline of Western Australia. *Source:* © 2016 DigitalGlobe. Scale bar 1812 m.

ductivity combined with decreases in sediment input. This may make them more susceptible to the effects of rising sea levels. More generally, mangroves may respond rather differently from other marshes in that they are composed of relatively long-lived trees and shrubs which means that the speed of zonation change will be less (Woodroffe, 1990). With increasing temperatures and fewer coastal freezes, mangroves may expand their latitudinal range (Comeaux et al., 2012). Like salt marshes, however, mangroves trap sediment to construct a depositional terrace in the upper intertidal zone. Where there is only a modest sediment supply, submergence by rising sea level may cause dieback of vegetation and erosion of their seaward margins. As their seaward margin erodes backwards, the mangroves will attempt to spread landward, displacing existing freshwater swamps or forest. As with normal salt marshes this would not be possible if they were backed by walls or embankments.

The degree of disruption is likely to be greatest in microtidal areas, where any rise in sea level represents a larger proportion of the total tidal range than in macrotidal areas. The setting of mangrove swamps will be very important in determining how they respond. River-dominated systems with large allochthonous sediment supply will have faster rates of shoreline progradation and deltaic plain accretion and so may be able to keep pace with relatively rapid rates of sea-level rise. By contrast in reef settings, in which sedimentation is primarily autochthonous, mangrove surfaces are less likely to be able to keep up with sea-level rises. This is the view

of Ellison and Stoddart (1990: 161), who argued that low island mangrove ecosystems (mangals) have in the past been able to keep up with a sea-level rise of up to 8–9 cm per hundred years, but that at rates over 12 cm per hundred years they had not been able to persist.

Snedaker (1995) found it difficult, however, to reconcile the Ellison and Stoddard view with what has happened in South Florida, where relative sea level rose by about 30 cm over 147 years (equivalent to 23 cm per hundred years). The mangrove swamps of the area did not for the most part appear to have been adversely stressed by this. Snedaker argued that precipitation and catchment runoff changes also need to be considered, as for any given sea-level elevation, reduced rainfall and precipitation would result in higher salinity and greater sea water–sulphate exposure. These in turn would be associated with decreased production and increased organic matter decomposition that would lead to subsidence. On the other hand, under conditions with higher rainfall and runoff the reverse would occur, so that mangrove production would increase and sediment elevations would be maintained.

The ability of mangrove propagules to take root and become established in intertidal areas subjected to a higher mean sea level is in part dependant on species (Ellison and Farnsworth, 1997). In general, the large propagule species (e.g. *Rhizophora* spp.) can become established in rather deeper water than can the smaller propagule species (e.g. *Avicennia* spp.). The latter has aerial roots which project only vertically above tidal muds for short distances (Snedaker, 1993).

In arid areas, such as the Arabian Gulf in the Middle East, extensive tracts of coastline are fringed by low-level salt-plains called sabkhas (Section 12.9). These features are generally regarded as equilibrium forms that are produced by depositional processes (e.g. wind erosion and storm surge effects). They tend to occur at or about high tide level. Because of the range of depositional processes involved in their development they might be able to adjust to a rising sea level but quantitative data on present and past rates of accretion are sparse. A large proportion of the industrial and urban infrastructure of the United Arab Emirates is located on or in close proximity to sabkhas.

Salt marsh, swamp, and sabkha regression caused by climatic and sea-level changes will compound the problems of wetland loss and degradation caused by other human activities (Wells, 1996; Kennish, 2001), including reclamation, ditching, diking, dredging, pollution, and sediment starvation. More than half of the original salt marsh habitat in the United States has already been lost, and Shriner and Street (1998: 298) suggest that a 50 cm rise in sea level would inundate approximately half of North American coastal wetlands in the twenty-first century. Park et al. (1986) also undertook a survey of coastal wetlands in the United States and suggested that sea-level change could, by 2100, lead to a loss of between 22 and 56% of the 1975 wetland area, according to the degree of sea-level rise that takes place. At a global scale, Nicholls et al. (1999) have suggested that by the 2080s sea-level rise could cause the loss of up to 22% of the world's coastal wetlands. When combined with other losses due to direct human action, up to 70% of the world's coastal wetlands could be lost by that date. More recently, Spencer et al. (2016) have postulated that with a 50 cm sea-level rise by 2100, losses of 46–59% of global coastal wetlands could occur, and that under a high sea-level rise (110 cm by 2100) scenario, global wetland losses may reach 78%.

9.11 River Deltas

Deltaic coasts and their environs are home to large numbers of people. Fifty-one of the world's deltas have a combined population of over 325 million, and the Nile Delta alone has a population of around 50 million (Syvitski, 2008). They are likely to be threatened by submergence as sea-levels rise, especially where prospects of compensating sediment accretion are not evident. Many deltas are currently zones of subsidence because of the isostatic effects of the sedimentation that caused them to form. This will compound the effects of eustatic sea-level rise (Milliman and Haq, 1996). The Niger Delta has rising rates of subsidence because of oil and gas

abstraction. Even without accelerating sea-level rise the Nile Delta has been suffering accelerated recession because of sediment retention by dams.

It needs to be remembered, however, that deltas will not solely be affected by sea-level changes. The delta lands of Bangladesh (Warrick and Ahmad, 1996), for example, receive very heavy sediment loads from the rivers that feed them so that it is the relative rates of accretion and inundation that will be crucial (Milliman et al., 1989). Land-use changes upstream, such as deforestation, could increase rates of sediment accumulation. Conversely, many deltas, such as the Mississippi, suffer because they have an insufficient sediment supply consequent upon the trapping of sediment by upstream dams (Ericson et al., 2006; Blum and Roberts, 2009). Deltas could also be affected by changing tropical cyclone activity, which might cause storm surge effects to be magnified (Karim and Mimura, 2008). Some deltas, such as the Mekong (Van Manh et al., 2015), now suffer from virtually no aggradation (because of upstream sediment trapping by dams and reservoirs), are undergoing accelerated compaction, and are sinking many times faster than the rate of sea-level increase, partly because of

Figure 9.11 Projected areas of flooding as a result of sea-level change in Bangladesh, for two scenarios (low = 1 metre and high = 3 metres). *Source:* adapted from Broadus et al. (1986: figure 7).

groundwater abstraction (Syvitski and Kettner, 2011; Schmitt et al., 2017).

Broadus et al. (1986) calculated that were the sea level to rise by just 1 m in 100 years, 12–15% of Egypt's arable land would be lost and 16% of the population would have to be relocated. With a 3 m rise the figures would be a 20% loss of arable land and a need to relocate 21% of the population. The cities of Alexandria, Rosetta, and Port Said are at particular risk and even a sea-level rise of 50 cm could mean that 2 million people would have to abandon their homes (El-Raey, 1997). In Bangladesh (Figure 9.11) a 1 m rise would inundate 11.5% of the total land area of the state and affect 9% of the population directly, while a 3 m rise in sea level would inundate 29% of the land area and affect 21% of the population. It is sobering to remember that at the present time approximately one-half of Bangladesh's rice production is in the area that is less than 1 m above sea level. Many of the world's major conurbations might be flooded in whole or in part, sewers and drains rendered inoperative, and peri-urban agricultural productivity reduced by saltwater incursion (Chen and Zong, 1999).

Bangkok is an example of a city that is being threatened by a combination of accelerated subsidence and accelerated sea-level rise (Nutalaya et al., 1996). More than 4550 km^2 of the city was affected by land subsidence between 1960 and 1988, and 20 to 160 cm of depression of the land surface occurred. The situation is critical because Bangkok is situated on a very flat, low-lying area, where the ground-level elevations range from only 0 to 1.5 m above mean sea level (Figure 9.12).

9.12 Estuaries

Estuaries, located between the land and the sea, are unique and sensitive ecosystems that are locations of many major ports and industrial concerns. They could be impacted upon by a range of climate-related variables, including the amount of fresh water and sediment coming from the land, the temperature and salinity of the estuarine water, and tidal range (Day et al., 2008).

The overall effect of sea-level rise has been summarized by Chappell et al. (1996: 224):

> In the earliest stages of sea-level rise, the extent of tidal flooding on high tide flats will increase and networks of small tidal creeks will expand into

Figure 9.12 Total subsidence (in cm), 1978–1987 (above) and ground elevation of Bangkok, 1987 (below). *Source:* adapted from Nutalaya et al. (1996: figures 3 and 9).

estuarine floodplains. Levees of tidal rivers will be breached and brackish water will invade freshwater floodplains. Eventually, tidal flow in main channels will increase to carry the enlarged tidal prism, and channels are likely to widen. In systems with extensive tidal floodplains, tidal regimes will shift towards ebb dominance and net sediment flux will tend to be offshore, except in macrotidal systems.

Salt-water intrusion could be a major change, with saline water extending far inland as sea-level rose. This in turn could affect swamp and marsh vegetation (Mulrennan and Woodroffe, 1998).

Attempts have been made to model the transgression rate for landward extending estuaries. For the Humber estuary in north-east England, Pethick (2001: 34) reports that the mean migration rate of the estuary as a whole would be 1.3 m per mm rise in sea- level (or 8 m per year assuming a 6 mm per year rise in sea level).

9.13 Cliffed Coasts

When sea level rises, near shore waters deepen, shore platforms become submerged, deeper water allows larger waves to reach the bases of cliffs, and the cliffs may suffer from accelerated rates of retreat, especially if they are made of susceptible materials (Ashton et al., 2011; Revell et al., 2011; Brooks and Spencer, 2012). In addition, sea-level rise is likely to cause increased frequencies of coastal landslides. Accelerated cliff retreat and land sliding may cause an augmented supply of sediment to adjacent and down-drift beaches. This could be beneficial. However, as Bray et al. (1992: 86) remarked:

> The location of the benefit will depend upon sediment transport conditions and their relation to sediment supply. Where littoral transport is poorly developed, beaches will accrete in front of cliffs as sea-level rises, and tend to offset any trend for increased retreat. Where littoral transport is efficient, cliff retreat is likely to increase significantly as sea-level rises because extra sediments yielded are rapidly removed from the eroding cliffs. Coasts of this type are likely to become increasingly valuable in the future because they are sensitive to sea-level rise and can supply large quantities of sediment to downdrift beaches. A further complicating factor is that cliff erosion products differ with respect to their mobility and coarse durable materials may be retained on the upper shoreface and provide natural armouring. Soft-rock cliffs yielding a high proportion of coarse durable products are therefore likely to be less sensitive to sea-level rise.

Cliffs on high latitude coasts (e.g. in Siberia, Alaska, and Canada) might be especially seriously affected by global change. On the one hand, coasts formed of weak sediments that are currently cemented by permafrost would lose strength if warming caused the permafrost to melt. On the other hand, melting of sea ice would expose them to greater wave affects from open water. This is discussed in further detail in Section 11.6.

9.14 Sandy Beaches

As sea level rises, many beaches, especially those in closed bays, often called pocket beaches, may suffer from accelerated erosion (Brunel and Sabatier, 2009) (Figure 9.13). Bruun (1962) developed a widely cited and elegantly simple model of the response of a sandy beach to sea-level rise in a situation where the beach was initially in equilibrium, neither gaining nor losing sediment (Figure 9.14). As Bird (1993: 56) has explained:

> Erosion of the upper beach would then occur, with removal of sand to the nearshore zone in such a way as to restore the previous transverse profile. In effect, there would be an upward and landward migration of the transverse profile, so that the coastline would recede beyond the limits of submergence. This restoration would be completed when the sea became stable at a higher level, and coastline recession would come to an end after a new equilibrium was achieved. The extent of recession was predicted by using a formula that translates into a 'rule of thumb' whereby the coastline retreats 50–100 times the

Figure 9.13 Malibu Beach, California, USA, is an example of a vulnerable beach. It is very narrow and is bounded on the landward side by properties (ASG).

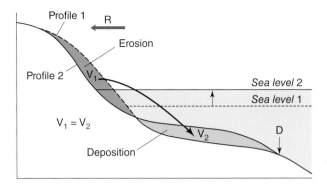

Figure 9.14 Sea-level rise and coastline changes. The Bruun Rule states that a sea-level rise will lead to erosion of the beach and removal of a volume of sand (V1) seaward to be deposited (V2) in such a way as to restore the initial transverse profile landward of D, the outer boundary of near shore sand deposits. The coastline will retreat (R) until stability is restored after the sea-level rise comes to an end. The coastline thus recedes further than it would if submergence were not accompanied by erosion.

dimensions of the rise in sea-level: a 1 m rise would cause the beach to retreat by 50–100 m. Since many seaside resort beaches are no more than 30 m wide, the implication is that these beaches will have disappeared by the time the sea has risen 15–30 cm (i.e. by the year 2030), unless they are artificially replaced.]/ex[

This influential model, often called the Bruun Rule, has been widely used. It is important to recognize, however, that there are some constraints on its applicability (Wells, 1995; Healy, 1996; Dean and Houston, 2016). The rule assumes that no sand is lost to longshore transport and that an offshore 'closure depth' exists beyond which there is no sediment exchange. Moreover, the rule does not allow for shoreward transport of sediment as overwash or for those situations where the slope of the coastal plain is too gentle for sufficient sand to be available as a source for supplying the offshore. In addition, the rule was originally proposed for beaches that were initially in equilibrium. However, as Bird (1993: 58) has pointed out, only a small proportion of the world's sandy beaches can in fact be considered to be in equilibrium. Beach erosion is widespread. Furthermore, there is a lack of established criteria to ascertain wherever the original shoreline really is in dynamic equilibrium (Healy, 1991).

In spite of these limitations the Bruun Rule remains widely used, and can be stated mathematically as follows (Gornitz et al., 2002: 68):

$$S = (A * B) / d$$

where S = shoreline movement, A = sea level rise, d = maximum depth of beach profile, measured from the berm elevation for each project location to the estimated depth of closure, B = horizontal length of the profile, measured from the beginning of the berm to the intersection with the estimated depth of closure. The depth of closure is taken as the minimum water depth at which no significantly measurable change occurs in bottom depth.

An example of the testing of the validity of the Bruun Rule is the study by List et al. (1997) of the barrier islands of Louisiana in the United States. Using bathymetric surveys over about a century, they found that only a portion of their studied profiles met the equilibrium criterion of the Bruun Rule. Furthermore, using those shore profiles that did meet the equilibrium criterion, they determined measured rates of relative sea-level rise so that they could hindcast shoreline retreat rates using the Bruun Rule formula. They found that the modelled and observed shoreline retreat rates showed no significant correlation. They suggested that if the Bruun Rule is inadequate for hindcasting it would also be inadequate for forecasting future rates of beach retreat. There are those who now suggest that use of the Bruun Rule should be abandoned (Cooper and Pilkey, 2004; Aagaard and Sorensen, 2012).

There are various other techniques that can be used to predict rates of shoreline retreat. One of these is historical trend analysis, which is based upon extrapolating the trend of shoreline change with respect to recorded sea-level rise over a given historical period:

$$R_2 = (R_1 / S_1) \cdot S_2$$

where S_1 = historical sea-level rise, S_2 = future sea-level rise, R_1 = historical retreat rate, and R_2 = future retreat rate.

Barrier islands, such as those that line the southern North Sea and the eastern seaboard of the United States are dynamic landforms that will tend to migrate inland with rising sea levels and increased intensity of overtopping by waves (Eitner, 1996; Ashton et al., 2008). If sea-level rise is not too rapid, and if they are not constrained by human activities (e.g. engineering structures and erosion control measures), they are moved inland by washover – a process similar to rolling up a rug (Titus, 1990); as the island rolls landward, it builds landwards and remains above sea level (Figure 9.15). Lagoons, lying to the landward of such barriers, will be modified depending on the speed of sea-level rise (Carrasco et al., 2016).

As sea level rises, barriers and other low-level coasts will be exposed to higher storm surges which will cause greater flooding (e.g. around the southern North Sea (Woth et al., 2006)) and the north-eastern US (Ashton et al., 2008)). In the New York area, Gornitz et al. (2002) calculated that by the 2080s, the return period

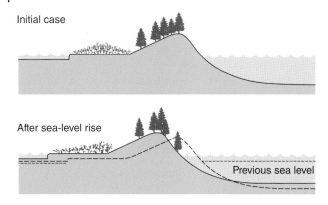

Initial case

After sea-level rise

Previous sea level

Figure 9.15 Overwash: the natural response of undeveloped barrier islands to sea-level rise. *Source:* Titus (1990: figure 2). Reproduced with permission from Taylor and Francis Publishers.

of the 100-year storm flood could be reduced to between 4 and 60 years. Lin et al. (2012) have made similar predictions, while in the case of Long Island, Shepard et al. (2012) have suggested that even a modest and likely SLR of 0.5 m by 2080, would hugely increase the numbers of people (47% increase) and property loss (73%) impacted by storm surges. Equally, if hurricanes become more frequent and widespread along the eastern and Gulf coasts of the US, wave heights would rise, as has happened during recent warming decades (Komar and Allan, 2008; Reed et al., 2015). As a result, flooding would become a greater hazard (Frazier et al., 2010), with flooding for Corpus Christi in Texas projected to increase by between 20% and 70% by the 2030s (Irish et al., 2010; Mousavi et al., 2011). Moreover, the effects of increased surge levels

will be amplified along the Atlantic coast of the US as this is an area where sea-level rise appears to have been faster than the global average (Sallenger et al., 2012). Sea-level rise, combined with greater typhoon intensity, also means that surges pose a growing threat to Tokyo, Japan, parts of which already lie below sea level (Hoshino et al., 2015).

Many beaches are currently eroding as they are no longer being replenished with sediment by rivers. This is because of the construction of dams, which trap much of the sediment that would otherwise go to the sea (Section 5.3.1).

9.15 Conclusions

Coastal environments are already suffering from many human impacts, including sediment starvation. However, these dynamic regions, at the interface between land and sea and home to many people, will also be subjected in the future to the combined effects of climate change and sea-level rise (Hoegh-Guldberg and Bruno, 2010). Plainly coastlines will be directly impacted by climatic change through such mechanisms as changes in storm surges and hurricanes, but they will also be impacted by sea-level changes resulting from global climatic change, local subsidence, and miscellaneous modifications of the hydrological cycle. If, on average, sea level rises by around half a meter during this century, it will greatly modify susceptible and sensitive coastlines, including marshes and swamps, estuaries, soft cliffs, barrier islands, and sandy beaches.

Guide to Reading

Bird, E.C.F. (1993) *Submerging Coasts.* Chichester: Wiley. A geomorphological overview of how coasts will respond to sea-level rise.

Douglas, B.C., Kearney, M.S. and Leatherman, S.P. (eds) (2001) *Sea-level Rise: History and Consequences.* San Diego: Academic Press. An edited volume, with a long time perspective, which considers some of the consequences of sea-level change.

Eisma, D. (ed.) (1995) *Climate Change: Impact on Coastal Habitation.* Boca Raton: Lewis Publishers. A study of the effects of climate change and sea-level rise.

Gattuso, J.-P. and Hansson, L. (eds) (2011) *Ocean Acidification.* Oxford: Oxford University Press. An

edited guide to the nature, causes, and impacts of ocean acidification.

Laffoley, D. and Baxter, J.M. (eds) (2016) *Exploring Ocean Warming.* Gland: IUCN. A big, international, multi-author survey of the pressures that are being exerted on the world's oceans, with a particular emphasis on the effects of ocean warming on biodiversity.

Milliman, J.D. and Haq, B.V. (eds) (1996) *Sea-level Rise and Coastal Subsidence.* Dordrecht: Kluwer. An edited discussion of the ways in which sea-level rise and land subsidence may impact upon coastal environments.

10

The Future: Hydrological and Geomorphological Impacts

CHAPTER OVERVIEW

In a warmer world, changes in the type, amount, and intensity of moisture received as precipitation, together with increased rates of evapotranspiration, will have major, though sometimes opposite, impacts on the hydrological environment. In addition, the presence of increased levels of carbon dioxide in the atmosphere may affect moisture transpiration by plants. There is evidence that some parts of the world will have more available moisture for stream flow and that other areas will have less. The chapter will consider the possible future runoff characteristics at a global scale, in cold regions, and also by considering regional examples from the UK, Europe, the USA, and elsewhere. It will also consider how such geomorphological processes as mass movements, soil erosion, and stone weathering may respond to changed environmental conditions.

10.1   Introduction

Global warming will affect hydrological systems in a whole range of ways (Arnell, 1996; Jones et al., 1996; Arnell et al., 2015). Extreme events may become more frequent and fierce (Naylor et al., 2017) and global mean precipitation will increase with global warming, a process referred to as 'hydrological cycle intensification'. As Fischer and Knutti (2015: 563) have written:

> Already today 75% of the moderate hot extremes and about 18% of the moderate precipitation extremes occurring worldwide are attributable to warming, of which the dominant part is extremely likely to be anthropogenic. The fraction increases nonlinearly with further warming such that the probability of hot extremes at 2°C, for example, is double that at 1.5°C global warming. With every degree of warming it is the rarest and the most extreme events and thereby the ones with typically the highest socio-economic impacts for which the largest fraction is due to human-induced greenhouse gas emissions.

There will be changes in the amount, intensity, duration, and timing of precipitation, which will affect river flows and groundwater recharge. Furthermore,

increasing temperatures will tend to melt snow and ice and promote greater losses through evapotranspiration. Vegetation cover will respond to temperature and precipitation changes, as will land use. Fire frequencies may also change and this too will have an effect on runoff. Fire significantly reduces the annual evapotranspiration loss of water over the global land surface and increases global total runoff (Li and Lawrence, 2016). Higher CO_2 levels may lead to changes in plant growth and physiology, which can lead to changes in transpiration. Higher atmospheric CO_2 levels may stimulate plant growth and lead to changes in plant water use efficiency and thus to transpiration and runoff (Eckhardt and Ulbrich, 2003; Morgan et al., 2004; Gedney et al., 2006). Global warming may also affect soil properties (such as organic matter content), which could alter runoff generation processes. Climate change will also lead to human interventions in the hydrological system with, for example, greater use of irrigation in areas subject to increased drought risk, and the continued spread of engineering controls on flooding and erosion.

The nature of the changes that will take place in fluvial systems depends to a certain extent on scale. As Ashmore and Church (2001: 5) explained:

> The nature of the changes caused by climatic change depends to some extent on the size of the

Human Impact on the Natural Environment: Past, Present and Future, Eighth Edition. Andrew S. Goudie.
© 2019 John Wiley & Sons Ltd. Published 2019 by John Wiley & Sons Ltd.
Companion website: www.wiley.com/go/goudie/human-impact-natural-environment

drainage basin in question. Drainage basin size also affects the relative impact of widespread climate change compared to local land-use change. The effects of land-use change are expected to dominate in smaller basins where a large proportion of the basin area may be affected, leading to substantial changes in runoff and erosion throughout the basin. In larger drainage basins, land use change is seldom sufficiently widespread to affect the entire basin and climatic effects will dominate. The impacts of climatic change will also vary with basin size. Thus, small basins will be affected by changes in local, high-intensity storms, whereas larger basins will show a greater response to cyclonic events or basin-wide snowmelt effects.

Equally, as Ashmore and Church (2001: 5) maintained, there are many ways in which river systems may change:

> Potential consequences of climatic change for river processes include changes to the magnitude of flood flows; modification of river channel dimensions and form; changes to bank stability, bank erosion rates, and channel migration; modification of in-channel erosion and deposition; onset of long term aggradation or degradation of river channels; changes to intensity and frequency of overbank flooding and ice-jams; and changes to the stability of valley sides. These changes in channel processes present a significant risk to structures both in and near streams including dams, bridges, water intakes, and outfalls. Structures on or near floodplains or valley margins are also at risk. Other environmental, scenic and economic attributes of streams will also be affected, especially in stream and riparian habitat.

10.2 Rainfall Intensity

Rainfall intensity is a major factor in controlling such phenomena as flooding, rates of soil erosion, and mass movements (Sidle and Dhakal, 2002). Under increased greenhouse gas concentrations some GCMs exhibit enhanced mid-latitude and global precipitation intensity and shortened return periods of extreme events (Jones and Reid, 2001; New et al., 2001). The IPCC (2007a: 91) suggested that 'Extremes of daily precipitation are *likely* to increase in many regions. The increase is considered to be *very likely* in northern Europe, south Asia, East Asia, Australia and New Zealand'. The IPCC (2013: 112) reported that 'Over most of the mid-latitude land masses and over wet tropical regions, extreme precipitation will *very likely* be more intense and more frequent in a

warmer world.' There are various reasons to expect increases in extreme precipitation if and when significant warming occurs. There will be more moisture in the atmosphere, and there is likely to be greater thermodynamic instability (Kunkel, 2003).

There is some evidence of increased rainfall events in various countries over recent warming decades, which lends support to this notion. Examples are known from the United States (Kunkel, 2003), Canada (Francis and Hengeveld, 1998), Australia (Suppiah and Hennessy, 1998), Japan (Iwashima and Yamamoto, 1993), South Africa (Mason et al., 1999), and Europe (Forland et al., 1998). In the UK there has been an upward trend in the heaviest winter rainfall events (Garner et al., 2017). Heavy precipitation events appear to have been intensified over very large parts of Northern Hemisphere land areas (Min et al., 2011).

Probabilistic analysis of GCMs by Palmer and Räisänen (2002), applied to Western Europe and the Asian Monsoon region, showed under global warming a clear increase in extreme winter precipitation for the former and for extreme summer precipitation for the latter. Increases in extreme winter precipitation are also likely in the western USA (Dominguez et al., 2012). Increased monsoonal rainfall events are widely predicted (Hsu et al., 2012) and would have potentially grave implications for flooding in places like Bangladesh.

In their analysis of flood records for 29 river basins from high and low latitudes with areas greater than 200,000 square kilometres, Milly et al. (2002) found that the frequency of great floods had increased substantially during the twentieth century, particularly during its warmer later decades. Their model suggested that this trend would continue.

10.3 Changes in Tropical Cyclones

Tropical cyclones (hurricanes) are highly important geomorphological agents, in addition to being notable natural hazards, and are closely related in their places of origin to sea temperature conditions. They only develop where sea surface temperatures (SSTs) are in excess of 26.5°C. Moreover, their frequency over the last century has changed in response to changes in temperature, and there is even evidence that their frequency was reduced during the Little Ice Age (see Spencer and Douglas, 1985). It is, therefore, possible that as the oceans warm up, so the geographical spread and frequency of hurricanes will increase (Figure 10.1). Furthermore, it is also likely that the intensity of these storms will be magnified (Figure 10.2). Emanuel (1987) used a GCM which predicted that with a doubling of present atmospheric concentrations of CO_2 there will be an increase of 40–50% in the destructive potential of hur-

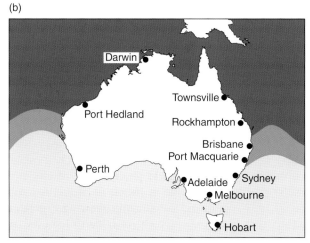

Figure 10.1 (a) The present frequency of cyclones crossing 500-km-long sections of the Australian coast, and an estimate of the frequency under conditions with a 2 °C rise in temperature. (b) The area where February sea surface temperatures around Australia are currently greater than 27 °C (stippled) and the additional area with such temperatures with a 2 °C rise in temperature (hatched). *Source:* modified after Henderson-Sellers and Blong (1989: figures 4.12 and 4.14). Reproduced with permission from New South Wales University Press.

Figure 10.2 (a) Scatter diagram of monthly mean sea surface temperature and best-track maximum wind speeds (after removing storm motion) for a sample of North Atlantic tropical cyclones. The line indicates the 99th percentile and provides an empirical upper bound on intensity as a function of ocean temperature. (b) The derived relationship between sea surface temperature and potential intensity of tropical cyclones. *Source:* adapted from Holland et al. (1988: figures 5 and 6). Reproduced with permission of American Geophysical Union.

ricanes. Subsequently, Knutson et al. (1998) and Knutson and Tuleya (1999) simulated hurricane activity for a sea surface temperature warming of 2.2°C and found that this yielded hurricanes that were more intense by 3–7 m per second for wind speed, an increase of 5–12%.

An increase in hurricane intensity and frequency would have numerous geomorphological consequences in low latitudes, including accentuated river flooding and coastal surges (Mousavi et al., 2011), severe coast erosion, accelerated land erosion and siltation, and the killing of corals (because of freshwater and siltation effects) (De Sylva, 1986). Mangroves are highly susceptible to hurricanes, being damaged by high winds and surges (Doyle and Girod, 1997).

Figure 10.1 indicates one scenario of the likely latitudinal change in the extent of warm, cyclone-generating sea water in the Australian region, using as a working threshold for cyclone genesis a summer (February) sea surface temperature of 27°C. Although cyclones do occur to the south of this line, they are considerably more frequent to the north of it. Under greenhouse conditions it is probable that on the margins of the Great Sandy Desert near Port Hedland the number of cyclones crossing the coast will approximately triple from around 4 per decade to 12 per decade (Henderson-Sellers and Blong, 1989).

Although some caution is necessary with regard to the extent to which warming will stimulate tropical cyclone activity (Walsh and Pittock, 1998), the relationship between sea surface temperature increase and increasing global hurricane activity has been confirmed by Hoyos et al. (2006) and Saunders and Lea (2008). Santer et al. (2006) have demonstrated that human factors have caused the increase in sea surface temperatures and cyclone development in both the Atlantic and Pacific regions, while Webster et al. (2005) and Elsner et al. (2008) have shown

ASKHAM BRYAN COLLEGE LEARNING RESOURCES

that the strongest tropical cyclones have become more intense in recent decades and this is likely to be the case in the future (Walsh et al., 2016a). There is also the possibility that tropical cyclones, at present relatively unimportant in South America, could become more significant, as presaged by Hurricane Catarina, which hit southern Brazil in March 2004 (Pezza and Simmonds, 2005). On the other hand, Knutson et al. (2008) argued that there might not be any great increase in hurricane frequency driven by increases in atmospheric greenhouse gas concentrations, and in some areas their frequency could even decrease (Walsh et al., 2016). The IPCC (2013: 113) reported that 'While projections indicate that it is *likely* that the global frequency of tropical cyclones will either decrease or remain essentially unchanged, concurrent with a *likely* increase in both global mean tropical cyclone wind speed and rainfall rates, there is lower confidence in region–region projections of frequency and intensity.'

Hurricane activity is linked to the ENSO phenomenon, so that if this was to be changed by global warming, as some models clearly demonstrate (Cai et al., 2014; Chand et al., 2017), then so might the frequency, distribution, and intensity of hurricanes. As Landsea (2000: 149) remarked, 'Perhaps the most dramatic effect that El Niño has upon the climate system is changing tropical cyclone characteristics around the world.' In some regions, an El Niño phase brings increases in tropical cyclone formation (e.g. the South Pacific and the North Pacific between 140°W and 160°E), while others tend to see decreases (e.g. the North Atlantic, the Northwest Pacific, and the Australian region). La Niña phases typically bring opposite conditions. Landsea envisaged a variety of reasons why ENSO should relate to cyclone activity: modulation of the intensity of the local monsoon trough, repositioning of the location of the monsoon trough, and alteration of the tropospheric vertical shear. Severe El Niños, like that of 1997/1998, can have a remarkable effect on rainfall amounts. This was shown with particular clarity in the context of Peru (Bendix et al., 2000), where normally dry locations suffered huge storms. At Paita (mean annual rainfall 15 mm), there was 1845 mm of rainfall, while at Chulucanas (mean annual rainfall 310 mm), there was 3803 mm. Major floods resulted (Magilligan and Goldstein, 2001).

10.4 Runoff Response

Studies of the sensitivity of runoff to climate changes have tended to indicate that annual runoff volume is more sensitive to changes in precipitation than to changes in potential evapotranspiration. Liu et al. (2011) have suggested that in the Yellow River Basin of China, the effects of increased evapotranspiration will be more than offset by increases in precipitation so that by 2080 that river's annual discharge could increase by 35–43%. A given percentage change in precipitation results in a greater percentage change in runoff (Arnell, 1996: 99; Najjar, 1999), with arid catchments showing a greater sensitivity than humid climates. As Table 10.1 shows, an

Table 10.1 Percentage change in annual runoff with different changes in annual precipitation and an increase in temperature of 2°C.

| River | Location | Percent change in precipitation | | | | |
		−20	−10	0	10	20
White	Colorado basin, USA	−23	−14	−4	7	19
East	Colorado basin, USA	−28	−19	−9	1	12
Animas	Colorado basin, USA	−26	−17	−7	3	14
Upper Colorado	Colorado basin, USA		−23	−12	1	
Lower Delaware	USA	−23		−5		−12
Saskatchewan	Canada	−51	−28	−15	11	40
Pease	Texas, USA	−76	−47	−12	40	100
Leaf	Mississippi, USA	−50	−30	−8	−16	40
Nzoia	Kenya	−65	−44	−13	17	70
Mesohora	Greece	−32	−18	−2	11	25
Pyli	Greece	−25	−13	−1	13	25
Jardine	North-east Australia	−32	−17	−1	11	28
Corang	South-east Australia	−38	−21	−3	16	33

Source: from various sources in Arnell (1996: table 5.1).

increase in annual precipitation of 10% is enough to offset the higher evaporation associated with a 2°C rise in temperature. The effects of increasing or decreasing precipitation are greatly amplified in those catchments with the lowest runoff coefficients (Pease, Nzoia, and Saskatchewan).

Another key aspect of the runoff response to climate change is that, as historical records show, higher average annual precipitation leads not only to higher stream flow but also to higher flood discharges. In Canada, for example, Ashmore and Church (2001) found that in the Southern Prairies and the Atlantic coast the magnitude of large floods (with a 10-year recurrence interval) increases by up to 50–100 % for only 5–15% increases in annual precipitation. Flood discharges increase proportionately much more than mean flows.

An attempt to map future runoff trends on a global basis was made by Arnell (2002). What is striking in this work is the large range there is in responses. Some areas will become very markedly prone to greatly reduced annual runoff, while others will see an enhancement of flows. The patterning at a global scale indicates that, by the 2080s, high latitudes in the Northern Hemisphere, together with parts of Central Africa and Central Asia, will have higher annual runoff levels, whereas Australia, southern Africa, north-west India, the Middle East, and the Mediterranean basin will show reduced runoff levels. There is some tendency, to which the Taklamakan of Central Asia appears to be a major exception, for some of the major deserts (e.g. Namib, Kalahari, Australian, Thar, Arabian, Patagonian, and North Sahara) to become even drier.

More recently, Sperna Weiland et al. (2011) analyzed available GCMs and suggested that there will be consistent decreases in discharge for southern Europe, southern Australia, parts of Africa, and south-western South America, while discharge will increase slightly in some monsoonal areas and in the Arctic. In the USA models tend to suggest substantial reductions in runoff the south-west and central USA, but increases in the north-east (Karl et al., 2009). Arnell and Gosling (2013) reported that more than two-thirds of climate models project a significant increase in average annual runoff across almost a quarter of the land surface, and a significant decrease over 14%, with considerably higher degrees of consistency in some regions. They also reported that most climate models project increases in runoff in Canada and high-latitude Eastern Europe and Siberia, and decreases in runoff in Central Europe, around the Mediterranean, the Levant, Central America, and Brazil. Another global assessment by van Vliet et al. (2013a) came up with a broadly similar picture of change, with an increase in mean annual river discharge in the high northern latitudes and large parts of the tropical (monsoon) region, and a decrease for the mid-northern latitude region (US,

Central America, Southern and Central Europe, South-East Asia) and the southern latitudes (southern parts of South America, Africa, and Australia). Schewe et al. (2014) projected that a global warming of 2°C above present would confront an additional approximate 15% of the global population with a severe decrease in water resources and would increase the number of people living under absolute water scarcity (<500 m^3 per capita per year) by another 40% (according to some models, more than 100%) compared with the effect of population growth alone.

On a global basis it is possible that runoff will increase in a warmer world because of a global increase in precipitation (Douville et al., 2002) and historical discharge records indicate that global runoff increases by c. 4% for each 1°C rise in temperature (Labat et al., 2004).

10.5 Cold Regions

There are many factors to be considered in an analysis of the response of cold region hydrological systems to climate change (Table 10.2), and good reviews are provided by Woo (1996) and Rouse et al. (1997). River channel forms are also likely to be transformed (Anisimov et al., 2008).

In the Arctic, overall the amount of moisture in the atmosphere is expected to increase as the atmosphere warms, leading to a general increase in precipitation and in river discharges. Peterson et al. (2002) analyzed discharge records for the six largest Eurasian rivers that flow into the Arctic Ocean and have shown that as surface air temperatures have increased so has the average annual discharge of fresh water. It grew by 7% from 1936 to 1999. They suggested that with increased levels of warming

Table 10.2 Potential hydrological changes in permafrost regions.

Changes in timing, extent, and duration of ice jams

Degradation of permafrost will add water during the transient phase of climatic change

Earlier melting of snow packs

Increase in surface ponding due to thermokarst development

Increased precipitation

Increased summer evaporative losses due to higher temperatures or replacement of lichens and mosses by transpiring plants

Less overland flow across impermeable permafrost

More groundwater storage in deeper active layers

Reduced proportion of snow, increased proportion of rain

Subterranean flow conduits may reopen

Source: author from information in Woo (1996).

(1.5 to 5.8° by 2100) there would be an 18 to 70% augmentation in Eurasian Arctic river discharge over present conditions. Wetherald and Manabe (2002) were of the view that by the middle of this century the runoff from such major rivers as the Mackenzie and Ob' could be increased by more than 20%. This analysis was largely confirmed by Wu et al. (2005) and McClelland et al. (2004), who believed that the main driver of the larger river discharge in the area is the increasing northward transport of moisture as a result of global warming. Prowse and Beltaos (2002) and Beltaos and Burrell (2003) explored the effects that climate change could have on ice jams and thus on the size and seasonality of floods and low flows, with the occurrence of ice break-up occurring earlier in the year, as appears to have been the case in the last several decades (Yoo and D'Odorico, 2002).

A particularly interesting analysis of recent temperature and stream-flow trends in the permafrost region of north-east China was provided by Liu et al. (2003). Warming has changed the depth of the active layer, enabling enhanced transport of subsurface water through unfrozen soils and a greater contribution of this flow to winter base flow. Stream-flow data for the period 1958 to 1998, indicated significantly greater runoff, with flow during February and March in the 1990s increasing by 80–100% over prior values.

The amount of snowpack accumulation is another major control on hydrological conditions in cold regions (Nijssen et al., 2001; Barnett et al., 2005), and winter snow accumulation in alpine watersheds provides most of the stream-flow runoff in western North America and similar regions of the world (Figure 10.3). Snow cover in the Northern Hemisphere has indeed shown a decline during recent warming decades (Stewart, 2009). Following a global analysis of future hydrological trends, Nijssen et al. (2001) suggested that the largest changes in the hydrological cycle are predicted for the snow-dominated basins of mid- to higher latitudes, and in particular there are likely to be marked changes in the amplitude and phase of the annual water cycle (Arora and Boer, 2001). Lapp et al. (2005) have modelled the likely response of snowpack accumulation to global warming in the Canadian Rockies, and have suggested that (a) there will be a substantial decline in the over-winter snow accumulation in most years, and (b) that spring runoff volumes may substantially decrease with the decline in snowpacks. This is confirmed by the work of Mote et al. (2005), who provide an historical analysis of changes in snowpack condition in recent warming decades, and who indicate that the losses in snowpack to date will continue and even accelerate, with faster losses in milder climates like the Cascades and the slowest losses in the high peaks of the Rockies and southern Sierra. In the south-west USA records show a recent increase in the fraction of precipitation falling as

Figure 10.3 Runoff in streams like this one in central Sweden depends greatly on the melting of snowpack (ASG).

rain rather than as snow. This is expected to continue with future warming, and decrease the natural high-mountain storage reservoir provided by snowpack. Bintanja and Andry (2017) reported that while climate models project a strong increase in Arctic precipitation over the coming century (primarily due to enhanced surface evaporation associated with sea-ice retreat), rain is projected to become the dominant form of precipitation in the Arctic region by the end of the century, as atmospheric warming causes a greater fraction of snowfall to melt before it reaches the surface, in particular over the North Atlantic and the Barents Sea. Warming also causes the snowmelt to peak earlier in the season than observed in historical records, and can reduce the water available to crops during the summer months. Records also indicate stream flow has shifted to earlier in the year, most notably in snow-dominated watersheds (Elias et al., 2016). Tree-ring chronologies for the North American cordillera have shown that the late twentieth-century snowpack reductions have been greater than at any time in the last millennium (Pederson et al., 2011). A 10–20% loss in the annual maximum amount of water contained in the snowpacks of the south-west USA occurred between the 1980s and the 2000s, and a further loss of 60% has been projected to occur within the next 30 years (Fyfe et al., 2017). However, it needs to be remembered that snowpack amounts will not only be affected by rising temperatures. Changes in precipitation totals may also be significant and in some areas may work in the same or opposite direction as warming (Adam et al., 2009; Stewart, 2009).

The other major control on future river flow in cold regions will be the melting of glaciers. Glaciers in areas like the Chinese mountains (Figure 10.4), the Karakorams, and Himalayas are important sources of flow to rivers

Figure 10.4 The melting of glaciers in high altitude areas like the Qialin Mountains of China is a major source of runoff in many of the great rivers of Asia (ASG).

like the Indus and the Ganga. If melting occurs, discharges may initially increase, but as the glacier mass declines through time, so will stream flows (Bradley et al., 2006; Rees and Collins, 2006; Immer Zeel et al., 2010). Some areas will show an initial increase in runoff, and there will also probably be a concomitant increase in flood frequency (Hirabayashi, et al., 2013). Bliss et al. (2014) undertook a global survey of stream-flow response to glacier melting from now to the end of the century. They suggested that the magnitude and sign of trends in annual runoff totals will differ considerably depending on the balance between enhanced melt and the reduction of the glacier reservoir by glacier retreat and shrinkage. In their analysis, most regions exhibited a fairly steady decline in runoff, demonstrating that they have passed their peak runoff. For example, runoff from glaciers in Western Canada and the US has been predicted to decline by 72% between 2003–2022 and 2080–2099. Low latitudes exhibited the fastest runoff decline (96%) due to the rapid and near complete volume loss of ice. In some regions, runoff will be stable for a few decades and then will decline (by 29% in Alaska and by 25% in the southern portion of Arctic Canada). Iceland, Svalbard, and South Asia will experience increasing runoff until the middle of the century, peaking 22%, 54%, and 27% higher than the initial period and declining thereafter, ending 30%, 10%, and 11% below their initial values, respectively. However, in the northern portion of Arctic Canada and the Russian Arctic, the runoff will steadily increase throughout most of the twenty-first century, ending 36% and 85% higher than it was at its start.

10.6 Changes in Runoff in the UK

Garner et al. (2017) have reviewed recent changes that have occurred in the hydrological environment in the UK and Arnell (1996, 1999a) has studied the likely changes that will occur in the UK as a result of global warming. With higher winter rainfalls and lower summer rainfalls (particularly in the south-east) he forecasts for the 2050s:

1) An increase in average annual runoff in the north of Britain of between 5 and 15%.
2) A decrease in the south of between 5 and 15%, but up to 25% in the south-east.
3) An increased seasonal variation in flow, with proportionately more of the total runoff occurring during winter.
4) High flows increased in northern catchments and decreased in the south.

Figure 10.5 shows the change in monthly stream flow under two climatic scenarios for six British catchments. As can be seen, in southern England, lower summer rainfall, coupled with increased evaporation, means that stream flows decrease during summer, whereas in the catchments in northern Britain, stream flow increases in winter, but changes little in summer. A more recent analysis by Prudhomme et al. (2012) confirmed that there are likely to be decreases in summer flows, especially in the south and east, but indicated that there remains uncertainty as to whether winter flows will increase or decrease.

Werritty (2002) looked specifically at Scottish catchments and noted a particularly marked increase in precipitation in the north and west in the winter half of the year. He predicted that by the 2050s Scotland as a whole will become wetter than at present and that average river flows will increase, notably in the autumn and winter months. He believed that high flows could become more frequent, increasing the likelihood of valley floor inundation. However, a study of the history of valley floors in upland Scotland suggests that they are relatively robust, so that although they may become subject to extensive reworking, they are unlikely to undergo large-scale destabilization (Werritty and Lees, 2001).

10.7 Europe

Arnell (1999b) modelled potential changes in hydrological regimes for Europe, using four different GCM-based climate scenarios. While there are differences between the four scenarios, each indicates a general reduction in annual runoff in Europe south of around 50°N and an increase polewards of that. The decreases could be as great as 50% and the increases up to 25%. The response of European rivers to climate change will, however, depend to a considerable degree on the amount of temperature rise and precipitation change that occurs in

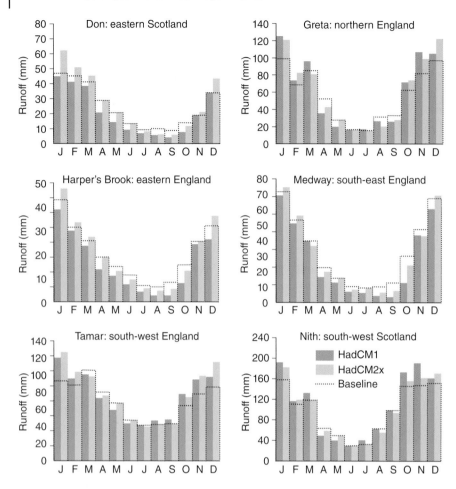

Figure 10.5 Monthly runoff by the 2050s under two scenarios for six British catchments. *Source:* adapted from Arnell and Reynard (2000: figure 7.19).

coming decades (Donnelly et al., 2017), with the impact of a 3°C temperature rise being much greater than that of 1.5 or 2°C.

Rising temperatures will affect snowfall and when it melts (Seidel et al., 1998). Under relatively mild conditions, even a modest temperature rise might mean that snow becomes virtually unknown, so that the spring snowmelt peak would be eliminated. It would be replaced by higher flows during the winter. Under more extreme conditions, all winter precipitation would still fall as snow, even with a rise in temperature. As a consequence, the snowmelt peak would still occur, although it might occur earlier in the year. In Figure 10.6, for instance, in the Polish example the snowmelt peak is eliminated by the 2050s, whereas in the Ukraine example it is brought forward.

One of the most important rivers in Europe is the Rhine. It stretches from the Swiss Alps to the Dutch coast

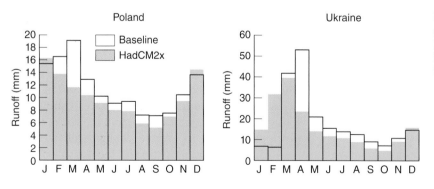

Figure 10.6 Effect of a climate change scenario on streamflow in two European snow-affected catchments by 2050s. *Source:* adapted from Arnell (2002: figure 7.20).

and its catchment covers 185,000 km^2 (Shabalova et al., 2003). Models suggest that the Rhine's discharge will become markedly more seasonal with mean discharge decreases of about 30% in summer and increases by about 30% in winter, by the end of the century. The increase in winter discharge will be caused by a combination of increased precipitation, reduced snow storage, and increased early melt. The decrease in the summer discharge is related mainly to a predicted decrease in precipitation combined with increases in evapotranspiration. Glacier melting in the Alps also contributes to the flow of the Rhine. Once these glaciers have wasted away, this contribution will diminish sharply.

In the Mediterranean region a number of processes operating in tandem may lead to a severe reduction in available water resources (García-Ruiz et al., 2011; Schneider et al., 2013). A general decrease in precipitation and a rise in evapotranspiration rates will lead to flow reductions, as will the presence of dams and reservoirs, over-exploitation of groundwater, and an expansion of the area that is forested following on from farm abandonment in upland regions. The low flows of Iberian rivers are set to become even lower (Guerreiro et al., 2017).

10.8 Geomorphological Consequences of Hydrological and Other Changes

Changes in river flow will cause changes in river morphology, particularly in sensitive systems, which include fine-grained alluvial streams. Bedrock streams will probably be less sensitive. Ashmore and Church (2001: 41) summarized some of the potential effects:

> The potential impacts of increased discharge include channel enlargement and incision, a tendency toward either higher sinuosity single channels or braided patterns, increased bank erosion, and more rapid channel migration. Increased magnitude of large floods will result in sudden changes to channel characteristics that may trigger greater long-term instability of rivers. Increased frequency of large floods will tend to keep rivers in the modified and unstable state. Decreased discharge often results in channel shrinkage, vegetation encroachment into the channel, sedimentation in side channels, and channel pattern change toward more stable, single-channel patterns. In entrenched or confined valleys there may be reductions in the stability of the valley walls and, hence, increases in the rate of erosion caused by a greater

tendency for streams to erode the valley walls. Increased valley-side erosion will increase sediment delivery to the streams with consequences for stream morphology.

One possible response of river basins to changes in runoff is that the channel length per unit area (i.e. drainage density) will change. After a consideration of the relationship between mean annual rainfall and drainage density in Africa, de Wit and Stankiewicz (2006) proposed that in areas with 500 mm per year, a 10% decrease in precipitation could reduce drainage density by as much as 50%.

Changes in river flow and direct inputs of water from precipitation may affect future lake levels (Section 12.8), including the Great Lakes of North America, which are likely to show modest falls (MacKay and Seglenieks, 2013). Ficklin et al. (2013) investigated the effects of future climate change on the state of Mono Lake in California. They predicted that annual total evapotranspiration would increase by 10 mm by the end of the century and there would be decreases in annual stream inflow by 15% compared to historical conditions, an advance of the peak snowmelt runoff to one month earlier (June to May), a decreased (10–15%) occurrence of 'wet' hydrologic years, and more frequent (7–22%) drought conditions.

Slope stability is another aspect of geomorphology which will be impacted upon by climate change (Gariano and Guzzetti, 2016), and Crozier (2010) provides a good general analysis of the factors that may alter future landslide activity (Table 8.7). Mass movements on slopes will also be impacted upon by changes in hydrological conditions. In particular, slope stability and landslide activity are greatly influenced by groundwater levels and pore-water pressure fluctuation in slopes.

In the south-east of England, Collison et al. (2000) sought to model the impact of climate change on the Lower Greensand escarpment of Kent. Using the Hadley Centre GCM (HADCMZ), combined with downscaling and a GIS-based combined slope hydrology/stability model, they found that because increases in rainfall would largely be matched by increases in evapotranspiration, the frequency of large landslides would be unchanged over the next 80 years. They argued that other factors, such as land-use change and human activity would be likely to have a greater impact than climate change.

Various other attempts have been made to model potential slope responses (Section 11.6). For example, in the Italian Dolomites, Dehn et al. (2000) suggested that future landslide activity would be reduced because there would be less storage of precipitation as snow. Therefore, the release of meltwater, which under present conditions contributes to high groundwater levels and strong landslide displacement in early spring, would be significantly diminished. However, because of the differences between GCMs and problems of downscaling, there are still great problems in modelling future landslide activity, and Dehn and Buma (1999), found that the use of three different GCM experiments for the assessment of the activity of a small landslide in south-east France did not show a consistent picture of future landslide frequencies. In the Swiss Alps, there is some evidence that debris flow activity has declined since the Little Ice Age, and if summer precipitation events occur less frequently in the future, their incidence could decline still further (Stoffel and Beniston, 2006). Comparable predictions have been made for the French Alps (Jomelli et al., 2009), where it is proposed that debris flow frequency could be reduced by 30% in the late twenty-first century. On the other hand, analysis of mass movement failures in high mountains during recent warm decades has provided no statistically rigorous evidence of a trend in activity (Huggel et al., 2012).

The peatlands of cold temperate regions are another landscape type that may be impacted by global change, though uncertainties exist about how they will respond (Moore, 2002). On the one hand, higher temperatures will tend to enhance plant productivity and organic matter accumulation but on the other will also lead to faster decomposition rates. Equally any decrease in water availability in the summer could cause peat loss and bog contraction.

Geomorphologists are starting to model changes in soil erosion that may occur as a consequence of changes in rainfall amounts and intensity (Nearing, 2001; Yang et al., 2003; Mullan et al., 2012), though it is difficult to determine the likely effects of climate change compared to future land-use management practices (Wilby et al., 1997). For example, Sun et al. (2002) calculated runoff erosivity changes for China. They adopted the UKMO Hadley climate scenario and produced a map of rainfall erosivity for 2061–2099 and suggested that for China as a whole, assuming current land-cover and land-management conditions, soil erosion rates will increase by 37–93%. For Brazil, Favis-Mortlock and Guerra (1999) used the Hadley Centre HADCM2 GCM and erosion model (WEPP – Water Erosion Predictions Project). They found that by 2050 the increase in mean annual sediment yield in their area in the Mato Grosso would be 27%. For the south-east of the UK, where winter rainfall is predicted to increase, albeit modestly, Favis-Mortlock and Boardman (1995) recognized that changes in rainfall not only impacted upon erosion rates directly, but also through their effects on rates of crop growth and on soil properties. Nonetheless, they showed that erosion rates were likely to rise, particularly in wet years.

In the USA, after analyzing a range of different models, Nearing et al. (2005: 151) remarked:

If rainfall amounts during the erosive times of the year were to increase roughly as they did during the last century in the United States, the increase in rainfall would be on the order of 10%, with greater than 50% of that increase due to increase in storm intensity. If these numbers are correct, and if no changes in land cover occurred, erosion could increase by something on the order of 25–55% over the next century … Both storm water runoff and soil erosion are likely to increase significantly under climate change unless offsetting amelioration measures are taken.

Sediment delivery by rivers may also be impacted by climate change. It has been suggested for example, that fire activity may increase in a warmer and drier environment, and that this could cause an increase in suspended loads as slopes are subjected to greater erosion and debris flow generation (Goode et al., 2012).

It is likely, of course, that climate change will cause farmers to change the ways in which they manage their crops and, in particular, to change the sorts of crops they plant in any particular area. This in turn may alter runoff and erosion. O'Neal et al. (2005) suggested, for example, that in the Midwest of the USA there might be a shift, because of price and yield advantages, from maize and wheat to soybean cultivation. Rates of runoff and erosion under soybeans would tend to be substantially greater than under the crops they replace.

There has also been interest recently in the role that global warming may play in accentuating or triggering various geohazards (McGuire, 2010) (Section 6.5). For example, the accelerated melting of submarine permafrost and the release of gas hydrates might promote submarine slope failures with consequent tsunami formation (Day and Maslin, 2010). Equally changes in the extent of ice sheets would alter the amount of loading on the Earth's crust and so might affect earthquake and volcanic activity.

10.9 Weathering

Remarkably little work has been done on how weathering rates of rock will change. Various attempts, however, deserve mention. The first of these is the study by Viles (2002) on stone deterioration in the UK. There she contrasted the likely impacts of climate change on building stones between the north-west and the south-east of the country (Table 10.3). She argued that in the north-west, which would have warmer and wetter winters, chemical weathering's importance might be increased, whereas in the south-east, which would have warmer, drier sum-

Table 10.3 Possible consequences of future climate change for building stone decay in the UK.

	Dominant building stone type	Process responses	Other threats	Overall response
NW – warmer, wetter winters	Siliceous sandstones and granites	Increased chemical weathering. Less freeze-thaw weathering. More organic growths contributing to soiling.	Increased storm activity may cause episodic damage. Increased wave heights may encourage faster weathering in coastal areas. Increased flooding may encourage decay.	Enhanced chemical decay processes and biological soiling, reduced physical decay processes.
SE – warmer, drier summers	Limestones	Less freeze-thaw weathering. Reduced chemical weathering as a result of less available water. Increased salt crystallization in summer. More deteriorating organic growths.	Increased drying of soils (especially clay-rich soils) will encourage subsidence and building damage. Low-lying coastal areas will be particularly prone to marine encroachment. Increased drought frequency may encourage decay.	Enhanced physical and biological weathering, more dust for soiling, reduced chemical weathering.

Source: Viles (2002: table 3).

mers, processes like salt weathering might become more important. Viles (2003) has also tried to model the impacts of climate change on limestone weathering and karstic processes in the UK (Figure 10.7), but the model has wider significance and could be applied to karst areas worldwide. Smith et al. (2011) suggested that higher winter rainfall amounts in the UK could cause the 'greening' of buildings by algal films, while deeper penetration of moisture might affect the operation of processes like salt

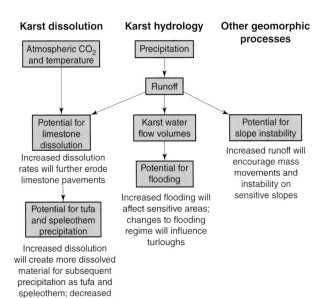

Figure 10.7 Conceptual model of the impacts of effective precipitation, air temperature, and atmospheric CO$_2$ concentration on karst dissolution, hydrology, and other geomorphic processes. *Source:* Viles (2003: figure 1). Reproduced with permission from Elsevier.

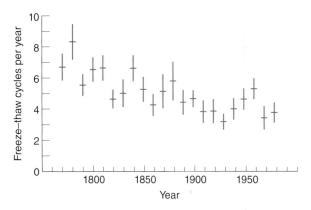

Figure 10.8 Decadal means of the freeze–thaw cycles in Central England. *Source:* Brimblecombe and Camuffo (2003: figure 3). Reproduced with permission from Imperial College.

weathering. Finally, as the climate warms, the number of freeze–thaw cycles to produce frost weathering in areas like Central England are likely to decrease, as they did during the warming of the nineteenth and twentieth centuries (Figure 10.8) (Brimblecombe and Camuffo, 2003). The possibility that salt weathering activity will change in drylands is a topic that is discussed in Section 12.10.

Guide to Reading

Arnell, N.W. (2002) *Hydrology and Global Environmental Change.* Harlow: Prentice Hall. A discussion of the responses of river systems to climate change.

Collier, M. and Webb, R.H. (2002) *Floods, Droughts and Climate Change.* Tucson: University of Arizona Press.

With a strong US focus, this accessible book discusses the relationship between climate change and the incidence of floods and droughts.

Sidle, R.C. (ed.) (2002) *Environmental Change and Geomorphic Hazards in Forests.* Wallingford: CABI.
A consideration of the ways in which mass movements and other hazards may change in the future.

Tang, Q. and Oki, T. (eds) (2016) *Terrestrial Water Cycle and Climate Change: Natural and Human-Induced Impacts.* Chichester: John Wiley & Sons.
A comprehensive volume that investigates the changes in the terrestrial water cycle and the natural and anthropogenic factors that cause these changes.

11

The Future: The Cryosphere

Chapter Overview

The cryosphere consists of ice sheets, ice caps, glaciers, sea, river and lake ice, and frozen ground (permafrost). Because of its very nature ice in its various forms will be susceptible to the effects of future warming. This chapter examines what may happen to the polar ice sheets and their associated ice shelves, the glaciers of mountainous regions, the sea ice of the Arctic and Antarctic, and the great spreads of permafrost that occupy around a quarter of Earth's land surface.

11.1 The Nature of the Cryosphere

The cryosphere is that part of the Earth's surface or subsurface environment that is composed of water in the solid state. It includes snow, sea ice, the polar ice sheets, mountain and valley glaciers, river and lake ice, and permafrost (permanently frozen subsoil). The cryosphere contains nearly 80% of all Earth's fresh water. Perennial ice covers about 11% of Earth's land surface and 7% of the world's oceans, while permafrost underlies about 25% of it. Seasonal snow has the largest area of any component of the global land surface; at its maximum in late winter it covers almost 50% of the land surface of the Northern Hemisphere. Because of the obvious role of temperature change in controlling the change of state of water to and from the liquid and solid states, global warming has the potential to cause very major changes in the state of the cryosphere.

11.2 The Polar Ice Sheets and Ice Caps

Ice sheets are ice masses that cover more than 50,000 km^2. The Antarctic ice sheet covers a continent that is a third bigger than Europe or Canada and twice as big as Australia. It attains a thickness that can be greater than 4000 m, thereby inundating entire mountain ranges. The Greenland ice sheet only contains 8% of the world's freshwater ice (Antarctica has 91%), but nevertheless covers an area 10 times that of the British Isles.

The Greenland ice fills a huge basin that is rimmed by ranges of mountains, and has depressed Earth's crust beneath. Ice caps have areas that are less than 50,000 km^2 in extent but which still bury the landscape.

Three main consequences of warming may be discerned for ice sheets (Drewry, 1991): ice temperature rise and attendant ice flow changes; enhanced basal melting beneath ice shelves and related dynamical response; and changes in mass balance. Temperatures of the ice sheets will rise due to the transfer of heat from the atmosphere above. However, because of the slow vertical conduction of heat through the thick ice column, the timescale for this process is relatively long (10^2–10^3 years). As the ice warms, it softens and can undergo enhanced deformation, which could increase the discharge of ice into the oceans. However, Drewry argued that it can be discounted as a major factor on a timescale of decades to a century.

The Antarctic ice sheet (Figure 11.1) is bounded over almost half of its extent by ice shelves. These are floating ice sheets nourished by the seaward extensions of the land-based glaciers or ice streams and by the accumulation of snow on their upper surfaces. Ice shelves would have enhanced basal melt rates if sea surface temperatures were to rise. This could lead to thinning and weakening of ice shelves (Warner and Budd, 1990). Combined with reduced underpinning from grounding points as sea level rose, this would result in a reduction of back-pressure on ice flowing from inland. Ice discharge through ice streams, the arteries of the ice sheets (Bennett, 2003), might therefore increase. There are some studies (e.g. De Angelis and Skvarca, 2003) that

Human Impact on the Natural Environment: Past, Present and Future, Eighth Edition. Andrew S. Goudie.
© 2019 John Wiley & Sons Ltd. Published 2019 by John Wiley & Sons Ltd.
Companion website: www.wiley.com/go/goudie/human-impact-natural-environment

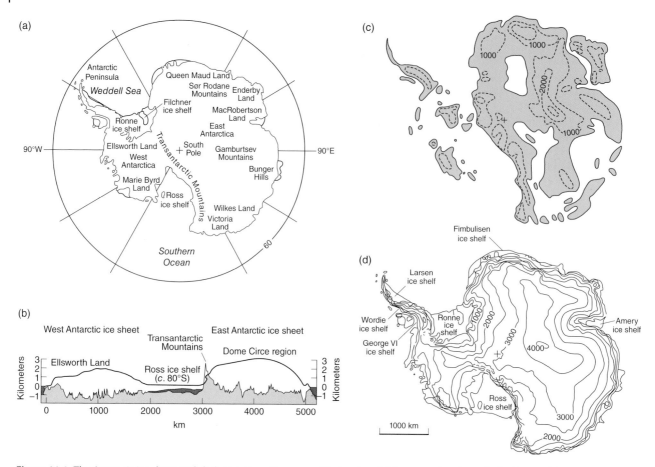

Figure 11.1 The Antarctic ice sheet and shelves. (a) Location map of Antarctica. (b) Cross-section through the East and West Antarctic ice sheets, showing the irregular nature of the bedrock surface, ice thickness, and the floating ice shelves. (c) Sub-glacial relief and sea level. The white areas are below sea level. (d) Surface elevations on the ice sheet in metres.

have indeed found evidence of ice streams increasing their velocities when ice shelves have collapsed, but this is not invariably the case (Vaughan and Doake, 1996). Nonetheless, following the disintegration of the Larsen B ice shelf in 2002, the glaciers that had previously been sheltered behind the ice shelf became tidewater glaciers and then flow rates increased greatly (Rott et al., 2010). Indeed, Cook and Vaughan (2010) have demonstrated the loss or substantial retreat of ice shelves around the Antarctic Peninsula in recent decades and the profound acceleration and thinning of ice streams that has occurred. Equally, Khazendar et al. (2015) have shown the accelerating change in glaciers following the collapse of the Larsen B Ice Shelf and they predict that the flow acceleration, ice front retreat, and enhanced fracture of the remnant Larsen B Ice Shelf presage its approaching demise.

The West Antarctic Ice Sheet (WAIS), because it is a marine ice sheet that rests on a bed well below sea level, is likely to be much more unstable than the East Antarctic Ice Sheet, from which it is separated by the Transantarctic Mountains. If the entire WAIS were discharged into the ocean, the sea level would rise by 5 or 6 m. Fears have been expressed over many years that it could be subject to rapid collapse, with disastrous consequences for coastal regions all over the world. One extreme view was postulated by Mercer (1978), who believed that predicted increases in temperature at 80°S would start a 'catastrophic' deglaciation of the area, leading to a sudden 5 m rise in sea level. A less extreme view was put forward by Thomas et al. (1979). They recognized that higher temperatures will weaken the ice sheets by thinning them, enhancing lines of weakness, and promoting calving, but they contended that deglaciation would be rapid rather than catastrophic, the whole process taking 400 years or so.

The WAIS has part of its ice grounded on land below sea level, and part in the form of floating extensions called ice shelves that move seaward but are confined horizontally by the rocky coast. The boundary between grounded and floating ice is called the grounding line (Oppenheimer, 1998; Ross et al., 2012). Weertman (1974) suggested that very rapid grounding line retreat could take place in the absence of ice shelf backpressure.

Figure 11.2 Cross-section of an ice stream and ice shelf of a marine ice sheet, indicating location of grounding line, bedrock rise on the ocean floor, and possible extent of deformable till. The thickness of the till layer, actually a few metres, is exaggerated for clarity. Sea-level rise due to collapse of WAIS was estimated by T. Hughes. *Source:* after Oppenheimer (1998: figure 2, p. 327 in *Nature,* volume 393, 28 May 1998). © Macmillan Publishers Ltd 1998.

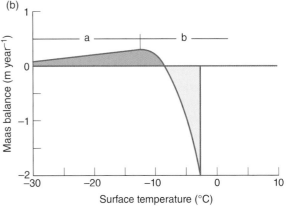

Figure 11.3 (a) and (b) Generalized curves of ablation and accumulation in dependence of (surface) temperature. Depending on which part of the *M-curve* applies, a climatic warming may lead to increasing (Antarctic) or decreasing (Greenland) mass balance. *Source:* after Oerlemans (1993: figure 9.4). Reproduced with permission from Springer.

He demonstrated (see Figure 11.2) that if the bedrock slopes downward in the inland direction away from the grounding line, as is the case with some of the WAIS ice streams, then if an ice shelf providing buttressing becomes unpinned owing to either melting or global sea-level rise, the grounded ice would accelerate its flow, become thinner, and rapidly float off its bed. Whether the WAIS will collapse catastrophically is still being debated (Oppenheimer, 1998; Joughlin and Alley, 2011), but there is some consensus that the WAIS will most probably not collapse in the next few centuries (Vaughan and Spouge, 2002). Bentley (1997) was amongst those who have expressed doubts about the imminence of collapse, believing 'that a rapid rise in sea level in the next century or two from a West Antarctic cause could only occur if a natural (not induced) collapse of the WAIS is imminent, the chances of which, based on the concept of a randomly timed collapse on the average of once every 100,000 years, are on the order of 0.1%' (see also Bentley, 1998).

Greenland and Antarctica will react very differently to global warming. This is in part because Antarctica, particularly in its interior, is very cold indeed. This means that the moisture content of the atmosphere over it is very low, ultimately suppressing the amount of snow and ice accumulation that can occur. An increase in temperature may therefore lead to more precipitation and greater accumulation of ice. With Greenland, the situation is different. Whereas in Figure 11.3 Antarctica lies to the left of the mass balance maximum, much of Greenland lies to the right of the maximum so that the total surface mass balance will decrease in the event of global warming (Oerlemans, 1993: 153). Indeed, Gregory et al. (2004b) argued that if the average temperature in Greenland increases by more than about 3°C, the ice

sheet would be eliminated, causing the global average sea level to rise by 7 m over a period of 1000 years or more.

However, the state of the Greenland ice sheet does not solely depend on the rate of surface ablation. Flow of the ice is enhanced by rapid migration of surface meltwater to the ice bedrock interface, and studies have shown that ice accelerates in summer (when melt occurs), that there is a near coincidence of ice acceleration with the duration of surface melting, and that interannual variations in ice acceleration are correlated with variations in the intensity of surface melting. This coupling between surface melting and ice sheet flow provides a mechanism for rapid response of ice sheets to warming (Zwally et al., 2002; Parizek and Alley, 2004). Some confirmation of this is provided by laser altimeter surveys, which show rapid ice thinning below 1500 m (Rignot and Thomas, 2002; Rignot and Kanagaratnam, 2006). They argue that the glaciers are thinning as a result of increased creep rates brought about by decreased basal friction consequent upon water penetrating to the bed of the glacier. They see this as a mechanism for transfer of ice sheet mass to the oceans that is potentially larger than could be achieved by surface melting alone. The overall loss of mass of the Greenland ice sheet has accelerated in recent years (Thomas et al., 2006; van den Broeke et al., 2009).

11.3 Valley Glaciers and Small Ice Caps

The world's alpine or mountain glaciers are numerous, and in all there are probably over 160,000 on the face of Earth. They are sensitive to climate change, and we have many examples of changes in glacier length of several kilometres since the end of the Little Ice Age (LIA) in the mid- to late nineteenth century (Oerlemans et al., 1998). Studies of the changes of snout positions obtained from cartographic, photogrammetric, and other data permit estimates to be made of the rate at which retreat can occur. The rate has not been constant, or the process uninterrupted. Indeed, some glaciers have shown a tendency to advance for some of the period. However, if one takes those glaciers that have shown a tendency for a fairly general retreat (Table 11.1) it becomes evident that as with most geomorphological phenomena there is a wide range of values, the variability of which is probably related to such factors as topography, slope, size, altitude, accumulation rate, and ablation rate. It is also evident, however, that rates of retreat can often be very high, being of the order of 20 to 70 m per year over extended periods of some decades in the case of the more active examples. It is therefore not unusual to find that over the last hundred or so years alpine glaciers in many areas have managed to retreat by some kilometres.

Fitzharris (1996: 246) suggested that since the end of the LIA, the glaciers of the European Alps have lost about 30 to 40% of their surface area and about 50% of their ice volume. In the Pyrenees, since the first half of the nineteenth century, about two-thirds of the ice cover has been lost. In Alaska (Arendt et al., 2002), glaciers appear to be thinning at an accelerating rate, which in the late 1990s amounted to 1.8 m per year. In North America glaciers have shown a general retreat after the LIA maximum, particularly at lower elevations and southern latitudes. In the Rocky Mountains the area lost since the LIA is about 25%. In China monsoonal temperate glaciers have lost an amount equivalent to 30% of their modern glacier area since the maximum of the LIA. New Zealand glaciers lost between one-quarter and almost half of their volume between the LIA maximum and the 1970s.

Not all glaciers have retreated in recent decades (Figure 11.4) and current glacier tendencies for selected

Table 11.1 Retreat of glaciers in metres per year in the twentieth century.

Location	Period	Rate
Abrekkbreen, Norway	–	17.7
Argentière, Mont Blanc, France	1900–1970	12.1
Austersdalbreen, Norway	–	21
Bossons, Mont Blanc France	1900–1970	6.4
Breidamerkurjökull, Iceland	1903–1948	30–40
	1945–1965	53–62
	1965–1980	48–70
Brikdalbreen, Norway	–	11.4
Carstenz, New Guinea	1936–1974	26.2
Franz Josef, New Zealand	1909–1965	40.2
Grosser Aletsch, Switzerland	1900–1980	52.5
Humo Glacier, Argentina	1914–1982	60.4
Lemon Creek, Alaska	1902–1919	4.4
	1919–1929	7.5
	1929–1948	32.9
	1948–1958	37.5
Nigardsbreen, Norway	1900–1970	26.1
Oztal Group, Switzerland	1910–1980	3.6–12.9
Tunsbergdalsbreen, Norway	–	11.4

Source: tables, maps, and text in Grove (1988).

Region	Period	Mean rate
Alps	1850–1988	15.6
Central Asia	1874–1980	9.9
Iceland	1850–1965	12.2
Irian Jaya	1936–1990	25.9
Kenya	1893–1987	4.8
New Zealand	1894–1990	25.9
Norway	1850–1990	28.7
Rocky Mountains	1890–1974	15.2
Spitzbergen	1906–1990	51.7

Source: Oerlemans (1994).

regions are shown. These are expressed in terms of their mass balance, which is defined as the difference between gains and losses (expressed in terms of water equivalent). In the European Alps (Figure 11.4a) a general trend toward mass loss, with some interruptions in the mid-1960s, late 1970s, and early 1980s, is observed. In Scandinavia (Figure 11.4b), glaciers close to the sea have seen a very strong mass gain since the 1970s, but mass losses have occurred with the more continental glaciers.

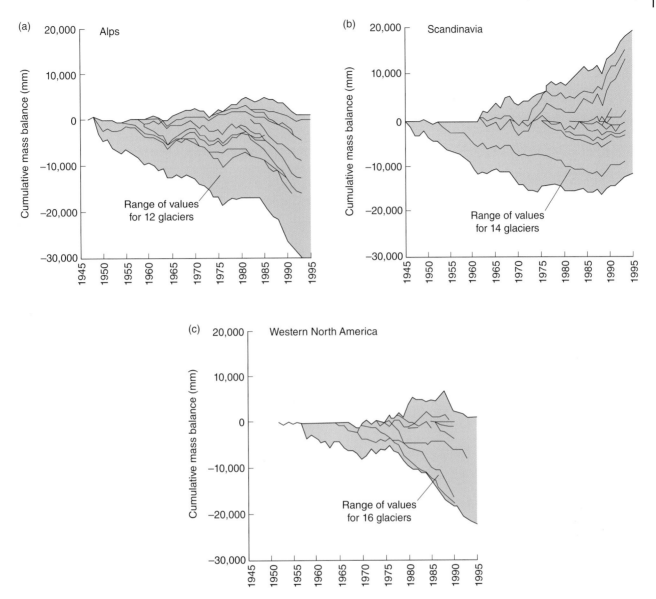

Figure 11.4 Cumulative mass balance for (a) the Alps, (b) Scandinavia, and (c) Western North America.

The mass gain in western Scandinavia could be explained by an increase in precipitation, which more than compensates for an increase in ablation caused by rising temperatures. Western North America (Figure 11.4c) shows a general mass loss near the coast and in the Cascade Mountains (Hoelzle and Trindler, 1998). The trend in cumulative mass balance of three US glaciers from 1958 to 2014 is shown in Figure 11.5, with the greatest changes taking place since c. 1990.

The positive mass balance (and advance) of some Scandinavian glaciers, notwithstanding rising temperatures, has been attributed to increased storm activity and precipitation inputs coincident with a high index of the NAO in winter months since 1980 (Nesje et al.,

2000; Zeeberg and Forman, 2001). In the case of Nigardsbreen (Norway), there is a strong correlation between mass balance and the NAO index (Reichert et al., 2001). A positive mass balance phase in the Austrian Alps between 1965 and 1981 has been correlated with a negative NAO index (Schoner et al., 2000). Indeed, the mass balances of glaciers in the north and south of Europe are inversely correlated (Six et al., 2001). However, since 2000, the Norwegian glaciers, which were still advancing in the 1990s, have started to retreat at a rapid rate. If this continues, then by 2100 about 98% of Norwegian glaciers are likely to disappear and the glacier area may be reduced by around a third (Nesje et al., 2008).

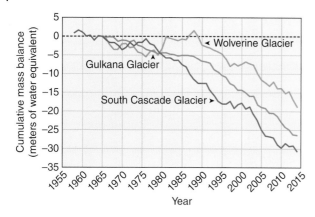

Figure 11.5 Changes in the cumulative mass balance of three US glaciers from 1958 to 2014. *Source:* https://www.epa.gov/climate-indicators/climate-change-indicators-glaciers (accessed January 2018).

Glaciers that calve into water can suffer from especially speedy retreat, which could be more than 1 km per year (Venteris, 1999). This rapid retreat is accomplished by iceberg calving, with icebergs detaching from glacier termini when the ice connection is no longer able to resist the upward force of flotation and/or the downward force of gravity. The rapid retreat is favoured by the thinning of ice near the termini, its flotation, and its weakening by bottom crevasses. Tidewater glaciers on the Antarctic Peninsula have been retreating and thinning fast (Pritchard and Vaughan, 2007).The Columbia tidewater glacier in Alaska (Figure 11.6) retreated around 13 km between 1982 and 2000, while the Mendenhall Glacier, which calves into a proglacial lake, has displayed 3 km of terminus retreat in the twentieth century (Motyka et al., 2002). Certainly, calving permits much larger volumes of ice to be lost to the glacier than would be possible through surface ablation alone (van der Ween, 2002) and great phases of calving in the past help to explain the Heinrich events of the Pleistocene and the rapid demise of the Northern Hemisphere ice sheets at the end of the last glacial period.

Some high-altitude glaciers in the tropics have also displayed fast rates of decay over the last hundred or so years, to the extent that some of them now only have around one-sixth to one-third of the area they had at the end of the nineteenth century (Table 11.2) (Kaser, 1999). In the mountains of New Guinea nearly all the ice caps have disappeared since the cessation of the LIA. In East Africa, the ice bodies of Mount Kilimanjaro have shrunk from c. 20 km^2 in 1880 to c. 2.5 km^2 in 2003. The rate of glacier loss on Kilimanjaro continues unabated (Thompson et al., 2009). At present rates of retreat the glaciers and ice caps of Mount Kilimanjaro in East Africa will have disappeared by in the next few years. The reasons for the retreat of the

East African glaciers include not only an increase in temperature. Also important may have been a relatively dry phase since the end of the nineteenth century (which led to less accumulation of snow) and a reduction in cloud cover (Mölg et al., 2003).

In the tropical Andes, the Quelccaya ice cap in Peru has also shown an accelerating and drastic loss over the last 40 years (Thompson, 2000). López-Moreno et al. (2014) showed that from 1984 to 2011, glaciers of the Cordillera Huaytapallana range in Peru experienced a 55% decrease in surface area. In neighbouring Bolivia, the Glacier Chacaltya lost 40% of its average thickness, two-thirds of its volume, and more than 40% of its surface area between 1992 and 1998. Complete extinction is expected within 10 to 15 years (Ramirez et al., 2001). In the Cordillera Real of Bolivia, between 1987 and 2010 glacier-covered areas were found to have diminished by more than 30% (Liu et al., 2013). In Patagonia, the calculated reduction in glacierized area between the LIA and 2011 was 4131 km^2 (15.4%) (Davies and Glasser, 2012).

The recent response of Himalayan and Tibetan Plateau glaciers shows great regional variations depending on such factors as the amount of debris cover that occurs on glacier surfaces (Ali et al., 2017) and also on differing precipitation trends (Yao et al., 2012). In the west of the region, around half of the westerlies-influenced Karakoram glaciers have been advancing or have been stable, showing a slight positive mass balance in recent years (Gardelle et al., 2012). This has been called 'the Karakoram anomaly' because it contrasts with glacier retreat worldwide (Minora et al., 2013). It is caused by a recent increase in snowfall, local temperature reductions, and the effects of thick debris mantles on some glaciers (Qureshi et al., 2017). The Pamir and Hindu Kush glaciers have also responded to recent increases in precipitation (Wang et al., 2017).

However, moving eastwards, the great bulk of the monsoon-influenced glaciers in the central Himalaya have been retreating, especially those with a limited debris cover (Scherler et al., 2011). Zhu et al. (2014), working on the Naimona'Nyi glaciers in the western Himalaya shows that the glacier retreat rate between 2003 and 2013 was five times of that in the previous 30 years (1973 to 2003). Since the early twentieth century, glaciers on the Tibetan Plateau have generally been retreating, and this trend has accelerated since the 1990s. In the central part, glaciers lost 22% of their coverage from 1977 to 2010 (Wang et al., 2013). In the Chinese Altai Mountains, analyses by Wang et al. (2015a) showed that the collective area of all 201 glaciers investigated was reduced by 30.4% from 1959 to 2008. Fifty-five glaciers disappeared entirely. Glacier area is estimated to have decreased by 20–25% in the Tien Shan, 30–35% in the

Figure 11.6 Changes in the state of the Columbia tidewater glacier as shown by satellite images (a) 1986 and (b) 2014. *Source:* NASA.

Pamirs and 50% in northern Afghanistan during the twentieth century. For the second part of the century, glacier area loss for the Polar Urals was 22.3% (Khromava et al., 2014). Fast rates of retreat have also been described for the Caucasus (Tielidze et al., 2015).

The situation in New Zealand is complex. Compilation of length-change records for Franz Josef and Fox Glaciers by Purdie et al. (2014) demonstrates that these glaciers have lost ~3 km in length and at least 3–4 km² in area

since the 1800s, with the greatest overall loss occurring between 1934 and 1983. Within this dramatic and ongoing retreat, however, both glaciers have experienced periods of re-advance. Mackintosh et al. (2017) have investigated the anomalous advance of some of these glaciers and have related it to local cooling rather than to any precipitation increase. Looking at a larger sample of glaciers, Chinn et al. (2012) showed that estimated ice volume (in water equivalents) for the Southern Alps had

Table 11.2 Area of tropical glaciers.

Location	Date	Area (km²)	Date	Area (km²)	%
Irian Jaya, Indonesia	c. 1850	19.3	c. 1990	3.0	15.5
Mount Kenya, Kenya	1899	1.563	1993	0.413	26.4
Lewis Glacier, Kenya	1899	0.63	1993	0.20	31.7
Kibo (Kilimanjaro), Tanzania	c. 1850	20.0	1989	3.3	16.5
Ruwenzori, Uganda	1906	6.509	c. 1990	1.674	25.7

Source: from data in Kaser (1999: table 2).

decreased from 54.5 km³ in 1976 to 46.1 km³ by 2008, a loss of 15% of the total ice volume.

The World Glacier Monitoring Service (WGMS) (2008) suggests that globally the average annual mass loss of glaciers during the warming decade from 1996 to 2005 was twice that of the previous decade (1986–1995) and over four times that from 1976 to 1985. Using WGMS data, Zemp et al. (2015) concluded that the rates of early twenty-first-century glacier mass loss are without precedent on a global scale. Figure 11.7, which is also based on WGMS data, shows the cumulative change in the mass balance of a set of 'reference' glaciers worldwide beginning in 1945. The accelerating rate, particularly over the last three decades, is clear.

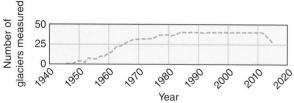

Figure 11.7 Cumulative changes in the mass balance of a set of 'reference' glaciers worldwide, beginning in 1945. The upper line represents the average of all glaciers that were measured and negative values indicate a net loss of ice and snow compared with the base year of 1945. *Source:* https://www.epa.gov/climate-indicators/climate-change-indicators-glaciers (accessed January 2018).

11.4 Predicted Rates of Glacier Retreat and Some Environmental Consequences

This response to the warming of recent decades suggests that with even greater warming in coming decades rates of recession and thinning may be very considerable. The monsoonal temperate glaciers of China, which occur in the south-eastern part of the Tibetan Plateau, are an example of glaciers that will suffer great shrinkage if temperatures rise. Indeed, Su and Shi (2002) have, using modelling studies, calculated that if temperatures rise by 2.1 °C, these glaciers will lose about 9900 km² of their total area of 13,203 km² (c. 75%) by the year 2100. The sub-polar and polar glaciers of China will shrink by c. 20% over the same period (Shi and Liu, 2000).

Oerlemans et al. (1998) attempted to model the responses of 12 glaciers (from Europe, New Zealand, and Antarctica) to three warming rates (0.01, 0.02, and 0.04 Kelvin per year), with and without concurrent changes in precipitation (Figure 11.8). For a warming rate of 0.04 Kelvin per year, without an increase in precipitation, they believed that few glaciers would survive until 2100. On the other hand with a low rate of warming (0.01 Kelvin per year) and an increase in precipitation of 10% per degree of warming, they predicted that overall loss of volume by 2100 would be 10 to 20% of the 1990 volume. On a global basis, mass balance modelling by Braithwaite and Zhang (1999) suggested that the most sensitive glaciers in terms of temperature change would be maritime and tropical glaciers. The latter, as in East Africa, are literally hanging on to high peaks, and so are very sensitive to quite modest changes in the height of the snowline. Radić and Hock (2011) tried to assess the glacier volume loss that will occur in various parts of the world by 2100. They suggested that for the Earth as a whole, the total glacier volume will be reduced by about a fifth, but that in some locations, notably New Zealand and the European Alps, the loss will be about three-quarters. In a more recent analysis, Radić et al. (2014) proposed that glaciers in Central Europe, low-latitude South America, the Caucasus Mountains, North Asia, and Western Canada and the USA will lose more than 80% of their volume by 2100. They suggested that the current global glacier volume will be reduced by between 29 and 41%, while Clarke et al. (2015) predicted that by 2100 the volume of glacier ice in western Canada will shrink by 70 ± 10% relative to 2005. According to their simulations, few glaciers will remain in the Interior and Rockies regions, but maritime glaciers, in particular those in north-western British Columbia, will survive in a diminished state.

Although an increase in glacier melting initially increases runoff, the eventual disappearance of glaciers will cause abrupt changes in stream flow because of the lack of a glacial buffer or reservoir during the dry season (Bradley et al., 2006; Vuille et al., 2008). Increased rates of glacier melting may for a period of years cause an increased incidence of summer meltwater floods (see, for example, the study by Liu et al. [2009] on the Yangtze), but when the glaciers have disappeared, river flow volumes may be drastically reduced (Braun et al., 2000), leading to severe water shortages.

The disappearance of glaciers can cause slope instability (Vilímek et al., 2005) by reducing their buttressing effect and by exposing rock slopes to severe weathering (Fischer et al., 2006) that produces rock falls. Such slopes (Holm et al., 2004) can become unstable, generating a risk of increased landsliding and debris avalanches (Kirkbride and Warren, 1999; Haeberli and Burn, 2002). It was one of the reasons for an apparent increase in landslides in the Austrian Alps (Kellerer-Pirklbauer et al., 2012), where substantial surface lowering and retreat of glacier tongues since the LIA have changed the stress and strain fields in the slopes.

One consequence of glacial down-wasting is that a variety of lakes have formed, which from time to time may drain catastrophically to give outburst floods (Harrison et al., 2006; Chen et al., 2010). There are numerous examples of accelerating lake formation. Working on western Greenland, Carrivick and Quincy (2014) used repeat remotely sensed imagery for the period from 1987 to 2010. During that time there was a c. 44% net increase in the number of lakes, and a c. 20% expansion in total lake surface area on a 1300 km length of ice margin. Similarly, in the Tibetan Plateau, in the 15 years from 1986, the total number of lakes increased by 11% and the total lake surface areas increased by 47%. Glacial lakes also expanded in the Mount Everest area (Benn et al., 2012) and on the border between Bhutan and China (Komori, 2008). In the Andes of Peru, Vilímek

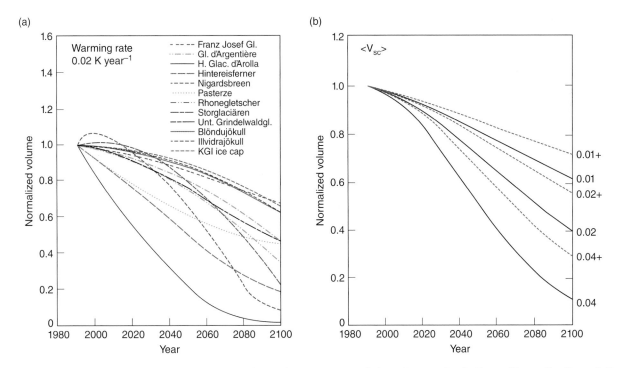

Figure 11.8 Changes in glacier volume 1980–2100 for 12 glaciers: Franz Josef Glacier (New Zealand), Glacier d'Argentière (France), Haut Glacier d'Arolla (Switzerland), Hintereisferner (Austria), Nigardsbreen (Norway), Pasterze (Austria), Rhonegletscher (Switzerland), Storglaciären (Sweden), Unt. Grindelwaldgl. (Switzerland), Blondujökull (Iceland), Illvidrajökull (Iceland), ice cap (Antarctica). *Source:* as modelled by Oerlemans et al. (1998). Reproduced with permission from Springer. (a) Ice volume change with a warming rate of 0.02 K a^{-1} without a change in precipitation. Volume is normalized with the 1990 volume. (b) Scaled ice volume change for six climate change scenarios. + refers to an increase in precipitation of 10% degree warming.

et al. (2005) showed that, following rapid deglaciation, the volume of Palcacocha Lake increased from 514,800 m^3 in 1972 to 3,690,000 m^3 in 2003, while in Patagonia, Mölg (2014) found that between 1985 and 2011 the number of proglacial lakes increased from 223 to 327 and their area expanded by 59%.

11.5 Sea Ice in the Arctic and Antarctic

Since the 1970s, sea ice in the Arctic has declined in area (Stocker, 2001: 446). Its thickness may also have become markedly less, with a near 40% decrease in its summer minimum thickness (Holloway and Sou, 2002; Maslowski et al., 2012). Figure 11.9 shows the decrease in area of Northern Hemisphere summer (as recorded in September each year) sea ice between 1979 and 2015. The average extent from 1979 to 2000 was 6.70 million km^2, whereas in 2012 it was just 3.41, which is a reduction by almost a half. The IPCC (2013: 9) reported that the annual mean Arctic sea ice extent decreased over the period 1979 to 2012 with a rate that was very likely in the range 3.5 to 4.1% per decade and very likely in the range 9.4 to 13.6% per decade for the summer sea ice minimum (perennial sea ice). The average decrease in decadal mean extent of Arctic sea ice has been most rapid in summer and the spatial extent has decreased in every season, and in every successive decade since 1979.

By contrast, changes in Antarctic sea ice were described by the IPCC as 'insignificant' (Stocker, 2001: 446). It has proved difficult to identify long-term trends because of the limited length of observations and the inherent interannual variability of Antarctic sea ice extent, but is possible that there has been some decline since the 1950s (Curran et al., 2003). Figure 11.10 shows the extent of Antarctic sea ice since 1979, and shows little evidence for any long-term change of the sort seen in the Arctic. The IPCC (2013: 9) believed that it is very likely that the annual mean Antarctic sea ice extent increased at a rate in the range of 1.2 to 1.8% per decade between 1979 and 2012.

Model projections tend to show a substantial future decrease of Arctic sea ice cover. The extent and volume of summer ice may be especially sensitive and it is possible that the Arctic could become free of summer sea ice at some point after 2050 (Zhang et al., 2010c). The IPCC (2013: 25) suggested that year-round reductions in Arctic sea ice extent by the end of the twenty-first century will range from 43% to 94% in September and from 8% to 34% for February. On the other hand, a decrease in sea ice extent and volume was projected for the Antarctic with only low confidence for the end of the twenty-first century.

Such a reduction in sea ice area in the Arctic would allow increased absorption of solar radiation so that a further increase in temperature could occur, though this might to some extent be mitigated by increasing cloud cover (Miller and Russell, 2002). However, the IPCC (Anisimov and Fitzharris, 2001: 819) believed that a sea ice albedo feedback, with amplified warming, means that 'At some point, with prolonged warming a transition to an Arctic Ocean that is ice free in summer – and perhaps even in the winter – could take place.'

Perversely, it is possible that one feedback of a decreasing Arctic sea ice cover will be an increase in winter snowfall is various parts of the Northern Hemisphere due to changes in the pattern of blocking anticyclones

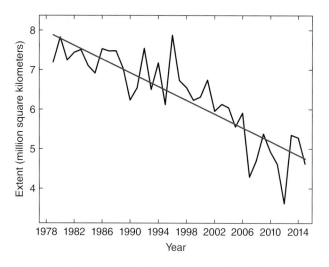

Figure 11.9 Decrease of Arctic sea ice extent since the late 1970s. *Source:* National Snow and Ice Data Center data in http://nsidc. org/arcticseaicenews/2015/10/2015-melt-season-in-review (accessed January 2018).

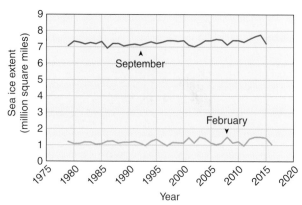

Figure 11.10 Antarctic sea ice extent since the late 1970s. No decrease is evident. *Source:* https://www.epa.gov/climate-indicators/climate-change-indicators-antarctic-sea-ice (accessed January 2018).

and an increase in available atmospheric moisture (Overland et al., 2011; Liu et al., 2012).

11.6 Permafrost Regions

Permafrost underlies large expanses of Siberia, Canada, Alaska, Greenland, Spitzbergen, and north-western Scandinavia (Figure 11.11). Permafrost also exists off-shore, particularly in the Beaufort Sea of the Western Arctic and in the Laptev and East Siberian Seas, and at high elevation in mid-latitudes, such as the Rocky Mountains of North America and the interior plateaux of Central Asia. It occurs not only in the tundra and polar desert environments poleward of the tree-line, but also in extensive areas of the boreal forest and forest-tundra environments.

Above the layer of permanently frozen ground there is usually a layer of soil in which temperature conditions vary seasonally, so that thawing occurs when tempera-tures rise sufficiently in summer but freeze in winter or on cold nights. This zone of freeze–thaw processes is called the active layer. It varies in thickness, ranging from 5 m where unprotected by vegetation to typical values of 15 cm in peat.

Conventionally, two main belts of permafrost are iden-tified. The first is the zone of continuous permafrost; in this area permafrost is present at all localities except for localized thawed zones, or taliks, existing beneath lakes, river channels, and other large water bodies which do not freeze to their bottoms in winter. In the discontinu-ous permafrost zone small, scattered unfrozen areas appear.

Regions underlain by permafrost may be especially prone to the effects of global climate change (Bowden, 2010; Guo and Wang, 2016). Firstly, the permafrost itself is by its very nature and definition susceptible to the effects of warming and thus to thermokarst subsidence (Section 6.4). Secondly, the amount of temperature increase predicted for high-latitude environments is greater than the global mean, and the loss of permafrost could have a direct effect on atmospheric conditions in the lower atmosphere. Thirdly, permafrost itself is an especially important control of a wide range of

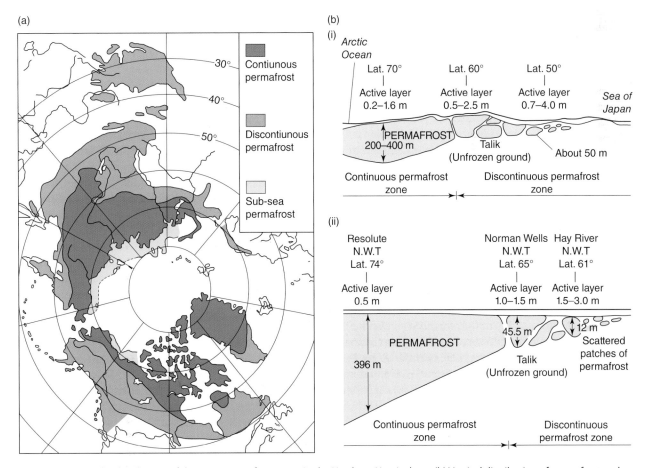

Figure 11.11 (a) The distribution of the main permafrost types in the Northern Hemisphere. (b) Vertical distribution of permafrost and active zones in longitudinal transects through (i) Eurasia and (ii) Northern America.

geomorphological processes and phenomena, including slope stability, rates of erosion, ground subsidence, and surface runoff. Fourthly, the nature (e.g. rain rather than snow) and amount of precipitation may also change substantially. Fifthly, the northern limits of some very important vegetation zones, including boreal forest, shrub-tundra, and tundra may shift latitudinally by some hundreds of kilometres (Section 8.2). Changes in snow cover and vegetation type may themselves have a considerable impact on the state of permafrost because of their role in insulating the ground surface. For example, if spring temperatures were to increase and early spring snowfall events were to become rain events, the duration of snow cover would decrease, surface albedo would also decrease, leading to an increase in air temperatures, and the snow might provide less insulation. This could cause relatively rapid permafrost degradation (Ling and Zhang, 2003). Conversely, if the warming were to occur in rather more severe periglacial climates, where temperatures are predicted to remain below or at freezing, the winters could become warmer, and wetter, producing an increase in the longevity and depth of the snowpack. This could lead to more insulation (retarding the penetration of the winter cold wave) and a reduction of warming because of an increase in surface albedo. A good general review of the likely consequences of climate change in the tundra of Canada is provided by Smith (1993).

There is some evidence that permafrost has been degraded by recent warming. For example, Kwong and Gan (1994) reported a northward migration of permafrost along the Mackenzie Highway in Canada. Here, between 1962 and 1988, the mean annual temperature rose by 1 °C. Over the same period the southern fringe of the discontinuous permafrost zone moved northwards by about 120 km. In Alaska, Osterkamp and Romanovsky (1999) found that in the late 1980s to mid-1990s some areas experienced warming of the permafrost table of 0.5 °C to 1.5 °C and that associated thawing rates were about 0.1 m per year. Recent permafrost degradation has also been identified in the Qinghai–Tibet Plateau (Jin et al., 2000), particularly in marginal areas.

Attempts have been made to assess future extents of permafrost (Figure 11.12). For the Northern Hemisphere, Nelson and Anisimov (1993) calculated the areas of continuous, discontinuous, and sporadic permafrost for the year 2050 (Table 11.3). They indicated an overall reduction of 16% by that date. Guo and Wang (2016) suggested that with a 2 °C rise in air temperatures about a quarter of Northern Hemisphere permafrost extent will be lost. In Canada, Woo et al. (1992: 297) predicted that if temperatures rise by 4–5 °C, as they may in this high latitude situation, 'Permafrost in over half of what is now the discontinuous zone could be eliminated'. They add:

The boundary between continuous and discontinuous permafrost may shift northwards by hundreds of kilometres but because of its links to the tree line, its ultimate position and the time taken to reach it are more speculative. It's possible that a warmer climate could ultimately eliminate continuous permafrost from the whole of the mainland of North America, restricting its presence only to the Arctic Archipelago.

Barry (1985) estimated that an average northward displacement of the southern permafrost boundary by 150 ± 50 km would be expected for each 1 °C warming so that a total *maximum* displacement of between 1000 and 2000 km is possible. Jin et al. (2000: 397) attempted to model the response of permafrost to different degrees of temperature rise in the Tibetan Plateau region (Table 11.4) and suggested that with a temperature rise of 2.91 °C by the end of the twenty-first century, the permafrost area will decrease by 58%. Similar estimates have been provided by Li et al. (2008). The IPCC (2013: 23) predicted that by the end of the twenty-first century the area of permafrost near the surface (upper 3.5 m) will decrease by between 37% and 81%.

In recent warming decades there has been a widespread, though not universal, increase in active layer thickness as permafrost has melted (IPCC, 2013: 364). For example, Sobota and Nowak (2013) investigated changes in the active layer of the high Arctic coastal area in north-west Spitsbergen (Svalbard). In 1996–2012 on a beach and on a moraine the trend of annual ALT increase was 1.3 cm and 2.5 cm respectively. Wu et al. (2015), working in the Tibetan Plateau, showed an increase in ALT between 2002 and 2012 that averaged ~4.26 cm per year, while Peng et al. (2015), working along the Qinghai–Tibet highway, found that between 1995 and 2011 the ALT increased about 0.44 m, with an average increasing annual rate of 3.42 cm in cold permafrost regions, while in warm permafrost regions the ALT increased about 0.68 m, with an average increasing annual rate of 5.72 cm. Streletskiy et al. (2106) measured changes in ALT at Barrow in Alaska between 2003 and 2015 and found subsidence trends of 0.4–1.0 cm per year, resulting in a net elevation change of 8–15 cm. Increasing temperatures are likely to cause the thickness of the seasonally thawed active layer to become deeper. A simulation by Stendel and Christensen (2002) indicated a 30–40% increase by the end of the twenty-first century for most of the permafrost area in the Northern Hemisphere.

Degradation of permafrost may lead to an increasing scale and frequency of slope failures (Gruber and Haeberli, 2007). Thawing reduces the strength of both ice-rich sediments and frozen jointed bedrock (Davies et al., 2001). Ice-rich soils undergo thaw consolidation

Figure 11.12 Projection of changes in permafrost with global warming for (a) North America and (b) Siberia. *Source:* modified after French (1996: figure 17.5) and Anisimov (1989). Reprinted with permission from *Physical Geography*, 10, 1989, © Bellweather Publishing Ltd., 8640 Guilford Road, Columbia, MD 21046, all rights reserved.

during melting, with resulting elevated pore-water pressures, so that formerly sediment-mantled slopes may become unstable. Equally, bedrock slopes may be destabilized if warming reduces the strength of ice-bonded open joints or leads to groundwater movements that cause pore pressures to rise (Harris et al., 2001). Increases in the thickness of the active layer may make more material available for debris flows. As a result of these trends,

Table 11.3 Calculated contemporary and future area of permafrost in the Northern Hemisphere by 2050.

Zone	Contemporary	2050	% change
Continuous	11.7	8.5	−27
Discontinuous	5.6	5.0	−11
Sporadic	8.1	7.9	−2
TOTAL	25.4	21.4	−16

Source: from Nelson and Anisimov (1993).

Table 11.4 Forecast permafrost degradation on the Qinghai–Tibet Plateau during the next 100 years.

Temperature increase (°C) (year)	Permafrost area (10^6 km²)	Percentage decrease
0.51 (2009)	1.190	8
1.10 (2049)	1.055	18
2.91 (2099)	0.541	58

Source: Jin et al. (2000: table 11). Reproduced with permission of Elsevier.

surface soils, sediments, and rock masses will become more mobile (Shan, 2015). Mass movements of soil and surface sediment occur along the base of the active layer. These slides, called active layer detachments (ALDs), take place when saturated overburden slides over the frozen substrate, and result in the downslope travel of material up to hundreds of metres over low slope angles (Lamoureux and Lafrenière, 2009). Rockfall activity has already increased in the Mont Blanc area as a consequence of this (Ravanel and Deline, 2011).

A combination of glacier retreat (Section 11.3) and permafrost degradation was championed by Deline et al. (2012) and by Stoffel et al. (2014) as the cause of slope instability. They argued that destabilized rock glaciers could lead to debris flows without historic precedents. That recent warming has caused some rock glaciers and associated debris flows to become more active has been confirmed in Alaska by Simpson et al. (2016) and in high Asia by Sorg et al. (2015). Geertsema et al. (2006) showed a recent increase in mass movement activity in British Columbia, Canada, and related this to the same sorts of mechanisms. Conversely, in the Tyrol of Italy, Sattler et al. (2011) failed to find a correlation between debris flows and degrading permafrost at the present time. In New Zealand, Allen et al. (2011) noted the prevalence of recent failures occurring from glacier-proximal slopes and from slopes near the lower permafrost limit, but uttered a word of caution to the effect that demonstrating any influence of atmospheric warming, permafrost degradation, and perennial ice melt on recent higher

elevation slope failures and, more importantly, distinguishing these influences from tectonic and other climatic forcing, is not yet possible. The thawing of permafrost can also lead to rapid river-bank erosion rates, as recorded by Kanevskiy et al. (2016) in Alaska.

Coastal bluffs may be subject to increased rates of erosion if they suffer from thermal erosion caused by permafrost decay (Obu et al., 2017). This would be accelerated still further if sea ice were to be less prevalent, for sea ice can protect coasts from wave erosion and debris removal (Carter, 1987). Wave action may become more vigorous (Thomson et al., 2016). Local erosional losses of up to 40 m per annum have been observed in locations in Siberia, Alaska, and Canada. Losses of up to 600 m over the past few decades have occurred in Alaska (Parson et al., 2001). The number and total area of thaw slumps along the Yukon coastline increased by as much as 160% between 1952 and 2000 (Lantuit and Pollard, 2008). Overeem et al. (2011) measured an average retreat of 14.4 m yr^{-1} over a 3 km stretch of Beaufort Sea coast in the two-year interval 2007–2009, with rates as high as 30 m yr^{-1} locally. They indicated that these rates had accelerated over the past 50 years synchronously with Arctic-wide declines in sea ice extent, suggesting a causal relationship between the two. Documentation by Jones et al. (2009) of erosion rates along a 75 km stretch of the Beaufort Sea revealed that the mean rate had doubled from ~7 m yr^{-1} for 1955–1979 to ~14 m yr^{-1} for 2002–2007. They found that the number of thermo-mechanical niche-forming episodes per annum, and thus the erosion rate, was a function of ice-free season duration, the number and type of storms impacting the coastline, sea level, and summertime sea surface temperature. Mars and Houseknecht (2007), working on the low-lying Arctic coastal plain north of Teshekpuk Lake in the National Petroleum Reserve in Alaska, established that erosion had more than doubled along a segment of that coast between 1955 and 1985 and 1985 and 2000. Some areas had undergone as much as 0.9 km of coastal erosion in the past 50 years. Coastal erosion had also breached numerous thermokarst lakes (see below), causing initial draining of the lakes followed by progressive flooding by marine water. By this process, freshwater lakes had evolved into marine bays over time. Vermaire et al. (2013) found that along the coastline of the Mackenzie Delta in Canada, warming has been increasing the frequency and intensity of storms. After ~1980, surge activity has increased sharply in response to the rapid rise in mean annual temperature and the dramatic reduction in Arctic sea ice.

One of the severest consequences of permafrost degradation is ground subsidence and the formation of thermokarst phenomena (Nelson et al., 2001, 2002), including multitudes of thaw lakes (Figure 11.13). This is

Figure 11.13 Thermokarst phenomena, including oriented thaw lakes, on the Arctic Ocean coast of Alaska. *Source* © Google Earth. Scale bar 36 km.

likely to be a particular problem in the zones of relatively warm permafrost (the discontinuous and sporadic zones), and where the permafrost is rich in ice. The excess ice content (EX) determines how much surface settlement will occur as a result of the thawing of permafrost, and it is the volume of water that exceeds the space available within the pores when the soil or sediment is thawed (Woo et al., 1992: 297):

$$EX = 100 \cdot (V_W / V_T)$$

where EX is the excess ice content (%), V_W is the volume of water that is released on thawing the sample (m^3), and V_T is the total volume of the thawed sample (m^3). Thus, to deepen an active layer by 0.5 m, 1.0 m of permafrost with an EX of 50% must thaw and this ultimately will result in surface settlement of 0.5 m (Figure 11.14).

Increasing thaw settlement was reported by Osterkamp et al. (2009) and Rowland et al. (2010), while Olthof et al. (2015) described lake expansion in the Tuktoyaktuk Coastal Plain of north-west Canada. Jones et al. (2011) noted an expansion of lakes in the continuous permafrost zone of the Seward Peninsula. Their assessment of lakes and ponds >0.1 ha using remotely sensed imagery from 1950/1951, 1978, and 2006/2007 revealed that the majority of thermokarst lakes were actively expanding as a result of surface permafrost degradation. However, as lakes expand the opportunity for drainage increases due to the encroachment towards a drainage gradient. Thus, total surface area of lakes in

their study region declined by 15% due to the lateral drainage of several large lakes. In the discontinuous

Surface settlement (cm)	25	12.5	6.25	0.05
Cumulative settlement (cm)	25	37.5	43.75	50

Additional thaw (cm)	50	25	12.5	0.1
Cumulative thaw (cm)	50	75	87.5	100
Year	1	2	3	10

Figure 11.14 Ground settlement in response to a thickening of the active layer in permafrost with an excess ice content of 50%. The active layer increases from 1.0 to 1.5 m and in so doing, 1.0 m of permafrost is thawed and the surface settles by 0.5. *Source:* after Woo et al. (1992: figure 8). Reproduced with permission from Bellwether Publishing Ltd.

permafrost zone in Alaska, complete thawing under a pond or lake may lead to drainage integration that causes the pond to be drained, thereby reducing the number of ponds (Yoshikawa and Hinzman, 2003). Sannel and Kuhry (2011) undertook studies in northern Canada, European Russia, and in northern Sweden and found that the most extensive lateral expansion along lake margins from the mid-1970s to the mid-2000s occurred in large lakes (>20,000 m^2) in the Hudson Bay Lowlands (Canada) and Rogovaya (Russia). They suggested that larger lakes are more likely to experience erosion as they have a longer fetch and thereby higher potential wave energy. They found that the maximum recorded lateral expansion rate was 7.3 m per decade in the Hudson Bay lowlands. Thermokarst degradation has also occurred in Siberia (Khvorostyanov, 2008),

where satellite monitoring (1973–2008) by Kirpotin et al. (2009) revealed that in the zone of continuous permafrost thermokarst lakes expanded their areas by about 10–12%, but that in the zone of discontinuous permafrost lake drainage prevailed, confirming observations made in Alaska.

Thawing ice-rich areas, such as ice-cored mounds (pingos), will settle more than those with lesser ice contents, thereby producing irregular hummocks and depressions. Water released from ice melt may accumulate in such depressions. The depressions may then enlarge into thaw lakes as a result of thermal erosion (Harris, 2002), which occurs because summer heat is transmitted efficiently through the water body into surrounding ice-rich material (Yoshikawa and Hinzman, 2003).

Guide to Reading

Benn, D.I. and Evans, D.J.A. (2010) *Glaciers and Glaciations* (2nd edn). London: Hodder. A very good summary of knowledge on glaciers and their effects on landscape.

French, H. (2007) *The Periglacial Environment* (3rd edn). Chichester: Wiley. An excellent survey of the nature of cold environments and the pressures that have been applied to them.

Hassol, S.J. (2004) *Impacts of a Warming Arctic*. Cambridge: Cambridge University Press. A report of the Arctic Climate Impact Assessment.

Knight, P.G. (1999) *Glaciers*. Cheltenham: Stanley Thornes. A useful introduction to glacial processes and landforms.

Nesje, A. and Dahl, S.O. (2000) *Glaciers and Environmental Change*. London: Arnold. A general text which is very strong on the changing mass balance of glaciers.

Slaymaker, O. and Kelly, R.E.J. (2007) *The Cryosphere and Global Environmental Change*. Oxford: Blackwell. This text considers all aspects of the cryosphere, including glaciers and permafrost, and their response to environmental changes.

Wadhams, P., Dowdeswell, J.A. and Schofield, A.N. (eds) (1996) *The Arctic and Environmental Change*. Amsterdam: Gordon and Breach. A collection of papers presented to the Royal Society and covering many aspects of cryospheric change in northern regions.

12

The Future: Drylands

CHAPTER OVERVIEW

Some components of desert landscapes are highly susceptible to environmental changes. They have demonstrated this in the ways they have responded to past climatic changes. Rainfall amounts and temperatures in coming decades will have an impact on a whole range of desert phenomena: wind erosion, dust storm emissions, dunes, runoff, lake levels, desert coastlines, and salt weathering.

12.1 Introduction

In the past, arid environments have been prone to rapid geomorphological and hydrological changes in response to apparently modest climatic stimuli, switching speedily from one state to another when a particular threshold has been reached (Goudie, 1994).

1) Desert valley bottoms appear to have been subject to dramatic alternations of cut-and-fill during the course of the Holocene and a large literature has developed on the arroyos (Section 6.10) of the American south-west (e.g. Cooke and Reeves, 1976) and debates have occurred about whether these alternations result from changes in rainfall characteristics or as a result of land-use changes (e.g. grazing pressure).

2) The heads of alluvial fans often display fan-head trenching, suggesting recent channel instability. There has been considerable debate in the literature about the trigger for such trenching, be it tectonic, extreme flood events, climatic change, or an inherent consequence of fluctuating sediment-discharge relationships during the course of a depositional cycle (e.g. Harvey, 1989).

3) Fluvial systems, as, for example, in the drier lands around the Mediterranean Basin, display a suite of terraces which demonstrate a complex record of cut-and-fill during the late Holocene (Van Andel et al., 1990). There has been prolonged debate as to whether the driving force has been climatic change or anthropogenic activities (Section 6.10).

4) Colluvial sections in sub-humid landscapes (including southern Africa) show complex consequences of deposition, stability, and incision (Watson et al., 1984).

5) Terminal lake basins (pans, playas, etc.) can respond dramatically, in terms of both their extent and the rapidity of change that can occur, to episodic rainfall events in their catchments. The history of Lake Eyre in Australia in the twentieth century bears witness to this fact (Figure 12.1).

6) West African dust storm activity has shown very marked shifts in the past half century in response to runs of dry years and increasing land-use pressures (Goudie and Middleton, 1992). The data for Nouakchott (Mauritania) are especially instructive, revealing a sudden acceleration in dust storm events since the 1960s. A broadly similar picture could be presented for the High Plains of the United States during the 'Dust Bowl years' of the 1930s (Section 4.29).

7) Some dune fields have been prone to repeated fluctuations in deposition and stabilization in the Holocene (Section 6.13), and as more optical dates become available, the situation is likely to prove to be even more complex than hitherto believed. A good illustration of this is provided by Gaylord's (1990) work in the Clear Creek area of south-central Wyoming where over the last 7500 years at least four episodes of enhanced aeolian activity and aridity are recorded.

Human Impact on the Natural Environment: Past, Present and Future, Eighth Edition. Andrew S. Goudie.
© 2019 John Wiley & Sons Ltd. Published 2019 by John Wiley & Sons Ltd.
Companion website: www.wiley.com/go/goudie/human-impact-natural-environment

(a)

(b)

Figure 12.1 The flooding of Lake Eyre. (a) Extent of flooding in 1949–1952. *Source:* after Bonython and Mason in Mabbutt (1977: figure 54). (b) Estimated annual inflows to Lake Eyre North for the period 1885–1989. *Source:* based on Kotwicki and Isdale (1991: figure 2). Both 1949–1952 and 1974 were strong La Niña events. *Source:* Viles and Goudie (2003). Reproduced with permission from Elsevier.

8) Studies have shown how rates of denudation (e.g. Langbein and Schumm, 1958) and drainage density (De Wit and Stankiewich, 2006) can change very rapidly in semi-arid areas either side of a critical rainfall or precipitation/evapotranspiration (P/E) value related to vegetation cover that constitutes a particular threshold between equilibrium states (Figures 12.2 and 12.3).

This apparent instability and threshold dependence of a range of arid-zone landforms, rates, and processes lead one to believe that such areas may be especially susceptible to the effects of future climate change (Figure 12.4).

12.2 Climate Changes in the Past

Past climatic changes have had dramatic effects on deserts (Goudie, 2002; Anderson et al., 2013) and this makes it likely that so will future ones. For example, fluctuations during the Holocene led to the expansion and contraction of lakes. In the Sahara there are huge numbers of Holocene pluvial lakes (Petit-Maire et al., 1999). In the Western Desert of Egypt and the Sudan there are also many closed depressions or playas, relict river systems, and abundant evidence of prehistoric human activity. Playa sediments indicate that they once contained substantial bodies of

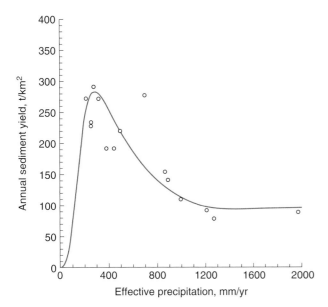

Figure 12.2 Variation of sediment yield with climate as based on data from small watersheds in the United States. *Source:* adapted from Langbein and Schumm (1958).

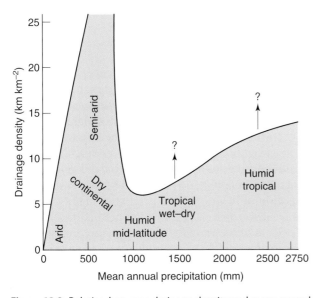

Figure 12.3 Relation between drainage density and mean annual precipitation. *Source:* after Gregory (1976). Copyright © 1976. Reprinted by permission of John Wiley & Sons.

water, which attracted Neolithic settlers. Many of these sediments indicate the ubiquity of an early to mid-Holocene wet phase, which has often been termed the 'Neolithic Pluvial'. A large lake, 'The West Nubian Palaeolake', formed in the north-west of Sudan (Hoelzmann et al., 2001). It was especially extensive between 9500 and 4000 years BP, and may have covered as much as 7000 km². If it was indeed that big, then a large amount of precipitation would have been needed to maintain it – possibly as much as 900 mm per year compared to the less than

15 mm it receives today. The Sahara may have largely disappeared during what has been called 'The Greening of Africa'. Conversely, some deserts experienced abrupt and relatively brief drought episodes in the Holocene which caused extensive dune mobilization in areas like the American High Plains (Forman et al., 2001, 2006).

At the present day, deserts continue to change, sometimes as a result of climatic fluctuations like the run of droughts that have afflicted the West African Sahel over recent decades. The changing vegetation conditions in the Sahel, which have shown marked fluctuations since the mid-1960s, have been mapped by Tucker et al. (1991). Inter-annual variability in the position of the southern boundary of the Sahara, as represented by the 200 mm isohyet, can be explained in large measure by changes in the North Atlantic Oscillation (NAO) and the El Niño Southern Oscillation (ENSO) (Oba et al., 2001). The drought also led to reductions in the flow of rivers like the Senegal and Niger, and to an increase in dust storm activity (Goudie and Middleton, 2006). The extent of Lake Chad's water surface has also fluctuated dramatically. It was particularly badly affected by the drought, which caused the lake surface area to fall from c. 25,000 km² in 1960 to just a tenth of that figure in the mid-1980s (Birkett, 2000).

We also know from recent centuries that ENSO fluctuations have had important consequences for such phenomena as droughts and dune reactivation (Forman et al., 2001), and through their effect on vegetation cover have had major impacts on slope stability and soil erosion (Viles and Goudie, 2003). Lake levels have responded to ENSO influences (Arpe et al., 2000), large floods have occurred, valleys have been trenched (Bull, 1997), erosivity patterns have altered (D'Odorico et al., 2001), and landslides and debris flows have been generated (Grosjean et al., 1997).

12.3 Future Changes in Climate in Drylands

The IPCC (2007a) suggested that in drylands temperatures could increase by between 1 and 7C by 2017–2100 compared to 1961–1990, and that precipitation levels could decrease by as much as 10–20% in the case of the Sahara but increase by as much as 10–15% in the Chinese deserts. Droughts may become more prevalent (Dai, 2011). The models of Sylla et al. (2010) suggested that this will be the case in the West African Sahel, partly because of a weaker monsoon flow and reduced easterly wave activity. While is likely that many areas that are currently dry may see enhanced aridity because of reductions in precipitation, even within an area such as the Middle East, some parts may become wetter and some may become drier. The Saudi Arabian desert may,

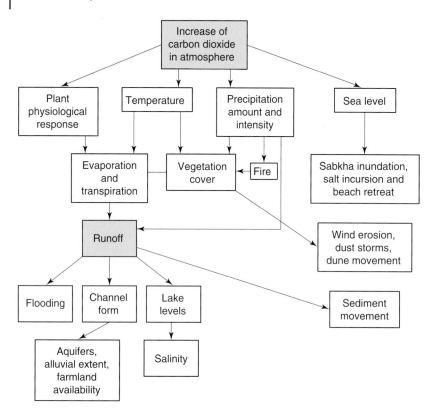

Figure 12.4 The potential responses of desert environments to increases of carbon dioxide in the atmosphere.

for instance, become wetter because of a more northerly intrusion by the Intertropical Convergence Zone (ITCZ) (Evans, 2010). There is a wide consensus that the south-western USA will become more arid (Seager et al., 2007; Seager and Vecchi, 2010). A review of global climate models for Australia suggests that over many areas droughts will become more intense and more frequent (Kirono et al., 2011). Zeng and Yoon (2009) have argued that as conditions become drier and vegetation cover is reduced, there may be vegetation–albedo feedbacks which will serve to enhance any aridity trend. By 2099 their model indicates that globally the warm desert area may expand by 8.5 million km^2 or 34%. However, some areas may experience more frequent hurricane activity and there may also be changes in ENSO frequency and intensity, though this latter aspect of climate change is still characterized by highly divergent model results (Latif and Keenlyside, 2009). Figure 12.5 shows those areas in the world where the IPCC (2007a) proposes that precipitation levels may fall by over 10%, and the increasing dryness forecast for the Sahara is clear.

12.4 Wind Erosivity and Erodibility

Changes in climate could affect wind erosion either through their impact on erosivity or through their effect on erodibility. The former is controlled by a range of wind variables including velocity, frequency, duration, magnitude, shear, and turbulence. For example, Bullard et al. (1996) have shown how dune activity varies in the South-West Kalahari in response to decadal scale variability in wind velocity, while over a longer timescale there is evidence that trade-wind velocities may have been elevated during the Pleistocene glacials. Unfortunately, General Circulation Models (GCMs) as yet give little indication of how these characteristics might be modified in a warmer world, so that prediction of future changes in wind erosivity is problematic. Erodibility is largely controlled by vegetation cover and surface type, both of which can be influenced markedly by climate. In general, vegetation cover, which protects the ground surface and modifies the wind regime, decreases as conditions become more arid. Likewise climate affects surface materials and their erodibility by controlling their moisture content, the nature and amount of clay mineral content (cohesiveness), and organic levels. However, modelling the response of wind erosion to climatic variables on farm land is vastly complex, not least because of the variability of soil characteristics, topographic variations, the state of plant growth and residue decomposition, and the existence of windbreaks. To this needs to be added the temporal variability of aeolian processes and moisture conditions and the effects of different land-management practices (Leys, 1999), which may themselves change with climate change.

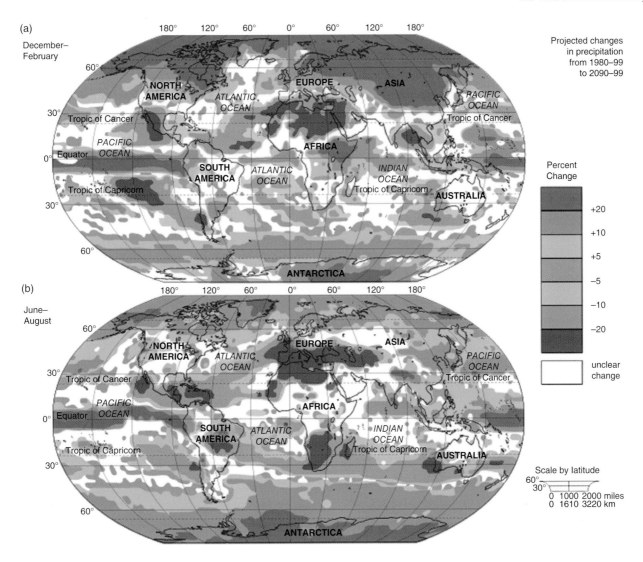

Figure 12.5 The global pattern of future precipitation change for this century as predicted by the IPCC (2007a) for (a) December, January, February and (b) June, July, August. The shaded areas are those where precipitation amounts will fall by 10% or greater. *Source:* IPCC 2007a: FAQ 2.1, figure 2. Reproduced with permission of Intergovernmental Panel on Climate Change.

12.5 Future Dust Storm Activity

The changes in temperature and precipitation conditions that occurred in the twentieth century (combined with land-cover changes) had an influence on the development of dust storms (Goudie and Middleton, 1992). These are events in which visibility is reduced to less than 1 km as a result of particulate matter, such as valuable topsoil, being entrained by wind. This is a process that is most likely to happen when there are high winds and large soil-moisture deficits. Probably the greatest incidence of dust storms occurs when climatic conditions and human pressures combine to make surfaces susceptible to wind attack, as with the Dust Bowl of the 1930s in the United States (Section 4.29). Attempts to relate past dust storm frequencies to simple climatic

parameters or antecedent moisture conditions have frequently demonstrated rather weak relationships (Bach et al., 1996), confirming the view that complex combinations of processes control dust emissions.

The nature of future dust activity will depend on three main factors: anthropogenic modification of desert surfaces (Mahowald and Luo, 2003; Mahowald et al., 2006); natural climatic variability (e.g. ENSO or the NAO); and changes in climate brought about by global warming.

If soil moisture levels decline as a result of changes in precipitation and/or temperature, there is the possibility that dust storm activity could increase in a warmer world (Wheaton, 1990; Routson et al., 2016). A comparison between the Dust Bowl years of the 1930s and model predictions of precipitation and temperature for the Great Plains of Kansas and Nebraska (Figure 12.6)

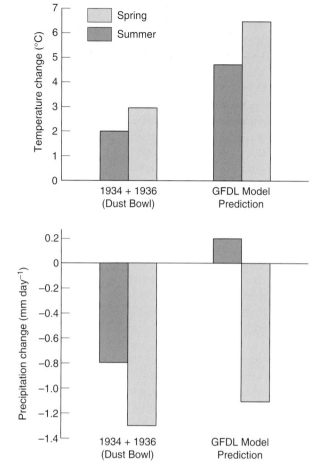

Figure 12.6 Comparison between two 'Dust Bowl years' (1934 and 1936) and the GFDL model prediction for a x 2 CO$_2$ situation for the Great Plains (Kansas and Nebraska). *Source:* adapted from Smith and Tirpak (1990: figure 7.3).

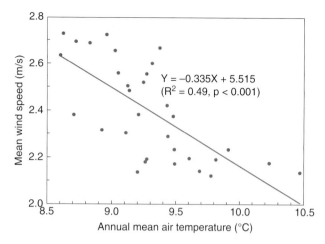

Figure 12.7 The relationship between annual mean wind speed and air temperature over China, 1969–2000. *Source:* adapted from Xu et al. (2006: figure 4), and courtesy of the AGU.

indicates that mean conditions could be similar to those of the 1930s under enhanced greenhouse conditions (Smith and Tirpak, 1990), or even worse (Rosenzweig and Hillel, 1993). Munson et al. (2011) also argued that with predicted increases in droughts in the western USA, perennial vegetation cover will be reduced and aeolian activity will be increased.

If dust storm activity were to increase as a response to global warming it is possible that this could have a feedback effect on precipitation that would lead to further decreases in soil moisture (Tegen et al., 1996; Miller and Tegen, 1998). It is also possible that increased dust delivery to the oceans could affect biogeochemical cycling, by providing nutrients to plankton, which in turn could draw down carbon dioxide from the atmosphere (Ridgwell, 2002). However, the impact and occurrence of dust storms will depend a great deal on land management practices, and recent decreases in dust storm activity in North Dakota have resulted from conservation measures (Todhunter and Cihacek, 1999).

Recent research in China has demonstrated that over the last five decades or so there have been changes in wind activity that have been related to warming trends. Various modelling studies have suggested that more generally in low latitudes extreme wind events will become less frequent with global warming, and this has been confirmed for the USA (Breslow and Sailor, 2002). The normally proposed explanation for this 'atmospheric stilling' is that according to GCMs, high latitudes will warm more than low (Section 8.1), that there will therefore be a smaller equator-to-pole difference in temperature, and that as a result weaker monsoonal wind speeds will prevail. The general message is that as warming has occurred wind velocities have fallen (e.g. Xu et al., 2006; Wang et al., 2007) (Figure 12.7). In northern China, there is some evidence that dust storm activity has indeed decreased in recent warming decades, partially in response to changes in the atmospheric circulation and associated wind conditions (Jiang et al., 2010) and might decrease therefore still further in a warming world (Zhu et al., 2008a). Another factor of potential importance in China is that dust activity could be reduced by the earlier spring greening of vegetation resulting from higher temperatures (Fan et al., 2014). It is by no means certain that wind velocities will decrease in all monsoonal regions and in one of the most important dust-generating areas – the Bodélé depression in the Central Sahara – gusty, high velocity winds may increase dust activity in coming decades (Washington et al., 2009).

12.6 Sand Dunes

Sand dunes, because of the intimate relationships between vegetation cover and sand movement, are highly susceptible to changes of climate, though there are huge

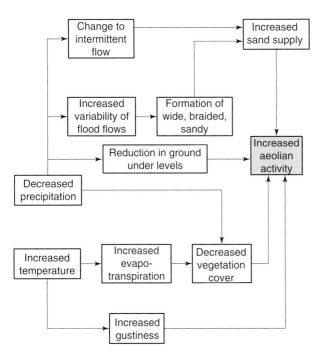

Figure 12.8 The influence of decreased precipitation and increased temperatures on aeolian activity.

Figure 12.9 These linear dunes in the south-west Kalahari have active crests at the present day, particularly in dry, windy years, but may become still more active in coming decades (ASG).

challenges in predicting just how much dune systems may be affected (Knight et al., 2004; Thomas and Wiggs, 2008). One problem is that active and stabilized dunes often coexist under the same climatic conditions (Yizhaq et al., 2007). There may also be lags in terms of response and these may be related to physical–biological interactions. So, for example, a dune may become vegetated when the wind power is sufficiently low, and once vegetated a much higher wind-stress is needed to destroy the vegetation and re-activate the dunes. Vegetation dynamics are a major consideration (Hugenholtz and Wolfe, 2005). In addition there are multiple environmental factors involved in determining dune activity: wind energy, rainfall, snow cover, soil moisture, groundwater conditions, vegetation cover, fire frequency, etc. (Figure 12.8).

Some areas, such as the south-west Kalahari (Stokes et al., 1997) or portions of the High Plains of the United States (Gaylord, 1990), may have been especially prone to changes in precipitation and/or wind velocity because of their location in climatic zones that are close to a climatic threshold between dune stability and activity (Figure 12.9). Development in the use of luminescence dating of sand grains and studies of explorers' accounts (Muhs and Holliday, 1995) have led to the realization that such marginal dune fields have undergone episodic and repeated phases of change at decadal and century timescales in response to extended drought events during the Holocene (Forman et al., 2006, 2008). In the Canadian Prairies, changes in precipitation amounts and decreases in wind velocity have led to increasing dune

stability since the mid-1900s (Hugenholtz and Wolfe, 2005), while over the last few hundreds of years relatively stable parabolic dunes have tended to replace active barchans (Wolfe and Hugenholtz, 2009).

The mobility of desert dunes *(M)* is directly proportional to the sand-moving power of the wind, but indirectly proportional to vegetation cover (Lancaster, 1995: 238). An index of the wind's sand-moving power is given by the percentage of the time *(W)* the wind blows above the threshold velocity (4.5 m per second) for sand transport. Vegetation cover is a function of the ratio between annual rainfall *(P)* and potential evapotranspiration *(PE)*. Thus, $M = W/(P/PE)$. Empirical observations in the United States and southern Africa indicate that dunes are completely stabilized by vegetation when M is <50, and are fully active when M is >200. Muhs and Maat (1993) used the output from GCMs combined with this dune mobility index to show that sand dunes and sand sheets on the Great Plains are likely to become reactivated over wide areas, particularly if the frequencies of wind speeds above the threshold velocity were to increase by even a moderate amount. For another part of the United States, Washington State, Stetler and Gaylord (1996) suggested that with a 4°C warming vegetation would be greatly reduced and that as a consequence dune mobility would increase by over 400%.

Scenarios for dune remobilization under conditions of global warming have been developed for the mega-Kalahari in southern Africa (Thomas et al., 2005) (Figure 12.10). Much of this vast thirstland is currently mostly vegetated and stable, but GCMs suggest that by 2099 all dune fields, from South Africa and Botswana in the south to Zambia and Angola in the north, will be reactivated. This could disrupt pastoral and agricultural systems and might lead to loss of agricultural land, the overwhelming of buildings, roads, canals, runways, and

Figure 12.10 Modelled dunefield activity by the end of the twenty-first century. *Source:* modified from Thomas et al. (2005: figure 8). Reproduced with permission from Macmillan.

the like, abrasion of structures and equipment, damage to crops, and the impoverishment of soil structure. However, Ashkenazy et al. (2012) criticized the work of Thomas and colleagues and argued that the Kalahari was unlikely to be subjected to sufficiently dry and windy conditions for wholesale mobilization to occur by the end of this century. Predictions of future dune state also require a consideration of fire management and grazing strategies (Mayaud et al., 2017).

For Tibet, Liu et al. (2016) suggested that a decline in surface wind-speed and an increase in precipitation would lead to a reduction in dune activity in coming decades. It has also been suggested that as a consequence of 'atmospheric stilling' dunes in northern China have become more stable (Wang et al., 2007), though this is not invariably true, partly because of human pressures. Thus it is possible that as warming continues and wind velocities decrease dunes may become still more stable in the region, but a great deal will also depend upon future soil moisture conditions which in turn will depend on precipitation amounts and levels of evapotranspiration. Another possible influence on future dune activity, as it has been in the past, may be changes in the frequency and severity of wildfires (Sankey et al., 2009).

Once again, however, it is important to stress that the activity of dunes and of dust storms may be dependent on drought interludes, but that the effects of such interludes, both in the past (see, for example, Cook et al., 2009; Seifan, 2009) and in the future, may be greatly affected by miscellaneous anthropogenic activities (Yizhaq et al., 2009): deforestation, overgrazing, dune removal, extension of irrigation, surface disturbance, mining, fire, etc.

12.7 Rainfall and Runoff

Some dry regions will suffer particularly large diminutions in soil moisture levels (Wetherald and Manabe, 2002) and annual runoff (sometimes 60% or more). Drylands appear to be more vulnerable than humid regions (Chiew et al., 1996; Guo et al., 2002). The sensitivity of runoff to changes in precipitation is complex, but in some environments quite small changes in rainfall can cause proportionally larger changes in runoff. As rainfall amounts decrease, the proportion that is lost to stream flow through evapotranspiration increases. Our modelling capability in this area is still imperfect and different types of model indicate differing degrees of sensitivity to climatic change (Nash and Gleick, 1991).

However, highly significant runoff changes and rates of aquifer recharge (Rosenberg et al., 1999) may be anticipated for the semi-arid environments of the south-west

United States (Thomson et al., 2005). Revelle and Waggoner (1983) argued that the effects of increased evapotranspiration losses as a result of a 2°C rise in temperature would be particularly serious in those regions where the mean annual precipitation is less than about 400 mm (Table 12.1). Projected summer dryness in such areas may be accentuated by a positive feedback process involving decreases in cloud cover and associated increases in radiation absorption on the ground consequent upon a reduction in soil moisture levels (Manabe and Wetherald, 1986). Shiklomanov (1999) suggested that in arid and semi–arid areas as a whole an increase in mean annual temperature by 1° to 2° and a 10% decrease in precipitation could reduce annual river runoff by up to 40–70% (Table 12.2).

One factor that makes estimates of rainfall-runoff relationships complicated is the possible effect of higher CO_2 concentrations on plant physiology and transpiration capacity. At higher CO_2 concentrations transpiration rates are less and this could lead to increases in runoff (e.g. Gedney et al., 2006). It is also important to remember that future runoff will be conditioned by nonclimatic factors, such as land-use and land-cover change, the construction of reservoirs, groundwater storage, and water demand (Conway et al., 1996).

River channels in arid regions are particularly sensitive to changes in precipitation characteristics and runoff (Nanson and Tooth, 1999). They can display rapid switches between incision and aggradation over short time periods in response to quite modest changes in climate. This is particularly true in the case of the arroyos of the American south-west, which have displayed major changes in form since the 1880s (Section 6.10). There has been considerable debate as to the causes of phases of trenching, and it is far from easy to disentangle

Table 12.1 Approximate percentage decrease in runoff for a 2 °C increase in temperatures.

Initial mean temperature (°C)	Precipitation (mm yr^{-1})					
	200	300	400	500	600	700
−2	26	20	19	17	17	14
0	30	23	23	19	17	16
2	39	30	24	19	17	16
4	47	35	25	20	17	16
6	100	35	30	21	17	16
8		53	31	22	20	16
10		100	34	22	22	16
12			47	32	22	19
14			100	38	23	19

Source: from data in Revelle and Waggoner (1983).

ASKHAM BRYAN
COLLEGE
LEARNING RESOURCES

Table 12.2 Results of assessments of impacts of climate change on annual river runoff (basins and areas of water deficit).

Region and basin	Temperature	Precipitation	Change in annual runoff (%)
Mean for seven large basins in the western USA	+2	−10	−40 to −76
Hypothetical arid basins	+1	−10	
Colorado River, USA	+1	−10	−50
Peace River, USA	+1	−10	−50
River basins in Utah and Nevada, USA	+2	−10	−60
River basins in the steppe zones of European Russia	+1	−10	−60

Source: after various sources in Shiklomanov (1999: table 2.1).

anthropogenic from climatic causes, but in many cases it is fluctuations in either rainfall amount or intensity that have been the controlling factor (Graf et al., 1991). Thus, the sorts of changes in runoff discussed here could have a profound influence on channel characteristics. These in turn impact on humans because they can lead to changes in the agricultural suitability of bottomlands, modify local aquifers, modify sediment inputs into reservoirs, and cut into engineering structures. Arroyo incision can also lead to the draining of riverbed marshes (cienegas) and to settlement abandonment (Hereford et al., 1995).

12.8 Lake Levels

Closed depressions are widespread in arid lands and their water levels and salinity characteristics respond rapidly and profoundly to climatic changes (Grimm et al., 1997). This generalization applies both to large and small lakes. In the twentieth century, for example, some of the largest arid-zone lakes (e.g. Chad, the Aral Sea, the Caspian, and the Great Salt Lake of Utah) have shown large variations in their extents, partly in some cases because of human activities, but also because of climatic fluctuations within their catchments.

In the early 1960s, prior to the development of the Sahel Drought, Lake Chad had an area of 23,500 km², but by the 1980s had split into two separate basins and had an area of only 1500 km². The Caspian Sea was -29.10 metres in 1977, but in 1995 had risen to -26.65 m, an increase of 2.45 m in just 17 years. Similarly impressive changes have occurred in recent decades in the level of the Great Salt Lake in Utah, with a particularly rapid rise taking place between 1964 and 1985 of nearly 6 m. Changes in lake level of these sorts of magnitude have an impact on a diverse range of human activities, ranging from fisheries and irrigation to recreation. Moreover, the drying-up of lake beds can have

adverse effects on air quality and human health through the liberation of dust, as has been found as a result of the humanly induced desiccation of the Aral Sea (Indoitu et al., 2012), Lake Urmia in Iran (Sotoudeheian et al., 2016), and Owens Lake, California (Reheis, 1997). Lakes will respond to the temperature and precipitation changes that may result from global warming. A fall of 9 m by the end of the present century has been predicted for the Caspian (Elguindi and Giorgi, 2006).

12.9 Sea-level Rise and Arid-zone Coastlines

One consequence of global warming will be a rise in sea level at around 5 mm per year (50 cm per century). Arid coastlines will be affected by this process, which could potentially be especially serious for low-lying shores such as the sabkhas of the United Arab Emirates and elsewhere in the Middle East (Figure 12.11a). Sabkhas result from the interaction of various depositional and erosional processes that create a low-angle surface in the zone of tidal influence. This means that they are subject to periodic inundation and might be vulnerable to modest sea-level rise and to any increase in storm-surge events. Given the degree of infrastructural development that has taken place in their proximity, this is a serious issue for cities like Abu Dhabi (Figure 12.11b). However, it is likely that many sabkhas will be able to cope with modestly rising sea levels, for a range of processes contribute to their accretion. These include algal stromatolite growth, faecal pellet deposition, aeolian inputs, and evaporite precipitation. Some of these can cause markedly rapid accretion (Schrieber, 1986), even in the absence of a very well-developed plant cover. Moreover, as sea level (and groundwater) rises, surface lowering by deflational processes will be reduced.

(a)

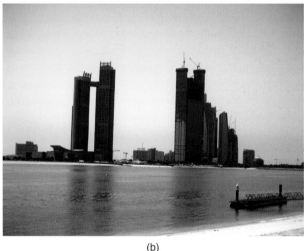

(b)

Figure 12.11 Sabkhas (a) in an undeveloped form on the coast of central Oman, and (b) after major urban development in Abu Dhabi, United Arab Emirates (ASG).

Among arid-zone coastal environments that may be particularly susceptible to sea-level rise are deltaic areas subject to subsidence and sediment starvation (e.g. the Nile) and areas where ground subsidence is occurring as a result of fluid abstraction (e.g. Long Beach, California). Whereas the IPCC prediction of sea-level rise is 30–100 cm per century, rates of deltaic subsidence in the Nile Valley are 35–50 cm per century, and in other parts of the world rates of land subsidence produced by oil, gas, or groundwater abstraction can be up to 500 cm per century (see Section 6.4). Rising sea levels can be expected to cause increased flooding, accelerated erosion, and accelerated incursion of saline water up estuaries and into aquifers. Coastal lagoon, spit, and barrier systems (such as those of Ras Al Khaimah in the United Arab Emirates) may be especially sensitive (Goudie et al., 2000), as will coastlines that have been deprived of

sediment nourishment by dam construction across rivers (see Section 6.14).

12.10 Salt Weathering and Salinization

Salt weathering is a major geomorphological process in many drylands and it poses a threat to many man-made structures, both ancient and modern (Goudie and Viles, 1997). Global warming could influence salt weathering in a variety of ways (Table 12.3). In low-lying coastal areas sea-level rise will impact upon groundwater conditions. The balance between fresh aquifers and sea-water incursion is a very delicate one. Recent modelling, using the Ghyben–Herzberg relationship, suggests that in the Nile Delta, where subsidence is occurring at a rate of 4.7 mm per year, over-pumping is taking place, and less freshwater flushing is being achieved by the dammed Nile, a 50 cm rise in Mediterranean level will cause an additional intrusion of salt water by 9.0 km into the Nile Delta aquifer (Sherif and Singh, 1999; Sušnik et al., 2015).

In addition, many arid areas may become still more arid. Moisture deficits will increase and stream flows will decrease, partly because of increased evaporative loss promoted by higher temperature, and partly because of decreased precipitation inputs. Lakes and reservoirs will suffer more evaporative losses and so could become more saline. In many areas stream flow will decline by 60–70%. Greater moisture stress may lead to an expansion in the quest for irrigation water, there may be less freshwater inputs to flush out estuarine zones, and rates of evaporative concentration of salt may increase (Utset and Borroto, 2001). Such tendencies could lead to an increase in salinization (Szabolcs, 1994). Conversely, in some areas falling groundwater levels may follow on from decreased recharge, and this could lead to improvements in the incidence of groundwater-induced salinization.

Table 12.3 Global warming and salinization.

Negative effects	Positive effects
Increased moisture stress will lead to a greater need for irrigation.	Groundwater levels may fall.
Higher evaporation losses will lead to increased salt concentrations.	
Lesser freshwater inputs will reduce estuarine flushing and decrease replenishment in coastal aquifers.	
Higher sea levels will cause change of salinity in estuaries and in coastal aquifers.	

Guide to Reading

Goudie, A.S. (2002) *Great Warm Deserts of the World: Landscapes and Evolution*. Oxford: Oxford University Press. A survey of the response of the world's deserts to past climatic changes.

Goudie, A.S. (2012) *Arid and Semi-arid Geomorphology*. Cambridge: Cambridge University Press.
A general treatment of the geomorphology of the world's drylands.

Williams, M.A.J. and Balling, R.C. Jr. (1996) *Interactions of Desertification and Climate*. London: Arnold.
A consideration of human impacts on desert environments, including a discussion of the effects of future climate changes.

Williams, M. (2014) *Climate Change in Deserts, Past, Present And Future*. Cambridge: Cambridge University Press. A masterful review of the evidence for, and effects of, climate changes in deserts, including those in the future.

13

Conclusion

CHAPTER OVERVIEW

This concluding chapter provides some general reflections on some of the issues that have been discussed elsewhere in the book. It stresses the role of non-industrial and pre-industrial societies in modifying the Earth's environment, discusses how human impacts have proliferated through time, considers to what extent the changes we have wrought are reversible, assesses to what extent some environments are particularly sensitive to change, explores the links between local changes and those in the whole Earth System, discusses environmental problems in China, examines the problems of deciding whether certain environmental changes are natural or anthropogenic, tries to place the significance of potential future global warming in the context of other anthropogenic pressures, and concludes by highlighting the uncertainties that remain with regard to predicting the future.

13.1 The Power of Non-industrial and Pre-industrial Civilizations

Marsh (1864) was correct, nearly a century and a half ago, to express his cogently argued views on the importance of human agency in environmental change. Since his time the impact that humans have had on the environment has increased, as has our awareness of this impact. There has been 'a screeching acceleration of so many processes that bring ecological change' (McNeill, 2000: 4) and particularly massive changes have taken place during the Great Acceleration of the past half-century (Waters et al., 2016). However, it is worth making the point here that although much of the concern expressed about the undesirable effects humans have tends to focus on the role played by sophisticated industrial societies, this should not blind us to the fact that many highly significant environmental changes were and are being achieved by non-industrial societies.

In recent years it has become evident that fire, in particular, enabled early societies to alter vegetation substantially, so that plant assemblages that were once thought to be natural climatic climaxes may in reality be in part anthropogenic fire climaxes. This applies to many areas of both savanna and mid-latitude grassland (Sections 2.12 and 2.15). Such alteration of natural vegetation has been shown to pre-date the arrival of European settlers in the Americas (Denevan, 1992), New Zealand, and elsewhere. The effects of fire may have been compounded by the use of the stone axe and by the grazing effects of domestic animals. In turn the removal and modification of vegetation would have led to adjustment in fauna. It is also apparent that soil erosion resulting from vegetation removal has a long history (Dotterweich, 2013) and that it was regarded as a threat by the classical authors.

Recent studies (Section 2.16) tend to suggest that some of the major environmental changes in highland Britain and similar parts of Western Europe that were once explained by climatic changes can be more effectively explained by the activities of Mesolithic and Neolithic peoples. This applies, for example, to the decline in the numbers of certain plants in the pollen record, to the development of peat bogs and podzolization (Section 4.12), to soil erosion and colluviation, and to coastal dune reactivation (Goudie and Viles, 2016). Even soil salinization started at an early date because of the adoption of irrigation practices in arid areas, and its effects on crop yields were noted in Iraq more than 4000 years ago (Section 4.3). Similarly (Section 3.7) there is an increasing body of evidence that the hunting practices of early civilizations may have caused great changes in the world's mega-fauna as early as 11,000 years ago – a phase called 'Pleistocene Overkill – though there is still a debate as to the role that severe and abrupt climatic changes played (Meltzer, 2015).

Human Impact on the Natural Environment: Past, Present and Future, Eighth Edition. Andrew S. Goudie.
© 2019 John Wiley & Sons Ltd. Published 2019 by John Wiley & Sons Ltd.
Companion website: www.wiley.com/go/goudie/human-impact-natural-environment

In spite of the increasing pace of world industrialization and urbanization, it is ploughing and pastoralism which are responsible for many of our most serious environmental problems and which are still causing some of our most widespread changes in the landscape. Thus, soil erosion brought about by agriculture is, it can be argued, a more serious pollutant of the world's waters than is industry: many of the habitat changes which so affect wild animals are brought about through agricultural expansion (Section 3.5); and soil salinization (Section 4.3) and desertification (Section 2.13) can be regarded as two of the most serious problems facing the human race. Land-use changes, such as the conversion of tropical forests (Figure 13.1) to fields, may be as effective in causing anthropogenic changes in climate as the more celebrated burning of fossil fuels and emission of industrial aerosols into the atmosphere. The liberation of CO_2 in the atmosphere through agricultural expansion, changes in surface albedo values, and the production of dust are all major ways in which agriculture may modify world climates. Perhaps most remarkably of all, humans, who only represent roughly 0.5% of the total heterotroph biomass on Earth, appropriate for their use something

Figure 13.1 Rainforest, such as this example in Sabah, Malaysia, is a repository of great biodiversity and also controls local erosion, runoff, and hydrological conditions (ASG).

around one third of the total amount of net primary production on land (Imhoff et al., 2004).

13.2 The Proliferation of Impacts

A further point one can make is that, with developments in technology, the number of ways in which humans are affecting the environment is proliferating. It is these recent changes, because of the uncertainty which surrounds them and the limited amount of experience we have of their potential effects, which have caused greatest concern. Thus it is only since the Second World War, for example, that humans have had nuclear reactors for electricity generation, that they have used powerful pesticides such as DDT, and that they have sent supersonic aircraft into the stratosphere. Likewise, it is only since around the end of the nineteenth century that the world's oil resources have been extensively exploited, that chemical fertilizers have become widely used, that CFCs have been manufactured, and that the internal combustion engine has revolutionized the scale and speed of transport and communications. Mass production of plastic products has only occurred since the 1950s and discarded plastic has a whole range of environmental consequences (Barnes et al., 2009), not least for the oceans (Moore, 2008), where much concern has been expressed about microbeads used in some cosmetic and household products (Rochman et al., 2015). New techniques to obtain gas from shale by hydraulic fracturing (fracking) are likely to be widely adopted in coming decades, but have implications for water quality and seismic activity (Rahm, 2011; Burton et al., 2014). The wholesale adoption of e-technology produces what is called 'e-waste' (Tripathy, 2010), which can contain many hazardous and polluting components (Wagner, 2009) including lithium from discarded batteries (Wanger, 2011). The world has seen a quadrupling in the production and consumption of rare earth elements (scandium, yttrium, and 15 lathanides) since the 1970s, for they have many uses in such areas as energy-efficient lighting systems, hybrid cars, wind turbines, and various low-carbon technologies. This creates environmental risks, including pollution by the acids used in the refining process, and the release of radioactivity from mine tailings and slurries (Migaszewski, and Gałuszka, 2015).

Above all, however, the complexity, frequency, and magnitude of impacts are increasing, partly because of steeply rising population levels and partly because of a general increase in *per capita* consumption (Figure 13.2). Thus some traditional methods of land use, such as shifting agriculture and nomadism, which have been thought to sustain some sort of environmental equilibrium, seem to break down and to cause environmental deterioration

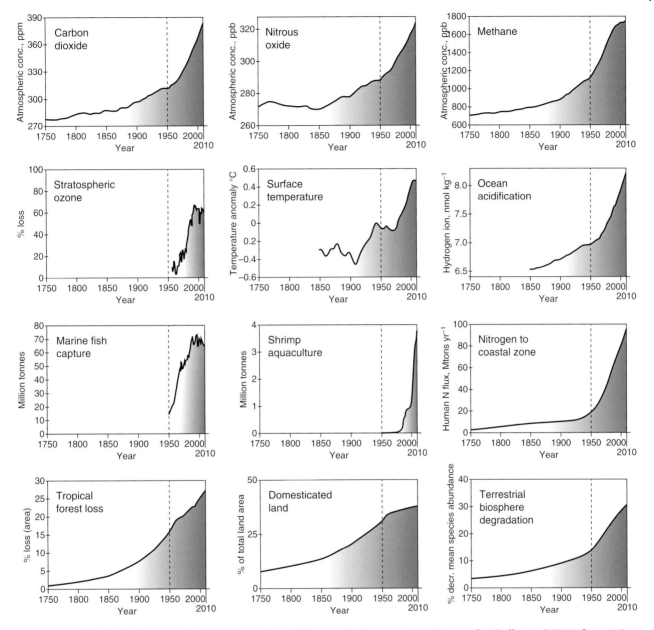

Figure 13.2 Global scale changes in the Earth System since 1750 caused by human activity. *Source:* after Steffen et al. (2010: figure 16). Reproduced with permission of John Wiley & Sons.

when population pressures exceed a particular threshold. For shifting agriculture systems fertility can be maintained under the long fallow cycles characteristic of low-density populations. However, as population levels increase, the fallow cycles necessarily become shorter, and soil fertility levels are not maintained, thereby imposing greater stresses on the land. In many areas shifting cultivation is being abandoned (Van Vliet et al., 2013b).

At the other end of the spectrum, increasing incomes, leisure, and ease of communication have generated a stronger demand for recreation and tourism in the developed nations (Table 13.1). Environmental degradation has, for example, been caused by the proliferation of off-road vehicle use in sensitive environments like deserts (Goossens et al., 2012; Webb and Wilshire, 2012; Westcott and Andrew, 2015; Dewidar et al., 2016). The number of these vehicles has increased more than sevenfold in the USA in the last three decades. Tourism development has created environmental problems, especially in coastal and mountain areas, and can have adverse effects on biodiversity (Pickering and Hill, 2007) and on a whole range of sensitive environments (Newsome et al., 2012). Some of the environmental consequences of

Table 13.1 World international tourist arrivals (in millions).

Year	Number
1950	25.3
1960	69.3
1970	165.8
1980	278.1
1990	439.5
2000	687.0
2005	806.8
2010	950.0
2015	1184.0
2020 (forecast)	1600.0

Source: UN World Tourism Organisation, http://media.unwto.org/press-release/2016-01-18/international-tourist-arrivals-4-reach-record-12-billion-2015 (accessed January 2018).

recreation, which are reviewed at length by Liddle (1997), can be listed as follows:

1) Desecration of cave formations by speleologists.
2) Trampling by human feet leading to soil compaction.

3) Nutrient additions at campsites by people and their pets.
4) Decrease in soil temperatures because of snow compaction by snowmobiles.
5) Footpath erosion and off-road vehicle erosion.
6) Dune reactivation by trampling.
7) Vegetation change due to trampling and collecting.
8) Creating of new habitats by cutting trails and clearing campsites.
9) Pollution of lakes and inland waterways by gasoline discharge from outboard motors and by human waste.
10) Creation of game reserves and protection of ancient domestic breeds.
11) Disturbance of wildlife by proximity of persons and by hunting, fishing, and shooting.
12) Conservation of woodland for pheasant shooting.

Table 13.1 indicates the remarkable growth in international tourism that has taken place since the middle of the twentieth century.

Likewise, it is apparent when considering the range of possible impacts of one major type of industrial development that they are significant. As Table 13.2 indicates,

Table 13.2 Qualitative environmental impacts of mineral industries with particular reference to an oilfield.

Facility	Direction of the impact and reaction to the environment			
	Land	Air	Water	Biocenosis
Well	Alienation of land surface Extraction of oil associated gas, groundwater Pollution by crude oil, refined products, drilling mud Disturbance of internal structure of soil and subsoil Destruction of soil	Pollution by associated gas and volatile hydrocarbons, productions of combustion	Withdrawal of surface water and groundwater Pollution by crude oil and refined products, salination of freshwater Disturbance of water balance of both subsurface and surface waters	Pollution by crude oil and refined products Disturbance and destruction over a limited surface area
Pipeline	Alienation of land Accidental oil spills Disturbance of landforms and internal structure of soil and subsoil	Pollution by volatile hydrocarbons	Disturbance and destruction over limited surface area	
Motor roads	Alienation of land Pollution by oil products Disturbance of landforms and internal structure of soil and subsoil	Pollution by combustion products, volatile hydrocarbons, sulphur dioxide, nitrogen oxides	Pollution by combustion products Disturbances and destruction over limited surface area	
Collection point	Alienation of land Pollution by crude oil and refined products (spills) Disturbance of internal structure of soil and subsoil	Pollution by volatile hydrocarbons	Disturbance and destruction over limited surface area	

Source: Denisova (1977: 650, table 2).

the exploitation of an oilfield and all the activities that it involves (for example, pipelines, new roads, refineries, drilling, etc.) have a wide range of likely effects on land, air, water, and organisms. These include damage to the land surface caused by seismic lines used in hydrocarbon exploration (Figure 13.3).

Conversely, if one takes one ecosystem type as an example – the coral reef – one can see the diversity of stresses to which they are now being exposed (Figure 13.4) as a result of a whole range of different human activities that include global warming, increased sedimentation and pollution from river runoff, and over-harvesting of fish and other organisms (Bellwood et al., 2004; Pendleton et al., 2016).

A very substantial amount of change has been achieved in recent decades. Table 13.3, based on the work of Kates et al. (1990), attempts to make quantitative comparisons of the human impact on ten 'component indicators of the biosphere'. For each component they defined total net change clearly induced by humans to be 0% for 10,000 years ago and 100% for 1985. They estimated dates by which each component had reached successive quartiles (i.e. 5, 50, and 75%) of its 1985 total change. They believe that about half of the components have changed more in the single generation since 1950 than in the whole of human history before that date. It is therefore appropriate to recognize the size and trajectory of what is now called 'The Great Acceleration'.

(a)

(b)

Figure 13.3 Desert surface disturbance caused by seismic lines in the oilfields of Oman (a) at Fahud anticline (ASG) and (b) from Google Earth. *Source:* ©CNES/Astrium. Scale bar 253 m.

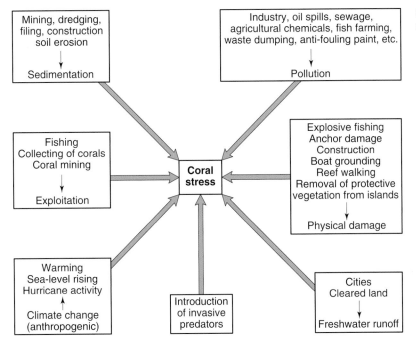

Figure 13.4 Some causes of anthropogenic stress on coral reef ecosystems.

Table 13.3 Chronologies of human-induced transformations.

(a) Quartiles of change from 10,000 BC to mid-1980s.

Form of transformation	Dates of quartiles		
	25%	50%	75%
Carbon releases	1815	1920	1960
Carbon tetrachloride production	1950	1960	1970
Deforested area	1700	1850	1915
Lead releases	1920	1950	1965
Nitrogen releases	1970	1975	1980
Phosphorus releases	1955	1975	1980
Population size	1850	1950	1970
Sulphur releases	1940	1960	1970
Terrestrial vertebrate diversity	1790	1880	1910
Water withdrawals	1925	1955	1975

(b) % change by time of Marsh and Princeton symposium.

Form of transformation	% change	
	1860	1950
Carbon releases	30	65
Carbon tetrachloride production	0	25
Deforested area	50	90
Lead releases	5	50
Nitrogen releases	<1	5
Phosphorus releases	<1	20
Population size	30	50
Sulphur releases	5	40
Terrestrial vertebrate diversity	25–50	75–100
Water withdrawals	15	40

Source: from Kates et al. (1990: table 1.3).

13.3 The Inter-relationships of Changes in the Earth System

It is clear that many environmental problems are now interrelated and trans-boundary in scope so that integrated approaches and international cooperation are required. Indeed, environmental issues and environmental

solutions have become globalized (Steffen et al. 2004: 290). The term Anthropocene was introduced by Crutzen (2002) as a name for a new epoch in Earth's history – an epoch when human activities have 'become so profound and pervasive that they rival, or exceed the great forces of Nature in influencing the functioning of the Earth System' (Steffen, 2010: 443). One can give many examples of how local actions can impact upon the whole global system. For instance, Goudie and Middleton (2006), Shao et al. (2011), and Mahowald et al. (2014) (Figure 13.5) have considered the impact of wind erosion-related dust-storm activity on the global system. Dust storms affect, *inter alia*, the albedo of ice bodies, radiation levels in the atmosphere, drought intensity, precipitation acidity, nutrient levels in the oceans, the draw-down of carbon dioxide by plankton, the state of coral reefs, the fertility of the Amazonian rainforest, and the transmission of pathogens. In turn, dust-storm activity may be influenced by other geomorphological changes such as desiccation of lakes (Gill, 1996) and the winnowing of fine material from reactivated dunes (Bhattachan et al., 2013, 2014). A second example is provided by permafrost degradation in high latitudes. Thermokarst development and the formation of thaw lakes, caused by global warming and land-cover changes, may play a crucial role in the liberation of a major greenhouse gas – methane (Schaefer et al., 2014), and climate change is expected to increase the initiation

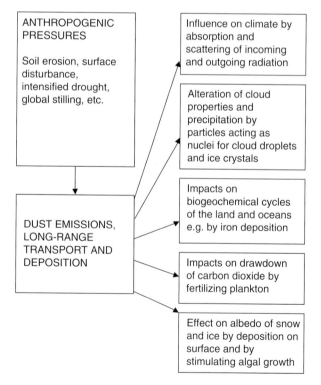

Figure 13.5 The effects of dust storm generation on the Earth system.

and expansion of abrupt thaw features accelerating its release (Schuur et al., 2015). A third example is provided by silica cycling. Land-use changes modify silica transport rates in rivers (Struyf et al., 2010), and so can have an impact on the productivity of coastal waters. While controls on chemical weathering, such as bedrock geology, runoff, and temperature, are the primary drivers of Si transport from the continents to the oceans, recent work has highlighted terrestrial vegetation as an important control over Si cycling. Carey and Fulweiler (2012) have shown that at the regional scale (southern New England, USA) land use and land cover are important variables controlling the net transport of Si from the land to the sea, accounting for at least 40% of dissolved Si fluxes. On the other hand, the post-war profusion of dams means that reservoirs trap biogenic and other forms of particulate, easily soluble silica, and thus starve downstream areas of dissolved Si, significantly reducing its flux to the ocean (Triplett et al., 2008; Tréguer and De La Rocha, 2013). Conversely, most 'natural filters' have either been removed or greatly reduced in their effectiveness by human pressures (Meybeck and Vörösmarty, 2005): wetlands have been drained for agriculture and other land uses, floodplains have become more and more isolated from river channels by dykes and levees, and many estuaries are channelized for navigation.

Related to this interest in Earth Systems and the inter-relationships that exist is the concept of ecosystem (or environmental) services. These form part of our Natural Capital – the wide range of benefits that we derive from nature. We have already mentioned this concept briefly in the context of soils (Section 4.31). De Groot et al. (2002: 395) attempted to give a fourfold classification of ecosystem functions and services:

1) *Regulation functions*: this group of functions relates to the capacity of natural and semi-natural ecosystems to regulate essential ecological processes and life-support systems through bio-geochemical cycles and other biospheric processes. In addition to maintaining ecosystem (and biosphere) health, these regulation functions provide many services that have direct and indirect benefits to humans (such as clean air, water, and soil, and biological control services).

2) *Habitat functions*: natural ecosystems provide refuge and reproduction habitat to wild plants and animals and thereby contribute to the (*in situ*) conservation of biological and genetic diversity and evolutionary processes.

3) *Production functions*: Photosynthesis and nutrient uptake by autotrophs converts energy, carbon dioxide, water, and nutrients into a wide variety of carbohydrate structures which are then used by secondary producers to create an even larger variety of living biomass. This broad diversity in carbohydrate structures provides many ecosystem goods for human consumption, ranging from food and raw materials to energy resources and genetic material.

4) *Information functions*: Because most of human evolution took place within the context of undomesticated habitat, natural ecosystems provide an essential 'reference function' and contribute to the maintenance of human health by providing opportunities for reflection, spiritual enrichment, cognitive development, recreation, and aesthetic experience.

There have now been numerous discussions of the loss of ecosystem services occasioned by the pressures on, for example, estuarine ecosystems (Barbier et al., 2011). In a consideration of wetlands, Zedler and Kercher (2005) divided their ecosystem services into biodiversity support, water quality improvement, flood abatement, and carbon sequestration. These are key functions that are impaired when wetlands are lost or degraded. Firstly, they noted that most efforts to protect wetlands are based on concern for biodiversity, especially waterfowl, shellfish, fish, and sometimes rare plants. Secondly, in tandem with better nutrient management on farms and in cities, wetlands can serve a major role in ameliorating the global problem of nutrient overloading. Thirdly, wetlands are also becoming appreciated for their role in storing and slowing the flow of floodwaters. Fourthly, although wetlands store vast quantities of carbon in their vegetation and in their soils, they also contribute more than 10% of the annual global emissions of the greenhouse gas methane (CH_4) and can also be a significant source of CO_2 under some conditions.

Soils also provide a series of ecosystem services. Dominati et al. (2010) classified their roles as follows:

Fertility role: soil nutrient cycles ensure fertility renewal and the delivery of nutrients to plants, therefore contributing to plant growth.

Filter and reservoir role: soils fix and store solutes passing through them and therefore they purify water. They also store water for plants to use and take part in flood mitigation.

Structural role: soils provide physical support to plants, animals, and human infrastructures.

Climate regulation role: soils take part in climate regulation through carbon sequestration and greenhouse gases (N_2O and CH_4) emissions regulation.

Biodiversity conservation role: soils are a reservoir of biodiversity. They provide habitat for thousands of species regulating, for instance, pest control or the disposal of wastes.

Resource role: soils can be a source of materials like peat and clay.

Coral reefs are another ecosystem type that provides many ecosystem services. Among those listed by Moberg and Folke (1999) are the following:

1) Coral reefs protect the shoreline from currents, waves, and storms.
2) Coral reefs function as important spawning, nursery, breeding, and feeding areas for a multitude of organisms.
3) Being one of the most species-rich habitats of the world, coral reefs are important in maintaining a vast biological diversity and genetic library for future generations.
4) Coral reefs function as nitrogen fixers in nutrient-poor environments.
5) Coral reefs can transform, detoxify, and sequester wastes released by humans, thus providing a cleansing service.
6) Biochemical processes on coral reefs play a significant role in the world's calcium and carbon balances.
7) Coral reefs support recreation and tourism.

A final example of the provision of ecosystem services is provided by the forests of Amazonia. As Foley et al. (2007: 25–26) wrote:

> Many of the ecosystem goods and services derived from the Amazon Basin (e.g. from timber, pasture, and soybean production), are easily recognized and are revealed on local scales – often within individual land parcels that are specifically managed for those purposes. Other ecosystem services, such as pollination and flood control, are somewhat less obvious and may appear over larger spatial scales, extending over complex landscapes and whole watersheds. Tropical rainforests also provide ecosystem services that are manifested at the scale of the whole Amazon Basin and, indeed, the planet. For example, rainforests in the Amazon sequester carbon from the global atmosphere, regulate the water balance and flow of the entire Amazon River system, influence the patterns of climate and air chemistry over much of the continent, and may even ameliorate the spread of vector-borne and water-borne diseases across the region.

Finally, it is important to appreciate that not all human impacts have adverse effects on all ecosystem services provision. Invasive species, though generally regarded as detrimental (Sections 2.18 and 3.2), also provide some valuable services, including erosion control and creating effective food sources for pollinating insects (Pejchar and Mooney, 2009). With regard to the future, it is evident that climate change will have a major impact on many types of ecosystem services – a theme investigated in the context of the USA by Nelson et al. (2013).

13.4 Human Impacts on the Environment in China

Some major countries have shown remarkable growth in recent decades (Table 13.4), notably China, India, and Brazil. One of the most interesting facets of the study of the human impact has been to study the speed and range of human impacts that have occurred as a result of this growth. This can be illustrated by China. This huge country has seen a dramatic increase in population, urban growth, energy consumption, industrial production, water abstraction, construction of great dams (e.g. the Three Gorges Project), car use, and the like. Figures 13.6 and 13.7 show the recent car and coal production. The former increased from 1.55 million units per year in 2000, to 21.1 million units between 2000 and 2015. Internal tourism has also grown and has set in train a whole suite of environmental concerns (Zhong et al., 2011). As a consequence of all these trends there has been a proliferation and intensification of many environmental problems. These are listed in Table 13.5. As we have seen for other parts of the world elsewhere in this book, there have been plant invasions, loss of habitats (including forests, wetlands, and mangrove swamps), extinction of mammals (most tragically the Yangtze dolphin), over-exploitation of groundwater, saltwater intrusion, decreases in river flows because of dam construction and water abstraction, accelerated wind and water erosion of soils, soil acidification, desertification, land subsidence, permafrost degradation, landslide generation, glacier retreat in the face of global warming, accelerated coastal retreat because of sediment starvation, eutrophication of water bodies, the growth of algal blooms offshore, the build-up of heat in cities as a result of the heat-island effect, and a wide range of types of air, water, and soil pollution, including those caused by rare earth elements, of which China is the world's biggest producer. Air pollution probably causes in excess of 400,000 premature deaths a year in China, a country which has been termed the 'air pollution capital of the world' (Watts, 2005). Steps are being taken to mitigate some of these problems (Yi et al., 2007), and not all environmental problems are getting worse, either because of legislation or because of more efficient use of energy sources. China has instituted a massive re-afforestation policy, though it is not always soundly based in ecological terms (Cao et al., 2011). In addition, some problems, such as increased fogs (Niu et al.,

Table 13.4 Some recent developments in Brazil, China, and India.

	1981	1991	2001	2009	2015
(a) Air transport. Passengers carried (in millions).					
Brazil	12.6	19.2	34.3	67.9	102
China	3.2	19.5	72.7	229.0	436
India	7.6	10.7	16.9	54.4	99
(b) Energy production (kt of oil equivalent).					
	1981	**1991**	**2001**	**2008**	**2013**
Brazil	66541	104779	152152	228127	2529000
China	612319	894968	1092157	1993306	2623700
India	200049	301567	374522	468307	523300
(c) Carbon dioxide emissions (kt).					
	1981	**1991**	**2001**	**2007**	**2012**
Brazil	171666	219151	339616	368016	298942
China	1450314	2582424	3484512	6533018	12454710
India	374516	737248	1202858	1611043	3002895

Source: World Bank, http://data.worldbank.org/indicator (accessed January 2018).

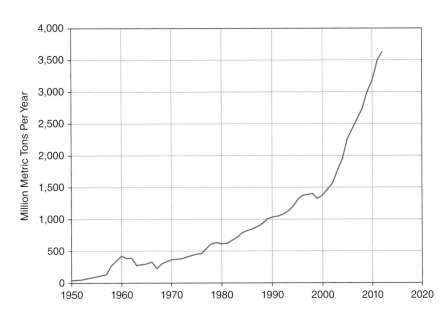

Figure 13.6 Trends in annual coal production in China since 1950. The figure for 2015 was 3.68 billion tonnes. *Source:* https://commons.wikimedia.org/wiki/File:China_Coal_Production.png (accessed January 2018).

2010) and dust storms, may at least in part be the result of natural climate changes. Nevertheless, through the burning of fossil fuels China is becoming an increasingly major source of global greenhouse gas emissions, its desire for wood drives deforestation in other countries, it is responsible for a substantial portion of world fish consumption, and it exports sulphur dioxide pollution (of which it is the world's largest culprit) to other parts of the Pacific rim (Liu and Diamond, 2005). It may also be the world's biggest emitter of nitrogen oxides (Vennemo et al., 2009).

13.5 Are Changes Reversible?

It is evident that while humans have imposed many undesirable and often unexpected changes on the environment, they often have the capacity to modify the rate of such changes or to reverse them. There are cases where this is not possible: once soil has been eroded from an area it cannot be restored; once a plant or animal has become extinct it cannot be brought back; and once a laterite iron pan has become established (Section 4.11) it is difficult to destroy.

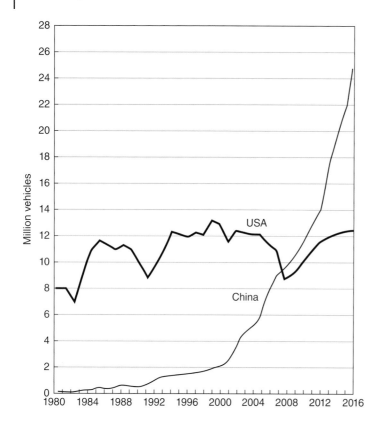

Figure 13.7 Trends in car production in China and the USA since 1980. Chinese production is now roughly double that of the USA.

However, through the work of Marsh and others, people became aware that many of the changes that had been set in train needed to be reversed or reduced in degree. Sometimes this has simply involved discontinuing a practice which has proved undesirable (such as the cavalier use of DDT or CFCs), or replacing it with another which is less detrimental in its effects. Often, however, specific measures have been taken which have involved deliberate decisions of management and conservation. Denson (1970), for example, outlined a sophisticated six-stage model for wildlife conservation:

1) Immediate physical protection from humans and from changes in the environment.
2) Educational efforts to awaken the public to the need for protection and to gain acceptance of protective measures.
3) Life-history studies of the species to determine their habitat requirements and the causes of their population decline.
4) Dispersion of the stock to prevent loss of the species by disease or by a chance event such as fire.

5) Captive breeding of the species to assure higher survival of young, to aid research, and to reduce the chances of catastrophic loss.
6) Habitat restoration or rehabilitation when this is necessary before introducing the species.

Many conservation measures have been successful, while others have created as many problems as they were intended to solve. This applies, for example, to certain schemes for the reduction of coast erosion (Section 6.14). On balance, however, there has been notable progress in dealing with such problems as the depletion of stratospheric ozone, urban smogs in Los Angeles (Section 7.14), and acid rain in Europe and North America (Section 7.15). With regard to these successful attempts to reduce pollution, the Kuznets Environmental Curve (Grossman and Krueger, 1995) models the relationship between economic development and environmental pollution (Figure 13.8). Some forms of local pollution (e.g. sulphur dioxide, lead) have declined significantly in developed industrial countries, despite economic growth. This follows a general pattern of poor countries being relatively unpolluted, middle-income countries being more polluted, and rich countries clean again. Many examples

Table 13.5 Examples of human impacts on the environment in China.

Acid rain	Tang et al., 2010
Acidification of soils	Guo et al., 2010
Acid mine drainage	Tao et al., 2012
Aeolian desertification	Hu et al., 2012
Aerosol pollution	Tie and Cao, 2009
Air pollution	Sheehan et al., 2014
Algal blooms	Wang et al., 2015b
Alien plant invasions	Weber et al., 2008
Coast erosion	Xu et al., 2009
Decreased sediment flux to coast	Chu et al., 2009
Delta erosion	Yang et al., 2011
Deforestation	Zhang and Song, 2006
Groundwater depletion	Grogan et al., 2015
Heavy metal pollution	Li et al., 2014
Karst rock desertification	Huang and Cai, 2007
Lake eutrophication	Le et al., 2010
Land degradation	Zhang et al., 2007
Land subsidence	Ye et al., 2016
Landslide generation	Huang and Chan, 2004
Lead pollution	Gottesfeld and Cherry, 2011
Mammal extinction	Turvey et al., 2007
Mangrove loss	Chen et al., 2009
Mercury pollution	Li et al., 2012
Municipal waste accumulation	Zhang et al., 2010a
Nitrate pollution	Gu et al., 2013
Nitrogen dioxide pollution	Richter et al., 2005
Organochloride pollution	Yu et al., 2013
Ozone pollution	Zhao et al., 2009
PCB pollution	Wu et al., 2015
Permafrost degradation	Yang et al., 2010b
Persistent organic pollutants	Nixdorf et al., 2015
Rare earth element pollution	Liang et al., 2014
Rocky desertification	Yang et al., 2011
Saltwater intrusion	An et al., 2009
Shrinking glaciers	Wang et al., 2016
Soil erosion	Liu et al., 2010
Soil nutrient loss	Zheng, 2005
Streamflow reduction	Xu and Milliman, 2009
Sulphur dioxide pollution	Lu et al., 2010
Sunshine hours depletion	Wang et al., 2012
Urban heat island build-up	Tan et al., 2010
Vehicular emissions	Wang et al., 2010
Water pollution	Miao et al., 2015
Wetland loss	Cui et al., 2015
Wind erosion	Du et al., 2015

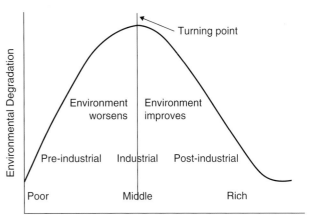

Figure 13.8 The Kuznets Environmental Curve models the relationship between economic development and environmental pollution.

have been given in this book of the introduction of means to address environmental problems (Table 13.6).

The concern with preservation and conservation has been longstanding, with many important landmarks, and the history of environmentalism is reviewed by Guha

Table 13.6 Some examples of means to reduce environmental problems.

Problem	Section reference
Fire occurrence	2.5
Mangrove loss	2.9
Smelter emissions	2.19
Rabbit predation	3.2
Wetland loss	3.5
Whale loss	3.6
Salinization	4.10
Soil erosion	4.30
Urban floods	5.3.6
River pollution	5.6
Acid rain	5.8, 13.6
Mass movements	6.11
Sand drifting	6.13
Beach erosion	6.14
Ozone depletion	7.3
Urban heat island	7.11
Global warming	7.13
Urban air pollution	7.14
Lead pollution	7.15
Species loss	13.5
Landscape degradation	13.5

(2014). Lowe (1983) identified four stages in the history of British nature conservation:

1. The natural history/humanitarium (1830–1890) period
2. The preservation period   (1870–1940)
3. The scientific period   (1910–1970)
4. The popular/political period   (1960–present)

The first of these stages was rooted in a strong enthusiasm for natural history, and the crusade against cruelty to animals. Although many Victorian naturalists were avid collectors, numerous clubs were established to study nature and some of them sought to preserve species to make them available for observation. As we shall see, certain acts were introduced at this time to protect birds. During the preservationist period, there was the formation of a spate of societies devoted to preserving open land and its associated wildlife (for example, the National Trust, 1894; and the Council for the Preservation of Rural England, 1926). There was a growing sense of the vulnerability of wildlife and landscapes to urban and industrial expansion and geographers like Vaughan Cornish (see Goudie, 1972) campaigned for the creation of national parks and the preservation of scenery, made possible through the National Parks and Access to Countryside Act of 1949. From the First World War onwards ecological research developed, and there arose an increasing understanding of ecological relationships. Scientists pressed for the regulation of habitats and species, and the Nature Conservancy was established in 1949. Popular interest in conservation and widespread media attention first developed in the 1960s. This was partly generated by pollution incidents (such as the wrecks of the *Torrey Canyon* and *Amoco Cadiz*) and a gathering sense of impending environmental doom, generated by such persuasive books as Rachel Carson's *Silent Spring* of 1962. Ecology became a political issue in various European nations, including the UK. In many countries major developments in land use, construction, and industrialization now have to be preceded by the production of an Environmental Impact Assessment, and the European Union has introduced measures such as the Landfill Directive (1999), the Water Framework Directive (2000), and the Marine Strategies Directive 2008) to improve the disposal of waste, the ecological status of water resources, and the state of the marine environment. A comprehensive list of international conventions on the environment is available at: https://en.wikipedia.org/wiki/List_of_international_environmental_agreements (accessed January 2018).

At a global scale, a 'Convention Concerning the Protection of the World Cultural and Natural Heritage'

was adopted by the General Conference of UNESCO on 16 November 1972 and came into force on 17 December 1975. It led to the establishment of World Heritage Sites (http://whc.unesco.org/en/list/, accessed January 2018), some of which are 'natural'. There are four criteria for their establishment:

1) 'contains superlative natural phenomena or areas of exceptional natural beauty and aesthetic importance';
2) 'is an outstanding example representing major stages of Earth's history, including the record of life, significant on-going geological processes in the development of landforms, or significant geomorphic or physiographic features';
3) 'is an outstanding example representing significant on-going ecological and biological processes in the evolution and development of terrestrial, fresh water, coastal and marine ecosystems, and communities of plants and animals';
4) 'contains the most important and significant natural habitats for in-situ conservation of biological diversity, including those containing threatened species of outstanding universal value from the point of view of science or conservation'.

Since 2001, UNESCO has also supported the establishment of Geoparks, which aim to help in the protection of our Earth Science heritage (http://www.unesco.org/new/en/natural-sciences/environment/earth-sciences/unesco-global-geoparks/, accessed January 2018).

The world's network of protected areas has grown steadily since the latter part of the nineteenth century (Figure 13.9), and particularly since the early 1960s. Indeed, there are now over 120,000 terrestrial sites world-wide and these cover about 15.4% of the land area, and have a combined area almost the size of South America.

In some countries, and in connection with particular species, conservation and protection have had a long and sometimes successful impact (see Hambler and Canney, 2013). In Britain, for example, the Wild Birds Protection Act dates back to 1880, and the Sea Birds Protection Act even further to 1869. The various acts have been modified and augmented over the years to outlaw egg-collecting, pole-trapping, plumage importation, and the capture or possession of a range of species.

One further ground which gives some basis for hope that humans may be soon reconciled with the environment is that there are some signs of a widespread shift in public attitudes to nature and the environment. We are now in what the supporters of the Anthropocene concept refer to as 'the era of stewardship'. Changing social values, combined with scientific facts, influence political

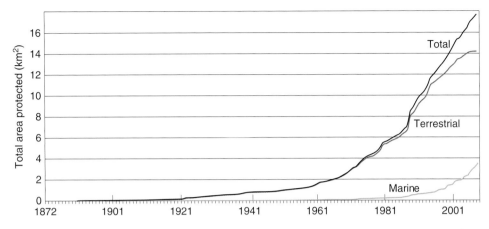

Figure 13.9 Global growth in nationally protected areas from 1872 to 2008. *Source:* based on data from UNEP and World Conservation Monitoring Centre.

action. This point of view, which acts as an antidote for some of the more pessimistic views of the world's future, was elegantly presented by Ashby (1978). He contended that the rudiments of a healthy environmental ethic are developing, and explained (pp. 84–85).

> Its premise is that respect for nature is more moral than lack of respect for nature. Its logic is to put the Teesdale Sandwort ... into the same category of value as a piece of Ming porcelain, the Yosemite Valley in the same category as Chartres Cathedral: a Suffolk landscape in the same category as a painting of the landscape by Constable. Its justification for preserving these and similar things is that they are unique, or irreplaceable, or simply part of the fabric of nature, just as Chartres and the painting by Constable are part of the fabric of civilisation; also that we do not understand how they have acquired their durability and what all the consequences would be if we destroy them.

Although there may be considerable controversy surrounding the precise criteria that can be used to select and manage sites that are particularly worthy of conservation (Goldsmith, 1983), there are nonetheless many motives behind the increasing desire to protect species and landscapes. These can be listed under the following general headings:

1) *The ethical*: It is asserted that wild species have a right to coexist with us on our planet, and that we have no right to exterminate them. Nature, it is maintained, is not simply there for humans to transform and modify as they please for their own utilitarian ends.

2) *The scientific*: We know very little about our surrounding environments, including, for example, the rich insect faunas of the tropical rain forest; therefore such environments should be preserved for future scientific study.

3) *The aesthetic*: Plants and animals, together with landscapes, may be beautiful and so enrich the life of humans.

4) *The need to maintain genetic diversity*: By protecting species we maintain the species diversity upon which future plant- and animal-breeding work will depend. Once genes have been lost (Section 2.22) they cannot be replaced.

5) *Environmental stability*: It is argued that in general the more diverse an ecosystem is, the more checks and balances there are to maintain stability. Thus environments that have been greatly simplified by humans may be inherently unstable, and prone to disease, etc.

6) *Recreational*: Preserved habitats and landscapes have enormous recreational value, and in the case of some game reserves and natural parks may have economic value as well (for example, the safari industry of East Africa).

7) *Economic*: Many of the species in the world are still little known, and there is the possibility that we have great storehouses of plants and animals, which, when knowledge improves, may become useful economic resources.

8) *Future generations*: One of the prime arguments for conservation, whether of beautiful countryside, rare species, soil or mineral resources, is that future generations (and possibly ourselves later in life) will require them, and may think badly of a generation that has squandered them.

9) *Unintended impacts*: As we have seen so often in this book, profligate or unwise actions can lead to

side-effects and consequences that may be disadvantageous to humans.

10) *Spiritual imperatives*: This includes a belief in the need for environmental stewardship.

Some of these arguments are more utilitarian than others (for example, 4, 5, 6, 7, and 9), and some may be subject to doubt – it could, for example, be argued that future generations will have technology to use new resources and may not need some of those we regard as essential – but overall they provide a broadly based platform for the conservation ideal (Myers, 1979).

One growing debate in conservation and restoration ecology is the question of rewilding. The concept was introduced in the late twentieth century as a large-scale conservation strategy. It seeks to restore ecosystem functions and services by reintroducing extirpated native keystone species (particularly megafauna) that drive these processes (Sandom et al., 2013a), and/or by changing land management by, for example, allowing land abandonment and subsequent forest regeneration (Navarro and Pereira, 2012), instigating naturalistic grazing and fire regimes on prairies or in boreal forests, or modifying flood patterns in river systems. Large animals are often important for ecosystem function and biodiversity via trophic cascades (Svenning et al., 2016) and they can be effective ecological engineers. The reintroduction of wolves in Yellowstone National Park (USA) is commonly seen as the flagship practical example of this approach, but schemes have been mooted to reintroduce animals such as wild boar into Scotland (Brown et al., 2011; Sandom et al., 2013b). The introduction of non-native species is, however, much more controversial (Caro and Sherman, 2009: 985), and 'there are no scientific grounds for introducing animals such as elephants, camels, cheetahs and lions into novel environments. Numerous scientifically driven concerns bear on these maverick programmes, including adverse effects of alien species on the ecosystems they are meant to foster; importation of diseases that may leap to native species; escapes that lead to hybridization; and predators jumping fences to endanger livestock.' Moreover, the experimental nature of rewilding means it is largely unproven, and opposition to rewilding is particularly likely where projects are perceived as being imposed from 'outside', with little consideration for local interests (Lorimer et al., 2015).

Also highly controversial is the question of 'de-extinction' or 'resurrection ecology' (Adams, 2016). This is the recreation of extinct species such as: the auroch (*Bos primigenius*) – a large species of cattle previously prevalent throughout Europe; the once highly numerous North American passenger pigeon (*Ectopistes migratorius*); the dog-like marsupial of Australia – the thylacine (*Thylacinus cynocephalus*); or the woolly mammoth (*Mammuthus primigenius*). There are three main approaches to de-extinction. The first, called backbreeding, involves finding living species that have traits similar to the extinct species. These animals would then be bred to try to make a version that more closely resembles the extinct animal. A second option is cloning. Scientists would take a preserved cell from a recently extinct animal (ideally before the last of its kind died) and extract the nucleus. They would then swap this nucleus into an egg cell from the animal's closest living relative and implant the egg into a surrogate host. The latest option is genetic engineering. Here, scientists would line up the genome of an extinct animal with that of its closest living relative. They would then use gene-editing tools to swap relevant genes from the extinct animal into the living species and implant the hybrid genome into a surrogate (or grow it in an artificial womb). Opponents of de-extinction have claimed, firstly, that efforts and resources to resurrect extinct species could have been better used trying to conserve endangered species that might themselves become extinct. Secondly, a resurrected species, while being genetically the same as previously living specimens, will not have the same behaviour as its predecessors, as it would be raised by parents of a different species (the fetus's host), and not the one that died out. Thus it would be subjected to differing mothering techniques and this would lead to differing behavioural traits. Thirdly, introducing extinct species to environments may do harm to modern species should they prove to be invasive.

13.6 The Susceptibility to Change

Ecosystems respond in different ways to the human impact, and some are more vulnerable to human perturbation than others (Kasperson et al., 1995). It has often been thought, for example, that complex ecosystems are more stable than simple ones. Thus in Clements's Theory of Succession (Clements, 1916) the tendency towards community stabilization was ascribed in part to an increasing level of integration of community functions. As Goodman (1975: 238) expressed it:

> In general the predisposition to expect greater stability of complex systems was probably a combined legacy of eighteenth century theories of political economics, aesthetically and perhaps religiously motivated attraction to the belief that the wondrous variety of nature must have some purpose in an orderly work, and ageless folkwisdom regarding eggs and baskets.

Indeed, as Murdoch (1975) pointed out, it makes good intuitive sense that a system with many links, or 'multiple fail-safes', is more stable than one with few links or feedback loops. As an example, if a type of herbivore is attacked by several predatory species, the loss of any one of these species will be less likely to allow the herbivore to erupt or explode in numbers than if only one predator species was present and that single predator type disappeared. The basic idea therefore is that diverse groups of species are more stable because complementary species compensate for one another if one species suffers severe declines (Doak and Marvier, 2003). A diverse ecosystem will have a variety of species that help to insure it against a range of environmental upsets (Naeem, 2002).

Various other arguments have been marshalled to support the idea that great diversity and complexity affords greater ability to minimize the magnitude, duration, and irreversibility of changes brought about by some external perturbation such as humans (Noy-Meir, 1974). It has been stated that natural systems, which are generally more diverse than artificial systems such as crops or laboratory populations, are also more stable. Likewise, the tropical rain forest has been thought of as more diverse and more stable than less complex temperate communities, while simple Arctic ecosystems or oceanic islands have always appeared highly vulnerable to disturbance brought about by anthropogenic plant and animal introductions (see Section 3.2). The relationship between biodiversity and ecosystem stability continues to be a hot topic in ecology (Loreau et al., 2002; Kareiva and Levin, 2003; Tilman et al., 2006; Ives and Carpenter, 2007; Downing and Leibold, 2010; Loreau and Mazancourt, 2013; MacDougall et al., 2013; and Hautier et al., 2015). Some studies continue to throw doubt upon any simple relationship between biodiversity and stability (e.g. Pfisterer and Schmid, 2002), but there is perhaps an emerging consensus that diversity is crucial to ecosystem operation (McCann, 2000). As Loreau et al. (2001: 807) wrote,

> There is consensus that at least some minimum number of species is essential for ecosystem functioning under constant conditions and that a larger number of species is probably essential for maintaining the stability of ecosystem processes in changing environments.

However, it is worth noting that considerable doubt has been expressed in the past as to whether the classic concept of the causal linkage between diversity/complexity and stability is entirely valid. Murdoch (1975) indicated that there is not convincing field evidence that diverse natural communities are generally more stable than simple ones. He cited various papers which show that fluctuations of microtine rodents (lemmings, field voles, etc.) are as violent in relatively complex temperate zone ecosystems as they are in the less complex Arctic zone ecosystems. Goodman (1975) queried the sufficiency of the argument in its reference to the apparent instability of island ecosystems, suggesting that islands, being evolutionary backwaters and dead-ends, may accumulate species that are especially susceptible to competitive or exploitative displacement. In this case, lack of diversity may not necessarily be the sole or prime cause of instability.

Some systems tend to be *vulnerable*. Lakes, for example, are natural traps and sinks and are thus more vulnerable to the effect of disadvantageous inputs than are rivers (which are continually receiving new inputs) or oceans (which are so much larger). Other systems display the property of *elasticity* – the ability to recover from damage. This may be because nearby epicentres exist to provide organisms to re-invade a damaged system. Small, isolated systems will often tend to possess low elasticity. Two of the most important properties, however, are *resilience* (Folke et al., 2004; Gunderson et al., 2012) (being a measure of the number of times a system can recover after stress), and *inertia* (the ability to resist displacement of structural and functional characteristics).

Two systems which display resilience and inertia are deserts and estuaries. In both cases their indigenous organisms are highly accustomed to variable environmental conditions. Thus most desert fauna and flora evolved in an environment where the normal pattern is one of more or less random alternations of short favourable periods and long stress periods. They have pre-adapted resilience (Noy-Meir, 1974) so that they can tolerate extreme conditions, have the ability for rapid recovery, have various delay and trigger mechanisms (in the case of plants), and have flexible and opportunistic eating habits (in the case of beasts). Estuaries, on the other hand, though the subject of increasing human pressures (Lotze et al., 2006), also display some resilience. The vigour of their water circulation continuously and endogenously renews the supply of water, food, larvae, etc.; this aids recovery. Also, many species have biological characteristics which provide special advantages in estuarine survival. These characteristics usually protect the species against the natural violence of estuaries and are often helpful in resisting external forces such as humans.

Some environments are *fragile* (e.g. polar habitats and upland bogs). These have relatively simple food chains and the productivity of their plants is low on account of the cold. Slow growth makes them vulnerable to many disturbances and recovery from them is often slow. Thus vehicle tracks in the tundra may last for many decades.

13.7 Human Influence or Nature?

From many of the examples given in this book it is apparent that in many cases of environmental change it is impossible to state, without risk of contradiction, that people rather than nature are responsible. Most systems are complex and human agency is but one component of them, so that many human actions can lead to end results which are intrinsically similar to those that may be produced by natural forces. How to distinguish between human-induced perturbations and ill-defined natural oscillations is a crucial question when considering issues like coral reef degradation (Sapp, 1999). Humans are not always responsible for some of the changes with which they are credited. This book has given many examples of this problem, and a selection is presented in Table 13.7. Deciphering the cause is often a ticklish problem, given the intricate interdependence of different components of ecosystems, the frequency and complexity of environ-

mental changes, and the varying relaxation times that different ecosystem components may have when subject to a new impulse. It has proved to be especially difficult to attribute the occurrence of extreme events, such as severe droughts, massive floods, or extreme cold spells, to anthropogenic climate change rather than inherent natural climate variability (National Academies of Sciences, Engineering, and Medicine, 2016). This problem of causation and attribution plainly does not apply to the same extent to changes which have been brought about deliberately and knowingly by humans, but it does apply to the many cases where humans may have initiated change inadvertently and unintentionally.

This fundamental difficulty means that environmental impact statements of any kind are extremely difficult to make. As we have seen in Chapter 1, humans have been living on Earth and modifying it in different degrees for several millions of years, so that it is problematical to reconstruct any picture of the environment before human intervention. We seldom have any clear baseline against which to measure changes brought about by human society. Moreover, even without human interference, the environment would be in a perpetual state of

Table 13.7 Human influence or nature? Some examples, with section references to this book where applicable.

Change	Causes		Section reference
	Natural	Anthropogenic	
Death of savanna trees	Soil salinization through climatically induced groundwater rise	Overgrazing	2.12
Delta subsidence	Tectonics, sediment compaction, sediment loading	Fluid abstraction, drainage, water management	6.4
Desertification of semi-arid areas	Climatic change	Overgrazing, etc.	2.13
Dust storm frequency	Droughts, wind storms	Over-exploitation of land	4.29
Forest decline	Drought	Air, soil, and water pollution	2.20
Ground collapse	Karstic process	Dewatering by over-pumping	6.4
Gully development	Climatic change	Land-use change	6.10
Holocene elm and linden decline	Climatic change	Feeding and stalling of animals	2.16
Holocene peat-bog development in highland Britain	Climatic change and progressive soil deterioration	Deforestation and ploughing	4.28
Increasing coast recession	Rising sea level	Disruption of sediment supply	6.14
Increasing coastal flood risk	Rising sea level, natural subsidence	Pumping of aquifers creating subsidence	9.14
Increasing river flood intensity	Higher intensity rainfall	Creation of drainage ditches	5.3.4
Late Pleistocene animal extinction	Climate	Hunting	3.7
Late twentieth-century climatic warming	Changes in solar emission and volcanic activity	CO_2-generated greenhouse effect	8.1
Tree encroachment into alpine pastures in USA and Europe	Temperature amelioration	Cessation of burning and agriculture	8.2

flux on a great many different timescales. In addition, there are spatial and temporal discontinuities between cause and effect. For example, erosion in one locality may lead to deposition in another, while destruction of key elements of an animal's habitat may lead to population declines throughout its range. Likewise, in a time context, a considerable interval may elapse before the full implications of an activity are apparent. Also, because of the complex interaction between different components of different environmental systems and subsystems it is almost impossible to measure total environmental impact. For example, changes in soil may lead to changes in vegetation, which in turn may trigger changes in water quality and in animal populations. Primary impacts give rise to a myriad of successive repercussions throughout ecosystems which may be impracticable to trace and monitor. Quantitative cause-and-effect relationships can seldom be established.

13.8 Global Warming and Other Pressures

As has been made clear in Chapters 8–12, future climate changes, and in particular global warming, will have many impacts on the environment. However, global warming is not the only major human driver of future change. Also of immense, and in many cases more immediate, importance are other aspects of global change, particularly those brought about by modifications of land use and land cover (Mahmood et al., 2014; Pelletier et al., 2015). The response of species to climate change, as Oliver et al. (2017) have pointed out in the context of the changes in range of birds and butterflies in Britain over recent decades, may be mediated by other types of habitat changes wrought by humans. Biodiversity loss, problems of water shortage and quality, the undermining of the value of our soil resources because of such processes as accelerated erosion and accelerated salinization, and the impacts of many types of pollution, remain of huge significance. Deforestation and land-cover change may cause climate changes at the regional scale which may be of comparable dimensions to those predicted to arise from global warming (e.g. Werth and Avissar, 2002; Sampaio et al., 2007; Deo et al., 2009; Avila et al., 2012); changes in stream runoff and sediment loads caused by land-cover change or dam construction may far exceed those caused by future changes in rainfall amounts (e.g. Ericson et al., 2006; Xu et al., 2007) and in particular, in irrigation-rich areas in Asia and in the western United States, the effect of current anthropogenic interventions on mean annual runoff is stronger than the projected changes for a 2 or 3 K increase in temperature (Haddeland et al., 2014); loss of coastal wetlands

due to direct human action may exceed those caused by sea-level rise (Nicholls et al., 1999); shifts in alpine tree-lines may owe more to cessation of agricultural activities than to warming (Ameztegui et al., 2016); landslide activity may owe more to changes in human activity than to changes in climate (Crozier, 2010); and over-exploitation of groundwater may be a more potent cause of saltwater intrusion in coastal areas than sea-level rise caused by global warming (Ferguson and Gleeson, 2012).

Secondly, it is important to recognize that global warming is going to act on an Earth that has already been transformed by other human activities. If it works in the same direction as these other processes, then the compound effect will be greater than individual effects in isolation. Global warming may already be working on 'a groggy Earth'. For example, many of the world's coastlines are eroding quickly at the present day (Bird and Lewis, 2015) because of sediment starvation, but this rate of erosion may almost certainly be accelerated further as a result of sea-level rise. Equally, sea-level rise will be especially threatening in areas that are subsiding because of groundwater or hydrocarbon extraction (Section 9.8). Deserts are suffering today from land degradation and desertification and this could be exacerbated if droughts become more prevalent and severe in a warmer world. The state of the Amazonian rain forest is being threatened by deforestation which, though serious in itself, may also cause regional rainfall declines that could be rendered still greater if global warming is associated with greater drought incidence (Zhang et al., 2015).

Thirdly, as discussed in Chapter 8, some environments may be especially sensitive to future climate change, either because they will be subjected to particularly severe impacts, or because they are inherently weak (e.g. sandy coastlines), or because they are close to some environmental threshold (e.g. at the edge of their temperature tolerance like some permafrost areas), or because, as discussed above, they have already been adversely impacted by other environmental changes.

Fourthly, some attempts at reducing greenhouse gas emissions may, perversely, have adverse environmental effects. This is, for example, the case with biofuel development. The increase in the production of ethanol derived from such crops as sugar cane and maize has been remarkable: global production in 1980 was around 1 billion gallons, and by 2015 had jumped to over 25 billion gallons. Biomass production that places additional demands on land and water resources, and increases nutrient, pesticide, and water use can have negative implications for environmental quality. Also, conversion of forests into biofuel production could lead to an increase rather than a decrease in greenhouse gas emissions (Searchinger et al., 2008). Production of biofuels may mean that grasslands, wetlands, or forests are transformed. There are also the effects of indirect land-use changes. For instance, if increased US maize production for ethanol were to reduce soybean production and exports, changes in world prices might provide an incentive to increase soybean production on land previously used as pasture in Brazil which in turn might push cattle farming into Amazonia (Marshall et al., 2011). Similarly, wind turbines (Figure 13.10) have various adverse environmental consequences, including noise, visual intrusion, and the killing of birds (Leung and Yang, 2012). Tidal barrage schemes have also been opposed because of their influence on sediment budgets, mud-flat exposure, and migration routes for fish (Kadiri et al., 2012), while wave energy schemes can create barriers, electromagnetic waves, noise, and other problems for organisms (Gill, 2005; Frid et al., 2012). Photovoltaic energy systems may add to lead pollution risks (Gottesfeld and Cherry, 2011), while the use of geothermal energy might increase seismic activity (Majer et al., 2007). Geoengineering to reduce global warming (Section 7.13) would also have an array of environmental implications (Vaughan and Lenton, 2011).

13.9 Into the Unknown

During the last three decades the full significance of possible future environmental changes has become apparent, and national governments and international institutions have begun to ponder whether the world is entering a spasm of unparalleled humanly induced modification. For example, Steffen et al. (2004) have suggested that the Earth is currently operating in a no-analogue state. They remark (p. 262):

> In terms of key environmental parameters, the Earth System has recently moved well outside the range of the natural variability exhibited over at least the last half million years. The nature of changes now occurring simultaneously in the Earth System, their magnitudes and rates of change are unprecedented.

Likewise, the Amsterdam Declaration of 2001 pointed to the role of thresholds and surprises (see Steffen et al., 2004: 298):

> Global change cannot be understood in terms of a simple cause-effect paradigm. Human-driven changes cause multiple effects that cascade through the Earth System in complex ways. These effects interact with each other and with local- and regional-scale changes in multidimensional

Figure 13.10 Wind turbines in the suburbs of Palm Springs, California, USA (ASG).

patterns that are difficult to understand and even more difficult to predict. Surprises abound.

> Earth System dynamics are characterised by critical thresholds and abrupt changes. Human activities could inadvertently trigger such changes with severe consequences for Earth's environment and inhabitants.

Many of the land-cover changes and associated shifts driven by altered global atmospheric and hydrologic processes are, according to some scientists, resulting in novel (no-analogue) vegetation and faunal types which have had no previous history on Earth (Hobbs et al., 2013; Young, 2016). According to Morse at al. (2014: 1):

> A novel ecosystem is a unique assemblage of biota and environmental conditions that is the direct result of intentional or unintentional alteration by humans, i.e., human agency, sufficient to cross an ecological threshold that facilitates a new ecosystem trajectory and inhibits its return to a previous trajectory regardless of additional human intervention. The resulting ecosystem must also be self-sustaining in terms of species composition, structure, biogeochemistry, and ecosystem services. A defining characteristic of a novel ecosystem is a change in species composition relative to ecosystems present in the same biome prior to crossing a threshold.

Novel ecosystems include urban environments (Francis et al., 2012) and many current coral reefs, which are changing in unprecedented ways (Graham et al., 2014). However, some scientists largely reject the concept, and believe that many of its suppositions, including those relating to thresholds, are unproven (Murcia et al., 2014).

Our models and predictions are still highly inadequate (see Chapter 8), and there are great ranges in some of the values we give for such crucial changes as sea-level rise and global climatic warming, but the balance of scientific argument favours the view that change will occur and that change will be substantial. Some of the changes may be advantageous for humans or for particular ecosystems; others will be extremely disadvantageous.

Some environments will change very substantially during the twenty-first century in response to a rise of land-use changes and climatic changes, with some predictions suggesting that the world's grasslands and Mediterranean biomes will be particularly impacted (Sala et al., 2000). Marine ecosystems will also be impacted and Jenkins (2003: 1176) suggested that by 2050: 'If present trends … continue, the world's marine ecosystems in 2050 will look very different from those of today's. Large species, and particularly top predators, will be by and large extremely scarce and some will have disappeared entirely …'.

But all change, if it is rapid and of a great magnitude, is likely to create uncertainties and instabilities, and there is always the risk that critical thresholds or boundaries will be crossed (Rockström et al., 2009; Lynas, 2011). The study of future events will not only become a major concern for the environmental sciences but will also become a major concern for economists, sociologists, lawyers, and political scientists. George Perkins Marsh was a lawyer and politician, but it is only now, over a century since he wrote *Man and Nature*, that the wisdom, perspicacity, and prescience of his ideas have begun to be given the praise and attention they deserve. The human population will probably by greater by 2 to 4 billion people by 2050 (Cohen, 2003), so that the human impact can only become yet more important.

Guide to Reading

Gillson, L. (2015) *Biodiversity Conservation and Environmental Change*. Oxford: Oxford University Press. A study of conservation in the light of palaeoecological studies.

Hambler, C. and Canney, S.M. (2013) *Conservation*. Cambridge: Cambridge University Press. A first-class introduction to all aspects of nature conservation.

Ladle, R.J. and Whittaker, R.J. (2011) *Conservation Biogeography*. Chichester: Wiley Blackwell. A survey of conservation issues.

Lynas, M. (2011) *The God Species*. London: Fourth Estate. A discussion of how humans may be transgressing various environmental thresholds or boundaries.

Steffen, W. and 10 others (2004) *Global Change and the Earth System*. Berlin: Springer. Chapter 6 of this multi-author volume addresses ways of global management for global sustainability.

References

Aagaard, T. and Sorensen, P. (2012) Coastal profile response to sea level rise: a process-based approach. *Earth Surface Processes and Landforms*, 37, 354–362.

Abbasi, S.A. and Abbasi, T. (eds) (2017) *Ozone Hole*. New York: Springer.

Abbo, S., Lev-Yadun, S. and Gopher, A. (2010) Agricultural origins: centers and noncenters; a Near Eastern appraisal. *Critical Reviews in Plant Sciences*, 29, 317–328.

Abul-Atta, A.A. (1978) *Egypt and the Nile after the Construction of the High Aswan Dam*. Cairo: Ministry of Irrigation and Land Reclamation.

Aby, S.B. (2017) Date of arroyo cutting in the American southwest and the influence of human activities. *Anthropocene*, 18, 76–88.

Achard, F., Eva, H.D., Stibig, H.-J., et al. (2002) Determination of deforestation rates of the world's humid tropical forests. *Science*, 297, 999–1002.

Acksel, A., Kappenberg, A., Kühn, P. and Leinweber, P. (2017) Humus-rich topsoils around the Baltic Sea, a product of human activity. *Geoderma Regional*, 10, 93–101.

Adam, J.C., Hamlet, A.F. and Lettenmaier, D.P. (2009) Implications of global climate change for snowmelt hydrology in the twenty-first century. *Hydrological Processes*, 23, 962–972.

Adams, J.W., Rodriguez, D. and Cox, R.A. (2005) The uptake of SO_2 on Saharan dust: a flow tube study. *Atmospheric Chemistry and Physics*, 5, 2679–2689.

Adams, W.M. (2016) Geographies of conservation: de-extinction and precision conservation. *Progress in Human Geography*, doi:10.1177/0309132516646641.

Aeschbach-Hertig, W. and Gleeson, T. (2012) Regional strategies for the accelerating global problem of groundwater depletion. *Nature Geoscience*, 5, 853–861.

Ågren, C. and Elvingson, P. (1996) *Still with Us: The Acidification of the Environment Is Still Going On*. Göteborg: Swedish NGO Secretariat on Acid Rain.

Aich, S., McVoy, C.W., Dreschel, T.W. and Santamaria, F. (2013) Estimating soil subsidence and carbon loss in the Everglades Agricultural Area, Florida using geospatial techniques. *Agriculture, Ecosystems & Environment*, 171, 124–133.

Aislabie, J., and Deslippe, J.R. (2013) Soil microbes and their contribution to soil services. In J.R. Dymond (ed.), *Ecosystem Services in New Zealand – Conditions and Trends*. Lincoln, NZ: Manaaki Whenua Press, 143–161.

Alabaster, J.S. (1972) Suspended solids and fisheries. *Proceedings of the Royal Society of London. Series B. Biological Sciences*, 180, 395–406.

Albert, R.M. (2015) Anthropocene and early human behavior. *The Holocene*, 25, 1542–1552.

Aldridge, D.C., Ho, S. and Froufe, E. (2014) The Ponto-Caspian quagga mussel, Dreissena rostriformis bugensis (Andrusov, 1897), invades Great Britain. *Aquatic Invasions*, 9 (4), 529–535.

Alemayehu, T., Furi, W. and Legesse, D. (2007) Impact of water overexploitation on highland lakes of eastern Ethiopia. *Environmental Geology*, 52, 147–154.

Ali, I., Shukla, A. and Romshoo, S.A. (2017) Assessing linkages between spatial facies changes and dimensional variations of glaciers in the upper Indus Basin, western Himalaya. *Geomorphology*, 284, 115–129.

Al-Ibrahim, A.A. (1991) Excessive use of ground-water resources in Saudi Arabia: impacts and policy options. *Ambio*, 20, 34–37.

Allchin, B., Goudie, A.S. and Hegde, K.T.M. (1977) *The Prehistory and Palaeogeography of the Great Indian Desert*. London: Academic Press.

Allen, C.D., Macalady, A.K., Chenchouni, H., et al. (2010) A global overview of drought and heat-induced tree mortality reveals emerging climate change risks for forests. *Forest Ecology and Management*, 259, 660–684.

Allen, R.J., Sherwood, S.C., Norris, J.R. and Zender, C.S. (2012) Recent northern hemisphere tropical expansion primarily driven by black carbon and tropospheric ozone. *Nature*, 485, 350–354.

Allen, S.K., Cox, S.C. and Owens, I.F. (2011) Rock avalanches and other landslides in the central Southern

Human Impact on the Natural Environment: Past, Present and Future, Eighth Edition. Andrew S. Goudie.
© 2019 John Wiley & Sons Ltd. Published 2019 by John Wiley & Sons Ltd.
Companion website: www.wiley.com/go/goudie/human-impact-natural-environment

Alps of New Zealand: a regional study considering possible climate change impacts. *Landslides*, 8, 33–48.

Alley, W.M. and Alley, R. (2017) *High and Dry: Meeting the Challenges of the World's Growing Dependence on Groundwater*. New Haven: Yale University Press.

Allis, R.G., Bromley, C. and Currie, S. (2009) Update on subsidence at the Wairakei–Tauhara geothermal system, New Zealand. *Geothermics*, 38, 169–180.

Allsop, N., Colville, J.F. and Verboom, G.A. (eds) (2014) *Fynbos*. Oxford: Oxford University Press.

Almer, B., Dickson, W., Ekstrom, C., et al. (1974) Effects of acidification on Finnish lakes. *Ambio*, 3, 30–36.

Altieri, A.H., Harrison, S.B., Seemann, J., Collin, R., Diaz, R.J. and Knowlton, N. (2017) Tropical dead zones and mass mortalities on coral reefs. *Proceedings of the National Academy of Sciences*, 114 (14), 3660–3665.

Ameztegui, A., Coll, L., Brotons, L. and Ninot, J.M. (2016) Land-use legacies rather than climate change are driving the recent upward shift of the mountain tree line in the Pyrenees. *Global Ecology and Biogeography*, doi:10.1111/geb.12407.

Amick, D.S. (2016) Evolving views on the Pleistocene colonization of North America. *Quaternary International*, 431, 125–151.

Amills, M. (2011) Biodiversity and origin of pig breeds. *Bulletin UASVM Animal Science and Biotechnologies*, 68, 1–5.

An, Q., Wu, Y., Taylor, S. and Zhao, B. (2009) Influence of the Three Gorges Project on saltwater intrusion in the Yangtze River estuary. *Environmental Geology*, 56, 1679–1686.

An, S.-I., Kug, J.-S., Ham, Y.-G., and Kang, I.-S. (2008) Successive modulation of ENSO to the future greenhouse warming. *Journal of Climate*, 21, 3–21.

Anadon, J.D., Sala, O.E. and Maestre, F.T. (2014) Climate change will increase savannas at the expense of forests and treeless vegetation in tropical and subtropical Americas. *Journal of Ecology*, 102 (6), 1363–1373.

Andela, N., Morton, D.C., Giglio, L., et al. (2017) A human-driven decline in global burned area. *Science*, 356 (6345), 1356–1362.

Anderson, A. (2009) The rat and the octopus: initial human colonization and the prehistoric introduction of domestic animals to remote Oceania. *Biological Invasions*, 11, 1503–1519.

Anderson, D.E., Goudie, A.S. and Parker, A.G. (2013) *Global Environments through the Quaternary* (2nd edn). Oxford: Oxford University Press.

Anderson, D.M. (1994) Red tides. *Scientific American*, 271 (2), 52–58.

Anderson, J.M. and Spencer, T. (1991) Carbon, nutrient and water balances of tropical rainforest ecosystems subject to disturbance: management implications and research proposals, *MAB Digest*, 7, UNESCO, Paris, France.

Anderson, R.C. (2006) Evolution and origin of the Central Grassland of North America: climate, fire, and mammalian grazers. *The Journal of the Torrey Botanical Society*, 133, 626–647.

Angelakis, A.N. and Zheng, X.Y. (2015) Evolution of water supply, sanitation, wastewater, and stormwater technologies globally. *Water*, 7 (2), 455–463.

Anisimov, O.A. (1989) Changing climate and permafrost distribution in the Soviet Arctic. *Physical Geography*, 10, 282–293.

Anisimov, O.A. and Fitzharris, B. (2001) Polar regions (Arctic and Antarctic). In J.J. McCarthy (ed.), *Climate Change 2001: Impacts, Adaptation, and Vulnerability*. Cambridge: Cambridge University Press, 801–841.

Anisimov, O., Vandenberghe, J., Lobanov, V. and Kondratiev, A. (2008) Predicting changes in alluvial channel patterns in North-European Russia under conditions of global warming. *Geomorphology*, 98, 262–274.

Anthony, E.J. (2015) Wave influence in the construction, shaping and destruction of river deltas: a review. *Marine Geology*, 361, 53–78.

Anthony, K.R.N., Kline, D.I., Diaz-Pulido, G., et al. (2008) Ocean acidification causes bleaching and productivity loss in coral reef builders. *Proceedings of the National Academy of Sciences*, 105, 17442–17446.

Araujo, B.B., Oliveira-Santos, L.G.R., Lima-Ribeiro, M.S., et al. (2015) Bigger kill than chill: the uneven roles of humans and climate on late Quaternary megafaunal extinctions. *Quaternary International*, 431B, 216–222.

Archer, D. (2007) *Global Warming: Understanding the Forecast*. Oxford: Blackwell.

Archer, S., MacKay, W., Mott, J., et al. (1999) Arid and semi-arid land community dynamics in a management context. In T.W. Hoekstra and M. Schachak (eds), *Arid Lands Management*. Urbana and Chicago: University of Illinois Press, 48–74.

Arendt, A.A., Echelmeyer, K.A., Harrison, W.D., et al. (2002) Rapid wastage of Alaska glaciers and their contribution to rising sea level. *Science*, 297, 382–385.

Armitage, A.R., Highfield, W.E., Brody, S.D. and Louchouarn, P. (2015) The contribution of mangrove expansion to salt marsh loss on the Texas Gulf Coast. *PloS one*, 10 (5), e0125404–e0125404.

Arnell, N.W. (1996) *Global Warming, River Flows and Water Resources*. Chichester: Wiley.

Arnell, N.W. (1999a) The impacts of climate change on water resources. In Meteorological Office (ed.), *Meteorological Office, Climate Change and Its Impacts*. Bracknell: Hadley Centre, 14–18.

Arnell, N.W. (1999b) The effect of climate change on hydrological regimes in Europe: a continental prospective. *Global Environmental Change*, 9, 5–23.

Arnell, N.W. (2002) *Hydrology and Global Environmental Change*. Harlow: Prentice Hall.

Arnell, N.W. and Gosling, S.N. (2013) The impacts of climate change on river flow regimes at the global scale. *Journal of Hydrology*, 486, 351–364.

Arnell, N.W., Halliday, S.J., Battarbee, R.W., et al. (2015) The implications of climate change for the water environment in England. *Progress in Physical Geography*, 39 (1), 93–120.

Aron, W.I. and Smith, S.H. (1971) Ship canals and aquatic ecosystems. *Science*, 174, 13–20.

Aronson, M.F., La Sorte, F.A., Nilon, C.H., et al. (2014) A global analysis of the impacts of urbanization on bird and plant diversity reveals key anthropogenic drivers. *Proceedings of the Royal Society B*, 281, No. 1780, 20133330.

Arora, V.K. and Boer, G.J. (2001) Effects of simulated climate change on the hydrology of major river basins. *Journal of Geophysical Research*, 106 (D4), 3335–3348.

Arpe, K., Bengtsson, L., Golitsyn, G.S., et al. (2000) Connection between Caspian Sea level variability and ENSO. *Geophysical Research Letters*, 27, 2693–2696.

Arzarello, M., Marcolini, F., Pavia, G., et al. (2007) Evidence of earliest human occurrence in Europe: the site of Pirro Nord (Southern Italy). *Die Naturwissenschaften*, 94, 107–112.

Ashby, E. (1978) *Reconciling Man with the Environment*. Oxford: Oxford University Press.

Ashkenazy, Y., Yizhaq, H. and Tsoar, H. (2012) Sand dune mobility under climate change in the Kalahari and Australian deserts. *Climatic Change*, 112, 901–923.

Ashley, W.S., Bentley, M.L. and Stallins, J.A. (2012) Urban-induced thunderstorm modification in the Southeast United States. *Climatic Change*, 113, 481–498.

Ashmore, P. and Church, M. (2001) The impact of climate change on rivers and river processes in Canada. *Geological Survey of Canada Bulletin*, 555.

Ashton, A.D., Donnelly, J.P. and Evans, R.L. (2008) A discussion of the potential impacts of climate change on the shorelines of the northeastern USA. *Mitigation and Adaptation Strategies for Global Change*, 13, 719–743.

Ashton, A.D., Walkden, M.J.A. and Dickson, M.E. (2011) Equilibrium responses of cliffed coasts to changes in the rate of sea level rise. *Marine Geology*, 284, 217–229.

Atkinson, B.W. (1968) A preliminary examination of the possible effect of London's urban area on the distribution of thunder rainfall, 1951–60. *Transactions of the Institute of British Geographers*, 44, 97–118.

Atkinson, B.W. (1975) *The Mechanical Effect of an Urban Area on Convective Precipitation*. Occasional Paper 3. London: Department of Geography, Queen Mary College, University of London.

Atkinson, G., Assatourians, K., Cheadle, B. and Greig, W. (2015) Ground motions from three recent earthquakes in Western Alberta and Northeastern British Columbia and their implications for induced-seismicity hazard in Eastern Regions. *Seismological Research Letters*, 86, 1022–1031.

Atlas, P. (1977) The paradox of hail suppression. *Science*, 195, 139–145.

Atwood, T.B., Connolly, R.M., Almahasheer, H., et al. (2017) Global patterns in mangrove soil carbon stocks and losses. *Nature Climate Change*, 7 (7), 523–528.

Aubault, H., Webb, N.P., Strong, C.L., et al. (2015) Grazing impacts on the susceptibility of rangelands to wind erosion: the effects of stocking rate, stocking strategy and land condition. *Aeolian Research*, 17, 89–99.

Aubertin, G.M. and Patric, J.H. (1974) Water quality after clearcutting a small watershed in West Virginia. *Journal of Environmental Quality*, 3, 243–249.

Aubréville, A. (1949) *Climats, forêts et désertification de L'Afrique tropicale*. Paris: Societé d'Edition Géographiques Maritimes et Coloniales.

Aulinger, A., Matthias, V., Zeretzke, M., et al. (2016) The impact of shipping emissions on air pollution in the greater North Sea region. Part 1: current emissions and concentrations. *Atmospheric Chemistry and Physics*, 16, 739–758.

Avila, F.B., Pitman, A.J., Donat, M.G., et al. (2012) Climate model simulated changes in temperature extremes due to land cover change. *Journal of Geophysical Research*, 117, D04108.

Ayenew, T. and Legesse, D. (2007) The changing face of the Ethiopian rift lakes and their environs: call of the time. *Lakes & Reservoirs: Research and Management*, 12, 149–165.

Ayres, M.C. and Lombardero, M.J. (2000) Assessing the consequences of global change for forest disturbance from herbivores and pathogens. *Science of the Total Environment*, 262, 263–286.

Baccari, N., Boussema, M.R., Lamachère, J.-M. and Nasri, S. (2008) Efficiency of contour benches, filling-in and silting-up of a hillside reservoir in a semi-arid climate in Tunisia. *Comptes Rendus Geoscience*, 340, 38–48.

Baccini, A., Goetz, S.J., Walker, W.S., et al. (2012) Estimated carbon dioxide emissions from tropical deforestation improved by carbon-density maps. *Nature Climate Change*, 2, 182–185.

Bach, A.J., Brazel, A.J. and Lancaster, N. (1996) Temporal and spatial aspects of blowing dust in the Mojave and Colorado Deserts of southern California, 1973–1994. *Physical Geography*, 17, 329–353.

Badescu, V. and Cathcart, R.B. (2011) Aral Sea partial restoration. 1. A Caspian importation macroproject. *International Journal of Environment and Waste Management*, 7, 161–182.

Baillie, J.E.M., Griffiths, J., Turvey, S.T., et al. (2010) *Evolution Lost. Status and Trends of the*

World's Vertebrates. London: Zoological Society of London.

Baine, M. (2001) Artificial reefs: a review of their design, application, management and performance. *Ocean & Coastal Management*, 44, 241–259.

Bakan, S., Chlono, A., Cubasch, U., et al. (1991) Climate response to smoke from the burning oil wells in Kuwait. *Nature*, 351, 367–371.

Baker, A. and Simms, M.J. (1998) Active deposition of calcareous tufa in Wessex, UK, and its implications for the 'late-Holocene tufa decline'. *The Holocene*, 8, 359–365.

Baker, A.C., Glynn, P.W. and Riegl, B. (2008) Climate change and coral reef bleaching: an ecological assessment of long-term impacts, recovery trends and future outlook. *Estuarine, Coastal and Shelf Science*, 80, 435–471.

Bakoariniaina, L.N., Kusky, T. and Raharimahefa, T. (2006) Disappearing Lake Alaotra: monitoring catastrophic erosion, waterway silting, and land degradation hazards in Madagascar using Landsat imagery. *Journal of African Earth Sciences*, 44, 241–252.

Balling, R.C. and Wells, S.G. (1990) Historical rainfall patterns and arroyo activity within the Zuni river drainage basin, New Mexico. *Annals of the Association of American Geographers*, 80, 603–617.

Balme, J. (2013) Of boats and string: the maritime colonisation of Australia. *Quaternary International* 285, 68–75.

Balter, M. (2010) The tangled roots of agriculture. *Science*, 327, 404–406.

Balter, M. (2013) Archaeologists say the 'Anthropocene' is here – but it began long ago. *Science*, 340 (6130), 261–262.

Barbante, C., Spolaor, A., Cairns, W.R. and Boutron, C. (2017) Man's footprint on the Arctic environment as revealed by analysis of ice and snow. *Earth-Science Reviews*, 168, 218–231.

Barberi, F., Brondi, F., Carapezza, M.L., et al. (2003) Earthen barriers to control lava flows in the 2001 eruption of Mt. Etna. *Journal of Volcanology and Geothermal Research*, 123, 231–243.

Barbier, E.B., Hacker, S.D., Kennedy, C., et al. (2011) The value of estuarine and coastal ecosystem services. *Ecological Monographs*, 81 (2), 169–193.

Barends, F.B.J., Brouwer, F.J.J. and Schröder, F.H. (1995) *Land Subsidence*. IAHS publication 234. Wallingford: International Association of Hydrological Sciences.

Bari, M.A. and Scholfield, N.J. (1992) Lowering of a shallow, saline water table by extensive eucalypt reforestation. *Journal of Hydrology*, 133, 273–291.

Barker, G. (2006) *The Agricultural Revolution in Prehistory: Why Did Foragers Become Farmers?* Cambridge: Cambridge University Press.

Barker, G. and Goucher, C. (eds) (2015) *The Cambridge World History: Volume 2, A World with Agriculture, 12,000 BCE–500 ce*. Cambridge: Cambridge University Press.

Barlow, P.M. and Reichard, E.G. (2010) Saltwater intrusion in coastal regions of North America. *Hydrogeology Journal*, 18, 246–270.

Barnard, P.L., Owen, L.A., Sharma, M.C. and Finkel, R.C. (2001) Natural and human-induced landsliding in the Garhwal Himalaya of northern India. *Geomorphology*, 40, 21–35.

Barnes, D.K.A., Galgani, F., Thompson, R.C. and Barlaz, M. (2009) Accumulation and fragmentation of plastic debris in global environments. *Philosophical Transactions of the Royal Society of London: Series B, Biological Sciences*, 364, 1985–1998.

Barnett, T.P., Adam, J.C. and Lettenmaier, D.P. (2005) Potential impacts of a warming climate on water availability in snow-dominated regions. *Nature*, 438, 303–309.

Barnston, A.G. and Schickedanz, P.T. (1984) The effect of irrigation on warm season precipitation in the southern Great Plains. *Journal of Climate and Applied Meteorology*, 23, 865–888.

Barreiro-Lostres, F., Moreno, A., González-Sampériz, P., et al. (2017) Erosion in Mediterranean mountain landscapes during the last millennium: a quantitative approach based on lake sediment sequences (Iberian Range, Spain). *Catena*, 149, 782–798.

Barrett, S.E. and Watmough, S.A. (2015) Factors controlling peat chemistry and vegetation composition in Sudbury peatlands after 30 years of pollution emission reductions. *Environmental Pollution*, 206, 122–132.

Barry, R.G. (1985) The cryosphere and climate change. In M.C. MacCraken and F.M. Luther (eds), *Detecting the Climatic Effects of Increasing Carbon Dioxide*. Washington, DC: US Dept of Energy, 111–148.

Bar-Yosef, O. (1998) On the nature of transitions: the Middle to Upper Palaeolithic and the Neolithic Revolution. *Cambridge Archaeological Journal*, 8, 141–163.

Bateman, P.W. and Fleming, P.A. (2012) Big city life: carnivores in urban environments. *Journal of Zoology*, 287 (1), 1–23.

Batey, T. (2009) Soil compaction and soil management – a review. *Soil Use and Management*, 25, 335–345.

Battarbee, R.W. (1977) Observations in the recent history of Lough Neagh and its drainage basin. *Philosophical Transactions of the Royal Society of London: Series B, Biological Sciences*, 281, 303–345.

Battarbee, R.W., Appleby, P.G., Odel, K. and Flower, R.J. (1985b) 210Pb dating of Scottish Lake sediments, afforestation and accelerated soil erosion. *Earth Surface Processes and Landforms*, 10, 137–142.

Battarbee, R.W., Flower, R.J., Stevenson, A.C. and Rippey, B. (1985a) Lake acidification in Galloway: a palaeoecological test of competing hypotheses. *Nature*, 314, 350–352.

Battarbee, R.W., Shilland, E.M., Kernan, M., et al. (2014) Recovery of acidified surface waters from acidification in the United Kingdom after twenty years of chemical and biological monitoring (1988–2008). *Ecological Indicators*, 37, 267–273.

Bautista, S., Bellot, J. and Ramón Vallejo, V. (1996) Mulching treatment for postfire soil conservation in a semi-arid ecosystem. *Arid Soil Research and Rehabilitation*, 10, 235–242.

Baxter, R.M. (1977) Environmental effects of dams and impoundments. *Annual Review of Ecology and Systematics*, 8, 255–283.

Beach, T., Dunning, N., Luzzadder-Beach, S., et al. (2006) Impacts of the ancient Maya on soils and soil erosion in the central Maya lowlands. *Catena*, 65, 166–178.

Beach, T., Luzzadder-Beach, S., Cook, D., et al. (2015) Ancient Maya impacts on the Earth's surface: an Early Anthropocene analog? *Quaternary Science Reviews*, 124, 1–30.

Beamish, R.J., Lockhart, W.L., Van Loon, J.C. and Harvey, H.H. (1975) Long-term acidification of a lake and resulting effects on fishes. *Ambio*, 4, 98–102.

Beaumont, P.B. (2011) The edge: more on fire-making by about 1.7 million years ago at Wonderwerk Cave in South Africa. *Current Anthropology*, 52, 585–594.

Beck, M.W., Brumbaugh, R.D., Airoldi, L., et al. (2011b) Oyster reefs at risk and recommendations for conservation, restoration, and management. *Bioscience*, 61, 107–116.

Beck, P.S.A., Juday, G.P., Alix, C., et al. (2011a) Changes in forest productivity across Alaska consistent with biome shift. *Ecology Letters*, 14 (4), 373–379.

Beckers, B., Berking, J. and Schütt, B. (2013) Ancient water harvesting methods in the drylands of the Mediterranean and Western Asia. *Journal for Ancient Studies*, 2, 145–164.

Beerten, K., Vandersmissen, N., Deforce, K. and Vandenberghe, N. (2014) Late Quaternary (15 ka to present) development of a sandy landscape in the Mol area, Campine region, north-east Belgium. *Journal of Quaternary Science*, 29, 433–444.

Beerung, D.J. and Osborne, C.P. (2006) The origin of the savanna biome. *Global Change Biology*, 12, 2023–2031.

Behnke, R. and Mortimore, M. (eds) (2016) *The End of Desertification? Disputing Environmental Change in the Drylands*. Heidelberg: Springer.

Behre, K.-E. (ed.) (1986) *Anthropogenic Indicators in Pollen Diagrams*. Rotterdam: Balkema.

Beja-Pereira, A., England, P.R., Ferrand, N., et al. (2004) African origins of the domestic donkey. *Science*, 304, 1781.

Belay, A.A. (2010) Impacts of chromium from tannery effluent and evaluation of alternative treatment options. *Journal of Environmental Protection*, 1, 53–58.

Belayneh, A. and Tessema, Z.K. (2017) Mechanisms of bush encroachment and its inter-connection with rangeland degradation in semi-arid African ecosystems: a review. *Journal of Arid Land*, 9, 299–312.

Bell, F.G., Stacey, T.R. and Genske, D.D. (2000) Mining subsidence and its effect on the environment: some differing examples. *Environmental Geology*, 40, 135–152.

Bell, M.L. (1982) The effect of land-use and climate on valley sedimentation. In A.F. Harding (ed.), *Climatic Change in Later Prehistory*. Edinburgh: Edinburgh University Press, 127–142.

Bell, M.L. and Nur, A. (1978) Strength changes due to reservoir-induced pore pressure and stresses and application to Lake Oroville. *Journal of Geophysical Research*, 83, 4469–4483.

Bell, T.L., Rosenfeld, D., Kim, K.-M., et al. (2008) Midweek increase in U.S. summer rain and storm heights suggests air pollution invigorates rainstorms. *Journal of Geophysical Research*, 113, D02209.

Bellard, C., Bertelsmeier, C., Leadley, P., et al. (2012) Impacts of climate change on the future of biodiversity. *Ecology Letters*, 15 (4), 365–377.

Bellwood, D.R., Hughes, T.P., Folke, C. and Nyström, M. (2004) Confronting the coral reef crisis. *Nature*, 429, 827–833.

Belsky, A.J. (1996) Viewpoint: western juniper expansion: is it a threat to arid northwest ecosystems? *Journal of Range Management*, 49, 53–59.

Beltaos, S. and Burrell, B.C. (2003) Climatic change and river ice breakup. *Canadian Journal of Civil Engineering*, 30, 145–155.

Bendell, J.F. (1974) Effects of fire on birds and mammals. In T.T. Kozlowski and C.C. Ahlgren (eds), *Fire and Ecosystems*. New York: Academic Press, 73–138.

Bendix, J., Bendix, A. and Richter, M. (2000) El Niño 1997/1998 in Nordperu: anzeichen eines Ökosystem – Wandels? *Petermanns Geographische Mitteilungen*, 144, 20–31.

Benn, D.I., Bolch, T., Hands, K., et al. (2012) Response of debris-covered glaciers in the Mount Everest region to recent warming, and implications for outburst flood hazards. *Earth-Science Reviews*, 114, 156–174.

Benn, D.I. and Evans, D.J.A. (2010) *Glaciers and Glaciations* (2nd edn). London: Hodder.

Bennett, H.H. (1938) *Soil Conservation*. New York: McGraw-Hill.

Bennett, M.R. (2003) Ice streams as the arteries of an ice sheet: their mechanics, stability and significance. *Earth-Science Reviews*, 61, 309–339.

Bentley, C.R. (1997) Rapid sea-level rise soon from West Antarctic ice sheet collapse? *Science*, 275, 1077–1078.

Bentley, C.R. (1998) Rapid sea-level rise from a West Antarctic ice-sheet collapse: a short-term perspective. *Journal of Glaciology*, 44, 157–163.

Benz, S.A., Bayer, P. and Blum, P. (2017) Identifying anthropogenic anomalies in air, surface and groundwater temperatures in Germany. *Science of the Total Environment*, 584, 145–153.

Berbet, M.L.C. and Costa, M.H. (2003) Climate change after tropical deforestation: seasonal variability of surface albedo and its effects on precipitation change. *Journal of Climate*, 16, 2099–2104.

Berg, R.D. and Carter, D.L. (1980) Furrow erosion and sediment losses on irrigated cropland. *Journal of Soil and Water Conservation*, 35, 267–270.

Beringer, J.E. (2000) Releasing genetically modified organisms: will any harm outweigh any advantage? *Journal of Applied Ecology*, 37, 207–214.

Berna, F., Goldberg, P., Horwitz, L.K., et al. (2012) Microstratigraphic evidence of in situ fire in the Acheulean strata of Wonderwerk Cave, Northern Cape province, South Africa. *Proceedings of the National Academy of Sciences*, 109 (20), E1215–1220.

Bernabo, J.C. and Webb, T., III (1977) Changing patterns in the Holocene pollen record of northeastern North America: mapped summary. *Quaternary Research*, 8, 64–96.

Bertness, M.D. and Silliman, B.R. (2008) Consumer control of salt marshes driven by human disturbance. *Conservation Biology*, 22, 618–623.

Besnard, G., Khadari, B., Navascués, M., et al. (2013) The complex history of the olive tree: from Late Quaternary diversification of Mediterranean lineages to primary domestication in the northern Levant. *Proceedings of the Royal Society* B, 280, doi:10.1098/rspb.2012.2833.

Betts, R.A. (2000) Offset of the potential carbon sink from boreal forestation by decreases in surface albedo. *Nature*, 408, 187–190.

Betts, R.A. (2001) Biogeophysical impacts of land use on present-day climate: near surface temperature change and radiative forcing. *Atmospheric Science Letters*, 2 (1–4), 39–51.

Betts, R.A., Malhi, Y. and Roberts, J.T. (2008) The future of the Amazon: new perspectives from climate, ecosystem and social sciences. *Philosophical Transactions of the Royal Society of London: Series B, Biological Sciences*, 363, 1729–1735.

Beysens, D., Mongruel, A. and Acker, K. (2017) Urban dew and rain in Paris, France: occurrence and physico-chemical characteristics. *Atmospheric Research*, 189, 152–161.

Bhagwat, S.A., Breman, E., Thekaekara, T., et al. (2012) A battle lost? Report on two centuries of invasion management of Lantana camara L. in Australia, India and South Africa. *PLoS ONE*, 7 (3), e32407.

Bhark, E.W. and Small, E.E. (2003) Association between plant canopies and the spatial patterns of infiltration in shrubland and grassland of the Chihuahuan Desert, New Mexico. *Ecosystems*, 6, 185–196.

Bhattachan A., D'Odorico, P., Dintwe, K., et al. (2014) Resilience and recovery potential of duneland vegetation in the southern Kalahari. *Ecosphere*, 5 (1), 1–14.

Bhattachan, A., D'Odorico, P., Okin, G.S., and Dintwe, K. (2013) Potential dust emissions from the southern Kalahari's dunelands. *Journal of Geophysical Research: Earth Surface*, 118, 307–314.

Bidwell, O.W. and Hole, F.D. (1965) Man as a factor of soil formation. *Soil Science*, 99, 65–72.

Bigg, E.K. (2008) Trends in rainfall associated with sources of air pollution. *Environmental Chemistry*, 5, 184–193.

Bindler, R. (2011) Contaminated lead environments of man: reviewing the lead isotopic evidence in sediments, peat and soils for the temporal and spatial patterns of atmospheric lead pollution in Sweden. *Environmental Geochemistry and Health*, 33, 311–329.

Binford, M.W., Brenner, M., Whitmore, T.J., et al. (1987) Ecosystems, palaeoecology, and human disturbance in subtropical and tropical America. *Quaternary Science Reviews*, 6, 115–128.

Bini, M., Pappalardo, M., Rossi, V., et al. (2017) Deciphering the effects of human activity on urban areas through morphostratigraphic analysis: the case of Pisa, Northwest Italy. *Geoarchaeology*, doi:10.1002/gea.21619.

Bintanja, R. and Andry, O. (2017) Towards a rain-dominated Arctic. *Nature Climate Change*, 7, 263–267.

Bird, E.C.F. (1979) Coastal processes. In K.J. Gregory and D.E. Walling (eds), *Man and Environmental Processes*. Folkestone: Dawson, 82–101.

Bird, E.C.F. (1993) *Submerging Coasts*. Chichester: Wiley.

Bird, E.C.F. (1996) *Beach Management*. Chichester: Wiley.

Bird, E.C F. and Lewis, N. (2015) *Beach Renourishment*. Heidelberg: Springer.

Birken, A.S. and Cooper, D.J. (2006) Processes of Tamarix invasion and floodplain development along the lower Green River, Utah. *Ecological Applications*, 16, 1103–1120.

Birkett, C.M. (2000) Synergist remote sensing of Lake Chad: variability of basin inundation. *Remote Sensing of Environment*, 72, 218–236.

Birkinshaw, S.J., Bathurst, J.C. and Robinson, M. (2014) 45 years of non-stationary hydrology over a forest plantation growth cycle, Coalburn catchment, Northern England. *Journal of Hydrology*, 519, 559–573.

Birks, H.J.B. (1986) Late-Quaternary biotic changes in terrestrial and lacustrine environments, with particular reference to north-west Europe. In B.E. Berglund (ed.),

Handbook of Holocene Palaeoecology and Palaeohydrology. Chichester: Wiley, 3–65.

Birks, H.J.B. (1988) Long-term ecological change in the British uplands. *British Ecological Society Special Publication*, 7, 37–56.

Bischoff, M., Cete, A., Fritschen, R. and Meier, T. (2009) Coal mining induced seismicity in the Ruhr area, Germany. *Pure and Applied Geophysics*, 167, 63–75.

Black, J.L., MacLeod, I.D. and Smith, B.W. (2017) Theoretical effects of industrial emissions on colour change at rock art sites on Burrup Peninsula, Western Australia. *Journal of Archaeological Science: Reports*, 12, 457–462.

Blainey, G. (1975) *Triumph of the Nomads. A History of Ancient Australia.* Melbourne: Macmillan.

Blank, I.W. (1985) A new type of forest decline in Germany. *Nature*, 314, 311–314.

Blanton, P. and Marcus, W.A. (2013) Transportation infrastructure, river confinement, and impacts on floodplain and channel habitat, Yakima and Chehalis rivers, Washington, USA. *Geomorphology*, 189, 55–65.

Bledsoe, B.P. and Watson, C.C. (2001) Effects of urbanization on channel instability. *Journal of the American Water Resources Association*, 37, 255–270.

Bliss, A., Hock, R. and Radić, V. (2014) Global response of glacier runoff to twenty-first century climate change. *Journal of Geophysical Research: Earth Surface*, 119, 717–730.

Blum, M.D. and Roberts, H.H. (2009) Drowning of the Mississippi delta due to insufficient sediment supply and global sea-level rise. *Nature Geoscience*, 2, 488–491.

Blum, M.D. and Törnqvist, T.E. (2000) Fluvial responses to climate and sea-level change: a review and look forward. *Sedimentology*, 47 (Suppl. 1), 2–48.

Blume, H.-P. and Leinweber, P. (2004) Plaggen soils: landscape history, properties, and classification. *Journal of Plant Nutrition and Soil Science*, 167, 319–327.

Boakes, E.H., Mace, G.M., McGowan, P.J.K. and Fuller, R.A. (2010) Extreme contagion in global habitat clearance. *Proceedings of the Royal Society*, B, 277, 1081–1085.

Boardman, J. (1998) An average soil erosion rate for Europe: myth or reality. *Journal of Soil and Water Conservation*, 53, 46–50.

Boardman, J. (2013) The hydrological role of 'sunken lanes' with respect to sediment mobilization and delivery to watercourses with particular reference to West Sussex, southern England. *Journal of Soils and Sediments*, 13, 1636–1644.

Boardman, J. and Foster, I.D.L. (2011) The potential significance of the breaching of small farm dams in the Sneeuberg region. *South Africa. Journal of Soils and Sediments*, 11, 1456–1465.

Boardman, J., Foster, I.D., Rowntree, K.M., Favis-Mortlock, D.T., Mol, L., Suich, H. and Gaynor, D. (2017) Long-term studies of land degradation in the Sneeuberg uplands, eastern Karoo, South Africa: a synthesis. *Geomorphology*, 285, 106–120.

Bochet, E., Rubio, J.L. and Poesen, J. (1998) Relative efficiency of three representative matorral species in reducing water erosion at the microscale in a semi-arid climate (Valencia, Spain). *Geomorphology*, 23, 139–150.

Bock, L. and Burkhardt, U. (2016) The temporal evolution of a long-lived contrail cirrus cluster: simulations with a global climate model. *Journal of Geophysical Research: Atmospheres*, 121 (7), 3548–3565.

Böckh, A. (1973) Consequences of uncontrolled human activities in the Valencia lake basin. In M.T. Farvar and J.P. Milton (eds), *The Careless Technology*. London: Tom Stacey, 301–317.

Boenzi, F., Caldara, M., Capolongo, D., et al. (2008) Late Pleistocene–Holocene landscape evolution in Fossa Bradanica, Basilicata (southern Italy). *Geomorphology*, 102, 297–306.

Bogaard, A., Fraser, R., Heaton, T.H., et al. (2013) Crop manuring and intensive land management by Europe's first farmers. *Proceedings of the National Academy of Sciences*, 110 (31), 12589–12594.

Bogaart, P.W., Van Balen, R.T., Kasse, C. and Vandenberghe, J. (2003) Process-based modeling of fluvial system response to rapid climate change – I: model formulation and generic applications. *Quaternary Science Reviews*, 22, 2077–2095.

Bollasina, M.O., Yi, M. and Ramaswamy, V. (2011) Anthropogenic aerosols and the weakening of the South Asian Summer Monsoon. *Science*, 334, 502–505.

Bomford, M. and Hart, Q. (2002) Non-indigenous vertebrates in Australia. In D. Pimentel (ed.), *Biological Invasions*. Boca Raton: CRC Press, 25–44.

Bonan, G.B. (1997) Effects of land use on the climate of the United States. *Climatic Change*, 37, 449–486.

Bond, W.J. and Midgley, G.F. (2012) Carbon dioxide and the uneasy interactions of trees and savannah grasses. *Philosophical Transactions of the Royal Society of London: Series B, Biological Sciences*, 367, 601–612.

Bonhomme, D., Boudouresque, C.F., Astruch, P., et al. (2015) Typology of the reef formations of the Mediterranean seagrass Posidonia oceanica, and the discovery of extensive reefs in the Gulf of Hyères (Provence, Mediterranean). *Scientific Report of Port-Cros National Park*, 29, 41–73.

Bonneau, J., Fletcher, T.D., Costelloe, J.F. and Burns, M.J. (2017) Stormwater infiltration and the 'urban karst' – a review. *Journal of Hydrology*, 552, 141–150.

Bonnell, T.R., Reyna-Hurtado, R. and Chapman, C.A. (2011) Post-logging recovery time is longer than expected in an East African tropical forest. *Forest Ecology and Management*, 261, 855–864.

Bonnichsen, T.M., Bonnichsen, M., Anderson, K., et al. (1999) Native American influences on the development of forest ecosystems. In R.C. Szaro, N.C. Johnson, W.T. Sexton and A.J. Malle (eds), *Ecological Stewardship* (Vol. 2). Amsterdam: Elsevier Science, 439–470.

Boorman, L.A. (1977) Sand-dunes. In R.S.K. Barnes (ed.), *The Coastline*. Chichester: Wiley, 161–197.

Boorman, L.A. and Hazelden, J. (2017) Managed re-alignment: a salt marsh dilemma? *Wetlands Ecology and Management*, doi:10.1007/s11273-017-9556-9.

Booysen, P. de V. and Tainton, N.M. (eds) (1984) *Ecological Effects of Fire in South African Ecosystems*. Berlin: Springer-Verlag.

Borella, J.W., Quigley, M. and Vick, L. (2016) Anthropocene rockfalls travel farther than prehistoric predecessors. *Science Advances*, 2 (9), doi:10.1126/sciadv.1600969.

Bormann, F.H., Likens, G.E., Fisher, D.W. and Pierce, R.S. (1968) Nutrient loss accelerated by clear cutting of a forest ecosystem. *Science*, 159, 882–884.

Boulanger, M.T. and Lyman, R.L. (2014) Northeastern North American Pleistocene megafauna chronologically overlapped minimally with Paleoindians. *Quaternary Science Reviews*, 85, 35–46.

Boulanger, Y., Taylor, A.R., Price, D.T., et al. (2016) Climate change impacts on forest landscapes along the Canadian southern boreal forest transition zone. *Landscape Ecology*, doi:10.1007/s10980-016-0421-7.

Bouraouni, F. and Grizzetti, B. (2011) Long term change of nutrient concentrations of rivers discharging in European seas. *Science of the Total Environment*, 409, 4899–4916.

Bourgeon, L., Burke, A. and Higham, T. (2017) Earliest human presence in North America dated to the Last Glacial Maximum: new radiocarbon dates from Bluefish Caves, Canada. *PloS one*, 12 (1), e0169486.

Bourscheidt, V., Pinto, O. and Naccarato, K.P. (2016) The effects of Sao Paulo urban heat island on lightning activity: decadal analysis (1999–2009). *Journal of Geophysical Research: Atmospheres*, 121 (9), 4429–4442.

Boussingault, J.B. (1845) *Rural Economy* (2nd edn). London: Baillière.

Boutron, C.F., Görlach, U., Candelone, J.-P., et al. (1991) Decrease in anthropogenic lead, cadmium and zinc in Greenland snows since the late 1960s. *Nature*, 353, 153–156.

Bouwman, A.F., van Vuuren, D.P., Derwent, R.G. and Posch, M. (2002) A global analysis of acidification and eutrophication of terrestrial ecosystems. *Water, Air, and Soil Pollution*, 141, 349–382.

Bowden, W.B. (2010) Climate change in the Arctic – permafrost, thermokarst, and why they matter to the non-Arctic world. *Geography Compass*, 4, 1553–1566.

Bowen, M.W. and Johnson, W.C. (2017) Anthropogenically accelerated sediment accumulation within playa wetlands as a result of land cover change on the High Plains of the central United States. *Geomorphology*, 168, 135-145.

Bowes, M.J., Smith, J.T., Neal, C., et al. (2011) Changes in water quality of the River Frome (UK) from 1965 to 2009: is phosphorus mitigation finally working? *Science of the Total Environment*, 409, 3418–3430.

Bowman, D.M. (2014) What is the relevance of pyrogeography to the Anthropocene? *The Anthropocene Review*, 2, 73–76.

Bowman, D.M., Balch, J., Artaxo, P., et al. (2011) The human dimension of fire regimes on Earth. *Journal of Biogeography*, 38, 2223–2226.

Boyd, M. (2002) Identification of anthropogenic burning in the paleoecological record of the Northern Prairies: a new approach. *Annals of the Association of American Geographers*, 92, 471–487.

Boyle, J.F., Gaillard, M.-J., Kaplan, J.O. and Dearing, J.A. (2011) Modelling prehistoric land use and carbon budgets: a critical review. *The Holocene*, 21, 715–722.

Bradley, R. (1985) *Quaternary Palaeoclimatology*. London: Chapman and Hall.

Bradley, R.S., Vuille, M., Diaz, H.F. and Vergara, W. (2006) Threats to water supplies in the tropical Andes. *Science*, 312, 1755–1756.

Bradshaw, C.J.A., Sodhi, N.T., Peh, K.S.H. and Brook, B.W. (2007) Global evidence that deforestation amplifies flood risk and severity in the developing world. *Global Change Biology*, 13, 2379–2395.

Braithwaite, R.J. and Zhang, Y. (1999) Modelling changes in glacier mass balance that may occur as a result of climate changes. *Geografiska Annaler. Series A, Physical Geography*, 81, 489–496.

Braje, T.J. (2015) Earth systems, human agency, and the Anthropocene: planet Earth in the human age. *Journal of Archaeological Research*, 23, 369–396.

Braje, T.J., Leppard, T.P., Fitzpatrick, S.M. and Erlandson, J.M. (2017) Archaeology, historical ecology and anthropogenic island ecosystems. *Environmental Conservation*, doi:10.1017/S0376892917000261.

Brander, K.E., Owen, K.E. and Potter, K.W. (2004) Modelled impacts of development type on runoff volume and infiltration performance. *Journal of the American Water Resources Association*, 40, 961–969.

Brandt, S.A. (2000) Classification of geomorphological effects downstream of dams. *Catena*, 40, 375–401.

Brassington, F.C. and Rushton, K.R. (1987) A rising water table in central Liverpool. *Quarterly Journal of Engineering Geology and Hydrogeology*, 20, 151–158.

Brattebo, B.O. and Booth, D.B. (2003) Long-term stormwater quantity and quality performance of permeable pavement systems. *Water Research*, 37, 4369–4376.

Braun, L.N., Weber, M. and Schulz, M. (2000) Consequences of climate change for runoff from alpine regions. *Annals of Glaciology*, 31, 19–25.

Bravard, J.-P., and Petts, G.E. (1996) Human impacts on fluvial hydrosystems. In G.E. Petts and C. Amoros (eds), *Fluvial Hydrosystems*. London: Chapman and Hall, 242–262.

Braverman, M. and Quinton, W.L. (2015) Hydrological impacts of seismic lines in the wetland-dominated zone of thawing, discontinuous permafrost, Northwest Territories, Canada. *Hydrological Processes*, 30, 2627–2627.

Bray, H.J., Carter, D.J. and Hooke, J.M. (1992) *Sea level rise and global warming: scenarios, physical impacts and policies*. Report to SCOPAC, University of Portsmouth.

Brazel, A.J. and Idso, S.B. (1979) Thermal effects of dust on climate. *Annals of the Association of American Geographers*, 69, 432–437.

Brecht, H., Dasgupta, S., Laplante, B., et al. (2012) Sea-level rise and storm surges: high stakes for a small number of developing countries. *Journal of Environment and Development*, 21, 120–138.

Bredenkamp, G.J., Spada, F. and Kazmierczak, E. (2002) On the origin of northern and southern hemisphere grasslands. *Plant Ecology*, 163, 209–229.

Breslow, P.B. and Sailor, D.J. (2002) Vulnerability of wind power resources to climate change in the continental United States. *Renewable Energy*, 27, 585–598.

Breuer, G. (1980) *Weather Modification: Prospects and Problems*. Cambridge: Cambridge University Press.

Brewer, S. (2008) Declines in plant species richness and endemic plant species in longleaf pine savannas invaded by Imperata cylindrica. *Biological Invasions*, 10, 1257–1264.

Brimblecombe, P. (1977) London air pollution 1500–1900. *Atmospheric Environment*, 11, 1157–1162.

Brimblecombe, P. and Camuffo, D. (2003) Long term damage to the built environment. In P. Brimblecombe (ed.), *The Effects of Air Pollution on the Built Environment*. London: Imperial College Press, 1–30.

Broadus, J.G. (1990) Greenhouse effects, sea level rise and land use. *Land Use Policy*, 7, 138–153.

Broadus, J.G., Milliman, J., Edwards, S., et al. (1986) Rising sea level and damming of rivers: possible effects in Egypt and Bangladesh. In J.G. Titus (ed.), *Effects of Changes in Stratospheric Ozone and Global Climate*. Washington, DC: UNEP/USEPA, 165–189.

Broodbank, C. (2006) The origins and early development of Mediterranean maritime history. *Journal of Mediterranean Archaeology*, 19, 199–230.

Brook, B.W. and Bowman, D.M.J.S. (2002) Explaining the Pleistocene megafaunal extinction: models, chronologies, and assumptions. *Proceedings of the National Academy of Sciences*, 99, 14624–14627.

Brookes, A. (1985) River channelization: traditional engineering methods, physical consequences, and alternative practices. *Progress in Physical Geography*, 9, 44–73.

Brookes, A. (1987) The distribution and management of channelized streams in Denmark. *Regulated Rivers: Research & Management*, 1, 3–16.

Brooks, A.P. and Brierly, G.J. (1997) Geomorphic responses of lower Bega River to catchment disturbance, 1851–1926. *Geomorphology*, 18, 291–304.

Brooks, M.L. and Matchett, J.R. (2006) Spatial and temporal patterns of wildfires in the Mojave Desert, 1980–2004. *Journal of Arid Environments*, 67, 148–164.

Brooks, S.M. and Spencer, T. (2012) Shoreline retreat and sediment release in response to accelerating sea level rise: measuring and modelling cliffloine dynamics on the Suffolk coast, UK. *Global and Planetary Change*, 80–81, 165–179.

Brouns, K., Eikelboom, T., Jansen, P.C., et al. (2015) Spatial analysis of soil subsidence in peat meadow areas in Friesland in relation to land and water management, climate change, and adaptation. *Environmental Management*, 55, 360–372.

Brown, B.E. (1997) Coral bleaching: causes and consequences. *Coral Reefs*, 16, S129–S138.

Brown, B.E., Dunne, R.P., Goodson, H.S. and Douglas, A.G. (2000) Bleaching patterns in coral reefs. *Nature*, 404, 142–143.

Brown, C., Mcmorran, R. and Price, M.F. (2011) Rewilding – a new paradigm for nature conservation in Scotland? *Scottish Geographical Journal*, 127 (4), 288–314.

Brown, J.H. (1989) Patterns, modes and extents of invasions by vertebrates. In J. A. Drake (ed.), *Biological Invasions: A Global Perspective*. Chichester: Wiley, 85–109.

Brown, S. and Lugo, A.E. (1990) Tropical secondary forests. *Journal of Tropical Ecology*, 6, 1–32.

Browning, K.A., Allah, R.J., Ballard, B.P., et al. (1991) Environmental effects from burning oil wells in Kuwait. *Nature*, 351, 363–367.

Bruijnzeel, L.A. (1990) *Hydrology of Moist Tropical Forests and Effects of Conversion: A State of Knowledge Review*. Amsterdam: Free University for UNESCO International Hydrological Programme.

Bruins, H.J. (2012) Ancient desert agriculture in the Negev and climate-zone boundary changes during average, wet and drought years. *Journal of Arid Environments*, 86, 28–42.

Brunel, C. and Sabatier, F. (2009) Potential influence of sea-level rise in controlling shoreline position on the French Mediterranean Coast. *Geomorphology*, 107, 47–57.

Brunet, M., Guy, F., Pilbeam, D., Mackay, H.T., et al. (2002) A new hominid from the upper Miocene of Chad, central Africa. *Nature*, 418, 145–151.

Brunhes, J. (1920) *Human Geography*. London: Harrap.

Bruno, J.F. and Selig, E.R. (2007) Regional decline of coral cover in the Indo-Pacific: timing, extent and subregional comparisons. *PLoS ONE*, 8, e711.

Brunsden, D. (2001) A critical assessment of the sensitivity concept in geomorphology. *Catena*, 42, 83–98.

Brusca, R.C., Wiens, J.F., Meyer, W.M., et al. (2013) Dramatic response to climate change in the Southwest: Robert Whittaker's 1963 Arizona Mountain plant transect revisited. *Ecology and Evolution*, 3 (10), 3307–3319.

Bruun, P. (1962) Sea level rise as a cause of shore erosion. *American Society of Civil Engineers Proceedings: Journal of the Waterways and Harbors Division*, 88, 117–130.

Bryan, G.W. (1979) Bioaccumulation of marine pollutants. *Philosophical Transactions of the Royal Society of London: Series B, Biological Sciences*, 286, 483–505.

Bryan, K. (1928) Historic evidence of changes in the channel of Rio Puerco, a tributary of the Rio Grande in New Mexico. *Journal of Geology*, 36, 265–282.

Bryant, R.G., Bigg, G.R., Mahowald, N.M., et al. (2007) Dust emission response to climate in southern Africa. *Journal of Geophysical Research*, 112, D09207, doi:10.1029/2005JD007025.

Buckley, S.M. and Mitchell, M.J. (2010) Improvements in urban air quality: case studies from New York State, USA. *Water, Air, and Soil Pollution*, 214, 93–106.

Buddemeier, R.W. and Smith, S.V. (1988) Coral reef growth in an era of rapidly rising sea level: predictions and suggestions for long-term research. *Coral Reefs*, 7, 51–56.

Buendia, C., Batalla, R.J., Sabater, S., Palau, A. and Marcé, R. (2016) Runoff trends driven by climate and afforestation in a Pyrenean Basin. *Land Degradation and Development*, 27 (3), 823–838.

Bugalho, M.N., Caldeira, M.C., Pereira, J.S., Aronson, J. and Pausas, J.G. (2011) Mediterranean cork oak savannas require human use to sustain biodiversity and ecosystem services. *Frontiers in Ecology and the Environment*, 9 (5), 278–286.

Buitenwerf, R., Bond, W.J., Stevens, N. and Trollope, W.S.W. (2012) Increased tree densities in South African savannas: >50 years of data suggests CO_2 as a driver. *Global Change Biology*, 18, 675–684.

Bull, W.B. (1997) Discontinuous ephemeral streams. *Geomorphology*, 19, 227–276.

Bullard, J.E., Thomas, D.S.G., Livingstone, I. and Wiggs, G. (1996) Wind energy variations in the south-western Kalahari Desert and their implications for linear dunefield activity. *Earth Surface Processes and Landforms*, 21, 263–278.

Burian, S.J. and Shepherd, J.M. (2005) Effect of urbanization on the diurnal rainfall pattern in Houston. *Hydrological Processes*, 19, 1089–1103.

Burjachs, F., Pérez-Obiol, R., Picornell-Gelabert, L., et al. (2017) Overview of environmental changes and human colonization in the Balearic Islands (Western Mediterranean) and their impacts on vegetation composition during the Holocene. *Journal of Archaeological Science: Reports*, 12, 845–849.

Burke, R. (1972) Stormwater runoff. In R.T. Oglesby, C.A. Carlson and J.A. McCann (eds), *River Ecology and Man*. New York: Academic Press, 727–733.

Burney, A.D. (1993) Recent animal extinctions: recipes for disaster. *American Scientist*, 81, 530–541.

Burrin, P.J. (1985) Holocene alluviation in southeast England and some implications for palaeohydrological studies. *Earth Surface Processes and Landforms*, 10, 257–271.

Burroughs, B.A., Hayes, D.B., Klomp, K.D., et al. (2009) Effects of Stronach Dam removal on fluvial geomorphology in the Pine River, Michigan, United States. *Geomorphology*, 110, 96–107.

Burt, T.P. (1994) Long-term study of the natural environment – perceptive science or mindless monitoring? *Progress in Physical Geography*, 18, 475–496.

Burt, T.P., Donohoe, M.A. and Vann, A.R. (1983) The effect of forestry drainage operations on upland sediment yields: the results of a stormbased study. *Earth Surface Processes and Landforms*, 8, 339–346.

Burt, T.P. and Haycock, N.E. (1992) Catchment planning and the nitrate issue: a UK perspective. *Progress in Physical Geography*, 16, 379–404.

Burt, T.P., Howden, N.J.K., Worrall, F., et al. (2010) Nitrate in United Kingdom rivers: policy and its outcomes since 1970. *Environmental Science & Technology*, 24, 2657–2662.

Burt, T.P., Howden, N.J.K., Worrall, F. and Whelan, M.J. (2008) Importance of long-term monitoring for detecting environmental change: lessons from a lowland river in south east England. *Biogeosciences*, 5 (6), 1529–1535.

Burton, G.A., Basu, N., Ellis, B.R., et al. (2014) Hydraulic 'fracking': are surface water impacts an ecological concern? *Environmental Toxicology and Chemistry*, 33 (8), 1679–1689.

Bush, M.B. (1988) Early Mesolithic disturbance: a force on the landscape. *Journal of Archaeological Science*, 15, 453–462.

Butchart, S.H., Walpole, M., Collen, B., et al. (2010) Global biodiversity: indicators of recent declines. *Science*, 328 (5982), 1164–1168.

Butler, D.R. (2006) Human-induced changes in animal populations and distributions, and the subsequent effects on fluvial systems. *Geomorphology*, 79 (3), 448–459.

Butzer, K.W. (1972) *Environment and Archaeology – An Ecological Approach to Prehistory*. London: Methuen.

Butzer, K.W. (1974) Accelerated soil erosion: a problem of man–land relationships. In I.R. Manners and M.W. Mikesell (eds), *Perspectives on Environments*. Washington, DC: Association of American Geographers, 55–77.

Butzer, K.W. (1976) *Early Hydraulic Civilization in Egypt*. Chicago: University of Chicago Press.

Buyanovsky, G.A. and Wagner, G.H. (1998) Carbon cycling in cultivated land and its global significance. *Global Change Biology*, 4, 131–141.

Buynevich, I., Bitinas, A. and Pupienis, D. (2007) Reactivation of coastal dunes documented by subsurface imaging of the Great Dune Ridge, Lithuania. *Journal of Coastal Research*, 50, 226–230.

Buytaert, W., Cuesta-Camacho, F. and Tobón, C. (2011) Potential impacts of climate change on the environmental services of humid tropical alpine regions. *Global Ecology and Biogeography*, 20, 19–33.

Cabanes, C., Cazanave, A. and Le Provost, C. (2001) Sea level rise during past 40 years determined from satellite and in situ observations. *Science*, 294, 840–842.

Cahill, A.E., Aiello-Lammens, M.E., Fisher-Reid, M.C., et al. (2012) How does climate change cause extinction? *Proceedings of the Royal Society*, B, doi:10.1098/rspb.2012.1890.

Cai, W., Borlace, S., Lengaigne, M., Van Rensch, P., et al. (2014) Increasing frequency of extreme El Niño events due to greenhouse warming. *Nature Climate Change*, 4 (2), 111–116.

Cai, Y., Zhang, H., Zheng, P. and Pan, W. (2016) Quantifying the impact of land use/land cover changes on the urban heat island: a case study of the natural wetlands distribution area of Fuzhou City, China. *Wetlands*, 36 (2), 285–298.

Caldararo, N. (2002) Human ecological intervention and the role of forest fires in human ecology. *Science of the Total Environment*, 292, 141–165.

Caldeira, K. and Wickett, M.G. (2003) Anthropogenic carbon and ocean pH. *Nature*, 425, 365.

Calef, M.P. (2010) Recent climate change impacts on the boreal forest of Alaska. *Geography Compass*, 4, 67–80.

Callaway, R.M. and Aschehoug, E.T. (2000) Invasive plants versus their new and old neighbors: a mechanism for exotic invasion. *Science*, 290, 521–523.

Cannon, S.H., Bigio, E.R. and Mine, E. (2001a) A process for fire-related debris flow initiation, Cerro Grande fire, New Mexico. *Hydrological Processes*, 15, 3011–3023.

Cannon, S.H., Kirkham, R.M. and Parise, M. (2001b) Wild-fire-related debris-flow initiation processes, Storm King Mountains, Colorado. *Geomorphology*, 39, 171–188.

Cao, S., Chen, L., Shankman, D., Wang, C., et al. (2011) Excessive reliance on afforestation in China's arid and semi-arid regions: lessons in ecological restoration. *Earth-Science Reviews*, 104, 240–245.

Cao, S., Tian, T., Chen, L., Dong, X., et al. (2010) Damage caused to the environment by reforestation policies in arid and semi-arid areas of China. *Ambio*, 39, 279–283.

Capra, G.F., Ganga, A., Grilli, E., et al. (2015) A review on anthropogenic soils from a worldwide perspective. *Journal of Soils and Sediments*, 15 (7), 1602–1618.

Carbognin, L., Teatini, P., Tomasin, A. and Tosi, L. (2010) Global change and relative sea level rise at Venice: what impact in term of flooding? *Climate Dynamics*, 35, 1039–1047.

Carbonell, E., De Castro, J.M.B., Parés, J.M., et al. (2008) The first hominim of Europe. *Nature*, 452, 465–469.

Carey, J.C. and Fulweiler, R.W. (2012) Human activities directly alter watershed dissolved silica fluxes. *Biogeochemistry*, 111, 125–138.

Carmona, P. and Ruiz, J.M. (2011) Historical morphogenesis of the Turia River coastal flood plain in the Mediterranean littoral of Spain. *Catena*, 86, 139–149.

Carnec, C. and Fabriol, H. (1999) Monitoring and modeling land subsidence at the Cerro Prieto geothermal field, Baja California, Mexico, using SAR interferometry. *Geophysical Research Letters*, 26, 1211–1214.

Caro, T. and Sherman, P. (2009) Rewilding can cause rather than solve ecological problems. *Nature*, 462 (7276), 985–985.

Carpenter, S.R., Stanley, E.H. and Zanden, M.J.V. (2011) State of the world's freshwater ecosystems: physical, chemical, and biological changes. *Annual Review of Environment and Resources*, 36, 75–99.

Carrara, P.E. and Carroll, T.R. (1979) The determination of erosion rates from exposed tree roots in the Piceance Basin, Colorado. *Earth Surface Processes*, 4, 407–417.

Carrasco, A.R., Ferreira, Ó. and Roelvink, D. (2016) Coastal lagoons and rising sea level: a review. *Earth-Science Reviews*, 154, 356–368.

Carrivick, J.L. and Quincey, D.J. (2014) Progressive increase in number and volume of ice-marginal lakes on the western margin of the Greenland Ice Sheet. *Global and Planetary Change*, 116, 156–163.

Carson, M., Köhl, A., Stammer, D., et al. (2016) Coastal sea level changes, observed and projected during the 20th and 21st century. *Climatic Change*, 134 (1–2), 269–281.

Carter, L.D. (1987) Arctic lowlands: introduction. In W.L. Graf (ed.), *Geomorphic Systems of North America* (centennial special Vol. 2). Boulder: Geological Society of America, 583–615.

Castree, N. (2014a) The Anthropocene and geography I: the back story. *Geography Compass*, 8 (7), 436–449.

Castree, N. (2014b) Geography and the Anthropocene II: current contributions. *Geography Compass*, 8 (7), 450–463.

Castree, N. (2014c) The Anthropocene and geography III: future directions. *Geography Compass*, 8 (7), 464–476.

Castree, N. (2015) Geography and global change science: relationships necessary, absent, and possible. *Geographical Research*, 53 (1), 1–15.

Catford, J.A., Vesk, P.A., Richardson, D.M. and Pyšek, P. (2012) Quantifying levels of biological invasion: towards the objective classification of invaded and invasible ecosystems. *Global Change Biology*, 18, 44–62.

Cathcart, R.B. (1983) Mediterranean Basin – Sahara reclamation. *Speculations in Science and Technology*, 6, 150–152.

Cattle, S.R. (2016) The case for a southeastern Australian Dust Bowl, 1895–1945. *Aeolian Research*, 21, 1–20.

Cavanaugh, K.C., Kellner, J.R., Forde, A.J., et al. (2014) Poleward expansion of mangroves is a threshold response to decreased frequency of extreme cold events. *Proceedings of the National Academy of Sciences*, 111, 723–727.

Cazenave, A. and Llovel, W. (2010) Contemporary sea level rise. *Annual Review of Marine Science*, 2, 145–173.

Ceballos, G. and Ehrlich, P.R. (2002) Mammal population losses and the extinction crisis. *Science*, 296, 904–907.

Ceballos, G., Ehrlich, P.R., Barnosky, A.D., García, A., Pringle, R.M. and Palmer, T.M. (2015) Accelerated modern human-induced species losses: entering the sixth mass extinction. *Science Advances*, 1 (5), e1400253.

Ceballos, G., Ehrlich, P.R. and Dirzo, R. (2017) Biological annihilation via the ongoing sixth mass extinction signaled by vertebrate population losses and declines. *Proceedings of the National Academy of Sciences*, doi:10.1073/pnas.1704949114.

Cerda, A. (1998) Post-fire dynamics of erosional processes under Mediterranean climatic conditions. *Zeitschrift für Geomorphologie*, 42, 373–398.

Cerdan, O., Govers, G., Le Bissonnais, Y., et al. (2010) Rates and spatial variations of soil erosion in Europe: a study based on erosion plot data. *Geomorphology*, 122, 167–177.

Cerney, D.L. (2010) The use of repeat photography in contemporary geomorphic studies: an evolving approach to understanding landscape change. *Geography Compass*, 4, 1339–1357.

Certini, G. and Scalenghe, R. (2011) Anthropogenic soils are the golden spikes for the Anthropocene. *The Holocene*, 21, 1269–1274.

Cervera, T., Pino, J., Marull, J., et al. (In press) Understanding the long-term dynamics of forest transition: from deforestation to afforestation in a Mediterranean landscape (Catalonia, 1868–2005). *Land Use Policy*.

Chai, J.-C., Shen, S.-L., Zhu, H.H. and Zhang, X.L. (2004) Land subsidence due to groundwater drawdown in Shanghai. *Géotechnique*, 54, 143–147.

Chai, S.-L. and Tanner, E.V.J. (2011) 150-year legacy of land use on tree species composition in old-secondary forests of Jamaica. *Journal of Ecology*, 99, 113–121.

Chambers, F.M., Dresser, P.Q. and Smith, A.G. (1979) Radio-carbon dating evidence on the impact of atmospheric pollution on upland peats. *Nature*, 282, 829–831.

Chand, S.S., Tory, K.J., Ye, H. and Walsh, K.J. (2017) Projected increase in El Niño-driven tropical cyclone frequency in the Pacific. *Nature Climate Change*, 7, 123–127.

Chandler, T.J. (1976) The climate of towns. In T.J. Chandler and S. Gregory (eds), *The Climate of the British Isles*. London: Longman, 307–329.

Changnon, S.A. (1973) Atmospheric alterations from manmade biospheric changes. In W.R.D. Sewell (ed.), *Modifying the Weather: A Social Assessment*. Adelaide: University of Victoria, 135–184.

Changnon, S.A. (1978) Urban effects on severe local storms at St Louis. *Journal of Applied Meteorology*, 17, 578–586.

Changnon, S.A., Kunkel, K.E. and Winstanley, D. (2003) Climate factors that caused the unique tall grass prairie in the Central United States. *Physical Geography*, 23, 259–280.

Chapin, F.S. and Danell, K. (2001) Boreal forest. In F.S. Chapin, O.E. Sala and E. Huber-Sannwald (eds), *Global Biodiversity in a Changing Environment*. New York: Springer, 101–120.

Chapin, F.S., McGuire, A.D., Ruess, R.W., et al. (2010) Resilience of Alaska's boreal forest to climatic change. *Canadian Journal of Forest Research*, 40, 1360–1370.

Chapin, F.S., Sala, O.E. and Huber-Sannwald, E. (2001) *Global Biodiversity in a Changing Environment*. Berlin: Springer.

Chappell, A., Baldock, J. and Sanderman, J. (2016) The global significance of omitting soil erosion from soil organic carbon cycling schemes. *Nature Climate Change*, 6 (2), 187–191.

Chappell, J., Cowell, P.J., Woodroffe, C.D. and Eliot, I.G. (1996) Coastal impacts of enhanced greenhouse climate change in Australia: implications for coal use. In W.J. Bouma, G.I. Pearman and M.R. Manning (eds), *Greenhouse*. Melbourne: Commonwealth Scientific and Industrial Research Organisation (CSIRO), 220–234.

Charles-Dominique, T., Davies, T.J., Hempson, G.P., et al. (2016) Spiny plants, mammal browsers, and the origin of African savannas. *Proceedings of the National Academy of Sciences*, 113 (38), E5572–E5579.

Charlson, R.J., Lovelock, J.E., Andreae, M.O. and Warren, S.G. (1987) Oceanic phytoplankton, atmospheric sulphur, cloud albedo and climate. *Nature*, 326, 655–661.

Charney, J., Stone, P.H. and Quirk, W.J. (1975) Drought in the Sahara: a bio-geophysical feedback mechanism. *Science*, 187, 434–435.

Chase, T.N., Pielke, R.A., Kittle, T.G.F., et al. (2000) Simulated impacts of historical land cover changes on global climate in northern winter. *Climate Dynamics*, 16, 93–105.

Chazdon, R.L., Letcher, S.G., van Breugel, M., et al. (2007) Rates of change in tree communities of secondary Neotropical forests following major disturbances. *Philosophical Transactions of the Royal Society of London: Series B, Biological Sciences*, 362, 273–289.

Chen, H.Y. and Luo, Y. (2015) Net aboveground biomass declines of four major forest types with forest ageing and climate change in western Canada's boreal forests. *Global Change Biology*, 21 (10), 3675–3684.

Chen, J., Theller, L., Gitau, M.W., et al. (2016) Urbanization impacts on surface runoff of the contiguous United States. *Journal of Environmental Management*, 187, 470–481.

Chen, L., Wang, W., Zhang, Y. and Lin, G. (2009) Recent progresses in mangrove conservation, restoration and research in China. *Journal of Plant Ecology*, 2, 45–54.

Chen, X. and Zong, Y. (1999) Major impacts of sea-level rise on agriculture in the Yangtze Delta area around Shanghai. *Applied Geography*, 19, 69–84.

Chen, Y., Xu, C., Chen, Y., et al. (2010) Response of glacial-lake outburst floods to climate change in the Yarkant River basin on northern slope of Karakoram Mountains, China. *Quaternary International*, 226, 75–81.

Cheng, F. and Granata, T. (2007) Sediment transport and channel adjustments associated with dam removal: field observations. *Water Resources Research*, 43, W03444.

Chester, D.K. and James, P.A. (1991) Holocene alluviation in the Algarve, southern Portugal: the case for an anthropogenic cause. *Journal of Archaeological Science*, 18, 73–87.

Chew, M.K. (2009) The monstering of tamarisk: how scientists made a plant into a problem. *Journal of the History of Biology*, 42, 231–266.

Chi, S.C. and Reilinger, R.E. (1984) Geodetic evidence for subsidence due to groundwater withdrawal in many parts of the United States of America. *Journal of Hydrology*, 67, 155–182.

Chiew, F.H.S., Wang, Q.J., McMahon, T.A., et al. (1996) Potential hydrological responses to climate change in Australia. In J.A.A. Jones, E. Liu, M.-K. Woo and H.-T. Kung (eds), *Regional Hydrological Response to Climate Change*. Dordrecht: Kluwer, 337–350.

Childe, V.G. (1936) *Man Makes Himself*. London: Watts.

Chin, A. (2006) Urban transformation of river landscapes in a global context. *Geomorphology*, 79, 460–487.

Chinn, T., Fitzharris, B.B., Willsman, A. and Salinger, M.J. (2012) Annual ice volume changes 1976–2008 for the New Zealand Southern Alps. *Global and Planetary Change*, 92, 105–118.

Chiverrell, R.C., Foster, G.C., Marshall, P., et al. (2009) Coupling relationships: hillslope-fluvial linkages in the Hodder catchment, NW England. *Geomorphology*, 109, 222–235.

Chiverrell, R.C., Harvey, A.M. and Foster, G.C. (2007) Hillslope gullying in the Solway Firth—Morecambe Bay region, Great Britain: responses to human impact and/or climatic deterioration? *Geomorphology*, 84, 317–343.

Chiverrell, R.C., Oldfield, F., Appleby, P.G., et al. (2008) Evidence for changes in Holocene sediment flux in Semer Water and Raydale, North Yorkshire, UK. *Geomorphology*, 100, 70–82.

Chorley, R.J. and More, R.J. (1967) The interaction of precipitation and man. In R.J. Chorley (ed.), *Water, Earth and Man*. London: Methuen, 157–166.

Chu, Z.X., Zhai, S.K., Lu, X.X., et al. (2009) A quantitative assessment of human impacts on decrease in sediment flux from major Chinese rivers entering the western Pacific Ocean. *Geophysical Research Letters*, 36, L19603.

Church, J.A. (2001) How fast are sea levels rising? *Science*, 294, 802–803.

Church, J.A., Gregory, J.M., Huybrechts, P., et al. (2001) Changes in sea level. In J.T. Houghton (ed.), *Climate Change 2001: The Scientific Basis*. Cambridge: Cambridge University Press, 639–693.

Ciccarelli, D. (2014) Mediterranean coastal sand dune vegetation: influence of natural and anthropogenic factors. *Environmental Management*, 54, 194–204.

Clark, J.R. (1977) *Coastal Ecosystem Management*. New York: Wiley.

Clark, J.S., Cachier, H., Goldammer, J.G. and Stocks, B. (eds) (1997) *Sediment Records of Biomass Burning and Global Change*. Berlin: Springer.

Clark, R.B. (2001) *Marine Pollution* (5th edn). Oxford: Clarendon Press.

Clarke, G.K., Jarosch, A.H., Anslow, F.S., et al. (2015) Projected deglaciation of western Canada in the twenty-first century. *Nature Geoscience*, 8, 372–377.

Clarke, M.A. and Walsh, R.P.D. (2006) Long-term erosion and surface roughness change of rain-forest terrain following selective logging, Danum Valley, Sabah, Malaysia. *Catena*, 68, 109–123.

Clarke, M.L. and Rendell, H.M. (2009) The impact of North Atlantic storminess on western European coasts: a review. *Quaternary International*, 195, 31–41.

Clarke, R.T. and McCulloch, J.S.G. (1979) The effect of land use on the hydrology of small upland catchments. In G.E. Hollis (ed.), *Man's Impact on the Hydrological Cycle in the United Kingdom*. Norwich: Geo Abstracts, 71–78.

Clarkson, C., Jacobs, Z., and Marwick, B., et al. (2017) Human occupation of northern Australia by 65,000 years ago. *Nature*, 547, 306–310.

Claudet, J. and Fraschetti, S. (2010) Human-driven impacts on marine habitats: a regional meta-analysis in the Mediterranean Sea. *Biological Conservation*, 143, 2195–2206.

Clay, G.D., Dixon, S., Evans, M.G., Rowson, J.G. and Worrall, F. (2012) Carbon dioxide fluxes and DOC concentrations of eroding blanket peat gullies. *Earth Surface Processes and Landforms*, 37, 562–571.

Clay, J. (2004) *World Agriculture and the Environment.* Washington, DC: Island Press.

Clements, F.E. (1916) *Plant Succession.* Carnegie Institution Publication, 242. Washington DC: Carnegie Institution of Washington.

Closson, D., LaMoreaux, P.E., Karaki, N.A. and Al-Fugha, H. (2007) Karst system developed in salt layers of the Lisan Peninsula, Dead Sea, Jordan. *Environmental Geology*, 52, 155–172.

Clout, M.N. and Williams, P.A. (eds) (2009) *Invasive Species Management.* New York: Oxford University Press.

Coe, M. (1981) Body size and the extinction of the Pleistocene megafauna. *Palaeoecology of Africa*, 13, 139–145.

Coe, M. (1982) The bigger they are. *Oryx*, 16, 225–228.

Coffin, A.W. (2007) From roadkill to road ecology: a review of the ecological effects of roads. *Journal of Transport Geography*, 15, 396–406.

Cohen, J.E. (2003) Human population: the next half century. *Science*, 302, 1172–1175.

Cohen, T.J., Jansen, J.D., Gliganic, L.A., et al. (2015) Hydrological transformation coincided with megafaunal extinction in central Australia. *Geology*, 43 (3), 195–198.

Cole, K.L., Ironside, K., Eischeid, J., Garfin, G., Duffy, P.B. and Toney, C. (2011) Past and ongoing shifts in Joshua tree distribution support future modeled range contraction. *Ecological Applications*, 21 (1), 137–149.

Cole, M.M. and Smith, R.F. (1984) Vegetation as an indicator of environmental pollution. *Transactions of the Institute of British Geographers*, 9, 477–493.

Cole, S. (1970) *The Neolithic Revolution* (5th edn). London: British Museum (Natural History).

Collier, M. and Webb, R.H. (2002) *Floods, Droughts and Climate Change.* Tucson: University of Arizona Press.

Collins, P.M., Davis, B.A.S. and Kaplan, J.O. (2012) The mid-Holocene vegetation of the Mediterranean region and southern Europe, and a comparison with the present day. *Journal of Biogeography*, 39 (10), 1848–1861.

Collison, A., Wade, S., Griffiths, J. and Dehn, M. (2000) Modelling the impact of predicted climate change on landslide frequency and magnitude in S.E. England. *Engineering Geology*, 55, 205–218.

Colls, J. and Tiwary, A. (2009) *Air Pollution: Measurement, Modelling and Mitigation* (3rd edn). London: Routledge.

Comeaux, R.S., Allison, M.A. and Bianchi, T.S. (2012) Mangrove expansion in the Gulf of Mexico with climate change: implications for wetland health and resistance to rising sea levels. *Estuarine, Coastal and Shelf Science*, 96, 81–95.

Conacher, A.J. and Conacher, J. (1995) *Rural Land Degradation in Australia.* Melbourne: Oxford University Press.

Conacher, A.J. and Sala, M. (eds) (1998) *Land Degradation in Mediterranean Environments of the World.* Chichester: Wiley.

Conley, D.J., Carstensen, J., Aigars, J., et al. (2011) Hypoxia is increasing in the coastal zone of the Baltic Sea. *Environmental Science & Technology*, 45, 6777–6783.

Conway, D., Kroi, M., Alcamo, J. and Hulme, M. (1996) Future availability of water in Egypt: the interaction of global, regional and basin scale driving forces in the Nile Basin. *Ambio*, 25, 336–342.

Conway, V.M. (1954) Stratigraphy and pollen analysis of southern Pennine blanket peats. *The Journal of Ecology*, 42, 117–147.

Cook, A.J. and Vaughan, D.G. (2010) Overview of areal changes of the ice shelves on the Antarctic Peninsula over the past 50 years. *The Cryosphere*, 4, 77–98.

Cook, B.I., Miller, R.L. and Seager, R. (2009) Amplification of the North American 'Dust Bowl' drought through human-induced land degradation. *Proceedings of the National Academy of Sciences*, 106, 4997–5001.

Cook, B.I., Seager, R., Miller, R.L. and Mason, J.A. (2013) Intensification of North American megadroughts through surface and dust aerosol forcing. *Journal of Climate*, 26 (13), 4414–4430.

Cook, H., Stearne, K. and Williamson, T. (2003) The origins of water meadows in England. *The Agricultural History Review*, 51, 155–162.

Cook, K.H. and Vizy, E.K. (2008) Effects of twenty-first-century climate change on the Amazon rain forest. *Journal of Climate*, 21, 542–560.

Cooke, R.U. and Doornkamp, J.C. (1990) *Geomorphology in Environmental Management* (2nd edn). Oxford: Clarendon Press.

Cooke, R.U., Brunsden, D., Doornkamp, J.C. and Jones, D.K.C. (1982) *Urban Geomorphology in Drylands*. Oxford: Oxford University Press.

Cooke, R.U. and Reeves, R.W. (1976) *Arroyos and Environmental Change in the American South-West*. Oxford: Clarendon Press.

Coones, P. and Patten, J.H.C. (1986) *The Landscape of England and Wales*. Harmondsworth: Penguin Books.

Cooper, A.H. and Saunders, J.M. (2002) Road and bridge construction across gypsum karst in England. *Engineering Geology*, 65 (2), 217–223.

Cooper, A.R., Infante, D.M., Daniel, W.M., Wehrly, K.E., Wang, L. and Brenden, T.O. (2017) Assessment of dam effects on streams and fish assemblages of the conterminous USA. *Science of the Total Environment*, 586, 879–889.

Cooper, C.F. (1961) The ecology of fire. *Scientific American*, 204 (4), 150–160.

Cooper, D.M. and Jenkins, A. (2003) Response of acid lakes in the UK to reductions in atmospheric deposition of sulphur. *Science of the Total Environment*, 313, 91–100.

Cooper, J.A.G. and Pilkey, O.H. (2004) Sea-level rise and shoreline retreat: time to abandon the Bruun Rule. *Global and Planetary Change*, 43, 157–171.

Corlett, R.T. (1995) Tropical secondary forests. *Progress in Physical Geography*, 19, 159–172.

Corlett, R.T. (2011) Impacts of warming on tropical lowland rainforests. *Trends in Ecology & Evolution*, 26, 606–613.

Corlett, R.T. (2016) Plant diversity in a changing world: status, trends, and conservation needs. *Plant Diversity*, 38, 10–16.

Cornell, J. D. and Miller, M. (2007) Slash and burn. *Encyclopedia of Earth*, 31, http://www.eoearth.org/view/article/156045 (accessed January 2018).

Costa, A., Pereira, H. and Madeira, M. (2009) Landscape dynamics in endangered cork oak woodlands in Southwestern Portugal (1958–2005). *Agroforestry Systems*, 77 (2), 83–96.

Costa, A., Pereira, H. and Madeira, M. (2010) Analysis of spatial patterns of oak decline in cork oak woodlands in Mediterranean conditions. *Annals of Forest Science*, 67 (2), article 204.

Costa, J.E. (1975) Effects of agriculture on erosion and sedimentation in the Piedmont province, Maryland. *Geological Society of America Bulletin*, 86, 1281–1286.

Cotton, W.R. and Pielke, R.A. (2007) *Human Impacts on Weather and Climate* (2nd edn). Cambridge: Cambridge University Press.

Coumou, D. and Rahmstorf, S. (2012) A decade of weather extremes. *Nature Climate Change*, 2, 491–496.

Cowell, E.B. (1976) Oil pollution of the sea. In R. Johnson (ed.), *Marine Pollution*. London: Academic Press, 353–401.

Cox, R., Zentner, D.B., Rakotondrazafy, A.F.M. and Rasoazanamparany, C.F. (2010) Shakedown in Madagascar: occurrence of lavakas (erosional gullies) associated with seismic activity. *Geology*, 38, 179–182.

Crawford, S.S. and Muir, A.M. (2008) Global introductions of salmon and trout in the genus Oncorhynchus: 1870–2007. *Reviews in Fish Biology and Fisheries*, 18, 313–344.

Crick, H.Q.P. (2004) The impact of climate change on birds. *Ibis*, 146 (Suppl. 1), 48–56.

Crisp, D.T. (1977) Some physical and chemical effects of the Cow Green (Upper Teesdale) impoundment. *Freshwater Biology*, 7, 109–120.

Critchley, W.R.S., Reij, C. and Willcocks, T.J. (1994) Indigenous soil and water conservation: a review of the state of knowledge and prospects for building on traditions. *Land Degradation and Rehabilitation*, 5, 293–314.

Croke, J., Hairsine, P. and Fogarty, P. (2001) Soil recovery from track construction and harvesting changes in surface infiltration, erosion and delivery rates with time. *Forest Ecology and Management*, 143, 3–12.

Cronk, Q.C.B. and Fuller, J.L. (1995) *Plant Invaders*. London: Chapman and Hall.

Crowley, B.E. (2010) A refined chronology of prehistoric Madagascar and the demise of the megafauna. *Quaternary Science Reviews*, 29, 2591–2603.

Croxall, J.P., Butchart, S.H.M., Lascelles, B., et al. (2012) Seabird conservation status, threats and priority actions: a global assessment. *Bird Conservation International*, 22, 1–34.

Crozier, M.J. (2010) Deciphering the effect of climate change on landslide activity: a review. *Geomorphology*, 124, 260–267.

Crozier, M.J., Marx, S.L. and Grant, I.J. (1978) Impact of off-road recreational vehicles on soil and vegetation. *Proceedings of the 9th New Zealand Geography Conference*, Dunedin, 76–79.

Crutzen, P.J. (2002) Geology of mankind. *Nature*, 415, 23.

Crutzen, P.J., Aselmann, I. and Sepler, W. (1986) Methane production by domestic animals, wild ruminants, other herbivores, fauna and humans. *Tellus*, 38B, 271–284.

Crutzen, P.J. and Goldammer, J.G. (1993) *Fire in the Environment*. Chichester: Wiley.

ASKHAM BRYAN
COLLEGE
LEARNING RESOURCES

Csiki, S. and Rhoads, B.L. (2010) Hydraulic and geomorphological effects of run-of-river dams. *Progress in Physical Geography*, 34, 755–780.

Cuadra, P.E. and Vidon, P. (2011) Storm nitrogen dynamics in tile-drain flow in the US Midwest. *Biogeochemistry*, 104, 293–308.

Cuff, D.J. and Goudie, A.S. (eds) (2009) *The Oxford Companion to Global Change*. New York: Oxford University Press.

Cui, L., Ge, Z., Yuan, L. and Zhang, L. (2015) Vulnerability assessment of the coastal wetlands in the Yangtze Estuary, China to sea-level rise. *Estuarine, Coastal and Shelf Science*, 156, 42–51.

Cui, Y., Xu, X., Dong, J. and Qin, Y. (2016) Influence of urbanization factors on surface urban heat island intensity: a comparison of countries at different developmental phases. *Sustainability*, 8 (8), doi:10.3390/su8080706 DOI:10.3390/su8080706#_blank.

Cumberland, K.B. (1961) Man in nature in New Zealand. *New Zealand Geographer*, 17, 137–154.

Cunningham, D.A., Collins, J.F. and Cummins, T. (2001) Anthropogenically-triggered iron pan formation in some Irish soils over various time spans. *Catena*, 43, 167–176.

Curran, M.A.J., van Ommen, T.D., Morgan, V.I., et al. (2003) Ice core evidence for Antarctic sea ice decline since the 1950s. *Science*, 302, 1203–1206.

Curtis, C.J., Battarbee, R.W., Monteith, D.T. and Shilland, E.M. (2014) The future of upland water ecosystems of the UK in the 21st century: a synthesis. *Ecological Indicators*, 37, 412–430.

Cushman, G.T. (2011) Humboldtian science, creole meteorology, and the discovery of human-caused climate change in South America. *Osiris*, 26, 19–44.

Custodio, E., Iribar, V., Manzano, B.A. and Galofre, A. (1986) Evolution of sea water chemistry in the Llobregat Delta, Barcelona, Spain. In *Proceedings of the 9th Salt Water Chemistry Meeting*, Delft.

Dadson, S.J., Hall J.W., Murgatroyd, A., et al. (2017) A restatement of the natural science evidence concerning catchment-based 'natural' flood management in the UK. *Proceedings of the Royal Society*, A. doi:10.1098/rspa.2016.0706.

Dagar, J.C. and Minhas, P.S. (eds.) (2016) *Agroforestry for the Management of Waterlogged Saline Soils and Poor-quality Waters*. Heidelberg: Springer.

Dai, A. (2011) Drought under global warming: a review. *Wiley Interdisciplinary Reviews: Climate Change*, 2, 45–65.

Dalby, S. (2016) Framing the Anthropocene: the good, the bad and the ugly. *The Anthropocene Review*, 3 (1), 33–51.

Daliakopoulos, I.N., Tsanis, I.K., Koutroulis, A., et al. (2016) The threat of soil salinity: a European scale review. *Science of the Total Environment*, 573, 727–739.

Dallmeyer, A. and Claussen, M. (2011) The influence of land cover change in the Asian monsoon region on present-day and mid-Holocene climate. *Biogeosciences*, 8, 1499–1519.

Dalzell, B.J., King, J.Y., Mulla, D.J., et al. (2011) Influence of subsurface drainage on quantity and quality of dissolved organic matter export from agricultural landscapes. *Journal of Geophysical Research*, 116, G02023.

Damp, J.E., Hall, S.A. and Smith, S.J. (2002) Early irrigation on the Colorado Plateau near Zuni Pueblo, New Mexico. *American Antiquity*, 67 (4), 665–676.

Daniel, T.C., McGuire, P.E., Stoffel, D. and Millfe, B. (1979) Sediment and nutrient yield from residential construction sites. *Journal of Environmental Quality*, 8, 304–308.

Dapples, F., Lotter, A.F., van Leeuwen, J.F.N., et al. (2002) Paleolimnological evidence for increased landslide activity due to forest clearing and land-use since 3600 cal bp in the western Swiss Alps. *Journal of Paleolimnology*, 27, 239–248.

Darby, H.C. (1956) The clearing of the woodland in Europe. In W.L. Thomas (ed.), *Man's Role in Changing the Face of the Earth*. Chicago: University of Chicago Press, 183–216.

Darling, F.F. (1956) Man's ecological dominance through domesticated animals on wild lands. In W.L. Thomas (ed.), *Man's Role in Changing the Face of the Earth*. Chicago: University of Chicago Press, 778–787.

Dasgupta, S., Laplante, B., Meisner, C., et al. (2009) The impact of sea level rise on developing countries: a comparative analysis. *Climatic Change*, 93, 379–388.

Davidson, A.D., Boyer, A.G., Kim, H., et al. (2012) Drivers and hotspots of extinction risk in marine mammals. *Proceedings of the National Academy of Sciences*, 109, 3395–3400.

Davies, B.J and Glasser, N.F. (2012) Accelerating shrinkage of Patagonian glaciers from the Little Ice Age (∼ AD 1870) to 2011. *Journal of Glaciology*, 58, 1063–1084.

Davies, M.C.R., Hamza, O. and Harris, C. (2001) The effect of rise in mean annual temperature on the stability of rock slopes containing ice-filled discontinuities. *Permafrost and Periglacial Processes*, 12, 137–144.

Davis, J.L. and Vinogradova, N.T. (2017) Causes of accelerating sea level on the East Coast of North America. *Geophysical Research Letters*, 44 (10), 5133–5141.

Davis, M.A. (2009) *Invasion Biology*. Oxford: Oxford University Press.

Dawson, Q., Kechavarzi, C., Leeds-Harrison, P.B. and Burton, R.G.O. (2010) Subsidence and degradation of agricultural peatlands in the Fenlands of Norfolk, UK. *Geoderma*, 154, 181–187.

Dawson, W., Moser D., van Kleunen, M., et al. (2017) Global hotspots and correlates of alien species richness across taxonomic groups. *Nature Ecology & Evolution*, 1, article number: 0186, doi:10.1038/s41559-017-0186.

Day, J.W., Christian, R.R., Boesch, D.M., et al. (2008) Consequences of climate change on the ecogeomorphology of coastal wetlands. *Estuaries and Coasts*, 31, 477–491.

Day, S.J. and Maslin, M. (2010) Gas hydrates: a hazard for the twenty-first century? *Philosophical Transactions: Series A, Mathematical, Physical, and Engineering Sciences*, 368, 2579–2583.

Dazzi, C. and Papa, G.L. (2015) Anthropogenic soils: general aspects and features. *Ecocycles*, 1 (1), 3–8.

Deák, B., Tóthmérész, B., Valkó, O., et al. (2016) Cultural monuments and nature conservation: a review of the role of kurgans in the conservation and restoration of steppe vegetation. *Biodiversity and Conservation*, 25, 2473–2490.

Dean, C., Kirkpatrick, J.B. and Friedland, A.J. (2017) Conventional intensive logging promotes loss of organic carbon from the mineral soil. *Global Change Biology*, 23, 1–11.

Dean, D.J. and Schmidt, J.C. (2011) The role of feedback mechanisms in historic channel changes of the lower Rio Grande in the Big Bend region. *Geomorphology*, 126, 333–349.

Dean, R.G. and Houston, J.R. (2016) Determining shoreline response to sea level rise. *Coastal Engineering*, 114, 1–8.

De Angelis, H. and Skvarca, P. (2003) Glacier surge after ice shelf collapse. *Science*, 299, 1560–1562.

De Feo, G., Angelakis, A.N., Antoniou, G.P., et al. (2013) Historical and technical notes on aqueducts from prehistoric to medieval times. *Water*, 5 (4), 1996–2025.

DEFRA (2011) https://www.gov.uk/government/statistics/wild-bird-populations-in-the-uk (accessed January 2018).

De Groot, R.S., Wilson, M.A. and Boumans, R.M. (2002) A typology for the classification, description and valuation of ecosystem functions, goods and services. *Ecological Economics*, 41 (3), 393–408.

Degu, A.M., Hossain, F., Niyogi, D., et al. (2011) The influence of large dams on surrounding climate and precipitation patterns. *Geophysical Research Letters*, 38, L044405.

Dehn, M. and Buma, J. (1999) Modelling future landslide activity based on general circulation models. *Geomorphology*, 30, 175–187.

Dehn, M., Gurger, G., Buma, J. and Gasparetto, P. (2000) Impact of climate change on slope stability using expanded downscaling. *Engineering Geology*, 55, 193–204.

de Jong, C., Carletti, G. and Previtali, F. (2015) Assessing impacts of climate change, ski slope, snow and hydraulic engineering on slope stability in ski resorts (French and

Italian Alps). *Engineering Geology for Society and Territory*, I, 51–55.

Deline, P., Gardent, M., Magnin, F. and Ravanel, L. (2012) The morphodynamics of the Mont Blanc massif in a changing cryosphere: a comprehensive review. *Geografiska Annaler*, 94 A, 265–283.

De Meyer, A., Poesen, J., Isabirye, M., et al. (2011) Soil erosion rates in tropical villages: a case study from Lake Victoria Basin, Uganda. *Catena*, 84, 89–98.

de Nascimento, L., Nogué, S., Criado, C., et al. (2015) Reconstructing Holocene vegetation on the island of Gran Canaria before and after human colonization. *The Holocene*, 26, 113–125.

Denevan, W.M. (1992) The pristine myth: the landscapes of the Americas in 1492. *Annals of the Association of American Geographers*, 82, 369–385.

Denevan, W.M. (2001) *Cultivated Landscapes of Native Amazonia and the Andes*. Oxford: Oxford University Press.

Denisova, T.B. (1977) The environmental impact of mineral industries. *Soviet Geography*, 18, 646–659.

Dennis, D.B., Morgan, B.J.T., Roy, D.B. and Brereton, T.M. (2017) Urban indicators of butterflies. *Ecological Indicators*, 76, 184–193.

Denson, E.P. (1970) The trumpeter swan, Olor Buccinator: a conservation success and its lessons. *Biological Conservation*, 2, 251–256.

Dent, D.L. and Pons, L.J. (1995) A world perspective on acid sulphate soils. *Geoderma*, 67, 263–276.

Deo, R.C., Syktus, J.I., McAlpine, C.A., et al. (2009) Impact of historical land cover change on daily indices of climate extremes including droughts in eastern Australia. *Geophysical Research Letters*, 36, L08705.

Derraik, J.G.B. (2002) The pollution of the marine environment by plastic debris: a review. *Marine Pollution Bulletin*, 44, 842–852.

De Sylva, D. (1986) Increased storms and estuarine salinity and other ecological impacts of the greenhouse effect. In J.G. Titus (ed.), *Effects of Changes in Stratospheric Ozone and Global Climate* (Vol. 4, Sea Level Rise). Washington, DC: UNEP/USEPA, 153–164.

Detwyler, T.R. (ed.) (1971) *Man's Impact on Environment*. New York: McGraw-Hill.

Detwyler, T.R. and Marcus, M.G. (1972) *Urbanisation and Environment: The Physical Geography of the City*. Belmont: Duxbury Press.

Deverel, S.J., Ingrum, T. and Leighton, D. (2016) Present-day oxidative subsidence of organic soils and mitigation in the Sacramento-San Joaquin Delta, California, USA. *Hydrogeology Journal*, 24 (3), 569–586.

De Vos, J.M., Joppa, L.N., Gittleman, J.L., et al. (2015) Estimating the normal background rate of species extinction. *Conservation Biology*, 29 (2), 452–462.

Dewidar, K., Thomas, J. and Bayoumi, S. (2016) Detecting the environmental impact of off-road vehicles on Rawdat Al Shams in central Saudi Arabia by remote sensing. *Environmental Monitoring and Assessment*, 188 (7), 1–12.

De Wit, M. and Stankiewicz, J. (2006) Changes in surface water supply across Africa with predicted climate change. *Science*, 311, 1917–1921.

Dialynas, Y.G., Bastola, S., Bras, R.L., et al. (2016) Topographic variability and the influence of soil erosion on the carbon cycle. *Global Biogeochemical Cycles*, 30, doi:10.1002/2015GB005302.

Diamond, J. (1997) *Guns, Germs and Steel*. London: Chatto and Windus.

Diamond, J. (2002) Evolution, consequences and future of plant and animal domestication. *Nature*, 418, 700–707.

Diaz, R.J. and Rosenberg, R. (2008) Spreading dead zones and consequences for marine ecosystems. *Science*, 321, 926–929.

Di Castri, F. (1989) History of biological invasions with special emphasis on the old world. In J.A. Drake (ed.), *Biological Invasions: A Global Perspective*. Chichester: Wiley, 1–30.

Dickinson, W.R. (1999) Holocene sea-level record on Funafuti and potential impact of global warming on Central Pacific atolls. *Quaternary Research*, 51, 124–132.

Diem, J. (2003) Potential impact of ozone on coniferous forests of the interior southwestern United States. *Annals of the Association of American Geographers*, 93, 265–280.

Diffenbaugh, N.S. and Field, C.B. (2013) Changes in ecologically critical terrestrial climate conditions. *Science*, 341 (6145), 486–492.

Dillehay, T.D., Rossen, J., Andres, T.C. and Williams, D.E. (2007) Preceramic adoption of peanut, squash and cotton in Northern Peru. *Science*, 316, 1890–1893.

Dimbleby, G.W. (1974) The legacy of prehistoric man. In A. Warren and F.B. Goldsmith (eds), *Conservation in Practice*. London: Wiley, 179–189.

Dinerstein, E., Loucks, C., Wikramanayake, E., et al. (2007) The fate of wild tigers. *Bioscience*, 57, 508–514.

Dirnböck, T., Essl, F. and Rabitsch, W. (2011) Disproportional risk for habitat loss of high-altitude endemic species under climate change. *Global Change Biology*, 17, 990–996.

Dirzo, R. and Raven, P.H. (2003) Global state of biodiversity and loss. *Annual Review of Environment and Resources*, 28, 137–167.

Dixon, S.J., Viles, H.A. and Garrett, B.L. (2017) Ozymandias in the Anthropocene: the city as an emerging landform. *Area*, doi:10.1111/area.12358.

Doak, T. and Marvier, M. (2003) Predicting the effects of species loss on community stability. In P. Kareiva and S.A. Levin (eds), *The Importance of Species*. Princeton: Princeton University Press, 140–160.

Dobson, A., Borner, M. and Sinclair, T. (2010) Road will ruin Serengeti. *Nature*, 467, 272–273.

Dobson, M.C. (1991) *De-icing Salt Damage to Trees and Shrubs*. Forestry Commission Bulletin 101. London: HMSO.

Dodd, A.P. (1959) The biological control of the prickly pear in Australia. In A. Keast, R.L. Crocker and C.S. Christian (eds), *Biogeography and Ecology in Australia*. The Hague: Junk, 565–577.

D'Odorico, P., Yoo, J.C. and Over, T.M. (2001) An assessment of ENSO-induced patterns of rainfall erosivity in the southwestern United States. *Journal of Climate*, 14, 4230–4242.

Dolman, S.J. and Jasny, M. (2015) Evolution of marine noise pollution management. *Aquatic Mammals*, 41 (4), 357–374.

Dominati, E., Patterson, M. and Mackay, A. (2010) A framework for classifying and quantifying the natural capital and ecosystem services of soils. *Ecological Economics*, 69 (9), 1858–1868.

Dominguez, F., Rivera, E., Lettenmaier, D.P. and Castro, C.L. (2012) Changes in winter precipitation extremes for the western United States under a warmer climate as simulated by regional climate models. *Geophysical Research Letters*, 39, L05803.

Donchyts, G., Baart, F., Winsemius, H., et al. (2016) Earth's surface water change over the past 30 years. *Nature Climate Change*, 6 (9), 810–813.

Doney, S.C. (2006) The dangers of ocean acidification. *Scientific American*, 294 (3), 38–45.

Dong, Z., Chen, G., He, X., Han, Z. and Wang, X. (2004) Controlling blown sand along the highway crossing the Taklimakan Desert. *Journal of Arid Environments*, 57, 329–344.

Donkin, R.A. (1979) Agricultural terracing in the Aboriginal New World. *Viking Fund Publications in Anthropology*, 561.

Donnelly, C., Greuell, W., Andersson, J., et al. (2017) Impacts of climate change on European hydrology at 1.5, 2 and 3 degrees mean global warming above preindustrial level. *Climatic Change*, doi:10.1007/s10584-017-1971-7.

Donnely, L.J. (2009) A review of international cases of fault reactivation during mining subsidence and fluid abstraction. *Quarterly Journal of Engineering Geology and Hydrogeology*, 42, 73–94.

Donner, S.D. (2009) Coping with commitment: projected thermal stress on coral reefs under different future scenarios. *PLoS ONE*, 4, e5712, 1–9.

Doody, J.P. (ed.) (1984) *Spartina Anglica in Great Britain.* Shrewsbury: Nature Conservancy Council.

Doody, J.P. (1989) Management for nature conservation. *Proceedings of the Royal Society of Edinburgh. Section B. Biological Sciences*, 96, 247–265.

Doody, J.P. (2013) Coastal squeeze and managed realignment in southeast England, does it tell us anything about the future? *Ocean and Coastal Management*, 79, 34–41.

Doolittle, W. (2000) *Cultivated Landscapes of Native North America.* Oxford: Oxford University Press.

Dörries, M. (2011) The politics of atmospheric sciences: 'Nuclear Winter' and global climate change. *Osiris*, 26, 198–223.

Dotterweich, M. (2008) The history of soil erosion and fluvial deposits in small catchments of central Europe: deciphering the long-term interaction between humans and the environment – a review. *Geomorphology*, 101, 192–208.

Dotterweich, M. (2013) The history of human-induced soil erosion: geomorphic legacies, early descriptions and research, and the development of soil conservation – a global synopsis. *Geomorphology*, 201, 1–34.

Doughty, C.E., Loarie, S.R. and Field, C.B. (2012) Theoretical impact of changing albedo on precipitation at the southernmost boundary of the ITCZ in South America. *Earth Interactions*, 16, 1–14.

Doughty, C.E., Wolf, A, and Field, C.B. (2010) Biophysical feedbacks between the Pleistocene megafauna extinction and climate: the first human-induced global warming? *Geophysical Research Letters*, 37, doi:10.1029/2010GL043985.

Doughty, R.W. (1974) The human predator: a survey. In I.R. Manners and M.V. Mikesell (eds), *Perspectives on Environment.* Washington, DC: Association of American Geographers, 152–180.

Doughty, R.W. (1978) *The English Sparrow in the American Landscape: A Paradox in Nineteenth Century Wildlife Conservation.* School of Geography, Research Paper 19. Oxford: School of Geography, University of Oxford.

Dougill, A.J., Akanyang, L., Perkins, J.S., et al. (2016) Land use, rangeland degradation and ecological changes in the southern Kalahari, Botswana. *African Journal of Ecology*, 54 (1), 59–67.

Douglas, I. (1983) *The Urban Environment.* London: Arnold.

Douglas, I. (1996) The impact of land-use changes, especially logging, shifting cultivation, mining and urbanization on sediment yields in humid tropical Southeast Asia: a review with special reference to Borneo. *IAHS Publications – Series of Proceedings and Reports – Intern Association of Hydrological Sciences*, 236, 463–472.

Douglas, I., Goode, D., Houck, C. and Wang, R. (eds) (2011) *The Routledge Handbook of Urban Ecology.* New York: Routledge.

Douglas, I. and James, P. (2014) *Urban Ecology: An Introduction.* London: Routledge.

Douglas, I. and Lawson, N. (2001) The human dimensions of geomorphological work in Britain. *Journal of Industrial Ecology*, 4, 9–33.

Douglas-Mankin, K.R., Srinivasan, R. and Arnold, J.G. (2010) Soil and Water Assessment Tool (SWAT) model: current developments and applications. *Transactions of the American Society of Agricultural and Biological Engineers*, 53, 1423–1431.

Douville, H., Chauvin, F., Planton, S., et al. (2002) Sensitivity of the hydrological cycle to increasing amounts of greenhouse gases and aerosols. *Climate Dynamics*, 20, 45–68.

Downing, A. and Leibold, M.A. (2010) Species richness facilitates ecosystem resilience in aquatic food webs. *Freshwater Biology*, 55, 2123–2137.

Downs, P.W. and Gregory, K.J. (2004) *River Channel Management.* London: Arnold.

Doyle, M.W., Stanley, E.H. and Habor, J.M. (2003) Channel adjustments following two dam removals in Wisconsin. *Water Resources Research*, 39, W1011.

Doyle, T.W. and Girod, G.F. (1997) The frequency and structure of Atlantic hurricanes and their influence on the structure of the South Florida mangrove communities. In H.F. Diaz and R.S. Pulwarty (eds), *Hurricane.* Berlin: Springer, 109–120.

Dragovich, D. and Morris, R. (2002) Fire intensity, slopewash and bio-transfer of sediment in eucalypt forest, Australia. *Earth Surface Processes and Landforms*, 27, 1309–1319.

Draut, A.E. (2012) Effects of river regulation on aeolian landscapes, Colorado River, southwestern USA. *Journal of Geophysical Research*, 117, F02022.

Dregne, H.E. and Tucker, C.J. (1988) Desert encroachment. *Desertification Control Bulletin*, 16, 16–19.

Dreibrodt, S., Lubos, C., Terhorst, B., et al. (2010) Historical soil erosion by water in Germany: scales and archives, chronology, research perspectives. *Quaternary International*, 222, 80–95.

Drewry, D.J. (1991) The response of the Antarctic ice sheet to climate change. In C.M. Harris and B. Stonehouse (eds), *Antarctica and Global Climatic Change.* London: Belhaven Press, 90–106.

Drexler, J.Z., de Fontaine, C.S. and Deverel, S.J. (2009) The legacy of wetland drainage on the remaining peat in the Sacramento-San Joaquin Delta, California, USA. *Wetlands*, 29, 372–386.

Drijfhout, S., Bathiany, S., Beaulieu, C., et al. (2015) Catalogue of abrupt shifts in Intergovernmental Panel on Climate Change climate models. *Proceedings of the National Academy of Sciences*, 112 (43), E5777–E5786.

Driscoll, C.A., Macdonald, D.W. and O'Brien, S.J. (2009) From wild animals to domestic pets, an evolutionary view of domestication. *Proceedings of the National Academy of Sciences*, 106, 9971–9978.

Driscoll, R. (1983) The influence of vegetation on the swelling and shrinkage of clay soils in Britain. *Géotechnique*, 33, 293–326.

Du Toit, G. van N., Snyman, H.A. and Malan, P.J. (2009) Physical impact of grazing by sheep on soil parameters in the Nama Karoo subshrub/grass rangeland of South Africa. *Journal of Arid Environments*, 73, 804–810.

Du, H., Xue, X., Wang, T. and Deng, X. (2015) Assessment of wind-erosion risk in the watershed of the Ningxia-Inner Mongolia Reach of the Yellow River, northern China. *Aeolian Research*, 17, 193–204.

Dullinger, S., Gattringer, A., Thuiller, W., et al. (2012) Extinction debt of hig-mountain plants under twenty-first-century climate change. *Nature Climate Change*, 2, 619–622.

Duncan, R.P., Blackburn, T.M. and Sol, D. (2003) The ecology of bird introductions. *Annual Review of Environment and Resources*, 28, 359–399.

Dunne, J., Evershed, R.P., Salque, M., et al. (2012) First dairying in green Saharan Africa in the fifth millennium BC. *Nature*, 486 (7403), 390–394.

Dunne, T. and Leopold, L.B. (1978) *Water in Environmental Planning*. San Francisco: Freeman.

Durá-Gómez, I. and Talwani, P. (2010) Reservoir-induced seismicity associated with the Itoiz Reservoir, Spain: a case study. *Geophysical Journal International*, 181, 343–356.

Durán Zuazo, V.H., Francia Martínez, J.R. and Martínez Raya, A. (2004) Impact of vegetative cover on runoff and soil erosion at hillslope scale in Lanjaron, Spain. *The Environmentalist*, 24, 39–48.

Durant, A.J., Harrison, S.P., Watson, I.M. and Balkanski, Y. (2009) Sensitivity of direct radiative forcing by mineral dust to particle characteristics. *Progress in Physical Geography*, 33, 80–102.

Durant, S.M., Becker, M.S., Creel, S., et al. (2015) Developing fencing policies for dryland ecosystems. *Journal of Applied Ecology*, 52 (3), 544–551.

Durant, S.M., Mitchell, N., Groom, R., et al. (2017) Disappearing spots, the global decline of cheetah and what it means for conservation. *Proceedings of the National Academy of Sciences*, 114, 528–533.

Dusar, B., Verstraeten, G., Notebaert, B. and Bakker, J. (2011) Holocene environmental change and its impact on sediment dynamics in the Eastern Mediterranean. *Earth-Science Reviews*, 108, 137–157.

Duvall, C.S. (2011) Biocomplexity from the ground up: vegetation patterns in a West African savanna landscape.

Annals of the Association of American Geographers, 101, 497–522.

D'Yakanov, K.N. and Reteyum, A.Y. (1965) The local climate of the Rybinsk reservoir. *Soviet Geography*, 6, 40–53.

Eckhardt, K. and Ulbrich, U. (2003) Potential impacts of climate change on groundwater recharge and streamflow in a central European low mountain range. *Journal of Hydrology*, 284, 244–252.

Eden, M.J. (1974) Palaeoclimatic influences and the development of savanna in southern Venezuela. *Journal of Biogeography*, 1, 95–109.

Edlin, H.L. (1976) The Culbin Sands. In J. Leniham and W.W. Fletcher (eds), *Reclamation*. Glasgow: Blackie, 1–31.

Edwards, A.J., Clark, S., Zahir, H., et al. (2001) Coral bleaching and mortality on artificial and natural reefs in Maldives in 1998, sea surface temperature anomalies and initial recovery. *Marine Pollution Bulletin*, 42, 7–15.

Edwards, G.P., Zeng, B., Saalfield, W.K. and Vaarzon-Morel, P. (2010) Evaluation of the impacts of feral camels. *The Rangeland Journal*, 32, 43–54.

Edwards, K.J. (1985) The anthropogenic factor in vegetational history. In K.J. Edwards and W.P. Warren (eds), *The Quaternary History of Ireland*. London: Academic Press, 187–200.

Edwards, P.J., Fletcher, M.R. and Berny, P. (2000) Review of the factors affecting the decline of the European brown hare, Lepus europeaus (Pallas, 1778) and the use of wildlife incident data to evaluate the significance of paraquat. *Agriculture, Ecosystems & Environment*, 79, 95–103.

Ehrenfeld, D.W. (1972) *Conserving Life on Earth*. New York: Oxford University Press.

Ehrlich, P.R. and Ehrlich, A.H. (1970) *Population, Resources, Environment: Issues in Human Ecology*. San Francisco: Freeman.

Ehrlich, P.R. and Ehrlich, A.H. (1982) *Extinction*. London: Gollancz.

Ehrlich, P.R., Ehrlich, A.H. and Holdren, J.P. (1977) *Ecoscience: Population, Resources, Environment*. San Francisco: Freeman.

Eitner, V. (1996) Geomorphological response to the East Frisian barrier islands to sea level rise: an investigation of past and future evolution. *Geomorphology*, 15, 57–65.

El Banna, M.M. and Frihy, O.E. (2009) Human-induced changes in the geomorphology of the northeastern coast of the Nile delta, Egypt. *Geomorphology*, 107, 72–78.

Eldridge, D.J. (1998) Trampling of microphytic crusts on calcareous soils, and its impact on erosion under rain-impacted flow. *Catena*, 33, 221–239.

Eldridge, D.J., Bowker, M.A., Maester, F.T., et al. (2011) Impacts of shrub encroachment on ecosystem structure and functioning: towards a global synthesis. *Ecology Letters*, 14, 709–722.

Eldridge, D.J. and Robson, A.D. (1997) Bladeploughing and exclosure influence soil properties in a semi-arid Australian woodland. *Journal of Range Management*, 50, 191–198.

Elguindi, N. and Giorgi, F. (2006) Projected changes in the Caspian Sea level for the 21st century based on the latest AOGCM simulations. *Geophysical Research Letters*, 33, L08706.

Elias, E., Rango, A., Smith, R., et al. (2016) Climate change, agriculture and water resources in the southwestern United States. *Journal of Contemporary Water Research & Education*, 158 (1), 46–61.

Elling, W., Dittmar, C., Pfaffelmoser, K. and Rötzer, T. (2009) Dendroecological assessment of the complex causes of decline and recovery of the growth of silver fir (Abies alba Mill) in Southern Germany. *Forest Ecology and Management*, 257, 1175–1187.

Elliott, J.G., Gillis, A.C. and Aby, S.B. (1999) Evolution of arroyos: incised channels of the southwestern United States. In S.E. Darby and A. Simon (eds), *Incised River Channels*. Chichester: Wiley, 153–185.

Elliott, J.M. (1989) Wild brown trout Salmon trutta: an important national and international resource. *Freshwater Biology*, 21, 1–5.

Ellis, E.C. (2011) Anthropogenic transformation of the terrestrial biosphere. *Philosophical Transactions: Series A, Mathematical, Physical, and Engineering Sciences*, 369, 1010–1035.

Ellis, E.C., Kaplan, J.O., Fuller, D.Q., et al. (2013) Used planet: a global history. *Proceedings of the National Academy of Sciences*, 110, 7978–7985.

Ellison, A.M. and Farnsworth, E.J. (1997) Simulated sea level change alters anatomy, physiology, growth and reproduction of red mangrove (Rhizophora mangle L.). *Oecologia*, 112, 435–446.

Ellison, J.C. and Stoddart, D.R. (1990) Mangrove ecosystem collapse during predicted sea level rise: Holocene analogues and implications. *Journal of Coastal Research*, 7, 151–165.

Ellsworth, W.L. (2013) Injection-induced earthquakes. *Science*, 341, doi:10.1126/science.1225942.

El-Raey, M. (1997) Vulnerability assessment of the coastal zone of the Nile delta of Egypt to the impact of sea level rise. *Ocean and Coastal Management*, 37, 29–40.

Elsner, J.B., Kossin, J.P. and Jagger, T.H. (2008) The increasing intensity of the strongest tropical cyclones. *Nature*, 455, 92–95.

Elton, C.S. (1958) *The Ecology of Invasions by Plants and Animals*. London: Methuen.

Emanuel, K.A. (1987) The dependence of hurricane intensity on climate. *Nature*, 326, 483–485.

Emmanuel, W.R., Shugart, H.H. and Stevenson, M.P. (1985) Climatic change and the broad-scale distribution of terrestrial ecosystem complexes. *Climatic Change*, 7, 29–43.

Engelhardt, F.R. (ed.) (1985) *Petroleum Effects in the Arctic Environment*. London: Elsevier Applied Science.

Engelhart, S.E., Horton, B.P., Douglas, B.C., et al. (2009) Spatial variability of late Holocene and 20th century sea-level rise along the Atlantic coast of the United States. *Geology*, 37, 1115–1118.

Engelstaedter, S., Tegen, I. and Washington, R. (2006) North African dust emissions and transport. *Earth-Science Reviews*, 79, 73–100.

Engler, R., Randin, C.F., Thuiller, W., et al. (2011) 21st century climate change threatens mountain flora unequally across Europe. *Global Change Biology*, 17, 2330–2341.

Environment Agency (2010) *Fifth otter survey of England 2009–2010. Summary report*. Bristol: Environment Agency.

Ericson, J.P., Vorosmarty, C.J., Dingham, L., et al. (2006) Effective sea-level rise and deltas: causes of change and human dimension implications. *Global and Planetary Change*, 50, 63–82.

Erlandson, J.M. (2010) A deep history for the Pacific: where past, present, and future meet. *Journal of Pacific Archaeology*, 1, 111–114.

Erlandson, J.M. (2013) Shell middens and other anthropogenic soils as global stratigraphic signatures of the Anthropocene. *Anthropocene*, 4, 24–32.

Erlandson, J.M., Rick, T.C., Braje, T.J., et al. (2011) Paleoindian seafaring, maritime technologies, and coastal foraging on California's Channel Islands. *Science*, 331, 1181–1185.

Erlandson J.M., Rick, T.C. and Peterson, C. (2005) A geoarchaeological chronology of Holocene dune building on San Miguel Island, California. *The Holocene*, 15, 1227–1235.

Escalente, S.A. and Pimentel, A.S. (2008) Coastal dune stabilization using geotextile tubes at Las Colorados. *Geosynthetics*, 26, 16–24.

Esteves, L.S. (2014) *Managed Realignment: A Viable Long-Term Coastal Management Strategy?* Dordrecht: Springer.

Etienne, D., Ruffaldi, P., Goepp, S., et al. (2011) The origin of closed depressions in Northeastern France: a new assessment. *Geomorphology*, 126, 121–131.

European Environment Agency (2001) *Eutrophication in Europe's Coastal Waters*. Copenhagen: European Environment Agency.

Evan, A.T., Dunion, J., Foley, J.A., et al. (2006) New evidence for a relationship between Atlantic tropical cyclone activity and African dust outbreaks. *Geophysical Research Letters*, 33, L19813.

Evan, A.T., Flamant, C., Gaetani, M. and Guichard, F. (2016) The past, present and future of African dust. *Nature*, 531 (7595), 493–495.

Evans, C.D., Cullen, J.M., Alewell, C., et al. (2001) Recovery from acidification in European surface waters. *Hydrology and Earth System Sciences*, 5, 283–297.

Evans, C.D. and Jenkins, A. (2000) Surface water acidification in the South Pennines II. Temporal trends. *Environmental Pollution*, 109, 21–34.

Evans, D.M. (1966) Man-made earthquakes in Denver. *Geotimes*, 10, 11–18.

Evans, G. (2008) Man's impact on the coastline. *Journal of Iberian Geology*, 34, 167–190.

Evans, J.P. (2010) Global warming impact on the dominant precipitation processes in the Middle East. *Theoretical and Applied Climatology*, 99, 389–402.

Evans, M. and Warburton, J. (2007) *Geomorphology of Upland Peat*. Oxford: Blackwell.

Evans, M., Warburton, J. and Yang, J. (2006) Eroding blanket peat catchments: global and local implications of upland organic sediment budgets. *Geomorphology*, 79, 45–57.

Eve, M.D., Sperow, M., Paustian, K. and Follett, R.F. (2002) National-scale estimation of changes in soil carbon stocks on agricultural lands. *Environmental Pollution*, 116, 431–438.

Evenari, M., Shanan, L. and Tadmor, N.H. (1971) Runoff agriculture in the Negev Desert of Israel. In W.G. McGinnies, R.J. Goldman and P. Paylore (eds), *Food, Fiber and the Arid Lands*. Tucson: University of Arizona Press, 312–322.

Fabricius, K.E. (2005) Effects of terrestrial runoff on the ecology of corals and coral reefs: review and synthesis. *Marine Pollution Bulletin*, 50, 125–146.

Faeth, S.H., Bang, C. and Saari, S. (2011) Urban biodiversity: patterns and mechanisms. *Annals of the New York Academy of Sciences*, 1223, 69–81.

Fahrig, L. (2003) Effects of habitat fragmentation on biodiversity. *Annual Review of Ecology, Evolution, and Systematics*, 34, 487–515.

Fairbridge, R.W. (1983) Isostasy and eustasy. In D.E. Smith and A.G. Dawson (eds), *Shorelines and Isostasy*. London: Academic Press, 3–25.

Fairhead, J. and Leach, M. (1996) *Misreading the African Landscape: Society and Ecology in a Forest-Savanna Mosaic*. Cambridge: Cambridge University Press.

Faith, J.T. and Surovell, T.A. (2009) Synchronous extinction of North America's Pleistocene mammals. *Proceedings of the National Academy of Sciences*, 106, 20641–20645.

Fan, B., Guo, L., Li, N., et al. (2014) Earlier vegetation green-up has reduced spring dust storms. *Scientific Reports*, 4, article number: 6749, doi:10.1038/srep06749.

Fan, J., Rosenfeld, D., Yang, Y., et al. (2015) Substantial contribution of anthropogenic air pollution to catastrophic floods in Southwest China. *Geophysical Research Letters*, 42 (14), 6066–6075.

Farias, W.R.G., Pinto, O., Naccarato, K.P. and Pinto, I.R.C.A. (2009) Anomalous lightning activity over the metropolitan region of São Paulo due to urban effects. *Atmospheric Research*, 91, 485–490.

Farley, K.A., Jobbágy, E.G. and Jackson, R.B. (2005) Effects of afforestation on water yield: a global synthesis with implications for policy. *Global Change Biology*, 11, 1565–1576.

Favis-Mortlock, D. and Boardman, J. (1995) Non-linear responses of soil erosion to climate change: modelling study on the UK South Downs. *Catena*, 25, 365–387.

Favis-Mortlock, D.T. and Guerra, A.J.T. (1999) The implications of general circulation model estimates of rainfall for future erosion: a case study from Brazil. *Catena*, 37, 329–354.

Fearnside, P.M. and Laurance, W.F. (2003) Comment on 'Determination rates of the world's humid tropical forests'. *Science*, 299, 1015.

Feeley, K.J. and Silman, M.R. (2016) Disappearing climates will limit the efficacy of Amazonian protected areas. *Diversity and Distributions*, 22 (11), 1081–1084.

Feldstein, S.B. (2011) Subtropical rainfall and the Antarctic ozone hole. *Science*, 332, 925–926.

Fenger, J. (1999) Urban air quality. *Atmospheric Environment*, 33, 4877–4900.

Fenn, M.E., Baron, J.S., Allen, E.B., et al. (2003) Ecological effects of nitrogen deposition in the western United States. *Bioscience*, 53, 404–420.

Feola, S., Carranza, M.L., Schaminée, J.H.J., et al. (2011) EU habitats of interest: an insight into Atlantic and Mediterranean beach and foredunes. *Biodiversity and Conservation*, 20, 1457–1468.

Ferguson, G. and Gleeson, T. (2012) Vulnerability of coastal aquifers to groundwater use and climate change. *Nature Climate Change*, 2, 342–345.

Fernandes, G.W., Coelho, M.S., Machado, R.B., et al. (2016) Afforestation of savannas: an impending ecological disaster. *Natureza & Conservação*, 14 (2), 146–151.

Fichtner, A., Von Oheimb, G., Härdtle, W., et al. (2014) Effects of anthropogenic disturbances on soil microbial communities in oak forests persist for more than 100 years. *Soil Biology and Biochemistry*, 70, 79–87.

Ficklin, D.L., Stewart, I.T. and Maurer, E.P. (2013) Effects of projected climate change on the hydrology in the Mono Lake Basin, California. *Climatic Change*, 116 (1), 111–131.

Fiedel, S.J. (2005) Man's best friend – mammoth's worst enemy? A speculative essay on the role of dogs in Paleoindian colonization and magafaunal extinction. *World Archaeology*, 37, 11–25.

Field, J. and Wroe, S. (2012) Aridity, faunal adaptations and Australian Late Pleistocene extinctions. *World Archaeology*, 44, 56–74.

Field, M.E., Ogston, A.S. and Storlazzi, C.D. (2011) Rising sea level may cause decline of fringing coral reefs. *Eos*, 92, 273–280.

Filin, S., Avni, Y., Baruch, A., et al. (2014) Characterization of land degradation along the receding Dead Sea coastal zone using airborne laser scanning. *Geomorphology*, 206, 403–420.

Fillenham, L.F. (1963) Holme Fen Post. *Geographical Journal*, 129, 502–503.

Finegan, B. (1996) Pattern and process in neotropical secondary rain forests: the first 100 years of succession. *Trends in Ecology & Evolution*, 11, 119–124.

Fire regime, Forest Change indicators, Canadian Forest Service. Reproduced with the permission of the Minister of Natural Resources Canada (2017). http://www.nrcan.gc.ca/forests/climate-change/forest-change/17780 (Accessed August 29th, 2016)

Fischer, E.M. and Knutti, R. (2015) Anthropogenic contribution to global occurrence of heavy-precipitation and high-temperature extremes. *Nature Climate Change*, 5 (6), 560–564.

Fischer, L., Kääb, A., Huggel, C. and Noetzli, J. (2006) Geology, glacier retreat and permafrost degradation as controlling factors of slope instabilities in a high-mountain rock wall: the Monte Rosa east face. *Natural Hazards and Earth System Sciences*, 6, 761–772.

Fisher, I., Pain, D.J. and Thomas, V.G. (2006) A review of lead poisoning from ammunition sources in terrestrial birds. *Biological Conservation*, 131, 421–432.

Fisher, J., Simon, N. and Vincent, J. (1969) *The Red Book – Wildlife in Danger*. London: Collins.

Fitt, W.K., Brown, B.E., Warner, M.E. and Dunne, R.P. (2001) Coral bleaching: interpretation of thermal tolerance limits and thermal thresholds in tropical corals. *Coral Reefs*, 20, 51–65.

Fitton, J.M., Hansom, J.D. and Rennie, A.F. (2016) A national coastal erosion susceptibility model for Scotland. *Ocean & Coastal Management*, 132, 80–89.

FitzGerald, D.M., Fenster, M.S., Argow, B.A. and Buynevich, I.V. (2008) Coastal impacts due to sea-level rise. *Annual Review of Earth and Planetary Sciences*, 36, 601–647.

Fitzharris, B. (1996) The cryosphere: changes and their impacts. In R.T. Watson, M.C. Zinyowera, R.H. Moss and D.J. Dokken (eds), *Climate Change 1995. Impacts, Adaptation and Mitigation of Climate Change: Scientific and Technical Analyses*. Cambridge: Cambridge University Press, 241–265.

Fitzhugh, T.W. and Vogel, R.M. (2011) The impact of dams on flood flows in the United States. *River Research and Applications*, 27, 1192–1115.

Flannery, J. (2005) *The Weather Makers*. London: Allen Lane.

Flannery, M.G., Shell, K.M., Barlage, M., et al. (2011) Radiative forcing and albedo feedback from the Northern Hemisphere cryosphere between 1979 and 2008. *Nature Geoscience*, 4, 151–155.

Flannigan, M.D., Logan, K.A., Amiro, B.D., et al. (2005) Future area burned in Canada. *Climatic Change*, 72, 1–16.

Flannigan, M.D., Stocks, B.J. and Wotton, B.M. (2000) Climate change and forest fires. *Science of the Total Environment*, 262, 221–230.

Flenley, J.R. (1979) *The Equatorial Rain Forest: A Geological History*. London: Butterworth.

Flenley, J.R., King, A.S.M., Jackson, J., et al. (1991) The late Quaternary vegetational and climatic history of Easter Island. *Journal of Quaternary Science*, 6, 85–115.

Foley, J.A., Asner, G.P., Costa, M.H., et al. (2007) Amazonia revealed: forest degradation and loss of ecosystem goods and services in the Amazon Basin. *Frontiers in Ecology and the Environment*, 5 (1), 25–32.

Foley, S.F., Gronenborn, D., Andreae, M.O., et al. (2013) The Palaeoanthropocene – the beginnings of anthropogenic environmental change. *Anthropocene*, 3, 83–88.

Folke, C., Carpenter, S., Walker, B., et al. (2004) Regime shifts, resilience, and biodiversity in ecosystem management. *Annual Review of Ecology, Evolution, and Systematics*, 35, 557–581.

Fölster, J. and Wilander, A. (2002) Recovery from acidification in Swedish forest streams. *Environmental Pollution*, 117, 389–399.

Food and Agriculture Organisation (FAO) (2001) *The State of the World's Forests*. Rome: FAO.

Food and Agriculture Organization (FAO) (2009) *The State of World Fisheries and Aquaculture 2008*. Rome: FAO.

Forbes, B.C., Kumpula, T., Meschtyb, N., et al. (2016) Sea ice, rain-on-snow and tundra reindeer nomadism in Arctic Russia. *Biology Letters*, doi:10.1098/rsbl.2016.0466.

Ford, C.C. (2016) *Natural Interest: The Contest over Environment in Modern France*. Cambridge, MA: Harvard University Press.

Forister, M.L., Cousens, B., Harrison, J.G., et al. (2016) Increasing neonicotinoid use and the declining butterfly fauna of lowland California. *Biology Letters*, 12 (8), 20160475.

Forland, E.J., Alexandersson, H., Drebs, A., et al. (1998) Trends in maximum 1-day precipitation in the Nordic region. *DNMI report 14/98, Klima*. Oslo: Norwegian Meteorological Institute, 1–55.

Forman, R.T.T. (2003) *Road Ecology: Science and Solutions*. Washington, DC: Island Press.

Forman, R.T.T. (2014) *Urban Ecology: Science of Cities*. Cambridge: Cambridge University Press.

Forman, S.L., Oglesby, R. and Webb, R.S. (2001) Temporal and spatial patterns of Holocene dune activity on the Great Plains of North America: megadroughts and climate links. *Global and Planetary Change*, 29 (1), 1–29.

Forman, S.L., Sagintayev, Z., Sultan, M., et al. (2008) The twentieth-century migration of parabolic dunes and wetland formation at Cape Cod National Sea Shore, Massachusetts, USA: landscape response to a legacy of environmental disturbance. *The Holocene*, 18, 765–774.

Forman, S.L., Spaeth, M., Márin, L.O., et al. (2006) Episodic Late Holocene dune movements on the sand-sheet area, Great Sand Dunes National Park and Preserve, San Luis Valley, Colorado, USA. *Quaternary Research*, 66, 97–108.

Foster, G.C., Chiverrell, R.C., Thomas, G.S.P., et al. (2009) Fluvial development and the sediment regime of the lower Calder, Ribble catchment, northwest England. *Catena*, 77, 81–95.

Foster, I.D.L., Dearing, J.A. and Appleby, R.G. (1986) Historical trends in catchment sediment yields: a case study in reconstruction from lake-sediment records in Warwickshire, UK. *Hydrological Sciences Journal*, 31, 427–443.

Foulds, S.A. and Macklin, M.G. (2006) Holocene land-use change and its impact on river basin dynamics in Great Britain and Ireland. *Progress in Physical Geography*, 30, 589–604.

Fox, H.L. (1976) The urbanizing river: a case study in the Maryland piedmont. In D.R. Coates (ed.), *Geomorphology and Engineering*. Stroudsburg: Dowden, Hutchinson and Ross, 245–271.

Foxcroft, L.C., Richardson, D.M., Rejmánek, M. and Pyšek, P. (2010) Alien plant invasions in tropical and sub-tropical savannas: patterns, processes and prospects. *Biological Invasions*, 12, 3913–3933.

Francis, D. and Hengeveld, H. (1998) *Extreme Weather and Climate Change*. Downsview, ON: Environment Canada.

Francis, R.A., Lorimer, J. and Raco, M. (2012) Urban ecosystems as 'natural' homes for biogeographical boundary crossings. *Transactions of the Institute of British Geographers*, 37 (2), 183–190.

Frankel, O.H. (1984) Genetic diversity, ecosystem conservation and evolutionary responsibility. In F.D. Castri, F.W.G. Baker and M. Hadley (eds), *Ecology in Practice* (Vol. I). Dublin: Tycooly, 4315–4327.

Frankl, A., Nyssen, J., De Dapper, M., et al. (2011) Linking long-term gully and river channel dynamics to environmental change using repeat photography (Northern Ethiopia). *Geomorphology*, 129, 238–251.

Frans, C., Istanbulluoglu, E., Mishra, V., et al. (2013) Are climatic or land cover changes the dominant cause of runoff trends in the Upper Mississippi River Basin? *Geophysical Research Letters*, 40, 1104–1110.

Frantz, L.A., Mullin, V.E., Pionnier-Capitan, M., et al. (2016) Genomic and archaeological evidence suggest a dual origin of domestic dogs. *Science*, 352 (6290), 1228–1231.

Frazier, T.G., Wood, N., Yarnal, B. and Bauer, D.H. (2010) Influence of potential sea level rise on societal vulnerability to hurricane storm-surge hazards, Sarasota County, Florida. *Applied Geography*, 30, 490–505.

Freedman, B. (1995) *Environmental Ecology* (2nd edn). San Diego: Academic Press.

Freeland, W.J. (1990) Large herbivorous mammals: exotic species in northern Australia. *Journal of Biogeography*, 17, 445–449.

Freeman, M.A., Turnbull, J.F., Yeomans, W.E. and Bean, C.W. (2010) Prospects for management strategies of invasive crayfish populations with an emphasis on biological control. *Aquatic Conservation: Marine and Freshwater Ecosystems*, 20 (2), 211–223.

French, H.M. (1976) *The Periglacial Environment*. London: Longman.

French. H.M. (2007) *The Periglacial Environment* (3rd edn). Chichester: Wiley.

French, J.R., Spencer, T. and Reed, D.J. (eds) (1995) Geomorphic responses to sea level rise: existing evidence and future impacts. *Earth Surface Processes and Landforms*, 20, 1–6.

French, P.W. (1997) *Coastal and Estuarine Management*. London: Routledge.

French, P.W. (2001) *Coastal Defences. Processes, Problems and Solutions*. London: Routledge.

Frenkel, R.E. (1970) Ruderal vegetation along some California roadsides. *University of California Publications in Geography*, 20.

Frid, C., Andonegi, E., Depestele, J., et al. (2012) The environmental interactions of tidal and wave energy generation devices. *Environmental Impact Assessment Review*, 32, 133–139.

Friess, D.A. (2016) Mangrove forests. *Current Biology*, 26 (16), R746–R748.

Friess, D.A., Möller, I., Spencer, T., et al. (2014) Coastal saltmarsh managed realignment drives rapid breach inlet and external creek evolution, Freiston Shore (UK). *Geomorphology*, 208, 22–33.

Frohlich, C., DeShon, H., Stump, B., et al. (2016) A historical review of induced earthquakes in Texas. *Seismological Research Letters*, 87, doi:10.1785/0220160016.

Fu, C. (2003) Potential impacts of human-induced land cover change on East Asia monsoon. *Global and Planetary Change*, 37, 219–229.

Fullen, M.A. (2003) Soil erosion and conservation in northern Europe. *Progress in Physical Geography*, 27 (3), 331–358.

Fuller, D.O. and Ottka, C. (2002) Land cover, rainfall and land-surface albedo in West Africa. *Climate Change*, 54, 181–204.

Fuller, D.Q., Denham, T., Arroyo-Kalin, M., et al. (2014) Convergent evolution and parallelism in plant domestication revealed by an expanding archaeological record. *Proceedings of the National Academy of Sciences*, 111 (17), 6147–6152.

Fuller, D.Q., Qin, L., Zheng, Y., et al. (2009) The domestication process and domestication rate in rice: spikelet bases from the lower Yangtze. *Science*, 323, 1607–1610.

Fuller, R., Hill, D. and Tucker, G. (1991) Feeding the birds down on the farm: perspectives from Britain. *Ambio*, 20, 232–237.

Furley, P.A. (2016) *Savannas. A Very Short Introduction.* Oxford: Oxford University Press.

Fyfe, J.C., Derksen, C., Mudryk, L., et al. (2017) Large near-term projected snowpack loss over the western United States. *Nature communications*, 8, doi:10.1038/ncomms14996.

Gabler, C.A., Osland, M.J., Grace, J.B., et al. (2017) Macroclimatic change expected to transform coastal wetland ecosystems this century. *Nature Climate Change*, 7, 142–147.

Gabunia, L. and Vekua, A. (1995) A Plio-Pleistocene hominid from Dmanisi, East Georgia, Caucasus. *Nature*, 373, 509–512.

Gadd, M.E. (2012) Barriers, the beef industry and unnatural selection: a review of the impact of veterinary fencing on mammals in Southern Africa. In M.J. Somers and M. Hayward (eds), *Fencing for Conservation*. New York: Springer, 153–186.

Gade, D.W. (1976) Naturalization of plant aliens: the volunteer orange in Paraguay. *Journal of Biogeography*, 3, 269–279.

Gaertner, M., Breeyen, A.D., Hui, C. and Richardson, D.M. (2009) Impact of alien plant invasions on species richness in Mediterranean-type ecosystems: a meta-analysis. *Progress in Physical Geography*, 33, 319–338.

Galay, V.J. (1983) Causes of river bed degradation. *Water Resources Research*, 19, 1057–1090.

Gale, S.J. and Hoare, P. G. (2012) The stratigraphic status of the Anthropocene. *The Holocene*, 22, 1491–1494.

Galibert, F., Quignon, P., Hitte, C. and André, C. (2011) Toward understanding dog evolutionary and domestication history. *Comptes Rendus Biologies*, 334, 190–196.

Gallego-Sala, A.V. and Prentice, I.C. (2012) Blanket peat biome endangered by climate change. *Nature Climate Change*, 3, 152–155.

Galloway, J.N., Townsend, A.R., Erisman, J.W., et al. (2008) Transformation of the nitrogen cycle: recent trends, questions, and potential solutions. *Science*, 320, 889–892.

Gambolati, G., Ricceri, G., Bertoni, W., et al. (1991) Mathematical simulation of the subsidence of Ravenna. *Water Resources Research*, 27, 2899–2918.

Gameson, A.L.H. and Wheeler, A. (1977) Restoration and recovery of the Thames Estuary. In J. Cairns, K.L. Dickson and E.E. Herricks (eds), *Recovery and Restoration of Damaged Ecosystems*. Charlottesville: University Press of Virginia, 92–101.

Ganguly, D., Rasch, P.J., Wang, H. and Yoon, J.-H. (2012) Climate response of the South Asian monsoon system to anthropogenic aerosols. *Journal of Geophysical Research*, 117, D13209.

Ganteaume, A., Camia, A., Jappiot, M., et al. (2013) A review of the main driving factors of forest fire ignition over Europe. *Environmental Management*, 51 (3), 651–662.

Gao, H. and Washington, R. (2010) Arctic oscillation and the interannual variability of dust emissions from the Tarim Basin: a TOMS AI based study. *Climate Dynamics*, 35, 511–522.

Gao, X. and Giorgi, F. (2008) Increased aridity in the Mediterranean region under greenhouse gas forcing estimated from high resolution simulations with a regional climate model. *Global and Planetary Change*, 62, 195–209.

Garcia, X.-F., Schnauder, I. and Pusch, M.T. (2012) Complex hydromorphology of meanders can support benthic invertebrate diversity in rivers. *Hydrobiologia*, 685, 49–68.

García-Ruiz, J.M. (2010) The effects of land uses on soil erosion in Spain: a review. *Catena*, 81, 1–11.

García-Ruiz, J.M., Lasanta, T. and Alberto, F. (1997) Soil erosion by piping in irrigated fields. *Geomorphology*, 20, 269–278.

García-Ruiz, J.M., López-Moreno, J.I., Vincente-Serrano, S.M., et al. (2011) Mediterranean water resources in a global change scenario. *Earth-Science Reviews*, 105, 121–139.

Gardelle, J., Bertier, E. and Arnaud, Y. (2012) Slight mass gain of Karakoram glaciers in the early twenty-first century. *Nature Geoscience*, 5, 322–325.

Gardner, C.M.K., Cooper, D.M. and Hughes, S. (2002) Phosphorous in soils and field drainage water in the Thame catchment, UK. *Science of the Total Environment*, 282–283, 253–262.

Gardner, R. (2009) Trees as technology: planting shelterbelts on the Great Plains. *History and Technology*, 25, 325–341.

Gariano, S.L. and Guzzetti, F. (2016) Landslides in a changing climate. *Earth-Science Reviews*, 162, 227–252.

Garner, G., Hannah, D.M. and Watts, G. (2017) Climate change and water in the UK: recent scientific evidence for past and future change. *Progress in Physical Geography*, p.0309133316679082.

Gates, D.M. (1993) *Climate Change and Its Biological Consequences*. Sunderland, MA: Sinauer.

Gattuso, J.-P., Frankignoulle, M., Bourge, I., et al. (1998) Effect of calcium carbonate saturation of seawater on coral calcification. *Global and Planetary Change*, 18, 37–46.

Gattuso, J.-P. and Hansson, L. (eds) (2011) *Ocean Acidification*. Oxford: Oxford University Press.

Gauthier, S., Bernier, P., Kuuluvainen, T., et al. (2015) Boreal forest health and global change. *Science*, 349 (6250), 819–822.

Gautney, J.R. and Holliday, T.W. (2015) New estimations of habitable land area and human population size at the last glacial maximum. *Journal of Archaeological Science*, 58, 103–112.

Gaylord, D.R. (1990) Holocene palaeoclimatic fluctuations revealed from dune and interdune strata in Wyoming. *Journal of Arid Environments*, 18, 123–138.

Gedan, K.B., Altieri, A.H. and Bertness, M.D. (2011) Uncertain future of New England salt marshes. *Marine Ecology Progress Series*, 434, 229–237.

Gedan, K.B., Silliman, B.R. and Bertness, M.D. (2009) Centuries of human-driven change in salt marsh ecosystems. *Annual Review of Marine Science*, 1, 117–141.

Gedney, N., Cox, P.M., Betts, R.A., et al. (2006) Detection of a direct carbon dioxide effect in continental river runoff records. *Nature*, 439, 835–838.

Geertsema, M., Clague, J.J., Schwab, J.W. and Evans, S.G. (2006) An overview of recent large catastrophic landslides in northern British Columbia, Canada. *Engineering Geology*, 83, 120–143.

Geertz, C. (1963) *Agricultural Involution. The Process of Ecological Change in Indonesia*. Berkeley: University of California Press.

Gehring, C., Denich, M. and Vlek, P.L.G. (2005) Resilience of secondary forest regrowth after slash-and-burn agriculture in central Amazonia. *Journal of Tropical Ecology*, 21, 519–527.

Genevois, R. and Ghirotti, M. (2005) The 1963 Vaiont landslide. *Giornale di Geologia Applicata*, 1, 41–52.

Germer, S., Neill, C., Krusche, A.V. and Elsenbeer, H. (2010) Influence of land-use on near-surface hydrological processes: undisturbed forest to pasture. *Journal of Hydrology*, 380, 473–480.

Gero, A.F., Pitman, A.J., Narisma, G.T., et al. (2006) The impact of land cover change on storms in the Sydney Basin, Australia. *Global and Planetary Change*, 54, 57–78.

GESAMP (IMO/FAO/UNESCO/WMO/IAEA/UN/UNEP Joint Group of Experts on the Scientific Aspects of Marine Pollution) (1990) *The state of the marine environment*. UNEP Regional Seas Reports and Studies, 115, Nairobi.

Geyer, R., Jambeck, J.R. and Law, K.R. (2017) Production, use, and fate of all plastics ever made. *Science Advances*, 3 (7), doi:10.1126/sciadv.1700782.

Ghassemi, F., Jakeman, A.J. and Nix, H.A. (1995) *Salinisation of Land and Water Resources*. Wallingford: CAB International.

Ghersa, C.M., de la Fuente, E., Suarez, S. and Leon, R.J.C. (2002) Woody species invasion in the Rolling Pampa grasslands, Argentina. *Agriculture, Ecosystems & Environment*, 88, 271–278.

Giani, L., Makowsky, L. and Mueller, K. (2014) Plaggic Anthrosol: Soil of the Year 2013 in Germany: an overview on its formation, distribution, classification, soil function and threats. *Journal of Plant Nutrition and Soil Science*, 177 (3), 320–329.

Gil, D. and Brumm, H. (eds) (2014) *Avian Urban Ecology. Behavioural and Physiological Adaption*. Oxford: Oxford University Press.

Gilbert, G.K. (1917) *Hydraulic mining debris in the Sierra Nevada*. United States Geological Survey professional paper, 105.

Gilbert, O.L. (1975) Effects of air pollution on landscape and land-use around Norwegian aluminium smelters. *Environmental Pollution*, 8, 113–121.

Gill, A.B. (2005) Offshore renewable energy: ecological implications of generating electricity in the coastal zone. *Journal of Applied Ecology*, 42, 605–615.

Gill, R. and Fuller, R.J. (2007) The effects of deer browsing on woodland structure and songbirds in lowland Britain. *Ibis*, 149 (s2), 119–127.

Gill, T.E. (1996) Eolian sediments generated by anthropogenic disturbance of playas: human impacts on the geomorphic system and geomorphic impacts on the human system. *Geomorphology*, 17, 207–228.

Gillon, D. (1983) The fire problem in tropical savannas. In F. Bourlière (ed.), *Tropical Savannas*. Oxford: Elsevier Scientific, 617–641.

Gillson, L. (2015) *Biodiversity Conservation and Environmental Change*. Oxford: Oxford University Press.

Gillson, L., Dawson, T.P., Jack, S. and McGeoch, M.A. (2013) Accommodating climate change contingencies in conservation strategy. *Trends in Ecology & Evolution*, 28 (3), 135–142.

Gil-Romera, G., Turton, D. and Sevilla-Callejo, M. (2011) Landscape change in the lower Omo valley, southwestern Ethiopia: burning patterns and woody encroachment in the savanna. *Journal of Eastern African Studies*, 5, 108–128.

Gimingham, C.H. (1981) Conservation: European heathlands. In R.L. Spect (ed.), *Heathlands and Related Shrublands*. Amsterdam: Elsevier Scientific, 249–259.

Gimingham, C.H. and de Smidt, I.T. (1983) Heaths and natural and semi-natural vegetation. In W. Holzner, M.J.A. Werger and I. Ikusima (eds), *Man's Impact on Vegetation*. The Hague: Junk, 185–199.

Ginoux, P., Prospero, J.M., Gill, T.E., et al. (2012) Global-scale attribution of anthropogenic and natural dust sources and their emission rates based on MODIS deep blue aerosol products. *Reviews of Geophysics*, 50, RG3005, doi:10.1029/2012RG000388.

Giorgi, F. (2006) Climate change hot-spots. *Geophysical Research Letters*, 33, L08707.

Girardin, M.P., Hogg, E.H., Bernier, P.Y., et al. (2016) Negative impacts of high temperatures on growth of black spruce forests intensify with the anticipated climate warming. *Global Change Biology*, 22 (2), 627–643.

Givati, A. and Rosenfeld, D. (2004) Quantifying precipitation suppression due to air pollution. *Journal of Applied Meteorology*, 43, 1038–1056.

Glacken, C. (1967) *Traces on the Rhodian Shore. Nature and Culture in Western Thought from Ancient Times to the End of the Eighteenth Century*. Berkeley: University of California Press.

Glade, T. (2003) Landslide occurrence as a response to land use change: a review of evidence from New Zealand. *Catena*, 51, 297–314.

Gleick, P.H. (ed.) (1993) *Water in Crisis: A Guide to the World's Freshwater Resources*. New York: Oxford University Press.

Gleick, P.J. (2002) Dams. In A.S. Goudie (ed.), *Encyclopedia of Global Change*. New York: Oxford University Press, 229–234.

Glikson, A. (2013) Fire and human evolution: the deep-time blueprints of the Anthropocene. *Anthropocene*, 3, 89–92.

Global Invasive Species Network (2011) http:www.gisin. org?cwis438/Websites/GISNDirectory/SpeciesStatus_ Topoinvasives.php? (accessed January 2018).

Goddard, M.A., Dougill, A.J. and Benton, T.G. (2010) Scaling up from gardens: biodiversity conservation in urban environments. *Trends in Ecology & Evolution*, 25, 90–98.

Goebel, T., Waters, M.R. and O'Rourke, D.H. (2008) The late Pleistocene dispersal of modern humans in the Americas. *Science*, 319, 1497–1502.

Goldewijk, K.K. (2001) Estimating global land use change over the past 300 years: the HYDE database. *Global Biogeochemical Cycles*, 15, 417–433.

Goldsmith, F.B. (1983) Evaluating nature. In A. Warren and F.B. Goldsmith (eds), *Conservation in Perspective*. Chichester: Wiley, 233–246.

Goldsmith, V. (1978) Coastal dunes. In R.A. Davis (ed.), *Coastal Sedimentary Environments*. New York: Springer, 171–235.

Goldstein, M.C., Rosenberg, M. and Cheng, L. (2012) Increased oceanic microplastic debris enhances oviposition in an endemic pelagic insect. *Biology Letters*, doi:10.1098/rsbl.2012.0298.

Golomb, B. and Eder, H.M. (1964) Landforms made by man. *Landscape*, 14, 4–7.

Gómez, S., Gonda-King, L., Orians, C.M., et al. (2015) Interactions between invasive herbivores and their long-term impact on New England hemlock forests. *Biological Invasions*, 17 (2), 661–673.

Gonzalez, M.A. (2001) Recent formation of arroyos in the Little Missouri Badlands of southwestern Dakota. *Geomorphology*, 38, 63–84.

Goode, J.R., Luce, C.H. and Buffington, J.M. (2012) Enhanced sediment delivery in a changing climate in semi-arid mountain basins: implications for water resource management and aquatic habitat in the northern Rocky Mountains. *Geomorphology*, 139–140, 1–15.

Goodman, D. (1975) The theory of diversity-stability relationships in ecology. *The Quarterly Review of Biology*, 50, 237–266.

Goosem, M., Paz, C., Fensham, R., Preece, N., et al. (2016) Forest age and isolation affect the rate of recovery of plant species diversity and community composition in secondary rain forests in tropical Australia. *Journal of Vegetation Science*, 27, 504–514.

Goossens, D., Buck, B. and McLaurin, B. (2012) Contributions to atmospheric dust production of natural and anthropogenic emissions in a recreational area designated for off-road vehicular activity (Nellis Dunes, Nevada, USA). *Journal of Arid Environments*, 78, 80–99.

Goreau, T.J. and Hayes, R.L. (1994) Coral bleaching and ocean 'hot spots'. *Ambio*, 23, 176–180.

Gorman, M. (1979) *Island Ecology*. London: Chapman and Hall.

Gornitz, V., Couch, S. and Hartig, E.K. (2002) Impacts of sea level rise in the New York City metropolitan area. *Global and Planetary Change*, 32, 61–88.

Gornitz, V., Rosenzweig, C. and Hillel, D. (1997) Effects of anthropogenic intervention in the land hydrologic cycle on global sea level rise. *Global and Planetary Change*, 14, 147–161.

Gottesfeld, P. and Cherry, C.R. (2011) Lead emissions from solar voltaic energy systems in China and India. *Energy Policy*, 39, 4939–4946.

Gottschalk, L.C. (1945) Effects of soil erosion on navigation in Upper Chesapeake Bay. *Geographical Review*, 35, 219–238.

Goudie, A.S. (1972) Vaughan Cornish: geographer. *Transactions of the Institute of British Geographers*, 55, 1–16.

Goudie, A.S. (1973) *Duricrusts of Tropical and Subtropical Landscapes*. Oxford: Clarendon Press.

Goudie, A.S. (1977) Sodium sulphate weathering and the disintegration of Mohenjo-Daro, Pakistan. *Earth Surface Processes*, 2, 75–86.

Goudie, A.S. (1983) Dust storms in space and time. *Progress in Physical Geography*, 7, 502–530.

Goudie, A.S. (ed.) (1990) *Techniques for Desert Reclamation*. Chichester: Wiley.

Goudie, A.S. (1994) Deserts in a warmer world. In A.C. Millington and K. Pye (eds), *Environmental Change in Drylands. Biogeographical and Geomorphological Perspectives*. Chichester: Wiley, 1–24.

Goudie, A.S. (2002) *Great Warm Deserts of the World. Landscape and Evolution.* Oxford: Oxford University Press.

Goudie, A.S. (2006) Global warming and fluvial geomorphology. *Geomorphology*, 79, 384–394.

Goudie A.S. (2013) *Arid and Semi-arid Geomorphology.* Cambridge: Cambridge University Press.

Goudie, A.S. (2017) The integration of Human and Physical Geography revisited. *The Canadian Geographer/Le Géographe canadien*, 6 (1), 19–27.

Goudie, A.S. and Middleton, N.J. (1992) The changing frequency of dust storms through time. *Climate Change*, 20, 197–225.

Goudie, A.S. and Middleton, N.J. (2006) *Desert Dust in the Global System.* Berlin: Springer and Heidelberg.

Goudie, A.S. and Viles, H.A. (1997) *Salt Weathering Hazards.* Chichester: Wiley.

Goudie, A.S. and Viles, H.A. (2016) *Geomorphology in the Anthropocene.* Cambridge: Cambridge University Press.

Goudie, A.S., Parker, A.G. and Al-Farraj, A. (2000) Coastal change in Ras Al Khaimah (United Arab Emirates): a cartographic analysis. *Geographical Journal*, 166, 14–25.

Goudie, A.S., Viles, H.A. and Pentecost, A. (1993) The late-Holocene tufa decline in Europe. *The Holocene*, 3, 181–186.

Goudie, A.S. and Wilkinson, J.C. (1977) *The Warm Desert Environment.* Cambridge: Cambridge University Press.

Goulson, D. (2003) Effects of introduced bees on native ecosystems. *Annual Review of Ecology, Evolution, and Systematics*, 34, 1–26.

Gourou, P. (1961) *The Tropical World* (3rd edn). London: Longman.

Goutal, N., Keller, T., Défossez, P. and Ranger, J. (2013) Soil compaction due to heavy forest traffic: measurements and simulations using an analytical soil compaction model. *Annals of Forest Science* 70 (5), 545–556.

Govorushko, S.M. (2011) *Natural Processes and Human Impacts.* Heidelberg: Springer.

Gowlett, J.A.J. (2016) The discovery of fire by humans: a long and convoluted process. *Philosophical Transactions of the Royal Society B*, 371 (1696), 20150164.

Gowlett, J.A.J., Harris, J.W.K., Walton, D. and Wood, B.A. (1981) Early archaeological sites, hominid remains and traces of fire from Chesowanja, Kenya. *Nature*, 284, 125–129.

Grabherr, G., Gottfried, M. and Pauli, H. (2010) Climate change impacts in alpine environments. *Geography Compass*, 4, 1133–1153.

Grable, J.L. and Harden, C.P. (2006) Geomorphic response of an Appalachian Valley and Ridge stream to urbanization. *Earth Surface Processes and Landforms*, 31, 1707–1720.

Graedel, T.E. and Crutzen, P.J. (1995) *Atmosphere, Climate and Change.* New York: Scientific American Library.

Graetz, D. (1994) Grasslands. In W.B. Meyer and B.L. Turner II (eds), *Changes in Land Use and Land Cover: A Global Perspective.* Cambridge: Cambridge University Press, 125–147.

Graf, J.B., Webb, R.H. and Hereford, R. (1991) Relation of sediment load and flood-plain formation to climatic variability, Paria River drainage basin, Utah and Arizona. *Geological Society of America Bulletin*, 103, 1405–1415.

Graf, W.L. (1978) Fluvial adjustments to the spread of tamarisk in the Colorado Plateau region. *Geological Society of America Bulletin*, 86, 1491–1501.

Graf, W.L. (1981) Channel instability in a sand-river bed. *Water Resources Research*, 17, 1087–1094.

Graf, W.L. (1988) *Fluvial Processes in Dryland Rivers.* Berlin: Springer.

Graf, W.L. (2001) Damage control: restoring the physical integrity of America's rivers. *Annals of the Association of American Geographers*, 91, 1–27.

Graham, N.A., Cinner, J.E., Norström, A.V. and Nyström, M. (2014) Coral reefs as novel ecosystems: embracing new futures. *Current Opinion in Environmental Sustainability*, 7, 9–14.

Grainger, A. (1990) *The Threatening Desert: Controlling Desertification.* London: Earthscan.

Grainger, A. (1992) *Controlling Tropical Deforestation.* London: Earthscan.

Grainger, A. (2008) Difficulties in tracking the long-term global trend in tropical forest area. *Proceedings of the National Academy of Sciences*, 105, 818–823.

Grant, M.J., Waller, M.P. and Groves, J.A. (2011) The Tilia decline: vegetation change in lowland Britain during the mid and late Holocene. *Quaternary Science Reviews*, 30, 394–408.

Grattan, J.P., Adams, R.B., Friedman, H., et al. (2016) The first polluted river? Repeated copper contamination of fluvial sediments associated with Late Neolithic human activity in southern Jordan. *Science of the Total Environment*, 573, 247–257.

Grattan, J.P., Gilbertson, D.D. and Hunt, C.O. (2007) The local and global dimensions of metalliferous pollution derived from a reconstruction of an eight thousand year record of copper smelting and mining at a desert-mountain frontier in southern Jordan. *Journal of Archaeological Science*, 34, 83–110.

Grayson, D.K. (1977) Pleistocene avifaunas and the overkill hypothesis. *Science*, 195, 691–693.

Green, F.H.W. (1978) Field drainage in Europe. *Geographical Journal*, 144, 171–174.

Green, J. and Trett, M.W. (eds) (2012) *The Fate and Effects of Oil in Freshwater.* Heidelberg: Springer Science & Business Media.

Green, P.A., Vörösmarty, C.J., Galloway, J.N., et al. (2004) Pre-industrial and contemporary fluxes of nitrogen through rivers: a global assessment based on typology. *Biogeochemistry*, 68, 71–105.

Greene, R., Timms, W., Rengasamy, P., et al. (2016) Soil and aquifer salinization: toward an integrated approach for salinity management of groundwater. In A. Jakeman, O. Barreteau, R.J. Hunt, et al. (eds), *Integrated Groundwater Management*. Heidelberg: Springer, 377–412.

Greenfield, H.J. (2010) The secondary products revolution: the past, the present and the future. *World Archaeology*, 42, 29–54.

Greenland, D.J. and Lal, R. (1977) *Soil Conservation and Management in the Humid Tropics*. Chichester: Wiley.

Gregory, J.M., Church, J.A., Boer, G.J., et al. (2001) Comparisons of results from several AOGCMs for global and regional sea level change 1900–100. *Climate Dynamics*, 18, 225–240.

Gregory, J.M., Huybrechts, P. and Raper, S.C.B. (2004b) Threatened loss of the Greenland ice-sheet. *Nature*, 428, 616.

Gregory, J.M. and Oerlemans, J. (1998) Simulated future sea-level rise due to glacier melt based on regionally and seasonally resolved temperature changes. *Nature*, 391, 474–476.

Gregory, K.J. (1976) Drainage networks and climate. In E. Derbyshire (ed.), *Geomorphology and Climate*. Chichester: Wiley, 289–315.

Gregory, K.J. (1985) The impact of river channelization. *Geographical Journal*, 151, 53–74.

Gregory, K.J. and Walling, D. (1973) *Drainage Basin Form and Process: A Geomorphological Approach*. London: Arnold.

Gregory, R.D., Noble, D.G. and Custance, J. (2004a) The state of play of farmland birds: population trends and conservation status of lowland farmland birds in the United Kingdom. *Ibis*, 146 (Suppl. 2), 1–13.

Gregory, R.D., Vorisek, P., Van Strien, A., et al. (2007) Population trends of widespread woodland birds in Europe. *Ibis*, 149 (Suppl. 2), 78–97.

Grieve, I.C. (2001) Human impacts on soil properties and their implications for the sensitivity of soil systems in Scotland. *Catena*, 42, 361–374.

Griffith, M.B., Norton, S.B., Alexander, L.C., et al. (2012) The effects of mountaintop mines and valley fills on the physicochemical quality of stream ecosystems in the central Appalachians: a review. *Science of the Total Environment*, 417, 1–12.

Griffiths, J.F. (1976) *Applied Climatology, an Introduction* (2nd edn). Oxford: Oxford University Press.

Grill, G., Lehner, B., Lumsdon, A.E., et al. (2015) An index-based framework for assessing patterns and trends in river fragmentation and flow regulation by global dams at multiple scales. *Environmental Research Letters*, 10 (1), doi:10.1088/1748-9326/10/1/015001.

Grimley, D.A., Anders, A.M., Bettis, E.A., et al. (2017) Using magnetic fly ash to identify post-settlement alluvium and its record of atmospheric pollution, Central USA. *Anthropocene*, doi:10.1016/j.ancene.2017.02.001 DOI:10.1016/j.ancene.2017.02.001#doilink.

Grimm, N.B., Chacon, A., Dahm, C.N., et al. (1997) Sensitivity of aquatic ecosystems to climatic and anthropogenic changes: the Basin and Range, American south-west and Mexico. In C.E. Cushing (ed.), *Freshwater Ecosystems and Climate Change in North America: A Regional Assessment*. Chichester: Wiley, 205–223.

Grogan, D.S., Zhang, F., Prusevich, A., et al. (2015) Quantifying the link between crop production and mined groundwater irrigation in China. *Science of the Total Environment*, 511, 161–175.

Grosjean, M., Núñez, L., Castajena, I. and Messerli, B. (1997) Mid-Holocene climate and culture change in the Atacama Desert, northern Chile. *Quaternary Research*, 48, 239–246.

Gross, A., Holdenrieder, O., Pautasso, M., et al. (2014) Hymenoscyphus pseudoalbidus, the causal agent of European ash dieback. *Molecular Plant Pathology*, 15, 5–21.

Grossman, G. and Krueger, A. (1995) Economic growth and the environment. *Quarterly Journal of Economics*, 110, 353–377.

Grove, A.T. and Rackham, O. (2001) *The Nature of Mediterranean Europe: An Ecological History*. New Haven: Yale University Press.

Grove, J.M. (1988) *The Little Ice Age*. London: Routledge.

Grove, R.H. (1983) *The Future for Forestry*. Cambridge: British Association of Nature Conservationists.

Grove, R.H. (1997) *Ecology, Climate and Empire: Colonialism and Global Environmental history, 1400–1940*. Cambridge: White Horse Press.

Grove, R.H. and Damodaran, V. (2006) Imperialism, intellectual networks and environmental change. *Economic and Social Weekly*, 14 October, 4345–4354.

Grover, H.D. and Musick, H.B. (1990) Shrubland encroachment in southern New Mexico, USA: an analysis of desertification processes in the American southwest. *Climatic Change*, 17, 305–330.

Gruber, S. and Haeberli, W. (2007) Permafrost in steep bedrock slopes and its temperature-related destabilization following climate change. *Journal of Geophysical Research*, 112, F02S18.

Gu, B., Ge, Y., Chang, S.X., Luo, W. and Chang, J. (2013) Nitrate in groundwater of China: sources and driving forces. *Global Environmental Change*, 23 (5), 1112–1121.

Guerreiro, S.B., Birkinshaw, S., Kilsby, C., Fowler, H.J. and Lewis, E. (2017) Dry getting drier – the future of transnational river basins in Iberia. *Journal of Hydrology: Regional Studies*, 12, 238–252.

Guha, R. (2014) *Environmentalism: A Global History.* Harmondsworth: Penguin.

Guha, S.K. (ed.) (2000) *Induced Earthquakes.* Dordrecht: Kluwer.

Guicherit, R. and Roemer, M. (2000) Tropospheric ozone trends. *Chemosphere – Global Change Science*, 2, 167–183.

Guida, R.J., Abella, S.R., Smith Jr, W.J., et al. (2014) Climatic change and desert vegetation distribution: assessing thirty years of change in southern Nevada's Mojave Desert. *Professional Geographer*, 66 (2), 311–322.

Guiot, J. and Cramer, W. (2016) Climate change: the 2015 Paris Agreement thresholds and Mediterranean basin ecosystems. *Science* 354 (6311), 465–468.

Guitart, R., Sachana, M., Caloni, F., et al. (2010) Animal poisoning in Europe. Part 3: wildlife. *Veterinary Journal*, 183, 260–265.

Gunderson, L.H., Allen, C.R. and Holling, C.S. (eds) (2012) *Foundations of Ecological Resilience.* Washington, DC and London: Island Press.

Gunn, J.M. (ed.) (2012) *Restoration and Recovery of an Industrial Region: Progress in Restoring the Smelter-damaged Landscape near Sudbury, Canada.* New York: Springer Science & Business Media.

Guo, D. and Wang, H. (2016) Permafrost degradation and associated ground settlement estimation under 2°C global warming. *Climate Dynamics*, doi:10.1007/s00382-016-3469-9.

Guo, J.H., Liu, X.J., Zhang, Y., et al. (2010) Significant acidification of major Chinese croplands. *Science*, 327, 1008–1010.

Guo, M., Wu, W., Zhou, X., et al. (2015) Investigation of the dramatic changes in lake level of the Bosten Lake in northwestern China. *Theoretical and Applied Climatology*, 119, 341–351.

Guo, S., Wang, J., Xiang, L., Ying, A. and Li, D. (2002) A macro-scale and semi-distributed monthly water balance model to predict climate change impacts in China. *Journal of Hydrology*, 268, 1–15.

Guo, X. and Zheng, G. (2009) Advances in weather modification from 1997 to 2007 in China. *Advances in Atmospheric Sciences*, 26, 240–252.

Gupta, H.K. (2002) A review of recent studies of triggered earthquakes by artificial water reservoirs with special emphasis on earthquakes in Koyna, India. *Earth-Science Reviews*, 58, 279–310.

Gurnell, A., Lee, M. and Souch, C. (2007) Urban rivers: hydrology, geomorphology, ecology and opportunities for change. *Geography Compass*, 1, 1118–1137.

Guthrie, R.D. (2003) Rapid body size decline in Alaskan Pleistocene horses before extinction. *Nature*, 426, 169–171.

Gutiérrez, F., Parise, M., De Waele, J. and Jourde, H. (2014) A review on natural and human-induced geohazards and impacts in karst. *Earth-Science Reviews*, 138, 61–88.

Gutierrez-Elorza, M. (2001) *Geomorfología climática.* Barcelona: Omega.

Haase, D., Larondelle, N., Andersson, E., et al. (2014) A quantitative review of urban ecosystem service assessments: concepts, models, and implementation. *Ambio* 43 (4), 413–433.

Haberl, H., Erb, K.H., Krausmann, F., et al. (2007) Quantifying and mapping the human appropriation of net primary production in earth's terrestrial ecosystems. *Proceedings of the National Academy of Sciences*, 104, 12942–12947.

Haberlie, A.M., Ashley, W.S., Fultz, A.J. and Eagan, S.M. (2016) The effect of reservoirs on the climatology of warm-season thunderstorms in Southeast Texas, USA. *International Journal of Climatology*, 36 (4), 1808–1820.

Haberlie, A.M., Ashley, W.S. and Pingel, T.J. (2015) The effect of urbanisation on the climatology of thunderstorm initiation. *Quarterly Journal of the Royal Meteorological Society*, 141 (688), 663–675.

Haddeland, I., Heinke, J., Biemans, H., et al. (2014) Global water resources affected by human interventions and climate change. *Proceedings of the National Academy of Sciences*, 111 (9), 3251–3256.

Haeberli, W. and Burn, C.R. (2002) Natural hazards in forests: glacier and permafrost effects as related to climate change. In R.C. Sidle (ed.), *Environmental Change and Geomorphic Effects in Forests.* Wallingford: CABI, 167–202.

Haff, P.K. (2010) Hillslopes, rivers, plows and trucks: mass transport on Earth's surface by natural and technological processes. *Earth Surface Processes and Landforms*, 35, 1157–1166.

Haghani, S., Leroy, S.A., Wesselingh, F.P. and Rose, N.L. (2016) Rapid evolution of coastal lagoons in response to human interference under rapid sea level change: a south Caspian Sea case study. *Quaternary International*, 408, 93–112.

Hails, J.R. (ed.) (1977) *Applied Geomorphology.* Amsterdam: Elsevier.

Haine, T.W., Curry, B., Gerdes, R., et al. (2015) Arctic freshwater export: status, mechanisms, and prospects. *Global and Planetary Change*, 125, 13–35.

Hall, S.R. and Mills, E.L. (2000) Exotic species in large lakes of the world. *Aquatic Ecosystem Health and Management*, 3, 105–135.

Halligan, J.J., Waters, M.R., Perrotti, A., et al. (2016) Pre-Clovis occupation 14,550 years ago at the Page-Ladson site, Florida, and the peopling of the Americas. *Science Advances*, 2 (5), e1600375, doi:10.1126/sciadv.1600375.

Halpern, B.S., Selkoe, K.A., Micheli, F. and Kappel, C.V. (2007) Evaluating and ranking the vulnerability of global marine ecosystems to anthropogenic threats. *Conservation Biology*, 21, 1301–1315.

Hambler, C. and Canney, S.M. (2013) *Conservation*. Cambridge: Cambridge University Press.

Hamel, A. and Dansereau, P. (1949) *L'aspect ecologique du probleme des mauvaises herbes*. Paris: Service de Biogéographie.

Hamilton, C. (2015) Getting the Anthropocene so wrong. *The Anthropocene Review*, 2, 102–107.

Hammer, S., Nager, R.G., Alonso, S., et al. (2016) Legacy pollutants are declining in Great Skuas (*Stercorarius skua*). *Bulletin of Environmental Contamination and Toxicology*, 97 (2), 184–190.

Han, Z., Wang, T., Dong, Z., et al. (2007) Chemical stabilization of mobile dunefields along a highway in the Taklimakan desert of China. *Journal of Arid Environments*, 68, 260–270.

Hand, J.L., White, W.H., Gebhart, K.A., et al. (2016) Earlier onset of the spring fine dust season in the southwestern United States. *Geophysical Research Letters*, 43 (8), 4001–4009.

Hanley, M.E., Hoggart, S.P.G., Simmonds, D.J., et al. (2014) Shifting sands? Coastal protection by sand banks, beaches and dunes. *Coastal Engineering*, 87, 136–146.

Hansen, J., Johnson, D., Lacis, A., et al. (1981) Climatic impact of increasing atmospheric carbon dioxide. *Science*, 213, 957–966.

Hansen, J., Sato, M., Hearty, P., Ruedy, R., et al. (2016) Ice melt, sea level rise and superstorms: evidence from paleoclimate data, climate modeling, and modern observations that 2°C global warming could be dangerous. *Atmospheric Chemistry and Physics*, 16, 3761–3812.

Hansen, M.C., Potapov, P.V., Moore, R., et al. (2013) High-resolution global maps of 21st-century forest cover change. *Science*, 342 (6160), 850–853.

Hanson, P.J. and Weltzin, J.F. (2000) Drought disturbance from climate change: response of United States forests. *Science of the Total Environment*, 262, 205–220.

Hapke, C.J., Kratzmann, M.G. and Himmelstoss, E.A. (2013) Geomorphic and human influence on large-scale coastal change. *Geomorphology*, 199, 160–170.

Happ, S.C. (1944) Effect of sedimentation on floods in the Kickapoo Valley, Wisconsin. *Journal of Geology*, 52, 53–68.

Harlan, J.R. (1975) Our vanishing genetic resources. *Science*, 188, 617–622.

Harlan, J.R. (1976) The plants and animals that nourish man. *Scientific American*, 235 (3), 88–97.

Harmand, S., Lewis, J.E., Feibel, C.S., et al. (2015) 3.3-million-year-old stone tools from Lomekwi 3, West Turkana, Kenya. *Nature*, 521, 310–315.

Harnischmacher, S. (2010) Quantification of mining subsidence in the Ruhr District (Germany). *Géomorphologie*, 3, 261–274.

Harper, G.A. and Bunbury, N. (2015) Invasive rats on tropical islands: their population biology and impacts on native species. *Global Ecology and Conservation*, 3, 607–627.

Harper, K.C. (2008) Climate control: United States weather modification in the cold war and beyond. *Endeavour*, 32, 20–26.

Harris, C., Davies, M.C.R. and Etzelmüller, B. (2001) The assessment of potential geotechnical hazards associated with mountain permafrost in a warming global climate. *Permafrost and Periglacial Processes*, 12, 145–156.

Harris, D.R. (1966) Recent plant invasions in the arid and semi-arid southwest of the United States. *Annals of the Association of American Geographers*, 56, 408–422.

Harris, D.R. (ed.) (1980) *Human Ecology in Savanna Environments*. London: Academic Press.

Harris, D.R. 1996 (ed.) *The Origins and Spread of Agriculture and Pastoralism in Eurasia*. London: UCL Press.

Harris, G., Thirgood, S., Hopcraft, J.G.C., et al. (2009) Global decline in aggregated migrations of large terrestrial mammals. *Endangered Species Research*, 7, 55–76.

Harris, J.M., Oltmans, S.J., Bodeker, G.E., et al. (2003) Long-term variations in total ozone derived from Dobson and satellite data. *Atmospheric Environment*, 37, 3167–3175.

Harris, S.A. (2002) Causes and consequences of rapid thermokarst development in permafrost or glacial terrain. *Permafrost and Periglacial Processes*, 13, 237–242.

Harrison, S., Glasser, N., Winchester, V., et al. (2006) A glacial lake outburst flood associated with recent mountain glacier retreat, Patagonian Andes. *The Holocene*, 16, 611–620.

Hartemink, A. (2006) Soil erosion: perennial crop plantations. In R. Lal (ed.), *Encolpedia of Soil Science*. New York: Taylor and Francis, 1613–1617.

Harvey, A.M. (1989) The occurrence and role of arid zone alluvial fans. In D.S.G. Thomas (ed.), *Arid Zone Geomorphology*. London: Belhaven Press, 136–158.

Harvey, A.M., Oldfield, F., Baron, A.F. and Pearson, G.W. (1981) Dating of post-glacial landforms in the central Howgills. *Earth Surface Processes and Landforms*, 6, 401–412.

Harvey, A.M. and Renwick, W.H. (1987) Holocene alluvial fan and terrace formation in the Bowland Fells, Northwest England. *Earth Surface Processes and Landforms*, 12, 249–257.

Harvey, L.D.D. (2000) *Global Warming: The Hard Science*. Harlow: Prentice Hall.

Hassol, S.J. (2004) *Impacts of a Warming Arctic.* Cambridge: Cambridge University Press.

Hathaway, J.M., Winston, R.J., Brown, R.A., et al. (2016) Temperature dynamics of stormwater runoff in Australia and the USA. *Science of the Total Environment*, 559, 141–150.

Hauck, M., Zimmermann, J., Jacob, M., et al. (2012) Rapid recovery of stem increment in Norway spruce at reduced SO$_2$ levls in the Harz Mountains, Germany. *Environmental Pollution*, 164, 132–141.

Hautier, Y., Tilman, D., Isbell, F., et al. (2015) Anthropogenic environmental changes affect ecosystem stability via biodiversity. *Science*, 348 (6232), 336–340.

Hawass, Z. (1993) The Egyptian monuments: problems and solutions. In M.J. Thiel (ed.), *Conservation of Stone and Other Material*. London: Spon, 19–25.

Hawksworth, D.L. (1990) The long-term effects of air pollutants on lichen communities in Europe and North America. In G.M. Woodwell (ed.), *The Earth in Transition: Patterns and Processes of Biotic Impoverishment*. Cambridge: Cambridge University Press, 45–64.

Hawksworth, D.L. and Rose, F. (1976) *Lichens as Pollution Monitors*. London: Edward Arnold.

Hawley, R.J., MacMannis, K.R. and Wooten, M.S. (2013) Bed coarsening, riffle shortening, and channel enlargement in urbanizing watersheds, northern Kentucky, USA. *Geomorphology*, 201, 111–126.

Hay, J. (1973) Salt cedar and salinity on the Upper Rio Grande. In M.T. Farver and J.P. Milton (eds), *The Careless Technology*. London: Tom Stacey, 288–300.

Hayden, B. (1995) A new review of domestication. In T.D. Price and A.B. Gebauser (eds), *Last Hunters, First Farmers*. Santa Fe: School of American Research, 273–299.

Hayhow D.B. and 49 others (2016) *State of Nature 2016.* UK: The State of Nature Partnership, http://www.rspb.org.uk/Images/State%20of%20Nature%20UK%20report%20pages_1%20Sept_tcm9-424984.pdf (accessed September 2016).

Haynes, C.V. (1991) Geoarchaeological and palaeohydrological evidence for a Clovis-age drought in North America and its bearing on extinction. *Quaternary Research*, 35, 438–450.

Haynes, G. (2012) Elephants (and extinct relatives) as earth-movers and ecosystem engineers. *Geomorphology*, 157, 99–107.

He, F., Vavrus, S.J., Kutzbach, J.E., et al. (2014) Simulating global and local surface temperature changes due to Holocene anthropogenic land cover change. *Geophysical Research Letters*, 41, 623–631.

Healy, T. (1991) Coastal erosion and sea level rise. *Zeitschrift für Geomorphologie, Supplementband*, 81, 15–29.

Healy, T. (1996) Sea level rise and impacts on nearshore sedimentation. *Geologische Rundschau*, 85, 546–553.

Heathwaite, A.L., Johnes, P.J. and Peters, N.E. (1996) Trends in nutrients. *Hydrological Processes*, 10, 263–293.

Heberger, M., Cooley, H., Herrera, P., et al. (2011) Potential impacts of increasing coastal flooding in California due to sea-level rise. *Climatic Change*, 109 (Suppl.), S229–S249.

Heberling, J.M., Jo, I., Kozhevnikov, A., et al. (2017) Biotic interchange in the Anthropocene: strong asymmetry in East Asian and eastern North American plant invasions. *Global Ecology and Biogeography*, 26, 447–458.

Heever, S.C. and Cotton, W.R. (2007) Urban aerosol impacts on downwind convective storms. *Journal of Applied Meteorology and Climatology*, 46, 828–850.

Heine, K., Niller, H.P., Nuber, T. and Scheibe, R. (2005) Slope and valley sediments as evidence of deforestation and land-use in prehistporic and historic Eastern Bavaria. *Zeitschrift für Geomorphologie, Supplementband*, 139, 147–171.

Helbig, M., Pappas, C. and Sonnentag, O. (2016) Permafrost thaw and wildfire: equally important drivers of boreal tree cover changes in the Taiga Plains, Canada. *Geophysical Research Letters*. doi:10.1002/2015GL067193.

Helldén, U. (1985) Land degradation and land productivity monitoring – needs for an integrated approach. In A. Hjört (ed.), *Land Management and Survival*. Uppsala: Scandinavian Institute of African Studies, 77–87.

Helliwell, D.R. (1974) The value of vegetation for conservation. II: M1 motorway area. *Journal of Environmental Management*, 2, 75–78.

Henderson, S., Dawson, T.P. and Whittaker, R.J. (2006) Progress in invasive plants research. *Progress in Physical Geography*, 30, 25–46.

Henderson-Sellers, A. and Blong, R. (1989) *The Greenhouse Effect: Living in a Warmer Australia*. Kensington: New South Wales University Press.

Henderson-Sellers, A. and Gornitz, V. (1984) Possible climatic impacts of land cover transformation with particular emphasis on tropical deforestation. *Climatic Change*, 6, 231–257.

Hendrix, P.F. (2006) Biological invasions belowground – earthworms as invasive species. *Biological Invasions*, 8, 1201–1204.

Henkner, J., Ahlrichs, J.J., Downey, S., Fuchs, M., James, B.R., Knopf, T., Scholten, T., Teuber, S. and Kühn, P. (2017) Archaeopedology and chronostratigraphy of colluvial deposits as a proxy for regional land use history (Baar, southwest Germany). *Catena*, 155, 93–113.

Henley, W.F., Patterson, M.A., Neves, R.J. and Lemly, A.D. (2000) Effects of sedimentation and turbidity on lotic food webs: a concise review for natural resource managers. *Reviews in Fisheries Science*, 8 (2), 125–139.

Henry, D.O., Cordova, C.E., Portillo, M., et al. (2017) Blame it on the goats? Desertification in the Near East during the Holocene. *The Holocene*, 27, 625–637.

Henry, J., Beguin, M., Requier, F., et al. (2012) A common pesticide decreases foraging success and survival in honey bees. *Science*, 336, 348–350.

Herb, W.R., Janke, B., Mohseni, O. and Stefan, H.G. (2008) Thermal pollution of streams by runoff from paved surfaces. *Hydrological Processes*, 22, 987–999.

Hereford, R., Jacoby, G.C. and McCord, V.A.S. (1995) Geomorphic history of the Virgin River in the Zion National Park area, southweset Utah. *US Geological Survey Circular*, 95–515.

Herms, D.A. and McCullough, D.G. (2014) Emerald ash borer invasion of North America: history, biology, ecology, impacts, and management. *Annual Review of Entomology*, 59, 13–30.

Hess, W.N. (ed.) (1974) *Weather and Climate Modification.* New York: Wiley.

Hester, E.T. and Doyle, M.W. (2011) Human impacts to river temperature and their effects on biological processes: a quantitative analysis. *Journal of the American Water Resources Association*, 47, 571–587.

Hewlett, J.D., Post, H.E. and Doss, R. (1984) Effect of clear-cut silviculture on dissolved ion export and water yield in the Piedmont. *Water Resources Research*, 20 (7), 1030–1038.

Heyvaert, V.M.A. and Walstra, J. (2016) The role of long-term human impact on avulsion and fan development. *Earth Surface Processes and Landforms*, 41 (14), 2137–2152.

Heywood, V.H. (1989) Patterns, extents and modes of invasions by terrestrial plants. In J.A. Drake (ed.), *Biological Invasions: A Global Perspective*. Chichester: Wiley, 31–55.

Heywood, V.H. and Watson, R.T. (eds) (1995) *Global Biodiversity Assessment.* Cambridge: Cambridge University Press.

Hicke, J.A., Allen, C.D., Desai, A.R., et al. (2012) Effects of biotic disturbanvces on forest carbon cycling in the United States and Canada. *Global Change Biology*, 18, 7–34.

Hickler, T., Vohland, K., Feehan, J., et al. (2012) Projecting the future distribution of European potential natural vegetation zones with a generalized, tree species-based dynamic vegetation model. *Global Ecology and Biogeography*, 21, 50–63.

Hidy, G.M. and Blanchard, C.L. (2016) The changing face of lower tropospheric sulfur oxides in the United States. *Elementa*, 4, doi:10.12952/journal.elementa.000138.

Hilborn, R., Branch, T.A., Ernst, B., et al. (2003) State of the world's fisheries. *Annual Review of Environment and Resources*, 28, 359–399.

Hills, T.L. (1965) Savannas: a review of a major research problem in tropical geography. *The Canadian Geographer*, 9, 216–228.

Hinkel, J., Nicholls, R.J., Tol, R.S., et al. (2013) A global analysis of erosion of sandy beaches and sea-level rise: an application of DIVA. *Global and Planetary Change*, 111, 150–158.

Hirabayashi, Y., Mahendran, R., Koirala, S., et al. (2013) Global flood risk under climate change. *Nature Climate Change*, 3, 816–821.

Hiscock, K.M., Lister, D.H., Boar, R.R. and Green, F.M.L. (2001) An integrated assessment of long-term changes in the hydrology of three lowland rivers in eastern England. *Journal of Environmental Management*, 61, 195–214.

Hobbs, P.V. and Radke, L.F. (1992) Airborne studies of the smoke from the Kuwait oil fires. *Science*, 256, 987–991.

Hobbs, R.J., Higgs, E.S. and Hall, C. (2013) *Novel Ecosystems: Intervening in the New Ecological World Order.* Chichester: John Wiley & Sons.

Hoegh-Guldberg, O. (1999) Climate change, coral bleaching and the future of the world's coral reefs. *Marine and Freshwater Research*, 50, 839–866.

Hoegh-Guldberg, O. (2001) Sizing the impact: coral reef ecosystems as early casualties of climate change. In G.R. Walther, C.A. Burga and P.J. Edwards (eds), *Fingerprints of Climate Change*. New York: Kluwer/Plenum, 203–228.

Hoegh-Guldberg, O. (2011) Coral reef ecosystems and anthropogenic climate change. *Regional Environmental Change*, 11 (Suppl. 1), S215–S227.

Hoegh-Guldberg, O. and Bruno, J.F. (2010) The impact of climate change on the world's marine ecosystems. *Science*, 328, 1523–1528.

Hoegh-Guldberg, O., Mumby, P.J., Hooten, A.J., et al. (2007) Coral reefs under rapid climate change and ocean acidification. *Science*, 318, 1737–1742.

Hoeksema, R.J. (2007) Three stages in the history of land reclamation in the Netherlands. *Irrigation and Drainage*, 56 (S1), S113–S126.

Hoelzle, M. and Trindler, M. (1998) Data management and application. In W. Haeberli (ed.), *Into the Second Century of Worldwide Glacier Monitoring: Prospects and Strategies*. Paris: UNESCO, 53–64.

Hoelzmann, P., Keding, B., Berke, H., et al. (2001) Environmental change and archaeology: lake evolution and human occupation in the eastern Sahara during the Holocene. *Palaeogeography, Palaeoclimatology, Palaeoecology*, 169, 193–217.

Hofman, C.A. and Rick, T.C. (2017) Ancient biological invasions and island ecosystems: tracking translocations of wild plants and animals. *Journal of Archaeological Research*, doi:10.1007/s10814-017-9105-3.

Hoffmann, M., Belant, J.L., Chanson, J.S., et al. (2011) The changing fate of the world's mammals. *Philosophical*

Transactions of the Royal Society of London: Series B, Biological Sciences, 366, 2598–2610.

Hogsden, K.L. and Harding, J.S. (2012) Consequences of acid mine drainage for the structure and function of benthic stream communities: a review. *Freshwater Science*, 31, 108–120.

Hohner, S.M. and Dreschel, T.W. (2015) Everglades peats: using historical and recent data to estimate predrainage and current volumes, masses and carbon contents. *Mires and Peat*, 16, 1–15.

Holden, J., Chapman, P.J. and Labadz, J.C. (2004) Artificial drainage of peatlands: hydrological and hydrochemical process and wetland restoration. *Progress in Physical Geography*, 28, 95–123.

Holden, J., Evans, M.G., Burt, T.P. and Horton, M. (2006) Impact of land drainage on peatland hydrology. *Journal of Environmental Quality*, 35, 1764–1778.

Holen, S.R., Deméré, T.A., Fisher D.C., et al. (2017) A 130,000-year-old archaeological site in southern California, USA. *Nature*, 465, 479–483.

Holland, G.J., McBridge, J.L. and Nicholls, N. (1988) Australian region tropical cyclones and the greenhouse effect. In G.I. Pearman (ed.), *Greenhouse, Planning for Climate Change*. Leiden: Brill, 438–455.

Holliday, V.T. (2004) *Soils in Archaeological Research*. New York: Oxford University Press.

Holliday, V.T. (2017) Anthrosols. In A.S. Gilbert (ed.), *Encyclopedia of Geoarchaeology*. Dordrecht: Springer, 24–27.

Hollis, G.E. (1975) The effects of urbanization on floods of different recurrence interval. *Water Resources Research*, 11, 431–435.

Hollis, G.E. (1988) Rain, roads, roofs and runoff: hydrology in cities. *Geography*, 73, 9–18.

Holloway, G. and Sou, T. (2002) Has Arctic sea ice rapidly thinned? *Journal of Climate*, 15, 1691–1701.

Holm, K., Bovis, M. and Jacob, M. (2004) The landslide response of alpine basins to post-Little Ice Age glacial thinning and retreat in southwestern British Columbia. *Geomorphology*, 57, 201–216.

Holmgren, K., Degerman, E., Petersson, E. and Bergquist, B. (2016) Long term trends of fish after liming of Swedish streams and lakes. *Atmospheric Environment*, 146, 245–251.

Holz, A. and Veblen, T.T. (2011) The amplifying effects of humans on fire regimes in temperate rainforests in western Patagonia. *Palaeogeography, Palaeoclimatology, Palaeoecology*, 311, 82–92.

Holzer, T.L. (1979) Faulting caused by groundwater extraction in South-central Arizona. *Journal of Geophysical Research*, 84, 603–612.

Holzmueller, E.J. and Jose, S. (2010) Invasion success of cogongrass, an alien C4 perennial grass, in the southeastern United States: exploration of the ecological basis. *Biological Invasions*, 13, 435–442.

Hoogland, T., Van Den Akker, J.J.H. and Brus, D.J. (2012) Modeling the subsidence of peat soils in the Dutch coastal area. *Geoderma*, 171, 92–97.

Hooijer, A., Page, S., Jauhiainen, J., et al. (2012) Subsidence and carbon loss in drained tropical peatlands. *Biogeosciences*, 9, 1053–1071.

Hooke, J. (ed.) (1998) *Coastal Defence and Earth Science Conservation*. Bath: Geological Society of London.

Hooke, R.L. (1994) On the efficacy of humans as geomorphic agents. *USA Today*, 4, 224–225.

Hope, G. (1999) Vegetation and fire response to late Holocene human occupation in island and mainland north west Tasmania. *Quaternary International*, 59, 47–60.

Hopkins, G.R., French, S.S. and Brodie, E.D. (2013b) Increased frequency and severity of developmental deformities in rough-skinned newt (Taricha granulosa) embryos exposed to road deicing salts (NaCl & MgCl$_2$). *Environmental Pollution*, 173, 264–269.

Hopkins, K.G., Morse, N.B., Bain, D.J., et al. (2015) Type and timing of stream flow changes in urbanizing watersheds in the Eastern US. *Elementa: Science of the Anthropocene*, 3 (1), doi:10.12952/journal.elementa.000056.

Hopkins, R.L., Altier, B.M., Haselman, D., et al. (2013a) Exploring the legacy effects of surface coal mining on stream chemistry. *Hydrobiologia*, 713, 87–95.

Horn, R., van der Akker, J.J.H. and Arvidsson, J. (eds) (2000) *Subsoil Compaction: Distribution, Processes and Consequences*. Reiskirchen: Catena Verlag.

Horrocks, M., Nichol, S.L., D'Costa, D.M., et al. (2007) A late Quaternary record of natural change and human impact from Rangihoua Bay, Bay of Islands, northern New Zealand. *Journal of Coastal Research*, 23, 592–604.

Hoshino, S., Esteban, M., Mikami, T., et al. (2016) Estimation of increase in storm surge damage due to climate change and sea level rise in the Greater Tokyo area. *Natural Hazards*, 80, 539–565.

Hossain, F. (2009) Empirical relationship between large dams and the alteration in extreme precipitation. *Natural Hazards Review*, 11 (3), 97–101.

Hossaini, R., Chipperfield, M.P., Montzka, S.A., et al. (2017) The increasing threat to stratospheric ozone from dichloromethane. *Nature Communications*, 8, 15962, doi:10.1038/ncomms15962.

Hough, S.E. and Page, M. (2016) Potentially induced earthquakes during the early twentieth century in the Los Angeles Basin. *Bulletin of the Seismological Society of America*, 106 (6), 2419–2435.

Houghton, J.T. (2009) *Global Warming: The Complete Briefing* (4th edn). Cambridge University Press Cambridge.

Houghton, J.T., Callander, B.A. and Varney, S.K. (eds) (1992) *Climate Change 1992: The Supplementary Report of the IPCC Scientific Assessment.* Cambridge: Cambridge University Press.

Houghton, J.T., Jenkins, G.J. and Ephraums, J.J. (eds) (1990) *Climate Change: The IPCC Scientific Assessment.* Cambridge: Cambridge University Press.

Houghton, R.A. and Nassikas, A.A. (2017) Global and regional fluxes of carbon from land use and land-cover change 1850–2015. *Global Biogeochemical Cycles*, 31, 455–472.

Houghton, R.H. and Skole, D.L. (1990) Carbon. In B.L. Turner II (ed.), *The Earth Transformed by Human Action.* Cambridge: Cambridge University Press, 393–408.

Houston, S.L., Houston, W.N., Zapata, C.E. and Lawrence, C. (2001) Geotechnical engineering practice for collapsible soils. *Geotechnical and Geological Engineering*, 19, 333–355.

Howard, J. (2017) *Anthropogenic Soils.* New York: Springer International Publishing.

Howarth, R., Chan, F., Conley, D.J., et al. (2011) Coupled biogeochemical cycles: eutrophication and hypoxia in temperate estuaries and coastal marine ecosystems. *Frontiers in Ecology and the Environment*, 9, 18–26.

Howden, N.J., Burt, T.P., Worrall, F., et al. (2013) Farming for water quality: balancing food security and nitrate pollution in UK river basins. *Annals of the Association of American Geographers*, 103 (2), 397–407.

Howe, G.M., Slaymaker, H.O. and Harding, D.M. (1966) Flood hazard in mid-Wales. *Nature*, 212, 584–585.

Hoyos, C.D., Agudelo, P.A., Webster, P.J. and Curry, J.A. (2006) Deconvolution of the factors contributing to the increase in global hurricane intensity. *Science*, 312, 94–97.

Hsu, P.-C., Li, T., Luo, J.-L., et al. (2012) Increase of global monsoon area and precipitation under global warming: a robust signal? *Geophysical Research Letters*, 39, L06701.

Hu, G., Dontg, Z., Lu, J. and Yan, C. (2012) Driving forces responsible for aeolian desertification in the source region of the Yangtze River from 1975 to 2005. *Environmental Earth Sciences*, 66, 257–263.

Hu, R. (2006) *Urban land subsidence in China.* IAEG2006 Paper 786. London: Geological Society of London.

Huang, Q.H. and Cai, Y.L. (2007) Spatial pattern of karst rock desertification in the middle of Guizhou Province, southwestern China. *Environmental Geology*, 52, 1325–1330.

Huang, R. and Chan, L. (2004) Human-induced landslides in China: mechanism study and its implications on slope management. *Chinese Journal of Rock Mechanics and Engineering*, 23, 2766–2777.

Huang, W., Clochon, R., Gu, Y., et al. (1995) Early homo and associated artefacts from Asia. *Nature*, 378, 275–278.

Hübner, R., Herbert, R.J.H. and Astin, K.B. (2010) Cadmium release caused by the die-back of the saltmarsh cord grass Spartina anglica in Poole Harbour (UK). *Estuarine, Coastal and Shelf Science*, 87, 553–560.

Hudson, N. (1987) Soil and water conservation in semi-arid areas. *FAO Soils Bulletin*, 55.

Hugenholtz, C.H. and Wolfe, S.A. (2005) Biogeomorphic model of dunefield activation and stabilization on the northern Great Plains. *Geomorphology*, 70, 53–70.

Huggel, C., Clague, J.J. and Korup, O. (2012) Is climate change responsible for changing landslide activity in high mountains? *Earth Surface Processes and Landforms*, 37, 77–91.

Hughes, A.C. (2017) Understanding the drivers of Southeast Asian biodiversity loss. *Ecosphere*, 8 (1), e01624.

Hughes, R.G. and Paramor, O.A.L. (2004) On the loss of saltmarshes in south-east England and methods for their restoration. *Journal of Applied Ecology*, 41, 440–448.

Hughes, R.J., Sullivan, M.E. and Yok, D. (1991) Human-induced erosion in a highlands catchment in Papua New Guinea: the prehistoric and contemporary records. *Zeitschrift für Geomorphologie, Supplementband*, 83, 227–239.

Hughes, T.P. (1994) Catastrophes, phase shifts, and large-scale degradation of a Caribbean coral reef. *Science*, 265, 1547–1551.

Hughes, T.P., Barnes, M.L., Bellwood, D.R., et al. (2017) Coral reefs in the Anthropocene. *Nature*, 546 (7656), 82–90.

Hughes, T.P., Bellwood, D.R., Baird, A.H., et al. (2011) Shifting base-lines, declining coral cover, and the erosion of reef resilience: comment on Sweatman et al. (2011). *Coral Reefs*, 30, 653–660.

Hughes, T.P., Linares, C., Dakos, V., et al. (2013) Living dangerously on borrowed time during slow, unrecognized regime shifts. *Trends in Ecology & Evolution*, 28, 149–155.

Hull, S.K. and Gibbs, J.N. (1991) Ash dieback: a survey of nonwoodland trees. *Forestry Commission Bulletin*, 93.

Hultine, K.R. and Bush, S.E. (2011) Ecohydrological consequences of non-native riparian vegetation in the southwestern United States: a review from an ecophysiological perspective. *Water Resources Research*, 47, W07542.

Humphries, M.S. (2013) DDT residue contamination in sediments from Lake Sibaya in northern KwaZulu-Natal, South Africa: implications for conservation in a World Heritage Site. *Chemosphere*, 93 (8), 1494–1499.

Huntington, E. (1914) *The Climatic Factor as Illustrated in Arid America*. Carnegie Institution of Washington publication, 192.

Hupp, C.R. and Osterkamp, W.R. (1996) Riparian vegetation and fluvial geomorphic processes. *Geomorphology*, 14 (4), 277–295.

Hupp, C.R., Pierce, A.R. and Noe, G.B. (2009) Floodplain geomorphic processes and environmental impacts of human alteration along coastal plain rivers, USA. *Wetlands*, 29, 413–429.

Hupp, C.R., Noe, G.B., Schenk, E.R. and Benthem, A.J. (2013) Recent and historic sediment dynamics along Difficult Run, a suburban Virginia Piedmont stream. *Geomorphology*, 180, 156–169.

Hupy, J.P. and Koehler, T. (2012) Modern warfare as a significant form of zoogeomorphic disturbance upon the landscape. *Geomorphology*, 157, 169–182.

Hupy, J.P. and Schaetzl, R.J. (2006) Introducing 'bombturbation', a singular type of soil disturbance and mixing. *Soil Science*, 171, 823–836.

Ibisate, A., Ollero, A., Ballarín, D., et al. (2016) Geomorphic monitoring and response to two dam removals: rivers Urumea and Leitzaran (Basque Country, Spain). *Earth Surface Processes and Landforms*, 41 (15), 2239–2255.

Ikawa-Smith, F. (1982) Current issues in Japanese archaeology. *American Scientist*, 68, 134–145.

Illies, J. (1974) *Introduction to Zoogeography*. London: Macmillan.

Imeson, A. (1971) Heather burning and soil erosion on the North Yorkshire Moors. *Journal of Applied Ecology*, 8, 537–541.

Imeson, A. (2012) *Desertification, Land Degradation and Sustainability*. Chichester: Wiley Blackwell.

Imfeld, G. and Vuilleumier, S. (2012) Measuring the effects of pesticides on bacterial communities in soil: a critical review. *European Journal of Soil Biology*, 49, 22–30.

Imhoff, M.L., Bounoua, L., Ricketts, T., et al. (2004) Global patterns in human consumption of net primary productivity. *Nature*, 429, 870–873.

Imhoff, M.L., Zhang, P., Wolfe, R.E. and Bounoua, L. (2010) Remote sensing of the urban heat island effect across biomes in the continental USA. *Remote Sensing of Environment*, 114, 504–513.

Immer Zeel, W.W., van Beek, L.P.H. and Bierkens, M.F.P. (2010) Climate change will affect the Asian water towers. *Science*, 328, 1382–1385.

Inbar, A., Lado, M., Sternberg, M., et al. (2014) Forest fire effects on soil chemical and physicochemical properties, infiltration, runoff, and erosion in a semiarid Mediterranean region. *Geoderma*, 221, 131–138.

Inbar, M. and Llerena, C. A. (2000) Erosion processes in high mountain agricultural terraces in Peru. *Mountain Research and Development*, 20, 72–79.

Indoitu, R., Orlovsky, L. and Orlovsky, N. (2012) Dust storms in Central Asia: spatila and temporal variations. *Journal of Arid Environments*, 85, 62–70.

Inkpen, R.J., Viles, H.A., Moses, C., et al. (2012) Thirty years of erosion and declining atmospheric pollution at St Paul's Cathedral, London. *Atmospheric Environment*, 62, 521–529.

Innes, J.L. (1983) Lichenometric dating of debris-flow deposits in the Scottish Highlands. *Earth Surface Processes and Landforms*, 8, 579–588.

Innes, J.L. (1987) Air pollution and forestry. *Forestry Commission Bulletin*, 70.

Innes, J.L. (1992) Forest decline. *Progress in Physical Geography*, 16, 1–64.

Innes, J.L., Blackford, J. and Simmons, I. (2010) Woodland disturbance and possible land-use regimes during the Late Mesolithic in the English uplands: pollen, charcoal and non-pollen palynomorph evidence from Bluewath Beck, North York Moors, UK. *Vegetation History and Archaeobotany*, 19, 439–452.

Innes, J.L. and Boswell, R.C. (1990) Monitoring of forest condition in Great Britain 1989. *Forestry Commission Bulletin*, 98, 1–54.

Intergovernmental Panel on Climate Change (IPCC) (2001) *Climate Change 2001: The Scientific Basis*. Cambridge: Cambridge University Press.

Intergovernmental Panel on Climate Change (IPCC) (2007a) *Climate Change 2007: The Physical Science Basis*. Cambridge: Cambridge University Press.

Intergovernmental Panel on Climate Change (IPCC) (2007b) *Climate Change 2007; Impacts, Adaptation and Vulnerability*. Cambridge: Cambridge University Press.

IPCC (Intergovernmental Panel on Climate Change) (2013) *Climate Change 2013: The Physical Science Basis: Contribution of Working Group I to the Fifth Assessment Report of the Intergovernmental Panel on Climate Change*, ed. T.F. Stocker, D. Qin, G.-K. Plattner, M. Tignor, S.K. Allen, J. Boschung, A. Nauels, Y. Xia, V. Bex and P.M. Midgley. Cambridge: Cambridge University Press.

International Tanker Owners Pollution Federation (ITOPF) http://www.itopf.co.uk/information-services/data-and-statistics/statistics/ (accessed January 2018).

Irabien, M. J., García-Artola, A., Cearreta, A. and Leorri, E. (2015) Chemostratigraphic and lithostratigraphic signatures of the Anthropocene in estuarine areas from the eastern Cantabrian coast (N. Spain). *Quaternary International*, 364, 196–205.

Irish, J.L., Frey, A.E., Rosati, J.D., et al. (2010) Potential implications of global warming and barrier island degradation on future hurricane inundation, property damages, and population impacted. *Ocean and Coastal Management*, 53, 645–657.

Irvine, P.J., Kravitz, B., Lawrence, M.G. and Muri, H. (2016) An overview of the Earth system science of solar geoengineering. *Wiley Interdisciplinary Reviews: Climate Change*, 7 (6), 815–833.

Isaac, E. (1970) *Geography of Domestication*. Englewood Cliffs: Prentice Hall.

Ives, A.R. and Carpenter, S.R. (2007) Stability and diversity of ecosystems. *Science*, 317, 58–62.

Ives, J.D. and Messerli, B. (1989) *The Himalayan Dilemma: Reconciling Development and Conservation*. London: Routledge.

Iwase, A., Hashizume, J., Izulo, M., et al. (2012) Timing of megafaunal extinction in the Late Pleistocene on the Japanese Archipelago. *Quaternary International*, 255, 114–124.

Iwashima, T. and Yamamoto, R. (1993) A statistical analysis of the extreme events: long-term trend of heavy daily precipitation. *Journal of the Meteorological Society of Japan*, 71, 637–640.

Jaboyedoff, M., Michoud, M., Derron, M.-H., et al. (2016) Human-induced landslides: toward the analysis of an-thropogenic changes of the slope environment. In S. Avresa, L. Cascini, L. Picarelli, and C. Scavia (eds), *Landslides and Engineering Slopes – Experiences, Theory and practices*. Boca Raton: CRC Press, 217–232.

Jacks, G.V. and Whyte, R.O. (1939) *The Rape of the Earth: A World Survey of Soil Erosion*. London: Faber & Faber.

Jackson, R.B. and Jobbágy, E.G. (2005) From icy roads to salty streams. *Proceedings of the National Academy of Sciences*, 102, 14487–14488.

Jacobs, J. (1969) *The Economy of Cities*. New York: Random House.

Jacobs, J. (1975) Diversity, stability and maturity in ecosystems influenced by human activities. In W.H. Van Dobben and R.H. Lowe-McConnell (eds), *Unifying Concepts in Ecology*. The Hague: Junk, 187–207.

Jacobsen, T. and Adams, R.M. (1958) Salt and silt in ancient Mesopotamian agriculture. *Science*, 128, 1251–1258.

Jaeger, K.L. (2015) Reach-scale geomorphic differences between headwater streams draining mountaintop mined and unmined catchments. *Geomorphology*, 236, 25–33.

Jalowska, A.M., Rodriguez, A.B. and McKee, B.A. (2015) Responses of the Roanoke Bayhead Delta to variations in sea level rise and sediment supply during the Holocene and Anthropocene. *Anthropocene*, 9, 41–55.

James, L.A. (1989) Sustained storage and transport of hydraulic gold mining sediment in the Bear River, California. *Annals of the Association of American Geographers*, 79, 570–592.

James, L.A. (2011) Contrasting geomorphic impacts of pre- and post-Columbian land-use changes in Anglo America. *Physical Geography*, 32, 399–422.

James, L.A. and Marcus, W.A. (eds) (2006) 37th Binghamton Geomorphology Symposium: the human role in changing fluvial systems. *Geomorphology*, 79, 1–506.

James, L.A., Phillips, J.D. and Lecce, S.A. (2017) A centennial tribute to G.K. Gilbert's 'Hydraulic-Mining Débris in the Sierra Nevada'. *Geomorphology*, 294, 4–19.

Jarvie, H.P., Neal, C. and Withers, P.J. (2006) Sewage-effluent phosphorus: a greater risk to river eutrophication than agricultural phosphorus? *Science of the Total Environment*, 360 (1), 246–253.

Jarvis, P.H. (1979) The ecology of plant and animal introductions. *Progress in Physical Geography*, 3, 187–214.

Jeffries, M.J. (2012) Ponds and the importance of their history: an audit of pond numbers, turnover and the relationship between the origins of ponds and their contemporary plant communities in south-east Northumberland, UK. *Hydrobiologia*, 689, 11–21.

Jenkins, M. (2003) Prospects for biodiversity. *Science*, 302, 1175–1177.

Jenkins, M.E., Davies, T.J. and Stedman, J.R. (2002) The origin and day-of-week dependence of photochemical ozone episodes in the UK. *Atmospheric Environment*, 36, 999–1012.

Jennings, J.N. (1952) *The Origin of the Broads*. Royal Geographical Society Research Series, 2.

Jenny, H. (1941) *Factors of Soil Formation*. New York: McGraw-Hill.

Jernelöv, A. (2010) The threats from oil spills: now, then, and in the future. *Ambio*, 39, 353–366.

Ji, R., Cui, P., Ding, F., et al. (2009) Monophyletic origin of domestic bactrian camel (Camelus bactrianus) and its evolutionary relationship with the extant wild camel (Camelus bactrianus ferus). *Animal Genetics*, 40 (4), 377–382.

Jiang, Y., Luo, Y., Zhao, Z. and Tao, S. (2010) Changes in wind speed over China during 1956–2004. *Theoretical and Applied Climatology*, 99, 421–430.

Jiang, Z., Lian, Y. and Qin, X. (2014) Rocky desertification in Southwest China: impacts, causes, and restoration. *Earth-Science Reviews*, 132, 1–12.

Jiao, W., Chen, W., Chang, A.C. and Page, A.L. (2012) Environmental risks of trace elements associated with long-term phosphate fertilizers applications: a review. *Environmental Pollution*, 168, 44–53.

Jickells, T.D., Carpenter, R. and Liss, P.S. (1991) Marine environment. In B.L. Turner, W.C. Clark, R.W. Kates, J.F., et al. (eds), *The Earth as Transformed by Human Action*. Cambridge: Cambridge University Press, 313–334.

Jilbert, T., Reichard, G.-J., Aeschlimann, B., et al. (2010) Climate-controlled multidecadal variability in North

African dust transport to the Mediterranean. *Geology*, 38, 19–22.

Jim, C.Y. (1998) Urban soil characteristics and limitations for landscape planting in Hong Kong. *Landscape and Urban Planning*, 40, 235–249.

Jin, H., Li, S., Cheng, G., Shaoling, W. and Li, X. (2000) Permafrost and climatic change in China. *Global and Planetary Change*, 26, 387–404.

Joern, A. and Keeler, K.H. (eds) (1995) *The Changing Prairie*. New York: Oxford University Press.

Johannessen, C.L. (1963) Savannas of interior Honduras. *Ibero-Americana*, 46, 160.

Johnson, A.I. (ed.) (1991) *Land subsidence*. International Association of Hydrological Sciences Publication, 200.

Johnson, C.N. (2005) What can the date on late survival of Australian megafauna tell us about the cause of their extinction? *Quaternary Science Reviews*, 24, 2167–2172.

Johnson, C.N. (2009) Ecological consequences of Late Quaternary extinctions of megafauna. *Proceedings of The Royal Society, Biological Sciences*, 276, 2509–2519.

Johnson, C.N., Balmford, A., Brook, B.W., Buettel, J.C., Galetti, M., Guangchun, L. and Wilmshurst, J.M. (2017) Biodiversity losses and conservation responses in the Anthropocene. *Science*, 356 (6335), 270–275.

Johnson, C.N. and Wroe, S. (2003) Causes of extinction of vertebrates during the Holocene of mainland Australia: arrival of the dingo, or human impact? *The Holocene*, 13, 941–948.

Johnson, D.B. and Hallberg, K.B. (2005) Acid mine drainage remediation options: a review. *Science of the Total Environment*, 338, 3–14.

Johnson, D.L. and Lewis, L.A. (1995) *Land Degradation: Creation and Destruction*. Oxford: Blackwell.

Johnson, K.S. (2008) Gypsum-karst problems in constructing dams in the USA. *Environmental Geology*, 53 (5), 945–950.

Johnson, N.M. (1979) Acid rain: neutralization within the Hubbard Brook ecosystem and regional implications. *Science*, 204, 497–499.

Johnston, A., Ausden, M., Dodd, A.M., et al. (2013) Observed and predicted effects of climate change on species abundance in protected areas. *Nature Climate Change*, 3 (12), 1055–1061.

Johnston, D. W. (1974) Decline of DDT residues in migratory songbirds. *Science*, 186, 841–842.

Johnston, D.W., Turner, J. and Kelly, J.M. (1982) The effects of acid rain on forest nutrient status. *Water Resources Research*, 18, 448–461.

Jolly, W.M., Cochrane, M.A., Freeborn, P.H., et al. (2015) Climate-induced variations in global wildfire danger from 1979 to 2013. *Nature Communications*, 6, doi:10.1038/ncomms8537.

Jomelli, V., Brunstein, D., Déqué, M., et al. (2009) Impacts of future climatic change (2070–2099) on the potential occurrence of debris flows: a case study in the Massif des Ecrins (French Alps). *Climatic Change*, 97, 171–191.

Jonard, M., Legout, A., Nicolas, M., et al. (2012) Deterioration of Norway spruce vitality despite a sharp decline in acid deposition: a long-term integrated study. *Global Change Biology*, 18, 711–725.

Jones, B.M., Arp, C.D., Jorgenson, M.T., et al. (2009) Increase in the rate and uniformity of coastline erosion in Arctic Alaska. *Geophysical Research Letters*, 36, doi:10.1029/2008GL036205.

Jones, B.M., Grosse, G., Arp, C.D., et al. (2011) Modern thermokarst lake dynamics in the continuous permafrost zone, northern Seward Peninsula, Alaska. *Journal of Geophysical Research: Biogeosciences*, 116 (G2), doi:10.1029/2011JG001666.

Jones, H.P. and Schmitz, O.J. (2009) Rapid recovery of damaged ecosystems. *PLoS ONE*, 4, e5653.

Jones, J.A.A., Liu, C., Woo, M.-K. and Kung, H.-T. (eds) (1996) *Regional Hydrological Response to Climate Change*. Dordrecht: Kluwer.

Jones, J.D.G. (2011) Why genetically modified crops? *Philosophical Transactions: Series A, Mathematical, Physical, and Engineering Sciences*, 369, 1807–1815.

Jones, M.D., Djamali, M., Holmes, J., et al. (2015) Human impact on the hydroenvironment of Lake Parishan, SW Iran, through the late Holocene. *The Holocene*, 25, 1651–1661.

Jones, M.P., Hunt, W.F. and Winston, R.J. (2012) Effect of urban catchment composition on runoff temperature. *Journal of Environmental Engineering*, 138 (12), 1231–1236.

Jones, P.D. and Lister, D.H. (2009) The urban heat island in Central London and urban-related warming trends in Central London since 1900. *Weather*, 64, 323–327.

Jones, P.D. and Reid, P.A. (2001) Assessing future changes in extreme precipitation over Britain using regional climate model integrations. *International Journal of Climatology*, 21, 1337–1356.

Jones, R., Benson-Evans, K. and Chambers, F.M. (1985) Human influence upon sedimentation in Llangorse Lake, Wales. *Earth Surface Processes and Landforms*, 10, 227–235.

Jordà, G., Marbà, N. and Duarte, C.M. (2012) Mediterranean seagrass vulnerable to regional climate warming. *Nature Climate Change*, 2, 821–824.

Joughlin, I. and Alley, R.B. (2011) Stability of the West Antarctic ice sheet in a warming world. *Nature Geoscience*, 4, 506–513.

Joyce, L., Aber, J., McNulty, S., et al. (2001) Potential consequences of climate variability and change for the forests of the United States. In National Assessment Synthesis Team (ed.), *Climate Change Impacts on the United States: The Potential Consequences of Climate*

Variability and Change. Cambridge: Cambridge University Press, 489–521.

Julian, M. and Anthony, E. (1996) Aspects of landslide activity in the Mercantour Massif and the French Riviera, southeastern France. *Geomorphology*, 15, 275–289.

Jürgens, M.D., Crosse, J., Hamilton, P.B., et al. (2016) The long shadow of our chemical past – high DDT concentrations in fish near a former agrochemicals factory in England. *Chemosphere*, 162, 333–344.

Justine, J.L., Winsor, L., Gey, D., et al. (2014) The invasive New Guinea flatworm Platydemus manokwari in France, the first record for Europe: time for action is now. *PeerJ*, 2, e297, doi:org/10.7717/peerj.297.

Kabakci, H., Chevalier, P.M. and Papendick, R.I. (1993) Impact of tillage and residue management on dryland spring wheat development. *Soil and Tillage Research*, 26, 127–137.

Kadiri, M., Ahmadian, R., Bockelmann-Evans, B., et al. (2012) A review of the potential water quality impacts of tidal renewable energy systems. *Renewable and Sustainable Energy Reviews*, 16, 329–341.

Kadomura, H. (1983) Some aspects of large-scale land transformation due to urbanization and agricultural development in recent Japan. *Advances in Space Research*, 2 (8), 169–178.

Kai, F.M., Tyler, S.C., Randerson, J.T. and Blake, D.R. (2011) Reduced methane growth rate explained by decreased Northern Hemisphere microbial sources. *Nature*, 476, 194–197.

Kanevskiy, M., Shur, Y., Strauss, J., et al. (2016) Patterns and rates of riverbank erosion involving ice-rich permafrost (yedoma) in northern Alaska. *Geomorphology*, 253, 370–384.

Kang, S.M., Polvani, L.M., Fyfe, J.C. and Sigmond, M. (2011) Impact of polar ozone depletion on subtropical precipitation. *Science*, 332, 951–954.

Kapfer, J. and Grytnes, J.A. (2017) Large climate change, large effect? Vegetation changes over the past century in the European High Arctic. *Applied Vegetation Science*, 20, 204–214.

Kaplan, J.O., Krumhardt, K.M. and Zimmermann, N. (2009) The prehistoric and preindustrial deforestation of Europe. *Quaternary Science Reviews*, 28, 3016–3034.

Kar, S.K., Liou, Y.-A. and Ha, K.-J. (2009) Aerosol effects on the enhancement of cloud-to-ground lightning over major urban areas of South Korea. *Atmospheric Research*, 92, 80–87.

Karakurt, I., Aydin, G. and Aydiner, K. (2012) Sources and mitigation of methane emissions by sectors: a critical review. *Renewable Energy*, 39, 40–48.

Kareiva, P. and Levin, S.A. (eds) (2003) *The Importance of Species.* Princeton: Princeton University Press.

Karim, M.F. and Mimura, N. (2008) Impacts of climate change and sea-level rise on cyclonic storm surge floods in Bangladesh. *Global Environmental Change*, 18, 490–500.

Karl, T.R., Melillo, J.M. and Peterson, T.C. (2009) *Global Climate Change Impacts in the United States.* Cambridge: Cambridge University Press.

Karnosky, D.F. (2003) Impacts of elevated atmospheric CO_2 on forest trees and forest ecosystems: knowledge gaps. *Environment International*, 29, 161–169.

Karnosky, D.F., Ceulemans, R., Scarascia-Mugnozza, G.E. and Innes, J.L. (2001) *The Impact of Carbon Dioxide and Other Greenhouse Gases on Forest Ecosystems.* Wallingford: CABI Publishing.

Karnosky, D.F., Skelly, J.M., Percy, K.E. and Chappelka, A.H. (2007) Perspectives regarding 50 years of research on effects of tropospheric ozone air pollution on US forests. *Environmental Pollution*, 147, 489–506.

Kaser, G. (1999) A review of the modern fluctuations of tropical glaciers. *Global and Planetary Change*, 22, 93–103.

Kasischke, E.S., Verbyla, D.L., Rupp, T.S., et al. (2010) Alaska's changing fire regime – implications for the vulnerability of its boreal forests. *Canadian Journal of Forest Research*, 40, 1313–1324.

Kasperson, V.X., Kasperson, R.E. and Turner, B.L. II (1995) *Regions at Risk: Comparisons of Threatened Environments.* Tokyo: United Nations University Press.

Kassam, A., Derpsch, R. and Friedrich, T. (2014) Global achievements in soil and water conservation: the case of conservation agriculture. *International Soil and Water Conservation Research*, 2, 5–13.

Kates, R.W., Turner, B.L.I and Clark, W.C. (1990) The great transformation. In B.L. Turner, W.C. Clark, R.W. Kates, et al. (eds), *The Earth as Transformed by Human Action.* Cambridge: Cambridge University Press, 1–17.

Kaufmann, R.K., Seto, K.C., Schneider, A., Liu, Z., Zhou, L. and Wang, W. (2007) Climate response to rapid urban growth: evidence of a human-induced precipitation deficit. *Journal of Climate*, 20, 2299–2306.

Kaushal, S.S., Duan, S., Doody, T.R., et al. (2017) Human-accelerated weathering increases salinization, major ions, and alkalinization in fresh water across land use. *Applied Geochemistry*, 83, 121–135.

Kaushal, S.S., Groffman, P.M., Likens, G.E., et al. (2005) Increased salinization of fresh water in the northeastern United States. *Proceedings of the National Academy of Sciences*, 102, 13517–13520.

Kaushal, S.S., Likens, G.E., Utz, R.M., et al. (2013) Increased river alkalinization in the Eastern US. *Environmental Science & Technology*, 47, 10302–10311.

Kayanne, H. (2016) Response of coral reefs to global warming. *Coral Reef Science* 5, 81–94.

Kean, J.W., Staley, D.M. and Cannon, S.H. (2011) In situ measurements of post-fire debris flows in southern California: comparisons of the timing and magnitude of

24 debris-flow events with rainfall and soil moisture conditions. *Journal of Geophysical Research*, 116, F04019.

Kearney, M.S. and Turner, R.E. (2016) Microtidal marshes: can these widespread and fragile marshes survive increasing climate-sea level variability and human action? *Journal of Coastal Research*, 32 (3), 686–699.

Keatley, B.E., Bennett, E.M., MacDonald, G.K., et al. (2011) Land-use legacies are important determinants of lake eutrophication in the Anthropocene. *PLoS ONE*, 6, e15913.

Keefer, D.K., de France, S.D., Mosely, M.E., et al. (1998) Early maritime economy and El Niño events at Quebrada Tachuay, Peru. *Science*, 281, 1833–1835.

Keller, E.A. (1976) Channelisation: environmental, geomorphic and engineering aspects. In D.R. Coates (ed.), *Geomorphology and Engineering*. Stroudsburg: Dowden, Hutchinson and Ross, 115–140.

Kellerer-Pirklbauer, A. Lieb, G.K., Avian, M. and Carrivick, J. (2012) Climate change and rock fall events in high mountain areas: numerous and extensive rock falls in 2007 at Mittlerer Burgstall, Central Austria. *Geografiska Annaler: Series A, Physical Geography*, 94, 59–78.

Kelleway, J.J., Cavanaugh, K., Rogers, K., et al. (2017) Review of the ecosystem service implications of mangrove encroachment into salt marshes. *Global Change Biology*, doi:10.1111/gcb.13727.

Kemp, D.D. (2004) *Exploring Environmental Issues: An Integrated Approach*. London: Routledge.

Kemp, W.M., Boynton, W.R. and Adolf, J.E., et al. (2005) Eutrophication of Chesapeake Bay: historical trends and ecological interactions. *Marine Ecology Progress Series*, 303, 1–29.

Kench, P.S., Smithers, S.G., McLean, R.F. and Nichol, S.L. (2009) Holocene reef growth in the Maldives: evidence of a mid-Holocene sea-level highstand in the central Indian Ocean. *Geology*, 37, 455–458.

Kennish, M.J. (2001) Coastal salt marsh systems in the US: a review of anthropogenic impacts. *Journal of Coastal Research*, 17, 731–748.

Kent, M. (1982) Plant growth problems in colliery spoil reclamation. *Applied Geography*, 2, 83–107.

Kernan, M., Battarbee, R.W., Curtis, C.J., et al. (2010) *UK Acid Waters Monitoring Network 20 year interpretative report*. London: Environmental Change Research Centre, University College London.

Keshkamat, S.S., Tsendbazar, N.-E., Zuidgeest, M.H.P., et al. (2012) The environmental impact of not having paved roads in arid regions: an example from Mongolia. *Ambio*, 41, 202–205.

Khalil, M.A.K. and Rasmussen, R.A. (1987) Atmospheric methane: trends over the last 10,000 years. *Atmospheric Environment*, 21, 2445–2452.

Khazendar, A., Borstad, C. P., Scheuchl, B., et al. (2015) The evolving instability of the remnant Larsen B Ice Shelf and its tributary glaciers. *Earth and Planetary Science Letters*, 419, 199–210.

Khromova, T., Nosenko, G., Kutuzov, S., et al. (2014) Glacier area changes in Northern Eurasia. *Environmental Research Letters*, 9, doi:10.1088/1748-9326/9/1/015003.

Khvorostyanov, D.V., Ciais, P., Krinner, G. and Zimov, S.A. (2008) Vulnerability of east Siberia's frozen carbon stores to future warming. *Geophysical Research Letters*, 35, L10703, doi:10.1029/2008GL033639.

Kibler, K., Tullos, D. and Kondolf, M. (2011) Evolving expectations of dam removal outcomes: downstream geomorphic effects following removal of a small, gravel-filled dam. *Journal of the American Water Resources Association*, 47, 408–422.

Kiepe, P. (1996) Cover and barrier effect of Cassia siamea hedgerows on soil conservation in semi-arid Kenya. *Soil Technology*, 9, 161–171.

Kim, D., Chin, M., Remer, L.A., et al. (2016) Role of surface wind and vegetation cover in multi-decadal variations of dust emission in the Sahara and Sahel. *Atmospheric Environment*, 148, 282–296.

Kimura, B., Marshall, F.B., Chen, S., et al. (2011) Ancient DNA from Nubian and Somali wild asses provides insights into donkey ancestry and domestication. *Proceedings of The Royal Society, Biological Sciences*, 278, 50–57.

King, C.A.M. (1975) *Introduction to Physical and Biological Oceanography*. London: Edward Arnold.

Kingston, P.F. (2002) Long-term environmental impact of oil spills. *Spill Science and Technology Bulletin*, 7, 53–61.

Kinoshita, A.M., Chin, A., Simon, G.L., et al. (2016) Wildfire, water, and society: toward integrative research in the 'Anthropocene'. *Anthropocene*, 16, 16–27.

Kinouchi, T., Yagi, H. and Miyamoto, M. (2007) Increase in stream temperature related to anthropogenic heat input from urban wastewater. *Journal of Hydrology*, 335, 78–88.

Kinsey, D.W. and Hopley, D. (1991) The significance of coral reefs as global carbon sinks – response to greenhouse. *Palaeogeography, Palaeoclimatology, Palaeoecology*, 89, 363–377.

Kirby, C. (1995) Urban air pollution. *Geography*, 80, 375–392.

Kirch, P.V. (1982) Advances in Polynesian prehistory: three decades in review. *Advances in World Archaeology*, 2, 52–102.

Kirk, S. and Herbert, A.W. (2002) Assessing the impact of groundwater abstractions on river flows. *Geological Society, London, Special Publications*, 193, 211–233.

Kirkbride, M.P. and Warren, C.R. (1999) Tasman Glacier, New Zealand: 20th century thinning and predicted calving retreat. *Global and Planetary Change*, 22, 11–28.

Kirono, D.G.C., Kent, D.M., Hennessy, K.J. and Mpelasoka, F. (2011) Characteristics of Australian droughts under enhanced greenhouse conditions: results from 14 global climate models. *Journal of Arid Environments*, 75, 566–575.

Kirpotin, S.N., Polishchuk, Y. and Bryksina, N. (2009) Abrupt changes of thermokarst lakes in Western Siberia: impacts of climatic warming on permafrost melting. *International Journal of Environmental Studies*, 66, 423–431.

Kirschke, S., Bousquet, P., Ciais, P., et al. (2013) Three decades of global methane sources and sinks. *Nature Geoscience*, 6 (10), 813–823.

Kirwan, M.L., Murray, A.B., Donnelly, J.P. and Corbett, D.R. (2011) Rapid wetland expansion during European settlement and its implication for marsh survival under modern sediment delivery rates. *Geology*, 39, 507–510.

Kirwan, M.L., Temmerman, S., Skeehan, E.E., et al. (2016) Overestimation of marsh vulnerability to sea level rise. *Nature Climate Change*, 6 (3), 253–260.

Kiss, T., Sipos, G., Mauz, B. and Mezösi, G. (2012) Holocene aeolian sand mobilization, vegetation history and human impact on the stabilized sand dune area of the southern Nyírség, Hungary. *Quaternary Research*, 78, 492–501.

Kittredge, J.H. (1948) *Forest Influences*. New York: McGraw-Hill.

Klein, R.G. (1983) The stone age prehistory of southern Africa. *Annual Review of Anthropology*, 12, 25–48.

Kleunen, M. van, Dawson, W., Essl, F., et al. (2015) Global exchange and accumulation of non-native plants. *Nature*, 525 (7567), 100–103.

Kleypas, J.A., Buddemeier, R.W., Archer, D., et al. (1999) Geochemical consequences of increased atmospheric carbon dioxide on coral reefs. *Science*, 284, 118–120.

Klingmüller K., Pozzer, A., Metzger, S., et al. (2016) Aerosol optical depth trend over the Middle East. *Atmospheric Chemistry and Physics* 16 (8), 5063–5073.

Knapp, A.B. (2010) Cyprus's earliest prehistory: seafarers, foragers and settlers. *Journal of World Prehistory*, 23, 79–120.

Knight, M., Thomas, D.S.G. and Wiggs, G.F.S. (2004) Challenges of calculating dunefield mobility over the 21st century. *Geomorphology*, 59, 197–213.

Knight, P.G. (1999) *Glaciers*. Cheltenham: Stanley Thornes.

Knighton, A.D. (1991) Channel bed adjustment along mine-affected rivers of northeast Tasmania. *Geomorphology*, 4, 205–219.

Knox, J.C. (1972) Valley alluviation in southwestern Wisconsin. *Annals of the Association of American Geographers*, 62, 401–410.

Knox, J.C. (1977) Human impacts on Wisconsin stream channels. *Annals of the Association of American Geographers*, 67, 323–342.

Knox, J.C. (1987) Historical valley floor sedimentation in the Upper Mississippi Valley. *Annals of the Association of American Geographers*, 77, 224–244.

Knox, J.C. (1993) Large increase in flood magnitude in response to modest changes in climate. *Nature*, 361, 430–432.

Knox, J.C. (2002) Agriculture, erosion and sediment yields. In A.R. Orme (ed.), *The Physical Geography of North America*. Oxford: Oxford University Press, 482–500.

Knutson, T.R., Sirutis, J.J., Garner, S.T., et al. (2008) Simulated reduction in Atlantic hurricane frequency under twenty-first-century warming conditions. *Nature Geoscience*, 1, 359–364.

Knutson, T.R. and Tuleya, R.E. (1999) Increased hurricane intensities with CO_2-induced warming as simulated using the GFDL hurricane prediction system. *Climate Dynamics*, 15, 503–519.

Knutson, T.R., Tuleya, R.E. and Kurihara, Y. (1998) Simulated increase of hurricane intensities in a CO_2-warmed climate. *Science*, 279, 1018–1020.

Koch, P.L. and Barnovsky, A.D. (2006) Late Quaternary extinctions: state of the debate. *Annual Review of Ecology, Evolution, and Systematics*, 37, 215–250.

Kohen, J. (1995) *Aboriginal Environmental Impacts*. Sydney: University of New South Wales Press.

Kok, J.F., Ridley, D.A., Zhou, Q., et al. (2017) Smaller desert dust cooling effect estimated from analysis of dust size and abundance. *Nature Geoscience*, 10, 274–278.

Kolk, H.J.V.D., Heijmans, M.M., Huissteden, J.V., et al. (2016) Potential Arctic tundra vegetation shifts in response to changing temperature, precipitation and permafrost thaw. *Biogeosciences*, 13 (22), 6229–6245.

Komar, P.D. and Allan, J.C. (2008) Increasing hurricane-generated wave heights along the US East Coast and their climate controls. *Journal of Coastal Research*, 24, 479–488.

Komar, P.D., McManus, J. and Styllas, M. (2004) Sediment accumulation in Tillamook Bay, Oregon: natural processes versus human impacts. *Journal of Geology*, 112, 455–469.

Komori, J. (2008) Recent expansions of glacial lakes in the Bhutan Himalayas. *Quaternary International*, 184, 177–186.

Kornis, M.S., Mercado-Silva, N. and Vander Zanden, M.J. (2012) Twenty years of invasion: a review of round goby Neoglobius melanstomus biology, spread and ecological implications. *Journal of Fish Biology*, 80, 238–285.

Kort, E.A., Wofsy, S.C., Daube, B.C., et al. (2012) Atmospheric observations of Arctic Ocean methane emissions up to 82° north. *Nature Geoscience*, 5 (5), 318–321.

Kotb, T.H.S., Watanabe, T., Ogino, Y. and Tanji, K.K. (2000) Soil salinization in the Nile Delta and related policy issues in Egypt. *Agricultural Water Management*, 43, 239–261.

Kotwicki, V. and Isdale, P.J. (1991) Hydrology of Lake Eyre, Australia: El Niño link. *Palaeogeography, Palaeoclimatology and Palaeoecology*, 84, 87–98.

Kratzmann, M.G. and Hapke, C.J. (2012) Quantifying anthropogenically driven morphological changes on a barrier island: Fire Island National Seashore, New York. *Journal of Coastal Research*, 28, 76–88.

Kravtsova, V.I. and Tarasenko, T.V. (2010) Space monitoring of Aral Sea degradation. *Water Resources*, 37, 285–296.

Krhoda, G.O. and Kwambuke, A.M. (2016) Impact of urbanization on morphology of Motoine/Ngong River channel, Nairobi River, Kenya. *Journal of Geography and Regional Planning*, 9 (4), 36–46.

Kriegler, E., Hall, J.W., Held, H., et al. (2009) Imprecise probability assessment of tipping points in the climate system. *Proceedings of the National Academy of Sciences*, 106, 5041–5046.

Krug, E.C. and Frink, C.R. (1983) Acid rain on acid soil: a new perspective. *Science*, 221, 520–525.

Kühn, I. and Klotz, S. (2006) Urbanization and homogenization – comparing the floras of urban and rural areas in Germany. *Biological Conservation*, 127, 292–300.

Kühn, P., Lehndorff, E. and Fuchs, M. (2017) Lateglacial to Holocene pedogenesis and formation of colluvial deposits in a loess landscape of Central Europe (Wetterau, Germany). *Catena*, 154, 118–135.

Kullman, L. (2001) 20th century climate warming and tree-limit rise in the southern Scandes of Sweden. *Ambio*, 30, 72–80.

Kumar, S., Merwade, V., Kam, J. and Thurner, K. (2009) Streamflow trends in Indiana: effects of long term persistence, precipitation and subsurface drains. *Journal of Hydrology*, 374, 171–183.

Kunkel, K.E. (2003) North American trends in extreme precipitation. *Natural Hazards*, 29, 291–305.

Küster, M., Fülling, A., Kaiser, K. and Ulrich, J. (2014) Aeolian sands and buried soils in the Mecklenburg Lake District, NE Germany: Holocene land-use history and pedo-geomorphic response. *Geomorphology*, 211, 64–76.

Kustu, M.D., Fan, Y. and Robock, A. (2010) Large-scale water cycle perturbation due to irrigation pumping in the US High Plains: a synthesis of observed streamflow changes. *Journal of Hydrology*, 390, 222–244.

Kuttippurath, J. and Nair, P.J. (2017) The signs of Antarctic ozone hole recovery. *Scientific Reports*, 7 (1), paper 585, doi:10.1038/s41598-017-00722-7.

Kwong, Y.T.J. and Gan, T.Y. (1994) Northward migration of permafrost along the Mackenzie Highway and climatic warming. *Climatic Change*, 26, 399–419.

L'Homer, A. (1992) Sea level changes and impact on the Rhône Delta coastal lowlands. In M.J. Tooley and S. Jelgersma (eds), *Impacts of Sea Level Rise on European Coastal Lowlands*. Oxford: Blackwell, 136–152.

Labadz, J.C., Burt, T.P. and Potter, A.W.L. (1991) Sediment yield and delivery in the blanket peat moorlands of the southern Pennines. *Earth Surface Processes and Landforms*, 16, 255–271.

Labat, D., Goddéris, Y., Probst, J.L. and Guyot, J.L. (2004) Evidence for global runoff increase related to climate warming. *Advances in Water Resources*, 27, 631–642.

Labrière, N., Locatelli, B., Laumonier, Y., et al. (2015) Soil erosion in the humid tropics: a systematic quantitative review. *Agriculture, Ecosystems & Environment*, 203, 127–139.

Lacombe, G., Ribolzi, O., De Rouw, A., et al. (2016) Contradictory hydrological impacts of afforestation in the humid tropics evidenced by long-term field monitoring and simulation modelling. *Hydrology and Earth System Sciences*, doi:10.5194/hess-20-2691-2016.

Ladle, R.J. and Whittaker, R.J. (2011) *Conservation Biogeography*. Chichester: Wiley Blackwell.

Laffoley, D. and Baxter, J.M. (eds) (2016) *Explaining Ocean Warming: Causes, Scale, Effects and Consequences*. Gland, Switzerland: IUCN.

Lal, R. (2002) Soil carbon dynamics in cropland and range land. *Environmental Pollution*, 116, 353–362.

Lamb, H.H. (1977) *Climate: Present, Past and Future. 2: Climatic History and the Future*, London: Methuen.

Lambeck, K. (1988) *Geological Geodesy*. Oxford: Clarendon Press.

Lambert, J.H., Jennings, J.N., Smith, C.T., et al. (1970) *The making of the Broads: a reconsideration of their origin in the light of new evidence*. Royal Geographical Society Research Series, 3.

Lamoureux, S.F. and Lafrenière, M.J. (2009) Fluvial impact of extensive active layer detachments, Cape Bounty, Melville Island, Canada. *Arctic, Antarctic, and Alpine Research*, 41 (1), 59–68.

Lamprey, H. (1975) The integrated project on arid lands. *Nature and Resources*, 14, 2–11.

Lancaster, N. (1995) *Geomorphology of Desert Dunes*. London: Routledge.

Land, P.E., Shutler, J.D., Bell, T.G. and Yang, M. (2014) Exploiting satellite earth observation to quantify current global oceanic DMS flux and its future climate sensitivity. *Journal of Geophysical Research: Oceans*, 119 (11), 7725–7740.

Landsberg, H.E. (1981) *The Urban Climate*. New York: Academic Press.

Landsea, C.W. (2000) El Niño/Southern Oscillation and the seasonal predictability of tropical cyclones. In H.F. Diaz and V. Markgraf (eds), *El Niño and the Southern Oscillation*. Cambridge: Cambridge University Press, 148–181.

Langbein, W.B. and Schumm, S.A. (1958) Yield of sediment in relation to mean annual precipitation. *Transactions of the American Geophysical Union*, 39, 1076–1118.

Langford, T.E.L. (1990) *Ecological Effects of Thermal Discharges*. London: Elsevier Applied Science.

Lanly, J.P., Singh, K.D. and Janz, K. (1991) FAO's 1990 reassessment of tropical forest cover. *Nature and Resources*, 27, 21–26.

Lantuit, H. and Pollard, W.H. (2008) Fifty years of coastal erosion and retrogressive thaw slump activity on Herschel Island, southern Beaufort Sea, Yukon Territory, Canada. *Geomorphology*, 95, 84–102.

Lapp, S., Byrjne, J., Townshend, I. and Kienzle, S. (2005) Climate warming impacts on snowpack accumulation in an alpine watershed. *International Journal of Climatology*, 25, 521–536.

Laris, P. (2011) Humanizing savanna biogeography: linking human practices with ecological patterns in a frequently burned savanna of southern Mali. *Annals of the Association of American Geographers*, 101, 1067–1088.

Larsen, R., Bell, J.N.B., James, P.W., et al. (2007) Lichen and bryophyte distribution on oak in London in relation to air pollution and bark acidity. *Environmental Pollution*, 146, 332–340.

Larson, E.R. and Kipfmueller, K.F. (2012) Ecological disaster on the limits of observation? Reconciling modern declines with the long-term dynamics of Whitebark pine communities. *Geography Compass*, 6, 189–214.

Larson, F. (1940) The role of bison in maintaining the short grass plains. *Ecology*, 21, 113–121.

Larson, G. and Fuller, D.Q. (2014) The evolution of animal domestication. *Annual Review of Ecology, Evolution, and Systematics*, 45, 115–136.

Larson, G., Piperno, D.R., Allaby, R.G., et al. (2014) Current perspectives and the future of domestication studies. *Proceedings of the National Academy of Sciences*, 111 (17), 6139–6146.

Lasanta, T., García-Ruez, J.M., Pérez-Rontomé, C. and San-cho-Marcén, C. (2000) Runoff and sediment yield in a semi-arid environment: the effect of land management after farmland abandonment. *Catena*, 38, 265–278.

Latif, M. and Keenlyside, N.S. (2009) El Niño/Southern oscillation response to global warming. *Proceedings of the National Academy of Sciences*, 106, 20578–20583.

Latrubesse, E.M., Arima, E.Y., Dunne, T., et al. (2017) Damming the rivers of the Amazon basin. *Nature*, 546, 363–369.

Läuchli, A. and Grattan, S.R. (2007) Plant growth and development under salinity stress. In M.A. Jenks, P.M. Hasegawa, P.M. and S.M. Jain (eds), *Advances in Molecular Breeding Toward Drought and Salt Tolerant Crops*. Dordrecht: Springer, 1–32.

Lawrence, S., Davies, P. and Turnbull, J. (2016) The archaeology of Anthropocene rivers: water management and landscape change in 'Gold Rush' Australia. *Antiquity*, 90 (353), 1348–1362.

Lazarus, R.S., Rattner, B.A., McGowan, P.C., et al. (2015) Decadal re-evaluation of contaminant exposure and productivity of ospreys (Pandion haliaetus) nesting in Chesapeake Bay regions of concern. *Environmental Pollution*, 205, 278–290.

Le, C., Zha, Y., Li, Y., et al. (2010) Eutrophication of lake waters in China: cost, causes and control. *Environmental Management*, 45, 662–668.

Lean, J. and Warrilow, D.A. (1989) Simulation of the regional climatic impact of Amazon deforestation. *Nature*, 342, 126–133.

Learmonth, J.A., Macleod, C.D., Santos, M.B., et al. (2006) Potential effects of climate change on marine mammals. *Oceanography and Marine Biology: An Annual Review*, 44, 431–464.

Leatherman, S.P. (2001) Social and economic costs of sea level rise. In B.C. Douglas, M.S. Kearney and S.P. Leatherman (eds), *Sea Level Rise: History and Consequences*. San Diego: Academic Press, 181–223.

Lecce, S., Pavlowsky, R. and Schlomer, G. (2008) Mercury contamination of active channel sediment and floodplain deposits from historic gold mining at Gold Hill, North Carolina, USA. *Environmental Geology*, 55, 113–121.

Leclercq, N., Gattuso, J.-P. and Jaubert, J. (2000) CO_2 partial pressure controls the calcification rate of a coral community. *Global Change Biology*, 6, 329–334.

Leduc, C., Favreau, G. and Schoreter, P. (2001) Long term rise in a Sahelian water-table: the Continental Terminal in South-West Niger. *Journal of Hydrology*, 243, 43–54.

Lee, A.T. and Barnard, P. (2016) Endemic birds of the Fynbos biome: a conservation assessment and impacts of climate change. *Bird Conservation International*, 26 (1), 52–68.

Lee, D.O. (1992) Urban warming – an analysis of recent trends in London's heat island. *Weather*, 47, 50–56.

Lee, D.S., Pitari, G., Grewe, V., et al. (2010) Transport impacts on atmosphere and climate: aviation. *Atmospheric Environment*, 44, 4678–4734.

Lee, E., Sacks, W.J., Chase, T.N. and Foley, J.A. (2011) Simulated impacts of irrigation on the atmospheric circulation over Asia. *Journal of Geophysical Research*, 116, D08114.

Lee, R.B. and DeVore, I. (1968) *Man the Hunter*. Chicago: Aldine.

Lehmann, J. and Joseph, S. (eds) (2015) *Biochar for Environmental Management: Science, Technology and Implementation.* Abingdon: Routledge.

Le Houérou, H.N. (1977) Biological recovery versus desertization. *Economic Geography*, 63, 413–420.

Leifeld, J., Muller, M. and Fuhrer, J. (2011) Peatland subsidence and carbon loss from drained temperate fens. *Soil Use and Management*, 27, 170–176.

Le Maitre, D.C., Versfeld, D.B. and Chapman, R.A. (2000) The impact of invading alien plants on surface water resources in South Africa: a preliminary assessment. *Water SA*, 26, 397–408.

Lently, A.D. (1994) Agriculture and wildlife: ecological implications of subsurface irrigation drainage. *Journal of Arid Environments*, 28, 85–94.

Lenton, T.M. (2012) Arctic climate tipping points. *Ambio*, 41, 10–22.

Lenton, T.M., Held, H., Kriegler, E., et al. (2008) Tipping elements in the Earth's climate system. *Proceedings of the National Academy of Sciences*, 105, 1786–1793.

Lents, J.M. and Kelly, W.J. (1993) Clearing the air in Los Angeles. *Scientific American*, October, 18–25.

Leopold, L.B. (1951) Rainfall frequency: an aspect of climatic variation. *Transactions of the American Geophysical Union*, 32, 347–357.

Leopold, L.B., Wolman, M.G. and Miller, J.P. (1964) *Fluvial Processes in Geomorphology.* San Francisco: Freeman.

Lerner, D. (1990) *Groundwater recharge in urban areas.* IAHS Publication, 198, 59–65.

Letourneau, D.K. and Burrows, B.E. (eds) (2001) *Genetically Engineered Organisms: Assessing Environmental and Human Health Effects.* Washington, DC: CRC Press.

Leung, D.Y.C. and Yang, Y. (2012) Wind energy development and its environmental impact: a review. *Renewable and Sustainable Energy Reviews*, 16, 1031–1039.

Levine, J.M., Vila, M., D'Antonio, C.M., et al. (2003) Mechanisms underlying the impacts of exotic plant invasions. *Proceedings ofThe Royal Society, Biological Sciences*, 270, 775–781.

Levis, C., Costa, F.R.C., Bongers, F.M., et al. (2017) Persistent effects of pre-Columbian plant domestication on Amazonian forest composition. *Science*, 355, 925–931.

Lewin, J., Bradley, S.B. and Macklin, M.G. (1983) Historical valley alluviation in mid-Wales. *Geological Journal*, 18, 331–350.

Lewis, S.L. and Maslin, M.A. (2015) Defining the Anthropocene. *Nature*, 519, 171–180.

Leys, J. (1999) Wind erosion on agricultural land. In A.S. Goudie, I. Livingstone and S. Stokes (eds), *Aeolian Environments, Sediments and Landforms.* Chichester: Wiley, 143–166.

Li, C., Bosch, C., Kang, S., et al. (2016b) Sources of black carbon to the Himalayan–Tibetan Plateau glaciers. *Nature Communications*, 7, doi:10.1038/ncomms12574.

Li, F. and Lawrence, D.M. (2016) Role of fire in the global land water budget during the 20th century due to changing ecosystems. *Journal of Climate*, doi:10.1175/JCLI-D-16-0460.1.

Li, P., Feng, X., Qiu, G., et al. (2012) Mercury pollution in Wuchuan mercury mining area, Guizhou, southwestern China: the impacts from large scale and artisanal mercury mining. *Environment International*, 42, 59–66.

Li, X., Cheng, G., Jin, H., et al. (2008) Cryospheric change in China. *Global and Planetary Change*, 62, 210–218.

Li, X., Sun, N., Dodson, J., et al. (2011) The impact of early smelting on the environment of Huoshiliang in Hexi Corridor, NW China, as recorded by fossil charcoal and chemical elements. *Palaeogeography, Palaeoclimatology, Palaeoecology*, 305 (1), 329–336.

Li, Y., Cui, J., Zhang, T., et al. (2009) Effectiveness of sand-fixing measures on desert land restoration in Kerqin Sandy Land, northern China. *Ecological Engineering*, 35, 118–127.

Li, Y., Zhao, M., Mildrexler, D.J., et al. (2016a) Potential and actual impacts of deforestation and afforestation on land surface temperature. *Journal of Geophysical Research: Atmospheres*, doi:10.1002/2016JD024969.

Li, Z., Ma, Z., van der Kuijp, T.J., et al. (2014) A review of soil heavy metal pollution from mines in China: pollution and health risk assessment. *Science of the Total Environment*, 468, 843–853.

Liang, P. and Ding, Y. (2017) The long-term variation of extreme heavy precipitation and its link to urbanization effects in Shanghai during 1916–2014. *Advances in Atmospheric Sciences*, 34 (3), 321–334.

Liang, T., Li, K. and Wang, L. (2014) State of rare earth elements in different environmental components in mining areas of China. *Environmental Monitoring and Assessment*, 186 (3), 1499–1513.

Liddle, M. (1997) *Recreation Ecology.* London: Chapman and Hall.

Liébault, F. and Piégay, H. (2002) Causes of 20th century channel narrowing in mountain and piedmont rivers of southeastern France. *Earth Surface Processes and Landforms*, 27, 425–444.

Liebhold, A.M., Brockerhoff, E.G., Garrett, L.J., et al. (2012) Live plant imports: the major pathway for forest insect and pathogen invasions of the US. *Frontiers in Ecology and the Environment*, 10, 135–143.

Liebsch, D., Marques, M.C.M. and Goldenberg, R. (2008) How long does the Atlantic Rain Forest take to recover after a disturbance? Changes in species composition and ecological features during secondary succession. *Biological Conservation*, 141, 1717–1725.

Lienert, J. (2004) Habitat fragmentation effects on fitness of plant populations – a review. *Journal for Nature Conservation*, 12, 53–72.

Lightfoot, K.G. and Cuthrell, R.Q. (2015) Anthropogenic burning and the Anthropocene in late Holocene California. *The Holocene*, 25, 1581–1587.

Likens, G.E. (2010) Acid rain. In *Encyclopedia of Earth*, http:/www.eoearth.org/article/Acid_rain?topic=49506 (accessed January 2018).

Likens, G.E. and Bormann, F.H. (1974) Acid rain: a serious regional environmental problem. *Science*, 184, 1176–1179.

Likens, G.E., Wright, R.F., Galloway, J.N. and Butler, T.J. (1979) Acid rain. *Scientific American*, 241 (4), 39–47.

Lin, N., Emanuel, K., Oppenheimer, M. and Vanmarcke, E. (2012) Physically based assessment of hurricane surge threat under climate change. *Nature Climate Change*, 2, 462–467.

Lindberg, T.T., Bernhardt, E.S., Bier, R., et al. (2011) Cumulative impacts of mountaintop mining on an Appalachian watershed. *Proceedings of the National Academy of Sciences*, 108, 20929–20934.

Ling, F. and Zhang, T. (2003) Impact of the timing and duration of seasonal snow cover on the active layer and permafrost in the Alaskan Arctic. *Permafrost and Periglacial Processes*, 14, 141–150.

Ling, S.D. (2008) Range expansion of a habitat-modifying species leads to loss of taxonomic diversity: a new and impoverished reef state. *Oecologia*, 156, 883–894.

Lioy, P.J. and Georgopoulos, P.G. (2011) New Jersey: a case study for the reduction in urban and suburban air pollution for the 1950s to 2010. *Environmental Health Perspectives*, 119, 1351–1355.

List, J.H., Sallenger, A.H., Hansen, M.E. and Jaffe, B.E. (1997) Accelerated sea level rise and rapid coastal erosion: testing a causal relationship for the Louisiana barrier islands. *Marine Geology*, 140, 437–465.

Liu, B., Qu, J. and Kang, S. (2016) Response of dune activity on the Tibetan Plateau to near future climate change. *Climate Research*, 69 (1), 1–8.

Liu, J., Curry, J.A., Wang, H., et al. (2012) Impact of declining Arctic sea ice on winter snowfall. *Proceedings of the National Academy of Sciences*, 109, 4074–4079.

Liu, J. and Diamond, J. (2005) China's environment in a globalizing world. *Nature*, 435, 1179–1186.

Liu, J., Hayakawa, N., Lu, M., et al. (2003) Hydrological and geocryological response of winter streamflow to climate warming in Northeast China. *Cold Regions Science and Technology*, 37, 15–24.

Liu, L., Lee, G.-A., Jiang, L. and Zhang, J. (2007) The earliest rice domestication in China. *Antiquity*, 81, 1–2.

Liu, L., Liu, Z., Ren, X., et al. (2011) Hydrological impacts of climate change in the Yellow River Basin for the 21st century using hydrological model and statistical downscaling model. *Quaternary International*, 244, 211–220.

Liu, S., Zhang, Y. and Ding, Y. (2009) Estimation of glacier runoff and future trends in the Yangtze River source region, China. *Journal of Glaciology*, 55, 353–362.

Liu, T., Kinouchi, T. and Ledezma, F. (2013) Characterization of recent glacier decline in the Cordillera Real by LANDSAT, ALOS, and ASTER data. *Remote Sensing of Environment*, 137, 158–172.

Liu, X.B., Zhang, X.Y., Wang, Y.X., et al. (2010) Soil degradation: a problem threatening the sustainable development of agriculture in northeast China. *Plant, Soil and Environment*, 56, 87–97.

Liu, Y.-P., Wu, G.S., Yao, Y.G., et al. (2006) Multiple maternal origins of chickens: out of the Asian jungles. *Molecular Phylogenetics and Evolution*, 38, 12–19.

Lloyd, J.W. (1986) A review of aridity and groundwater. *Hydrological Processes*, 1, 63–78.

Loehle, C. and Eschenbach, W. (2012) Historical bird and terrestrial mammal extinction rates and causes. *Diversity & Distributions*, 18, 84–91.

Loidi, J., Biurrun, I., Campos, J.A., et al. (2010) A biogeographical analysis of the European Atlantic lowland heathlands. *Journal of Vegetation Science*, 21, 832–842.

Lomborg, B. (2001) *The Skeptical Environmentalist*. Cambridge: Cambridge University Press.

López-Moreno, J.I., Beguería, S. and García-Ruiz, J.M. (2006) Trends in high flows in the central Spanish Pyrenees: response to climatic factors or to land-use change? *Hydrological Sciences Journal*, 51, 1039–1050.

López-Moreno, J.I., Fontaneda, S., Bazo, J., et al. (2014) Recent glacier retreat and climate trends in Cordillera Huaytapallana, Peru. *Global and Planetary Change*, 112, 1–11.

Loreau, M. and Mazancourt, C. (2013) Biodiversity and ecosystem stability: a synthesis of underlying mechanisms. *Ecology Letters*, 16 (s1), 106–115.

Loreau, M., Naeem, S. and Inchausti, P. (eds) (2002) *Biodiversity and Ecosystem Functioning. Synthesis and Perspectives*. Oxford: Oxford University Press.

Loreau, M., Naeem, S., Inchausti, P., et al. (2001) Biodiversity and ecosystem functioning: current knowledge and future challenges. *Science*, 294, 804–808.

Lorimer, J., Sandom, C., Jepson, P., et al. (2015) Rewilding: science, practice, and politics. *Annual Review of Environment and Resources*, 40, 39–62.

Lotze, H.K., Lenihan, H.S., Bourque, B.J., et al. (2006) Depletion, degradation, and recovery potential of estuaries and coastal seas. *Science*, 312 (5781), 1806–1809.

Lovelock, J. (2006) *The Revenge of Gaia*. London: Allen Lane.

Lovelock, J. (2008) A geophysiologist's thoughts on geoengineering. *Philosophical Transactions: Series A*,

Mathematical, Physical, and Engineering Sciences, 366, 3883–3890.

Lovett, G.M., Weiss, M., Liebhold, A.M., et al. (2016) Nonnative forest insects and pathogens in the United States: impacts and policy options. *Ecological Applications*, 26 (5), 1437–1455.

Lowdermilk, W.C. (1935) Man-made deserts. *Pacific Affairs*, 8, 409–419.

Lowe, D.J. (2008) Polynesian settlement of New Zealand and the impacts of volcanism on early Maori society: an update. In D.J. Lowe (ed.), *Guidebook for Pre-Conference North Island Field Trip*. New Zealand: Massey University, Palmerston North, New Zealand Society of Soil Science, 142–147.

Lowe, P.D. (1983) Values and institutions in the history of British nature conservation. In A. Warren and F.B. Goldsmith (eds), *Conservation in Perspective*. Chichester: Wiley, 329–352.

Lowe-McConnell, R.H. (1975) Freshwater life on the move. *Geographical Magazine*, 47, 768–775.

Lowenthal, D. (2000) *George Perkins Marsh, Prophet of Conservation*. Seattle: University of Washington Press.

Lowenthal, D. (2013) Marsh and Sauer: reexamining the rediscovery. *Geographical Review*, 103, 409–414.

Loya, Y., Sakai, K., Yamazato, K., et al. (2001) Coral bleaching: the winners and the losers. *Ecology Letters*, 4, 122–132.

Lu, H., Zhang, J., Liu, K.B., et al. (2009) Earliest domestication of common millet (Panicum miliaceum) in East Asia extended to 10,000 years ago. *Proceedings of the National Academy of Sciences*, 106, 7367–7372.

Lu, Q., Jürgens, M.D., Johnson, A.C., et al. (2017b) Persistent Organic Pollutants in sediment and fish in the River Thames catchment (UK). *Science of the Total Environment*, 576, 78–84.

Lu, Y., Waldmann, N., Nadel, D. and Marco, S. (2017a) Increased sedimentation following the Neolithic Revolution in the Southern Levant. *Global and Planetary Change*, 152, 199–208.

Lu, Z., Streets, D.G., Zhang, Q., et al. (2010) Sulfur dioxide emissions in China and sulphur trends in East Asia since 2000. *Atmospheric Chemistry and Physics*, 10, 6311–6331.

Luce, C.H. and Black, T.A. (1999) Sediment production from forest roads in western Oregon. *Water Resources Research*, 35, 2561–2570.

Luce, C.H., Vose, J.M., Pederson, N., et al. (2016) Contributing factors for drought in United States forest ecosystems under projected future climates and their uncertainty. *Forest Ecology and Management*, 380, 299–308.

Lugo, A.E. (2000) Effects and outcomes of Caribbean hurricanes in a climate change scenario. *Science of the Total Environment*, 262, 243–251.

Lugo, A.E., Cintron, G. and Goenaga, C. (1981) Mangrove ecosystems under stress. In G.W. Barrett and R. Rosenberg (eds), *Stress Effects on Natural Ecosystems*. Chichester: John Wiley, 129–153.

Lupo, K.D., Schmitt, D.N., Kiahtipes, C.A., et al. (2015) On intensive Late Holocene iron mining and production in the northern Congo Basin and the environmental consequences associated with metallurgy in Central Africa. *PloS one*, 10 (7), e0132632.

Lupton, M.K., Rojas, C., Drohan, P. and Bruns, M.A. (2013) Vegetation and soil development in compost-amended iron oxide precipitates at a 50-year-old acid mine drainage barrens. *Restoration Ecology*, 21 (3), 320–328.

Lyell, C. (1835) *Principles of Geology* (4th edn, Vol. III). London: Murray.

Lyell, C. (1875) *Principles of Geology* (12th edn). London: Murray.

Lynas, M. (2011) *The God Species*. London: Fourth Estate.

Lynch, J.A., Rishel, G.B. and Corbett, E.S. (1984) Thermal alteration of streams draining clearcut watersheds: quantification and biological implications. *Hydrobiologia*, 111, 161–169.

Lyons, S.K., Smith, F.A., Wagner, P.J., et al. (2004) Was a 'hyperdisease' responsible for the late Pleistocene megafaunal extinction? *Ecology Letters*, 7, 859–868.

Mabbutt, J.A. (1977) *Desert Landforms*. Cambridge, MA: MIT Press.

Mabbutt, J.A. (1985) Desertification of the world's rangelands. *Desertification Control Bulletin*, 12, 1–11.

MacDonald, D. and Burnham, D. (2011) *The State of Britain's Mammals 2011*. London: People's Trust for Endangered Mammals.

MacDougall, A.S., McCann, K.S., Gellner, G. and Turkington, R. (2013) Diversity loss with persistent human disturbance increases vulnerability to ecosystem collapse. *Nature*, 494 (7435), 86–89.

Macfarlane, M.J. (1976) *Laterite and Landscape*. London: Academic Press.

Machowski, R., Rzetala, M.A., Rzetala, M. and Solarski, M. (2016) Geomorphological and hydrological effects of subsidence and land use change in industrial and urban areas. *Land Degradation & Development*, 27, 1740–1752.

Macias-Fauria, M., Forbes, B.C., Zetterberg, P. and Kumpula, T. (2012) Eurasian Arctic greening reveals teleconnections and the potential for structurally novel ecosystems. *Nature Climate Change*, 2, 613–618.

MacKay, M. and Seglenieks, F. (2013) On the simulation of Laurentian Great Lakes water levels under projections of global climate change. *Climatic Change*, 117, 55–67.

Mackintosh, A.N., Anderson, B.M., Lorrey, A.M., et al. (2017) Regional cooling caused recent New Zealand glacier advances in a period of global warming. *Nature Communications*, 8, 14202.

Macklin, M.G., Jones, A.F. and Lewin, J. (2010) River response to rapid Holocene environmental change: evidence and explanation in British catchments. *Quaternary Science Reviews*, 29, 1555–1576.

Macklin, M.G. and Lewin, J. (1986) Terraced fills of Pleistocene and Holocene age in the Rheidol Valley, Wales. *Journal of Quaternary Science*, 1, 21–34.

Macklin, M.G., Lewin, J. and Jones, A.F. (2014) Anthropogenic alluvium: an evidence-based meta-analysis for the UK Holocene. *Anthropocene*, 6, 26–38.

Macklin, M.G., Passmore, D.G., Stevenson, A.C., et al. (1991) Holocene alluviation and land-use change on Callaly Moor, Northumberland, England. *Journal of Quaternary Science*, 6, 225–232.

Macklin, M.G. and Woodward, J.C. (2009) River systems and environmental change. In J.C. Woodward (ed.), *The Physical Geography of the Mediterranean*. Oxford: Oxford University Press, 319–52.

Mader, H.J. (1984) Animal habitat isolation by roads and agricultural fields. *Biological Conservation*, 29, 81–96.

Maestre, F.T., Delgado-Baquerizo, M., Jeffries, T.C., et al. (2015) Increasing aridity reduces soil microbial diversity and abundance in global drylands. *Proceedings of the National Academy of Sciences*, 112 (51), 15684–15689.

Magdaleno, F., Fernández, J.A. and Merino, S. (2012) The Ebro River in the 20th century or the ecomorphological transformation of a large and dynamic Mediterranean channel. *Earth Surface Processes and Landforms*, 37 (5), 486–498.

Magilligan, F.J. and Goldstein, P.S. (2001) El Niño floods and culture change: a late Holocene flood history for the Rio Moquegua, Southern Peru. *Geology*, 29, 431–434.

Mahmood, R., Foster, S.A., Keeling, T., et al. (2006) Impacts of irrigation on 20th century temperature in the northern Great Plains. *Global and Planetary Change*, 54, 1–18.

Mahmood, R., Pielke, R.A., Hubbard, K.G., et al. (2014) Land cover changes and their biogeophysical effects on climate. *International Journal of Climatology*, 34 (4), 929–953.

Mahowald, N.M., Albani, S., Kok, J.F., et al. (2014) The size distribution of desert dust aerosols and its impact on the Earth system. *Aeolian Research*, 15, 53–71.

Mahowald, N.M., Kloster, S., Engelstaedter, S., et al. (2010) Observed 20th century desert dust variability: impact on climate and biogeochemistry. *Atmospheric Chemistry and Physics*, 10, 10875–10893.

Mahowald, N.M. and Luo, C. (2003) A less dusty future? *Geophysical Research Letters*, doi:10.1029/2003GL017880.

Mahowald, N.M., Muhs, D.R., Levis, S., et al. (2006) Change in atmospheric mineral aerosols in response to climate: last glacial period, preindustrial, modern and doubled carbon dioxide climates. *Journal of Geophysical Research*, doi:10.1029/2005JD006653.

Mainguet, M. (1995) *L'Homme et la Sécheresse*. Paris: Masson.

Majer, E.L., Baria, R., Start, M., et al. (2007) Induced seismicity associated with Enhanced Geothermal Systems. *Geothermics*, 36, 185–222.

Major, J.J., Spicer, K.R., Rhode, A., et al. (2008) Initial fluvial response to the removal of Oregon's Marmot Dam. *Eos*, 27, 241–243.

Major, J., O'Connor, J., Podolak, J.E., et al. (2012) *Geomorphic response of the Sandy River, Oregon, to removal of Marmot Dam*. US Geological Survey professional paper, 1792.

Malamud, B.D., Morein, G. and Turcotte, D.L. (1998) Forest fires: an example of self-organized critical behavior. *Science*, 281, 1840–1842.

Malingreau, J.P., Eva, H.D. and de Miranda, E.E. (2012) Brazilian Amazon: a significant five year drop in deforestation rates but figures are on the rise again. *Ambio*, 41, 309–314.

Malkisnon, D., Wittenberg, L., Beeri, O. and Barzilai, R. (2011) Effects of repeated fires on the structure, composition, and dynamics of Mediterranean maquis: short- and long-term perspectives. *Ecosystems*, 14, 478–488.

Malm, W.C., Schichtel, B.A., Ames, R.B. and Gebhart, K.A. (2002) A 10-year spatial and temporal trend of sulfate across the United States. *Journal of Geophysical Research*, 107 (D22), 4627.

Manabe, S. and Stouffer, R.J. (1980) Sensitivity of a global climate model to an increase of CO_2 concentration in the atmosphere. *Journal of the Atmospheric Sciences*, 37, 99–118.

Manabe, S. and Wetherald, R.T. (1986) Reduction in summer soil wetness by an increase in atmospheric carbon dioxide. *Science*, 232, 626–628.

Manney, G.L., Santee, M.L., Rex, M., et al. (2011) Unprecedented Arctic ozone loss in 2011. *Nature*, 478, 469–475.

Mannion, A.M. (1992) Acidification and eutrophication. In A.M. Mannion and S.R. Bowlby (eds), *Environmental issues in the 1990s*. Chichester: Wiley, 177–195.

Marden, M. (2012) Effectiveness of reforestation in erosion mitigation and implications for future sediment yields, East Coast catchments, New Zealand: a review. *New Zealand Geographer*, 68, 24–35.

Marden, M., Arnold, G., Seymour, A. and Hambling, R. (2012) History and distribution of steepland gullies in response to land use change, East Coast Region, North Island, New Zealand. *Geomorphology*, 153–154, 81–90.

Mark, A.F. and McSweeney, G.D. (1990) Patterns of impoverishment in natural communities: case studies in forest ecosystems – New Zealand. In G.M. Woodwell (ed.), *The Earth in Transition: Patterns and Processes of Biotic Impoverishment.* Cambridge: Cambridge University Press, 151–176.

Marlon, J.R., Bartlein, P.J., Gavin, D.G., et al. (2012) Long-term perspective on wildfires in the western USA. *Proceedings of the National Academy of Sciences*, 109, E535–E543.

Marquiss, M., Newton, I. and Ratcliffe, D.A. (1978) The decline of the raven, *Corvus corax*, in relation to afforestation in southern Scotland and northern England. *Journal of Applied Ecology*, 15, 129–144.

Marriner, N., Morhange, C., Flaux, C. and Carayon, N. (2017) Harbors and ports, ancient. In A.S. Gilbert (ed.), *Encyclopedia of Geoarchaeology*. Dordrecht: Springer, 382–403.

Mars, J.C. and Houseknecht, D.W. (2007) Quantitative remote sensing study indicates doubling of coastal erosion rate in past 50 yr along a segment of the Arctic coast of Alaska. *Geology*, 35, 583–586.

Marsh, G.P. (1864) *Man and Nature.* New York: Scribner.

Marsh, G.P. (1965) *Man and Nature.* D. Lowenthal (ed.). Cambridge, MA: Belknap Press.

Marshall, E., Weinberg, M., Wunder, S. and Kaphengst, T. (2011) Environmental dimensions of bioenergy development. *EuroChoices*, 10, 43–48.

Marshall, L.G. (1984) Who killed Cock Robin? An investigation of the extinction controversy. In P.S. Martin and R.G. Klein (eds), *Quaternary Extinctions*. Tucson: University of Arizona Press, 785–806.

Marston, R.A. and Dolan, L.S. (1999) Effectiveness of sediment control structures relative to spatial patterns of upland soil loss in an arid watershed, Wyoming. *Geomorphology*, 31, 313–323.

Marszałek, M., Alexandrowicz, Z. and Rzepa, G. (2014) Composition of weathering crusts on sandstones from natural outcrops and architectonic elements in an urban environment. *Environmental Science and Pollution Research*, 21, 14023–14036.

Martin, P.S. (1967) Prehistoric overkill. In P.S. Martin and H.E. Wright (eds), *Pleistocene Extinctions*. New Haven: Yale University Press, 75–120.

Martin, P.S. (1974) Palaeolithic players on the American stage: man's impact on the Late Pleistocene megafauna. In J.D. Ives and R.G. Barry (eds), *Arctic and Alpine Environments*. London: Methuen, 669–700.

Martin, P.S. (1982) The pattern and meaning of Holarctic mammoth extinction. In D.M. Hopkins, J.V. Matthews, C.S. Schweger and S.B. Young (eds), *Paleoecology of Beringia*. New York: Academic Press, 399–408.

Martin, P.S. and Klein, R.G. (1984) *Pleistocene Extinctions*. Tucson: University of Arizona Press.

Martin, Y.E., Johnson, E.A., Gallaway, J.M. and Chaikina, O. (2011) Negligible soil erosion in a burned mountain watershed, Canadian Rockies: field and modelling investigations considering the role of duff. *Earth Surface Processes and Landforms*, 36, 2097–2113.

Martinez Raya, A., Duran Zuazo, V.H. and Francia Martinez, J.R. (2006) Soil erosion and runoff response to plant-cover strips on semiarid slopes (SE Spain). *Land Degradation and Development*, 17, 1–11.

Maskell, L.C., Smart, S.M., Bullock, J.M., et al. (2010) Nitrogen deposition causes widespeard loss of species richness in British habitats. *Global Change Biology*, 16, 671–679.

Maslowski, W., Kinney, J.C., Higgins, M. and Roberts, A. (2012) The future of Arctic Sea Ice. *Annual Review of Earth and Planetary Sciences*, 40, 625–654.

Mason, I.M., Guzkowska, M.A.J., Rapley, C.G. and Street-Perrott, F.A. (1994) The response of lake levels and areas to climatic change. *Climatic Change*, 27, 161–197.

Mason, S.J., Waylen, P.R., Mimmack, G.M., et al. (1999) Changes in extreme rainfall events in South Africa. *Climatic Change*, 41, 249–257.

Massonnet, D., Holzer, T. and Vadon, H. (1997) Land subsidence caused by the East Mesa geothermal field, California, observed using SAR interferometry. *Geophysical Research Letters*, 24, 901–904.

Mather, A.S. (1983) Land deterioration in upland Britain. *Progress in Physical Geography*, 7, 210–228.

Mather, A.S. (2007) Recent Asian forest transitions in relation to transition theory. *International Forestry Review*, 9, 491–502.

Matisoo-Smith, E. (2015) Ancient DNA and the human settlement of the Pacific: a review. *Journal of Human Evolution*, 79, 93–104.

Mattheus, C.R., Rodriguez, A.B., McKee, B.A. and Curring, C.A. (2010) Impact of land-use change and hard structures on the evolution of fringing marsh shorelines. *Estuarine, Coastal and Shelf Science*, 88, 365–376.

Matthews, J., Van der Velde, G., De Vaate, A.B., et al. (2014) Rapid range expansion of the invasive quagga mussel in relation to zebra mussel presence in the Netherlands and Western Europe. *Biological Invasions*, 16 (1), 23–42.

Mavruk, S. and Avsar, D. (2008) Non-native fishes in the Mediterranean from the Red Sea, by way of the Suez Canal. *Reviews in Fish Biology and Fisheries*, 18, 251–262.

May, L., Defew, L.H., Bennion, H. and Kirika, A. (2012) Historical changes (1905–2005) in external phosphorus loads to Loch Leven, Scotland, UK. *Hydrobiologia*, 681, 11–21.

May, T. (1991) Südspanische matorrales als Kulturofolge-vegetation. *Geoökodynamik*, 12, 87–107.

Mayaud, J.R., Bailey, R.M. and Wiggs, G.F. (2017) Modelled responses of the Kalahari Desert to 21st century climate and land use change. *Scientific Reports*, 7, doi:10.1038/s41598-017-04341-0

Mayle, B.A. and Broome, A.C. (2013) Changes in the impact and control of an invasive alien: the grey squirrel (Sciurus carolinensis) in Great Britain, as determined from regional surveys. *Pest Management Science*, 69 (3), 323–333.

Mays, L.W. (2014) Use of cisterns during antiquity in the Mediterranean region for water resources sustainability. *Water Science and Technology: Water Supply*, 14 (1), 38–47.

McCann, K.S. (2000) The diversity-stability debate. *Nature*, 405, 228–233.

McCarney-Castle, K., Voulgaris, G. and Kettner, A.J. (2010) Analysis of fluvial suspended sediment load contribution through Anthropoecne history to the South Atlantic Bight coastal zone, USA. *Journal of Geology*, 118, 399–416.

McCarthy, T.S. (2011) The impact of acid mine drainage in South Africa. *South African Journal of Science*, 107, 1–7.

McClanahan, T.R. (2000) Bleaching damage and recovery potential of Maldivian coral reefs. *Marine Pollution Bulletin*, 40, 587–597.

McClelland, J.W., Holmes, R.M., Peterson, B.J. and Stieglitz, M. (2004) Increasing river discharge in the Eurasian Arctic: consideration of dams, permafrost thaw, and fires as potential agents of change. *Journal of Geophysical Research*, 109, D18102.

McConnell, J.R., Aristarain, A.J., Banta, J.R., et al. (2007) 20th-century doubling in dust archived in an Antarctic Peninsula ice core parallels climate change and desertification in South America. *Proceedings of the National Academy of Sciences*, 104, 5743–5748.

McCormack, C.G., Born, W., Irvine, P.J., et al. (2016) Key impacts of climate engineering on biodiversity and ecosystems, with priorities for future research. *Journal of Integrative Environmental Sciences*, 13, 103–128.

McCulloch, M., Fallon, S., Wyndham, T., et al. (2003) Coral record of increased sediment flux to the inner Great Barrier Reef since European settlement. *Nature*, 421, 727–730.

McDermid, S.S. and Winter, J. (2017) Anthropogenic forcings on the climate of the Aral Sea: a regional modeling perspective. *Anthropocene*, 20, 48–60.

McDowell, N.G., Williams, A.P., Xu, C., et al. (2016) Multi-scale predictions of massive conifer mortality due to chronic temperature rise. *Nature Climate Change*, 6, 295–300.

McGarr, A., Bekins, B., Burkardt, N., et al. (2015) Coping with earthquakes induced by fluid injection. *Science*, 347, 830–831.

McGlone, M.S. and Wilmshurst, J.M. (1999) Dating initial Maori environmental impact in New Zealand. *Quaternary International*, 59, 5–16.

McGuire, B. (2010) Climate forcing of geological and geomorphological hazards. *Philosophical Transactions: Series A, Mathematical, Physical, and Engineering Sciences*, 368, 2311–2315.

McGuire, B. (2012) *Waking the Giant: How a Changing Climate Triggers Earthquakes, Tsunamis, and Volcanoes*. Oxford: Oxford University Press.

McKinney, M.L. (2002) Urbanization, biodiversity, and conservation. *Bioscience*, 52, 883–890.

McKinney, M.L. (2008) Effects of urbanization on species richness: a review of plants and animals. *Urban Ecosystems*, 11, 161–176.

McKnight, T.L. (1959) The feral horse in Anglo-America. *Geographical Review*, 49, 506–525.

McKnight, T.L. (1971) Australia's buffalo dilemma. *Annals of the Association of American Geographers*, 61, 759–773.

McLennan, S.M. (1993) Weathering and global denudation. *Journal of Geology*, 101, 295–303.

McNeall, D., Halloran, P.R., Good, P. and Betts, R.A. (2011) Analyzing abrupt and nonlinear climate changes and their impacts. *Wiley Interdisciplinary Reviews: Climate Change*, 2, 663–686.

McNeill, J.R. (2000) *Something New under the Sun: An Environmental History of the Twentieth Century*. London: Allen Lane.

McNeill, J.R. (2003) Resource exploitation and over-exploitation: a look at the 20th century. In T.S. Benzing and B. Herrmann (eds), *Exploitation and Overexploitation in Societies Past and Present*. Münster: LIT Verlag, 1–60.

McNeill, J.R. (2005) Modern global environmental history. IHDP Global Update, 2–7.

McNeill, J.R. and Engelke, P. (2016) *The Great Acceleration*. Cambridge, MA: Harvard University Press.

McPherron, S.P., Alemseged, Z., Marean, C.W., et al. (2010) Evidence for stone-tool-assisted consumption of animal tissues before 3.39 million years ago at Dikika, Ethiopia. *Nature*, 466, 857–860.

McWethy, D.B., Whitlock, C., Wilmshurst, J.M., et al. (2009) Rapid deforestation of South Island, New Zealand, by early Polynesian fires. *The Holocene*, 19, 883–897.

Meade, R.H. (1991) Reservoirs and earthquakes. *Engineering Geology*, 30, 245–262.

Meade, R.H. (1996) River-sediment input to major deltas. In J.D. Milliman and B.V. Haq (eds), *Sea-Level Rise and Coastal Subsidence*. Dordrecht: Kluwer, 63–85.

Meade, R.H. and Moody, J.A. (2010) Causes for the decline of suspended-sediment discharge in the Mississippi River system, 1940–2007. *Hydrological Processes*, 24, 35–49.

Meade, R.H. and Parker, R.S. (1985) *Sediment in rivers in the United States*. United States Geological Survey water supply paper, 2276, 49–60.

Meade, R.H. and Trimble, S.W. (1974) Changes in sediment loads in rivers of the Atlantic drainage of the United States since 1900. *Publication of the International Association of Hydrological Science*, 113, 99–104.

Meadows, A. and Meadows P.S. (eds) (1999) *The Indus River: Biodiversity, Resources, Humankind.* Karachi: Oxford University Press.

Meadows, M.E. and Linder, H.P. (1993) A palaeoecological perspective on the origin of Afromontane grasslands. *Journal of Biogeography*, 20, 345–355.

Mee, L.D. (1992) The Black Sea in crisis: a need for concerted international action. *Ambio*, 21, 278–286.

Meehl, G.A., Arblaster, J.M. and Collins, W.D. (2008) Effects of black carbon aerosols on the Indian Monsoon. *Journal of Climate*, 21, 2869–2882.

Mekonnen, M.M., Hoekstra, A.Y. and Becht, R. (2012) Mitigating the water footprint of export cut flowers from the Lake Naivasha Basin, Kenya. *Water Resources Management*, 26, 3725–3742.

Melillo, J., Janetos, A., Schimel, D. and Kittel, T. (2001) Vegetation and biogeochemical scenarios. In National Assessment Synthesis Team (ed.), *Climate Change Impacts on the United States: The Potential Consequences of Climate Variability and Change.* Cambridge: Cambridge University Press, 74–91.

Meltzer, D.J. (2015) Pleistocene Overkill and North American mammalian extinctions. *Annual Review of Anthropology*, 44, 33–53.

Menze, B.H. and Ur, J.A. (2012) Mapping patterns of long-term settlement in Northern Mesopotamia at a large scale. *Proceedings of the National Academy of Sciences*, 109, E778–E787.

Mercer, J.H. (1978) West Antarctic ice sheet and CO_2 greenhouse effect: a threat of disaster. *Nature*, 271, 321–325.

Meriläinen, J.J., Kustula, V. and Witick, A. (2011) Lead pollution history from 256 BC to AD 2005 inferred from the Pb isotope ratio (206Pb/207Pb) in a varve record of Lake Korttajärvi in Finland. *Journal of Paleolimnology*, 45, 1–8.

Messier, M.S., Shatford, J.P.A. and Hibbs, D.E. (2012) Fire exclusion effects on riparian forest dynamics in southwestern Oregon. *Forest Ecology and Management*, 264, 60–71.

Metcalfe, S. and Derwent, D. (2005) *Atmospheric Pollution and Environmental Change.* London: Hodder Arnold.

Meusberger, K. and Alewell, C. (2008) Impacts of anthropogenic and environmental factors on the occurrence of shallow landslides in an alpine catchment (Urseren Valley, Switzerland). *Natural Hazards and Earth System Sciences*, 8, 509–520.

Meybeck, M. (1979) Concentration des eaux fluviales en éléments majeurs et apports en solution aux océans.

Revue de Géographie Physique et de Géologie Dynamique, 21, 215–246.

Meybeck, M. (2001a) Global alteration of riverine geochemistry under human pressure. In E. Ehlers (ed.), *Understanding the Earth System: Compartments, Processes and Interactions.* Heidelberg: Springer, 97–113.

Meybeck, M. (2001b) River basins under anthropocene conditions. In B. von Bodungen and R.K. Turner (eds), *Science and Integrated Coastal Management.* Dahlem: Dahlem University Press, 275–294.

Meybeck, M. and Vörösmarty, C. (2005) Fluvial filtering of land-to-ocean fluxes: from natural Holocene variations to Anthropocene. *Comptes Rendus Geoscience*, 337, 107–123.

Meyer, R.S., DuVal, A.E. and Jensen, H.R. (2012) Patterns and processes in crop domestication: an historical review and quantitative analysis of 203 global food crops. *The New Phytologist*, 196, 29–48.

Meyer, W.B. (1996) *Human Impact on the Earth.* Cambridge: Cambridge University Press.

Meyer, W.B. and Turner, B.L. II (eds) (1994) *Changes in Land Use and Land Cover: A Global Perspective.* Cambridge: Cambridge University Press.

Meyfroidt, P. and Lambin, E. (2008) Forest transition in Vietnam and its environmental impacts. *Global Change Biology*, 14, 1319–1336.

Meyfroidt, P. and Lambin, E. (2009) Geographic and historical patterns of reforestation. *Bulletin des Séances de l'Academie Royale des Sciences d'outre-mer*, 55, 477–502.

Miao, X., Tang, Y., Wong, C.W. and Zang, H. (2015) The latent causal chain of industrial water pollution in China. *Environmental Pollution*, 196, 473–477.

Micheletti, N., Lane, S.N and Chandler, J.H. (2015) Application of archival aerial photogrammetry to quantify climate forcing of Alpine landscapes. *The Photogrammetric Record*, 30, 143–165.

Micklin, P. (1972) Dimensions of the Caspian Sea problem. *Soviet Geography*, 13, 589–603.

Micklin, P. (2010) The past, present and future Aral Sea. *Lakes and Reservoirs: Research and Management*, 15, 193–213.

Micklin, P. (2016) The future Aral Sea: hope and despair. *Environmental Earth Sciences*, 75 (9), 1–15.

Middleton, N.J. (2013) *The Global Casino.* London: Routledge.

Middleton, N.J. (2016) Rangeland management and climate hazards in drylands: dust storms, desertification and the overgrazing debate. *Natural Hazards*, doi:10.1007/s11069-016-2592-6.

Middleton, N.J. and Thomas, D.S.G. (1997) *World Atlas of Desertification* (2nd edn). London: Edward Arnold.

Midgley, G.F., Hannah, L., Millar, D., et al. (2003) Developing regional and species-level assessments of climate change impacts on biodiversity in the Cape Floristic Region. *Biological Conservation*, 112, 87–97.

Miesel, J.R., Hockaday, W.C., Kolka, R.K. and Townsend, P.A. (2015) Soil organic matter composition and quality across fire severity gradients in coniferous and deciduous forests of the southern boreal region. *Journal of Geophysical Research: Biogeosciences*, 120 (6), 1124–1141.

Miettingen, J., Shi, C. and Soo, C.L. (2011) Deforestation rates in insular southeast Asia between 2000 and 2010. *Global Change Biology*, 17, 2261–2270.

Mietton, M., Cordier, S., Frechen, M., et al. (2014) New insights into the age and formation of the Ankarokaroka lavaka and its associated sandy cover (NW Madagascar, Ankarafantsika natural reserve). *Earth Surface Processes and Landforms*, 39, 1467–1477.

Migaszewski, Z.M. and Gałuszka, A. (2015) The characteristics, occurrence, and geochemical behavior of rare earth elements in the environment: a review. *Critical Reviews in Environmental Science and Technology*, 45 (5), 429–471.

Mikesell, M.W. (1969) The deforestation of Mount Lebanon. *Geographical Review*, 59, 1–28.

Millennium Ecosystem Assessment (MA) (2005) *Ecosystems and Human Well-Being: Synthesis*. Washington, DC: Island Press.

Miller, J.D., Kim, H., Kjeldsen, T.R., et al. (2014) Assessing the impact of urbanization on storm runoff in a peri-urban catchment using historical change in impervious cover. *Journal of Hydrology*, 515, 59–70.

Miller, J.D., Safford, H.D., Crimmins, M. and Thode, A.E. (2009) Quantitative evidence for increasing fire severity in the Sierra Nevada and southern Cascade Mountains, California and Nevada, USA. *Ecosystems*, 12, 16–32.

Miller, J.R. (2017) Causality of historic arroyo incision in the southwestern United States. *Anthropocene*, 18, 69–75.

Miller, J.R. and Russell, G.L. (2002) Projected impact of climate change on the energy budget of the Arctic Ocean Global Climate Model. *Journal of Climate*, 15, 3028–3042.

Miller, L. and Douglas, B.C. (2004) Mass and volume contribution to twentieth-century global sea level rise. *Nature*, 428, 406–409.

Miller, R.L. and Tegen, I. (1998) Climate response to soil dust aerosols. *Journal of Climate*, 11, 3247–3267.

Miller, R.S. and Botkin, D.B. (1974) Endangered species: models and predictions. *American Scientist*, 62, 172–181.

Milliman, J.D. (1990) Fluvial sediment in coastal seas: flux and fate. *Nature and Resources*, 26, 12–22.

Milliman, J.D., Broadus, J.M. and Gable, F. (1989) Environmental and economic impacts of rising sea level

and subsiding deltas: the Nile and Bengal examples. *Ambio*, 18, 340–345.

Milliman, J.D. and Haq, B.U. (eds) (1996) *Sea Level Rise and Coastal Subsidence*. Dordrecht: Kluwer.

Milliman, J.D., Qin, Y.S., Ren, M.E. and Saita, Y. (1987) Man's influence on erosion and transport of sediment by Asian rivers: the Yellow River (Huanghe) example. *Journal of Geology*, 95, 751–762.

Mills, K., Schillereff, D., Saulnier-Talbot, É., et al. (2017) Deciphering long-term records of natural variability and human impact as recorded in lake sediments: a palaeolimnological puzzle. *Wiley Interdisciplinary Reviews: Water*, 4, doi:10.1002/wat2.1195.

Milly, P.C.D., Wetherald, R.T., Dunne, K.A. and Delworth, T.L. (2002) Increasing risk of great floods in a changing climate. *Nature*, 415, 514–517.

Milne, W.G. (1976) Induced seismicity. *Engineering Geology*, 10, 83–88.

Min, S.-K., Zhang, X., Zwiers, F.W. and Hegerl, G.C. (2011) Human contribution to more-intense precipitation extremes. *Nature*, 470, 378–381.

Minassian, V.T. (2011) The Green Wall of Africa. *CNRS International Magazine*, 23, 6–7.

Minora, U., Bocchiola, D., D'Agata, C., et al. (2013) 2001–2010 glacier changes in the Central Karakoram National Park: a contribution to evaluate the magnitude and rate of the 'Karakoram anomaly'. *The Cryosphere Discussions*, 7 (3), 2891–2941.

Mistry, J. (2000) *World Savannas: Ecology and Human Use*. Harlow: Prentice Hall.

Mitchell, R.M., Campbell, S.K. and Qin, Y. (2010) Recent increase in aerosol loading over the Australian arid zone. *Atmospheric Chemistry and Physics*, 10, 1689–1699.

Mithen, S. (2007) Did farming arise from a misapplication of social intelligence? *Philosophical Transactions of the Royal Society of London: Series B, Biological Sciences*, 362, 705–718.

Mithen, S. (2012) *Thirst: Water and Power in the Ancient World*. London: Weidenfeld and Nicholson.

Mitra, A., Chatterjee, C. and Mandal, F.B. (2011) Synthetic chemical pesticides and their effects on birds. *Research Journal of Environmental Toxicology*, 5, 81–96.

Moberg, F. and Folke, C. (1999) Ecological goods and services of coral reef ecosystems. *Ecological Economics*, 29 (2), 215–233.

Moleele, N.M., Ringrose, S., Matheson, W. and Vanderpost, C. (2002) More woody plants? The status of bush encroachment in Botswana's grazing areas. *Journal of Environmental Management*, 64, 3–11.

Moles, A.T., Flores-Moreno, H., Bonser, S.P., et al. (2012) Invasions: the trail behind, the path ahead, and a test of a disturbing idea. *Journal of Ecology*, 100, 116–127.

Mölg, N. (2014) Hasty retreat of glaciers in northern Patagonia from 1985–2011. *Journal of Glaciology*, 60, 1033–1043.

Mölg, T., Georges, C. and Kaser, G. (2003) The contribution of increased incoming shortwave radiation to the retreat of the Rwenzori Glaciers, East Africa, during the 20th century. *International Journal of Climatology*, 23, 291–303.

Møller, A.P., Díaz, M., Grim, T., et al. (2015) Effects of urbanization on bird phenology: a continental study of paired urban and rural populations. *Climate Research*, 66 (3), 185–199.

Monceau, K., Bonnard, O. and Thiéry, D. (2014) Vespa velutina: a new invasive predator of honeybees in Europe. *Journal of Pest Science*, 87 (1), 1–16.

Moncel, M.-H. (2010) Oldest human expansions in Eurasia: favouring and limiting factors. *Quaternary International*, 223–224, 1–9.

Montgomery, D.R. (1997) What's best on the banks? *Nature*, 388, 328–329.

Montgomery, D.R. (2007) *Dirt: The Erosion of Civilizations*. Berkeley: University of California Press.

Moody, J.A. and Martin, D.A. (2001) Initial hydrologic and geomorphic response following a wildfire in the Colorado Front Range. *Earth Surface Processes and Landforms*, 26, 1049–1070.

Moore, C.J. (2008) Synthetic polymers in the marine environment: a rapidly increasing, long-term threat. *Environmental Research*, 108, 131–139.

Moore, D.M. (1983) Human impact on island vegetation. In W. Holzner, M.J.A. Werger and I. Ikusima (eds), *Man's Impact on Vegetation*. The Hague: Junk, 237–248.

Moore, J. (2000) Forest fire and human interaction in the early Holocene woodlands of Britain. *Palaeogeography, Palaeoclimatology, Palaeoecology*, 164, 125–137.

Moore, N. and Rojstaczer, S. (2001) Irrigation-induced rainfall and the Great Plains. *Journal of Applied Meteorology*, 40, 1297–1309.

Moore, N.W., Hooper, M.D. and Davis, B.N.K. (1967) Hedges, I. Introduction and reconnaissance studies. *Journal of Applied Ecology*, 4, 201–220.

Moore, P.D. (1973) Origin of blanket mires. *Nature*, 256, 267–269.

Moore, P.D. (1986) Unravelling human effects. *Nature*, 321, 204.

Moore, P.D. (2002) The future of cool temperate bogs. *Environmental Conservation*, 29, 3–20.

Moore, T.R. (1979) Land use and erosion in the Machakos Hills. *Annals of the Association of American Geographers*, 69, 419–431.

Morgan, J.A., Pataki, D.E., Körner, C., et al. (2004) Water relations in grassland and desert ecosystems exposed to elevated atmospheric CO_2. *Oecologia*, 140, 11–25.

Morgan, R.P.C. (1977) *Soil erosion in the United Kingdom: field studies in the Silsoe area, 1973–75*. National College of Agricultural Engineering, occasional paper, 4.

Morgan, R.P.C. (1995) *Soil Erosion and Conservation* (2nd edn). Harlow: Longman.

Morgan, R.P.C. (2005) *Soil Erosion and Conservation* (3rd edn). Oxford: Blackwell.

Moridnejad A., Karimi, N., and Ariya, P.A. (2015) Newly desertified regions in Iraq and its surrounding areas: significant novel sources of global dust particles. *Journal of Arid Environments*, 116, 1–10.

Morris, I. (2010) *Why the West Rules – For Now*. London: Profile Books.

Morse, N.B., Pellissier, P.A., Cianciola, E.N., et al. (2014) Novel ecosystems in the Anthropocene: a revision of the novel ecosystem concept for pragmatic applications. *Ecology and Society*, 19 (2), 12, doi:org/10.5751/ES-06192-190212.

Morton, R.A., Bernier, J.C. and Barras, J.A. (2006) Evidence of regional subsidence and associated wetland loss induced by hydrocarbon production, Gulf Coast region, USA. *Environmental Geology*, 50, 261–274.

Morton, R.A., Bernier, J.C., Barras, J.A. and Ferina, N.F. (2005) Historical subsidence and wetland loss in the Mississippi delta Plain. *Gulf Coast Association of Geological Societies Transactions*, 55, 555–571.

Morzaria-Luna, H.N., Turk-Boyer, P., Rosemartin, A. and Camacho-Ibar, V.F. (2014) Vulnerability to climate change of hypersaline salt marshes in the Northern Gulf of California. *Ocean & Coastal Management*, 93, 37–50.

Mote, P.W., Hamlet, A.F., Clark, M.P. and Lettenmaier, D.P. (2005) Declining mountain snowpack in western North America. *Bulletin of the American Meteorological Society*, 86, 39–49.

Motyka, R.J., O'Neal, S., Connor, C.L. and Echelmeyer, K.A. (2002) Twentieth century thinning of Mendenhall Glacier, Alaska, and its relationship to climate, lake calving and glacier run-off. *Global and Planetary Change*, 35, 93–112.

Moulherat, C., Tengberg, M., Haquet, J.-F. and Mille, B. (2002) First evidence of cotton at Neolithic Mehrgarh, Pakistan: analysis of mineralized fibres from a copper bead. *Journal of Archaeological Science*, 29, 1393–1401.

Mousavi, M.E., Irish, J.L., Frey, A.E., et al. (2011) Global warming and hurricanes: the potential impact of hurricane intensification and sea level rise on coastal flooding. *Climatic Change*, 104, 575–597.

Moyle, P.B. (1976) Fish introductions in California: history and impact on native fishes. *Biological Conservation*, 9, 101–118.

Muhly, J.D. (1997) Artifacts of the Neolithic, Bronze and Iron Ages. In E.M. Myers (ed.), *The Oxford Encyclopaedia of Archaeology in the Near East* (Vol. 4). New York: Oxford University Press, 5–15.

Muhs, D.R. and Holliday, V.T. (1995) Evidence of active dune sand in the Great Plains in the 19th century from accounts of early explorers. *Quaternary Research*, 43, 198–208.

Muhs, D.R. and Maat, P.B. (1993) The potential response of eolian sands to greenhouse warming and precipitation reduction on the Great Plains of the United States. *Journal of Arid Environments*, 25, 351–361.

Mulitza, S., Heslop, D., Pittauerova, D., et al. (2010) Increase in African dust flux at the onset of commercial agriculture in the Sahel region. *Nature*, 466, 226–228.

Mullan, D., Favis-Mortlock, D. and Fealy, R. (2012) Addressing key limitations associated with modelling soil erosion under the impacts of future climate change. *Agricultural and Forest Meteorology*, 156, 18–30.

Mulrennan, M.E. and Woodroffe, C.D. (1998) Saltwater intrusion into the coastal plains of the lower Mary River, Northern Territory, Australia. *Journal of Environmental Management*, 54, 169–188.

Munson, S., Belnap, J. and Okin, G.S. (2011) Responses of wind erosion to climate-induced vegetation changes on the Colorado Plateau. *Proceedings of the National Academy of Sciences*, 108, 3854–3859.

Murcia, C., Aronson, J., Kattan, G.H., et al. (2014) A critique of the 'novel ecosystem' concept. *Trends in Ecology & Evolution*, 29 (10), 548–553.

Murdoch, W.W. (1975) Diversity, complexity, stability and pest control. *Journal of Applied Ecology*, 12, 795–807.

Murozumi, M., Chow, T.J. and Paterson, C. (1969) Chemical concentrations of pollutant lead aerosols, terrestrial dusts and sea salt in Greenland and Antarctic snow strata. *Geochimica et Cosmochimica Acta*, 33, 1247–1294.

Murphy, B.P. and Bowman, D.M. (2012) What controls the distribution of tropical forest and savanna? *Ecology Letters*, 15 (7), 748–758.

Murthy, A.C., Fristoe, T.S. and Burger, J.R. (2016) Homogenizing effects of cities on North American winter bird diversity. *Ecosphere*, 7 (1), doi:10.1002/ecs2.1216.

Murton, R.K. (1971) *Man and Birds*. London: Collins.

Musk, L.F. (1991) The fog hazard, In A.H. Perry and L.J. Symons (eds), *Highway Meteorology*. London: Spon, 91–130.

Muturi, G.M., Mohren, G.M.J. and Kimani, J.N. (2009) Prediction of Prosopis species invasion in Kenya using geographical information system techniques. *African Journal of Ecology*, 48, 628–636.

Myers, N. (1979) *The Sinking Ark: A New Look at the Problem of Disappearing Species*. Oxford: Pergamon Press.

Myers, N. (1983) Conversion rates in tropical moist forests. In F.B. Golley (ed.), *Tropical Rain Forest Ecosystems*. Amsterdam: Elsevier Scientific, 289–300.

Myers, N. (1984) *The Primary Source: Tropical Forests and Our Future*. New York: Norton.

Myers, N. (1988) *Natural resource systems and human exploitation systems: physiobiotic and ecological linkages*. World Bank policy planning and research staff, environment department working paper, 12.

Myers, N. (1990) The biodiversity challenge: expanded hotspots analysis. *The Environmentalist*, 10 (4), 243–256.

Myers, N. (1992) Future operational monitoring of tropical forests: an alert strategy. In J.P. Mallingreau, R. da Cunha and C. Justice (eds), *Proceedings World Forest Watch Conference*. Brazil: Sao Jose dos Campos, 9–14.

Myers, N. and Kent, J. (2003) New consumers: the influence of affluence on the environment. *Proceedings of the National Academy of Sciences*, 100, 4963–4968.

Myers, N., Mittermeier, R.A., Mittermeier, C.G., da Fonseca, G.A.B. and Kent, J. (2000) Biodiversity hotspots for conservation priorities. *Nature*, 403, 853–858.

Myers-Smith, I.H., Elmendorf, S.C., Beck, P.S., et al. (2015) Climate sensitivity of shrub growth across the tundra biome. *Nature Climate Change*, 5 (9), 887–891.

Myles, S., Boyko, A.R., Owens, C.L., et al. (2011) Genetic structure and domestication history of the grape. *Proceedings of the National Academy of Sciences*, 108, 3530–3535.

Mylne, M.F. and Rowntree, P.R. (1992) Modelling the effects of albedo change associated with tropical deforestation. *Climatic Change*, 21, 317–343.

Nadal-Romero, E., Lasanta, T. and García-Ruiz, J.M. (2013) Runoff and sediment yield from land under various uses in a Mediterranean mountain area: long-term results from an experimental station. *Earth Surface Processes and Landforms*, 38, 346–355.

Naden, P., Bell, V., Carnell, E., et al. (2016) Nutrient fluxes from domestic wastewater: a national-scale historical perspective for the UK 1800–2010. *Science of the Total Environment*, 572, 1471–1484.

Naeem, S. (2002) Biodiversity equals instability? *Nature*, 416, 23–24.

Naidoo, V., Wolter, K., Cuthbert, R. and Duncan, N. (2009) Veterinary diclofenac threatens Africa's endangered vulture species. *Regulatory Toxicology and Pharmacology*, 53, 205–208.

Naik, M. and Abiodun, B.J. (2016) Potential impacts of forestation on future climate change in Southern Africa. *International Journal of Climatology*, 36 (14), 456–476.

Naik, P.K. and Jay, D.A. (2011) Distinguishing human and climate influences on the Columbia River: changes in mean flow and sediment transport. *Journal of Hydrology*, 404, 259–277.

Najjar, R.G. (1999) The water balance of the Susquehanna River Basin and its response to climate change. *Journal of Hydrology*, 219, 7–19.

Nakagawa, K. (1996) Recent trends of urban climatological studies in Japan, with special emphasis on the thermal environments of urban areas. *Geographical Review of Japan, Series B*, 69, 206–224.

Nakano, T. and Matsuda, I. (1976) A note on land subsidence in Japan. *Geographical Reports of Tokyo Metropolitan University*, 11, 147–162.

Nanson, G.C. and Tooth, S. (1999) Arid-zone rivers as indicators of climate change. In A.K. Singhvi and E. Derbyshire (eds), *Paleoenvironmental Reconstruction in Arid Lands*. New Delhi and Calcutta: Oxford and IBH, 75–216.

Napieralski, J.A. and Carvalhaes, T. (2016) Urban stream deserts: mapping a legacy of urbanization in the United States. *Applied Geography*, 67, 129–139.

Nash, L.L. and Gleick, P.H. (1991) Sensitivity of streamflow in the Colorado Basin to climatic changes. *Journal of Hydrology*, 125, 221–241.

Natalini, F., Alejano, R., Vázquez-Piqué, J., et al. (2016) The role of climate change in the widespread mortality of holm oak in open woodlands of Southwestern Spain. *Dendrochronologia*, 38, 51–60.

Nath, A.J. and Lal, R. (2017) Effects of tillage practices and land use management on soil aggregates and soil organic carbon in the North Appalachian Region, USA. *Pedosphere*, 27 (1), 172–176.

National Academies of Sciences, Engineering, and Medicine (2016) *Attribution of Extreme Weather Events in the Context of Climate Change*. Washington, DC: National Academies Press, doi:10.17226/21852.

National Research Council (2014) *Responding to Oil Spills in the US Arctic Marine Environment*. Washington, DC: National Academies Press.

Nature Conservancy Council (1977) *Nature Conservation and Agriculture*. London: Her Majesty's Stationery Office.

Nature Conservancy Council (1984) *Nature Conservation in Great Britain*. Shrewsbury: Nature Conservancy Council.

Navarro, L.M. and Pereira, H.M. (2012) Rewilding abandoned landscapes in Europe. *Ecosystems*, 15 (6), 900–912.

Navratil, O., Breil, P., Schmitt, L., et al. (2013) Hydrogeomorphic adjustments of stream channels disturbed by urban runoff (Yzeron River basin, France). *Journal of Hydrology*, 485, 24–36.

Nawaz, M.F., Bourrie, G. and Trolard, F. (2013) Soil compaction impact and modelling. A review. *Agronomy for Sustainable Development*, 33 (2), 291–309.

Naylor, L.A., Spencer, T., Lane, S.N., et al. (2017) Stormy geomorphology: geomorphic contributions in an age of climate extremes. *Earth Surface Processes and Landforms*, 42 (1), 166–190.

Nearing, M.A. (2001) Potential changes in rainfall erosivity in the US with climate change during the 21st century. *Journal of Soil and Water Conservation*, 56, 229–232.

Nearing, M.A., Xie, Y., Liu, B. and Ye, Y. (2017) Natural and anthropogenic rates of soil erosion. *International Soil and Water Conservation Research*, 5, 77–84.

Nearing, W., Jetten, V., Baffaut, C., et al. (2005) Modeling response of soil erosion and runoff to changes in precipitation and cover. *Catena*, 61, 131–154.

Neave, M., Rayburg, S. and Swan, A. (2009) River channel change following dam removal in an ephemeral stream. *Australian Geographer*, 40, 235–246.

Needham, J., Merow, C., Butt, N., et al. (2016) Forest community response to invasive pathogens: the case of ash dieback in a British woodland. *Journal of Ecology*, 104 (2), 315–330.

Neff, J.C., Ballantyne, A.P., Farmer, G.L., et al. (2008) Increasing eolian dust deposition in the western United States linked to human activity. *Nature Geosciences*, 1, 189–195.

Nelson, E.J., Kareiva, P., Ruckelshaus, M., et al. (2013) Climate change's impact on key ecosystem services and the human well-being they support in the US. *Frontiers in Ecology and the Environment*, 11 (9), 483–893.

Nelson, F.E. (2002) Climate change and hazard zonation in the Circum-Arctic Permafrost regions. *Natural Hazards*, 26, 203–225.

Nelson, F.E. and Anisimov, O.A. (1993) Permafrost zonation in Russia under anthropogenic climate change. *Permafrost and Periglacial Processes*, 4, 137–148.

Nelson, F.E., Anisimov, O.A. and Shiklomanov, N.I. (2001) Subsidence risk from thawing permafrost. *Nature*, 410, 889–890.

Nepstad, D.C., Stickler, C.M., Soares-Filho, B. and Merry, F. (2008) Interactions among Amazon land use, forests and climate: prospects for a near-term forest tipping point. *Philosophical Transactions of the Royal Society of London: Series B, Biological Sciences*, 363, 1737–1746.

Neris, J., Tejedor, M., Fuentes, J. and Jiménez, C. (2013) Infiltration, runoff and soil loss in Andisols affected by forest fire (Canary Islands, Spain). *Hydrological Processes*, 27 (19), 2814–2824.

Nesje, A., Bakke, J., Dahl, S.O., et al. (2008) Norwegian mountain glaciers in the past, present and future. *Global and Planetary Change*, 60, 10–27.

Nesje, A. and Dahl, S.O. (2000) *Glaciers and Environmental Change*. London: Arnold.

Nesje, A., Lie, O. and Dahl, S.O. (2000) Is the North Atlantic Oscillation reflected in glacier mass balance records? *Journal of Quaternary Science*, 15, 587–601.

Neudorf, C.M., Smith, N., Lepofsky, D., et al. (2017) Between a rock and a soft place: using optical ages to date ancient clam gardens on the Pacific Northwest. *PloS one*, 12 (2), e0171775.

Neves, E.G., Petersen, J.B., Bartone, R.N. and da Silva, C.A. (2003) Historical and socio-cultural origins of Amazonian Dark earths. In J. Jehmann (ed.), *Amazonian*

Dark Earths: Origin, Properties, Management. Dordrecht: Kluwer, 29–50.

New, M., Liverman, D., Schroeder, H. and Anderson, K. (2011) Four degrees and beyond: the potential for a global temperature increase of four degrees and its implications. *Philosophical Transactions: Series A, Mathematical, Physical, and Engineering Sciences,* 369, 6–19.

New, M., Todd, M., Hulme, M. and Jones, P. (2001) Precipitation measurements and trends in the twentieth century. *International Journal of Climatology,* 21, 1899–1922.

Newbold, T., Hudson, L.N., Hill, S.L., et al. (2015) Global effects of land use on local terrestrial biodiversity. *Nature,* 520 (7545), 45–50.

Newman, J.R. (1979) Effects of industrial pollution on wildlife. *Biological Conservation,* 15, 181–190.

Newman, W.S. and Fairbridge, R.W. (1986) The management of sealevel rise. *Nature,* 320, 319–321.

Newsome, D., Moore, S.A. and Dowling, R.K. (2012) *Natural Area Tourism: Ecology, Impacts and Management.* Bristol: Channel View Publications.

Newton, J. G. (1976) Induced and natural sinkholes in Alabama: continuing problem along highway corridors. In F.R. Zwanig (ed.), *Subsidence over Mines and Caverns.* Washington, DC: National Academy of Sciences, 9–16.

Nichol, S.L., Augustinus, P.L., Gregory, M.R., Creese, R. and Horrocks, M. (2000) Geomorphic and sedimentary evidence of human impact on the New Zealand landscape. *Physical Geography,* 21, 109–132.

Nicholls, R.J., Hoozemans, F.M.J. and Marchand, M. (1999) Increasing flood risk and wetland losses due to global sea level rise: regional and global analyses. *Global Environmental Change,* 9, S69–S87.

Nicholls, R.J., Marinova, N., Lowe, J.A., et al. (2011) Sea-level rise and its possible impacts given a 'beyond 4°C world' in the twenty-first century. *Philosophical Transactions: Series A, Mathematical, Physical, and Engineering Sciences,* 369, 161–181.

Nicholls, R.J., Wong, P.P., Burkett, V.R., et al. (2007) Coastal systems and low-lying areas. In M.L. Parry (ed.), *Climate Change 2007: Impacts, Adaptation and Vulnerability.* Cambridge: Cambridge University Press, 315–356.

Nicholson, S.E. (1988) Land surface atmosphere interaction: physical processes and surface changes and their impact. *Progress in Physical Geography,* 12, 36–65.

Nicod, J. (1986) Facteurs physico-chimiques de l'accumulation des formations travertineuses. *Méditerranée,* 10, 161–164.

Nicolay, A., Raab, A., Raab, T., et al. (2014) Evidence of (pre-) historic to modern landscape and land use history near Jänschwalde (Brandenburg, Germany). *Zeitschrift für Geomorphologie,* 58, Suppl. 2, 7–31.

Nihlgård, B.J. (1997) Forest decline and environmental stress. In D. Brune, D.V. Chapman, M.D. Gwynne and J.M. Pacyna (eds), *The Global Environment.* Weinheim: VCH, 422–440.

Nijssen, B., O'Donnell, G.M., Hamlet, A.F. and Lettenmaier, D.P. (2001) Hydrologic sensitivity of global rivers to climate change. *Climatic Change,* 50, 143–175.

Nikolaou, T.G., Christodoulakos, I., Piperidis, P.G. and Angelakis, A.N. (2016) Evolution of Cretan, Greece aqueducts. In *Proceedings of the 4th IWA International Symposium on Water and Wastewater Technologies in Ancient Civilizations, Coimbra,* Portugal, 17–19.

Nikolskiy, P.A., Sulerzhitsky, L.D. and Pitulko, V.V. (2011) Last straw versus Blitzkrieg overkill: climate-driven changes in the Arctic Siberian mammoth population and the Late Pleistocene extinction problem. *Quaternary Science Reviews,* 30, 2309–2328.

Nikonov, A.A. (1977) Contemporary technogenic movements of the Earth's crust. *International Geology Review,* 19, 1245–1258.

Nir, D. (1983) *Man, a Geomorphological Agent: An Introduction to Anthropic Geomorphology.* Jerusalem: Keter.

Nitschke, C.R. and Innes, J.L. (2013) Potential effect of climate change on observed fire regimes in the Cordilleran forests of South-Central Interior, British Columbia. *Climatic Change,* 116 (3–4), 579–591.

Niu, F., Li, Z., Li, C., et al. (2010) Increase of wintertime fog in China: potential impacts of weakening of the Eastern Asian monsoon circulation and increased aerosol loading. *Journal of Geophysical Research,* 115, D00k20.

Nixdorf, E., Chen, C., Sun, Y. and Kolditz, O. (2015) Persistent organic pollutants contaminate Chinese water resources: overview of the current status, challenges and European strategies. *Environmental Earth Sciences,* 74 (2), 1837–1843.

Nobre, C.A. and Borma, L.D.S. (2009) 'Tipping points' for the Amazon forest. *Current Opinion in Environmental Sustainability,* 1, 28–36.

Nobre, C.A., Dias, M.A.S., Culf, A.D., et al. (2004) The Amazonian climate. In P. Kabat, M. Claussen, P.A. Dirmeyer, et al. (eds), *Vegetation, Water, Humans and the Climate.* New York: Springer, 79–92.

Nordstrom, K.F. (1994) Beaches and dunes of human-altered coasts. *Progress in Physical Geography,* 18, 497–516.

Nordstrom, K.F. (2014) Living with shore protection structures: a review. *Estuarine, Coastal and Shelf Science,* 150, 11–23.

Nordstrom, K.F. and Hotta, S. (2004) Wind erosion from cropland in the USA: a review of problems, solutions and prospects. *Geoderma,* 121, 157–167.

Norris, S. (2001) Thanks for all the fish. *New Scientist,* 29 September, 36–39.

Noss, R.F. (2011) Between the devil and the deep blue sea: Florida's unenviable position with respect to sea level rise. *Climatic Change*, 107, 1–16.

Notebaert, B. and Verstraeten, G. (2010) Sensitivity of West and Central European river systems to environmental changes during the Holocene: a review. *Earth-Science Reviews*, 103, 163–182.

Noti, R., van Leeuwen, J.F.N., Colombaroli, D., et al. (2009) Mid- and late-Holocene vegetation and fire history at Biviere di Gela, a coastal lake in southern Sicily, Italy. *Vegetation History and Archaeobotany*, 18, 371–387.

Novotny, E.V., Murphy, D. and Stefan, H.G. (2008) Increase of urban lake salinity by road deicing salt. *Science of the Total Environment*, 406, 131–144.

Nowlis, J.S., Roberts, C.M., Smith, A.H. and Siirila, E. (1997) Human-enhanced impacts of a tropical storm on nearshore coral reefs. *Ambio*, 26, 515–521.

Noy-Meir, I. (1974) Stability in arid ecosystems and effects of men on it. *Proceedings of the 12th International Congress of Ecology*, Wageningen, 220–225.

Nriagu, J.O. (1979) Global inventory of natural and anthropogenic emissions of trace metals in the atmosphere. *Nature*, 279, 409–411.

Nriagu, J.O. and Pacyna, J.M. (1988) Quantitative assessment of worldwide contamination of air, water and soils by trace metals. *Nature*, 337, 134–139.

Nuckolls, A.E., Wurzburger, N., Ford, C.R., et al. (2009) Hemlock declines rapidly with hemlock wooly adelgid infestation: impacts on the carbon cycle of southern Appalachian forests. *Ecosystems*, 12, 179–190.

Nunn, P.D. (1991) *Human and natural impacts on Pacific island environments*. Occasional paper of the East West Environment and Policy Institute, 13, Honolulu.

Nutalaya, P. and Rau, J.L. (1981) Bangkok: the sinking metropolis. *Episodes*, 4, 3–8.

Nutalaya, P., Yong, R.N., Chumnankit, T. and Buapeng, S. (1996) Land subsidence in Bangkok during 1978–1988. In J.D. Milliman and B.U. Haq (eds), *Sea Level Rise and Coastal Subsidence*. Dordrecht: Kluwer, 105–130.

Nyssen, J., Haile, M., Naudts, J., et al. (2009) Desertification? Northern Ethiopia re-photographed after 140 years. *Science of the Total Environment*, 407, 2749–2755.

O'Connor, C.D., Garfin, G.M., Falk, D.A. and Swetnam, T.W. (2011) Human pyrogeography: a new synergy of fire, climate and people is reshaping ecosystems across the globe. *Geography Compass*, 5, 329–350.

Oba, G., Post, E. and Stenseth, N.C. (2001) Sub-Saharan desertification and productivity are linked to hemispheric climate variability. *Global Change Biology*, 7, 241–246.

Oberle, M. (1969) Forest fires: suppression policy has its ecological drawbacks. *Science*, 165, 568–571.

Obu, J., Lantuit, H., Grosse, G., et al. (2017) Coastal erosion and mass wasting along the Canadian Beaufort Sea based on annual airborne LiDAR elevation data. *Geomorphology*, 293, 331–346.

Ochoa-Tocachi, B.F., Buytaert, W., De Bièvre, B., et al. (2016) Impacts of land use on the hydrological response of tropical Andean catchments. *Hydrological Processes*, 30 (22), 4074–4089.

O'Connor, C.D., Garfin, G.M., Falk, D.A. and Swetnam, T.W. (2011) Human pyrogeography: a new synergy of fire, climate and people is reshaping ecosystems across the globe. *Geography Compass*, 5, 329–350.

O'Connor, T.G. (2017) Demography of woody species in a semi-arid African savanna reserve following the re-introduction of elephants. *Acta Oecologica*, 78, 61–70.

O'Donnell, A.G., Seasman, M., Macrae, A., et al. (2001) Plants and fertilisers as drivers of change in microbial community structure and function in soils. *Plant and Soil*, 232 (1–2), 135–145.

Oechel, J.W.C., Hastings, S.J., Vourlitis, G.L., et al. (1995) Direct effects of elevated CO_2 in Chaparral and Mediterranean-type ecosystems. In J.M. Moreno and W.C. Oechel (eds), *Global Change and Mediterranean-Type Ecosystems*. New York: Springer, 58–75.

Oerlemans, J. (1993) Possible changes in the mass balance of the Greenland and Antarctic ice sheets and their effects on sea level. In R.A. Warwick, E.M. Barrows and T.M.L. Wigley (eds), *Climatic and Sea Level Change: Observations, Projections and Implications*. Cambridge: Cambridge University Press, 144–161.

Oerlemans, J. (1994) Quantifying global warming from the retreat of glaciers. *Science*, 264, 243–245.

Oerlemans, J., Anderson, B., Hubbard, A., et al. (1998) Modelling the response of glaciers to climate warming. *Climate Dynamics*, 14, 267–274.

O'Hara, S.L., Street-Perrott, F.A. and Burt, T.P. (1993) Accelerated soil erosion around a Mexican highland lake caused by prehispanic agriculture. *Nature*, 362, 48–51.

Oke, T.R. (1978) *Boundary Layer Climates*. London: Methuen.

Olden, J.D., Lockwood, J.L. and Parr, C.L. (2011) Biological invasions and the homogenization of faunas and floras. In R.J. Ladle and R.J. Whittaker (eds), *Conservation Biogeography*. Chichester: Wiley Blackwell, 224–243.

Oliveira, P.T.S., Nearing, M.A. and Wendland, E. (2015) Orders of magnitude increase in soil erosion associated with land use change from native to cultivated vegetation in a Brazilian savannah environment. *Earth Surface Processes and Landforms*, 40, 1524–1533.

Oliver, T.H., Gillings, S., Pearce-Higgins, J.W., et al. (2017) Large extents of intensive land use limit community reorganization during climate warming. *Global Change Biology*, 23, 2272–2283.

Olley, J.M. and Wasson, R.J. (2003) Changes in the flux of sediment in the Upper Murrumbidgee catchment, southeastern Australia, since European settlement. *Hydrological Processes*, 17, 3307–3320.

Olsson, L., Eklundh, L. and Ardö, J. (2005) A recent greening of the Sahel – trends, patterns and potential causes. *Journal of Arid Environments*, 63, 556–566.

Olthof, I., Fraser, R.H. and Schmitt, C. (2015) Landsat-based mapping of thermokarst lake dynamics on the Tuktoyaktuk Coastal Plain, Northwest Territories, Canada since 1985. *Remote Sensing of Environment*, 168, 194–204.

Oltmans, S.J., Lefohn, A.S., Harris, J.M., et al. (2006) Long-term changes in tropospheric ozone. *Atmospheric Environment*, 40, 3156–3173.

O'Neal, M.R., Nearing, M.A., Vining, R.C., et al. (2005) Climate change impacts on soil erosion in Midwest United States with changes in crop management. *Catena*, 61, 165–184.

Oppenheimer, M. (1998) Global warming and the stability of the West Antarctic ice sheet. *Nature*, 393, 325–332.

Oppenheimer, S. (2003) *Out of Eden: The Peopling of the World*. London: Constable.

Orlando, L. (2016) Back to the roots and routes of dromedary domestication. *Proceedings of the National Academy of Sciences*, 113 (24), 6588–6590.

Orr, J.C., Fabry, V.J., Aumont, O., et al. (2005a) Anthropogenic ocean acidification over the twenty-first century and its impact on organisms. *Nature*, 437, 681–686.

Orr, J.C., Pantoja, S. and Pörtner, H.-O. (2005b) Introduction to special section: the ocean in a high-CO2 world. *Journal of Geophysical Research*, 110 (C), doi:10 1029/2005 JC 003086.

Orts, W.J., Roa-Espinosa, A., Sojka, R.E., et al. (2007) Use of synthetic polymers and biopolymers for soil stabilization in agricultural, construction and military applications. *Journal of Materials in Civil Engineering*, 19, 58–66.

Osterkamp, T.E., Jorgenson, M.T., Schuur, T., et al. (2009) Physical and ecological changes associated with warming permafrost and thermokarst in interior Alaska. *Permafrost and Periglacial Processes*, 20, 235–236.

Osterkamp, T.E. and Romanovsky, V.E. (1999) Evidence for warming and thawing of discontinuous permafrost in Alaska. *Permafrost and Periglacial Processes*, 10, 17–37.

O'Sullivan, P.E., Coard, M.A. and Pickering, D.A. (1982) The use of laminated lake sediments in the estimation and calibration of erosion rates. *Publication of the International Association of Hydrological Science*, 137, 385–396.

Otterman, J. (1974) Baring high albedo soils by overgrazing: a hypothesised desertification mechanism. *Science*, 186, 531–533.

Otu, M.K., Ramlal, P., Wilkinson, P., et al. (2011) Paleolimnological evidence for the effects of recent cultural eutrophication during the last 200 years in Lake Malawi, East Africa. *Journal of Great Lakes Research*, 37 (Suppl. 1), 61–74.

Outram, A.K., Stear, N.A., Bendrey, R., et al. (2009) The earliest horse harnessing and milking. *Science*, 323 (5919), 1332–1335.

Ovchinnikova, A., Krylova, E., Gavrilenko, T., et al. (2011) Taxonomy of cultivated potatoes (Solanum section Petota: Solanaceae). *Botanical Journal of the Linnean Society*, 165 (2), 107–155.

Overeem, I., Anderson, R.S., Wobus, C.W., et al. (2011) Sea ice loss enhances wave action at the Arctic coast. *Geophysical Research Letters*, 38, doi:10.1029/2011GL048681.

Overland, J.E., Wood, K.R. and Wang, M. (2011) Warm Arctic – cold continents: climate impacts of the newly open Arctic Sea. *Polar Research*, doi:10.3402/polar. v30i0.15787.

Overpeck, J.T., Rind, D. and Goldberg, R. (1990) Climate-induced changes in forest disturbance and vegetation. *Nature*, 343, 51–53.

Owen, L.A., Kamp, U., Khattak, G.A., et al. (2008) Landslides triggered by the 8 October 2005 Kashmir earthquake. *Geomorphology*, 94, 1–9.

Oxley, D.J., Fenton, M.B. and Carmody, G.R. (1974) The effects of roads on populations of small mammals. *Journal of Applied Ecology*, 11, 51–59.

Ozenda, P. and Borel, J.L. (1990) The possible responses of vegetation to a global climatic change. In M.M. Boer and R.S. de Groot (eds), *Landscape – Ecological Impact of Climatic Change*. Amsterdam: IOS Press, 221–249.

Özkan, H., Willcox, G., Graner, A., et al. (2011) Geographic distribution and domestication of wild emmer wheat (Triticum dicoccoides). *Genetic Resources and Crop Evolution*, 58, 11–53.

Pacifici, M., Foden, W.B., Visconti, P., et al. (2015) Assessing species vulnerability to climate change. *Nature Climate Change*, 5 (3), 215–224.

Pacifici, M., Visconti, P., Butchart, S.H.M., et al. (2017) Species' traits influenced their response to recent climate change. *Nature Climate Change*, doi:10.1038/ nclimate3223.

Padonou, E.A., Bachmann, Y., Kakaï, R.G., et al. (2015) Spatial distribution of bowal and differences in physicochemical characteristics between bowal and woodland soils in Benin, West Africa. *Catena*, 124, 45–52.

Page, M.J. and Trustrum, N.A. (1997) A late Holocene lake sediment record of the erosion response to land use change in a steepland catchment, New Zealand. *Zeitschrift für Geomorphologie*, 41, 369–392.

ASKHAM BRYAN
COLLEGE
LEARNING RESOURCES

Pakeman, R.J., Marrs, R.H., Howard, D.C., et al. (1996) The bracken problem in Great Britain: its present extent and future changes. *Applied Geography*, 16, 65–86.

Palmer, T.N. and Räisänen, J. (2002) Quantifying the risk of extreme seasonal precipitation events in a changing climate. *Nature*, 415, 512–514.

Palumbi, S.R., Barshis, D.J., Traylor-Knowles, N. and Bay, R.A. (2014) Mechanisms of reef coral resistance to future climate change. *Science*, 344, 895–898.

Pandolfi, J.M., Jackson, J.B.X.C., Baron, N., et al. (2005) Are US coral reefs on the slippery slope to slime? *Science*, 307, 1725–1726.

Panel on Weather and Climate Modification (1966) *Weather and Climate Modification Problems and Prospects*. Washington, DC: National Academy of Sciences.

Pang, J.-F., Kluetsch, C., Zou, X.J., et al. (2009) mtDNA data indicate a single origin for dogs south of Yangtze River, less than 16,300 years ago, from numerous wolves. *Molecular Biology and Evolution*, 26, 2849–2864.

Parfitt, S.A., Ashton, N.M., Lewis, S.G., et al. (2010) Early Pleistocene human occupance at the edge of the boreal zone in northwest Europe. *Nature*, 466, 229–233.

Parizek, B.R. and Alley, R.B. (2004) Implications of increased Greenland surface melt under global-warming scenarios: ice-sheet simulations. *Quaternary Science Reviews*, 23, 1013–1027.

Park, C.C. (1987) *Acid Rain: Rhetoric and Reality*. London: Methuen.

Park, J.H., Meusburger, K., Jang, I., Kang, H. and Alewell, C. (2014) Erosion-induced changes in soil biogeochemical and microbiological properties in Swiss Alpine grasslands. *Soil Biology and Biochemistry*, 69, 382–392.

Park, R.A., Armentano, T.V. and Cloonan, C.L. (1986) Predicting the effects of sea level rise on coastal wetlands. In J.G. Titus (ed.), *Effects of Changes in Stratospheric Ozone and Global Climate* (Vol. 4, *Sea Level Rise*). Washington, DC: UNEP/USEPA, 129–152.

Parker, A.G., Goudie, A.S., Anderson, D.E., et al. (2002) A review of the mid-Holocene elm decline in the British Isles. *Progress in Physical Geography*, 26, 1–45.

Parris, K.M. (2016) *Ecology of Urban Environments*. Chichester: Wiley Blackwell.

Parshall, T. and Foster, D.R. (2002) Fire on the New England landscape: regional and temporal variation, cultural and environmental controls. *Journal of Biogeography*, 29, 1305–1317.

Parson, E.A., Carter, L., Anderson, P., et al. (2001) Potential consequences of climate variability and change for Alaska. In National Assessment Synthesis Team (ed.), *Climate Change Impacts on the United States: The Potential Consequences of Climate Variability and Change*. Cambridge: Cambridge University Press, 283–312.

Parsons, A.J., Abrahams, A.D. and Wainwright, J. (1996) Responses of interrill runoff and erosion rates to vegetation change in southern Arizona. *Geomorphology*, 14, 311–317.

Pasternack, G.B., Brush, G.S. and Hilgartner, W.B. (2001) Impact of historic land-use change on sediment delivery to a Chesapeake Bay subestuarine delta. *Earth Surface Processes and Landforms*, 26, 409–427.

Paul, K.I., Poglase, P.J., Nyakuengama, J.G. and Khanna, P.K. (2002) Change in soil carbon following afforestation. *Forest Ecology and Management*, 168, 241–257.

Paulson, A.K., Sanders, S., Kirschbaum, J. and Waller, D.M. (2016) Post-settlement ecological changes in the forests of the Great Lakes National Parks. *Ecosphere*, 7 (10), doi:10.1002/ecs2.1490.

Pauly, D. and Zeller, D. (2016) Catch reconstructions reveal that global marine fisheries catches are higher than reported and declining. *Nature Communications*, 7, doi:10.1038/ncomms10244.

Pautasso, M., Döring, T.F., Garbelotto, M., et al. (2013) Impact of climate change on plant diseases – opinions and trends. *European Journal of Plant Pathology*, 133, 295–313.

Pearson, A.J., Snyder, N.P. and Collins, M.J. (2011) Rates and processes of channel response to dam removal with a sand-filled impoundment. *Water Resources Research*, 47, W08504.

Pearson, R.G. and Dawson, T.P. (2003) Predicting the impacts of climate change on the distribution of species: are biocli mate envelope models useful? *Global Ecology and Biogeography*, 12, 361–371.

Pechony, O. and Shindell, D.T. (2010) Driving forces of global wildfires over the past millennium and the forthcoming century. *Proceedings of the National Academy of Sciences*, 107, 19167–19170.

Peck, A.J. (1983) Response of groundwaters to clearing in Western Australia. In *Papers of the International Conference on Groundwater and Man, Sydney*. Canberra: Australian Government Publishing Service, 2: 327–335.

Peck, A.J. and Halton, T. (2003) Salinity and the discharge of salts from catchments in Australia. *Journal of Hydrology*, 272, 191–202.

Pederson, G.T., Gray, S.T., Woodhouse, C.A., et al. (2011) The unusual nature of recent snowpack declines in the North American cordillera. *Science*, 333, 332–335.

Peet, R.K., Glenn-Lewin, D.C. and Wolf, J.W. (1983) Prediction of man's impact on plant species diversity. In W. Holzner, M.J.A. Werger and I. Ikusima (eds), *Man's Impact on Vegetation*. The Hague: Junk, 41–54.

Peglar, S.M. and Birks, H.J.B. (1993) The mid-Holocene Ulmus fall at Diss Mere, Norfolk, south-east England – disease and human impact? *Vegetation History and Archaeology*, 2, 61–68.

Peierls, B.L., Caraco, N.F., Pace, M.L. and Cole, J.J. (1991) Human influence on river nitrogen. *Nature*, 350, 386–387.

Pejchar, L. and Mooney, H.A. (2009) Invasive species, ecosystem services and human well-being. *Trends in Ecology & Evolution*, 24 (9), 497–504.

Pelejero, C., Calvo, E. and Hoegh-Guldberg, O. (2010) Paleoperspectives on ocean acidification. *Trends in Ecology & Evolution*, 25, 332–344.

Pelletier, J.D., Brad Murray, A., Pierce, J.L., et al. (2015) Forecasting the response of Earth's surface to future climatic and land use changes: a review of methods and research needs. *Earth's Future*, 3 (7), 220–251.

Pendleton, L.H., Hoegh-Guldberg, O., Langdon, C. and Comte, A. (2016) Multiple stressors and ecological complexity require a new approach to coral reef research. *Frontiers in Marine Science*, 3, article 36.

Peng, S., Piao, S., Ciais, P., et al. (2012) Surface urban heat island across 419 global big cities. *Environmental Science & Technology*, 46, 696–703.

Peng, H., Ma, W., Mu, Y.H., Jin, L. and Yuan, K. (2015) Degradation characteristics of permafrost under the effect of climate warming and engineering disturbance along the Qinghai–Tibet Highway. *Natural Hazards*, 75 (3), 2589–2605.

Pennington, W. (1981) Records of a lake's life in time: the sediments. *Hydrobiologia*, 79, 197–219.

Pereira, H.C. (1973) *Land Use and Water Resources in Temperate and Tropical Climates*. Cambridge: Cambridge University Press.

Perkol-Finkel, S., Shashar, N. and Benayahu, Y. (2006) Can artificial reefs mimic natural reef communities? The roles of structural features and age. *Marine Environmental Research*, 61, 121–135.

Perrins, C.M. and Overall, R. (2001) Effect of increasing numbers of deer on bird populations in Wytham Woods, central England. *Forestry*, 74 (3), 299–309.

Perry, C.T., Murphy, N., Kench, P.S., et al. (2013) Caribbean-wide decline in carbonate production threatens coral reef growth. *Nature Communications*, 4, 1402.

Peters, J.H. (ed.) (1998) *Artificial Recharge of Groundwater*. Amsterdam: Swetzs and Zeitlinger.

Peters, R.L. (1988) The effect of global climatic change on natural communities. In E.O. Wilson (ed.), *Biodiversity*. Washington, DC: National Academy Press, 450–461.

Peterson, B.J., Homes, R.M., McClelland, J.W., et al. (2002) Increasing river discharge to the Arctic Ocean. *Science*, 298, 2171–2173.

Peterson, C.J. (2000) Catastrophic wind damage to North American forests and the potential impact of climate change. *Science of the Total Environment*, 262, 287–311.

Pethick, J. (1993) Shoreline adjustments and coastal management: physical and biological processes under accelerated sea level rise. *Geographical Journal*, 159, 162–168.

Pethick, J. (2001) Coastal management and sea level rise. *Catena*, 42, 307–322.

Petit-Maire, N., Burollet, P.F., Ballais, J.-L., et al. (1999) Paléoclimats Holocènes du Sahara septentionale. Dépôts lacustres et terrasses alluviales en bordure du Grand Erg Oriental à l'extrême – Sud de la Tunisie. *Comptes Rendus Académie des Sciences*, Series 2, 312, 1661–1666.

Petley, D.N., Hearn, G.J., Hart, A., et al. (2007) Trends in landslide occurrence in Nepal. *Natural Hazards*, 43, 23–44.

Petts, G.E. (1979) Complex response of river channel morphology subsequent to reservoir construction. *Progress in Physical Geography*, 3, 329–362.

Petts, G.E. (1985) *Impounded Rivers: Perspectives for Ecological Management*. Chichester: Wiley.

Petts, G.E. and Lewin, J. (1979) Physical effects of reservoirs on river systems. In G.E. Hollis (ed.), *Man's Impact on the Hydrological Cycle in the United Kingdom*. Norwich: Geo-books, 79–91.

Pezza, A.B. and Simmonds, I. (2005) The first South Atlantic hurricane: unprecedented blocking, low shear and climate change. *Geophysical Research Letters*, 32, L15712.

Pfisterer, A.B. and Schmid, B. (2002) Diversity-dependent production can decrease the stability of ecosystem functioning. *Nature*, 416, 84–86.

Phan, L.K., van Thiel de Vries, J.S.M. and Stive, M.J.F. (2015) Coastal mangrove squeeze in the Mekong Delta. *Journal of Coastal Research*, 31, 233–243.

Phelan, P.E., Kaloush, K., Miner, M., et al. (2015) Urban heat island: mechanisms, implications, and possible remedies. *Annual Review of Environment and Resources*, 40, 285–307.

Phien-Wej, N., Giao, P.H. and Nutalaya, P. (2006) Land subsidence in Bangkok, Thailand. *Engineering Geology*, 82, 187–201.

Phillips, B.L., Brown, G.P., Greenlees, M., Webb, J.K. and Shine, R. (2007) Rapid expansion of the cane toad (Bufo marinus) invasion front in tropical Australia. *Austral Ecology*, 32 (2), 169–176.

Pickering, C.M. and Hill, W. (2007) Impacts of recreation and tourism on plant biodiversity and vegetation in protected areas of Australia. *Journal of Environmental Management*, 85, 791–800.

Pickersgill, B. (2007) Domestication of plants in the Americas: insights from Mendelian and molecular genetics. *Annals of Botany*, 100, 925–940.

Pierson, F.B., Carlson, D.H. and Spaeth, K.E. (2002) Impacts of wildfire on soil hydrological properties of steep sage-brush-steepe rangeland. *International Journal of Wildland Fire*, 11, 145–151.

Pierson, F.B., Williams, C.J., Hardegree, S.P., et al. (2011) Fire, plant invasions, and erosion events on Western Rangelands. *Rangeland Ecology and Management*, 64, 439–449.

Pimentel, D. (1976) Land degradation: effects on food and energy resources. *Science*, 194, 149–155.

Pimentel, D. (2003) *Biological Invasions*. Washington, DC: CRC Press.

Pimentel, D., Harvey, C., Resosuddarmo, P., et al. (1995) Environmental and economic costs of soil erosion and conservation benefits. *Science*, 267, 1117–1122.

Pimm, S.L., Jenkins, C.N., Abell, R., et al. (2014) The biodiversity of species and their rates of extinction, distribution, and protection. *Science*, 344 (6187), doi:10.1126/science.1246752.

Pinker, R.T., Zhang, B. and Dutton, E.G. (2005) Do satellites detect trends is surface solar radiation? *Science*, 308, 850–854.

Piotto, D., Montagnini, F., Thomas, W., et al. (2009) Forest recovery after swidden cultivation across a 40-year chronosequence in the Atlantic forest of southern Bahia, Brazil. *Plant Ecology*, 205, 261–272.

Piperno, D.R., McMichael, C. and Bush, M.B. (2015) Amazonia and the Anthropocene: what was the spatial extent and intensity of human landscape modification in the Amazon Basin at the end of prehistory? *The Holocene*, 25, 1588–1597.

Pirazzoli, P.A. (1996) *Sea Level Changes: The Last 20,000 Years*. Chichester: Wiley.

Pittock, A.B. and Wratt, D. (2001) Australia and New Zealand. In J.J. McCarthy, O.F. Canziani, N.A. Leary, et al. (eds), *Climate Change 2001: Impacts, Adaptation and Vulnerability*. Cambridge: Cambridge University Press, 591–639.

Pluhowski, E.J. (1970) *Urbanization and its effects on the temperature of the streams on Long Island, New York*. United States Geological Survey professional paper, 627–D.

Poeppl, R.E., Keesstra, S.D. and Maroulis, J. (2017) A conceptual connectivity framework for understanding geomorphic change in human-impacted fluvial systems. *Geomorphology*, 277, 237–250.

Poesen, J.W., Nachtergaele, J., Verstraeten, G. and Valentin, C. (2003) Gully erosion and environmental change: importance and research needs. *Catena*, 50, 91–133.

Poesen, J.W., Torri, D. and Bunte, K. (1994) Effects of rock fragments on soil erosion by water and different spatial scales: a review. *Catena*, 23, 141–166.

Pohlner, H. (2016) Institutional change and the political economy of water megaprojects: China's south–north water transfer. *Global Environmental Change*, 38, 205–216.

Poirier, C., Chaumillon, E. and Arnaud, F. (2011) Siltation of river-influenced coastal environments: respective impact of late Holocene land use and high-frequency climate changes. *Marine Geology*, 290, 51–62.

Pokhrel, Y.N., Hanasaki, N., Yeh, P.J.-F., et al. (2012) Model estimates of sea-level change due to anthropogenic impacts on terrestrial water storage. *Nature Geoscience*, 5, 389–392.

Polidoro, B.A., Carpenter, K.E., Collins, L., et al. (2010) The loss of species: mangrove extinction risk and geographic areas of global concern. *PLoS ONE*, 5, e10095.

Pollack, I.B., Ryerson, T.B., Trainer, M., Neuman, J.A., Roberts, J.M. and Parrish, D.D. (2013) Trends in ozone, its precursors, and related secondary oxidation products in Los Angeles, California: a synthesis of measurements from 1960 to 2010. *Journal of Geophysical Research: Atmospheres*, 118 (11), 5893–5911.

Poloczanska, E.S., Limpus, C.J. and Hays, G.C. (2010) Vulnerability of marine turtles to climate change. *Advances in Marine Biology*, 56, 151–211.

Polvani, L.M., Waugh, D.W., Correa, G.J.P. and Son, S.-W. (2011) Stratospheric ozone depletion: the main driver of twentieth-century atmospheric circulation changes in the Southern Hemisphere. *Journal of Climate*, 24, 795–812.

Ponting, C. (1991) *A Green History of the World*. London: Penguin.

Ponting, C. (2007) *A New Green History of the World*. London: Penguin.

Poole, G.C. and Berman, C.H. (2001) An ecological prespective on in-stream temperature: natural heat dynamics and mechanisms of human-caused thermal degradation. *Environmental Management*, 27, 787–802.

Poore, M.E.D. (1976) The values of tropical moist forest ecosystems. *Unasylva*, 28, 127–143.

Por, F.D. (2012) *Lessepsian Migration: The Influx of Red Sea Biota into the Mediterranean by Way of the Suez Canal*. Heidelberg: Springer Science & Business Media.

Portenga, E.W., Westaway, K.E. and Bishop, P. (2016) Timing of post-European settlement alluvium deposition in SE Australia: a legacy of European land-use in the Goulburn Plains. *The Holocene*, 26, 1472–1485.

Post, W.M. and Kwon, K.C. (2000) Soil carbon sequestration and land-use change: processes and potential. *Global Change Biology*, 6, 317–327.

Potter, D.A. and Held, D.W. (2002) Biology and management of the Japanese beetle. *Annual Review of Entomology*, 47 (1), 175–205.

Potter, G.L., Ellsaesser, H.W., MacCracken, M.C. and Luther, F.M. (1975) Possible climatic impact of tropical deforestation. *Nature*, 258, 697–698.

Potter, G.L., Ellsaesser, H.W., MacCracken, M.C. and Ellis, J.C. (1981) Albedo change by man: test of climatic effects. *Nature*, 291, 47–49.

Powell, M. (1985) Salt, seed and yields in Sumerian agriculture: a critique of progressive salinization.

Zeitschrift für Assyrologie and Vorderasiatische Archaologie, 75, 7–38.

Powers, S.M., Bruulsema, T.W., Burt, T.P., et al. (2016) Long-term accumulation and transport of anthropogenic phosphorus in three river basins. *Nature Geoscience*, 9 (5), 353–356.

Powlesland, R.G. (2009) Impacts of wind farms on birds: a review. *Science for Conservation*, 289, 1–51.

Prats, J., Val, R., Armengol, J. and Dolz, J. (2010) Temporal variability in the thermal regime of the lower Ebro River (Spain) and alteration due to anthropogenic factors. *Journal of Hydrology*, 387, 105–118.

Price, M. and Reed, D.W. (1989) The influence of mains leakage and urban drainage on groundwater levels beneath conurbations in the United Kingdom. *Proceedings of the Institution of Civil Engineers*, 86, 31–39.

Price, M.F. (1989) Global change: defining the ill-defined. *Environment*, 31 (8), 18–20, 42–44.

Price, S.J., Ford, J.R., Cooper, A.H. and Neal, C. (2011) Humans as major geological and geomorphological agents in the Anthropocene: the significance of artificial ground in Great Britain. *Philosophical Transactions: Series A, Mathematical, Physical, and Engineering Sciences*, 369, 1056–1084.

Prince, H.C. (1959) Parkland in the Chilterns. *Geographical Review*, 49, 18–31.

Prince, H.C. (1962) Pits and ponds in Norfolk. *Erdkunde*, 16, 10–31.

Prince, H.C. (1964) The origin of pits and depressions in Norfolk. *Geography*, 49, 15–32.

Prince, H.C. (1979) Marl pits or dolines of the Dorset Chalk-lands? *Transactions of the Institute of British Geographers*, 4, 116–117.

Pritchard, H.D. and Vaughan, D.G. (2007) Widespread acceleration of tidewater glaciers on the Antarctic Peninsula. *Journal of Geophysical Research*, 112, F03S29.

Proffitt, M.H., Margitan, J.J., Kelly, K.K., et al. (1990) Ozone loss in the Arctic polar vortex inferred from high-altitude aircraft measurements. *Nature*, 347, 31–33.

Proffitt, T., Luncz, L.V., Falotico, T., et al. (2016) Wild monkeys flake stone tools. *Nature*, 539, 85–88.

Prokopovich, N.P. (1972) Land subsidence and population growth. *24th International Geological Congress Proceedings*, 13, 44–54.

Provoost, S., Jones, M.L.M. and Edmondson, S.E. (2011) Changes in landscape and vegetation of coastal dunes in northwest Europe: a review. *Journal of Coastal Conservation*, 15, 207–226.

Prowse, T.D. and Beltaos, S. (2002) Climatic control of riverice hydrology: a review. *Hydrological Processes*, 16, 805–822.

Prudhomme, C., Young, A., Watts, G., et al. (2012) The drying up of Britain? A national estimate of changes in seasonal river flows from 11 Regional Climatic Model simulations. *Hydrological Processes*, 26, 1115–1118.

Puddu, G., Falucci, A. and Maiorano, L. (2012) Forest changes over a century in Sardinia: implications for conservation in a Mediterranean hotspot. *Agroforestry Systems*, 85, 319–330.

Purdie, H., Anderson, B., Chinn, T., et al. (2014) Franz Josef and Fox Glaciers, New Zealand: historic length records. *Global and Planetary Change*, 121, 41–52.

Purich, A. and Son, S.-W. (2012) Impact of Antarctic ozone depletion and recovery on Southern Hemisphere precipitation, evaporation, and extreme changes. *Journal of Climate*, 25, 3145–3154.

Pushkina, D. and Raia, P. (2008) Human influence on distribution and extinctions of the late Pleistocene Eurasian megafauna. *Journal of Human Evolution*, 54, 769–782.

Pye, K. and Blott, S.J. (2014) The geomorphology of UK estuaries: the role of geological controls, antecedent conditions and human activities. *Estuarine, Coastal and Shelf Science*, 150B, 196–214.

Pyne, S.J. (1982) *Fire in America – A Cultural History of Wildland and Rural Fire.* Princeton: Princeton University Press.

Qadir, M., Ghafoor, A. and Murtaza, G. (2000) Amelioration strategies for saline soils: a review. *Land Degradation and Development*, 11, 501–521.

Qadir, M., Noble, A.D., Kureshi, A.S., et al. (2009) Salt-induced land and water degradation in the Ara Sea basin: a challenge to sustainable agriculture in Central Asia. *Natural Resources Forum*, 33, 134–149.

Qiao, X., Du, J., Lugli, S., Ren, J., et al. (2016) Are climate warming and enhanced atmospheric deposition of sulfur and nitrogen threatening tufa landscapes in Jiuzhaigou National Nature Reserve, Sichuan, China? *Science of the Total Environment*, 562, 724–731.

Qiu, J. (2012) Evidence mounts for dam-quake link. *Science*, 336, 291.

Qiu, X. and Fenton, C. (2015) Factors controlling the occurrence of reservoir-induced seismicity. *Engineering Geology for Society and Territory*, 6, 567–570.

Quataert, E., Storlazzi, C., Rooijen, A., et al. (2015) The influence of coral reefs and climate change on wave-driven flooding of tropical coastlines. *Geophysical Research Letters*, 42 (15), 6407–6415.

Quinton, J.N., Edwards, G.M. and Morgan, R.P.C. (1997) The influence of vegetation species and plant properties on runoff and soil erosion: results from a rainfall simulation study in south east Spain. *Soil Use and Management*, 13, 143–148.

Qureshi, M.A., Yi, C., Xu, X. and Li, Y. (2017) Glacier status during the period 1973–2014 in the Hunza Basin,

Western Karakoram. *Quaternary International*, 444 (A), 125–136.

Raabe, E.A. and Stumpf, R.P. (2015) Expansion of tidal marsh in response to sea-level rise: Gulf Coast of Florida, USA. *Estuaries and Coasts*, 39, 145–157.

Rackham, O. (1980) *Ancient Woodland*. London: Arnold.

Rackham, O. and Moody, J. (1996) *The Making of the Cretan Landscape*. Manchester: Manchester University Press.

Radić, V., Bliss, A., Beedlow, A.C., et al. (2014) Regional and global projections of twenty-first century glacier mass changes in response to climate scenarios from global climate models. *Climate Dynamics*, 42, 37–58.

Radić, V. and Hock, R. (2011) Regionally differentiated contribution of mountain glaciers and ice caps to future sea-level rise. *Nature Geoscience*, 4, 91–94.

Radivojević, M., Rehren, T., Pernicka, E., et al. (2010) On the origins of extractive metallurgy: new evidence from Europe. *Journal of Archaeological Science*, 37, 2775–2787.

Radley, J. (1962) Peat erosion on the high moors of Derbyshire and west Yorkshire. *East Midland Geographer*, 3, 40–50.

Rahi, K.A. and Halihan, T. (2010) Changes in the salinity of the Euphrates River system in Iraq. *Regional Environmental Change*, 10 (1), 27–35.

Rahm, D. (2011) Regulating hydraulic fracturing in shale gas plays: the case of Texas. *Energy Policy*, 39, 2974–2981.

Rahmstorf, S. (2007) A semi-empirical approach to projecting future sea-level rise. *Science*, 315, 368–370.

Raison, R.J. (1979) Modification of the soil environment by vegetation fires with particular reference to nitrogen transformation: a review. *Plant and Soil*, 51, 73–108.

Raji, B.A., Utovbisere, E.O. and Momodu, A.B. (2004) Impact of sand dune stabilization structures on soil and yield of millet in the semi-ard region of NW Nigeria. *Environmental Monitoring and Assessment*, 99, 181–196.

Ramamurthy, P. and Sangobanwo, M. (2016) Inter-annual variability in urban heat island intensity over 10 major cities in the United States. *Sustainable Cities and Society*, 26, 65–75.

Ramanathan, V. and Carmichael, G. (2008) Global and regional climate changes due to black carbon. *Nature Geoscience*, 1, 221–227.

Ramankutty, N. and Foley, A. (1999) Estimating historical changes in global land cover: croplands from 1700 to 1992. *Global Biogeochemical Cycles*, 13, 997–1027.

Ramankutty, N., Heller, E. and Rhemtulla, J. (2010) Prevailing myths about agricultural abandonment and forest regrowth in the United States. *Annals of the Association of American Geographers*, 100, 502–512.

Ramirez, E., Francou, B., Ribstein, P., et al. (2001) Small glaciers disappearing in the tropical Andes: a case study of Bolivia: Glacier Chacaltya (16°S). *Journal of Glaciology*, 47, 187–194.

Ramirez-Llodra, E., Tyler, P.A., Baker, M.C., et al. (2011) Man and the Last Great Wilderness: human impact on the deep sea. *PLoS ONE*, 6 (8), e22588.

Ran, L., Lu, X.X., Xin, Z. and Yang, X. (2013) Cumulative sediment trapping by reservoirs in large river basins: a case study of the Yellow River basin. *Global and Planetary Change*, 100, 308–319.

Ranta, P. (2001) Changes in urban lichen diversity after a fall in sulphur dioxide levels in the city of Tampere, SW Finland. *Annales Botanici Fennici*, 38, 295–304.

Ranwell, D.S. (1964) *Spartina* salt marshes in southern England, II: rate and seasonal pattern of sediment accretion. *The Journal of Ecology*, 52, 79–94.

Ranwell, D.S. and Boar, R. (1986) *Coast Dune Management Guide*. Monks Wood: Institute of Terrestrial Ecology.

Rao, K.N., Subraelu, P., Naga Kumar, K.C.V., et al. (2010) Impacts of sediment retention by dams on delta shoreline recession: evidences from the Krishna and Godavari deltas, India. *Earth Surface Processes and Landforms*, 35, 817–827.

Rapp, A. (1974) *A review of desertization in Africa – water, vegetation and man*. Secretariat for International Ecology, Stockholm, report no. 1.

Rapp, A., Le Houérou, H.N. and Lundholm, B. (1976) *Can desert encroachment be stopped? Ecological Bulletins*, 24. Stockholm: Swedish Natural Science Research Council.

Rapp, A., Murray-Rust, D.H., Christansson, C. and Berry, L. (1972) Soil erosion and sedimentation in four catchments near Dodoma, Tanzania. *Geografiska Annaler*, 54A, 255–318.

Raptis, C.E., van Vliet, M.T. and Pfister, S. (2016) Global thermal pollution of rivers from thermoelectric power plants. *Environmental Research Letters*, 11 (10), doi:10.1088/1748-9326/11/10/104011.

Rasid, H. (1979) The effects of regime regulation by the Gardiner Dam on downstream geomorphic processes in the South Saskatchewan River. *The Canadian Geographer*, 23, 140–158.

Rasmussen, K., Fog, B. and Masden, J.E. (2001) Desertification in reverse? Observations from northern Burkina Faso. *Global Environmental Change*, 11, 271–282.

Ratcliffe, D.A. (1974) Ecological effects of mineral exploitation in the United Kingdom and their significance to nature conservation. *Proceedings of the Royal Society of London*, 339A, 355–372.

Ratnam, J., Tomlinson, K.W., Rasquinha, D.N. and Sankaran, M. (2016) Savannahs of Asia: antiquity, biogeography, and an uncertain future. *Philosophical*

Transactions of the Royal Society B, 371 (1703), 20150305.

Ravanel, L. and Deline, P. (2011) Climate influence on rockfalls in high-Alpine steep rockwalls: the north side of the Aiguilles de Chamonix (Mont Blanc massif) since the end of the 'Little Ice Age'. *The Holocene*, 21, 357–65.

Ravi, S., D'Odorico, P., Breshears, D.D., et al. (2011) Aeolian processes and the biosphere. *Review of Geophysics*, 49, RG3001, doi:10.1029/2010RG000328.

Ravi, S., D'Odorico, P., Wang, J., et al. (2009) Post-fire resource redistribution in desert grasslands: a possible negative feedback on land degradation. *Ecosystems*, 12, 434–444.

Ray, C., Hayden, B.P., Bulger, A.J. and McCormick-Ray, G. (1992) Effects of global warming on the biodiversity of coastal-marine zones. In R.L. Peters and T.E. Lovejoy (eds), *Global Warming and Biological Diversity*. New Haven: Yale University Press, 91–102.

Raymond, P.A. and Oh, N.H. (2009) Long term changes of chemical weathering products in rivers heavily impacted from acid mine drainage: insights on the impact of coal mining on regional and global carbon and sulfur budgets. *Earth and Planetary Science Letters*, 284, 50–56.

Reale, O. and Dirmeyer, P. (2000) Modeling the effects of vegetation on Mediterranean climate during the Roman Classical Period: Part I: climate history and model sensitivity. *Global and Planetary Change*, 25 (3), 163–184.

Reclus, E. (1871) *The Earth* (2 vols). London: Chapman and Hall.

Reclus, E. (1873) *The Ocean, Atmosphere and Life*. New York: Harper and Brothers.

Redfern, T., Macdonald, N., Kjeldsen, T., et al. (2016) Current understanding of hydrological processes on common urban surfaces. *Progress in Physical Geography*, 40, 699–713.

Reed, A.J., Mann, M.E., Emanuel, K.A., et al. (2015) Increased threat of tropical cyclones and coastal flooding to New York City during the anthropogenic era. *Proceedings of the National Academy of Sciences*, 112, 12610–12615.

Reed, C.A. (1970) Extinction of mammalian megafauna in the old world late Quaternary. *Bioscience*, 20, 284–288.

Reed, D.J. (1990) The impact of sea level rise on coastal salt marshes. *Progress in Physical Geography*, 14, 465–481.

Reed, D.J. (1995) The response of coastal marshes to sea level rise: survival or submergence? *Earth Surface Processes and Landforms*, 20, 39–48.

Reed, D.J. (2002) Sea-level rise and coastal marsh sustainability: geological and ecological factors in the Mississippi delta plain. *Geomorphology*, 48, 233–243.

Reed, L.A. (1980) *Suspended-sediment discharge in five streams near Harrisburg, Pennsylvania, before, during and after highway construction*. United States Geological Survey Water Supply Paper, 2072.

Rees, H.G. and Collins, D.N. (2006) Regional differences in response of flow in glacier-fed Himalayan rivers to climatic warming. *Hydrological Processes*, 20, 2157–2169.

Rees, W.G. (2012) Automated spaceborne detection of degraded vegetation around Monchegorsk, Kola Peninsula, Russia. *Polar Record*, 48 (1), 107–112.

Reeve, D., Chadwick, A. and Fleming, C. (2012) *Coastal Engineering* (2nd edn). London: Spon Press.

Regalado, A. (2010) Brazil says rate of deforestation in Amazon continues to plunge. *Science*, 329, 1270–1271.

Reheis, M.C. (1997) Dust deposition downwind of Owens (dry) Lake, 1991–1994: preliminary findings. *Journal of Geophysical Research*, 102, 25998–26008.

Reichert, B.K., Bengston, L. and Oerlemans, J. (2001) Midlatitude forcing mechanism for glacier mass balance investigated using general circulation models. *Journal of Climate*, 14, 3767–3784.

Reid, D. and Church, M. (2015) Geomorphic and ecological consequences of riprap placement in river systems. *JAWRA Journal of the American Water Resources Association*, 51 (4), 1043–1059.

Reij, C., Scoones, I. and Toulmin, C. (eds) (1996) *Sustaining the Soil: Indigenous Soil and Water Conservation in Africa*. London: Earthscan.

Remini, B., Achour, B. and Albergel, J. (2011) Timimoun's foggara (Algeria): An heritage in danger. *Arabian Journal of Geosciences*, 4, 495–506.

Remondi, F., Burlando, P. and Vollmer, D. (2016) Exploring the hydrological impact of increasing urbanisation on a tropical river catchment of the metropolitan Jakarta, Indonesia. *Sustainable Cities and Society*, 20, 210–221.

Remondo, J., Soto, J., González-Díez, A., et al. (2005) Human impact on geomorphic processes and hazards in mountain areas in northern Spain. *Geomorphology*, 66, 69–84.

Renberg, I. and Hellberg, T. (1982) The pH history of lakes in SW Sweden, as calculated from the subfossil diatom flora of the sediments. *Ambio*, 11, 30–33.

Renfrew, C. (2006) Inception of agriculture and rearing in the Middle East. *Comptes Rendus Palevol*, 5, 395–404.

Restrepo, J.D. and Escobar, H.A. (2016) Sediment load trends in the Magdalena River basin (1980–2010): Anthropogenic and climate-induced causes. *Geomorphology*, 10.1016/j.geomorph.2016.12.013. In press.

Revell, D.L., Battalio, R., Spear, B., et al. (2011) A methodology for predicting future coastal hazards due to sea-level rise on the California Coast. *Climatic Change*, 109 (Suppl.), S251–S276.

Revelle, R.R. and Waggoner, P.E. (1983) Effect of a carbon dioxide-induced climatic change on water supplies in the western United States. In Carbon Dioxide Assessment Committee (ed.), *Changing Climate*. Washington, DC: National Academy Press, 419–432.

Rhemtulla, J.M., Mladenoff, D.J. and Clayton, M.K. (2009) Legacies of historical land use on regional forest composition and structure in Wisconsin, USA (mid-1800s–1930s–2000s). *Ecological Applications*, 19, 1061–1078.

Rhoades, J.D. (1990) Soil salinity – causes and controls. In A.S. Goudie (ed.), *Techniques for Desert Reclamation*. Chichester: Wiley, 109–134.

Rhodes, S.E., Walker, M.J., López-Jiménez, A., et al. (2016) Fire in the Early Palaeolithic: evidence from burnt small mammal bones at Cueva Negra del Estrecho del Río Quípar, Murcia, Spain. *Journal of Archaeological Science: Reports*, 9, 427–436.

Rice, J., Rosenberg, A. and Simcock, A. (2016) *Overall Assessment of Human Impact on the Oceans*. New York: United Nations.

Richards, J.F. (1991) Land transformation. In B.L. Turner, W.C. Clark, R.W. Kates, et al. (eds), *The Earth as Transformed by Human Action*. Cambridge: Cambridge University Press, 163–178.

Richardson, J.A. (1976) Pit heap into pasture. In J. Lenihan and W.W. Fletcher (eds), *Reclamation*. Glasgow: Blackie, 60–93.

Richardson, K., Steffen, W. and Liverman, D. (eds) (2011) *Climate Change: Global Risks, Challenges and Decisions*. Cambridge: Cambridge University Press.

Richter, A., Burrows, J.P., Nüss, H., et al. (2005) Increase in tropospheric nitrogen dioxide over China observed from space. *Nature*, 437, 129–132.

Richter, D. (2007) Humanity's transformation of Earth's soil: pedology's new frontier. *Soil Science*, 172, 957–967.

Richter, D.D. and Babbar, L.I. (1991) Soil diversity in the tropics. *Advances in Ecological Research*, 21, 315–389.

Richter D., Grün, R., Joannes-Boyau, R., et al. (2017) The age of the hominin fossils from Jebel Irhoud, Morocco, and the origins of the Middle Stone Age. *Nature*, 546, 293–296.

Rickson, R.J. (2006) Controlling sediment at source: an evaluation of erosion control geotextiles. *Earth Surface Processes and Landforms*, 31, 550–560.

Riddle, B.R., Ladle, R.J., Lourie, S.A. and Whittaker, R.J. (2011) Basic biogeography: estimating biodiversity and mapping nature. In R.J. Ladle and R.J. Whittaker (eds), *Conservation Biogeography*. Chichester: Wiley Blackwell, 47–92.

Ridgwell, A.J. (2002) Dust in the Earth system: the biogeochemical linking of land, sea and air. *Philosophical Transactions: Series A, Mathematical, Physical, and Engineering Sciences*, 360, 2905–2924.

Ridgwell, A.J. (2003) Implications of the glacial CO_2 'iron hypothesis' for Quaternary climate change.

Geochemistry, Geophysics, Geosystems, 4, doi:10.1029/2003GC000563.

Ries, J.B., Andres, K., Wirtz, S., et al. (2014) Sheep and goat erosion–experimental geomorphology as an approach for the quantification of underestimated processes. *Zeitschrift für Geomorphologie*, Supplement, 58, 23–45.

Rignot, E. and Kanagaratnam, P. (2006) Changes in the velocity structure of the Greenland Ice Sheet. *Science*, 311, 986–990.

Rignot, E. and Thomas, R.H. (2002) Mass balance of polar ice sheets. *Science*, 297, 1502–1506.

Rignot, E., Velicogna, I., van der Broejke, M.R., et al. (2011) Acceleration of the contribution of the Greenland and Antarctica ice sheets to sea level rise. *Geophysical Research Letters*, 38, L05503.

Rijnsdorp, A.D., Peck, M.A., Engelhard, G.H., et al. (2009) Resolving the effect of climate change on fish populations. *ICES Journal of Marine Science*, 66, 1570–1583.

Rinaldi, M., Wyzga, B. and Surian, N. (2005) Sediment mining in alluvial channels: physical effects and management perspectives. *River Research and Applications*, 21, 805–828.

Rinderer, T.E., Oldroyd, R.P. and Sheppard, W.S. (1993) Africanized bees in the US. *Scientific American*, 269 (6), 52–58.

Ripley, E.A. (1976) Drought in the Sahara: insufficient geophysical feedback? *Science*, 191, 100–102.

Ripple, W.J., Newsome, T.M., Wolf, C., et al. (2015) Collapse of the world's largest herbivores. *Science Advances*, 1 (4), doi:10.1126/sciadv.1400103.

Ripple, W.J., Abernethy, K., Betts, M.G., et al. (2016) Bushmeat hunting and extinction risk to the world's mammals. *Royal Society Open Science*, doi:10.1098/rsos.160498.

Robb, G.A. and Robinson, J.D.F. (1995) Acid drainage from mines. *Geographical Journal*, 161, 47–54.

Roberts, B.W., Thornton, C.P. and Pigott, V.C. (2009) Development of metallurgy in Eurasia. *Antiquity*, 83, 1012–1022.

Roberts, N. (1998) *The Holocene: An Environmental History* (2nd edn). Oxford: Basil Blackwell.

Roberts, N. (2014) *The Holocene: An Environmental History* (3rd edn). Chichester: Wiley Blackwell.

Roberts, N. and Barker, P. (1993) Landscape stability and biogeomorphic response to past and future climatic shifts in intertropical Africa. In D.S.G. Thomas and R.J. Allison (eds), *Landscape Sensitivity*. Chichester: Wiley, 65–82.

Roberts, R.G., Flannery, T.F., Ayliffe, L.K., et al. (2001) New ages for the least Australian megafauna: continent-wide extinction about 46,000 years ago. *Science*, 292, 1888–1892.

Robinson, M. (1979) *The effects of pre-afforestation ditching upon the water and sediment yields of a small upland catchment.* Working Paper 252. Leeds: School of Geography, University of Leeds.

Robinson, M. (1990) *Impact of improved land drainage on river flows.* Wallingford: Institute of Hydrology, Report 113.

Robinson, M.A. and Lambrick, G.H. (1984) Holocene alluviation and hydrology in the Upper Thames Basin. *Nature*, 308, 809–814.

Rochman, C.M., Kross, S.M., Armstrong, J.B., et al. (2015) Scientific evidence supports a ban on microbeads. *Environmental Science & Technology*, 49 (18), 10759–10761.

Rockström, J., Steffen, W., Noone, K., et al. (2009) Planetary boundaries: exploring the safe operating space for humanity. *Ecology and Society*, 14, http://www.ecologyandsociety.org/vol14/iss2/art32/ (accessed January 2018).

Rodda, J.C., Downing, R.A. and Law, F.M. (1976) *Systematic Hydrology.* London: Newnes-Butterworth.

Rodell, M., Velicogna, I. and Famiglietti, J.S. (2009) Satellite-based estimates of groundwater depletion in India. *Nature*, 460, 999–1001.

Rodway-Dyer, S.J. and Walling, D.E. (2010) The use of ^{137}Cs to establish longer-term soil erosion rates on footpaths in the UK. *Journal of Environmental Management*, 91, 1952–1962.

Rogers, R.D. and Schumm, S. (1991) The effect of sparse vegetative cover on erosion and sediment yield. *Journal of Hydrology*, 123, 19–24.

Rogers, S., Barnett, J., Webber, M., Finlayson, B. and Wang, M. (2016) Governmentality and the conduct of water: China's South–North Water Transfer Project. *Transactions of the Institute of British Geographers*, 41 (4), 429–441.

Rojas-Soto, O.R., Sosa, V. and Ornelas, J.F. (2012) Forecasting cloud forest in eastern and southern Mexico: conservation insights under future climate change scenarios. *Biodiversity and Conservation*, 21 (10), 2671–2690.

Rolett, B.V., Zheng, Z. and Yue, Y. (2010) Holocene sea-level change and the emergence of Neolithic seafaring in the Fuzhou Basin (Fujian, China). *Quaternary Science Reviews*, 30, 788–797.

Roman, J. and Palumbi, S.R. (2003) Whales before whaling in the North Atlantic. *Science*, 301, 508–510.

Romero, A., González, I. and Galán, E. (2011) Stream water geochemistry from mine wastes in Peña de Hierro, Riotinto area, SW Spain: a case of extreme acid mine drainage. *Environmental Earth Sciences*, 62, 645–656.

Romero-Diaz, A., Belmonte-Serrato, F. and Ruiz-Sinoga, J.D. (2010) The geomorphic impact of afforestations on soil erosion in southeast Spain. *Land Degradation and Development*, 21, 188–195.

Romm, J. (2016) *Climate Change: What Everyone Needs to Know.* Oxford: Oxford University Press.

Romme, W.H. and Despain, D.G. (1989) The Yellowstone fires. *Scientific American*, 261, 21–29.

Roques, K.G., O'Connor, T.G. and Watkinson, A.R. (2001) Dynamics of shrub encroachment in an African savanna: relative influences of fire, herbivory, rainfall and density dependence. *Journal of Applied Ecology*, 38, 268–280.

Rösch, M. and Lechterbeck, J. (2016) Seven millennia of human impact as reflected in a high resolution pollen profile from the profundal sediments of Litzelsee, Lake Constance region, Germany. *Vegetation History and Archaeobotany*, 25 (4), 339–358.

Rose, L.S., Stallins, J.A. and Bentley, M.L. (2008) Concurrent cloud-to-ground lightning and precipitation enhancement in the Atlanta, Georgia (United States), urban region. *Earth Interactions*, doi:10.1175/2008EI265.1.

Rose, N.L. (2015) Spheroidal carbonaceous fly-ash particles provide a globally synchronous stratigraphic marker for the Anthropocene. *Environmental Science & Technology*, 49, 4155–4162.

Rosenberg, N.J., Epstein, D.J., Wang, D., et al. (1999) Possible impacts of global warming on the Ogallala Aquifer Region. *Climatic Change*, 42, 677–692.

Rosenbom, S., Costa, V., Al-Araimi, N., et al. (2015) Genetic diversity of donkey populations from the putative centers of domestication. *Animal Genetics*, 46 (1), 30–36.

Rosenzweig, C. and Hillel, D. (1993) The dust bowl of the 1930s: analog of greenhouse effect in the Great Plains? *Journal of Environmental Quality*, 22, 9–22.

Rosenzweig, C., Solecki, W. and Slosberg, R. (2009) Mitigating New York City's heat island. *Bulletin of the American Meteorological Society*, 90, 1297–1312.

Rosepiler, M.J. and Reilinger, R. (1977) Land subsidence due to water withdrawal in the vicinity of Pecos, Texas. *Engineering Geology*, 11, 295–304.

Roskin, J., Katra, I., and Blumberg, D.G. (2013) Late Holocene dune mobilizations in the northwestern Negev dunefield, Israel: a response to combined anthropogenic activity and short-term intensified windiness. *Quaternary International*, 303, 10–23.

Ross, N., Bingham, R.G., Corr, H.F., et al. (2012) Steep reverse bed slope at the grounding line of the Weddell Sea sector in West Antarctica. *Nature Geoscience*, 5, 393–396.

RoTap (2012) *Review of Transboundary Air Pollution: Acidification, Eutrophication, Ground Level Ozone and Heavy Metals in the UK.* Wallingford: Centre for Ecology and Hydrology.

Rott, H., Müller, F., Nagler, T. and Floricioiu, D. (2010) The imbalance of glaciers after disintegration of Larsen B ice shelf, Antarctic Peninsula. *The Cryosphere Discussions*, 4, 1607–1633.

Rouse, W.R., Douglas, M.S., Hecky, R.E., et al. (1997) Effects of climate change on the freshwaters of Arctic and Subarctic North America. *Hydrological Processes*, 11, 873–902.

Routson, C.C., Overpeck, J.T., Woodhouse, C.A. and Kenney, W.F. (2016) Three millennia of Southwestern North American dustiness and future implications. *PloS one*, 11 (2), e0149573.

Rowland, J.C., Jones, C.E., Altmann, G., et al. (2010) Arctic landscapes in transition: responses to thawing permafrost. *Eos, Transactions American Geophysical Union*, 91 (26), 229–230.

Royal Society (2005) *Ocean Acidification due to Increased Atmospheric Carbon Dioxide*. London: Royal Society.

Royal Society (2008) *Ground-Level Ozone in the 21st Century: Future Trends, Impacts and Policy Implications*. London: Royal Society.

Royal Society (2009) *Geoengineering the Climate*. London: Royal Society.

Royal Society (2010) Climate change: a summary of the science, http://royalsociety.org/policy/publications/2010/climate-change-summary-science/ (accessed January 2018).

Ruddiman, W.F. (2005) *Plows, Plagues and Petroleum: How Humans Took Control of Climate*. Princeton and Oxford: Princeton University Press.

Ruddiman, W.F. (2014) *Earth Transformed*. New York: W.H. Freeman and Company.

Ruddiman, W.F., Kutzbach, J.E. and Vavrus, S.J. (2011) Can natural or anthropogenic explanations of late-Holocene CO_2 and CH_4 increases be falsified? *The Holocene*, 21, 865–879.

Ruddiman, W.F. and Thomson, J.S. (2001) The case for human causes of increased atmospheric CH_4 over the last 5000 years. *Quaternary Science Reviews*, 20, 1769–1777.

Rudel, T.K., Coomes, O.T., Moran, E., et al. (2005) Forest transitions: towards a global understanding of land use change. *Global Environmental Change*, 15, 23–31.

Rudel, T.K., Schneider, L. and Uriarte, M. (2010) Forest transitions: an introduction. *Land Use Policy*, 27, 95–97.

Rugel, K., Jackson, C.R., Romeis, J.J., et al. (2012) Effects of irrigation withdrawals on streamflows in a karst environment: lower Flint River Basin, Georgia, USA. *Hydrological Processes*, 26, 523–534.

Ruiz-Labourdette, D., Nogués-Bravo, D., Ollero, H.S., et al. (2012) Forest composition in Mediterranean mountains is projected to shift along the entire elevational gradient under climate change. *Journal of Biogeography*, 39 (1), 162–176.

Rule, S., Brook, B.W., Haberle, S.G., et al. (2012) The aftermath of megafaunal extinction: ecosystem transformation in Pleistocene Australia. *Science*, 335, 1483–1486.

Rumschlag, J.H. and Peck, J.A. (2007) Short-term sediment and morphologic response of the Middle Cuyahoga River to the removal of the Munroe Falls Dam, Summit County, Ohio. *Journal of Great Lakes Research*, 33, 142–153.

Rutherford, I. (2000) Some human impacts on Australian stream channel morphology. In S. Brizga and B. Finlayson (eds), *River Management: The Australian Experience*. Chichester: Wiley, 11–47.

Rutherford, M.C. and Westfall, R.H. (1994) Biomes of southern Africa: an objective characterization. *Memoir Botanical Survey of South Africa*, 63, 1–94.

Ryan, P.A. and Blackford, J.J. (2010) Late Mesolithic environmental change at Black Heath, south Pennines, UK: a test of Mesolithic woodland management models using pollen, charcoal and non-pollen palynomorph data. *Vegetation History and Archaeobotany*, 19, 545–558.

Ryder, M.L. (1966) The exploitation of animals by man. *Advancement of Science*, 23, 9–18.

Ryken, N., Vanmaercke, M., Wanyama, J., et al. (2015) Impact of papyrus wetland encroachment on spatial and temporal variabilities of stream flow and sediment export from wet tropical catchments. *Science of the Total Environment*, 511, 756–66.

Saalfield, W.K. and Edwards, G.P. (2010) Distribution and abundance of the feral camel (*Camelus dromedarius*) in Australia. *The Rangeland Journal*, 32, 1–9.

Sabadini, R. (2002) Ice sheet collapse and sea level change. *Science*, 295, 2376–2377.

Sahagian, D. (2000) Global physical effects of anthropogenic hydrological alterations: sea level and water redistribution. *Global and Planetary Change*, 25, 38–48.

Saiko, T.A. and Zonn, I.S. (2000) Irrigation expansion and dynamics of desertification in the Circum-Aral region of Central Asia. *Applied Geography*, 20, 349–367.

Saintilan, N., Wilson, N.C., Rogers, K., Rajkaran, A. and Krauss, K.W. (2014) Mangrove expansion and salt marsh decline at mangrove poleward limits. *Global Change Biology*, 20, 147–157.

Saito, H., Murakami, W., Daimaru, H. and Oguchi, T. (2017) Effect of forest clear-cutting on landslide occurrences: analysis of rainfall thresholds at Mt. Ichifusa, Japan. *Geomorphology*, 276, 1–7.

Sakals, M.E., Innes, J.L., Wilford, D.J., et al. (2006) The role of forests in reducing hydrogeomorphic hazards. *Forest Snow Landscape Research*, 80, 11–22.

Sala, O.E., Chapin, F.S., Armesto, J.J., et al. (2000) Global biodiversity scenarios for the years 2100. *Science*, 287, 1770–1774.

Salazar, L.F., Nobre, C.A. and Oyama, M.D. (2007) Climate change consequences on the biome distribution in tropical South America. *Geophysical Research Letters*, 34, L09709.

Salby, M., Titova, E. and Deschamps, L. (2011) Rebound of Antarctic ozone. *Geophysical Research Letters*, 38, L09702.

Sallenger, A.H., Doranm, K.S. and Howd, P.A. (2012) Hotspot of accelerated sea-level rise on the Atlantic coast of North America. *Nature Climate Change*, 2, 884–888.

Salmoral, G., Willaarts, B.A., Troch, P.A. and Garrido, A. (2015) Drivers influencing streamflow changes in the Upper Turia basin, Spain. *Science of the Total Environment*, 503, 258–268.

Salque, M., Bogucki, P.I., Pyzel, J., et al. (2013) Earliest evidence for cheese making in the sixth millennium BC in northern Europe. *Nature*, 493 (7433), 522–525.

Saltré, F., Rodríguez-Rey, M., Brook, B.W., et al. (2016) Climate change not to blame for late Quaternary megafauna extinctions in Australia. *Nature Communications*, 7, doi:10.1038/ncomms10511.

Sampaio, G., Nobre, C., Costa, M.H., et al. (2007) Regional climate change over eastern Amazonia caused by pasture and soybean cropland expansion. *Geophysical Research Letters*, 34, L17709.

Sanchez, P.A. and Buol, S.W. (1975) Soils of the tropics and the world food crisis. *Science*, 188, 598–603.

Sanchez-Lorenzo, A., Wild, M., Brunetti, M., et al. (2015) Reassessment and update of long-term trends in downward surface shortwave radiation over Europe (1939–2012). *Journal of Geophysical Research: Atmospheres*, 120 (18), 9555–9569.

Sand, M., Berntsen, T.K., Seland, Ø. and Kristjánsson, J.E. (2013) Arctic surface temperature change to emissions of black carbon within Arctic or midlatitudes. *Journal of Geophysical Research: Atmospheres*, 118 (14), 7788–7798.

Sanders, W.M. (1972) Nutrients. In R.T. Oglesby, C.A. Carlson and J.A. McCann (eds), *River Ecology and Man*. New York: Academic Press, 389–415.

Sandom, C.J., Donlan, C.J., Svenning, J.C. and Hansen, D. (2013a) Rewilding. *Key Topics in Conservation Biology*, 2, 430–451.

Sandom, C.J., Hughes, J. and Macdonald, D.W. (2013b) Rewilding the Scottish highlands: do wild boar, Sus scrofa, use a suitable foraging strategy to be effective ecosystem engineers? *Restoration Ecology*, 21 (3), 336–343.

Sankaran, M., Ratnam, J. and Hanan, N. (2008) Woody cover in African savannas: the role of resources, fire and herbivory. *Global Ecology and Biogeography*, 17, 236–245.

Sankey, J.B., Germino, M.J. and Glenn, N.F. (2009) Relationships of post-fire aeolian transport to soil and atmospheric conditions. *Aeolian Research*, 1, 75–85.

Sannel, A.B.K. and Kuhry, P. (2011) Warming-induced destabilization of peat plateau/thermokarst lake complexes. *Journal of Geophysical Research: Biogeosciences* 116 (G3), doi:10.1029/2010JG001635.

Santer, B.D., Wigley, T.M.L., Gleckler, P.J., et al. (2006) Forced and unforced ocean temperature changes in Atlantic and Pacific tropical cyclogenesis regions. *Proceedings of the National Academy of Sciences*, 103, 13905–13910.

Santín, C. and Doerr, S.H. (2016) Fire effects on soils: the human dimension. *Philosophical Transactions of the Royal Society B*, 371 (1696), 20150171.

Sapozhnikov, V.V., Mordasova, N.V. and Metreveli, M.P. (2010) Transformations in the Caspian Sea ecosystem under the fall and rise of the sea level. *Oceanology*, 50, 488–497.

Sapp, J. (1999) *What Is Natural? Coral Reef Crisis*. New York: Oxford University Press.

Sarmiento, G. and Monasterio, M. (1975) A critical consideration of the environmental conditions associated with the occurrence of savanna ecosystems in tropical America. *Ecological Studies*, 11, 233–250.

Sarre, P. (1978) The diffusion of Dutch elm disease. *Area*, 10, 81–85.

Sattler, K., Keiler, M., Zischg, A. and Schrott, L. (2011) On the connection between debris flow activity and permafrost degradation: a case study from the Schnalstal, South Tyrolean Alps, Italy. *Permafrost and Periglacial Processes*, 22, 254–265.

Sauer, C.O. (1938) *Destructive exploitation in modern colonial expansion*. International Geographical Congress, Amsterdam, Vol. III, sect. IIIC, 494–499.

Sauer, C.O. (1952) *Agricultural Origins and Dispersals*. New York: American Geographical Society.

Sauer, C.O. (1969) *Seeds, Spades, Hearths and Herds*. Cambridge, MA: MIT Press.

Saunders, M.A. and Lea, A.S. (2008) Large contribution of sea surface warming to recent increase in Atlantic hurricane activity. *Nature*, 451, 557–560.

Saunois, M., Bousquet, P., Poulter, B., et al. (2016) The global methane budget: 2000–2012. *Earth System Science Data Discussions*, 8, 697–751.

Savage, M. (1991) Structural dynamics of a southwestern pine forest under chronic human influence. *Annals of the Association of American Geographers*, 81, 271–289.

Savini, J. and Kammerer, J.C. (1961) *Urban growth and the water regime*. United States Geological Survey water supply paper, 159.

Sax, F.F. and Gaines, S.D. (2008) Species invasions and extinction: the future of native biodiversity on islands. *Proceedings of the National Academy of Sciences*, 105, 11490–11497.

Saye, S.E., Van der Wal, D., Pye, K. and Blott, S.J. (2005) Beach–dune morphological relationships and erosion/ accretion: an investigation at five sites in England and Wales using LIDAR data. *Geomorphology*, 72 (1), 128–155.

Sayer, E.J., Oliver, A.E., Fridley, J.D., et al. (2017) Links between soil microbial communities and plant traits in a species-rich grassland under long-term climate change. *Ecology and Evolution*, 7, 855–862.

Sazakli, E., Sazaklie, E. and Leotsinidis, M. (2015) Rainwater harvesting: from ancient Greeks to modern times. The case of Kefalonia Island. *International Journal of Global Environmental Issues*, 14 (3–4), 286–295.

Scanlon, B.R., Faunt, C.C., Longuevergne, L., et al. (2012) Groundwater depletion and sustainability of irrigation in the US High Plains and Central Valley. *Proceedings of the National Academy of Sciences*, 109, 9320–9325.

Scarborough V.L. and Tankersley, K.B. (2017) Wells and reservoirs. In A.S. Gilbert (ed.), *Encyclopedia of Geoarchaeology*. Dordrecht: Springer Science and Business Media, 1007–1017.

Scarre, C. (ed.) (2005) *The Human Past: World History and the Development of Human Societies*. London: Thames & Hudson.

Schaefer, K., Lantuit, H., Romanovsky, V.E., Schuur, E.A. and Witt, R. (2014) The impact of the permafrost carbon feedback on global climate. *Environmental Research Letters*, 9, doi:10.1088/1748-9326/9/8/085003.

Scherler, D., Bookhagen, B. and Strecker, M.R. (2011) Spatially variable response of Himalayan glaciers to climate change affected by debris cover. *Nature Geoscience*, 4, 156–159.

Schewe, J., Heinke, J., Gerten, D., et al. (2014) Multimodel assessment of water scarcity under climate change. *Proceedings of the National Academy of Sciences*, 111 (9), 3245–3250.

Schiermeier, Q. (2007) What we don't know about climate change. *Nature*, 445, 580–581.

Schilling, K.E., Chan, K.-S., Liu, H. and Zhang, Y.-K. (2010) Quantifying the effect of land use land cover change on increasing discharge in the Upper Mississippi River. *Journal of Hydrology*, 387, 343–345.

Schimper, A.F.W. (1903) *Plant-Geography upon a Physiological Basis*. Oxford: Clarendon Press.

Schipper, J., Chanson, J.S., Chiozza, F., et al. (2008) The status of the world's land and marine mammals: diversity, threat and knowledge. *Science*, 322, 225–230.

Schlünzen, K.H., Hoffmann, P., Rosenhagen, G. and Riecke, W. (2010) Long-term changes and regional differences in temperature and precipitation in the metropolitan area of Hamburg. *International Journal of Climatology*, 30, 1121–1136.

Schmieder, O. (1927a) The Pampa – a natural or culturally induced grassland? *University of California Publications in Geography*, 2, 255–270.

Schmieder, O. (1927b) Alteration of the Argentine Pampa in the colonial period. *University of California Publications in Geography*, 2, 303–321.

Schmitt, R.J.P., Rubin, Z. and Kondolf, G.M. (2017) Losing ground: scenarios of land loss as consequence of shifting sediment budgets in the Mekong Delta. *Geomorphology*, 294, 58–69.

Schneider, C., Laizé, C.L.R., Acreman, M.C. and Florke, M. (2013) How will climate change modify river flow regimes in Europe? *Hydrology and Earth System Sciences*, 17 (1), 325–339.

Schneider, H., Höfer, D., Irmler, R. and Mäusbacher, R. (2010) Correlation between climate, man and debris flow events – a palynological approach. *Geomorphology*, 120, 48–55.

Schneider, S.H. and Thompson, S.L. (1988) Simulating the effects of nuclear war. *Nature*, 333, 221–227.

Scholz, N.L., Fleishman, E., Brown, L., et al. (2012) A perspective on modern pesticides, pelagic fish declines, and unknown ecological resilience in highly managed ecosystems. *Bioscience*, 62, 428–434.

Schoner, W., Auer, I. and Bohm, R. (2000) Climate variability and glacier reaction in the Austrian Eastern Alps. *Annals of Glaciology*, 23, 31–38.

Schottler, S.P., Ulrich, J., Belmont, P., et al. (2014) Twentieth century agricultural drainage creates more erosive rivers. *Hydrological Processes*, 28, 1951–1961.

Schrieber, B.C. (1986) Arid shorelines and evaporates. In H.G. Reading (ed.), *Sedimentary Environments and Facies*. Oxford: Blackwell Scientific, 189–228.

Schumm, S.A. (1977) *The Fluvial System*. New York: Wiley.

Schumm, S.A., Harvey, M.D. and Watson, C.C. (1984) *Incised Channels: Morphology, Dynamics and Control*. Littleton, CO: Water Resources Publications.

Schuur, E.A.G. and Abbott, B. (2011) High risk of permafrost thaw. *Nature*, 480, 32–33.

Schuur, E.A.G., McGuire, A.D., Schädel, C., et al. (2015) Climate change and the permafrost carbon feedback. *Nature*, 520, 171–179.

Schwarz, E.H.L. (1923) *The Kalahari or Thirstland Redemption*. Cape Town and Oxford: Oxford University Press.

Schwarz, H.E., Emel, J., Dickens, W.J., Rogers, P. and Thompson, J. (1991) Water quality and flows. In B.L. Turner, W.C. Clark, R.W. Kates, J.F. Richards, J.T. Matthews and W.B. Meyer (eds), *The Earth as Transformed by Human Action*. Cambridge: Cambridge University Press, 253–270.

Scott, D.F. (1997) The contrasting effects of wildfire and clear felling on the hydrology of a small catchment. *Hydrological Processes*, 11, 543–555.

Scott, D.M., Berg, M.J., Tolhurst, B.A., et al. (2014) Changes in the distribution of red foxes (Vulpes vulpes) in urban areas in Great Britain: findings and limitations of a media-driven nationwide survey. *PloS one*, 9 (6), e99059.

Seager, R., Ting, M., Held, I., et al. (2007) Model projections of an imminent transition to a more arid climate in southwestern North America. *Science*, 316, 1181–1184.

Seager, R. and Vecchi, G.A. (2010) Greenhouse warming and the 21st century hydroclimate of southwestern North America. *Proceedings of the National Academy of Sciences*, 107, 21277–21282.

Searchinger, T., Heimlich, R., Houghton, R.A., et al. (2008) Use of US croplands for biofuels increase greenhouse gases through emissions from land-use change. *Science*, 319, 1238–1240.

Sears, P.B. (1957) Man the newcomer: the living landscape and a new tenant. In L.H. Russwurm and E. Sommerville (eds.), *Man's Natural Environment, a System Approach*. North Scituate: Duxbury, 43–55.

Seddon, A.W., Macias-Fauria, M., Long, P.R., et al. (2016) Sensitivity of global terrestrial ecosystems to climate variability. *Nature*, 531 (7593), 229–232.

Segall, P. (1989) Earthquakes triggered by fluid extraction. *Geology*, 17, 942–946.

Seidel, K., Ehrler, C. and Martinec, J. (1998) Effects of climate change on water resources and runoff in an alpine basin. *Hydrological Processes*, 12, 1659–1669.

Seifan, N. (2009) Long-term effects of anthropogenic activities on semi-arid sand dunes. *Journal of Arid Environments*, 73, 332–337.

Selman, M., Greenhalgh, S., Diaz, R. and Sugg, Z. (2008) Eutrophication and hypoxia in coastal areas: a global assessment of the state of knowledge. *World Resources Institute Policy Note*, 1, 6 pp.

Semaw, S., Renne, P., Harris, J.W.K., et al. (1997) 2.5-million-year-old stone tools from Gona, Ethiopia. *Nature*, 385, 333–336.

Semtner, A.J. (1984) The climate response of the Arctic Ocean to Soviet river diversions. *Climatic Change*, 6, 109–130.

Senter, J. (2003) Live dunes and ghost forests: stability and change in the history of North Carolina's maritime forests. *North Carolina Historical Review*, 80, 334–371.

Serneels, V. (2017) Metals. In A.S. Gilbert (ed.), *Encyclopedia of Geoarchaeology*. Dordrecht: Springer, 521–532.

Setia, R., Gottschalk, P., Smith, P., et al. (2013) Soil salinity decreases global soil organic carbon stocks. *Science of the Total Environment*, 465, 267–272.

Seto, S., Nakamura, A., Noguchi, I., et al. (2002) Annual and seasonal trends in chemical composition of precipitation in Japan during 1989–1998. *Atmospheric Environment*, 31, 3505–3517.

Setterfield, S., Rossiter-Rachov, N.A., Hutley, L.B., et al. (2010) Turning up the heat: the impacts of *Andropogon gayanus* (gamba grass) invasion on fire behaviour in northern Australian savannas. *Diversity & Distributions*, 16, 854–861.

Seyoum, W.M., Milewski, A.M. and Durham, M.C. (2015) Understanding the relative impacts of natural processes and human activities on the hydrology of the Central Rift Valley lakes, East Africa. *Hydrological Processes*, 29 (19), 4312–4324.

Shabalova, M.V., van Deursen, W.P.A. and Buishand, T.A. (2003) Assessing future discharge of the river Rhine using regional climate model integrations and a hydrological model. *Climate Research*, 23, 233–246.

Shackleton, R.T., Witt, A.B., Piroris, F.M. and van Wilgen, B.W. (2017) Distribution and socio-ecological impacts of the invasive alien cactus Opuntia stricta in eastern Africa. *Biological Invasions*, doi:10.1007/s10530-017-1453-x.

Shakesby, R.A. (2011) Post-wildfire soil erosion in the Mediterranean: review and future research directions. *Earth-Science Reviews*, 105, 71–100.

Shakesby, R.A., Bento, C.P., Ferreira, C.S., et al. (2015) Impacts of prescribed fire on soil loss and soil quality: an assessment based on an experimentally-burned catchment in central Portugal. *Catena*, 128, 278–293.

Shakesby, R.A., Wallbrink, P.J., Doerr, S.H., et al. (2007) Distinctiveness of wildfire effects on soil erosion in south-east Australian eucalyptus forests assessed in a global context. *Forest Ecology and Management*, 238, 347–364.

Shaler, N.S. (1912) *Man and the Earth*. New York: Duffield.

Shan, W., Hu, Z., Guo, Y., Zhang, C., Wang, C., Jiang, H., Liu, Y. and Xiao, J. (2015) The impact of climate change on landslides in southeastern of high-latitude permafrost regions of China. *Frontiers in Earth Science*, 3, 7.

Shankman, D. and Smith, L.J. (2004) Stream channelization and swamp formation in the US coastal plain. *Physical Geography*, 25, 22–38.

Shannon, G., McKenna, M.F., Angeloni, L.M., et al. (2016) A synthesis of two decades of research documenting the effects of noise on wildlife. *Biological Reviews*, 91 (4) 982–1005.

Shannon, L.M., Boyko, R.H., Castelhano, M., et al. (2015) Genetic structure in village dogs reveals a Central Asian domestication origin. *Proceedings of the National Academy of Sciences*, 112 (44), 13639–13644.

Shao, Y. (2008) *Physics and Modelling of Wind Erosion*. Berlin: Springer Science & Business Media.

Shao, Y., Wyrwoll, K.H., Chappell, A., et al. (2011) Dust cycle: an emerging core theme in Earth system science. *Aeolian Research*, 2, 181–204.

Shaw, L.M., Chamberlain, D. and Evans, M. (2008) The House Sparrow *Passer domesticus* in urban areas: reviewing a possible link between post-decline distribution and human socio-economic status. *Journal of Ornithology*, 149, 293–299.

Sheail, J. (1971) *Rabbits and Their History*. Newton Abbot: David & Charles.

Sheehan, P., Cheng, E., English, A. and Sun, F. (2014) China's response to the air pollution shock. *Nature Climate Change*, 4 (5), 306–309.

Sheffield, A.T., Healy, T.R. and McGlone, M.S. (1995) Infilling rates of a steepland catchment estuary, Whangamata, New Zealand. *Journal of Coastal Research*, 11 (4), 1294–1308.

Sheffield, J. and Wood, E.F. (2008) Projected changes in drought occurrence under future global warming from multi-model, multi-scenario, IPCC AR4 simulations. *Climate Dynamics*, 31, 79–105.

Shehata, W. and Lotfi, H. (1993) Preconstruction solution for groundwater rise in sabkha. *Bulletin of the International Association of Engineering Geology*, 47, 145–150.

Shellberg, J.G., Spencer, J., Brooks, A.P. and Pietsch, T.J. (2016) Degradation of the Mitchell River fluvial megafan by alluvial gully erosion increased by post-European land use change, Queensland, Australia. *Geomorphology*, 266, 105–120.

Shem, W. and Shepherd, M. (2009) On the impact of urbanization on summertime thunderstorms in Atlanta: two numerical model case studies. *Atmospheric Research*, 92, 172–189.

Sheng, J. and Wilson, J.P. (2009) Watershed urbanization and changing flood behaviour across the Los Angeles metropolitan region. *Natural Hazards*, 48, 41–57.

Shepard, C.C., Agostini, V.N., Gilmer, B., et al. (2012) Assessing future risk: quantifying the effects of sea level rise on storm surge risk for the southern shores of Long Island, New York. *Natural Hazards*, 60, 727–745.

Sheppard, C.R.C. (2003) Predicted recurrences of mass coral morality in the Indian Ocean. *Nature*, 425, 294–297.

Sheppard, C.R.C., Davy, S.K. and Pilling, G.M. (2009) *The Biology of Coral Reefs*. Oxford: Oxford University Press.

Sherif, M.M. and Singh, V.P. (1999) Effect of climate change on sea water intrusion in coastal aquifers. *Hydrological Processes*, 13, 1277–1287.

Sherlock, R.L. (1922) *Man as a Geological Agent*. London: Witherby.

Sherratt, A. (1981) Plough and pastoralism: aspects of the secondary products revolution. In I. Hodder, G. Isaac and N. Hammond (eds), *Pattern of the Past*. Cambridge: Cambridge University Press, 261–305.

Sherratt, A. (1997) Climatic cycles and behaviour revolutions: the emergence of modern humans and the beginning of farming. *Antiquity*, 71, 271–287.

Sherriff, R.L. and Veblen, T.T. (2006) Ecological effects of changes in fire regimes in *Pinus ponderosa* ecosystems in the Colorado Front Range. *Journal of Vegetation Science*, 17, 705–718.

Sherwood, B., Cutler, D. and Burton, J. (eds) (2002) *Wildlife and Roads: The Ecological Impact*. London: Imperial College Press.

Shi, Y.F. and Liu, S.Y. (2000) Estimation on the response of glaciers in China to the global warming in the 21st century. *Chinese Science Bulletin*, 45, 668–672.

Shiklomanov, I.A. (1985) Large scale water transfers. In J.C. Rodda (ed.), *Facets of Hydrology II*. Chichester: Wiley, 345–387.

Shiklomanov, I.A. (1999) Climate change, hydrology and water resources: the work of the IPCC, 1988–1994. In J.C. van Dam (ed.), *Impacts of Climate Change and Climate Variability on Hydrological Regimes*. Cambridge: Cambridge University Press, 8–20.

Shimelmitz, R., Kuhn, S.L., Jelinek, A.J., et al. (2014) 'Fire at will': The emergence of habitual fire use 350,000 years ago. *Journal of Human Evolution*, 77, 196–203.

Shindell, D. and Faluvegi, G. (2009) Climate response to regional radiative forcing during the twentieth century. *Nature Geoscience*, 2, 294–300.

Shirahata, H., Elias, R.W., Patterson, C.C. and Koide, M. (1980) Chronological variations in concentrations and isotopic composition of anthropogenic atmospheric lead in sediments of a remote subalpine pond. *Geochimica et Cosmochimica Acta*, 44, 149–162.

Short, F.T., Polidoro, B., Livingstone, S.R., et al. (2011) Extinction risk assessment of the world's seagrass species. *Biological Conservation*, 144, 1961–1971.

Shriner, D.S. and Street, R.B. (1998) North America. In R.T. Watson (ed.), *The Regional Impacts of Climate Change*. Cambridge: Cambridge University Press, 253–330.

Shuman, J.K., Shugart, H.H. and O'Halloran, T.L. (2011) Sensitivity of Siberian larch forests to climate change. *Global Change Biology*, 17, 2370–2384.

Siakeu, J., Oguchi, T., Aoki, T., et al. (2004) Change in riverine suspended sediment concentration in central Japan in response to late 20th century human activities. *Catena*, 55, 231–254.

Sidle, R.C. and Dhakal, A.S. (2002) Potential effect of environmental change on landslide hazards in forest environments. In R.C. Sidle (ed.), *Environmental Change and Geomorphic Hazards in Forests*. Wallingford: CABI, 123–165.

Sidle, R.C., Furuichi, T. and Kono, Y. (2011) Unprecedented rates of landslide and surface erosion along a newly constructed road in Yunnan, China. *Natural Hazards*, 57, 31–26.

Sidle, R.C., Kamil, I., Sharma, A. and Yamashita, S. (2000) Stream response to subsidence from underground coal mining in central Utah. *Environmental Geology*, 39, 279–291.

Sidle, R.C., Ziegler, A.D., Negishi, J.N., et al. (2006) Erosion processes in steep terrain – truths, myths, and uncretainties related to forest management in Southeast Asia. *Forest Ecology and Management*, 224, 199–225.

Sidorchuk, A.Y. and Golosov, V.N. (2003) Erosion and sedimentation on the Russian Plain, II: the history of erosion and sedimentation during the period of intensive agriculture. *Hydrological Processes*, 17, 3347–3358.

Siebert, S., Burke, J., Faures, J.M., et al. (2010) Groundwater use for irrigation – a global inventory. *Hydrology and Earth System Sciences Discussions*, 7, 3977–4021.

Siegel, P.E., Jones, J.G., Pearsall, D.M., et al. (2015) Paleoenvironmental evidence for first human colonization of the eastern Caribbean. *Quaternary Science Reviews*, 129, 275–295.

Silveira, L. and Alonso, J. (2009) Runoff modifications due to the conversion of natural grasslands to forests in a large basin in Uruguay. *Hydrological Processes*, 23, 320–329.

Simas, T., Nunes, J.P. and Ferreira, J.G. (2001) Effects of global climate change on coastal salt marshes. *Ecological Modelling*, 139, 1–15.

Simberloff, D. (2000) Global climate change and introduced species in United States forests. *Science of the Total Environment*, 262, 253–261.

Simberloff, D., Nuñez, M.A., Ledgard, N.J., et al. (2010) Spread and impact of introduced conifers in South America: lessons from other southern hemisphere regions. *Austral Ecology*, 35, 489–504.

Simmons, I.G. (1993) *Environmental History: A Concise Introduction*. Oxford: Blackwell.

Simmons, I.G. (1996) *Changing the Face of the Earth: Culture, Environment and History* (2nd edn). Oxford: Blackwell.

Simpson, J.M., Darrow, M.M., Huang, S.L., Daanen, R.P. and Hubbard, T.D. (2016) Investigating movement and characteristics of a frozen debris lobe, South-central Brooks Range, Alaska. *Environmental & Engineering Geoscience*, 22 (3), 259–277, doi:org/10.2113/gseegeosci.22.3.259.

Sinclair, A.R.E. and Fryxell, J.M. (1985) The Sahel of Africa: ecology of a disaster. *Canadian Journal of Zoology*, 63, 987–994.

Singh, B.K., Quince, C., Macdonald, C.A., et al. (2014) Loss of microbial diversity in soils is coincident with reductions in some specialized functions. *Environmental Microbiology*, 16 (8), 2408–2420.

Siriwardena, L., Finlayson, B.L. and McMahon, T.A. (2006) The impact of land use change on catchment hydrology in large catchments: the Comet River, Central Queensland, Australia. *Journal of Hydrology*, 326, 199–214.

Sitoki, L., Gichuki, J., Ezekiel, C., et al. (2010) The environment of Lake Victoria (East Africa): current status and historical changes. *International Review of Hydrobiology*, 95, 209–223.

Six, D., Reynaud, L. and Letreguilly, A. (2001) Silans de masse des glaciers alpines et scandinaves, leurs relations avec l'oscillation due climat de l'Atlantique nord. *Comptes rendus Academie des Sciences, science de la terre et des planètes*, 333, 693–698.

Skagen, S.K., Burris, L.E. and Granfors, D.A. (2016) Sediment accumulation in prairie wetlands under a changing climate: the relative roles of landscape and precipitation. *Wetlands*, 36, 383–395.

Skeat, A.J., East, T.J. and Corbett, L.K. (2012) Impact of feral water buffalo. In C. M. Finlayson and I. von Oetzen (eds), *Landscape and Vegetation Ecology of the Kakadu Region, Northern Australia*. Dordrecht: Springer, 155–177.

Slaymaker, O. and Kelly, R.E.J. (2007) *The Cryosphere and Global Environmental Change*. Oxford: Blackwell.

Slaymaker, O., Spencer, T. and Embleton-Hamann, C. (eds) (2009) *Geomorphology and Global Environmental Change*. Cambridge: Cambridge University Press.

Sloan, B.P., Basu, N.B. and Mantilla, R. (2016) Hydrologic impacts of subsurface drainage at the field scale: climate, landscape and anthropogenic controls. *Agricultural Water Management*, 165, 1–10.

Smil, V. (2011) Harvesting the biosphere: the human impact. *Population and Development Review*, 37, 613–636.

Smith, B.D. and Zeder, M.A. (2013) The onset of the Anthropocene. *Anthropocene*, 4, 8–13.

Smith, B.J., McCabe, S., McAllister, D., et al. (2011) A commentary on climate change, stone decay dynamics and the 'greening' of natural stone buildings: new perspectives on 'deep wetting'. *Environmental Earth Sciences*, 63, 1691–1700.

Smith, G.D., Coughland, K.J., Yule, D.F., et al. (1992a) Soil management options to reduce runoff and erosion on a hardsetting Alfisol in the semi-arid tropics. *Soil and Tillage Research*, 25, 195–215.

Smith, J.B. and Tirpak, D.A. (eds) (1990) *The Potential Effects of Global Climate Change on the United States*. New York: Hemisphere.

Smith, J.E. (ed.) (1968) *Torrey Canyon Pollution and Marine Life*. Cambridge: Cambridge University Press.

Smith, K. (1975) *Principles of Applied Climatology*. London: McGraw-Hill.

Smith, M.W. (1993) Climate change and permafrost. In H.M. French and O. Slaymaker (eds), *Canada's Cold Environments*. Montreal and Kingston: McGill-Queens University Press, 292–311.

Smith, N. (1976) *Man and Water*. London: Davies.

Smith, P., House, J.I., Bustamante, M., et al. (2016) Global change pressures on soils from land use and management. *Global Change Biology*, 22 (3), 1008–1028.

Smith, S.J., Pitcher, H. and Wigley, T.M.L. (2001) Global and regional anthropogenic sulfur dioxide emissions. *Global and Planetary Change*, 29, 99–119.

Smith, T.M., Shugart, H.H., Bonan, G.B. and Smith, J.B. (1992b) Modelling the potential response of vegetation to global climate change. *Advances in Ecological Research*, 22, 93–116.

Smol, J.P. and Stoermer, E.F. (eds) (2010) *The Diatoms: Applications for the Environmental and Earth Sciences*. Cambridge: Cambridge University Press.

Smolikowski, B., Puig, H. and Roose, E. (2001) Influence of soil protection techniques on runoff, erosion and plant production on semi-arid hillslopes of Cabo Verde. *Agriculture, Ecosystems & Environment*, 87, 67–80.

Snedaker, S.C. (1993) Impact on mangroves. In G. Maul (ed.), *Climatic Change in the Intra-Americas Sea*. London: Edward Arnold, 282–305.

Snedaker, S.C. (1995) Mangroves and climate change in the Florida and Caribbean region: scenarios and hypotheses. *Hydrobiologia*, 295, 43–49.

Snelder, D.J. and Bryan, R.B. (1995) The use of rainfall simulation tests to assess the influence of vegetation density on soil loss on degraded rangelands in the Baringo District, Kenya. *Catena*, 25, 105–116.

Snover, A. (1997) *Impacts of global climate change on the Pacific Northwest*. Preparatory white paper for OSTP/USGCRP regional workshop on the Impacts of Global Climate Change on the Pacific Northwest, July 1997.

So, C.L. (1971) Mass movements associated with the rainstorm of 1966 in Hong Kong. *Transactions of the Institute of British Geographers*, 53, 55–65.

Sobota, I. and Nowak, M. (2014) Changes in the dynamics and thermal regime of the permafrost and active layer of the high Arctic coastal area in North-West Spitsbergen, Svalbard. *Geografiska Annaler: Series A, Physical Geography*, 96, 227–240.

Sodhi, N.S. and Ehrlich, P.R. (eds) (2010) *Conservation Biology for All*. Oxford: Oxford University Press.

Soja, A.J., Tchebakova, N.M., French, N.H., et al. (2007) Climate-induced boreal forest change: predictions versus current observations. *Global and Planetary Change*, 56, 274–296.

Solomon, D., Lehmann, J., Fraser, J.A., et al. (2016b) Indigenous African soil enrichment as a climate-smart sustainable agriculture alternative. *Frontiers in Ecology and the Environment*, 14 (2), 71–76.

Solomon, S., Ivy, D.J., Kinnison, D., et al. (2016a) Emergence of healing in the Antarctic ozone layer. *Science*, 353 (6296), 269–274.

Somers, K.A., Bernhardt, E.S., Grace, J.B., et al. (2013) Streams in the urban heat island: spatial and temporal variability in temperature. *Freshwater Science* 32 (1), 309–326.

Somerville, M. (1858) *Physical Geography* (4th edn). London: Murray.

Son, S.-W., Tandon, N.F., Polvani, L.M. and Waugh, D.M. (2009) Ozone hole and Southern Hemisphere climate change. *Geophysical Research Letters*, 36, L15705.

Sophocleous, M. (2010) Review: groundwater management practices, challenges, and innovations in the High Plains aquifer, USA – lessons and recommended actions. *Hydrogeology Journal*, 18, 559–575.

Sopper, W.E. (1975) Effects of timber harvesting and related management practices on water quality in forested watersheds. *Journal of Environmental Quality*, 4, 24–29.

Sorg, A., Kääb, A., Roesch, A., Bigler, C. and Stoffel, M. (2015) Contrasting responses of Central Asian rock glaciers to global warming. *Scientific Reports*, 5, doi:10.1038/srep08228.

Sorkin, A.J. (1982) *Economic Aspects of Natural Hazards*. Lexington: Lexington Books.

Sotoudeheian, S., Salim, R., and Arhami, M. (2016) Impact of Middle Eastern dust sources on PM10 in Iran: highlighting the impact of Tigris–Euphrates basin sources and Lake Urmia desiccation. *Journal of Geophysical Research – Atmospheres*, 121, 14,018–14,034.

Souch, C. and Grimmond, S. (2006) Applied climatology: urban climate. *Progress in Physical Geography*, 30, 270–279.

Soukopova, J. (2017) Central Saharan rock art: considering the kettles and cupules. *Journal of Arid Environments*, 143, 10–14.

Souter, D.W. and Linden, O. (2000) The health and future of coral reef systems. *Ocean and Coastal Management*, 43, 657–688.

Southon, G.E., Green, E.R., Jones, A.G., et al. (2012) Long-term nitrogen additions increase likelihood of climate stress and affect recovery from wildfire in a lowland heath. *Global Change Biology*, 18 (9), 2824–2837.

Spanier, E. and Galil, B.S. (1991) Lessepsian migration: a continuous biogeographical process. *Endeavour*, 15, 102–106.

Spate, O.H.K. and Learmonth, A.T.A. (1967) *India and Pakistan*. London: Methuen.

Speight, M.C.D. (1973) *Oudoor recreation and its ecological effects: a bibliography and review*. Discussion Papers in Conservation, 4, University College, London.

Spencer, T. (1995) Potentialities, uncertainties and complexities in the response of coral reefs to future sea level rise. *Earth Surface Processes and Landforms*, 20, 49–64.

Spencer, T. and Douglas, I. (1985) The significance of environmental change: diversity, disturbance and tropical ecosystems. In I. Douglas and T. Spencer (eds), *Environmental Change and Tropical Geomorphology*. London: Allen & Unwin, 13–33.

Spencer, T., Schuerch, M., Nicholls, R.J., et al. (2016) Global coastal wetland change under sea-level rise and related stresses: the DIVA Wetland Change Model. *Global and Planetary Change*, 139, 15–30.

Spencer, T., Teleki, K.A., Bradshaw, C. and Spalding, M.D. (2000) Coral bleaching in the Southern Seychelles during the 1997–1998 Indian Ocean warm event. *Marine Pollution Bulletin*, 40, 569–586.

Sperling, C.H.B., Goudie, A.S., Stoddart, D.R. and Poole, G.C. (1979) Origin of the Dorset dolines. *Transactions of the Institute of British Geographers*, 4, 121–124.

Sperna Weiland, F.C., van Beek, L.P.H., Kwadijk, K.C.J. and Blerkens, M.F.P. (2011) Global patterns of change in discharge rehgimes for 2100. *Hydrology and Earth System Sciences Discussions*, 8, 10973–11014.

Squire, G.R., Brooks, D.R., Bohan, D.A., et al. (2003) On the rationale and interpretation of the farm scale evaluations of genetically modified herbicide-tolerant crops. *Philosophical Transactions of the Royal Society of London: Series B, Biological Sciences*, 358, 1779–1799.

Staehelin, J., Harris, N.R.P., Appenzeller, C. and Ebeshard, J. (2001) Ozone trends: a review. *Reviews of Geophysics*, 39, 231–290.

Stanhill, G. and Cohen, S. (2001) Global dimming: a review of the evidence for a widespread and significant reduction in global radiation with discussion of its probable causes and possible agricultural consequences. *Agricultural and Forest Meteorology*, 107, 255–278.

Stanley, D.J. (1996) Nile delta: extreme case of sediment entrapment on a delta plain and consequent coastal land loss. *Marine Geology*, 129, 189–195.

Stanley, D.J. and Chen, Z. (1993) Yangtze delta, eastern China: I. Geometry and subsidence of Holocene depocenter. *Marine Geology*, 112, 1–11.

State of the Birds, United States of America (2009) *State of the Birds United States of America, 2009*. Washington, DC: US Department of the Interior.

Staver, A.C., Archibald, S. and Levin, S. (2011) Tree cover in sub-Saharan Africa: rainfall and fire constrain forest and savanna alternative stable states. *Ecology*, 92, 1063–1072.

Steadman, D.W., Stafford, T.W., Donahue, D.J. and Jull, A.J.T. (1991) Chronology of Holocene vertebrate extinction in the Galápagos Islands. *Quaternary Research*, 36, 126–133.

Steffen, W. (2010) Observed trends in Earth System behaviour. *Wiley Interdisciplinary Reviews: Climate Change*, 1, 428–449.

Steffen, W., Sanderson, R.A., Tyson, P.D., et al. (2004) *Global Change and the Earth System*. Berlin: Springer.

Steffen, W., Broadgate, W., Deutsch, L., et al. (2015) The trajectory of the Anthropocene: the Great Acceleration. *The Anthropocene Review*, 2, 81–98.

Steffen, W., Crutzen, P.J. and McNeill, J.R. (2007) The Anthropocene: are humans now overwhelming the great forces of nature? *Ambio*, 36, 614–621.

Steffen, W., Grinevald, J., Crutzen, P. and McNeill, J. (2011) The Anthropocene: conceptual and historical perspectives. *Philosophical Transactions of the Royal Society*, 369A, 842–867.

Stendel, M. and Christensen, J.H. (2002) Impact of global warming on permafrost conditions in a coupled GCM. *Geophysical Research Letters*, 29, 10–11.

Stephens, J.C. (1956) Subsidence of organic soils in the Florida Everglades. *Proceedings of the Soil Science Society of America*, 20, 77–80.

Sterk, G. (2003) Causes, consequences and control of wind erosion in Sahelian Africa: a review. *Land Degradation and Development*, 14, 95–108.

Sternberg, H.O.R. (1968) Man and environmental change in South America. *Monographiae Biologicae*, 18, 413–445.

Stetler, L.L. and Gaylord, D.R. (1996) Evaluating eolian-climate interactions using a regional climate model from Hanford, Washington (USA). *Geomorphology*, 17, 99–113.

Stevens, C.J., Dupre, C., Dorland, E., et al. (2010) Nitrogen deposition threatens species richness of grasslands across Europe. *Environmental Pollution*, 158, 2940–2945.

Stevens, C.J., Gowing, D.J.G., Wotherspoon, K.A., et al. (2011) Addressing the impact of atmospheric nitrogen deposition on Western European grasslands. *Environmental Management*, 48, 885–894.

Stevens, C.J., Lind, E.M., Hautier, Y., et al. (2015) Anthropogenic nitrogen deposition predicts local grassland primary production worldwide. *Ecology*, 96 (6), 1459–1465.

Stevens, N., Lehmann, C.E., Murphy, B.P. and Durigan, G. (2017) Savanna woody encroachment is widespread across three continents. *Global Change Biology*, 23 (1), 235–244.

Stevenson, A.C., Jones, V.J. and Battarbee, R.W. (1990) The cause of peat erosion: a palaeolimnological approach. *The New Phytologist*, 114, 727–735.

Stewart, D.C. (1956) Fire as the first great force employed by man. In W.L. Thomas (ed.), *Man's role in Changing the Face of the Earth*. Chicago: University of Chicago Press, 115–133.

Stewart, I.T. (2009) Changes in snowpack and snowmelt runoff for key mountain regions. *Hydrological Processes*, 23, 78–94.

Stiles, D. (1995) An overview of desertification as dryland degradation. In D. Stiles (ed.), *Social Aspects of Sustainable Dryland Management*. Chichester: Wiley, 3–20.

Stirling, I. and Derocher, A.E. (2012) Effects of climate warming on polar bears: a review of the evidence. *Global Change Biology*, 18 (9), 2694–2706.

Stock, F., Knipping, M., Pint, A., et al. (2016) Human impact on Holocene sediment dynamics in the Eastern Mediterranean–the example of the Roman harbour of Ephesus. *Earth Surface Processes and Landforms*, 41 (7), 980–996.

Stocker, T.F. (2001) Physical climate processes and feedbacks. In J.T. Houghton (ed.), *Climate Change 2001: The Scientific Basis*. Cambridge: Cambridge University Press, 417–470.

Stoddart, D.R. (1968) Catastrophic human interference with coral atoll ecosystems. *Geography*, 53, 25–40.

Stoddart, D.R. (1971) Coral reefs and islands and catastrophic storms. In J.A. Steers (ed.), *Applied Coastal Geomorphology*. London: Macmillan, 154–197.

Stoddart, J.L., Jeffries, D.S., Lükewille, A., et al. (1999) Regional trends in aquatic recovery from acidification in North America and Europe. *Nature*, 401, 575–578.

Stoffel, M. and Beniston, M. (2006) On the incidence of debris flows from the early Little Ice Age to a future greenhouse climate: a case study from the Swiss Alps. *Geophysical Research Letters*, 33, L16404.

Stoffel, M., Tiranti, D. and Huggel, C. (2014) Climate change impacts on mass movements – case studies from the European Alps. *Science of the Total Environment*, 493, 1255–1266.

Stoffel, M., Wyżga, B. and Marston, R.A. (2016) Floods in mountain environments: a synthesis. *Geomorphology*, 272, 1–9.

Stokes, A., Atger, C., Bengough, A.G., et al. (2009) Desirable plant root traits for protecting natural and engineered slopes against landslides. *Plant and Soil*, 324, 1–30.

Stokes, S., Thomas, D.S.G. and Washington, R. (1997) Multiple episodes of aridity in southern Africa since the last interglacial period. *Nature*, 388, 154–158.

Stone, B. (2007) Urban and rural temperature trends in proximity to large US cities: 1951–2000. *International Journal of Climatology*, 27, 1801–1807.

Stork, N.E. (2010) Re-assessing current extinction rates. *Biodiversity and Conservation*, 19, 357–371.

Stott, P. (2016) Physical geographies: past, present, and future. *Progress in Physical Geography*, 40 (1), 3–6.

Stott, T. and Marks, S. (2000) Effects of plantation forest clear-felling on stream temperatures in the Plynlimon experimental catchments, mid-Wales. *Hydrology and Earth System Sciences*, 4, 95–104.

Street, F.A. and Grove, A.T. (1979) Global maps of lake level fluctuation since 30,000 years ago. *Quaternary Research*, 12, 83–118.

Streets, D.G., Wu, Y. and Chin, M. (2006) Two-decadal aerosol trends as a likely explanation of the global dimming/brightening transition. *Geophysical Research Letters*, 33, L15806.

Streletskiy, D.A., Shiklomanov, N.I., Little, J.D., et al. (2016) Thaw subsidence in undisturbed tundra landscapes, Barrow, Alaska, 1962–2015. *Permafrost and Periglacial Processes*. doi:10.1002/ppp.1918.

Stringer, C. (2003) Out of Africa. *Nature*, 423, 692–699.

Strong, D.R. and Ayres, D.A. (2009) Spartina introduction and consequences in salt marshes. In B.R. Silliman, E.D. Grosholz and M.D. Bertness (eds), *Human Impacts on Salt Marshes: A Global Perspective*. Vancouver: University of British Columbia Press, 3–22.

Struyf, E., Smis, A., Van Damme, S., Garnier, J., et al. (2010) Historical land use change has lowered terrestrial silica mobilization. *Nature Communications*, 1, doi:10.1038/ncomms1128.

Stuart, A.J. (2015) Late Quaternary megafaunal extinctions on the continents: a short review. *Geological Journal*, 50 (3), 338–363.

Sturrock, F. and Cathie, J. (1980) *Farm modernisation and the countryside*. Occasional paper 12, Department of Land Economy, University of Cambridge.

Su, Z. and Shi, Y. (2002) Response of monsoonal temperate glaciers to global warming since The Little Ice Age. *Quaternary International*, 97–98, 123–131.

Suchodoletz, H., von Oberhänsli, H., Faust, D., et al. (2010) The evolution of Saharan dust input on Lanzarote (Canary Islands) – influenced by human activity during the early Holocene? *The Holocene*, 20, 169–179.

Suckale, J. (2010) Moderate-to-large seismicity induced by hydrocarbon production. *The Leading Edge*, 29, 310–319.

Summers-Smith, J.D. (2003) The decline of the House Sparrow: a review. *British Birds*, 96 (9), 439–446.

Sun, G.E., McNulty, S.G., Moore, J., et al. (2002) Potential impacts of climate change on rainfall erosivity and water availability in China in the next 100 years. *Proceedings of the 12th International Soil Conservation Conference*, Beijing, https://www.srs.fs.usda.gov/pubs/ja/ja_sun014.pdf (accessed January 2018).

Suppiah, R. and Hennessy, K.J. (1998) Trends in total rainfall, heavy rain events and number of dry days in Australia. *International Journal of Climatology*, 18, 1141–1164.

Sušnik, J., Vamvakeridou-Lyroudia, L.S., Baumert, N., et al. (2015) Interdisciplinary assessment of sea-level rise and climate change impacts on the lower Nile delta, Egypt. *Science of the Total Environment*, 503, 279–288.

Sutfin, N.A., Wohl, E.E. and Dwire, K.A. (2016) Banking carbon: a review of organic carbon storage and physical factors influencing retention in floodplains and riparian ecosystems. *Earth Surface Processes and Landforms*, 41 (1), 38–60.

Sutton, J.E.G. (1965) Sirikwa holes, stone houses and their makers in the western highlands of Kenya. *Man*, 65, 113–115.

Svenning, J.C., Pedersen, P.B., Donlan, C.J., et al. (2016) Science for a wilder Anthropocene: synthesis and future directions for trophic rewilding research. *Proceedings of the National Academy of Sciences*, 113 (4), 898–906.

Swank, W.T. and Douglass, J.E. (1974) Streamflow greatly reduced by converting deciduous hardwood stands to pine. *Science*, 185, 857–859.

Swann, A.L.S., Fung, I.Y. and Chiang, J.C.H. (2012) Mid-latitude afforestation shifts general circulation and tropical precipitation. *Proceedings of the National Academy of Sciences*, 109, 712–716.

Swanston, D.N. and Swanson, F.J. (1976) Timber harvesting, mass erosion and steepland forest geomorphology in the Pacific north-west. In D.R. Coates (ed.), *Geomorphology and Engineering*. Stroudsburg: Dowden, Hutchinson and Ross, 199–221.

Sweatman, H., Delean, S. and Syms, C. (2011) Assessing loss of coral cover on Australia's Great Barrier Reef over two decades, with implications for longer term trends. *Coral Reefs*, 30, 521–531.

Sweet, M. and Brown, B. (2016) Coral responses to anthropogenic stress in the twenty-first century: an ecophysiological perspective. *Oceanography and Marine Biology: An Annual Review*, 54, 271–314.

Swetnam, T.W. and Betancourt, J.L. Mesoscale Ecological Responses to Climatic Variability in the American Southwest. http://geochange.er.usgs.gov/sw/impacts/biology/fires_SOI/ 4/10/03.

Swift, L.W. and Messer, J.B. (1971) Forest cuttings raise temperatures of small streams in the southern Appalachians. *Journal of Soil and Water Conservation*, 26, 111–116.

Swift, M.J. and Sanchez, P.A. (1984) Biological management of tropical soil fertility for sustained productivity. *Nature and Resources*, 20, 2–10.

Swisher, C.C., Curtis, G.H., Jacob, T., et al. (1994) Age of the earliest known hominids in Java, Indonesia. *Science*, 263, 1118–1121.

Sylla, M.B., Gaye, A.T., Jenkins, G.S., et al. (2010) Consistency of projected drought over the Sahel with changes in the monsoon circulation and extremes in a regional climate model projections. *Journal of Geophysical Research*, 115, D16108.

Syvitski, J.P.M. (2008) Deltas at risk. *Sustainability Science*, 3, 23–32.

Syvitski, J.P.M. and Kettner, A. (2011) Sediment flux and the Anthropocene. *Philosophical Transactions: Series A, Mathematical, Physical, and Engineering Sciences*, 369, 957–975.

Syvitski, J.P.M., Kettner, A.J., Overeem, I., et al. (2009) Sinking deltas due to human activities. *Nature Geosciences*, 2, 681–686.

Syvitski, J.P.M. and Milliman, J.D. (2007) Geology, geography and humans battle for dominance over the delivery of fluvial sediment to the coastal ocean. *Journal of Geology*, 115, 1–19.

Syvitski, J.P.M. and Saito, Y. (2007) Morphodynamics of deltas under the influence of humans. *Global and Planetary Change*, 57, 261–282.

Syvitski, J.P.M., Vörösmarty, C.J., Kettner, A.J. and Green, P. (2005) Impact of humans on the flux of terrestrial sediment to the global coastal ocean. *Science*, 308, 376–380.

Szabó, J., Dávid, L. and Lóczy, D. (eds) (2010) *Anthropogenic Geomorphology*. Dordrecht: Springer.

Szabolcs, I. (1994) State and perspectives on soil salinity in Europe. *European Society for Soil Conservation Newsletter*, 3, 17–24.

Ta, W., Xiao, H. and Dong, Z. (2008) Long-term morphody-namic changes of a desert reach of the Yellow River following upstream large reservoirs' operation. *Geomorphology*, 97, 249–259.

Takacs-Santa, A. (2004) The major transitions in the history of human transformation of the biosphere. *Human Ecology Review*, 11, 51–66.

Tallis, J.H. (1965) Studies on southern Pennine peats, IV: evidence of recent erosion. *The Journal of Ecology*, 53, 509–520.

Tallis, J.H. (1985) Erosion of blanket peat in the southern Pennines: new light on an old problem. In R.H. Johnson (ed.), *The Geomorphology of North-West England*. Manchester: Manchester University Press, 313–336.

Tan, J., Zheng, Y., Tang, X., et al. (2010) The urban heat island and its impact on heat waves and human health in Shanghai. *International Journal of Biometeorology*, 54, 75–84.

Tang, J., Xu, X.B. and Wang, S.F. (2010) Trends of the precipitation acidity over China during 1992–2006. *Chinese Science Bulletin*, 55, 1800–1807.

Tang, Q. and Oki, T. (eds) (2016) *Terrestrial Water Cycle and Climate Change: Natural and Human-Induced Impacts*. Chichester: John Wiley & Sons.

Tang, Z., Gu, Y., Drahota, J., et al. (2015) Using fly ash as a marker to quantify culturally-accelerated sediment accumulation in playa wetlands. *JAWRA Journal of the American Water Resources Association*, doi:10.1111/1752-1688.12347.

Tao, X., Wu, P., Tang, C., et al. (2012) Effect of acid mine drainage on a karst basin: a case study on the high-As coal mining area in Guizhou province, China. *Environmental Earth Sciences*, 65, 631–638.

Tarolli, P., Preti, F. and Romano, N. (2014) Terraced landscapes: from an old best practice to a potential hazard for soil degradation due to land abandonment. *Anthropocene*, 6, 10–25.

Tasser, E., Leitinger, G. and Tappeiner, U. (2017) Climate change versus land-use change. What affects the mountain landscapes more? *Land Use Policy*, 60, 60–72.

Taylor, A.H. (2010) Fire disturbance and forest structure in an old-growth *Pinus ponderosa* forest, southern Cascades, USA. *Journal of Vegetation Science*, 21, 561–572.

Taylor, C.M., Lambin, E.F., Stephenne, N., et al. (2002) The influence of land use change on climate in the Sahel. *Journal of Climate*, 15, 3615–3629.

Taylor, J.A. (1985) Bracken encroachment rates in Britain. *Soil Use and Management*, 1, 53–56.

Taylor, K.E. and Penner, J.E. (1994) Response of the climatic system to atmospheric aerosols and greenhouse gases. *Nature*, 369, 734–737.

Taylor, M.P. and Little, J.A. (2013) Environmental impact of a major copper mine spill on a river and floodplain system. *Anthropocene*, 3, 36–50.

Tegen, I., Lacis, A.A. and Fung, I. (1996) The influence on climate forcing of mineral aerosols from disturbed soils. *Nature*, 380, 419–422.

Temmerman, S., Meire, P., Bouma, T.J., et al. (2013) Ecosystem-based coastal defence in the face of global change. *Nature*, 504, 79–83.

Teneva, L., Karnauskas, M., Logan, C.A., et al. (2012) Predicting coral bleaching hotspots: the role of regional variability in thermal stress and potential adaptation rates. *Coral Reefs*, 31, 1–12.

Tengberg, M. (2012) Beginnings and early history of date palm garden cultivation in the Middle East. *Journal of Arid Environments*, 86, 139–147.

Teo, E.A. and Marren, P.M. (2015) Interaction of ENSO-driven flood variability and anthropogenic changes in driving channel evolution: Corryong/Nariel Creek, Australia. *Australian Geographer*, 46, 339–362.

Terborgh, J. (1992) *Diversity and the Tropical Rain Forest*. New York: Freeman.

Ternan, J.L., Williams, A.G., Elmes, A. and Fitzjohn, C. (1996) The effectiveness of bench-terracing and afforestation for erosion control on Rana sediments in central Spain. *Land Degradation and Development*, 7, 337–351.

Terry, J.P. and Chui, T.F.M. (2012) Evaluating the fate of freshwater lenses on atoll islands after eustatic sea-level rise and cyclone-driven inundation: a modelling approach. *Global and Planetary Change*, 88, 76–84.

Tesdal, J.E., Christian, J.R., Monahan, A.H. and Salzen, K.V. (2016) Sensitivity of modelled sulfate aerosol and its radiative effect on climate to ocean DMS concentration and air–sea flux. *Atmospheric Chemistry and Physics*, 16 (17), 10847–10864.

Theodoropoulos, D.I. (2003) *Invasion Biology: Critique of a Pseudoscience*. Blythe, CA: Avvar Books.

Thirgood, J.V. (1981) *Man and the Mediterranean Forest – A History of Resource Depletion*. London: Academic Press.

Thomas, A.D., Walsh, R.P.D. and Shakesby, R.A. (2000) Solutes in overland flow following fire in eucalyptus and pine forests, northern Portugal. *Hydrological Processes*, 14, 971–985.

Thomas, C.D. (2015) Rapid acceleration of plant speciation during the Anthropocene. *Trends in Ecology & Evolution*, 30 (8), 448–455.

Thomas, C.D., Cameron, A., Green, R.E., et al. (2004) Extinction risk from climate change. *Nature*, 427, 145–148.

Thomas, D.S.G., Knight, M. and Wiggs, G.F.S. (2005) Remobilization of southern African desert dune systems by twenty-first century global warming. *Nature*, 435, 1218–1221.

Thomas, D.S.G. and Middleton, N.J. (1993) Salinisation: new perspectives on a major desertification issue. *Journal of Arid Environments*, 24, 95–105.

Thomas, D.S.G. and Middleton, N.J. (1994) *Desertification: Exploding the Myth*. Chichester: Wiley.

Thomas, D.S.G. and Wiggs, G.F.S. (2008) Aeolian system responses to global change: challenges of scale, process and temporal integration. *Earth Surface Processes and Landforms*, 33, 1396–1418.

Thomas, R., Frederick, E., Krabill, W., et al. (2006) Progressive increase in ice loss from Greenland. *Geophysical Research Letters*, 33, L10503.

Thomas, R.H., Sanderson, T.J.O. and Rose, K.E. (1979) Effect of climatic warming on the West Antarctic ice sheet. *Nature*, 277, 355–358.

Thomas, W.L. (ed.) (1956) *Man's Role in Changing the Face of the Earth*. Chicago: University of Chicago Press.

Thomas, Z.A. (2016) Using natural archives to detect climate and environmental tipping points in the Earth system. *Quaternary Science Reviews*, 152, 60–71.

Thompson, J.R. (1970) Soil erosion in the Detroit metropolitan area. *Journal of Soil and Water Conservation*, 25, 8–10.

Thompson, L.G. (2000) Ice core evidence for climate change in the Tropics: implications for our future. *Quaternary Science Reviews*, 19, 19–35.

Thompson, L.G., Brecher, H.H., Mosley-Thompson, E., et al. (2009) Glacier loss on Kilimanjaro continues unabated. *Proceedings of the National Academy of Sciences*, 106, 19770–19775.

Thomson, A.M., Brown, R.A., Rosenberg, N.J., et al. (2005) Climate change impacts for the conterminous USA: an integrated assessment. Part 4: water resources. *Climatic Change*, 69, 67–88.

Thomson, D.P., Shaffe, G.P. and McCorquodale, J.A. (2002) A potential interaction between sea level rise and global warming: implications for coastal stability on the Mississippi River Deltaic Plain. *Global and Planetary Change*, 32, 49–59.

Thomson, J., Fan, Y., Stammerjohn, S., et al. (2016) Emerging trends in the sea state of the Beaufort and Chukchi seas. *Ocean Modelling*, 105, 1–12.

Thornthwaite, C.W. (1956) Modification of the rural micro-climates. In W.L. Thomas (ed.), *Man's Role in Changing the Face of the Earth*. Chicago: University of Chicago Press, 567–583.

Thuiller, W., Broennimann, O., Hughes, G., et al. (2006) Vulnerability of African mammals to anthropogenic climate change under conservative land transformation assumptions. *Global Change Biology*, 12, 424–440.

Tiberi, R., Branco, M., Bracalini, M., et al. (2016) Cork oak pests: a review of insect damage and management. *Annals of Forest Science*, 73 (2), 219–232.

Tickner, D.P., Angold, P.G., Gurnell, A.M. and Mountford, J.O. (2001) Riparian plant invasions: hydrogeomorphological control and ecological impacts. *Progress in Physical Geography*, 25, 22–52.

Tie, X. and Cao, J. (2009) Aerosol pollution in China: present and future impact on environment. *Particuology*, 7, 426–431.

Tielidze, L.G., Lomidze, N. and Asanidze, L. (2015) Glaciers retreat and climate change effect during the last one century in the Mestiachala River Basin, Caucasus Mountains, Georgia. *Earth Sciences*, 4, 72–79.

Tiffen, M., Mortimore, M. and Gichuki, F.N. (1994) *More People, Less Erosion: Environmental Recovery in Kenya*. Chichester: Wiley.

Tilman, D., Reich, P.B. and Knops, M.H. (2006) Biodiversity and ecosystem stability in a decade-long grassland experiment. *Nature*, 441, 629–632.

Tipping, E., Bettney, R., Hurley, M.A., et al. (2000) Reversal of acidification in tributaries of the River Duddon (English Lake District) between 1970 and 1998. *Environmental Pollution*, 109, 183–191.

Tipping, R. (2008) Blanket peat in the Scottish Highlands: timing, cause, spread and the myth of environmental determinism. *Biodiversity and Conservation*, 17, 2097–2113.

Titus, J.G. (1990) Greenhouse effect, sea level rise, and barrier islands: case study of Long Beach Island, New Jersey. *Coastal Management*, 18, 65–90.

Titus, J.G. and Seidel, S. (1986) Overview of the effects of changing the atmosphere. In J.G. Titus (ed.), *Effects of Changes in Stratospheric Ozone and Global Climate*. Washington, DC: UNEP/USEPA, 3–19.

Tivy, J. (1971) *Biogeography: A Study of Plants in the Ecosphere*. Edinburgh: Oliver and Boyd.

Tiwari, V.M., Wahr, J. and Swenson, S. (2009) Dwindling groundwater resources in northern India, from satellite gravity observations. *Geophysical Research Letters*, 36, L18401.

Tixier-Boichard, M., Bed'hom, B. and Rognon, X. (2011) Chicken domestication: from archaeology to genomics. *Comptes Rendus Biologies*, 334, 197–204.

Tkachenko, K.S. (2017) Coral reefs in the face of ecological threats of the 21st century. *Biology Bulletin Reviews*, 7 (1), 64–83.

Tockner, K. and Stanford, J.A. (2002) Riverine flood plains: present state and future trends. *Environmental Conservation*, 29, 308–330.

Todd, V.L., Todd, I.B., Gardiner, J.C., et al. (2015) A review of impacts of marine dredging activities on marine mammals. *ICES Journal of Marine Science: Journal du Conseil*, 72 (2), 328–340.

Todhunter, P.E. and Chihacek, L.J. (1999) Historical reduction of airborne dust in the Red River Valley of the North. *Journal of Soil and Water Conservation*, 54, 543–551.

Tolba, M.K. and El-Kholy, O.A. (1992) *The World Environment, 1972–1992*. London: UNEP/Chapman and Hall.

Tolksdorf, J.F. and Kaiser, K. (2012) Holocene aeolian dynamics in the European sand-belt as indicated by geochronological data. *Boreas*, 41, 408–421.

Tölle, M.H., Engler, S. and Panitz, H.J. (2017) Impact of abrupt land cover changes by tropical deforestation on South-East Asian climate and agriculture. *Journal of Climate*, 30, 2587–2600.

Tomaselli, R. (1977) Degradation of the Mediterranean maquis. *UNESCO, MAB Technical Note*, 2, 33–72.

Tomkins, D.M., White, A.R. and Boots, M. (2003) Ecological replacement of native red squirrels by invasive greys driven by disease. *Ecology Letters*, 6, 189–196.

Toon, O.B. (2003) African dust in Florida clouds. *Nature*, 424, 623–624.

Törnqvist, T.E., Wallace, D.J., Storms, J.E., et al. (2008) Mississippi Delta subsidence primarily caused by compaction of Holocene strata. *Nature Geoscience*, 1 (3), 173–176.

Török, P., Ambarlı, D., Kamp, J., et al. (2016) Step(pe) up! Raising the profile of the Palaearctic natural grasslands. *Biodiversity and Conservation*, 25 (12), 2187–2195.

Tourian, M.J., Elmi, O., Chen, Q., et al. (2015) A spaceborne multisensor approach to monitor the desiccation of Lake Urmia in Iran. *Remote Sensing of Environment*, 156, 349–360.

Towns, D.R., Atkinson, I.A. and Daugherty, C.H. (2006) Have the harmful effects of introduced rats on islands been exaggerated? *Biological Invasions*, 8 (4), 863–891.

Townsend-Small, A., Pataki, D.E., Liu, H., et al. (2013) Increasing summer river discharge in southern California, USA, linked to urbanization. *Geophysical Research Letters*, 40, 4643–4647.

Tratalos, J., Fuller, R.A., Evans, K.L., et al. (2007) Bird densities are associated with household densities. *Global Change Biology*, 13 (8), 1685–1695.

Tréguer, P.J. and De La Rocha, C.L. (2013) The world ocean silica cycle. *Annual Review of Marine Science*, 5, 477–501.

Trimble, S.W. (1974) *Man-Induced Soil Erosion on the Southern Piedmont*. Ankeny, IA: Soil Conservation Society of America.

Trimble, S.W. (1976) Modern stream and valley sedimentation in the Driftless Area, Wisconsin, USA. *23rd International Geographical Congress*, sect. 1, 228–231.

Trimble, S.W. (1988) The impact of organisms on overall erosion rates within catchments in temperate regions. In H.A. Viles (ed.), *Biogeomorphology*. Oxford: Basil Blackwell, 83–142.

Trimble, S.W. (1997) Stream channel erosion and change resulting from riparian forests. *Geology*, 25, 467–469.

Trimble, S.W. (2003) Historical hydrographic and hydrologic changes in the San Diego Creek watershed, Newport Bay, California. *Journal of Historical Geography*, 29, 422–444.

Trimble, S.W. (2004) Effects of riparian vegetation on stream channel stability and sediment budgets. *Water Science and Application*, 8, 153–169.

Trimble, S.W. (2008a) *Man-Induced Soil Erosion on the Southern Piedmont* (2nd edn). Ankeny, IA: Soil Conservation Society of America.

Trimble, S.W. (2008b) The use of historical data and artifacts in geomorphology. *Progress in Physical Geography*, 32, 3–29.

Trimble, S.W. (2011) The historical decrease of soil erosion in the eastern United States – the role of geography and engineering. In S.D. Brunn (ed.), *Engineering Earth*. Dordrecht: Springer, 1383–1393.

Trimble, S.W. (2013) *Historical Agriculture and Soil Erosion in the Upper Mississippi Valley Hill Country*. Boca Raton: CRC Press.

Trimble, S.W. and Cooke, R.U. (1991) Historical sources for geomorphological research in the United States. *Professional Geographer*, 43, 212–228.

Trimble, S.W. and Crosson, S. (2000) US soil erosion rates – myth and reality. *Science*, 289, 248–250.

Trimble, S.W. and Lund, S.W. (1982) *Soil conservation and the reduction of erosion and sedimentation in the Coon Creek Basin, Wisconsin*. US Geological Survey professional paper, 1234.

Trimble, S.W. and Mendel, A.C. (1995) The cow as a geomorphic agent: a critical review. *Geomorphology*, 13, 233–253.

Tripathy, D.P. (2010) Environmentally sound management of e-wastes. *Ecology, Environment and Conservation*, 16, 641–649.

Triplett, L.D., Engstrom, D.R., Conley, D.J. and Schellhaass, S.M. (2008) Silica fluxes and trapping in two contrasting natural impoundments of the upper Mississippi River. *Biogeochemistry*, 87, 217–230.

Troels-Smith, J. (1956) Neolithic period in Switzerland and Denmark. *Science*, 124, 876–879.

Tryjanowski, P., Sparks, T.H., Biaduń, W., et al. (2015) Winter bird assemblages in rural and urban environments: a national survey. *PloS one*, 10 (6), e0130299.

Tsvetkov, N., Samson-Robert, O., Sood, K., et al. (2017) Chronic exposure to neonicotinoids reduces honey bee health near corn crops. *Science*, 356 (6345), 1395–1397.

Tubiello, F.N., Biancalani, R., Salvatore, M., et al. (2016) A worldwide assessment of greenhouse gas emissions from drained organic soils. *Sustainability*, 8 (4), doi:10.3390/su8040371 DOI:10.3390/su8040371#_blank.

Tucker, C.J., Dregne, H.E. and Newcomb, W.W. (1991) Expansion and contraction of the Sahara Desert from 1980 to 1990. *Science*, 253, 299–301.

Tuffen, H. (2013) Melting ice and volcanic hazards in the twenty-first century. In B. McGuire and M. Maslin (eds), *Climate Forcing of Geological Hazard*. Chichester: John Wiley & Sons, 78–107.

Turco, R.P., Toon, O.B., Ackermann, T.P., et al. (1983) Nuclear winter: global consequences of multiple nuclear explosions. *Science*, 222, 1283–1292.

Turnbull, L., Wainwright, J. and Brazier, R.E. (2010) Changes in hydrology and erosion over a transition from grassland to shrubland. *Hydrological Processes*, 24, 393–414.

Turner, B.L., Kasperson, R.E., Meyer, W.B., et al. (1990) Two types of global environmental change: definitional and spatial-scale issues in their human dimensions. *Global Environmental Change*, 1, 14–22.

Turner, I.M. (1996) Species loss in fragments of tropical rain forest: a review of the evidence. *Journal of Applied Ecology*, 33, 200–209.

Turvey, S.T. (ed.) (2009) *Holocene Extinctions*. Oxford: Oxford University Press.

Turvey, S.T., Pitman, R.L., Taylor, B.L., et al. (2007) First human-caused extinction of a cetacean species? *Biology Letters*, 3, 537–540.

Tweel, A.W. and Turner, R.E. (2012) Watershed land use and river eigineering drive wetland formation and loss in the Mississippi birdfoot delta. *Limnology and Oceanography*, 57, 18–28.

Tyldesley, J.A. and Bahn, P.G. (1983) The use of plants in the European palaeolithic: a review of the evidence. *Quaternary Science Reviews*, 2, 53–81.

Tyler, S.W., Kranz, S., Parlange, M.B., et al. (1997) Estimation of groundwater evaporation and salt flux from Owens Lake, California, USA. *Journal of Hydrology*, 200, 110–135.

UK Climate Impacts Programme (2001) *Climate Change and Nature Conservation in Britain and Ireland*. Oxford: UKCIP.

UNEP (1991) *United Nations Environment Programme Environmental Data Report* (3rd edn). Oxford: Basil Blackwell.

UNEP (2007) *Global Environment Outlook GEO₄*. Nairobi: UNEP.

Unger, P.W., Stewart, B.A., Parr, J.F. and Singh, R.P. (1991) Crop residue management and tillage methods for conserving soil and water in semi-arid regions. *Soil and Tillage Research*, 20, 219–240.

Urban, M.C. (2015) Accelerating extinction risk from climate change. *Science*, 348 (6234), 571–573.

US Department of Agriculture, Soil Conservation Service (1972) http://www.plant-materials.nrcs.usda.gov/pubs/ndpmcrnmama37midw.pdf (accessed January 2018).

US General Accounting Office (2000) *Acid Rain: Emissions Trends and Effects in the Eastern United States*. Washington, DC: US General Accounting Office.

Usher, M.B. (1973) *Biological Management and Conservation*. London: Chapman and Hall.

Utset, A. and Borroto, M. (2001) A modelling-GIS approach for assessing irrigation effects of soil salinisation under global warming conditions. *Agricultural Water Management*, 50, 53–63.

Vale, T.R. and Vale, G.R. (1976) Suburban bird population in westcentral California. *Journal of Biogeography*, 3, 157–165.

Valentin, C., Rajot, J.-L. and Mitja, D. (2004) Response of soil crusting, runoff and erosion to fallowing in the sub-humid and semi-arid regions of West Africa. *Agriculture, Ecosystems & Environment*, 104, 287–302.

van Andel, T.H., Zangger, E. and Demitrack, A. (1990) Land use and soil erosion in prehistoric and historical Greece. *Journal of Field Archaeology*, 17, 379–396.

van Auken, O.W. (2000) Shrub invasion of North American semiarid grasslands. *Annual Review of Ecology and Systematics*, 31, 197–215.

Van Cappellen, P. and Maavara, T. (2016) Rivers in the Anthropocene: global scale modifications of riverine nutrient fluxes by damming. *Ecohydrology & Hydrobiology*, 16 (2), 106–111.

van den Broeke, M., et al. (2009) Partitioning recent Greenland mass loss. *Science*, 326, 984–986.

Van Der Kaars, S., Miller, G.H., Turney, C.S., et al. (2017) Humans rather than climate the primary cause of Pleistocene megafaunal extinction in Australia. *Nature Communications*, 8, doi:10.1038/ncomms14142 DOI:10.1038%2Fncomms14142#pmc_ext.

Van der Ent, A. and Lambers, H. (2016) Plant-soil interactions in global biodiversity hotspots. *Plant and Soil*, 403 (1), 1–5.

van der Ween, C.J. (2002) Polar ice sheets and global sea level: how well can we predict the future? *Global and Planetary Change*, 32, 165–194.

Vanguelova, E.I., Benham, S., Pitman, R., et al. (2010) Chemical fluxes in time through forest ecosystems in the UK – soil response to pollution recovery. *Environmental Pollution*, 158, 1857–1869.

Van Herk, C.M., Mathijssen-Spiekman, E.A.M. and de Zwart, D. (2003) Long distance nitrogen effects on lichens in Europe. *Lichenologist*, 35, 347–359.

Van Manh, N., Dung, N.V., Hung, N.N., et al. (2015) Future sediment dynamics in the Mekong Delta floodplains: impacts of hydropower development, climate change and sea level rise. *Global and Planetary Change*, 127, 22–33.

Van Oost, K., Govers, G., de Alba, S. and Quine, T.A. (2006) Tillage erosion: a review of controlling factors and implica tions for soil quality. *Progress in Physical Geography*, 30, 443–466.

van Oudenhoven, A.P., Veerkamp, C.J., Alkemade, R. and Leemans, R. (2015) Effects of different management regimes on soil erosion and surface runoff in semi-arid to sub-humid rangelands. *Journal of Arid Environments*, 121, 100–111.

Van Vliet, M.T., Franssen, W.H., Yearsley, J., et al. (2013a) Global river discharge and water temperature under climate change. *Global Environmental Change*, 23, 450–464.

Van Vliet, N., Mertz, O., Birch-Thomsen, T. and Schmook, B. (2013b) Is there a continuing rationale for swidden cultivation in the 21st century? *Human Ecology*, 41 (1), 1–5.

Vaudour, J. (1986) Travertins holocènes et pression anthropique. *Méditerranée*, 10, 168–173.

Vaughan, D.G. and Doake, C.S.M. (1996) Recent atmospheric warming and retreat of ice shelves on the Antarctic Peninsula. *Nature*, 379, 328–331.

Vaughan, D.G. and Spouge, J.R. (2002) Risk estimation of collapse of the west Antarctic ice sheet. *Climate Change*, 52, 65–91.

Vaughan, N.E. and Lenton, T.M. (2011) A review of climate geoengineering proposals. *Climate Change*, 109, 745–790.

Veblen, T.T. and Stewart, G.H. (1982) The effects of introduced wild animals on New Zealand forests. *Annals of the Association of American Geographers*, 72, 372–397.

Vehrs, H.P. (2016) Changes in landscape vegetation, forage plant composition and herding structure in the pastoralist livelihoods of East Pokot, Kenya. *Journal of Eastern African Studies*, 10 (1), 88–110.

Veit, E. and Conrad, C.P. (2016) The impact of groundwater depletion on spatial variations in sea level change during the past century. *Geophysical Research Letters*, 43 (7), 3351–3359.

Vendrov, S.L. (1965) A forecast of changes in natural conditions in the northern Ob' basin in case of construction of the lower Ob' Hydro Project. *Soviet Geography*, 6, 3–18.

Vennemo, H., Aunan, K., Lindhjem, H. and Seip, H.M. (2009) Environmental pollution in China: status and trends. *Review of Environmental Economics and Policy*, 3, 209–230.

Venter, O., Sanderson, E.W., Magrach, A., et al. (2016) Sixteen years of change in the global terrestrial human footprint and implications for biodiversity conservation. *Nature Communications*, 7, doi:10.1038/ncomms12558.

Venteris, E.R. (1999) Rapid tidewater glacier retreat: a comparison between Columbia Glacier, Alaska and Patagonian calving glaciers. *Global and Planetary Change*, 22, 131–138.

Vermaire, J.C., Pisaric, M.F., Thienpont, J.R., et al. (2013) Arctic climate warming and sea ice declines lead to increased storm surge activity. *Geophysical Research Letters*, 40, 1386–1390.

Vermeer, M. and Rahmstorf, S. (2009) Global sea level linked to global temperature. *Proceedings of the National Academy of Sciences*, 106, 21527–21532.

Verstraeten, G., Broothaerts, N., Van Loo, M., et al. (2017) Variability in fluvial geomorphic response to anthropogenic disturbance. *Geomorphology*. doi:10.1016/j.geomorph.2017.03.027.

Verstraeten, G., Rommens, T., Peeters, I., et al. (2009) A temporarily changing Holocene sediment budget for a loess-covered catchment (central Belgium). *Geomorphology*, 108, 24–34.

Vesely, J., Majer, V. and Norton, S.A. (2002) Heterogeneous response of central European streams to decreased acid atmospheric deposition. *Environmental Pollution*, 120, 275–281.

Veth, P., Ward, I., Manne, T., et al. (2017) Early human occupation of a maritime desert, Barrow Island, North-West Australia. *Quaternary Science Reviews*, 168, 19–29.

Viana, M., Hamminghh, P., Colette, A., et al. (2014) Impact of maritime transport emissions on coastal air quality in Europe. *Atmospheric Environment*, 90, 96–105.

Vice, R.B., Guy, H.P. and Ferguson, G.E. (1969) *Sediment movement in an area of suburban highway construction, Scott Run Basin, Fairfax, County, Virginia, 1961–64*. United States Geological Survey water supply paper, 1591–E.

Viessman, W., Knapp, J.W., Lewis, G.L. and Harbaugh, T.E. (1977) *Introduction to Hydrology* (2nd edn). New York: IEP.

Viles, H.A. (2002) Implications of future climate change for stone deterioration. In S. Siegesmund, T. Weiss and J.A. Vollbrecht (eds), *Natural Stone, Weathering Phenomena, Conservation Strategies and Case Studies*. Geological Society of London special publication, 205, 407–418.

Viles, H.A. (2003) Conceptual modelling of the impacts of climate change on karst geomorphology in the UK and Ireland. *Journal for Nature Conservation*, 11, 59–66.

Viles, H.A. and Goudie, A.S. (2003) Interannual decadal and multidecadal scale climatic variability and geomorphology. *Earth-Science Reviews*, 61, 105–131.

Viles, H.A. and Spencer, T. (1995) *Coastal Problems: Geomorphology, Ecology and Society at the Coast*. London: Edward Arnold.

Vilímek, V., Zapata, M.L., Klimeš, J., et al. (2005) Influences of glacial retreat on natural hazards of the Palcacocha Lake area, Peru. *Landslides*, 2, 107–115.

Villmoare, B., Kimbel, W.H., Seyoum, C., et al. (2015) Early Homo at 2.8 Ma from Ledi-Geraru, Afar, Ethiopia. *Science*, 347, 1352–1355.

Vine, H. (1968) Developments in the study of soils and shifting agriculture in tropical Africa. In R.P. Moss (ed.), *The Soil Resources of Tropical Africa*. Cambridge: Cambridge University Press, 89–119.

Vita-Finzi, C. (1969) *The Mediterranean Valleys*. Cambridge: Cambridge University Press.

Vitousek, P.M., Gosz, J.R., Gruer, C.C., et al. (1979) Nitrate losses from disturbed ecosystems. *Science*, 204, 469–473.

Vitousek, P.M., Mooney, H.A., Lubchenco, J. and Melillo, J.M. (1997) Human Domination of Earth's Ecosystems. *Science*, 277, 494–499.

Vogl, R.J. (1977) Fire: a destructive menace or a rational process. In J. Cairns, K.L. Dickson and E.E. Herricks (eds), *Recovery and Restoration of Damaged Ecosystems*. Charlottesville: University Press of Virginia, 261–289.

von Broembsen, S.L. (1989) Invasions of natural ecosystems by plant pathogens. In J.A. Drake (ed.), *Biological Invasions: A Global Perspective*. Chichester: Wiley, 77–83.

Vörösmarty, C.J., Meybeck, M., Fekete, B., et al. (2003) Anthropogenic sediment retention: major global impact from registered river impoundments. *Global and Planetary Change*, 39, 169–190.

Vuille, M., Francou, B., Wagnon, P., et al. (2008) Climate change and tropical Andean glaciers: past, present and future. *Earth-Science Reviews*, 89, 79–96.

Vuorenmaa, J. and Forsius, M. (2008) Recovery of acidified Finnish lakes: trends, patterns and dependence of catchment characteristics. *Hydrology and Earth System Sciences*, 12, 465–478.

Wackernagel, M. and Rees, W. (1995) *Our Ecological Footprint: Reducing Human Impact on the Earth*. Gabriola Island: New Society Publishers.

Wada, Y., van Beek, L.P.H. and Bierkens, M.F.P. (2012a) Non-sustainable groundwater sustaining irrigation: a global assessment. *Water Resources Research*, 48, W00L06.

Wada, Y., van Beek, L.P.H., Sperna Weiland, F.C., et al. (2012b) Past and future contribution of global groundwater depletion to sea-level rise. *Geophysical Research Letters*, 39, L09402.

Wada, Y., van Beek, L.P.H., van Kempen, C.M., et al. (2010) Global depletion of groundwater resources. *Geophysical Research Letters*, 37, L20402, doi:10.1029/2010GL044571.

Wagner, T.P. (2009) Shared responsibility for managing electronic waste: a case study of Maine, USA. *Waste Management*, 29, 3014–3021.

Waguespack, N.M., Surovell, T.A., Denoyer, A., et al. (2009) Making a point: wood-versus stone-tipped projectiles. *Antiquity*, 83 (321), 786–800.

Waithaka, J.M. (1996) Elephants: a keystone species. In T.R. McClanahan and T. Young (eds), *East African Ecosystems and Their Conservation*. New York: Oxford University Press, 284–285.

Wakindiki, I.I.C. and Ben-Hur, M. (2002) Indigenous soil and water conservation techniques: effects on runoff, erosion, and crop yields under semi-arid conditions. *Australian Journal of Soil Research*, 40, 367–379.

Walker, G. (2006) The tipping point of the iceberg. *Nature*, 441, 802–805.

Walker, H.J. (1988) *Artificial Structures and Shorelines*. Dordrecht: Kluwer.

Walker, H.J., Coleman, J.M., Roberts, H.H. and Tye, R.S. (1987) Wetland loss in Louisiana. *Geografiska Annaler*, 69A, 189–200.

Walker, M., Gibbard, P., and Lowe, J. (2015) Comment on 'When did the Anthropocene begin? A mid-twentieth century boundary is stratigraphically optimal' by Jan Zalasiewicz et al. (2015). *Quaternary International*, 383, 204–207.

Walker, M.D., Gould, W.A. and Chapin, F.S. (2001) Scenarios of biodiversity changes in Arctic and alpine tundra. In F.S. Chapin, O.E. Sala and E. Huber-Sannwald (eds), *Global Biodiversity in a Changing Environment*. New York: Springer, 83–100.

Wall, D.H. and Bardgett, R.D. (eds) (2012) *Soil Ecology and Ecosystem Services*. Oxford: Oxford University Press.

Walling, D.E. (2006) Human impact on land-ocean sediment transfer by the world's rivers. *Geomorphology*, 79, 192–216.

Walling, D.E. and Gregory, K.J. (1970) The measurement of the effects of building construction on drainage basin dynamics. *Journal of Hydrology*, 11, 129–144.

Walling, D.E. and Quine, T.A. (1991) *Recent rates of soil loss from areas of arable cultivation in the UK. IAHS publication* 203, 123–131.

Wallwork, K.L. (1956) Subsidence in the mid-Cheshire industrial area. *Geographical Journal*, 122, 40–53.

Wallwork, K.L. (1974) *Derelict Land*. Newton Abbot: David & Charles.

Walsh, C.J., Fletcher, T.D. and Vietz, G.J. (2016b) Variability in stream ecosystem response to urbanization: unravelling the influences of physiography and urban land and water management. *Progress in Physical Geography*, 40 (5), 714–731.

Walsh, K. and Pittock, B. (1998) Potential changes in tropical storms, hurricanes, and extreme rainfall events as a result of climate change. *Climatic Change*, 39, 199–213.

Walsh, K.J., McBride, J.L., Klotzbach, P.J., et al. (2016a) Tropical cyclones and climate change. *Wiley Interdisciplinary Reviews: Climate Change*, 7 (1), 65–89.

Walsh, R.P.D., Clarke, M.A., Bidin, K., et al. (2006) Changes in the spatial distribution of erosion within a selectively logged rainforest in Borneo 1988–2003. In P.N. Owens and A.J. Collins (eds), *Soil Erosion and Sediment Redistribution in River Catchments*. Wallingford: CAB International, 239–253.

Walter, H. (1984) *Vegetation and the Earth* (3rd edn). Berlin: Springer.

Walter, R.C. and Merritts, D.J. (2008) Natural streams and the legacy of water-powered mills. *Science*, 319, 299–304.

Wan, D., Jin, Z., Zhang, F., Song, L. and Yang, J. (2016a) Increasing dust fluxes on the northeastern Tibetan Plateau linked with the Little Ice Age and recent human activity since the 1950s. *Aeolian Research*, 23, 93–102.

Wan, Z., Zhu, M., Chen, S. and Sperling, D. (2016b) Three steps to a green shipping industry. *Nature*, 530, 275–277.

Wang, F., Zhang, Y., Huo, Z., et al. (2008) Movement of the Shuping landslide in the first four years after the initial impoundment of the Three Gorges Dam Reservoir, China. *Landslides*, 5, 321–329.

Wang, H., Fu, L., Du, X. and Ge, W. (2010) Trends in vehicular emissions in China's mega cities from 1995–2005. *Environmental Pollution*, 158, 394–400.

Wang, P., Li, Z., Luo, S., et al. (2015a) Five decades of changes in the glaciers on the Friendship Peak in the Altai Mountains, China: changes in area and ice surface elevation. *Cold Regions Science and Technology*, 116, 24–31.

Wang, P., Li, Z., Yu, G., et al. (2016) Glacier shrinkage in the Daxue and Danghenan ranges of the western Qilian Mountains, China, from 1957 to 2010. *Environmental Earth Sciences*, 75 (2), 1–11.

Wang, Q., Yi, S. and Sun, W. (2017) Precipitation-driven glacier changes in the Pamir and Hindu Kush mountains. *Geophysical Research Letters*, 44, 2817–2824.

Wang, X., Eerdun, H., Zhou, Z. and Liu, X. (2007) Significance of variations in the wind energy environment over the past 50 years with respect to dune activity and desertification in arid and semiarid northern China. *Geomorphology*, 86, 252–266.

Wang, X., Siegert, F., Zhou, A.G. and Franke, J. (2013) Glacier and glacial lake changes and their relationship in the context of climate change, Central Tibetan Plateau 1972–2010. *Global and Planetary Change*, 111, 246–257.

Wang, Y., Yang, Y., Zhao, N., et al. (2012) The magnitude of the effect of air pollution on sunshine hours in China. *Journal of Geophysical Research*, 117, D00V14.

Wang, Z., Xiao, J., Fan, S., et al. (2015b) Who made the world's largest green tide in China? – an integrated study on the initiation and early development of the green tide in Yellow Sea. *Limnology and Oceanography*, 60 (4), 1105–1117.

Wanger, T.C. (2011) The lithium future – resources, recycling and the environment. *Conservation Letters*, 4, 202–206.

Ward, A.I. (2005) Expanding ranges of wild and feral deer in Great Britain. *Mammal Review*, 35 (2), 165–173.

Ward, D. (2005) Do we understand the causes of bush encroachment in African savannas? *African Journal of Range and Forage Science*, 22, 101–105.

Ward, P.J., Marfai, M.A., Yulianto, F.F., et al. (2011) Coastal inundation and damage exposure estimation: a case study for Jakarta. *Natural Hazards*, 56, 899–916.

Ward, R.D., Friess, D.A., Day, R.H. and MacKenzie, R.A. (2016) Impacts of climate change on mangrove ecosystems: a region by region overview. *Ecosystem Health and Sustainability*, 2 (4), doi:10.1002/ehs2.1211.

Ward, S.D. (1979) Limestone pavements – a biologist's view. *Earth Science Conservation*, 16, 16–18.

Warner, R.C. and Budd, W.F. (1990) Modelling the long-term response of the Antarctic Ice Sheet to global warming. *Annals of Glaciology*, 27, 161–168.

Warren, A. (ed.) (2002) *Wind Erosion on Agricultural Land in Europe*. Brussels: European Commission.

Warrick, J.A., Hatten, J.A., Pasternack, G.B., et al. (2012) The effects of wildfire on the sediment yield of a coastal California watershed. *Geological Society of America Bulletin*, 124 (7–8), 1130–1146.

Warrick, J.A., Madej, M.A., Goñi, M.A. and Wheatcroft, R.A. (2013) Trends in the suspended-sediment yields of coastal rivers of northern California, 1955–2010. *Journal of Hydrology*, 489, 108–123.

Warrick, R.A. and Ahmad, Q.K. (eds) (1996) *The Implications of Climate and Sea Level Change for Bangladesh*. Dordrecht: Kluwer.

Washington, R., Bouet, C., Cautenet, G., et al. (2009) Dust as a tipping element: the Bodélé Depression, Chad. *Proceedings of the National Academy of Sciences*, 106, 20564–20571.

Wasson, K., Jeppesen, R., Endris, C., et al. (2017) Eutrophication decreases salt marsh resilience through proliferation of algal mats. *Biological Conservation*, 212, 1–11.

Wasson, R.J. (2012) Geomorphic histories for river and catchment management. *Philosophical Transactions: Series A, Mathematical, Physical, and Engineering Sciences*, 370, 2240–2263.

Waters, C.N., Zalasiewicz, J., Summerhayes, C., et al. (2016) The Anthropocene is functionally and stratigraphically distinct from the Holocene. *Science*, 351 (6269), aad2622.

Waters, M.R. and Haynes, C.V. (2001) Late Quaternary arroyo formation and climate change in the American southwest. *Geology*, 29, 399–402.

Watkins, T. (2010) New light on Neolithic revolution in south-west Asia. *Antiquity*, 84, 621–634.

Watson, A. (1976) The origin and distribution of closed depressions in south-west Lancashire and north-west Cheshire. Unpublished BA dissertation, University of Oxford.

Watson, A., Price-Williams, D. and Goudie, A.S. (1984) The palaeoenvironmental interpretation of colluvial sediments and palaeosols of the Late Pleistocene hypothermal in southern Africa. *Palaeogeography, Palaeoclimatology, Palaeoecology*, 5, 225–249.

Watson, E.B., Raposa, K.B., Carey, J.C., et al. (2017) Anthropocene survival of southern New England's salt marshes. *Estuaries and Coasts*, 40, 617–625.

Watson, J.E., Shanahan, D.F., Di Marco, M., et al. (2017) Catastrophic declines in wilderness areas undermine global environment targets. *Current Biology*, 26, 2929–2934.

Watts, J. (2005) China: the air pollution capital of the world. *Lancet*, 366, 1761–1762.

Waycott, M., Duarte, C.M., Carruthers, T.J., et al. (2009) Accelerating loss of seagrasses across the globe threatens coastal ecosystems. *Proceedings of the National Academy of Sciences*, 106, 12377–12381.

Weart, S.R. (2003) *The Discovery of Global Warming*. Cambridge, MA: Harvard University Press.

Weaver, J.E. (1954) *North American Prairie*. Lincoln: Johnsen.

Webb, N.P., Herrick, J.E., Van Zee, J.W., et al. (2016) The National Wind Erosion Research Network: building a standardized long-term data resource for aeolian research, modeling and land management. *Aeolian Research*, 22, 23–36.

Webb, N.P. and McGowan, H.A. (2009) Approaches to modeling land erodibility by wind. *Progress in Physical Geography*, 33, 587–613.

Webb, R.H. (1982) Off-road motorcycle effects on a desert soil. *Environmental Conservation*, 9, 197–208.

Webb, R.H., Boyer, D.E. and Turner, R.M. (eds) (2010) *Repeat Photography: Methods and Applications in the Natural Sciences.* Washington, DC: Island Press.

Webb, R.H. and Wilshire, H.G. (eds) (2012) *Environmental Effects of Off-Road Vehicles: Impacts and Management in Arid Regions.* Heidelberg: Springer Science & Business Media.

Weber, E., Sun, S.-G. and Li, B. (2008) Invasive alien plants in China: diversity and ecological insights. *Biological Invasions*, 10, 1411–1429.

Weber, K.A. and Perry, R.G. (2006) Groundwater abstraction impacts on spring flow and base flow in the Hillsborough River Basin, Florida, USA. *Hydrogeology Journal*, 14, 1252–1264.

Weber, P. (1993) Reviving coral reefs. In L.R. Brown (ed.), *State of the World 1993.* London: Earthscan, 42–60.

Webster, P.J., Holland, G.J., Curry, J.A. and Chang, H.-R. (2005) Changes in tropical cyclone number, duration, and intensity in a warming environment. *Science*, 309, 1844–1846.

Weertman, J. (1974) Stability of the junction of an ice sheet and an ice shelf. *Journal of Glaciology*, 13 (67), 3–11.

Wehrli, M.N., Mitchell, E.A.D., van der Knaap, W.O., et al. (2010) Effects of climatic change and bog development on Holocene tufa formation in the Lorze Valley (central Switzerland). *The Holocene*, 20, 325–336.

Wein, R.W. and Maclean, D.A. (eds) (1983) *The Role of Fire in Northern Circumpolar Ecosystem.* Chichester: Wiley.

Weis, J.S. (2015) *Marine Pollution: What Everyone Needs to Know.* Oxford: Oxford University Press.

Weisrock, A. (1986) Variations climatiques et periodes de sedimentation carbonatée a l'Holocene – l'age des depôts. *Mediterranée*, 10, 165–167.

Weiss, E., Kislev, M.E. and Hartmann, A. (2006) Autonomous cultivation before domestication. *Science*, 312, 1608–1610.

Wellburn, A. (1988) *Air Pollution and Acid Rain: The Biological Impact.* London: Longman.

Wells, J.T. (1995) Effects of sea level rise on coastal sedimentation and erosion. In D. Eisma (ed.), *Climate Change Impact on Coastal Habitation.* Boca Raton: Lewis, 111–136.

Wells, J.T. (1996) Subsidence, sea level rise, and wetland loss in the lower Mississippi River Delta. In J.D. Milliman and B.V. Haq (eds), *Sea Level Rise and Coastal Subsidence.* Dordrecht: Kluwer.

Wells, N.A. and Andriamihaja, B. (1993) The initiation and growth of gullies in Madagascar: are humans to blame? *Geomorphology*, 8, 1–46.

Wells, P.V. (1965) Scarp woodlands, transported grass soils and concept of grassland climate in the Great Plains region. *Science*, 148, 246–249.

Wen, F. and Chen, X. (2006) Evaluation of the impact of groundwater irrigation on streamflow in Nebraska. *Journal of Hydrology*, 327, 603–617.

Werritty, A. (2002) Living with uncertainty: climate change, river flows and water resource management in Scotland. *Science of the Total Environment*, 294, 29–40.

Werritty, A. and Lees, K.F. (2001) The sensitivity of Scottish rivers and upland valley floors to recent environmental change. *Catena*, 42, 251–273.

Werth, D. and Avissar, R. (2002) The local and global effects of Amazon deforestation. *Journal of Geophysical Research – Atmospheres*, 107 (D20), 8087.

Westcott, F. and Andrew, M.E. (2015) Spatial and environmental patterns of off-road vehicle recreation in a semi-arid woodland. *Applied Geography*, 62, 97–106.

Westhoff, V. (1983) Man's attitude towards vegetation. In W. Holzner, M.J.A. Werger and I. Ikusima (eds), *Man's Impact on Vegetation.* The Hague: Junk, 7–24.

Westing, A. and Pfeiffer, E.W. (1972) The cratering of Indochina. *Scientific American*, 226 (5), 21–29.

Westing, A.H. (2013) Nuclear war: its environmental impact. *Springer Briefs on Pioneers in Science and Practice*, 1, 80–113.

Wetherald, R.T. and Manabe, S. (2002) Simulation of hydrologic changes associated with global warming. *Journal of Geophysical Research*, 107, D19.

Wheaton, E.E. (1990) Frequency and severity of drought and dust storms. *Canadian Journal of Agricultural Economics*, 38, 695–700.

Whitaker, J.R. (1940) World view of destruction and conservation of natural resources. *Annals of the Association of American Geographers*, 30, 143–162.

White, T., Asfaw, B., De Gusta, D., et al. (2003) Pleistocene *Homo sapiens* from Middle Awash, Ethiopia. *Nature*, 423, 742–747.

Whitehorn, P.R., O'Connor, S., Wackers, F.L. and Goulson, D. (2012) Neonicotinoid pesticide reduces bumble bee colony growth and queen production. *Science*, 336, 351–352.

Whitlock, C., Shafer, S.L. and Marlon, J. (2003) The role of climate and vegetation change in shaping past and future fire regimes in to northwestern US and the implications for ecosystem management. *Forest Ecology and Management*, 178, 5–21.

Whitmore, T.M., Turner, B.L., Johnson, D.L., et al. (1990) Long term population change. In B.L. Turner, W.C. Clark, R.W. Kates, et al. (eds), *The Earth as Transformed by Human Action.* Cambridge: Cambridge University Press, 26–39.

Whitney, G.G. (1994) *From Coastal Wilderness to Fruited Plain.* Cambridge: Cambridge University Press.

Whitten, A.J., Damanik, S.J., Anwar, J. and Nazaruddin, H. (1987) *The Ecology of Sumatra.* Yogyukarta: Gadjah Mada University Press.

Wicke, B., Sikkema, R., Dornburg, V. and Faaij, A. (2011) Exploring land use changes and the role of palm oil production in Indonesia and Malaysia. *Land Use Policy*, 28, 193–206.

Wigley, B.J., Bond, W.J. and Hoffmann, M.T. (2009) Bush encroachment under three contrasting land-use practices in a mesic South African savanna. *African Journal of Ecology*, 47 (Suppl. 1), 62–70.

Wilby, R.L. (2003) Past and projected trends in London's urban heat island. *Weather*, 58, 251–260.

Wilby, R.L. and Gell, P.A. (1994) The impact of forest harvesting on water yield: modelling hydrological changes detected by pollen analysis. *Hydrological Sciences Journal*, 39, 471–486.

Wilby, R.L., Dalgleish, H.Y. and Foster, I.D.L. (1997) The impact of weather patterns on historic and contemporary catchment sediment yields. *Earth Surface Processes and Landforms*, 22, 353–363.

Wild, M. (2009) Global dimming and brightening: a review. *Journal of Geophysical Research*, 114, D00D16.

Wild, M. (2012) Enlightening global dimming and brightening. *Bulletin of the American Meteorological Society*, 93, 27–37.

Wild, M., Gilgen, H., Roesch, A., et al. (2005) From dimming to brightening: decadal changes in solar radiation at Earth's surface. *Science*, 308, 847–850.

Wild, M., Ohmura, A. and Makowski, K. (2007) Impact of global dimming and brightening on global warming. *Geophysical Research Letters*, 34, L04702.

Wildman, L.A.S. and Macbroom, J.G. (2005) The evolution of gravel bed channels after dam removal: case study of the Anaconda and Union City dam removals. *Geomorphology*, 71, 245–262.

Wilken, G.C. (1972) Microclimate management by traditional farmers. *Geographical Review*, 62, 544–560.

Wilkinson, B.H. and McElroy, B.J. (2007) The impact of humans on continental erosion and sedimentation. *Geological Society of America Bulletin*, 119, 140–156.

Wilkinson, C., Linden, O., Cesar, H., et al. (1999) Ecological and socio-economic impacts of 1998 coral mortality in the Indian Ocean: an ENSO impact and a warning of future change? *Ambio*, 28, 188–196.

Wilkinson, J.C. (1977) *Water and Tribal Settlement in South-East Arabia: A Study of the Aflāj of Oman.* Oxford: Clarendon Press.

Wilkinson, T.J. and Rayne, L. (2010) Hydraulic landscapes and imperial power in the Near East. *Water History*, 2 (2), 115–144.

Wilkinson, T.J., French, C., Ur, J.A. and Semple, M. (2010) The geoarchaeology of route systems in northern Syria. *Geoarchaeology*, 25, 745–771.

Wilkinson, W.B. and Brassington, F.C. (1991) Rising groundwater levels – an international problem. In R.A. Downing and W.B. Wilkinson (eds), *Applied Groundwater Hydrology – A British Perspective.* Oxford: Clarendon Press, 35–53.

Williams, A.T., Giardino, A. and Pranzini, E. (2016) Canons of coastal engineering in the United Kingdom: seawalls/groynes, a century of change? *Journal of Coastal Research*, 32 (5), 1196–1211.

Williams, E.H. and Bunkley-Williams, L. (1990) The worldwide coral bleaching cycle and related sources of coral mortality. *Atoll Research Bulletin*, 335, 1–71.

Williams, G.P. (1978) The case of the shrinking channels – the North Platte and Platte rivers in Nebraska. *United States Geological Survey circular*, 781.

Williams, M. (1970) *The Draining of the Somerset Levels.* Cambridge: Cambridge University Press.

Williams, M. (1988) The death and rebirth of the American forest: clearing and reversion in the United States, 1900–1980. In J.F. Richards and R. Tucker (eds), *World Deforestation in the Twentieth Century.* Durham, NC: Duke University Press, 211–229.

Williams, M. (1989) *Americans and Their Forests.* Cambridge: Cambridge University Press.

Williams, M. (1990) *Wetlands: A Threatened Landscape.* Oxford: Basil Blackwell.

Williams, M. (1994) Forests and tree cover. In W.B. Meyer and B.L. Turner II (eds), *Changes in Land Use and Land Cover: A Global Perspective.* Cambridge: Cambridge University Press, 97–124.

Williams, M. (2000) Deforestation: general debates explored through local studies. *Progress in Environmental Science*, 2, 229–251.

Williams, M. (2003) *Deforesting the Earth: From Prehistory to Global Crisis.* Chicago: The University of Chicago Press.

Williams, M. (2014) *Climate Change in Deserts, Past, Present and Future.* Cambridge: Cambridge University Press.

Williams, P., Biggs, J., Crowe, A., et al. (2010) Ponds report from 2007. *Countryside Survey Technical Report* No. 7/07.

Williams, P.W. (ed.) (1993) Karst terrains: environmental changes and human impact. *Catena Supplement*, 25, 1–20.

Williams, R.S. and Moore, J.G. (1973) Iceland chills lava flow. *Geotimes*, 18, 14–17.

Williams, W.D. (1999) Salinisation: a major threat to water resources in the arid and semi-arid regions of the world. *Lakes and Reservoirs: Research and Management*, 4, 85–91.

Williamson, M. (1996) *Biological Invasions.* London: Chapman and Hall.

Willis, C.M. and Griggs, G.B. (2003) Reductions in fluvial sediment discharge by coastal dams in California and implications for beach sustainability. *Journal of Geology*, 111, 167–182.

Willis, K.J., Gillson, L. and Brncic, T.M. (2004) How 'virgin' is virgin rainforest? *Science*, 304, 402–403.

Wilshire, H.G. (1980) Human causes of accelerated wind erosion in California's deserts. In D.R. Coates and J.D. Vitek (eds), *Geomorphic Thresholds*. Stroudsburg: Dowden, Hutchinson & Ross, 415–433.

Wilshire, H.G., Nakata, J.K. and Hallet, B. (1981) Field observations of the December 1977 wind storm, San Joaquin Valley, California. In T.L. Péwé (ed.), *Desert Dust: Origin, Characteristics and Effects on Man*. Special Paper, Geological Society of America. Denver, CO: Geological Society of America, 233–251.

Wilson, C.J. (1999) Effects of logging and fire on runoff and erosion on highly erodible granitic soils in Tasmania. *Water Resources Research*, 35, 3531–3546.

Wilson, E.O. (1992) *The Diversity of Life*. Cambridge, MA: Harvard/Belknap.

Wilson, K.V. (1967) *A preliminary study of the effect of urbanization on floods in Jackson, Mississippi*. United States Geological Survey professional paper, 575-D, 259–261.

Wine, M.L. and Cadol, D. (2016) Hydrologic effects of large southwestern USA wildfires significantly increase regional water supply: fact or fiction? *Environmental Research Letters*, 11 (8), doi:10.1088/1748-9326/11/8/085006.

Winkler, E.M. (1965) Weathering rates as exemplified by Cleopatra's Needle in New York City. *Journal of Geological Education*, 13 (2), 50–52.

Winkler, E.M. (1970) The importance of air pollution in the corrosion of stone and metals. *Engineering Geology*, 4, 327–334.

Wishart, D. and Warburton, J. (2001) An assessment of blanket shire degradation and peatland gully development in the Cheviot Hills, Northumberland. *Scottish Geographical Magazine*, 117, 185–206.

Wohl, E., Hall, R.O., Lininger, K.B., Sutfin, N.A. and Walters, D.M. (2017a) Carbon dynamics of river corridors and the effects of human alterations. *Ecological Monographs*, doi:10.1002/ecm.1261.

Wohl, E., Lininger, K.B. and Barron, J. (2017b) Land before water: the relative temporal sequence of human alteration of freshwater ecosystems in the conterminous United States. *Anthropocene*, 18, 27–46.

Wolfe, S.A. and Hugenholtz, C.H. (2009) Barchan dunes stabilized under recent climate warming on the northern Great Plains. *Geology*, 37, 1039–1042.

Wolfe, S.A., Hugenholtz, C.H., Evans, C.P., et al. (2007) Potential aboriginal-occupation-induced dune activity, Elbow Sand Hills, northern Great Plains, Canada. *Great Plains Research*, 17, 173–192.

Wolman, M.G. (1967) A cycle of sedimentation and erosion in urban river channels. *Geografiska Annaler*, 49A, 385–395.

Wolman, M.G. and Schick, A.P. (1967) Effects of construction on fluvial sediment, urban and suburban areas of Maryland. *Water Resources Research*, 3, 451–464.

Wondzell, S.M. and King, J.G. (2003) Postfire erosional processes in the Pacific Northwest and Rocky Mountain regions. *Forest Ecology and Management*, 178, 75–87.

Wong, C.M. and Daniels, L.D. (2017) Novel forest decline triggered by multiple interactions among climate, an introduced pathogen and bark beetles. *Global Change Biology*, 23, 1926–1941.

Wong, S., Dessler, A.E., Mahowald, N., et al. (2008) Long-term variability in Saharan dust transport and its link to North Atlantic sea surface temperature. *Geophysical Research Letters*, 35, L07812, doi:10.1029/2007GL032297.

Woo, M.-K. (1996) Hydrology of northern North America under global warming. In J.A.A. Jones, C. Liu, M.-K. Woo, and H.-T. Kung (eds), *Regional Hydrological Response to Climate Change*. Dordrecht: Kluwer, 73–86.

Woo, M.-K., Lewkowicz, A.G. and Rouse, W.R. (1992) Response of the Canadian permafrost environment to climate change. *Physical Geography*, 13, 287–317.

Wood, B. (2002) Hominid revelations from Chad. *Nature*, 418, 133–135.

Woodcock, B.A., Isaac, N.J., Bullock, J.M., et al. (2016) Impacts of neonicotinoid use on long-term population changes in wild bees in England. *Nature Communications*, 7, doi:10.1038/ncomms12459.

Woodroffe, C.D. (1990) The impact of sea-level rise on mangrove shorelines. *Progress in Physical Geography*, 14, 483–520.

Woodroffe, C.D. (2008) Reef-island topography and the vulnerability of atolls to sea-level rise. *Global and Planetary Change*, 62, 77–96.

Woodroffe, C.D., Rogers, K., McKee, K.L., et al. (2016) Mangrove sedimentation and response to relative sea-level rise. *Annual Review of Marine Science*, 8, 243–266.

Woodson, M.K., Sandor, J.A., Strawhacker, C. and Miles, W.D. (2015) Hohokam Canal irrigation and the formation of irragric anthrosols in the Middle Gila River Valley, Arizona, USA. *Geoarchaeology*, 30 (4), 271–290.

Woodwell, G.M. (1992) The role of forests in climatic change. In N.P. Starman (ed.), *Managing the World's Forests*. Dubuque, IA: Kendall/Hunt, 75–91.

Woolf, D., Amonette, J.E., Street-Perrott, F.A., et al. (2010) Sustainable biochar to mitigate global climate change. *Nature Communications*, 1, doi:10.1038/ncomms1053.

Wooster, W.S. (1969) The ocean and man. *Scientific American*, 221, 218–223.

World Commission on Dams (2000) *Dams and Development.* London: Earthscan.

World Conservation Monitoring Centre (1992) *Global Biodiversity.* London: Chapman and Hall.

World Glacier Monitoring Service (2008) Global glacier changes: facts and figures, http://www.grid.unep.ch/glaciers/ (accessed January 2018).

World Meteorological Organization (1995) *Climate System Review.* Geneva: WMO.

World Resources Institute (1986) *World Resources 1986–7.* New York: Basic Books.

World Resources Institute (1987) *World Resources 1987.* New York: Basic Books.

World Resources Institute (1988) *World Resources 1988–9.* New York: Basic Books.

World Resources Institute (1992) *World Resources 1990–91.* New York and Oxford: Oxford University Press.

World Resources Institute (1996) *World Resources 1994–95.* New York and Oxford: Oxford University Press.

World Resources Institute (1998) *World Resources 1996–7.* New York and Oxford: Oxford University Press.

Woth, K., Weisse, R. and von Storch, H. (2006) Climate change and North Sea storm surge extremes: an ensemble study of storm surge extremes expected in a changed climate projected by four different regional climate models. *Ocean Dynamics*, 56, 3–15.

Wright, L.W. and Wanstall, P.J. (1977) The vegetation of Mediterranean France: a review. Occasional paper 9, Department of Geography, Queen Mary College, University of London.

Wright, S.A. and Schoellhamer, D.H. (2004) Trends in the sediment yield of the Sacramento River, California, 1957–2001. *San Francisco Estuary and Watershed Science* (on line serial), 2 (2), Article 2.

Wroe, S. and Field, J. (2006) A review of the evidence for a human role in the extinction of Australian megafauna and an alternative interpretation. *Quaternary Science Reviews*, 25, 2692–2703.

Wu, C., Zhu, H., Luo, Y., et al. (2015) Levels and potential health hazards of PCBs in shallow groundwater of an e-waste recycling area, China. *Environmental Earth Sciences*, 74 (5), 4431–4438.

Wu, J. (2014) Urban ecology and sustainability: the state-of-the-science and future directions. *Landscape and Urban Planning*, 125, 209–221.

Wu, P., Wood, R. and Stott, P. (2005) Human influence on increasing Arctic river discharges. *Geophysical Research Letters*, 32, L02703.

Wu, Q., Hou, Y., Yun, H. and Liu, Y. (2015) Changes in active-layer thickness and near-surface permafrost between 2002 and 2012 in alpine ecosystems, Qinghai–Xizang (Tibet) Plateau, China. *Global and Planetary Change*, 124, 149–155.

Wulf, A. (2015) *The Invention of Nature.* London: John Murray.

Wullschleger, S.D., Gunderson, C.A., Hanson, P.J., et al. (2002) Sensitivity of stomatal and canopy conductance to elevated CO_2 concentrations – interacting variables and perspective on scale. *The New Phytologist*, 153, 485–496.

WWF (2010) *Living Planet Report.* Gland, Switzerland: WWF.

Xu, K. and Milliman, J.D. (2009) Seasonal variations of sediment discharge from the Yangtze River before and after impoundment of the Three Gorges Dam. *Geomorphology*, 104, 276–283.

Xu, K., Milliman, J.D., Yang, Z. and Xu, H. (2007) Climatic and anthropogenic impacts on water and sediment discharges from the Yangtze River (Changjiang), 1950–2005. In A. Gupta (ed.), *Large Rivers: Geomorphology and Management.* Chichester: Wiley, 609–626.

Xu, L., Dai, F.C., Gong, Q.M., et al. (2012) Irrigation-induced loess flow failure in Heifangtai platform, North-West China. *Environmental Earth Sciences*, 66 (6), 1707–1713.

Xu, M., Chang, C.-P., Fu, C., et al. (2006) Steady decline of east Asian monsoon winds, 1969–2000: evidence from direct ground measuremenrs of wind speed. *Journal of Geophysical Research*, 111, D24111.

Xu, Y.S., Zhang, D.X., Shen, S.L. and Chen, L.Z. (2009) Geo-hazards with characteristics and prevention measures along the coastal regions of China. *Natural Hazards*, 49, 479–500.

Xue, Y.Q., Zhang, Y., Ye, S.J., et al. (2005) Land subsidence in China. *Environmental Geology*, 48, 713–720.

Yaalon, D.H. and Yaron, B. (1966) Framework for man-made soil changes – an outline of metapedogenesis. *Soil Science*, 102, 272–277.

Yamano, H., Sugihara, K. and Nomura, K. (2011) Rapid poleward range expansion of tropical reef corals in response to rising sea surface temperatures. *Geophysical Research Letters*, 38, L04601.

Yang, D., Kanae, S., Oki, T., et al. (2003) Global potential soil erosion with reference to land use and climate changes. *Hydrological Processes*, 17, 2913–2928.

Yang, D.Y., Liu, L., Chen, X. and Speller, C.F. (2008) Wild or domesticated: DNA analysis of ancient water buffalo remains from north China. *Journal of Archaeological Science*, 35, 2778–2785.

Yang, M., Nelson, F.E., Shiklomanov, N.I., et al. (2010b) Permafrost degradation and its environmental effects on the Tibetan Plateau. *Earth-Science Reviews*, 103, 31–44.

Yang, P., Hong, G. and Dessler, A.E. (2010a) Contrails and induced cirrus. *Bulletin of the American Meteorological Society*, 91, 473–478.

Yang, Q., Wang, K., Zhang, C., et al. (2011b) Spatio-temporal evolution of rocky desertification and its driving forces in karst areas of Northwestern Guangxi, China. *Environmental Earth Sciences*, 64, 383–393.

Yang, S.L., Milliman, J.D., Li, P. and Xu, K. (2011a) 50,000 dams later: erosion of the Yangtze River and its delta. *Global and Planetary Change*, 75, 14–20.

Yang, Y.H., Zhao, N., Hao, X.H. and Li, C.Q., et al. (2012) Decreasing trend of sunshine hours and related driving forces in southwestern China. *Theoretical and Applied Climatology*, 109, 305–321.

Yannopoulos, S.I., Lyberatos, G., Theodossiou, N., et al. (2015) Evolution of water lifting devices (pumps) over the centuries worldwide. *Water*, 7 (9), 5031–5060.

Yao, T., Thompson, L., Yang, W., et al. (2012) Different glacier status with atmospheric circulations in Tibetan Plateau and surroundings. *Nature Climate Change*, 2 (9), 663–667.

Yasunari, T.J., Tan, Q., Lau, K.M., et al. (2013) Estimated range of black carbon dry deposition and the related snow albedo reduction over Himalayan glaciers during pre-monsoon periods. *Atmospheric Environment*, 78, 259–267.

Ye, S., Xue, Y., Wu, J., et al. (2016) Progression and mitigation of land subsidence in China. *Hydrogeology Journal*, 24 (3), 685–693.

Yechieli, Y., Abelson, M., Bein, A., et al. (2006) Sinkhole 'swarms' along the Dead Sea coast: reflection of disturbance of lake and adjacent groundwater systems. *Geological Society of America Bulletin*, 118, 1075–1087.

Yi, H., Hao, J. and Tang, X. (2007) Atmospheric environmental protection in China: current status, development trend and research emphasis. *Energy Policy*, 35, 907–915.

Yizhaq, H., Ashkenazy, Y. and Tsoar, H. (2007) Why do active and stabilized dunes coexist under the same climatic conditions? *Physical Review Letters*, doi:10.1103/PhysRevLett.98.188001.

Yizhaq, H., Ashkenazy, Y. and Tsoar, H. (2009) Sand dune dynamics and climate change: a modelling approach. *Journal of Geophysical Research*, 114, F01023.

Yoo, J.-C. and D'Odorico, P. (2002) Trends and fluctuations in the dates of ice break-up of lakes and rivers in Northern Europe: the effect of the North Atlantic Oscillation. *Journal of Hydrology*, 268, 100–112.

Yorke, T.H. and Herb, W.J. (1978) *Effects of urbanization on streamflow and sediment transport in the Rock Creek and Anacostia basins, Montgomery County, Maryland, 1962– 74*. United States Geological Survey professional paper 1003.

Yoshikawa, K. and Hinzman, L.D. (2003) Shrinking thermokarst ponds and groundwater dynamics in discontinuous permafrost near Council, Alaska. *Permafrost and Periglacial Processes*, 14, 151–160.

Young, A.J., Guo, D., Desmet, P.G. and Midgley, G.F. (2016a) Biodiversity and climate change: risks to dwarf succulents in Southern Africa. *Journal of Arid Environments*, 129, 16–24.

Young, A.M., Higuera, P.E., Duffy, P.A. and Hu, F.S. (2016b) Climatic thresholds shape northern high-latitude fire regimes and imply vulnerability to future climate change. *Ecography*, 40, 606–617.

Young, J.E. (1992) *Mining the earth. Worldwatch Paper*, 109, 1–53.

Young, K.R. (2016) Biogeography of the Anthropocene: novel species assemblages. *Progress in Physical Geography*, 40, 161–174.

Yu, H.Y., Li, F.B., Yu, W.M., et al. (2013) Assessment of organochlorine pesticide contamination in relation to soil properties in the Pearl River Delta, China. *Science of the Total Environment*, 447, 160–168.

Yuill, B., Lavoie, D. and Reed, D. (2009) Understanding subsidence processes in coastal Louisiana. *Journal of Coastal Research*, 54, 23–36.

Yule, J.V. (2009) North American Late Pleistocene megafaunal extinctions: overkill, climate change or both? *Evolutionary Anthropology*, 18, 159–160.

Yunus, M. and Iqbal, M. (eds) (1996) *Plant Response to Air Pollution*. Chichester: Wiley.

Zabinski, C. and Davis, M.B. (1989) Hard times ahead for Great Lakes forests: a climate threshold model predicts responses to CO_2-induced climate change. In J.B. Smith and D. Tirpak (eds), *The Potential Effects of Global Climate Change on the United States*. Washington, DC: US Environmental Protection Agency, Appendix D, 5–1–5–19.

Zaimes, G.N. and Schultz, R.C. (2015) Riparian land-use impacts on bank erosion and deposition of an incised stream in north-central Iowa, USA. *Catena*, 125, 61–73.

Zalasiewicz, J., Waters, C., Williams, M., Aldridge, D.C. and Wilkinson, I.P. (2018) The stratigraphical signature of the Anthropocene in England and its wider context. *Proceedings of the Geologists' Association*. In press.

Zalasiewicz, J., Williams, M., Haywood. A. and Ellis, M. (2011) The Anthropocene: a new epoch of geological time? *Philosophical Transactions of the Royal Society*, 369A, 835–41.

Zanello, F., Teatini, P., Putti, M. and Gambolati, G. (2011) Long term peatland subsidence: experimental study and modeling scenarios in the Venice coastland. *Journal of Geophysical Research: Earth Surface*, 116 (F4), F04002, doi:10.1029/2011JF002010.

Zarfl, C., Lumsdon, A.E., Berlekamp, J., et al. (2015) A global boom in hydropower dam construction. *Aquatic Sciences*, 77, 161–170.

Zavada, M.S., Wang, Y., Rambolamanana, G., et al. (2009) The significance of human induced and natural erosion features (lavakas) on the central highlands of Madagascar. *Madagascar Conservation & Development*, 4, 120–127.

Zeder, M.A. (2008) Domestication and early agriculture in the Mediterranean Basin: origins, diffusion, and impact. *Proceedings of the National Academy of Sciences*, 105, 11597–11604.

Zedler, J.B. and Kercher, S. (2005) Wetland resources: status, trends, ecosystem services, and restorability. *Annual Review of Environment and Resources*, 30, 39–74.

Zeeberg, J. and Forman, S.L. (2001) Changes in glacier extent of north Novaya Zemlya in the twentieth century. *The Holocene*, 11, 161-175.

Zektser, S., Loáiciga, H.A. and Wolf, J.T. (2005) Environmental impacts of groundwater overdraft: selected case studies in the southwestern United States. *Environmental Geology*, 47, 396–404.

Zelazowski, P., Malhi, Y., Huntingford, C., et al. (2011) Changes in the potential distribution of humid tropical forests on a warmer planet. *Philosophical Transactions: Series A, Mathematical, Physical, and Engineering Sciences*, 369, 137–160.

Zemp, M., Frey, H., Gärtner-Roer, I., et al. (2015) Historically unprecedented global glacier decline in the early 21st century. *Journal of Glaciology*, 61 (228), 745–762.

Zeng, N. and Yoon, J. (2009) Expansion of the world's deserts due to vegetation-albedo feedback under global warming. *Geophysical Research Letters*, 36, L17401.

Zhang, D.Q., Tan, S.K. and Gersberg, R.M. (2010a) Municipal solid waste management in China: status, problems, and challenges. *Journal of Environmental Management*, 91, 1623–1633.

Zhang, G.L. and Gong, Z.-T. (2003) Pedogenic evolution of paddy soils in different soil landscapes. *Geoderma*, 115, 15–29.

Zhang, J., Gilbert, D., Gooday, A., et al. (2010d) Natural and human-induced hypoxia and consequences for coastal areas: synthesis and future development. *Biogeosciences*, 7, 1443–1467.

Zhang, J., Steele, M. and Schweifer, A. (2010c) Arctic sea ice response to atmospheric forcings with varying levels of anthropogenic warming and climate variability. *Geophysical Research Letters*, 37, L20505.

Zhang, K., Almeida Castanho, A.D., Galbraith, D.R., et al. (2015) The fate of Amazonian ecosystems over the coming century arising from changes in climate, atmospheric CO2, and land use. *Global Change Biology*, 21 (7), 2569–2587.

Zhang, K., Yu, Z., Li, X., et al. (2007) Land use change and land degradation in China from 1991–2001. *Land Degradation and Development*, 18, 209–219.

Zhang, T.-H., Zhao, H.-L., Li, S.-G., et al. (2004) A comparison of different measures for stabilizing moving sand dunes in the Horqin Sandy Land of Inner Mongolia, China. *Journal of Arid Environments*, 58, 203–214.

Zhang, Y., Lü, X., Isbell, F., et al. (2014) Rapid plant species loss at high rates and at low frequency of N addition in temperate steppe. *Global Change Biology*, 20 (11), 3520–3529.

Zhang, Y. and Song, C. (2006) Impacts of afforestation, deforestation and reforestation on forest cover in China from 1949 to 2003. *Journal of Forestry*, 104, 383–387.

Zhao, C., Wang, Y. and Zeng, T. (2009) East China Plains: a 'basin' of ozone pollution. *Environmental Science & Technology*, 43, 1911–1915.

Zheng, F.L. (2005) Effects of accelerated soil erosion on soil nutrient loss after deforestation on the loess plateau. *Pedosphere*, 15, 707–715.

Zhong, L., Deng, J., Song, Z. and Ding, P. (2011) Research on environmental impacts of tourism in China: progress and prospect. *Journal of Environmental Management*, 92, 2972–2983.

Zhu, A., Ramanathan, V., Li, F. and Kim, D. (2007) Dust plumes over the Pacific, Indian, and Atlantic Oceans: climatology and radiative impact. *Journal of Geophysical Research*, 112, D16208.

Zhu, C., Wang, B. and Qian, W. (2008a) Why do dust storms decrease in northern China concurrently with the recent global warming? *Geophysical Research Letters*, 35, L18702.

Zhu, D., Tian, L., Wang, J., et al. (2014) Rapid glacier retreat in the Naimona'Nyi region, western Himalayas, between 2003 and 2013. *Journal of Applied Remote Sensing*, 8, 083508–083508.

Zhu, R.X., Potts, R., Pan, Y.X., et al. (2008b) Early evidence of the genus Homo in East Asia. *Journal of Human Evolution*, 55, 1075–1085.

Zhuang, W. (2016) Eco-environmental impact of inter-basin water transfer projects: a review. *Environmental Science and Pollution Research*, 23 (13), 12867–12879.

Ziegler, A.D., Bruun, T.B., Guardiola-Claramonte, M., et al. (2009) Environmental consequences of the demise in swidden cultivation in montane mainland Southeast Asia: hydrology and geomorphology. *Human Ecology*, 37, 361–373.

Ziegler, A.D. and Giambelluca, T.W. (1997) Importance of rural roads as source areas for runoff in mountainous areas of northern Thailand. *Journal of Hydrology*, 196, 204–229.

Zizumbo-Villarreal, D. and Colunga-GarcíaMarín, P. (2010) Origin of agriculture and plant domestication in West Mesoamerica. *Genetic Resources and Crop Evolution*, 57, 813–825.

Zohary, D., Hopf, M. and Weiss, E. (2012) *Domestication of Plants in the Old World* (4th edn). Oxford: Oxford University Press.

Zwally, H.J., Abdalafi, W., Herring, T., et al. (2002) Surface melt-induced acceleration of Greenland ice-sheet flow. *Science*, 297, 218–221.

Index

Human Impact on the Natural Environment: Past, Present and Future, Eighth Edition. Andrew S. Goudie.
© 2019 John Wiley & Sons Ltd. Published 2019 by John Wiley & Sons Ltd.
Companion website: www.wiley.com/go/goudie/human-impact-natural-environment

ASKHAM BRYAN
COLLEGE
LEARNING RESOURCES